COOPERATIVE BUSINESS ENTERPRISE

Cooperative Business Enterprise

Martin A. Abrahamsen, Ph.D.

Visiting Professor
Department of Agricultural and Resource Economics
University of Maryland

McGRAW-HILL BOOK COMPANY

New York   St. Louis   San Francisco   Auckland   Düsseldorf
Johannesburg   Kuala Lumpur   London   Mexico   Montreal   New Delhi   Panama
Paris   São Paulo   Singapore   Sydney   Tokyo   Toronto

Library of Congress Cataloging in Publication Data

Abrahamsen, Martin Abraham, date
   Cooperative business enterprise.

   Includes index.
   1. Cooperation. 2. Cooperative societies. 3. Cooperation—United States. I. Title.
HD2965.A24   334   76-4588
ISBN 0-07-000151-0

COOPERATIVE BUSINESS ENTERPRISE

Copyright © 1976 by McGraw-Hill, Inc. All rights reserved. Printed in the United States of America. No part of this publication may be reproduced, stored in a retrieval system, or transmitted, in any form or by any means, electronic, mechanical, photocopying, recording, or otherwise, without the prior written permission of the publisher.

1234567890 KPKP 7832109876

This book was set in Times Roman by Creative Book Services, subsidiary of McGregor & Werner, Inc. The editors were Rose Orletti and Annette Hall; the cover was designed by Anne Canevari Green; the production supervisor was Milton J. Heiberg. The drawings were done by Danmark & Michaels, Inc.
Kingsport Press, Inc., was printer and binder.
Cover montage from photographs courtesy Cooperative Cotia and Farm Credit Administration.

*To
Joseph G. Knapp
Friend and distinguished
cooperative scholar*

Contents

Foreword	xiii
Preface	xv

1 Cooperatives: Nature and Place in the Economy — 1
- Cooperative Business Enterprise — 2
- Cooperatives in the Political Economy — 5
- Cooperatives and the Isms — 10
- Cooperatives in the Economy of the United States — 12
- Summary — 16

2 Types of Cooperatives — 19
- Problems of Classification — 20
- Groups Served — 21
- Areas Served — 35
- Functions Performed — 37
- Size of Cooperatives — 37
- Types of Membership — 39
- Legal Status — 40

	Financial Structure	41
	Quasi-Cooperatives	41
	Cooperative Service and Trade Associations	42
	Factors Influencing Types of Cooperatives Established	42
	Summary	44
3	**Cooperative Principles**	**47**
	Rochdale Contributions	47
	Evolutionary Development in the United States	51
	Basic Cooperative Principles Reexamined	53
	Other Principles or Practices Examined	63
	Summary	68
4	**The Evolution of Cooperative Thought**	**71**
	Pre-Rochdale	72
	The Rochdale Pioneers	74
	Early European Post-Rochdale Thinkers	74
	Early American Thinkers	76
	Recent Views Regarding Cooperatives	83
	Summary	85
5	**Historical Development of Cooperatives in the United States**	**88**
	Early Cooperative Explorations: Up to 1870	89
	The Age of Experimentation: 1870–1920	90
	Cooperative Commodity Marketing Gains: 1920–1933	94
	Business Performance Improvement: 1933–1945	95
	Adjustments to Change: 1945 to Date	98
	Summary	101
6	**Cooperative Growth**	**104**
	Farmers' Marketing and Purchasing Cooperatives	105
	Selected Industrial Comparisons	110
	General Service Cooperatives	117
	Consumer Cooperatives	121
	Growth Strategy	122
	Summary	124
7	**Cooperatives in Other Selected Countries**	**126**
	Early Cooperative Efforts	126
	Cooperative Business Efforts	127
	Factors Influencing Cooperative Development in Other Countries	155

CONTENTS ix

8	**Organizations That Serve Cooperatives**	**158**
	National Cooperative Organizations	159
	Cooperative Trade Organizations	165
	State Cooperative Councils	170
	General Farm Organizations	172
	International Cooperative Organizations	172

9	**Benchmarks in Cooperative Legislation**	**183**
	State Legislation	184
	Federal Legislation	190
	Summary	199

10	**Special Legal Problems**	**202**
	Legislative and Regulatory Environment	202
	Antitrust Decisions	205
	Status of Cooperatives under Antitrust Legislation	212
	Marketing Contracts and Marketing Agreements and Orders	216
	Summary	220

11	**Cooperative Taxation**	**223**
	Property Taxes	224
	Franchise, Sales, and Other Related Taxes	225
	Federal Income Taxes	225
	State Income Taxes	238
	Basic Income Tax Issues	239
	Summary	241

12	**Organizing a Cooperative**	**243**
	The Problem Identified: Solutions Explored	243
	Precautionary Organizational Measures	250
	Getting the Cooperative Underway	253
	Organizational Structures Compared	255
	Special Organizational Problems of Limited-Resource Cooperatives	258
	Summary	259

13	**Cooperative Management**	**261**
	Success as a Cooperative	262
	Success as a Business	267
	Special Considerations in Cooperative Management	269
	Summary	272

14 Cooperative Communications — 274
- Why Is Cooperative Communication Needed? — 275
- Who Should Communicate for Cooperatives? — 277
- With Whom Should Cooperatives Communicate? — 278
- How Do Cooperatives Communicate? — 280
- What Makes an Effective Communications Program? — 280
- Coordinating Communications and Member Relations — 283
- Summary — 287

15 Cooperative Finance — 289
- Cooperatives' Need for Capital — 290
- Leasing and Leveraged Leasing Financing — 298
- Financial Planning and Management — 300
- Financial Controls — 301
- Summary — 306

16 Patronage Refunds and Per Unit Capital Investments — 308
- Patronage Refunds — 309
- Per Unit Capital Investments — 312
- How Revolving Capital Financing Works — 313
- Summary — 319

17 Cooperative Finance Associations — 321
- Background Developments — 321
- The Cooperative Farm Credit System — 323
- The Banks for Cooperatives — 329
- Federal Land Banks — 332
- Production Credit Associations — 335
- National Rural Utilities Cooperative Finance Corporation (CFC) — 337
- Rural Telephone Bank — 339
- Cooperative Credit Corporations — 340
- Credit Unions — 341
- Savings and Loan Associations and Mutual Savings Banks — 341
- Summary — 342

18 Cooperative Bargaining — 344
- The Nature of Bargaining — 344
- Why Bargaining Has Become Important — 348
- The Extent of Bargaining — 349
- Operating Practices — 352
- Problem Areas — 355
- Summary — 361

CONTENTS

19	**Pooling**	**364**
	Early Pooling Efforts	365
	The Nature of Pooling	365
	The Pooling Operation Illustrated	367
	Advantages of Pooling	370
	Disadvantages of Pooling	371
	Comparing Pooling with Other Methods of Sale	373
	Summary	374
20	**Cooperative Mergers and Liquidations**	**376**
	External Merger Considerations	377
	Local and Internal Considerations	380
	Impact on Practices, Resources, and Functions	381
	Determining Merger Feasibility	383
	Merger Procedure	383
	Postmerger Considerations	384
	Cooperative Liquidations	386
	Summary	388
21	**Cooperatives and Government Policies**	**390**
	Early Notions	391
	Congressional-Cooperative Relationships	392
	Federal Government–Cooperative Relationships	394
	State Government–Cooperative Relationships	403
	Unfavorable Government Action	408
	Cooperatives and Government Policy: An Evaluation	415
22	**Limitations and Benefits**	**420**
	Limitations	421
	Benefits	426
	Summary	434
23	**Cooperative Opportunities**	**436**
	Increased Emphasis on Economic Integration	437
	Implications for Cooperatives	442
	Expansion of Foreign Trade	444
	Increased Attention to Cooperative Research	448
	Cooperatives as a Tool for Economic Development	456
	Summary	464
Appendix A	Terminology	468
Appendix B	Quotations from Leaders on Cooperatives	451
Index		475

Foreword

It may interest the reader to know about the various forces that have helped shape my ideas on business cooperation. They go back to my boyhood days on a small Wisconsin dairy farm. My father, whose uncle had managed a consumers' cooperative in Norway, was secretary of the local crossroads cooperative cheese factory and president of the local livestock shipping association. My experiences with the cooperative cheese factory were firsthand. I helped "figure the statements"—a job that involved adding the pounds of milk each patron delivered, finding out how much butterfat the milk contained, determining the price per pound that patrons received for this butterfat, and calculating the amount of money to pay the patrons for their specific milk deliveries. In my hometown, I also observed how the manager of the local consumers' cooperative bought shares of stock from the local villagers and farmers when times were hard. He quickly gained control of enough stock to own the business, and it soon no longer operated as a cooperative.

At the River Falls State Teachers College, River Falls, Wisconsin (now the University of Wisconsin—River Falls), Professor J. M. May's course in agricultural cooperation helped me understand what cooperatives could and could not do for their members. Moreover, this course enabled me to observe firsthand the operations of Land O'Lakes Creameries, Inc., and to see how such a large-scale cooperative business enterprise helped its members further to integrate their farm operations.

My subsequent graduate study at the University of Wisconsin, Madison, introduced me to the thinking of such nationally recognized cooperative teachers and authorities as Professors Bakken, Froker, Hobson, and Schaars. They did much to stimulate my growing interest in cooperatives. At Madison, too, I had an opportunity to observe in detail the functioning of some 100 farm supply cooperatives. This was in connection with my work on a research study conducted by the Department of Agricultural Economics of the university and Farmer Cooperative Service (FCS), which was then known as the Cooperative Research and Service Division of the Farm Credit Administration. Findings were published in FCS Bulletin 20, *Farmers' Purchasing Associations in Wisconsin* (1937).

At the University of Wisconsin, I wrote a master's thesis called "Land O'Lakes Creameries, Inc.: A Historical Account of a Large-Scale Butter Marketing Cooperative." Later, while on the staff of the Department of Agricultural Economics, West Virginia University, I wrote my doctoral thesis, "Farm Supply Cooperatives in West Virginia," which I submitted at the University of Wisconsin.

During the next thirteen years, I taught cooperative and marketing courses at West Virginia University and at North Carolina State University. At both these places, I had an opportunity to work with numerous graduate students who were interested in cooperatives.

My responsibilities with Farmer Cooperative Service did much to broaden my cooperative horizons. There, I did research and provided advisory and educational assistance on problems of farmers' marketing, purchasing, and related service cooperatives. I also taught the cooperative course at the U.S. Department of Agriculture Graduate School. Moreover, I had occasion to observe in action cooperatives in the Scandinavian countries, Great Britain, Ireland, India, Brazil, and Paraguay. During this period, too, stimulating contacts with the administrator, Dr. Joseph G. Knapp, and other associates in Farmer Cooperative Service, many of whom had achieved national and international recognition for their work with cooperatives, gave me a better insight into various significant aspects of cooperative enterprise. In addition, my thinking about cooperatives was strongly shaped by consultations with teachers of cooperation at land-grant universities and other colleges, as well as by contacts with many cooperative leaders in the United States and foreign countries.

The University of Maryland provided an ideal environment for the preparation of this book. There, I had an opportunity to test the contents of the text under actual classroom conditions. I also had an opportunity again to study cooperatives in Great Britain, as well as in Iceland, Austria, and Israel. In addition, I have benefited greatly from contacts with teachers and graduate students in the university's Department of Agricultural and Resource Economics.

Martin A. Abrahamsen

Preface

Teachers are increasingly reporting the need for new and updated educational materials to help them improve their teaching of cooperative enterprise. This book is designed as a basic college and university text to meet this need. It should also be useful to those teachers in colleges and high schools who are responsible for teaching selected aspects of cooperative enterprise as a part of various social science courses. Moreover, teachers of vocational agriculture, educational and training directors of regional and other large-scale cooperatives, and officials of cooperative service or trade associations will find it helpful in their teaching and training programs.

Cooperative enterprise covers a wide range of activities. It has application, for example, to farmers joining together to sell their crops and livestock, to buy their production supplies, and to obtain the services they need to carry on their farm operations. Cooperatives are also organized by consumers to help them buy items they use in their day-to-day living. Farmers and business owners may even insure their property in cooperative fire insurance companies. Similarly, they may be members of cooperative life insurance companies. More and more people in general are turning to the cooperative technique to provide health services; and grocers, hardware dealers, and others have organized cooperative wholesale associations to purchase the products they sell at retail. People may put their savings in mutual cooperative savings banks and may use cooperative credit unions both as savings institutions and as places to get loans.

In addition, cooperative members may be craftworkers in Appalachia, plywood workers in the Pacific states, fishboat captains on the East or West Coast, or, indeed, just about anyone who would join a cooperative to buy necessary supplies and to sell the products produced.

These are but a few of the many forms of business enterprise that cooperatives may take. They can, in fact, be organized to meet any legitimate need.

This book is written with all the many types of cooperative enterprise in mind. It places special emphasis on the basic and unique features that apply to all types of cooperatives, irrespective of the services they provide. This uniqueness has special application, for example, to cooperative principles, organization, management, financing, and communications. The various types of cooperatives have much in common when it comes to legal features, impact of government policies, and contributions to economic development. Although agricultural cooperatives predominate in the United States, the text also identifies the contributions of other types of cooperatives and illustrates how these organizations function in the business world.

The book begins by emphasizing the unique and distinct features of cooperatives—features that often are not fully recognized or understood. The role of cooperatives in the nation's economy is next explored. This investigation is followed by chapters that cover the historical development and growth of cooperatives, both in the United States and in foreign countries. Next we shall look at the organization techniques that apply to cooperatives. Special attention is again directed to the uniqueness of cooperative enterprise as we look at operating features—management, financing, patronage refunds and capital retain practices, member and public education, bargaining, pooling, integration, marketing contracts, mergers, and liquidations. Important legal benchmarks and aspects, as well as the cooperative taxation issue, are also examined. The relationships that cooperatives have with government, other forms of business enterprise, and other cooperatives are considered. Finally, cooperatives are appraised from the standpoint of their limitations, possibilities, and opportunities.

The text is developed in such a way that teachers can readily select from its contents the material necessary to meet their special needs. This form of presentation will enable them both to *add* supplementary educational materials that have special applications to their particular situations and to *omit* those sections that are less relevant to their needs. In addition, each chapter is supplemented with basic questions covering the material presented and with suggested references for students who wish to explore the subject in greater detail.

My experience in teaching cooperative courses had led me to conclude that a textbook on the subject cannot provide the teacher with all the information needed to teach the class. Teachers have a responsibility to personalize their teaching. This fact requires that they know the leaders of the various types of cooperatives that operate in the area. It suggests also the need for understanding just how the associations are organized and operated. Changes in operations and in the political, social, and economic environment in which cooperatives operate are likely to bring to the foreground new and distinct problems each year. The teacher will find it advantageous to relate these specific problems to the basic material covered in this book. To do so may require the preparation of special case studies, the development of individual assignments for students, and the

PREFACE

use of supplementary educational materials. Teachers also may want to supplement their classroom efforts by drawing not only on local cooperative leaders, but also on representatives of regional cooperatives, banks for cooperatives, national cooperative trade organizations, and state and federal government officials who work with cooperatives. In this way, teachers can keep abreast of the impacts of change in cooperative performance and offer a challenging and well-balanced course to their students.

This book was made possible by a research agreement between the Farmer Cooperative Service and the Department of Agricultural and Resource Economics of the University of Maryland. The agreement provided that, with the support of the Farmer Cooperative Service, the Department would

> develop a basic college text on cooperatives giving consideration to: distinctive features; highlights in development in the United States and in foreign countries; operations, including management, financing, nature of patronage refunds and capital retains, member and public education, bargaining, pooling, integration, contracts, and mergers and liquidations; legislative and legal aspects; relationships as they may apply to government, other business, and various types of cooperatives; problems and procedures in organization; and appraisal of limitations, possibilities, and opportunities.

The views expressed are those of the author and may or may not conform with the official views of the University of Maryland, the Farmer Cooperative Service, U.S. Department of Agriculture, or any other government agency.

Many persons have taken the time to read individual chapters of the manuscript and make helpful suggestions and pertinent observations. I particularly wish to thank:

- Glenn M. Anderson, Executive Secretary, Wisconsin Federation of Cooperatives (the section on state cooperative councils, Chapter 8)
- James Baarda, Agricultural Economist, Farmer Cooperative Service (the chapters on benchmarks in cooperative legislation, special legal problems, and cooperative taxation)
- Professors C. A. Becker, Department of Agricultural Economics and Sociology, Pennsylvania State University; E. Fred Koller, Department of Agricultural and Applied Economics, University of Minnesota; Robert Lytle, Division of Agriculture, Arizona State University; and Vernon E. Schneider, Department of Agricultural Economics and Rural Sociology, Texas A & M University, who tested selected chapters in their respective cooperative classes
- Gilbert Biggs and George Tucker, Agricultural Economist and Senior Agricultural Economist, respectively, and J. K. Samuels, Assistant Administrator (retired), Farmer Cooperative Service (the chapter on cooperative bargaining)
- Martin Blum, Senior Agricultural Economist, and William Hand and J. David Morressy, Agricultural Economists, Farmer Cooperative Service (many of the chapters)
- Wallace Campbell, formerly President, Foundation for Cooperative Housing (the section on that organization, Chapter 8)
- Margaret Digby, Consultant, The Plunkett Foundation for Cooperative Studies (the section on that organization, Chapter 8, and the section on Great Britain, Chapter 7)
- Professor Yeluda Don, Chairman, Department of Economics, Bar-Ilan University, Israel (the section on the International Research Center on Rural Cooperative Communities, Chapter 8, and the section on Israeli cooperatives, Chapter 7)

- Stanley Dreyer, President, Cooperative League of the U.S.A. (the section on that organization, Chapter 8)
- Allie C. Felder, Jr., Executive Vice President, Cooperative League of the U.S.A. (the section on India, Chapter 7)
- Herbert C. Fledderjohn (deceased), former Executive Vice President, Agricultural Cooperative Development International (the section on that organization, Chapter 8)
- Raymond L. Fox, Senior Agricultural Economist, Farmer Cooperative Service (the section on National Livestock Producers Association, Chapter 8)
- Nelda Griffin, Senior Agricultural Economist, Farmer Cooperative Service, and Gifford Hoag, formerly Assistant to the Governor, Farm Credit Administration (the chapters on cooperative financing, cooperative finance associations, and patronage refunds and per unit capital investments)
- Paul E. Hanson, Agricultural Attaché, Embassy of Denmark (the section on Denmark, Chapter 7)
- Patrick B. Healy, Secretary, National Milk Producers Federation (the section on that association, Chapter 8)
- Ross E. Heller, Director of Member Services, National Telephone Cooperative Association (the section on that association, Chapter 8)
- Gene Ingalsbe, Director of Information, Farmer Cooperative Service (the chapter on communications)
- Daniel Kellerhuls, Second Secretary, Embassy of Switzerland (the section on Switzerland, Chapter 7)
- Clark H. Kirkman, Agricultural Economist, Farmer Cooperative Service (the chapters on the nature of cooperative enterprise and communications)
- Professor Vesa Loakonew, Cooperating Institute of the University of Helsinki, Finland (the section on Finland, Chapter 7)
- Kenneth J. McCready, Cooperatives and Producer Marketing Institutions, Canadian Department of Agriculture (the section on international cooperative associations, Chapter 8)
- Signurdur Markusson, Samband Isl., Iceland (the section on Iceland, Chapter 7)
- Bert D. Miner, Senior Agricultural Economist, Farmer Cooperative Service (the section on Brazil, Chapter 7)
- Kenneth D. Naden, President, National Council of Farmer Cooperatives (the section on that organization, Chapter 8)
- Robert W. Nelson, Director of Public Relations, National Rural Electric Cooperative Association (the section on that association, Chapter 8)
- Professor Nils Nesheim, Royal College of Agriculture, Norway (the section on Norway, Chapter 7)
- Marvin A. Schaars (retired), Department of Agricultural Economics, University of Wisconsin (the chapter on cooperative principles)
- Professor Fred Swardstrum (retired), University of Uppsala, Sweden, and Carl Janér, Agricultural Attaché, Embassy of Sweden (the section on Sweden, Chapter 7)
- Beryle Stanton, Editor, and Owen K. Hallberg, President, American Institute of Cooperation (the section on that organization, Chapter 8)
- Dave Volkin, Senior Agricultural Economist, Farmer Cooperative Service (the chapters on cooperative mergers and liquidations, benchmarks in cooperative legislation, special legal problems, and cooperative taxation)

PREFACE

- Herb Wagner, Managing Director, Credit Union National Association, Inc. (the section on that association, Chapter 8)
- Hamil Kenney, for his highly valuable editorial assistance
- Abraham Avidor, graduate assistant, Department of Agriculture and Resource Economics, University of Maryland, who assisted on all aspects of the project and wrote the preliminary draft of the section, "Cooperatives as a Tool for Economic Development," Chapter 23
- Special thanks go to J. Warren Mather, Senior Agricultural Economist, Farmer Cooperative Service, who read the entire manuscript and offered many especially valuable suggestions
- Finally, my special thanks to Mrs. Gerri Smith and Mrs. Bonnie Buck who competently and painstakingly typed rough and final drafts of the manuscript.

Martin A. Abrahamsen

Chapter 1

Cooperatives: Nature and Place in the Economy

Cooperation—working together to achieve a common end—is a practice that has existed in this country since the days of the first colonists. Cooperative business enterprise, however, even in its most elementary forms, did not begin until the early 1800s. First attempts were sporadic, and it was not until the National Grange (Patrons of Husbandry) promoted cooperatives in the 1870s that cooperative businesses began to be numerous.

Notwithstanding the deep taproots that cooperatives have developed in American economic life, there is much misunderstanding as to what they are and how they operate. What people know or do not know about cooperatives reflects to a large degree their training, interests, biases, and job experience. This is why such terms as *cooperation* and *cooperative business enterprise* mean different things to different people. A need exists to clarify those terms.

Let us begin by examining "cooperation," a word that has been described as the "most powerful in the English language." Some examples of early and present-day cooperation are:

- Early colonists joined forces to clear land, build houses, and protect themselves against common enemies.
- Farmers got together for husking bees, threshing rings, barn raising, and home building.

- City people cooperated to build streets and bridges and to protect themselves against fire.
- State and federal agencies now cooperate to deal with problems of general social concern—health, crime, pollution, and education. We speak, for example, of cooperative meat-inspection programs and the Cooperative State Research Service, as well as of cooperative state extension services.
- Members of the business community cooperate to achieve common goals through various trade organizations.
- In striving for various goals, cooperation has become an "in" word for everyone from politicians to business persons and educators. They all entreat us to cooperate with them to further advance whatever objectives they have in mind. The performers in "Sesame Street" even join in the chorus.

The emphasis in cooperation is on self-help. Expressed in another way, people cooperate because they have learned that it is extremely difficult to achieve some future goal by working alone. Only by joining others who have common objectives can we advance not only our interests but theirs as well. Cooperation, then, involves working together for any purpose, laudatory or otherwise, depending on what the cooperators have in mind.

It is obvious, therefore, that in a broad sense the ways in which people cooperate may differ widely and may even be quite informal. The techniques used will depend on the specific activities undertaken, and uniform procedures and practices hardly exist.

COOPERATIVE BUSINESS ENTERPRISE

Now let us explore the meaning of the term *cooperative business enterprise*. Here, too, we find that the emphasis is on self-help. By joining together with people who have similar goals or objectives, cooperative members can achieve more than by working alone. Upon examining definitions of cooperative business enterprise, we observe that they reflect a wide range of economic, social, and legal views, depending upon the background and experience of whoever does the defining. Some definitions are limited to agricultural cooperatives; others are broad enough to cover any type of business activity.

Definitions of cooperative enterprise that illustrate a wide range of views are:

> A cooperative enterprise is one which belongs to the people who use its services, the control of which rests with all the members, and the gains of which are distributed to the members in proportion to the use they made of its services.[1]
>
> A cooperative is a democratic association of persons organized to furnish themselves an economic service under a plan that eliminates entrepreneur profit and that provides for substantial equality in ownership and control.[2]

---

[1] *Report of the Inquiry on Cooperative Enterprise in Europe,* U.S. Government Printing Office, Washington, 1937.

[2] Israel Packel, *The Organization and Operation of Cooperatives,* 4th ed., American Law Institute and the American Bar Association, Philadelphia, Pa., 1970, p. 2.

An agricultural cooperative is business organization, usually incorporated, owned and controlled by member agricultural producers, which operates for the mutual benefit of its members or stockholders, as producers or patrons, on a cost basis after allowing for the expenses of operation and maintenance and any other authorized deductions for expansion and necessary reserves.[3]

A "cooperative" is a form of business enterprise that enables a group of individuals, partnerships, or corporations to combine together for the purpose of producing or buying or selling a commodity or service. City consumers have gotten together to buy goods and sell them. Businessmen have formed mutual fire insurance companies. Individuals join together to buy life insurance through a mutual insurance company or merchandise through a mutual wholesale purchasing association. People who save money put their funds in a mutual savings bank. Farmers join together to buy goods they use in production or to sell the things they grow. All of these are "cooperatives." They are also legitimate forms of private enterprise.[4]

Cooperation is organized working together for mutual benefits. Economic cooperation is a form of business with democratic ownership and control by member-patrons having common needs, serving themselves on a nonprofit basis, and receiving benefits proportional to participation.[5]

A cooperative is a business voluntarily owned and controlled by its member-patrons and operated for them and by them on a non-profit or cost basis.[6]

A cooperative is a voluntary contractual organization of persons having a mutual ownership interest in providing themselves a needed service(s) on a nonprofit basis. It is usually organized as a legal entity to accomplish an economic objective through joint participation of its members. In a cooperative the investment and operational risks, benefits gained, or losses incurred are shared equitably by its members in proportion to their use of the cooperative's services. A cooperative is democratically controlled by its members on the basis of their status as member-users and not as investors in the capital structure of the cooperative.[7]

A review of these definitions gives us some clues as to cooperative objectives and the advantages members hope to gain by organizing such a business enterprise. It is clear, too, that certain basic features characterize cooperative business undertakings. These are:

- *Cooperative business enterprise is a commercial activity.* When members join together in a cooperative business venture, they do so mainly to increase or stretch their

---

[3]L. S. Hulbert, *Legal Phases of Cooperative Associations,* Farm Credit Administration Bulletin 50, U.S. Department of Agriculture, Washington, 1942, p. 1.
[4]National Association of Manufacturers, *NAM and Cooperatives,* privately published, New York, 1946, p. 7.
[5]Ward W. Fetrow and R. H. Elsworth, *Agricultural Cooperation in the United States,* Farm Credit Administration Bulletin 54, U.S. Department of Agriculture, Washington, 1947.
[6]Marvin A. Schaars, *Cooperatives, Principles and Practices,* University of Wisconsin Extension, Madison, 1973, p. 7.
[7]Job K. Savage and David Volkin, *Cooperative Criteria,* FCS Service Report 71, Farmer Cooperative Service, U.S. Department of Agriculture, Washington, 1965.

incomes. To farmers, this usually means buying supplies and related services for less and selling farm products for more than they could otherwise do. To consumers, it means buying food and clothing and securing credit, health protection, insurance, and other necessary services at lower costs. In some cases emphasis is placed primarily on providing better services, and in others it is on obtaining services hitherto unavailable. In all cases members seek to improve their economic status by organizing and operating their own cooperative business enterprise.

• *Cooperative business enterprise is a nonprofit enterprise.* A business cooperative is organized to perform services for its members and not to realize monetary gains as a separate legal entity. To maintain this status, it is necessary for the cooperative to distribute all net margins or savings to patrons after deduction of operating and other lawful expenses. This distribution is made in proportion to the business each patron does on a dollar or on a unit base.

When net margins from some operations are not distributed or allocated to patrons, the cooperative no longer operates along cooperative lines in that part of its business, and it is subject to an income tax on the profits realized. In a cooperative, however, such profits are incidental to its basic purposes.

The nonprofit nature of a business cooperative is often not well understood by its members or the general public. Those who argue that cooperative operations result in profits that should be taxed do not recognize that, to begin with, a true cooperative has no taxable profits since net margins or savings are distributed as refunds to patrons who include these patronage refunds in their taxable income. (The tax issue is discussed in detail in Chapter 11.)

• *Cooperative enterprises are owned by members who are the users.* This fact distinguishes cooperatives from other corporations whose owners primarily are investors. The fact that people form a cooperative to provide themselves with a needed service largely determines it objectives; how it is controlled, financed, and operated; and how its net savings are distributed. The extent to which a cooperative is successful in achieving its objectives explains why it is advantageous for its member-users to patronize it rather than investor-oriented corporations.

• *Cooperatives are organized in response to mutual interests and economic needs of members.* Experience has shown that a cooperative is most successful when members have a common interest in its operations. Such mutual interests may result when all members are the same kind of farmers, when they are all consumers, or when they all belong to the same ethnic or religious group. Many marketing cooperatives, for example, center their operations on providing services for one or more closely related products, such as milk, grain, cotton, livestock, or various fruits and vegetables. Similarly, supply cooperatives gear their operations toward users of feed, seed, fertilizer, petroleum products, and related items. Consumer cooperatives may specialize in providing services for members who are interested in buying groceries, dry goods, furniture, and drugs, or in obtaining medical, housing, credit, and insurance services.

• *Cooperatives emphasize member control.* The concept of member control, often referred to as democratic control (one member, one vote), is dear to many cooperators. It is relatively easy to realize this concept in local cooperatives. However, the idea of one member, one vote, regardless of the amount of business done with a cooperative, encounters difficulty as these organizations increase in size and complexity. The issue of how members can and should be represented in their cooperative is a moot point, and will be further examined in Chapter 3.

- *Cooperative business enterprise is voluntary.* One can join or leave a cooperative as he or she sees fit. Furthermore, neither cooperatives nor, in the United States, agencies of government have any authority to force people to join cooperatives. Although in some communities a cooperative may be the only business that provides a given service, the individual is still free to decide whether or not to trade in an adjoining community or to engage in the type of business that requires the services of the cooperative.
- *Cooperatives recognize the principle of proportionality.* In a cooperative business, members share risks, financial obligations, and benefits in proportion to the use that they make of their organization. This sharing usually is done on as equitable a basis as possible, with an emphasis on fair treatment for all patrons. Thus, the principle of proportionality is introduced. For example, a patron delivering 20,000 bushels of wheat through the cooperative is responsible for twice the risks, costs, and financial obligations of a patron delivering 10,000 bushels. Likewise, this patron realizes twice the returns and twice the patronage refunds if there are any. The reason is that returns and savings are distributed to members in proportion to the use that they make of their association. As indicated in the previous observations on democratic control, a point for further consideration is whether or not, and if so to what degree, the principle of proportionality should be applied to member voting rights.

COOPERATIVES IN THE POLITICAL ECONOMY

All business activity takes place within a political economy of some sort. When we examine such systems as capitalism (private enterprise), socialism, communism, and fascism, we find a varying mixture of political and economic ideologies. A very brief look at some of the essential features of these systems will help us better to understand how they relate to cooperatives.

Such a review also is desirable because of the many myths that have sprung up, and to some extent still prevail, as to how cooperatives relate to the various systems and ideologies as they have developed in other countries. We will examine each system from the standpoint of its views on (1) human nature, (2) the State, and (3) private property.

Capitalism (Private Enterprise)

View on Human Nature   "Men are more desirous of gain than honor." With this statement, Aristotle gave us an early view of human nature that has been accepted by many as a basic tenet of the capitalistic system. This idea was further buttressed by the contention that we all know our self-interests better than anyone else. It was only natural, therefore, to expect us to work harder and with greater effectiveness for ourselves than for others. Adam Smith examined how human nature influenced the economic actions of individuals. To him an "invisible hand" guided personal destinies and the entire economy. By acting rationally and pursuing their own interests, people fortunately contribute to the general welfare as servants of society.

View on the Role of the State   If we accept the idea that self-interest is at the same time public interest, it is obvious that the power of the State need be only minimal. In fact, one's inclination to assume risk and the opportunities for investment and profit are greatest when the power of the State is limited. It is, of course, true that security of expectations must prevail with respect to enforcement of contracts and protection of property and business opportunities. This fact requires the State to maintain a reasonable degree of law and order.

View on Private Property   Adam Smith pinpointed the prevailing emphasis on private property when he spoke of humanity's "propensity to truck, barter, and exchange." In the competitive economy of his day, this propensity largely related to one's ability to achieve wealth. A century or so later, the Carnegies, the Mellons, and the Rockefellers were recognized as "captains of industry" who came to the forefront in an era of relatively free competition and limited government intervention. More recently, their place has been taken by such industrial giants as General Motors, U.S. Steel, and Exxon (formerly Standard Oil).

Early economic thinking accepted the idea that competition would assure that market values would correspond to social values. To the extent that competition prevails, the things consumers desire will most likely be produced. When monopolistic practices prevail, however, there is no assurance that social (welfare) needs will be met. Moreover, many students of economics and psychology believe that individuals in the marketplace often act in a most irrational manner.

Socialism

Advocates of socialism have taken many divergent paths since Saint Simon and his contemporaries first expressed their socialistic views in the 1830s. Moreover, they have tended to be strong on theory, but weak and uncertain on its application to real-world problems.

View on Human Nature   Socialists differ dramatically from capitalists in their ideas of human nature. They believe that people, rather than being dominated by what critics of capitalism described as ethicless self-interest and gain, should be characterized by a strong sense of "brotherly love" in their day-to-day relations. Early socialistic leaders often included intellectuals who were willing to sacrifice such material things as income and physical well-being for the sake of humanitarian ideals.

Early socialists believed that a person exists to serve society and that only by doing so is it possible to achieve a "blessed harmonious culture." They emphasized associated efforts and altruism, and indeed they were called Socialistic Associationists. Some stressed a complete working-class culture, and others called for abolition of private property and the existing political system. These views explain why socialism never gained any appreciable support among land-owning European peasants and American farmers. Rather, its main source of support came from industrial workers and intellectuals. More recently, most socialists have come to believe that peaceful transition to socialism can be achieved through the electoral process. The more pragmatic ones even advocate that private ownership should be not only allowed, but also entitled to, government protection whenever such ownership contributes to a more just and equitable distribution of wealth and income.

View on the Role of the State Socialists believe that the basic needs of society should be met through planned and coordinated political economic action. Resources—labor, capital, materials, and management—should be allocated and controlled by the State in the public interest. Only in this way, they argue, can priorities be given to basic needs. This belief is in sharp contrast with the views of people in private business, who are largely concerned with balance sheets and operating statements. The socialists further believe that government-run or -supported productive enterprises would be more responsive to social needs. They view such things as waste in advertising, inequalities in income, and monopoly in production as inherent weaknesses of capitalism. The State ideally should be the servant of the people, and it can best serve social needs only through effective harnessing of resources. In addition, socialists believe that capitalism dominates our lives from "the pulpit to the press" and that it breeds imperialism and, through it, war.

View on Private Property Early socialists held a very negative view of private property—it was "the root of all evil." Public ownership and State control of productive industries were the socialists' answer. Especially selected for such ownership and control were public utilities, banking institutions, railroads, factories, mines, and various service industries. In some instances they agreed that it might be possible to achieve socialistic objectives by breaking up or limiting the size of private business undertakings. Small shops, retail establishments, and family-sized farms could be allowed if adequate controls were maintained.

In comparison with capitalism, socialism centers on such key questions as: Which system functions more effectively—the capitalistic system where individuals express their needs by voting with their dollars in the marketplace, or the socialistic system where they vote in the polling place on the productive enterprises they personally want the government to take over or regulate? Under which system can individuals make decisions that are most likely to best serve basic social needs? The problem of relations with labor poses other important questions for socialists to answer. For example, how should labor be paid—according to need or to performance? Moreover, which system is subject to a greater degree of corruption—private enterprise or government enterprise? Can cooperatives ("economic democracy") complement socialism ("social democracy"), or does the cooperative acceptance of the institution of private property create unsurmountable barriers between the two?

Communism

Students of political science have experienced as much difficulty in defining communism as they have in defining socialism. For a start they can go back as far as Plato's *Republic* and his description of a communal society. Then they can investigate Sir Thomas More who described communism as a condition in which ". . . no man has anything, yet they are all rich; for what can make a man so rich as to lead a serene and cheerful life, free from anxieties, neither apprehending want himself, or mixed with endless complaints of his wife." Another early definer of communism and its tenets was Charles Fourier, who inspired communal ventures such as Robert Owen's in New Harmony, Indiana, and Brook Farm in Massachusetts (see Chapter 4).

Modern communism dates back to Lenin in post-World War I Russia. Drawing on the theories of Karl Marx and capitalizing on the corruption of the czar's regime, the communists, through the Bolshevik Revolution of 1917, took over the country. It is worth noting, however, that it was a revolution against a feudal monarchy and not against the decadent capitalism which Marx predicted would be the seedbed for such a revolution.

View on Human Nature Soviet communism was introduced and led by a Marxist intelligentsia, and it strove to gain the support of the land-hungry peasants. The key features of the system are: concentration of power in an elite party, control from above, and a highly developed bureaucratic system maintained through authoritarian means. This system glorifies the State, an approach that was necessary because, in the words of Stalin, the "working class could not be trusted to discover their own interests." The worker soon found, however, that the State became all-powerful and that any resistance was met by liquidation or banishment to Siberia. Individuals were looked upon as "bees in a hive" making their contribution to the State. Infiltration, subjugation, purges, and the secret police were used to achieve party objectives.

View on the Role of the State The State assumed responsibility for all forms of business activity, and it nationalized all private property. This policy became even more pronounced in 1928 when the Russian government, committed to more rapid industrialization, confiscated private holdings and established State farms and so-called cooperative farms. Under the communist system, the government establishes controls over all forms of economic activity—production and distribution of consumer goods as well as the operation of capital goods industries. Management becomes highly centralized, and much emphasis is placed on the completion of five-year plans that are an integral part of the planned economy.

View on Private Property The parties engaged in production and consumption in a communistic economy are not the traditional buyers and sellers of the capitalistic system. Goods often are rationed by the State, and private property and profits do not exist. Moreover, as Aizsilnieks, a keen student of the Russian political system, reported, ". . . the Soviet Government and the Communistic Party actually control this (Cooperative) property without troubling themselves to obtain the consent of members. . . . The local authorities also used to confiscate cooperative properties."[8]

Resources are directed toward building the industrial sector of the economy and toward the production of certain goods in the amounts specified by the government plans. Production factors are apportioned under government direction, and prices are not determined by supply-and-demand conditions but, rather, reflect predetermined goals established by party policies. Two important exceptions to general communistic doctrine, however, have been adopted in Russia. Farm laborers are permitted to cultivate small parcels of land, which they do quite intensely, and to sell the products they produce

---

[8]Arnold P. Aizsilnieks, *Cooperation Behind the Iron Curtain*, Mimir Publications, Madison, Wis., 1952, p. 27.

on these parcels. In addition, wages and incentives have been instituted in order to recognize superior performance.

Fascism

The strong taproots of modern fascism developed out of the confused and seemingly hopeless conditions that prevailed in Italy and Germany following World War I. With its totalitarian techniques, dictatorial powers, and anarchistic leaning, fascism later spread to Spain, Turkey, and many African and South American countries. Weak democracies and confused socialistic and communistic political parties characterize the countries that turn to fascism.

View on Human Nature While capitalism and socialism recognize the importance of the individual in society, fascism, not unlike communism, makes the State all-powerful. The individual can be molded, coerced, and, if need be, liquidated to achieve desired ends. The press is controlled, and coercion is the cornerstone of the system. While ideology appears to be on shifting sands, the basic support, in varying degrees, usually comes from industrialists, middle-class business entrepreneurs, large landowners, and the military. Fascism assumes the role of restoring law and order, and it clamors for the achievement of national goals. Power is achieved, maintained, and concentrated through a firmly controlled political party. In general, fascism is autocratic, exploits ignorance and prejudice, and seeks conquests and expansion through military means.

View on the Role of the State Under the fascist State, society is tightly controlled. Key industrial and financial institutions are either owned or controlled by the government.

Cooperatives and corporations are taken over directly or infiltrated by appointed State representatives who serve on the board of directors and function as managers. The cooperative emphasis on democracy, voluntarism, personal freedom, and local leadership is considered dangerous to the State and hence suppressed. Regulation is the watchword of the day, and all efforts are directed toward the maintenance of the State and the achievement of party goals. In actual practice, there is usually little relationship between the productive efforts of fascism and the basic needs of society. Everything is done for the State, and the individual is subordinated accordingly.

View on Private Property Even in those instances where private property technically prevails, the tight controls that are enforced make ownership quite meaningless. These controls especially apply to banking, industrial activity, and agricultural production. The tightly State-controlled corporation is the principal vehicle for generating economic activity in the fascistic system. The State regulates and controls employment, wages, prices, and the direction of economic growth and development. The economy is run in the interest of the State, and profits are forcibly directed into new industries or expanded facilities as the State decrees. Aggressive international trade, likewise, is primarily carried on to support expanded military efforts, and imports and exports are rigidly controlled. Consequently, many of the smaller countries involved—usually producers of raw products—became economic satellites of the principal fascist countries.

COOPERATIVES AND THE ISMS

This review of some of the ideas that characterize the various systems of political economy brings into focus the basic differences between capitalism and the other isms. It also emphasizes the emergence of a mixed economy, because all systems are in a state of constant flux and actually deviate a great deal from the original ideologies propounded by early adherents. Pure capitalism has been evolving into a mixed economy, with both private and public property existing side by side in varying proportions. This economy has contributed to rapid and sustained economic growth in many countries.

The United States economy, for example, has changed considerably since the New Deal. Constraints on personal economic freedom have become more pronounced, and the government has become increasingly involved in protecting the interests of individuals. Social security legislation, health legislation, general welfare programs, controls of some agricultural prices, and sanctioning of collective bargaining all have become commonplace. Our educational system has even become largely socialized. At the same time, socialistic and communistic systems have borrowed some capitalistic ideas. As mentioned previously, differentiated salary schedules, for example, have become increasingly frequent under communism. To the extent that Russian peasants are granted the use of small plots of land, they now participate in a price-and-market economy.

Of special interest is the question, "How do cooperatives relate to the various political systems?" Let us consider, for example, Midwestern farmers and observe how their cooperatives relate to the capitalistic system. It is quite obvious that their reason for joining a cooperative is economic. They seek to get more for the products they sell and, consistent with reliable service and high quality, to pay less for the production supplies and services they buy. Farmers join cooperatives to maintain a position in a private enterprise economy where they can own, operate, and manage their own businesses—the farm. Through membership, farmers seek to improve their competitive position.

American farmers have rather complete freedom of choice as to whether or not they want to join a cooperative, how long they desire to remain members, and what type or types of farm activity they wish to pursue. As a member, the farmer has an obligation to patronize the cooperative, participate in the selection of its officials, and help finance it. Finally, the member is entitled to all the benefits and assumes all the risks that result from operations.

It is more difficult to determine how membership in a consumer cooperative would be influenced by the various isms. Members may be farmers, small urban business people, professional workers, or laborers. The farmer and the urban business person look upon any consumer cooperative to which they may belong primarily as an economic tool to help them stretch their income by getting goods and services at lower costs. Laborers, however, have a different motive for joining a cooperative. By patronizing the cooperative, they realize savings; but since they are not entrepreneurs, their interest in no way relates to furthering their status as small business owners. The same is true of professional workers who may be members of a cooperative.

Government policy toward cooperatives varies widely. In capitalistic countries it ranges all the way from discouragement to active support, with many countries officially adopting a policy of neutrality. Where support is provided, it may take the form of favorable legislation, grants, loans, technical assistance, research, and the use of cooperative services to achieve social, political, and national goals.

The support and encouragement that cooperatives receive in a socialistic economy likewise differ from one country to another. Worker and consumer cooperatives usually are encouraged and operate quite freely in most of these countries. How agricultural cooperatives are accepted by socialists also varies from country to country. Some socialists look upon these cooperatives as a part of the generally accepted agricultural system. Others view them with alarm, considering them as a tool used to prop up and support the capitalistic system, which they thoroughly despise. The success of all types of cooperative business enterprise in the Scandinavian countries—countries that are considered quite socialistic—suggests wide acceptance of all types of cooperatives in the economic systems of these countries.

Something close to a half-way situation may exist in developing countries that follow socialistic systems of political economy. Often the cooperative becomes an instrument of the State in carrying on its economic and social programs. In support of various government programs, it may function as the State trading agency. In so doing, cooperatives may serve the State in assembling and processing agricultural products, as well as in supplying farm inputs such as seeds, feeds, petroleum, and fertilizer. And consumer and worker cooperatives may, in effect, serve as an arm of government.

In communistic and fascistic countries, the situation is entirely different. Aizsilnieks, in commenting on the fate of cooperatives in Russia, stated: ". . . the consumer cooperatives were subjugated to the dictates of the Soviet State. . . . Their rights of self determination were practically abrogated . . . the whole population was commanded to join the consumer communes established instead of voluntary cooperative organizations."[9]

The so-called cooperative farms in the Soviet Union are not cooperatives as we understand them—rather, they are an instrument operated and controlled by the State, just like other "cooperative ventures" that have been organized in that country. The basic features of cooperatives in capitalistic countries—voluntary participation, member control, service at cost, proportionality of risks and benefits, and limited dividends on equity capital—do not exist in the Soviet's cooperative farms.

Cooperative enterprise in democratic countries is considered a part and parcel of the private enterprise system. People join cooperatives mainly to improve their income. Membership is a matter of freedom of choice, and risks and financial obligations assumed are directly related to the economic benefits realized. This is in the best traditions of a private enterprise economy and in direct contrast to the operations of

---

[9]Aizsilnieks, op. cit., pp. 15–16.

business enterprise in communism and fascism. Cooperatives are looked upon in these countries merely as tools to further the interests of the State. To the extent that these interests conflict with members' interests, cooperatives are not permitted to function freely, as they do in capitalistic economies. There is, therefore, no basis for comparing and identifying any phase of cooperative business activity as carried on in the United States and other democracies with that of the economic and political systems of communism and fascism.

Important, too, is the status of capital in the various economic systems. Laszlo Volko, now retired from Washington State University, emphasizes that all systems need capital. To him the big question is: "Who owns it?" Under systems based on communism and fascism, it is the State or the Party. Under a system based on private enterprise, it is the individual.

COOPERATIVES IN THE ECONOMY OF THE UNITED STATES

Three basic forms of business enterprise have developed in the economy of the United States. These are the individual proprietorship, the partnership, and the corporation. There are two types of corporations: cooperative corporations and other corporations. We will find it useful to examine the essential features of each form of business enterprise in order to determine how cooperatives fit into the established ways of doing business in this country. The essential features of each method of doing business are summarized in Table 1-1.

Individual Proprietorships

There are more individually owned businesses in the United States than any other type of business. In this type of business venture, the individual owner supplies the facilities, assumes all risks, makes all decisions, provides and arranges for all necessary capital, and realizes all profits or losses that may result. The owner is the entrepreneur, although often doing a great deal of the physical labor involved in carrying on the business enterprise. Farmers, small retail establishments, and many service industries are examples of the individual owners and operators of businesses.

Depending on the capabilities of the owner, the individual proprietorship has several advantages.

- The owner is self-motivated and is free to test whatever skills and ideas at will.
- The control problems are minimal. The owner's judgment is final, and he or she makes all the decisions. No prior approval by someone else is required.
- The owner encounters fewer rules and regulations and less resistance to change than do other forms of business.
- The owner gets all the benefits.

The individual proprietorship also has several disadvantages.

Table 1-1 Methods of Doing Business under Private Enterprise

Features compared	Types of business			
	Individual	Partnership	Cooperative	Corporation
				Other
1. Who uses the services?	Nonowner customers	Generally nonowner customers	Chiefly the member-patrons or -users	Generally nonowner customers
2. Who owns the business?	The individual	The partners	The member-patrons	The stockholders
3. Who votes?	None necessary	The partners	The member-patrons†	Common stockholders
4. How is voting done?	None necessary	Usually by partners' share in capital	Usually one-member, one-vote†	By shares of common stock
5. Who determines policies?	The individual	The partners	The member-patrons and directors	Common stockholders and directors
6. Are returns on ownership capital limited?	No	No	Yes—8% or less (usually less, if any)†	No
7. Who gets the operating proceeds?	The individual	The partners in proportion to interest in business	The partons on a patronage basis†	The stockholders in proportion to stock held

†Basic Cooperative characteristics.
Source: Adapted from Cooperatives in Agribusiness, Farmer Cooperative Service, U.S. Department of Agriculture, 1968, p. 6.

- The owner has no assurance that the business will operate profitably, and when it doesn't, she or he must assume all losses.
- The capital resources usually are so limited that the business venture generally is small and may not operate efficiently.
- The owner may lack the necessary competency in some lines of endeavor required of the modern entrepreneur. For example, the proprietor may be competent in dealing with people but poor in financial management and record keeping.
- The unlimited personal liability can be a great handicap, especially in case of a loss or debt.
- The business span is limited to the owner's period of productive life.

The individual business person performs essentially the same functions as partnerships and corporations. The owner buys and sells goods and services and makes many of the same decisions that are made by dozens of corporate officials. The difference primarily is in the scope of business and in market relationships.

Partnerships

Partnership is a form of business enterprise that is jointly owned for profit by two or more people. Partnerships become increasingly important as the complexity of operating a business enterprise expands beyond the abilities of a single individual. As co-owners, partners join together to provide capital, facilities, and management. Costs, responsibilities, and profits and losses are shared equally or in accordance with agreements that specifically state the share and the contribution assigned to each partner. Although partnerships continue to increase in number, their relative importance is declining as corporations gain in significance. They are becoming more and more common, however, in the ownership of farms, particularly as arranged between parent and child. Often such arrangements eventually lead to complete ownership and operation by the child.

Partnerships also are common in the broad range of retail and service establishments—grocery stores, hardware stores, dry goods and haberdashery, insurance, dry cleaning, and the like.

A partnership has a number of comparative advantages:

- Compared with corporations, the partnership requires minimal legal formality.
- It generally enables the development of a larger business venture than is possible for the individual business owner.
- Usually, financial resources are more readily available to partners than to individual business proprietors.
- The varying skills of the different partners may effectively complement one another and contribute substantially to better decision making and more effective division and specialization of labor than are available when one operates alone.
- Partners may act for one another and are thus able to do business with dispatch.

There are, however, definite disadvantages in the operation of a partnership. The most important ones are:

- Since partners may act for one another, a lack of information and judgment in one partner can result in disruption of the partnership and contribute to business instability.
- Because partnerships are based on the unlimited liability principle, each partner is liable for all debts.
- When a partner dies or leaves the organization, it may be necessary to dissolve the partnership, unless a new partner can be found. In some cases, however, a remaining partner may continue to operate as a single proprietor.

Corporations

The third form of business organization is the corporation. It is a voluntary association of people joined together in a separate, autonomous legal entity that is distinct from these people. Important features of the corporation are limited liability of owners to creditors and legal immortality, which lends stability to operations. Sporadic efforts to organize corporations occurred prior to the Revolutionary War, and by the time of the Civil War, many state constitutions and laws provided for corporate businesses. Since then, the corporate form of business enterprise has grown until it now encompasses the major share of the business activity of the nation. For our purposes, we will distinguish between the two forms of corporations—cooperative corporations and other corporations (frequently referred to as standard, regular, investor, or profit-oriented corporations).

Cooperative Corporations Business corporations have developed a high degree of flexibility in their operating practices. This explains why cooperatives, building on previous experience of various forms of business organization, have adopted some of the corporate features, discarded others, and invented new ones better to achieve their basic objectives. To help us get an understanding of what a cooperative corporation is like, let us visit the Farmers Mercantile Company on High Street of any rural county seat. From its outside appearance, one cannot possibly determine whether it operates as a cooperative or as another type of business. Both have the same type of facilities, do the same kinds of business, and are subject to much the same regulations. To determine if a given business is a cooperative, it will be necessary to examine in detail the corporate structure. Even here, many similarities exist. Both types of business maintain limited liability, provide legal immortality, and avail themselves of all the advantages of the corporate form of business enterprise.

A further examination of a cooperative corporation, however, indicates a difference in motivation, ownership, and certain operating practices. In the cooperative corporation, ownership, control, and patronage are vested in the same people. Emphasis is placed on providing members with service at cost. To achieve these objectives, special features are built into the corporate structure of the cooperative. As we shall see in Chapter 9, most cooperatives are incorporated under special state laws that enable members to achieve their objectives with respect to control, financing, and benefits.

The cooperative also has distinct provisions with respect to membership. Further details on cooperative organization and operation are given in Chapters 12 to 20.

These chapters should help bring into focus the possible advantages of cooperative participation as compared with the advantages of doing business with ordinary corporations.

Other Corporations Other corporations in the United States are characterized as large-scale business undertakings that are profit-oriented. Capital is raised by issuing shares of stock that generally are sold to investors on a stock exchange. The value of this stock may change daily, depending upon the general business conditions and on the appraisal of business prospects for the firm.

Corporations, investor- or cooperative-oriented, have distinct business advantages:

- All stockholders or members have limited liability to creditors. Thus, if the corporation should fail, stockholders would lose only their investment in the corporation.
- The corporation, through its broad ownership, is able to tap effectively wider and larger sources of capital than individual proprietorships and partnerships can do. It is in a position, therefore, to finance larger and more diversified business undertakings.
- A corporation is an artificial legal entity that is created by the state issuing a charter or articles of incorporation.
- The corporation has an indefinite existence. As such, it is able to continue operations regardless of the death of individual stockholders.

The corporation also has certain disadvantages:

- Incorporating costs for small or special types of business may be excessive when compared with volume of business.
- The corporation may become an instrument for manipulation and deceit when management lacks social responsibility and owners have little, if any, influence on operations.
- The activities of a corporation are subject to the laws of the state in which it incorporates, and in some instances, these may be too restrictive for certain specialized corporations to achieve their objectives.

SUMMARY

We have indicated that it is desirable to distinguish between cooperation and cooperatives. Cooperative business enterprise is a commercial activity; it realizes no profits as a separate business entity; it is organized in response to the mutual interests of members; it is controlled by member-users; and it is voluntary in nature.

A look at the relationship of cooperatives to the major political systems leads to two basic conclusions:

- Cooperatives are an integral part of the capitalistic system of business enterprise. They have unique characteristics that emphasize control by and benefits for members. The mere fact that they are organized and operated as a business corporation is an indication that cooperatives are capitalistic in nature and, as such, occupy an important place in the economic structure of the United States.

- Cooperatives, as we know them, cannot exist in communistic and fascistic political systems. The emphasis in these systems is on tight State control, subservience of the individual, and the use of force to achieve compliance. This is in sharp contrast with the cooperative that is voluntarily organized and operated by members and patrons for their mutual benefit.

There are three basic forms of business structure in the United States—the individual proprietorship, the partnership, and the corporation. The cooperative differs from other corporations in ownership, methods of control, the people who use it, and ways in which benefits from its operations are shared.

QUESTIONS

1. Distinguish between cooperation and cooperative business enterprise.
2. Develop your definition of a cooperative.
3. What are the basic or distinguishing features of cooperative business?
4. What are the essential features of (*a*) capitalism, (*b*) socialism, (*c*) communism, and (*d*) fascism? Identify similarities and differences among these systems.
5. In which systems of political economy are cooperatives found?
6. What basic forms of business enterprise have developed in the United States? What are the main features of each?
7. To which form of business enterprise do cooperatives belong?
8. Distinguish between cooperative corporations and other corporations.

REFERENCES

Aizsilnieks, Arnold P.: *Cooperation behind the Iron Curtain,* Mimir Publications, Madison, Wis., 1952, p. 49.

Beal, Daniel: "Socialism," *International Encyclopedia of the Social Sciences,* vol. 14, 1968, pp. 506–534.

Bergson, Abraham: "Communism: Economic Organization—Overview," *International Encyclopedia of the Social Sciences*, vol. 3, 1968, pp. 132–139.

Dallin, Alexander: "Communism: National Communism," *International Encyclopedia of the Social Sciences,* vol. 3, 1968, pp. 112–119.

Davidovic, G.: *Towards a Cooperative World,* Coady International Institute, St. Francis Xavier University, Antigonish, Nova Scotia, Canada, pp. 48–105.

Einaudi, Mario: "Fascism," *International Encyclopedia of the Social Sciences,* vol. 5, 1968, pp. 334–341.

Fainsod, Merle: "Communism: Soviet Communism," *International Encyclopedia of the Social Sciences,* vol. 3, 1968, pp. 102–111.

Hoover, Calvin B.: "Capitalism," *International Encyclopedia of the Social Sciences,* vol. 2, 1968, pp. 294–302.

Ice, John: *Economics,* Harper, 1946, chaps. 36–43, pp. 530–670.

Kirkman, C. H. Jr.: *Opportunities in the Co-Op Business World: A Leader's Program for Youth,* FCS Information 80, U.S. Department of Agriculture, Washington, 1971.

Knapp, Joseph G.: "Are Cooperatives Good Business?" *Harvard Business Review,* January–February 1957, pp. 57–64.

Mason, Edward S.: "Cooperation," *International Encyclopedia of the Social Sciences,* vol. 3, 1968, pp. 396–403.

Modelske, George: "Communism: The International System," *International Encyclopedia of the Social Sciences,* vol. 3, 1968, pp. 126-131.

Morris, Bernard S.: "Communism: The International Movement," *International Encyclopedia of the Social Sciences,* vol. 3, 1968, pp. 119–126.

National Education Association and American Institute of Cooperation, *How We Organize to Do Business in America*, Washington, 1973, p. 29.

Samuelson, Paul A.: *Economics,* 9th ed., McGraw-Hill, New York, 1970, chap. 43, pp. 818–835.

Savage, Job K., and David Volkin: *Cooperative Criteria,* FCS Service Report 71, U.S. Department of Agriculture, Washington, 1965.

Stanton, Beryle: *Farmer Cooperatives: Farm Business Tools,* FCS Agricultural Information Bulletin 275, U.S. Department of Agriculture, Washington, 1970.

Willett, Joseph W.: "Communism: Economic Organization—Agriculture," *International Encyclopedia of the Social Sciences,* vol. 3, 1968, pp. 139–151.

Chapter 2

Types of Cooperatives

Since cooperatives can be organized for any legal purpose, we can expect to find many different types in operation. Having gained a general understanding of the meaning of the term *cooperatives* in Chapter 1, we can now proceed to identify the various types that have developed. Cooperatives may be classified according to groups served, size, areas served, functions performed, types of membership, legal status, and financial structure. There are also a number of businesses known as quasi-cooperatives that, in varying degrees, have some cooperative features. In addition, most business cooperatives are members of one or more cooperative trade associations that provide advisory, educational, and other services for their members.

PROBLEMS OF CLASSIFICATION

There are many problems in classifying cooperatives. While neat and clear-cut classifications can be established, in reality we find that these associations often belong to several classifications. For example, a cooperative may be organized as an incorporated stock or nonstock (membership) association. It may perform a marketing service, operate as a regional association on a federated or a centralized basis, or engage in processing farm products.

A cooperative also may provide services for producers and consumers at the same time. The way it handles petroleum products serves as a case in point. When its operations are geared toward providing petroleum products that are used in tractors and for operating trucks and combines, it is providing production services. In contrast, when it supplies gasoline for automobiles used for shopping trips, for heating farm homes, or for vacation transportation, it functions as a consumer cooperative.

Recreation associations also illustrate the need for caution in classifying cooperatives. Usually they are user- (consumer-) oriented. It is possible, however, for them to be resource- (i.e., producer-) oriented and to represent owners who are organized to market the use of recreational land and related services. Examples are game land, vacation-farm, guide-service, and camping cooperatives.

Much the same situation exists with respect to service cooperatives. For example, they may provide insurance coverage for livestock, crops, farm buildings, and equipment. When they do so, they quite correctly may be classified as producers' service cooperatives. It is just as possible, however, for an insurance cooperative to provide protection for the house and household appliances of consumers or for the retail and wholesale facilities and stock of small business owners. Processing or manufacturing services also may be provided by agricultural, consumers', workers', fishing, or business owners' cooperatives.

Since the needs of each group differ widely, it is only natural that the cooperatives organized by groups will vary considerably in their operations. The forces which motivate people to organize a cooperative will, therefore, determine its type.

For example, let us consider a hypothetical cooperative, the Greenbelt Dairy Cooperative. From its name and its operations, we know only that it is engaged in the dairy business. We do not know what brought about its organization. This can be determined only by looking beyond its facilities and operations.

Greenbelt Dairy Cooperative could have been created by a group of farmers interested in improving their income by developing new or expanded markets for the dairy products they produce. Such a cooperative would be a most logical development, since dairy producers usually are scattered over a wide area. Only by organizing a cooperative can farmers combine their resources and extend their market influence beyond the immediate confines of their farm holdings.

But it is entirely possible that the motivation for organizing the Greenbelt Dairy Cooperative could have come from consumers. They might be dissatisfied with the quality and cost of the dairy products available. By organizing a cooperative to buy milk from dairy farmers, they could realize all the savings that would result from going into business for themselves. Moreover, they are now more likely to get the exact quality and kinds of dairy products they desire.

A group of workers could also have organized the Greenbelt Dairy Cooperative. Among them, the workers may have concluded that they have the capital, facilities, and the talents necessary to go into business for themselves. In all likelihood, they would buy raw milk from farmers at the going market price and, after processing, sell it to retailers or directly to consumers. The workers are the ones who would provide the necessary resources, assume the resulting risks, and share the net margins that would be realized.

Although not likely to do business under the name of Greenbelt Dairy Cooperative, a group of independent store owners engaged in retailing milk (business operators) might decide to organize and operate their own dairy plant on a cooperative basis. They would do this to assure themselves of quality dairy products and to realize any savings that would result from such operations.

In reviewing the functions that a service cooperative might perform, a hypothetical Greenbelt Transportation Cooperative could be organized by any one of such groups as farmers, consumers, laborers, or small business owners. The basic reason for setting up such a cooperative would be to provide services hitherto not available or to improve existing services. Any savings would accrue to patrons in proportion to the use they make of their cooperative.

GROUPS SERVED

Cooperatives have demonstrated that they can be useful economic tools for many different economic groups. Actually, they can serve farmers, consumers, workers, fishers, independent business people, and other groups in varied occupations. The principal types of cooperatives that serve each of these groups are here identified. Their operations are briefly described either in this chapter or in Chapter 17, which gives more detailed attention to specialized cooperative finance associations.

Agricultural Producers

By far the most important types of producer cooperatives in the United States are agricultural cooperatives. Farmers use them to market practically all types of crops and livestock and livestock products. These cooperatives also provide a substantial amount of the farm supplies and business services that farmers use in agricultural production. Some of these cooperatives are highly specialized and handle just one farm product. Others have diversified operations that include handling production supplies and services in addition to the marketing of one or more farm products. Still others provide only limited services such as assembling, processing, transporting, storing, financing, and giving wholesale and retail services.

Marketing Cooperatives At one stage or another in the marketing process, cooperatives in the United States market about 25 percent of all the products farmers sell. The proportion varies from a high of 90 percent or more for cranberries, 70 percent for milk, and 64 percent for California citrus to a low of 11 percent for tobacco and poultry.

As of 1971–1972, the Farmer Cooperative Service reported the number of cooperatives primarily engaged in marketing each of the principal farm products and their net volume of business to be:

Farm products marketed	Marketing cooperatives	Net volume of business (in thousands)
Beans and peas	53	$ 45,956
Cotton and cotton products	502	466,171
Dairy	719	5,852,097
Fruits and vegetables	437	1,696,323
Grain	2,566	3,806,121
Livestock	577	2,246,899
Nut	52	307,135
Poultry and poultry products	190	550,291
Rice	62	365,244
Sugar products	66	694,158
Tobacco	30	355,006
Wool and mohair	172	14,399
Miscellaneous marketing	97	63,265
Total	5,331*	$16,463,065

*Some cooperatives market more than one product.

Four kinds of marketing cooperatives—dairy, fruit and vegetable, grain, and livestock—are especially important, accounting for about 80 percent of the farm products marketed through cooperatives. Marketing cooperatives, however, can be organized to market any of the many types of products that farmers produce. For example, there are cooperatives that market tung oil, furs, rabbits, flowers, forest products, coffee, wild rice, turpentine, and other specialty products.

Following are four examples of large-scale marketing cooperatives. They represent each of the four main commodity areas:

DAIRY *Maryland and Virginia Milk Producers Association, Inc.,* Arlington, Virginia, was organized in 1920, and it serves 1,000 dairy owners located in Maryland, Virginia, West Virginia, and Pennsylvania. Sales in 1974 were reported at $54 million. Most of its members' milk is marketed as raw whole milk to fluid milk packaging and distributing firms. Milk not used as fluid goes to the cooperative's large milk manufacturing plant that processes condensed products, butter, dry milk, and other dairy products.

FRUITS AND VEGETABLES *Ocean Spray* (cranberries), Hanson, Massachusetts, organized in 1930, serves some 900 producers in Massachusetts, New Jersey, Wisconsin, Washington, and Oregon. Sales of fresh and frozen cranberries, as well as a wide range of processed cranberry products, amounted to approximately $109 million in 1974. All products are marketed under the Ocean Spray brand.

GRAIN *Farmers Grain Dealers Association,* Des Moines, Iowa, was organized in 1904. It serves 329 farmer cooperative grain-elevator associations in Iowa and reported an annual business of approximately $660 million in 1974. This association has two large loading facilities, and it operates a soybean-processing plant. It reports that 25 to 30 percent of its volume goes into export markets through the Farmers Export Company, a sales agency that is serving six other regional grain cooperatives.

"Milk train" of Michigan Milk Producers Association This modern 12,500-gallon refrigerated truck hauls enough milk to last a family of four for fifty years. It is in sharp contrast with early trucks that picked up the farmer's milk in cans from a stand in front of the farmstead. *(Courtesy Farmer Cooperative Service.)*

LIVESTOCK *Interstate Producers Livestock Association,* Peoria, Illinois, began operations in 1921. Present activities, following five mergers, include operation of about sixty local and terminal markets in Illinois, Iowa, and Missouri, in addition to contract production and marketing. In 1973, it served 47,500 producers and reported yearly sales of about $341 million.

Marketing cooperatives can sell their products in a number of ways. They may serve patrons by (1) purchasing products outright, (2) handling products on a separate account basis, (3) functioning on a commission basis, (4) bargaining with users for price and conditions of sale, and (5) pooling products according to market preferences. (Bargaining, pooling, and other methods of sale are discussed in further detail in Chapters 18 and 19.)

Production Supply Cooperatives Another type of agricultural producer cooperative is the production supply cooperative (sometimes referred to as farm supply purchasing cooperative or just supply cooperative) which provides farmer members with the many inputs they need for their farm operations. Nearly 75 percent of their business volume consists of feed, fertilizer, and petroleum products. Items of lesser importance include seed, pesticides, building materials, and farm machinery and equipment. Some of these cooperatives, especially petroleum associations, have specialty operations and handle only one supply item. Most of them, however, provide a wide range of supplies, and a number of them also market some farm products and handle a limited amount of consumer goods.

For the fiscal year of 1971–1972, the Farmer Cooperative Service reported the principal types of farm supplies handled, the number of cooperatives handling them, and their net volume of business as:

Farm supplies handled	Cooperatives involved	Net volume of business (in thousands)
Building materials	2,222	$ 192,525
Containers and packaging supplies	887	128,570
Farm machinery and equipment	1,319	137,271
Feed	3,898	1,430,122
Fertilizer	3,992	840,052
Meat and groceries	544	65,181
Petroleum products	2,667	1,080,835
Seed	3,701	169,876
Sprays and dusts (farm chemicals)	3,433	233,678
Miscellaneous supplies	4,412	461,493
Total	5,665*	$4,739,603

*Most production supply cooperatives handle more than one item.

Service Cooperatives There are two types of service cooperatives—related and general. Related service cooperatives provide those services that affect the form, quality, or location of the farm products or supplies handled by cooperatives. They include trucking, storage, grinding, drying, application of fertilizer and pesticides, and similar services. In addition to separate cooperatives performing those services, many marketing and purchasing cooperatives provide them as a part of their operations. As of 1971–1972, there were 151 such cooperatives, and they reported about 21,800 memberships and net business volume, mostly service receipts, of $462 million.

General service cooperatives provide a number of unique and distinct services related to the business operations of farming. The number of such cooperatives by type and their memberships for the years indicated were:

Type of cooperative	Cooperatives		
	Year	Number	Memberships
Federal land bank associations	1974	553	413,460
Production credit associations	1974	433	520,888
Banks for cooperatives	1974	13	3,059*
Rural credit unions	1974	357	478,270
Rural electric cooperatives	1974	915	7,200,000
Rural telephone cooperatives	1974	231	580,083
Farmers mutual fire insurance companies	1970	1,209	n.a.
Mutual irrigation companies	1969	6,756	156,361
Dairy-herd improvement associations	1973	1,129	33,146†
Artificial breeding cooperatives	1974	27	n.a.

*Cooperatives
†Member herds

The operations of general service cooperatives are here described briefly.

Southern States Frederick Cooperative Farm supply cooperatives now maintain modern retail distribution facilities to serve members. (*Courtesy Southern States Cooperative, Inc.*)

Credit Cooperatives Many types of credit cooperatives serve rural America. The most important ones are the following.

The Cooperative Farm Credit System The Cooperative Farm Credit System provides long- and short-term loans for farmers, as well as loan services for their cooperatives. Through 533 local Federal Land Bank Associations, mortgage credit is made available for periods of thirty-five to forty-two years. These cooperatives provide 20 to 25 percent of the long-term credit needs of farmers. Production Credit Associations (PCAs) are the units of the Farm Credit System that were set up to provide members with short-term (three to eighteen months) credit. Some 430 production associations provide about 15 percent of the short-term credit needs of farmers. An integral part of the Cooperative Farm Credit System are the twelve district Banks for Cooperatives and the central Bank for Cooperatives. These banks provide about 65 percent of the commodity, operating, and facility credit used by farmer marketing, purchasing, and related service cooperatives.

REA Electric and Telephone Cooperatives Electrical cooperatives came into being with the establishment of the Rural Electrification Administration (REA) in 1935. REA is a government lending agency that makes secured mortgage loans to the local REA cooperatives to finance the construction of facilities and operations. Some 900 rural electric cooperatives and 200 telephone cooperatives, financed in whole or in part by REA, now serve farmers and other rural people.

Rural Credit Unions Credit for rural residents is also provided by credit unions. Some operate in close conjunction with production supply cooperatives, while others are strictly independent and meet a wide range of local rural needs. (For additional information on cooperative credit associations, see Chapter 17.)

Mutual Insurance Companies Mutual insurance companies in the United States date back to Benjamin Franklin's efforts to organize the Workman's Protective Association in Philadelphia in 1743. With the encouragement of the Quakers, the Grange, and other interested groups, insurance companies provided members with a wide range of protection covering fire, flood, and, in some instances, windstorm, lightning, and other natural hazards.

These companies emphasize low-cost insurance protection and are distinctly local and rural in nature. In early days, many of them were known as township associations because they served approximate township areas. Since that time, many of them have consolidated and now operate on a county or multicounty basis. Some 1,200 farmers' mutual fire insurance companies, at least half of which were organized in the last fifty years, now operate in thirty-seven states and collect premiums amounting to $50 million a year. These companies account for at least 50 percent of the fire insurance written in rural communities. Mutual fire insurance companies have placed much emphasis on fire prevention. They have done so by encouraging the establishment of local volunteer and community fire departments, the inspection of properties for actual and potential fire hazards, and an active educational campaign designed to prevent and cut fire losses.

Mutual Irrigation Companies Indications are that at the time of the early Spanish settlements, the Pueblo Indians in the Southwest had already established what, in practice, were tribal cooperative irrigation systems. The first formally organized cooperative irrigation efforts in America, however, are generally traced to the Mormon pioneers in what was to become Utah. They established mutual irrigation companies that were characterized largely by simple operating practices, limited membership, and low-cost operation.

Mutual irrigation companies usually allocate water to members in proportion to the capital stock or financial equity they have invested in their cooperative. The U.S. Bureau of the Census reports that there were 6,856 mutual irrigation companies operating in the United States in 1969. They provided water for over 9 million acres. A total of 4,268 such companies were unincorporated, but, since they represented the smaller companies, they accounted for only about 30 percent of the irrigated acreage. About half the mutual irrigation companies were located in the states of Colorado, Montana, and Utah.

Dairy-Herd Improvement Associations Farmers have turned to cooperative cow-testing associations, usually referred to as dairy-herd improvement associations, to increase the productivity of their dairy herds. These associations operate in accordance with established practices for weighing and testing the milk in the herds of participating members. They were first organized some fifty years ago, and in 1970 there were 1,200 in operation.

Artificial Breeding Cooperatives Another cooperative development that has made important contributions in improving the quality of dairy cattle is artificial breeding. Farmer Cooperative Service reported the operation of twenty-two such cooperatives, through which an estimated 4.4 million cows were bred in 1969.

Dairy-herd improvement and artificial breeding cooperatives, together with improved feeding and management practices, are responsible for substantial increases in the productivity of dairy cattle in the past fifty years. In 1925, it was reported that the average American cow produced about 175 pounds of butterfat. That figure is in contrast to 353 pounds in 1971.

Farm Machinery-Use Cooperatives With the passage of the Economic Opportunity Act in 1964, the Farmers Home Administration, in the Department of Agriculture, obtained funds for the purpose of helping low-income farmers to organize and operate cooperatives. Although a number of the resulting cooperatives engaged in traditional operations such as providing production supplies and marketing farm products, some 100 local farm machinery-use cooperatives were also established. These are relatively simple associations, often providing for no more than a cotton picker, a tractor, or some other supplementary type of machinery. Most of these associations are unincorporated and serve only a limited number of farmers—often no more than four or five. When the cooperatively owned machine wears out, one farmer often undertakes to replace it and to provide custom machinery services.

Experience with this type of cooperative venture is somewhat limited, and indications are that they may be rather short-lived, since individual members often move or change farm operations. In any event, these cooperatives have demonstrated that more intensive use of machinery, especially by the smaller farmers, may be a realistic way of reducing machine costs.

Consumer Cooperatives

Members expect their consumer cooperatives to provide them with a wide range of the goods and services they use in everyday living. In the United States, these cooperatives have achieved varying degrees of success.

Some operate as retail stores and handle complete lines of food, clothing, appliances, hardware, and lawn and garden items. As a rule they own their own wholesaling and warehouse facilities. Others function as informal consumer buying clubs that meet occasionally and distribute specialty items, such as cases of canned and processed food and basic household supplies. Consumer cooperatives also have been organized to provide such services as credit, insurance, health care, housing, recreation, preschool day care, and travel.

Members hope to benefit from consumer cooperatives through favorable prices, high-quality products, and reliable services. Thus, the basic goal of these associations, not unlike that of agricultural cooperatives, is economic gain for members. The consumer cooperative is actually the economic agent of its members and an extension of their household operations. Its aim is to increase members' purchasing power and in this way to improve their standard of living.

The number of some of the more important types of consumer cooperatives and their memberships, classified according to type, was reported by the Cooperative League of the U.S.A. as follows for 1974:

Type of cooperative	Cooperatives	Members
Consumer goods	223	577,000
Credit unions	22,879	29,900,000
Group health	183	8,000,000
Housing	800	800,000
Insurance	2,034	7,607,000
Memorial societies	125	500,000
Nursery schools	1,700	68,000
Bookstores	12	350,000
Student housing	258	25,000

Cooperative Supermarket, New York City Consumer cooperatives are becoming established in some urban communities. *Courtesy Cooperative League of U.S.A.*

Consumer Goods Cooperatives The motivation for organizing consumer goods cooperatives stems largely from general dissatisfaction with prevailing retail prices and services. In the United States, these cooperatives often have found it somewhat difficult to compete effectively with established chain stores. They have, however, attained substantial prominence in many European and some Asian countries. Except in England, where early permanent consumer cooperatives began in 1844 with the Rochdale pioneers, and in the Scandinavian countries, most of their growth has occurred since World War I.

Examples of successful consumer cooperatives in the United States are: Consumer Cooperative Association, Eau Claire, Wisconsin; Hyde Park Cooperative Society, Chicago, Illinois; and Greenbelt Consumer Services, Greenbelt, Maryland. The third association was organized in 1937, and through thirteen retail outlets it reported a $53 million annual business in 1975. Operations were in Washington, D.C., and nearby suburbs. In addition to its retail grocery stores, Greenbelt operations included seven automobile service stations, three pharmacies, and eight furniture and gift stores that handled Scandinavian ("Scan") furniture.

In the Midwest, a number of cooperatives handle consumer goods, either separately or as departments of farm supply cooperatives. Motivation for the establishment of many of these can be traced to Finnish immigrants who settled in Wisconsin, Minnesota, and Michigan, following World War I. From 1919 until 1963, these local cooperatives maintained their own wholesale organization, Central Cooperative Wholesale. In 1963, it merged with Midland Cooperatives, Inc., Minneapolis, Minnesota, a major regional farm supply association.

Credit Cooperatives Credit unions are the most prevalent type of cooperative in the United States, with approximately 12 percent of the nation's population being members. The credit union functions both as a savings institution and as a loan agency. Member savings (shares) provide most of the funds that are loaned to members, often at rates of 1 percent or less per month on the unpaid balance. Loans are made for the purchase of cars, furniture, and appliances, and for financing education, vacation expenses, and household repairs.

It is generally agreed that the strength of credit unions stems from their close ties to labor union members, teachers, government workers (local, state, and federal), and other professional workers who constitute their membership. Credit unions, except for the 3 percent that are classified as rural, are urban-oriented.

Other cooperative credit institutions are (1) savings and loan associations that promote thrift by earning dividends on member investments and by purchasing mortgages on property, and (2) mutual saving banks that provide incentives for personal savings. Funds are usually invested in home mortgages and other long-term financing.

Health Care Cooperatives Skyrocketing medical, dental, and hospital costs are prime factors in motivating the organization of health cooperatives. These associations provide medical services under mostly prepayment plans, often supplemented with fixed fees by doctors who are frequently direct employees of the cooperatives. Health cooperatives are characterized by the special emphasis they place on preventive medical care.

Although no longer operating on a cooperative basis, the Farmer Union Hospital Association, Elk City, Oklahoma, was the largest cooperative hospital facility in the United States in 1949. It had a staff of nine doctors and two dentists, and a membership of 2,000.

Early health cooperatives faced strong opposition from organized medical groups. However, the United States Supreme Court upheld the legal status of medical cooperatives, and its decision has helped to assure their existence.

Currently, one of the largest health cooperatives is the Group Health Association, Inc., Washington, D.C. It was organized in 1937, survived "a fight to the finish" that was unsuccessfully undertaken by the District of Columbia Medical Society, and in 1975 it provided complete medical, dental, and hospital care for some 40,000 members who accounted for about 101,000 enrollees. It maintains a staff of about sixty-five full-time doctors, a number of consulting specialists, and a supporting nursing staff. It operates four clinics in the District of Columbia and suburban areas in Maryland and Virginia.

Housing Cooperatives   Early cooperative housing efforts are traced to Finnish artisans who, in 1918, organized the Finnish Home Building Association in Brooklyn, New York. By 1926, organized labor had become interested in cooperative housing. In that year the Amalgamated Clothing Workers of America built the Amalgamated Dwelling for members who primarily were recruited from labor unions. Emphasis was placed on "economy and good living." Recently completed was Co-op City, a development of 16,000 units in New York City, capable of housing 60,000 people. It contains three complete shopping centers and three schools built by the cooperative and turned over to the city. Other cooperative housing developments are located in Greenbelt, Maryland; Bridgeport, Connecticut; and (Luna Park Village) Brooklyn, New York.

The federal government, through the Housing Act of 1950, began to support cooperative housing through a mortgage insurance program. Presently 1 million people live in cooperatively owned homes, and 2,500 housing cooperatives report a mortgage value of $2.2 billion.

A recent development in housing is the condominium. Although it has some aspects of cooperative ownership, motivation and control come from the builder. There is one basic difference in ownership rights between a member of a housing cooperative and a condominium dweller. The owner of a condominium owns a specific lot or apartment and is usually free to mortgage it at will. The cooperative member, in contrast, owns a share of the entire development, not a specific dwelling, and the cooperative mortgage covers the entire development.

Mutual Insurance Companies   A wide range of cooperative mutual insurance services is available. They cover substantially all types of risk (car, fire, life, and general liability). They are characterized by operations on a cost basis, with receipts above cost being returned to policyholders. Perhaps the best known is Nationwide Corporation, Columbus, Ohio, a holding company for several insurance subsidiaries. Starting in 1925 as a farmer-oriented insurance company and serving largely Farm Bureau members in Ohio, it has expanded operations to include all basic types of insurance, annuities and pensions, mutual funds, and actuarial insurance. In 1974, it reported operations in forty-nine states, the District of Columbia, Puerto Rico, and the Virgin Islands. In that year its total insurance amounted to nearly $10 billion; combined assets were $1.04 billion, premium income was $193 million, and the number of employees was about 8,000.

Other types of cooperative insurance include several State Grange, Farm Bureau, and Farmers Union insurance companies.

A number of the large insurance companies also operate on a mutual basis. Although the nature of their operations is such that policyholders have only minimum control, they do follow the basic cooperative principle of operating at cost by refunding a large proportion of the excess premiums collected to policyholders in proportion to the size of the premiums they pay.

Recreation Cooperatives   Recreation cooperatives are a development that came to the foreground in the 1960s. According to Farmer Cooperative Service, over 600 recreation cooperatives are now in operation. These associations illustrate how the motivation for cooperative effort may come from people with widely differing interests. They are classified here as consumer associations because most of them are user-oriented. As such, they represent voluntary groups of people who are interested in using various recreational services. The associations serve their members by owning or leasing land and other supporting facilities for recreation.

Examples of user-controlled recreation cooperatives are golf clubs, flying clubs, swimming clubs, trapshooting clubs, fishing and hunting clubs, and toboggan runs. They are operated primarily for members' use on a nonprofit basis.

Other Consumer Cooperatives The wide range of services provided by consumer cooperatives is illustrated by the diverse activities that they undertake. These vary from nursery schools to memorial societies, and from student bookstores, eating clubs, and housing cooperatives to cooperatives that provide transportation, entertainment, and repair and maintenance services.

Worker Cooperatives

Workers may organize cooperatives to pursue any of a large number of occupational interests. At one extreme they may undertake industrial business ventures, while at the other they may join forces to operate a farm. Workers also may operate a cooperative to produce and market crafts or to provide any of the many services used in everyday living.

Industrial Worker Cooperatives Although some of the first cooperative efforts in the United States involved industrial workers, this type of business venture failed to gain much of a foothold. Early efforts can be traced to the encouragement of "cooperative workshops" by such labor organizations as the Knights of Labor and the Sovereigns of Industry. As a result of their support, worker cooperatives were organized by stove makers, furniture makers, shipwrights, boilermakers, hatters, glassblowers, printers, tailors, and needleworkers. Most of these efforts flourished briefly but foundered eventually on the shoals of poor business practices and mismanagement.

The most successful industrial worker cooperatives are now found in the western timber regions of the United States. Although the first workers cooperative, Plywood Manufacturing Association, was organized in 1921, it was not until after World War II that this type of cooperative made significant headway. As of the mid-sixties, some twenty associations were in operation, accounting for 15 to 20 percent of the plywood business in the Northwest. These cooperatives differ widely in their operating practices. Some restrict ownership and employment to workers only. They operate in full accordance with accepted cooperative principles, and workers in the plants are benefited. Others operate with varying amounts of labor and capital provided by outsiders who share in any net margins that may result from operations. They represent joint ventures, similar to early European copartnership production societies.

An unusual type of worker cooperative developed in the West Virginia hand-blown glass industry during the Depression years of the 1930s. Many long-established glass companies were forced to close, but workers at some plants joined together, leased the facilities, and hired the existing management in order to achieve job security. This arrangement enabled them to price their output at a level acceptable to buyers—something that could not be done when they were union employees. Although successful in achieving their initial objective, all these ventures discontinued operations as worker cooperatives after World War II when economic conditions improved.

Worker cooperatives have made substantially more progress in most European and Asiatic countries—particularly France, Italy, Israel, Yugoslavia, and India—than in the United States. Some worker cooperatives are also found in the Philippines and in Central American countries. Their limited success in this country is due in part to the many employment opportunities usually available to most workers. In other cases, even when workers' interest existed, opportunities to establish small-scale, joint cooperative ventures were limited once other business firms became well established.

Agricultural Worker Cooperatives Cooperative effort among agricultural workers has developed among two groups—those who jointly work the land they own and those who work for others. Cooperatives of farm workers, not unlike cooperatives of industrial workers, have achieved but limited success in America. Early efforts can be traced to the communal association idea developed by Charles Fourier, the French economist. In the United States some forty associations modeled on the Fourier plan were organized. Primarily agricultural in nature, they flourished briefly and then withered away. Another hundred or so cooperative farm ventures, many of them associated with religious groups, were established during the past century. A few continue to operate, largely among certain religious sects in the North Central states. A limited number of such ventures in Western Canada have achieved somewhat more success and stability.

Another cooperative farming development was that sponsored by the Farm Security Administration. In the late 1930s, twenty-two cooperative farms were organized. They had about 400 members and tilled some 27,000 acres. Title to the land remained with the Farm Security Administration, which also provided the operating capital. Member-operators leased the land they worked for a five-year period. After five years, most projects were liquidated. Failure was attributed to (1) selection of members largely from lower social strata of society, (2) inadequate training, (3) absence of a common bond that would hold the group together, and (4) lack of understanding of basic cooperative principles.

Cooperative farming in India and Israel has received considerable attention. The Israeli kibbutz (which gradually has become also industrial) is well known. It is a communal village controlled by functional committees, and it often serves as a defense outpost as well as a cooperative farming venture. (See Chapter 7 for further details.)

Cooperative farms vary in structure from one extreme, in which members own land but directors develop production and marketing plans and a hired manager executes them, to the other extreme of collective ownership, where plans and operations are worked out by the individual cooperative members. The latter cooperatives differ completely from the compulsory collective farms of communistic countries and should not be confused with them.

Labor cooperatives may also represent landless workers who join together in order to work for others. The Sequoia Farm Labor Association, Sequoia, California, is an example. Through an elected board of directors, members select their own boss and determine the type of work they can qualify for. By scheduling work, they seek increased employment and income. At the same time, the Sequoia Farm Labor Association assumes responsibility for supplying employers with experienced and dependable workers. The cooperative also serves members by conducting training programs, furnishing bus transportation, organizing a federal credit union, and qualifying them for unemployment insurance.

Handicraft Cooperatives While handicraft cooperatives have been in operation in the United States for more than fifty years, it is only within the past decade that they have become well established. Currently, some 250 are known to be in operation. Nearly half of them are in the five Appalachian states of West Virginia, Kentucky, Tennessee, Virginia, and North Carolina. Handicraft cooperatives also are important in New Mexico and New York.

These cooperatives strive to achieve quality production by furnishing necessary supplies and providing training programs. They follow up with a marketing program that emphasizes retail and/or wholesale sales. Members per association range from half a dozen or so to over 100.

In the Southwest, American Indians constitute the majority of the membership in craft cooperatives. They specialize in making jewelry from silver and semiprecious stones, baskets, beadware, and ceramic and pottery items. In Alaska, native members of handicraft cooperatives produce a large number of specialty items from local materials.

Special Service Cooperatives Workers also may organize cooperatives that provide many special services. They include transport, architectural, entertainment, and repair services.

Fishery Cooperatives

Membership in fishery cooperatives in the United States generally consists of people who own fishing boats. They usually hire a small crew that is paid either a straight salary or a percentage of the catch. Although the boat owners may also be workers, they essentially perform an entrepreneurial function.

These cooperatives usually perform one or more of three functions:

1 Processing and marketing of fish
2 Obtaining necessary supplies and equipment
3 Providing various related services needed in the fishery business, such as insurance

As of 1974, the Bureau of Fisheries reported 102 fishery cooperatives in the United States. Of these, thirty-seven were in Alaska; twenty were in the three Pacific states of Washington, Oregon, and California; and nineteen were in the New England states. These cooperatives reported 6,243 craft and 7,098 members. Fourteen are active along the East and Gulf Coasts, and four in the Great Lakes and inland areas.

There are several inland cooperatives engaged in the production, processing, and marketing of catfish. They have come into being since 1960 and are located in the Southern states. Actually, these cooperatives operate in much the same way that a farmer cooperative does, in that they provide their producer-members with marketing services and needed production supplies.

Business Persons' Cooperatives

Business persons' cooperatives usually develop in response to the needs of entrepreneurs and generally appear in retail businesses, light industry, and services. Illustrations of such cooperatives follow.

Cooperative Grocery Chains By far the most prevalent type of business persons' cooperative in the United States is the wholesale cooperative that is owned by the individual retailers who use its services. According to *Chain Store Guide,* in 1972 nearly 35,000 local retail distributors had established 134 cooperatively owned wholesale chains that provided and distributed a wide assortment of food-related products and services.

A somewhat similar development, known as the "voluntary chain," was largely motivated by wholesale grocers who, in order to meet strong competition, have made their services available to retail grocers more or less along cooperative lines. In 1972 there were some 730 voluntary chains serving some 65,000 stores.

Cooperative and voluntary chains varied in scope of operations from those handling specialty products to those providing a complete line of fresh and processed foods. As of 1975, these chains served about 43 percent of the 232,000 operating retail food stores in the United States.

Wholesale cooperatives also serve such groups as retail hardware merchants, druggists, bakery groups, and fish distributors.

Cooperative Business Services Not unlike workers, business executives sometimes come together to provide various services needed in their operations. The more important ones are transportation, insurance, engineering, architectural assistance, and repair services.

The Associated Press is a good example of how businesses join together on a cooperative basis to provide needed services. Organized in 1848 by six New York City newspapers, it currently provides news and picture services for over 8,000 newspapers and radio and television stations in more than 100 countries. It operates on an annual budget of over $50 million, leases about 475,000 miles of wire to carry its reports, and receives from members all the local and regional news they collect.

Railroads, to illustrate further, jointly own and operate the Railway Express Agency (REA) on a cooperative basis. Railroads also jointly own and operate railroad bridges on the same basis. Other examples of cooperative services established by businesses are merchants' credit bureaus, banks' clearing corporations, and florists' telegraphic delivery services.

AREAS SERVED

Cooperatives are also classified by the area they serve. Actually, four types of cooperatives may be identified in this way—local, regional, national, and international. The basis for this classification is not entirely clear-cut. It often reflects a mixture of the size of business operations and the various functions that cooperatives perform.

Local Cooperatives

When all types of local cooperatives are taken into consideration—farmers marketing, purchasing, and service associations; various types of consumer cooperatives; credit, insurance, and irrigation cooperatives; and miscellaneous associations—there are at least 45,000 local cooperatives operating in the United States. They generally operate from a trading center and have individuals as their members. Some variations, however, exist from area to area and among different types of cooperatives. In Ohio, Indiana, and Illinois, for example, the usual practice is for farm supply cooperatives to operate on a county basis. Since their coverage may include anywhere from one to ten trading centers, it is not uncommon for the cooperative to have a central facility located in the county seat, with a number of branch units serving local trading centers. In the upper Midwest, particularly in Wisconsin, Minnesota, and the Dakotas, as well as in the Far West, cooperatives tend to organize primarily around individual trading centers rather than on a county basis.

The Farmers Union Mercantile Company, Grinnell, Kansas, is an example of a local cooperative. Organized in 1944, it reported 1,528 members and 1,922 patrons in 1972. Business volume was nearly $3 million, just over half of which was due to grain and the rest to supplies and consumer goods, including carpets and furniture. The Grinnell cooperative operates grain elevators in three towns, and members have invested over $1.5 million in it. Savings refunded to patrons in 1972 were $313,000. The cooperative had a payroll of $205,000 for twenty-seven full-time employees. In 1972, it paid out $30,000 in real estate and property taxes, $20,000 for utilities, and $10,000 for insurance premiums.

Regional Cooperatives

Regional cooperatives operate in territories that range in size from several counties to several states. These cooperatives are primarily organized to provide wholesaling and manufacturing services that local associations, because of limited size and resources, are unable to provide. In other words, they enable members further to integrate their operations.

Regional cooperatives enable marketing cooperatives to move products closer to the eventual consumer. They do it by expanding their operations from performing simple assembling and storage functions to providing processing and merchandising services. Supply cooperatives, in turn, integrate back to sources of raw materials. They, like cooperative grocery regionals, provide wholesale manufacturing and service functions for their local members.

An example of a mixed type of regional cooperative is Southern States Cooperative, Inc., Richmond, Virginia. Organized in 1923 as the Virginia Seed Service, in

1973 it reported serving 243,000 members in Virginia, West Virginia, Kentucky, Delaware, and Maryland through some 475 affiliated distributive outlets. Net sales were $180 million. It markets grain, eggs, and wool; distributes a complete line of farm supplies; and operates feed mills, fertilizer plants, seed-cleaning plants, a petroleum terminal, and a number of wholesale warehouses.

National Cooperatives

Certain specialized services are so unique and so limited in nature that even regional cooperatives may not be able to provide them efficiently. This need has led to the establishment of national associations. Universal Cooperatives, Inc., Alliance, Ohio, which was recently formed by the merger of two national associations—United Cooperatives, Alliance, Ohio, and National Cooperatives, Albert Lea, Minnesota—serves as an example. This organization manufactures milking machines, mixes paints, blends lubricating oil, contracts for the manufacturing of tires and various automotive supplies, and handles certain grocery items for some of its members.

International Cooperatives

Cooperatives also operate on an international basis. Some have their headquarters in the United States; others, in foreign countries. Examples are:

International Cooperative Petroleum Association (ICPA) New York City. This association was organized in 1947 to provide lubricating oils and related services for national cooperatives in Belgium, Denmark, Egypt, France, Germany, Holland, Scotland, Sri-Lanka (Ceylon), Sweden, and Switzerland. The association emphasizes that it provides members with the services and products they need. Through its oil-blending plant in Dordrecht, Holland, it furnishes lubricating oil to members. It provides technical assistance to member associations for the construction of their own oil-blending facilities. ICPA also helps member associations obtain basic raw petroleum materials and a wide range of related goods and services. Two United States regional cooperatives are members and supply lubricating oil to other members. Sales for the 1974 fiscal year totaled $8.5 million, and savings before taxes—of which about 50 percent was distributed as patronage refunds—were $745,000.

The Scandinavian Cooperative Wholesale Society [*Nordisk Andelsforbund (NAF)*], *Copenhagen, Denmark.* This organization includes in its membership thirteen national wholesale societies located in the five Scandinavian countries—Denmark, Iceland, Finland, Norway, and Sweden. Starting in 1918, annual volume has grown until, in 1971, it approximated $120 million. Principal products handled or manufactured include lamps and light bulbs, TV appliances, washing powder, chocolate and other confectionery items, and aerosol products. In addition, some joint buying has developed among this society and wholesale societies of some of the ECA countries.

Cooperative Fertilizers International (CFI), Chicago. This organization is a somewhat different type of international venture. It started with a $1 million contribution by Americans to assist in the development of the Indian Farmers Fertilizer Cooperative (IFFCO). With the encouragement of the Cooperative League of the U.S.A. (CLUSA), the U.S. Agency for International Development (AID), the government of India, Indian cooperatives, U.N. Overseas Development Administration, and the Dutch government, resources were coordinated, financing was obtained, and construction was undertaken. The result is a $127 million investment in two plant complexes at Kalol and Kandla, in the state of Gujarat, that will ultimately be owned and operated by participating Indian cooperatives. The Kalol plant has a daily capacity of 910 metric tons of ammonia and 1,200 metric tons of urea, and the Kandla plant has a yearly capacity of 400,000 metric tons of mixed fertilizer.

FUNCTIONS PERFORMED

The preceding classification of groups and areas served also brings into focus the various functions that cooperatives may perform and how they perform them. They are marketing, purchasing, and the provision of services.

Marketing

Local marketing cooperatives are generally the point of contact with producer-members. These cooperatives assemble products and often serve as the transportation or forwarding agent in moving products on to central markets or direct to processors. Processing cooperatives, as the name implies, change the form of the product. For example, some dairy cooperatives convert raw milk to butter, cheese, ice cream, and pasteurized fluid milk. Other cooperatives can or freeze fresh fruits and vegetables. Central market wholesalers assemble products in large lots for sale to manufacturers, processors, jobbers, or international traders. Grain and cotton regional marketing associations demonstrate how cooperatives provide this marketing function.

Purchasing

Local retail cooperatives or branch units of regionals are local retail or distribution points for serving patrons. They are generally serviced by cooperative wholesalers that assemble the many production supplies and consumer items that local cooperatives distribute. These regional wholesale cooperatives also usually engage in manufacturing and processing. They, for example, may manufacture feed, refine petroleum products, process fertilizers, and manufacture appliances and equipment.

Services

Specialized cooperatives, for example, provide credit, insurance, health care, housing, irrigation, electrical and telephone, and any other of the many services required by patrons.

SIZE OF COOPERATIVES

There are many ways of measuring the size of cooperatives. This may be done, for example, by the volume of business, the number of members, or the dollars of assets. The most common way of measuring size, however, is by the annual volume of business. The Farmer Cooperative Service assembles information as to the gross and net annual business volume of marketing, purchasing, and related service cooperatives.

The percentage distribution of these cooperatives, according to the annual net volume of business, after eliminating intercooperative volume, in 1971–1972, was:

Annual net volume (in dollars, millions)	Percentage			
	Marketing	Farm supply	Related service	Total
Under 0.5	38.3	43.0	89.4	41.0
0.5–0.9	15.3	24.5	5.9	18.4
1.0–4.9	37.2	29.2	3.3	33.7
5.0–9.9	4.8	1.9	0.7	3.7
10.0–24.9	1.8	0.4	0.7	1.3
25.0–49.9	1.1	0.3	—	0.8
50.0–99.9	0.7	0.3	—	0.5
100.0 and over	0.8	0.4	—	0.6
Total	100.0	100.0	100.0	100.0

Even though annual volume per association has increased substantially since 1971–1972 because of price inflation, these data still indicate that the great majority of cooperative business firms are small. In 1971–1972, 41 percent did less than $0.5 million of business annually, 18 percent did between $0.5 million and $1 million of business annually, about 34 percent did $1 million to $5 million of business annually, and only about 7 percent did an annual business of over $5 million (see Figure 2-1). Compared with their counterparts in the business world, cooperatives are relatively small.

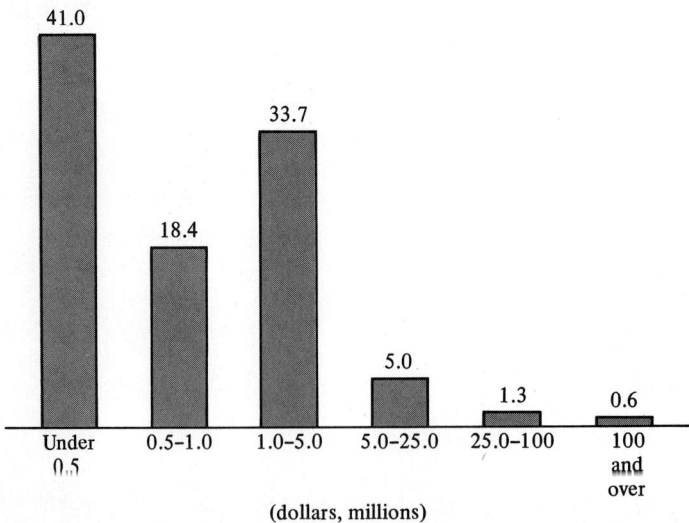

Figure 2-1 Percentage of cooperatives according to business volume, 1969–1970.

TYPES OF MEMBERSHIP

When cooperatives are classified according to type of membership, three types are recognized—federated, centralized, and mixed. This classification applies only to large-scale cooperatives that operate on a regional basis. Figure 2-2 illustrates the relations that characterize each type of membership.

Federated Cooperatives

In federated cooperatives, membership consists of local associations, and control rests with these locals. They have responsibility for electing directors and providing general operating guidance for their federation. All savings resulting from the operation of a federated cooperative are distributed to its local member associations in proportion to the volume of business they do with their federation. The Farmers Union Central Exchange, Inc. (CENEX), St. Paul, Minnesota, is an example of a federated cooperative. All its $300 million farm supply business in 1973 was distributed to about 1,150 local cooperative patrons.

Centralized Cooperatives

Centralized cooperatives are characterized by direct service to patron-users. The basis for distinguishing between local and centralized regional cooperatives generally is their size, methods of operation, and the functions they perform. National Grape Cooperative Association, Inc., Westfield, New York, is an example of a regional centralized cooperative. Farmer members own and operate all assembling, processing, and distributing facilities through their wholly owned subsidiary, Welch Foods Inc., formerly the nationally famous Welch Grape Juice Company, Inc. Another centralized cooperative is Agway, Inc., Syracuse, New York, in which 105,000 farmers are direct members. It owns and operates not only manufacturing and processing units, but more than 800 local branch distributing and marketing units as well.

Mixed Cooperatives

In actual practice, regional cooperatives often operate on a mixed basis. At the same time that a mixed regional cooperative provides wholesale services to its member local associations, it also supplies its individual members with retail services through its branch units. Southern States Cooperative, Inc., Richmond, Virginia—mentioned earlier as an example of a regional cooperative—also is an example of a mixed cooperative. Either an individual farmer or an agricultural cooperative can become a member through the purchase of a $1 par value share of common stock. As of 1973, Southern States operates on a federated basis through 150 local member farm supply associations, of which 48 are entirely independent and 124 operate on a management contract basis. On a centralized basis, it operates 73 retail branches, and in addition it distributes supplies to individual members through some 250 independently owned service agencies. Grain-marketing services are provided by a separate affiliate which is managed directly by Southern States Cooperative, Inc.

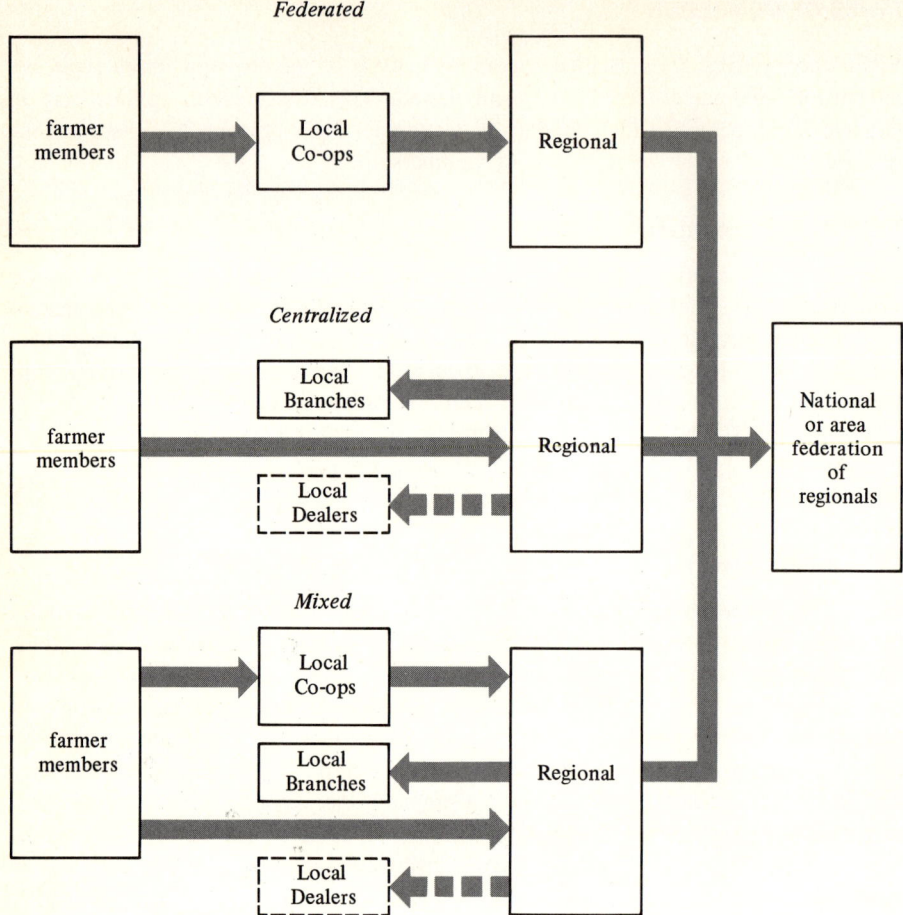

*Developed by J. Warren Mathers. See FCS Research Report 24, U.S. Department of Agriculture, Washington, p. 7.

Figure 2-2 Membership structure of cooperatives

LEGAL STATUS

Legally, cooperatives may be classified as incorporated or unincorporated. Such classification can be made regardless of size, areas and groups served, and types of membership.

Incorporated Cooperatives

Almost all the operating cooperatives are incorporated, generally under special cooperative state laws. While cooperatives are unique and distinct businesses, each one is as much a corporation as General Motors or Exxon. (The corporate nature of cooperatives is discussed in more detail in Chapters 1 and 9.)

TYPES OF COOPERATIVES

Unincorporated Cooperatives

Unincorporated associations are usually small, informally operated joint ventures that require little capital or facilities. Their basic feature is that, when they are organized for business purposes, members are individually liable for any debts and obligations. This feature makes them ill-suited for most cooperative business ventures. Machinery-use cooperatives are an example of unincorporated cooperatives. A typical machinery-use cooperative may consist of as few as three farmers who jointly own a cotton picker or a combine on the basis of mutually agreed-upon rules and regulations. Many of the early livestock shipping associations, car-door farm supply cooperatives, and the present wool pools that operate in the Appalachian mountain states are also examples of unincorporated cooperatives.

FINANCIAL STRUCTURE

Another way to classify cooperatives is according to their financial structure. Two types are recognized—stock and nonstock associations.

Stock Cooperatives

In a stock cooperative, equity is represented by ownership of shares of common or preferred stock by stockholders who are the owners. In contrast to corporations that have general provisions for the ready transfer of stock ownership, stock cooperatives usually have restrictions on the transferability of stock by members and on withdrawal from the association.

Nonstock Cooperatives

In nonstock (membership) associations, ownership is represented by membership certificates, often evidencing payment of a membership fee. Legislation providing for stock and nonstock cooperatives may be in separate legislative acts or may be a part of an overall cooperative statute. Except in the case of cooperatives, nonstock firms are not so likely to engage in business ventures. Nonstock associations that do not engage in commercial undertakings include churches, clubs, and most social organizations.

QUASI-COOPERATIVES

In actual practice, a number of business ventures may be undertaken that are only partially cooperative in nature. Such ventures exist either because of institutional limitations, such as a lack of adequate legislation, or because of the special interests of members. When such situations prevail, the resulting business enterprise frequently is referred to as a quasi-cooperative. Generally they operate in a way that enables members or users to receive many or all financial benefits from participation in them. However, members generally have limited control of operations. Proxy voting is often recognized, and quite generally the motivation for organizing this form of business comes from people other than the users of the service. Patrons participate or join primarily because experience has shown that belonging is a "good thing."

Examples of such types of joint undertaking are many. They include the large mutual insurance companies, mutual funds, condominiums, consumer rebate plans and discount bargaining organizations, and various health plans. Some government price-support or trading corporations may be classified in this category.

COOPERATIVE SERVICE AND TRADE ASSOCIATIONS

Cooperative business associations have found it desirable to establish special service and trade associations that further meet their members' specific needs and interests. For example: (1) The American Institute of Cooperation and the Cooperative League of the U.S.A. conduct educational programs for many types of associations; (2) the National Council of Farmer Cooperatives monitors national legislation and government programs of interest to cooperatives; and (3) various producer, commodity, and service cooperatives have national organizations that look after their specific legislative interests and service needs. (For details on these organizations, see Chapter 8.)

FACTORS INFLUENCING TYPES OF COOPERATIVES ESTABLISHED

The preceding observations on the types of cooperatives raise the question: What are the reasons for the different degree of success achieved by each? It is hard to give definitive answers, but it is possible to identify some interrelated and contributing factors.

Need

Most individuals have little interest in cooperatives unless they think that through them they can accomplish things that they cannot do alone. The need for cooperatives exists among many American farmers, for example, because their operations are relatively small and scattered, and market outlets and sources of needed production supplies often are far away. There are, however, other areas where the need for cooperatives has been great but progress at best has been modest. Examples are consumer goods, health services, and housing.

Capital Requirements

Financial requirements for different types of cooperatives vary widely. It takes comparatively little money to start a credit union or to run a mutual fire insurance company or a mutual grazing association. On the other hand, when an agricultural cooperative goes into the refining of petroleum products, the manufacture of fertilizer, or the refining of sugar beets, capital requirements become tremendous. In some cases, members may be able to raise the necessary funds; in other cases, such as the rural electric cooperatives, they have to obtain government assistance. (For further information, see Chapter 15.)

Management

Cooperative leaders have often failed to recognize the importance of qualified and competent management in achieving cooperative success. Furthermore, the unique nature of cooperative management, with its separate responsibilities for members, directors, and staff, sometimes is not well understood by those interested in establishing various types of cooperatives. (For further details, see Chapter 13.)

Understanding (Education)

A well-planned communication program is necessary if cooperatives are to achieve maximum effectiveness. Such a program helps members and directors understand the unique nature of cooperatives and the need for good business performance. Moreover, various publics need to understand how cooperatives are organized and operated if a favorable environment for cooperative growth is to prevail. The need for education applies specially to educators, legislators, and the general public.

While we pride ourselves in the United States on the degree of literacy we have achieved, realistically, we must agree that much economic and social illiteracy still prevails. Cooperative leaders too often have a limited understanding of the nature of business enterprise and the various socioeconomic forces—local, national, and international—that have a bearing on cooperative operations. (Cooperative communication problems are discussed in further detail in Chapter 14.)

Preemption of the Field

In many areas, cooperatives have failed to succeed because other forms of business were already well entrenched. These businesses may or may not be providing the desired services at a reasonable cost. If they are doing so, the need for a cooperative may not exist. But even if they are not, the competition cooperatives will encounter may prevent them from entering the field or cause them to fail if they do.

Institutional Factors

Institutional factors may be important in determining the success or failure of a cooperative venture. For example, are the legislature, courts, and government officials favorable, unfavorable, or neutral? Moreover, in any given country the stability and continuity of a favorable governmental policy will do much to assure successful cooperative business ventures.

Services Desired

From time to time there is speculation as to why farm supply cooperatives have grown faster and become relatively more important than consumer cooperatives. Officials of farm supply cooperatives have pointed out that to some extent this is so because farmers buy in larger lots than consumers, thereby having greater needs and achieving greater benefits. Under these circumstances, there is more inducement and opportunity to achieve successful operations. Another factor may be the greater stability of membership in farmer cooperatives in contrast with a large turnover among members of urban cooperatives.

Special Problems of Workers' Cooperatives

While it would appear that there are many inducements for workers to join forces to further their own business interests, there are certain built-in limitations. Workers often find themselves in the dual and conflicting role of laborer and entrepreneur at the same time. Moreover, members quite frequently are people who have had difficulty in getting employment elsewhere or in adjusting to accepted work and cultural patterns. This possibility suggests that careful selection of members is essential and that methods of remuneration must be given careful attention to achieve wage equitability.

SUMMARY

To summarize, the types of cooperatives discussed in this chapter are classified as follows:

    Groups served
      Agricultural producers
        Marketing cooperatives
        Production supply cooperatives
        Service cooperatives
        Credit cooperatives
        Mutual insurance cooperatives
        Mutual irrigation cooperatives
        Dairy-herd improvement cooperatives
        Artificial breeding cooperatives
        Machinery-use cooperatives
      Consumer cooperatives
        Consumer goods cooperatives
        Credit cooperatives
        Health cooperatives
        Housing cooperatives
        Insurance cooperatives
        Recreation cooperatives
        Other consumer cooperatives
      Worker cooperatives
        Industrial worker cooperatives
        Agricultural worker cooperatives
        Handicraft cooperatives
        Fishery cooperatives
        Business persons' cooperatives
          Grocery chains
          Cooperative business services
      Area served
        Local cooperatives
        Regional cooperatives
        National cooperatives
        International cooperatives
      Functions performed
        Marketing
        Purchasing
        Services

Size of business
Type of membership
  Federated cooperatives
  Centralized cooperatives
  Mixed cooperatives
Legal status
  Incorporated cooperatives
  Unincorporated cooperatives
Financial structure
  Stock cooperatives
  Nonstock cooperatives
Quasi-cooperatives
Trade and service cooperatives

QUESTIONS

1. Identify the various ways of classifying cooperatives, and indicate the principal kinds of cooperatives found in each type.
2. Identify the kinds of cooperatives operating in your home community. How would you classify them?
3. What is the basis for distinguishing between a production supply cooperative and a consumer cooperative?
4. Why is it difficult to classify cooperatives?
5. How can we account for differences in the relative progress of various types of cooperatives?
6. What factors have contributed to the increase in the number of multipurpose (mixed function) cooperatives in the United States?
7. Why are most local cooperatives affiliated with one or more regional associations?
8. Why do regional cooperatives establish federations of regionals?
9. What are the advantages and disadvantages of incorporating and of not incorporating cooperatives?
10. What are the advantages of stock and membership types of organization for cooperatives?
11. Why have handicraft, recreation, and machinery-use cooperatives achieved their greatest prominence since 1960? What is their probable future?
12. Compare opportunities for the further development of the two oldest types of producer cooperatives: farmers cooperatives and workers cooperatives.

REFERENCES

Berman, Katrina V.: *Worker Owned Plywood Companies,* Washington State University Press, Pullman, 1967, chaps. 6–8 and 13, pp. 95–128, 180–220.

Foundation for Cooperative Housing: *Cooperative Housing in the United States,* Washington, 1972, p. 24.

Knapp, Joseph G.: *The Rise of American Cooperative Enterprise: 1620–1920,* The Interstate, Danville, Ill., 1969, chaps. 1–4 and 21, pp. 5–98, 393–417.

McMillan, Leslie D.: *Organizing and Operating Fishery Cooperatives in the United States,* Circular 155, U.S. Department of Interior, Bureau of Commercial Fisheries, Washington, 1963.

Neely, Morrison D.: *Legal Phases of Farmer Cooperatives*, FCS Information 100, U.S. Department of Agriculture, Washington, 1976, p. 750.

Packel, Israel: *The Organization and Operation of Cooperatives,* 4th ed., American Law Institute and the American Bar Association, Philadelphia, Pa., 1970, chap. 1, pp. 6–23.

Parker, Florence E.: *The First 125 Years,* Cooperative League of the U.S.A., Washington, D.C., 1955, pp. 37–321.

Seymour, William R.: *The Cooperative Approach to Outdoor Recreation,* FCS Information 57, U.S. Department of Agriculture, Washington, 1968.

――――: *American Crafts: A Rich Heritage and a Rich Future,* FCS Program Aid 1026, U.S. Department of Agriculture, Washington, 1972, p. 16.

Thurston, Stanley K.: *35th Annual Report of the Regional Grain Cooperatives,* FCS Service Report 144, U.S. Department of Agriculture, Washington, 1975, p. 34.

Tucker, George C.: *Need for Restructuring Dairy Cooperatives,* FCS Service Report 125, U.S. Department of Agriculture, Washington, 1972.

U.S. Department of Agriculture: *Farmers Cooperatives in the United States,* FCS Bulletin 1, rev., Washington, 1965, pp. 87–333.

――――: *Major Regional Cooperative Supply Operations,* FCS Research Report 29, Washington, 1975.

――――: "Articles on Forestry Cooperatives," *News for Farmer Cooperatives,* Reprint No. 355, Washington, 1962–1968.

Williams, Raymond, and Lloyd C. Biser: *Analysis of Emerging Cooperatives, 1965–1970,* FCS Information 85, U.S. Department of Agriculture, Washington, 1972.

Chapter 3

Cooperative Principles

We shall now consider *how* cooperatives should be operated if members are to achieve the objectives they had in mind when they organized their cooperatives.

Webster's Third New International Dictionary (unabridged) in defining the word "principle" includes the definitions: "A governing law of conduct"; "a general or fundamental truth"; "a comprehensive or fundamental law."

We should expect, therefore, that cooperative principles would give us some useful clues as to how these associations are organized and operated. These indications are important because many cooperative scholars disagree on what does or does not constitute basic cooperative principles, especially as compared with sound or common operating practices. Understanding cooperative principles should help us to identify those characteristics that set cooperatives apart from other types of organizations or businesses.

ROCHDALE CONTRIBUTIONS

The Rochdale pioneers established the first permanent cooperative in England in 1844. They contributed both the principles and the results of practical operating experience to the development of cooperatives. They also drew on the experience of other cooperative pioneers in developing their ideas and operating practices.

Principles

Rochdale principles are accepted by many people as the distinguishing trademarks of cooperative business. Catherine Webb, in *Industrial Cooperation–The Story of a Peaceful Revolution* (5th ed., Cooperative Union, Ltd., Manchester, 1912), states that the Rochdale Society in its *Annual Almanac* of 1860 set forth the rules of conduct and points of organization relating to the business activities of the Society as:

1. That capital should be of their own providing and bear a fixed rate of interest
2. That only the purest provisions procurable should be supplied to members
3. That full weight and measure should be given
4. That market prices should be charged and no credit given nor asked
5. That "profits" should be divided *pro rata* upon the amount of purchases made by each member
6. That the principle of "one member one vote" should obtain in government and the equality of the sexes in membership
7. That the management should be in the hands of officers and committees elected periodically
8. That a definite percentage of profits should be allotted to education
9. That frequent statements and balance sheets should be presented to members

These rules of conduct, commonly called the Rochdale principles, therefore did not appear suddenly as a "revelation from on high." Rather, on a trial-and-error basis lasting more than sixteen years, they evolved as many amendments to practical rules for operating a small, local consumer cooperative under the conditions that prevailed in the middle of the nineteenth century. Their manner of development largely accounts for variations in the opinion of cooperative scholars as to the wording of the Rochdale principles, their number, and the time of their development.

Professor Paul Lambert, of the University of Liège, Belgium, for example, suggests that three additional principles are a part of the Rochdale kit of tools. These are: (1) disposal of net assets without profit to members in the event of dissolution; (2) promotion of member interests only if they are consistent with the interests of the community; and (3) achievement of a "cooperative commonwealth."[1]

Antecedent Cooperative Ideas

It is to the credit of the Rochdale pioneers that they drew on the experience of other cooperators in putting together a set of rules and practices that led to the establishment of a successful cooperative business—the first to stand the test of time.

The practical members of Rochdale would be the first to acknowledge that they benefited greatly from those who went before. Specifically:

- They built on the ideas of Robert Owen and Charles Fourier, whose cooperative views they accepted and whose basic objectives they also hoped eventually to achieve. From these men they adopted the concepts of voluntary and democratic types of associated business efforts that emphasized service instead of profits.

---

[1] Paul Lambert, *Studies in the Social Philosophy of Cooperation*, Cooperative League of the U.S.A., Washington, D.C., 1963, p. 63.

- They probably accepted the idea of distributing the yearly surplus among members on a patronage basis from the Lennoxtown Society of Scotland. This society was organized in 1812, and in 1826 was the first known consumers' society to put the patronage refund idea into practice.
- They were in agreement with the views of Dr. William King, who in 1827 organized a consumer cooperative at Brighton, England, that was to serve as a model for hundreds of local societies in the 1830s. He emphasized that (1) cooperation was voluntary and not compulsory, and (2) cooperatives should be neutral as to political and religious tenets.
- Observing that uncontrolled credit was responsible for the failure of a cooperative store at Rochdale in 1835 after only two years of operation, the Pioneers established a firm cash trading policy that contributed much to their success. This policy provided a sound basis for a later statement by Prof. Charles Gide, noted French cooperative scholar: "The cooperative societies which succumbed, did not die for nothing."[2]
- They built upon, and were influenced by, the experiences of the medieval guilds, friendly societies, and "penny capitalists." These groups all experimented with new ways of working together. Their experiences undoubtedly contributed to the fund of knowledge that went into the development of what have come to be known as the Rochdale principles.

Although the Rochdale pioneers were followers of Owen and Dr. William King and hoped eventually to establish an ideal cooperative communal society, they also were realists. Hence they were willing to take one step at a time, and their first objective was to obtain better-quality food and clothing at reasonable prices. The many aspects of running local stores, developing a federated wholesale service, and operating manufacturing plants took all their resources and energies. The idea of establishing a cooperative commonwealth could come later. Except for the writings of some cooperative idealists and social reformers, and excluding attempts to operate on a cooperative commonwealth basis by small isolated groups—mostly religious sects—this idea never again received serious consideration among students of cooperation.

Evaluation

Many people revered the Rochdale principles as the accepted catechism of fundamental cooperative thought. Professor Lambert tells us: "Far from becoming outmoded the Rochdale principles represent, in their essence, everything that is new and hopeful in our modern civilization."[3] But there were and are dissenters. These dissenters recognize the pragmatic traits of the Rochdale pioneers insofar as they built on the experience of others and adjusted their operations to changing conditions that confronted them. They point out, however, that the pioneers only sought to develop practical guidelines to run a local cooperative under conditions that prevailed more than 125 years ago. Those conditions were characterized by degrading mass poverty and the difficult adjustments required to meet the impact of the embryonic but fast-developing industrial revolution. Critics ask: "How can the Rochdale principles serve to guide cooperatives in the changing and complex economy in which they operate today?"

[2] Ibid., p. 13.
[3] Ibid., p. 90.

A practical question for cooperators, therefore, is whether or not these principles have application to conditions that will prevail in the 1970s and 1980s. Profound political, social, and economic development has recently occurred. Some cooperatives now operate on both a national and an international basis. Their operations often are highly integrated, and their business volume amounts to hundreds of millions of dollars annually. This is in sharp contrast to the initial efforts of the twenty-eight weavers at Rochdale.

Some of the principles developed by the Rochdale pioneers, however, have stood the test of time and are recognized as basic even today. Their contributions to cooperative development throughout Great Britain and the rest of the world have been far-reaching.

The first three Rochdale principles listed in Figure 3-1, with some refinements in terminology, provide the essential ideas that comprise what most cooperative scholars, even today, generally accept as the basic principles of cooperation. These are expressed as: (1) service at cost, (2) democratic control, and (3) limited returns on equity capital. Some thinkers have emphasized a fourth principle—education of members.

These principles, together with other cooperative concepts, will be examined in greater detail later in this chapter.

It is no discredit to the members of Rochdale that most of their remaining so-called principles are not uniquely cooperative but, in reality, are only sound operating practices that have application to most types of business venture. They were realistic guidelines that helped the Rochdale group to deal with practical problems of the day. Adherence to them, moreover, put the pioneers in the forefront in introducing improved business practices—especially charging market prices, operating on a cash purchase and sales basis, and insisting on purity and quality in the products they handled.

Political and religious neutrality, while desirable, are not universally followed. England, for instance, has a Cooperative Party, and in the Netherlands and Belgium many cooperatives are organized along Protestant and Catholic lines. Likewise, the practices of marketing cooperatives and some other types of associations suggest that open membership is frequently not a practical or necessary operating guideline. (These and other practices are examined in greater detail in a subsequent section of this chapter.)

Further questions arise about cooperative principles. Are they timeless, just waiting to be discovered, and do they have universal validity? This was a suggestion advanced by Prof. Henry H. Bakken, now retired from the University of Wisconsin, in a talk, "A Critique of the Rochdale Principles of Cooperation," given in 1961. Others see cooperative principles as flexible and responsive to various types of cooperative activity, stages of development, and changes in economic and political institutions.

We do not know how the Rochdale pioneers looked upon the permanency of the rules they established to guide their operations. Since they were realists, it seems reasonable to assume that they believed that changing conditions would lead to modifications. The reverence with which some admirers have adhered to Rochdale principles, however, suggests that they have considered the Principles to be of universal validity and subject to little change over time.

EVOLUTIONARY DEVELOPMENT IN THE UNITED STATES

Cooperative leaders have gradually distinguished between what may be termed cooperative principles and business practices. We have indicated that, at least in the United States, there seems to be reasonably general agreement that basic cooperative principles relate to who benefits from operations, who controls operations, and what the role of capital is. Figure 3-1 gives a comparative summary of the thinking on cooperative principles of the Rochdale pioneers, selected cooperative students in the United States, and the International Cooperative Alliance.

Edwin G. Nourse

In his benchmark article "The Economic Philosophy of Cooperation" in the *American Economic Review* (1922), Dr. Nourse emphasized: (1) democratic control, (2) minimum interest on invested capital, and (3) the distribution of savings as patronage refunds.

Henry H. Bakken and Marvin A. Schaars

In their well-known college textbook *The Economics of Cooperative Marketing*,[4] Professors Bakken and Schaars, both then with the University of Wisconsin, list nine principles of cooperative sales associations: (1) membership selection; (2) functional and commodity specialization; (3) democratic representation; (4) service at cost; (5) savings prorated to members on a patronage basis; (6) no unusual risk assumption; (7) attitude of nonpartisanship and nonsectarianism; (8) dissemination of information to membership; and (9) control and ownership of marketing facilities and institutions. They also list seven principles for cooperative purchasing associations: (1) open membership; (2) democratic control; (3) dividends on purchases; (4) limited interest on capital; (5) political and religious neutrality; (6) cash trading; and (7) promotion of education.

Ward W. Fetrow

Dr. Fetrow, in *Three Principles of Agricultural Cooperation*,[5] stresses the following as three basic cooperative principles: (1) democratic control; (2) limited returns on capital; and (3) sharing savings in proportion to patronage.

Marvin A. Schaars

Professor Schaars, in *American Cooperation*,[6] identifies (1) service at cost, (2) democratic control, and (3) limited returns on equity capital as "hard-core principles." In addition to these, he recognizes principles applicable to different types of cooperatives as (1) open or selective membership, (2) single or multiple commodity operation, and (3) cash trading. He further identifies eight "fringe principles." They are: (1) financ-

---

[4] McGraw-Hill, New York, 1937.
[5] FCS Circular E24, rev., U.S. Department of Agriculture, Washington, 1940.
[6] Marvin A. Schaars, "Basic Principles of Cooperatives—Their Growth and Development," *American Cooperation*, American Institute of Cooperation, Washington, D.C., 1951, pp. 835–852.

Figure 3-1 Cooperative Principles and Practices

Rochdale pioneers[a]	Nourse	Fetrow	Bakken	Schaars	International Cooperative Alliance
Profits divided pro rata on purchases	Savings distributed as patronage refunds[c]	Sharing savings in proportion to patronage	Service at cost	Service at cost	Earnings belong to members[g]
One man, one vote in government[b]	Democratic control	Democratic control	Democratic representation	Democratic control	Democratic control (one man, one vote in local cooperatives)
Capital provided by members and at a fixed rate	Limited returns on capital	Limited returns on capital	Deemphasis of capital	Limited interest on equity capital	Limited interest or none on shares of stock
Percentage of profits allocated to education	—	—	Promotion of education	Promotion of education[e]	Education of members, employees, and public
Equality of sexes in membership[b]	—	—	Selective vs. open membership and political, religious, and racial neutrality	Selective vs. open membership[f] and political and religious neutrality	Voluntary membership—no restrictions as to race, political views, and religious beliefs
—	Increased efficiency[d]	—	—	Striving for business efficiency[e]	—
—	—	—	Commodity and functional specialization	Single vs. multiple commodity operation[f]	—
—	—	—	Control and ownership of marketing facilities and service installations	Control and ownership of market facilities[e]	—
—	—	—	—	—	Cooperation among cooperatives on local, national and international levels

[a] In addition, the Rochdale pioneers listed the following principles which now are generally considered operating practices: (1) cash sales, (2) sales at market prices, (3) frequent statement of operations for members, (4) management in officers and a periodically elected committee, (5) provisions handled should be purest available, (6) full weights and measures given.
[b] Expressed as one combined principle.
[c] Discussed under the general concept of distribution.
[d] Achieved through open membership, prohibition of proxy voting, and maintenance of loan status of equity capital.
[e] "Fringe principles." Others include: (1) selling at market prices, (2) financing in proportion to patronage, (3) expanding operations through integration, and (4) disseminating information to members and patrons.
[f] Applicable to different types of cooperatives.
[g] Members may decide to: (1) provide for future cooperative development, (2) establish consumer services, or (3) distribute in proportion to patronage.

ing an association in proportion to patronage; (2) selling goods at market prices; (3) striving for business efficiency; (4) expanding operations—horizontal, vertical, and circular integration; (5) controlling or owning marketing facilities; (6) political, religious, and racial neutrality; (7) promotion of education in cooperatives—history, theory, philosophy, and principles; and (8) disseminating information to members and patrons.

Henry H. Bakken

Professor Bakken has grouped cooperative principles into three categories. They are:

Principles governing membership: (1) open membership; (2) selective membership; (3) democratic representation; and (4) commodity and functional specialization.

Principles affecting wealth accumulation and income distribution: (1) service at cost; (2) from each according to his capacity, to each according to his contribution; (3) deemphasis of capital; (4) no unusual risk assumption; and (5) control or ownership of marketing facilities and service institutions.

Principles relating to social advancement: (1) political, religious, and racial equality; and (2) promotion of education.[7]

International Cooperative Alliance

Cooperative principles no doubt have been subjected to more discussion and analysis by cooperative students abroad than in the United States. Although there are wide differences in their views, they approach a consensus in their general acceptance (with some reservations) of the principles approved by the International Cooperative Alliance.[8] The most recent version (1969) listed basic cooperative principles as (1) voluntary membership without restrictions as to race, political views, and religious beliefs; (2) democratic control; (3) limited interest or no interest on shares of stock; (4) earnings to belong to members, and method of distribution to be decided by them; (5) education of members, advisors, employees, and the public at large; and (6) cooperation among cooperatives on local, national, and international levels.

BASIC COOPERATIVE PRINCIPLES REEXAMINED

We have mentioned that three principles—service at cost (sometimes expressed as pro rata distribution of saving on the basis of patronage or benefits according to use),

---

[7]Henry H. Bakken, *Basic Concepts, Principles, and Practices of Cooperation,* Mimir Publications, Madison, Wis., 1963, pp. 38–77.

[8]An exception is Prof. Paul Lambert (op. cit., pp. 239–243), who discusses "the essential nature of cooperation" under the following headings: (1) self-help; (2) voluntary nature; (3) mutual aid; (4) democratic autonomy; (5) profit ruled out; (6) educational purposes; (7) the socialistic nature; and (8) striving to conquer. Professor Hans H. Munkner, in *Cooperative Principles and Cooperative Law* (Marburg/Lahn, West Germany, 1974), lists cooperative principles as: (1) mutual assistance through association; (2) member promotion; (3) identity; (4) democratic management and control; (5) economic efficiency; (6) voluntary association; (7) autonomy; (8) fair and just distribution of results; (9) open membership; (10) indivisible reserve fund; and (11) promotion of education.

member control, and limited returns on capital—have gained acceptance among American and other cooperators as basic cooperative principles. Two other concepts merit consideration as key cooperative principles. One, member ownership, while perhaps implied, generally has not been singled out for specific recognition as a principle. The other, duty to educate, has, in one form or another, been accepted more widely in many other countries than in the United States.

With the passage of time, the three basic principles also have been subjected to refinements and modifications which the International Cooperative Alliance Commission described in 1966 as "clearing up confusion and removing rigidity rooted in unbalanced or oversimplified interpretations. . . ." This statement suggests that the following terminology best describes the five principles that seem basic and that are in most common use in explaining how cooperatives must be organized and operated if members are to achieve the essential objectives they have in mind:

- Operation at cost
- Member control
- Member ownership
- Limited returns on equity capital
- Duty to educate

Operation at Cost

Operation or service at cost is a key feature of cooperative business enterprise. Other businesses that provide the same services as cooperatives seek to realize profits for the benefit of investors. Cooperatives, in contrast, are not operated to make profits from dealing with their members. Moreover, they seek to provide services that result in increased net income for their patrons.[9]

A good example of differences in the basic objectives of cooperatives and other businesses is found in the situation that prevailed when fertilizer prices in the United States were subject to federal price controls in 1973. Even though American farmers were short of fertilizers, business firms other than cooperatives increased their profits by selling substantial quantities in foreign markets not subject to price controls. Cooperatives, in contrast, being oriented to serve members, continued to channel their fertilizer production to patrons irrespective of the more favorable prices prevailing in foreign markets.

To operate at cost on patron business, cooperatives in the United States are obligated to distribute their net margins or savings to their patrons. Most state cooperative laws, for example, require that this distribution be done at least once annually. This provision assures operation on a cooperative basis, which is achieved through a binding agreement that requires an association to allocate all net margins or savings to

[9]Persons who use the services of cooperatives are known as patrons. Patrons may be either member-users or nonmember users. Thus, even though cooperatives start operations with an active membership, after years of operation, some members may no longer be users of the services their cooperatives provide. A member is interested in obtaining needed services and in this respect differs from a stockholder in other types of corporations whose interest is in returns on investment.

COOPERATIVE PRINCIPLES

patrons in proportion to the business they do with their cooperatives. Terms of this obligation generally are spelled out in bylaws, marketing contracts, or special resolutions. In a cooperative, all receipts above the actual costs of operation are the property of patrons. Net margins or savings, therefore, are returned to the patrons rather than remain as the unallocated property of their cooperative. It is this practice which gives rise to the often-repeated statement that a cooperative is a "nonprofit" organization. The net margins or savings, in effect, are profits of the patron rather than of the cooperative as a separate business entity.

The question may well arise: "If a cooperative operates on a cost basis with patrons, how can it have net margins or savings?" In actual practice, it is not possible for a farm supply, service, or consumer cooperative to determine what its day-to-day operating costs are. To be on the safe side, it usually charges current prices, and if it operates with reasonable efficiency, it will be "overcharging" patrons. To maintain its cooperative character, a cooperative returns these overcharges to its patrons in proportion to the volume of business each patron transacts with it.

Two things should be said about these overcharges. First, they obviously exist because costs cannot be determined when each individual transaction occurs. Second, they exist when cooperatives are successful in operating with a high degree of efficiency, and can thus actually handle farm supplies or consumer goods and provide services at costs that are as low as, or lower than, those charged by their competitors. As a general rule, both costs and returns are pooled and averaged over the period of the fiscal year. (See Chapter 19 for a discussion of pooling practices.)

Marketing cooperatives usually aim to pay patrons at least the current price for their products. Some make advance payments and the patronage refund is, in reality, a final price adjustment for their patrons.

The nature of the cooperative business transaction throws additional light on the relationship of the cooperative to its patrons. Many marketing cooperatives, in fact, operate on an agency basis and sell farm products only for their patrons. Even when a cooperative "buys" from or "sells" to a patron, the transaction is essentially a technical consideration that reflects prevailing market structures and operating conditions. The service-at-cost obligation of the cooperative is maintained through the patronage refund technique—a technique that assures that members benefit according to their use of their cooperative. This is a most important distinguishing feature that serves to set cooperatives apart from other businesses.

Although the Rochdale Society and other early cooperatives placed special stress on the pro rata division of net margins to patrons, this practice in reality is one of the techniques used to achieve service at cost. Those marketing cooperatives that pool products according to specific variety and/or grade make successive payments as the product is sold. The first payment or payments may be termed *price advances*. A final *price determination*, or return after all sales are made and all expenses taken into account, becomes the technique for operating on a service-at-cost basis.

The practice of charging lower prices at farm supply, consumer, or service cooperatives, or the payment of higher than current prices by marketing cooperatives (which will reduce patronage refunds), is also used by some cooperatives, especially those that operate in relatively stable markets or those that have achieved a position of industry leadership. This is another way cooperatives provide service at cost for patrons or, as some say, return "instant refunds."

Some cooperatives, however, operate only on a cost basis as far as member business is concerned. They may choose, for example, to treat nonmember patron business as a profit transaction. When they do this, they pay income taxes on the profit instead of returning savings to the nonmembers in the form of patronage refunds. This practice is sanctioned by federal and state statutes, provided that such nonmember business does not exceed member business.

Member Control

At the time of the Rochdale pioneers, most cooperative leaders emphasized one vote per member and no more, or democratic control as a basic cooperative principle. This practice seemed to owe its origin to the idea of political representation in which each voter is considered equal. Every voter had the same right as other citizens to speak and express views on public questions

We can easily recognize that the idea of democratic control worked quite satisfactorily for most local farm supply, consumer, or service cooperatives. Members live in reasonably close proximity, and even purchases of goods or services by each member may not vary greatly. There is little wonder that the idea of "people control," rather than "money control," gained universal recognition as a cooperative principle. It has been defended with fervor as a distinguishing cooperative characteristic.

As cooperatives became well established, however, certain complications arose. In the United States, especially in western states, the size of farm operations often varies widely and continues to become more differentiated. In response to member desire to achieve control in proportion to the business they do with their cooperative, laws in a dozen or more states sanction proportional voting in local associations. Such voting could be based on the dollar volume of business, the acres in a crop, the units of farm produce (e.g., bushels of apples, pounds of milk, number of livestock, and capital invested). Even where proportional voting is sanctioned, some cooperatives may specify the maximum number of votes each member may have.

Another complication centers on the establishment of regional or wholesale cooperatives. In the case of federated cooperatives, the question arises whether voting should be on the one-association, one-vote basis. Or should recognition be given to greater volume of business or larger membership numbers by techniques of proportionality? Likewise, large-scale centralized associations are confronted with the need for working out some means of electing directors to represent the members equitably.

The issue is further complicated in those regionals that have a mixed federated-centralized structure. For example, their supply operations may be federated through membership of affiliated local associations, while their grain or livestock operations may be centralized with direct farmer membership. In these cooperatives, it therefore becomes quite evident that the practice of voting in proportion to the business transacted, number of members, or capital invested may come closer to achieving equitable representation for members than the one of operating on the basis of one association, one vote, when memberships in associations may range from 5 to 5,000.

In actual practice, regional cooperatives with local affiliates that vary widely in business volume or number of members often provide for one vote per association plus additional votes for a specified volume of business or number of members. They often may set a maximum limit, such as five, ten, or twenty-five votes per association. Centralized regionals generally provide for directors to represent districts that approach having an equal volume of business or number of members. Mixed federated-centralized regional cooperatives often arrange for representation by each member association plus additional representation for individual members. For example, each 5,000 direct members or every $5 million of annual business may qualify a regional cooperative for an additional director.

This trend has proved extremely disturbing for some cooperative scholars. They hold that the only "true cooperative" is the one that operates on the one-member, one-vote principle. Others, with tongue in cheek, state that proportional or representative voting is voting according to the economic interests of people (members), and that this, in effect, also is democratic control. It would seem more realistic, however, to agree that, strictly speaking, democratic control is what the term implies it is, namely, one vote per member (equal representation). The idea of one member, one vote also enables many cooperatives to maintain the type of control they desire, and is one way of distinguishing cooperatives from other forms of business enterprise.

This is not to say, however, that variation from the one-member, one-vote principle is necessarily less cooperative in character or that it results in less member control. There are those who emphasize that democratic control is synonymous with people control as contrasted with capital control. They recognize, however, that pure democracy (one member, one vote) may be difficult to maintain and not even desirable unless a high degree of homogeneity exists in member needs and operations.

There is no evidence that a cooperative that operates with proportional, or weighted, voting is any less effective in giving members a complete say in its operations. Nor does weighted voting hinder members from following any of the other cooperative principles that assure that those who own and patronize the association are the ones who benefit from its operations. Control in an association that provides for proportional representation is simply exercised on a different basis.

Another variation in member control is found in a few states where cooperative statutes permit voting on the basis of the shares of capital stock owned. Some cooperatives attempt to keep such stock ownership in proportion to use or patronage. The Capper-Volstead Act, which is discussed in detail in Chapter 9, also authorizes agricultural cooperatives to provide for voting according to shares of stock owned. The act states that the cooperatives shall, among other things, either limit voting to one member, one vote, *or* limit dividends on capital to 8 percent per annum or the legal rate of the state, whichever is higher.

The key consideration seems to rest with how members wish their cooperative to operate. If they want proportional voting, and if they understand how such voting can be achieved and what it means in actual practice, should they not be permitted to make their own decisions as to how they wish to control their cooperative? If they have the necessary information to make sound decisions, they will still maintain control on the basis they have agreed upon. In their judgment, they may conclude, on a one-member, one-vote basis, that member control based on economic interests meets their needs better than the principle of one member, one vote. It is not a decision that should be left to government agencies or "cooperative intellectuals."

Cooperative members have long believed that control should be related to the needs of people and not to capital investments. Therefore, considerable attention has been given to making certain that, even though some method of proportional voting is adopted, one or a few individuals cannot buy themselves into a position of control simply because voting is permitted on the basis of shares of stock or some other form of financial investment. Some states' statutes limit members' stock ownership in a cooperative to not over 5 percent of the total amount of stock outstanding. We have indicated that most associations using some form of proportional voting have therefore developed techniques to limit the number of shares or the financial equity of members so as to achieve a broad membership base.

A more accurate description of this principle seems to be *member control*. This term recognizes that member control may be achieved either through the technique of one member, one vote, or through some system of proportional voting that relates to the economic participation of members in their cooperative with a limit as to the maximum number of votes any one member may cast. If we agree that member control correctly describes this basic cooperative concept, we avoid putting members under the strain of identifying control with a concept that, in practice and for good reasons, some cooperatives no longer follow.

To make certain that control remains in the hands of active members, some cooperatives provide that the voting privilege be denied to members who fail to patronize their cooperative during the past year or two. Also, many cooperatives permit voting by mail if the member has been previously notified of the exact motion or resolution to be voted on at a meeting. This is just another way of helping members maintain active control of their cooperative.

To achieve more effective member control, most cooperatives, through legislative action, also prohibit proxy voting. This restriction helps to prevent one individual or a limited number of members from gaining control of the cooperative. It is but another technique for assuring a broad membership base for control of the cooperative.

The voluntary nature of membership is also closely related to the concept of member control. We have mentioned that neither the state nor any other group should have the right to determine who can qualify for cooperative membership—which should be voluntary as far as the individual is concerned. There is no place in a cooperative for "obligatory membership." In other words, the question of membership should be independent of external control.

The decision to join a cooperative, provided an individual can qualify and meet such requirements as are specified, is therefore a prerogative of the individual. Likewise, a member has the right to withdraw, in accordance with established cooperative rules. Although this right has practically no qualifications as far as consumer, farm supply, and service cooperatives are concerned, marketing cooperatives often have found it advisable to designate certain periods when new members are accepted and old members may withdraw. Members of housing cooperatives are also subject to contractual arrangements as to withdrawal. It should be emphasized that, with the exception of rural electric cooperatives, no person can demand admittance as a member. Acceptance of an applicant is a matter for the board of directors to decide. "Open membership" does not mean that any and all applicants must be taken in.

The basic idea is that neither withdrawing members nor newly approved members should be permitted to jeopardize cooperative operations of other members while the cooperative is making necessary operating adjustments to changes in membership. Once having joined the cooperative, the members have obligations to other members to contribute to association stability by providing financial resources and patronage for a specified period of time. Freedom to withdraw is not absolute in cooperatives and cannot be exercised at the expense of members who remain. In marketing cooperatives that have marketing contracts with their members, a member can withdraw legally only at such times as specified in the marketing agreement.

Member Ownership

Member control and ownership are interrelated. In actual practice, it is difficult to have one without the other. It is generally accepted in business enterprise that ownership carries with it a substantial degree of control. Cooperatives are no exception. Control, however, relates to political considerations, whereas ownership has economic implications. For these reasons, they are considered separately in this section, even though it is recognized that, *ideally,* cooperative ownership and control should rest in the same individuals.

When members have substantial equity capital in their cooperative, they have an interest in having a say about how it should be organized and operated. Now they have a financial stake to protect and defend. This financial interest has an important psychological effect on how actively they will support their cooperative. It helps to make the cooperative "their" organization. It also may be a strong force in inducing members to patronize their cooperative. This is in sharp contrast to the emotions of most investors in other types of business. They feel little if any compunction to buy the products or control the operations of the companies in which they invest. Nor do they develop close personal identification with the firms whose stock they own.

We might question how realistic this principle is in developing countries where income is low and cooperative experience is limited. Under such conditions, grants and subsidies in the form of low interest rates for extended periods often may be a matter of national policy. This may be highly desirable. The important thing to recognize, however, is that until the cooperative can stand on its own feet, it really is a "pre-cooperative" or quasi-cooperative. It is not in a position legitimately to consider itself fully member-controlled and member-owned. The reason is that under such conditions, the state usually insists on representation—often majority representation—on the board of directors. Moreover, it is likely to specify, and correctly so, how any funds it provides are to be used. Until the organization is able to disengage itself from such arrangements, it is in reality a state-owned and -operated business.

It should also be recognized that, in some instances, member ownership may mean ownership of the business but not necessarily ownership of its facilities. Land, buildings, and equipment may be leased. This practice limits capital investment in physical facilities and leaves more capital available for support of basic operations. The best policy for an individual cooperative to follow can only be determined after careful evaluation of advantages and disadvantages of leasing.

To achieve a full-fledged cooperative status, emphasis should be directed to becoming self-sustaining as soon as possible. Government help, while it may subsidize initial stages of development, should always have as its basic objective the building of permanent self-help organizations. The vital role government can play is in helping to train management people to a degree of competency that will encourage them to assume greater responsibilities for cooperative management. Cooperators have learned, also, that financial responsibility ranks with patronage and membership responsibilities as key ingredients in cooperative success. This tenet has been well expressed by the statement: "Cooperative control, patronage, and ownership should rest with the same individuals."

Support appears substantial for the idea that *member ownership* is a basic cooperative principle. It seems important to emphasize that cooperatives should constantly seek to keep ownership in the hands of member-users. As to the three principles discussed so far—operation at cost, member control, and member ownership—the ideal situation prevails when the members who benefit from cooperative patronage are also the ones who own the cooperative and control its operations.

Limited Returns on Equity Capital

The principle of limited returns on equity capital complements the principle of services at cost. Cooperators recognize that capital, together with management, labor, and the products handled, are necessary resources in the operation of their business. Equity capital, however, is a means to an end and not an end in itself. In the case of the cooperative, that end is to provide services at reasonable prices and not to realize profits for capital.

Cooperative leaders have long emphasized that, as a factor of production, capital is entitled to the going rate of remuneration, but no more. The rationale of limiting returns on capital in the cooperative is that the patrons shall not benefit as investors. If such a situation were permitted, it is obvious that those in control might well seek to drastically change the character of the cooperative's operation. Emphasis then would likely be on protection of returns on investment rather than on service to members. This effort could destroy the basic purpose of the cooperative.

Limited returns on capital (member equity) is provided for in most state laws under which cooperatives are organized. It also is recognized in the Capper-Volstead Act.

In stating this principle, the International Cooperative Alliance in 1969 modified it to read: "Share capital should receive a limited rate of interest, *if any*." We have already discussed the idea of financing in proportion to the amount of business done through the cooperative. It is obvious that when such financing is possible, nothing is gained by dividing net margins or savings between patronage refunds and dividends on equity capital. Members would be treated equitably if all net margins or savings were distributed as patronage refunds. We have indicated, however, that, in practice, this ideal situation is seldom achieved. Hence, the payment for the use of equity capital at the going rate has become a widely accepted practice.

Limiting returns on equity capital also complements the principle of member control. By rewarding patronage rather than capital invested, there is an added inducement to build a broad base for membership participation in contrast to concentrating membership and control in the hands of the limited number of individuals who are in a position to make substantial capital contributions.

Duty to Educate

Robert Owen believed that through education it would be possible to achieve an "ideal society"—a society that would contribute much to human happiness. The Rochdale pioneers followed in his footsteps. In 1853, they changed their rules to provide that 2½ percent of profits would be set aside for educational purposes. Over the years, the Pioneers gradually developed an active and broad program of member enlightenment. Since that time, many consumer societies have stressed educational programs, and their spokespersons generally have looked on educational activities as a basic cooperative principle.

In the United States, early efforts to organize cooperatives by general farm organizations, such as the Grange, Equity, Farmers Union, and the Farm Bureau, virtually ignored educational programs. Much the same can be said about the commodity marketing programs promoted by Aaron Sapiro in the early 1920s. He relied on ironclad legal contracts and a highly charged emotional appeal, rather than a broad basis of understanding. The failure of these efforts focused attention on the need for informed membership and leaders. As a result, larger regional cooperatives started to train employees and establish member and public educational programs as early as the late 1920s. Land-grant universities, banks for cooperatives, and state cooperative councils also began to direct attention to various aspects of cooperative education.

Notwithstanding increased recognition of the importance of education, most cooperative leaders in the United States have not been inclined to think of education as a sufficiently distinct feature of cooperative enterprise to justify identifying it as a principle.

There are many problems. First, there are the nagging questions: Just what is meant by cooperative education, and what direction should it take? Should it, for example, relate only to members, or should it also include potential members, employees, and the general public? In other words, what publics should cooperatives try to reach in their educational programs? What educational techniques offer the greatest possibilities? Should cooperative education emphasize operations, ideology, or both? Considering these questions, one astute cooperative observer, when commenting on the rather uncoordinated educational program of a certain cooperative, stated that it "is doing too much of the kind of educating it is now doing."

There is also the more basic question of whether education, as applied to cooperatives, is sufficiently unique to justify including it as a basic cooperative principle or as a practice unique to cooperatives.

There are those who will argue that the duty to educate, while it is a desirable practice that improves operation, is really not distinct as far as cooperatives are concerned. Members of cooperatives, however, have responsibilities for financing, control, and patronage that are substantially different from what their obligations would be if they were only customers of a business. Therefore, sound reasons seem to exist for concluding that cooperatives have special and distinct obligations to educate their membership.

No less a dedicated cooperator than Jerry Voorhis, former executive director of the Cooperative League of the U.S.A., states: "The practices of continuous education are necessary to the success of cooperatives, but they are not essentially distinguishing characteristics." He believes this is so because it is possible to have a cooperative that carries on no education of its members, even though he concedes that "it is almost sure to be headed for economic problems and perhaps slow or sudden death. . . ." He further states that "where member education has been neglected—the cooperative has sooner or later suffered—sometimes fatally."[10]

President James Madison said: "To put the conduct of the affairs of the people in the hands of the people without first educating the people will prove to be the prelude to either a farce or a tragedy." Experience suggests that we are justified in raising the question: Is it possible for a successful cooperative to be far ahead of the general level of understanding of its patrons and the general public?

Among the millions of cooperative members in the United States, some are sophisticated and some are economically illiterate, or, as Professor Bonner has said, subject to "economic superstition and darkness."[11] What these members know or do not know about cooperatives, farming practices, agricultural policies, and general economic, social, and political forces will largely determine their understanding of and support for cooperatives. More specifically, what they know will also influence how they vote on key cooperative policy questions, their patronage of cooperatives, and the extent to which they are willing to assume responsibilities for meeting financial needs. Education may be the most effective tool to "awaken and renew" cooperative interest.

The knowledge that the general public has of cooperatives may be equally important. The views and actions of legislators, educators, the clergy, and, especially, competing business operators will be influenced by their understanding of cooperatives.

As far as employees are concerned, it has been stated on many occasions that "they are the cooperative" when it comes to contacts with local members. Quite obviously, what they know about cooperatives will greatly influence the members' attitude toward their cooperative. We must agree, however, that much the same can be said about the employees of other types of business enterprise.

The threefold audience for cooperative education that we identified previously—members, the general public, and employees—coupled with the unique nature of cooperatives, emphasizes the special needs that these organizations have for effective educational programs. The early experiences and frequent failure of cooperatives, when they did little or nothing to inform members or the general public about the nature of their operations, support the view that cooperative progress will go little farther than the knowledge of people with whom they have business relations.

Because members of cooperatives, their employees, and the general public are a continually changing parade, it seems quite reasonable to conclude that the *duty to*

---

[10]Jerry Voorhis, *A New Look at Principles and Practices of Cooperatives,* Cooperative League of the U.S.A., Washington, D.C., 1966, p. 11.

[11]Arnold Bonner, *British Cooperation,* Cooperative Union Ltd., Manchester, England, 1970, p. 325.

educate deserves the status of a basic cooperative principle. The evidence is preponderant that to avoid failure and achieve success, constant education of the various publics that can affect cooperatives is necessary. If we accept, also, the appraisal of some students of cooperation that not more than 25 percent of all United States cooperatives even approach operating at their full potential, we have further reason to accept the duty to educate as a basic concept that has special application to the unique nature of cooperative enterprise.

OTHER PRINCIPLES OR PRACTICES EXAMINED

Other cooperative ideas or concepts have been elevated to the status of principles by some cooperative writers. They merit examination, even though some no longer are considered to be basic principles and others generally are classified as operating practices. As such, they may be an important and useful business technique but are not distinctly cooperative in nature.

Open or Selective Membership

The idea of open membership was dear to the hearts of the Rochdale pioneers, and it has continued so among other groups—particularly leaders of consumer cooperatives. Some cooperative scholars have the impression that the concept of open membership was essential or highly desirable in getting people interested in changing the social order as it existed in the early nineteenth century. Owen's new moral world, his criticism of the established order, and his villages of cooperation called for adherents and converts. Hence, an open membership policy in cooperatives as a steppingstone to a socialistic order was a natural procedure.

This does not mean that under all circumstances anyone could become and remain a member. Even the Pioneers provided that a member who became three months' delinquent in weekly payments on shares would be fined. After being delinquent for six months, that person would be expelled. But consumer cooperatives and, for that matter, most farm supply and service cooperatives, have found that they usually can reduce operating costs if they can expand business volume. As a result, they have encouraged a policy of open membership to achieve this end. Exceptions have been made when facilities were limited, when supplies were short, or when a cooperative was unable to provide services over widely scattered areas. Therefore, the cooperative, a tool for self-help and improvement, may be expected to limit its membership to the specific groups it is organized to serve, and to restrict operations to providing the specific services members want.

It requires little imagination to recognize that open membership may not apply to a farmers' marketing cooperative. The areas in which it can provide services effectively may be restricted, facilities may be limited, and market outlets just may not exist for an unlimited number of members or for the particular quality of their products. A further restriction on membership in some marketing and farm supply cooperatives in the United States is found in those organizations that require membership in a general farm organization, such as the Farm Bureau or the Farmers Union, as a prerequisite for cooperative membership.

In general, if cooperatives are to protect the interests of their members, they may have every reason to limit membership to those farmers who can provide a specified quality and quantity of produce, and who can meet specific financial, patronage, and member obligations. Likewise, marketing cooperatives may wish to restrict membership to producers of specified types of farm products; mutual fire insurance companies may find it desirable to limit membership to those who meet certain fire prevention standards; and housing cooperatives may want to limit memberships to families of a specified size.

Some students of cooperation have taken the idea of open membership too literally. From the beginning of organized cooperative effort, mutuality of interests, economic considerations, and a willingness to assume responsibilities have been considerations that have determined who can and should be members. It was never intended that the door should be open to mavericks, nonconformists, or competitors whose interests might be detrimental to the self-help objectives of the group.

Political, Religious, and Racial Neutrality

From the standpoint of social advancement, it may be argued that there is no justification for limiting cooperative membership for political, religious, or racial reasons. Besides, many cooperatives pride themselves in taking stands on economic issues, on being "pacesetters," and on marching in the forefront when it comes to social consciousness. Even if other business firms are less socially conscious, there is no reason why cooperatives should be found wanting.

From a practical standpoint, at least as far as most types of consumer and farm supply purchasing cooperatives are concerned, cooperative experts generally recognize that it is just good business to build volume by leaving membership open to all, irrespective of political affiliation, religious beliefs, or racial characteristics. For these and other reasons, some people argue that "neutrality" is too passive a word. They believe that cooperatives, by example and by conscious effort, should aggressively seek to achieve political, religious, and racial involvement. Others argue that since the cooperative is a business enterprise, it will lose volume if it takes a strong stand on political, religious, or racial issues. (The question of degree of political involvement of cooperatives in the United States, for example, is examined in some detail in Chapter 21.)

In any event, it is difficult to see how the principle of neutrality can be identified as one having distinct application to cooperatives. It can be argued logically that neutrality has equal application to churches, clubs, and, for that matter, many other types of business firms. There now is general agreement that political neutrality does not exclude any interest in legislative matters and any stand on adverse legislative issues that concern the cooperative. On a given issue, a cooperative may approve the stand of a political party, but it does so on a nonpartisan basis and avoids alignment with any party.

Exclusive Trading with Members

The idea behind this concept seems to be that membership should be considered a privilege. One may ask why those who have not contributed much in the way of time or resources to the cooperative should be permitted to enjoy a "free ride." Requiring patrons to be members before they use the services of the cooperative, it is reasoned, helps to develop membership responsibility, makes for a better understanding of objectives and operations, and builds stronger financial support. Others, however, believe that, if handled realistically, nonmember business may be an effective way of building membership.

Farmers' marketing cooperatives often are faced with a quite different situation. They may have commitments to provide a certain amount of product of a given grade, at regular intervals. Drought, floods, or other calamities may make it impossible for members to meet these obligations from their own production efforts. When such situations occur, it seems reasonable that a cooperative be permitted to buy from nonmembers the products necessary to maintain its market outlets.

Cooperatives are far from agreement on exclusive trading with members. Rather than accept it as a general principle, many leaders believe that the advantages or disadvantages of exclusive trading with members stem from the particular conditions that confront a cooperative at any given time and place. Whether it should deal exclusively with members seems to be an issue that should be determined by the economic situation that prevails. The concept does not appear to merit recognition as a cooperative principle.

Indivisible Capital Reserves

The idea of indivisible capital reserves seems to have its origin in the belief that members are less inclined to adversely affect the operations of their cooperative if they know that they cannot get their hands on reserves during periods of misfortune. The idea that net assets should be considered indivisible or collective reserves in the event of dissolution, and in such an event should be given to various public causes, is also strongly supported by Professor Lambert and certain French and Italian cooperators. There is little justification for this very peculiar view other than that it was enunciated by Buchez in 1831.

In some countries, cooperatives have used reserves for such purposes as the construction and maintenance of libraries, hospitals, and other public facilities. An opposite point of view is taken in provisions of federal legislation in the United States as well as in the state cooperative statutes. They require that all net margins be allocated to member-patrons if such margins are not to be subject to income tax payments. Also, some state statutes require that 10 percent of net margins be placed in general reserves.

It seems reasonable to have members determine whether they wish to maintain indivisible reserves. The concept cannot be justified as a cooperative principle.

Financing in Proportion to Patronage

Most cooperative members perhaps would agree that there is merit in strongly urging, if not requiring, that the financial obligations of members to their cooperative be in proportion to the volume of business they do through it. In most instances, however, this is not practical, especially when starting a cooperative. Some members are in a position to make relatively greater contributions to cooperative financing than others, who may be able to meet only the minimum financial requirements for membership.

Also, there is the very practical problem of developing equitable techniques for maintaining this principle. Although it might easily be determined for an initial period, changes in individual patronage, as well as in overall volume from year to year, could cause problems in administering such a program.

The concept is in accord with established cooperative philosophy, but in practice it has not had general acceptance. The concept is sound because it takes the idea of member ownership one step farther by specifically identifying the extent of such ownership. The problem is to devise techniques for effectively making it work. The revolving plan of financing is one method of financing in proportion to the amount of business that individual patrons do with their cooperative. (This plan is discussed in detail in Chapter 16.)

Single or Multiple Business Services

Cooperators have discussed at length the relative merits of single versus multipurpose cooperatives. For example, should farmers' marketing cooperatives also handle farm supplies? Should farm supply cooperatives market farm products and/or provide such services as painting, applying fertilizers and pesticides, handling consumer goods, and selling insurance? Should consumer food cooperatives add dry goods, appliances, drugs, and furniture? Should housing cooperatives also provide insurance and run grocery, drug, and furniture stores?

It seems quite evident that these issues have little to do with special or distinctive cooperative features. The extent to which a cooperative, or other business firm, may diversify or integrate its operations will be influenced primarily by such factors as stage of development, capability of management, financial resources, nature of the services provided, the inclination of members, and the economic features of the territory serviced. In fact, the trend in this and many other countries is for large-scale cooperatives to provide multiple business services ranging all the way from selling cotton to processing catfish.

These considerations have application to cooperatives and to other kinds of businesses. There appears to be no justification for concluding that the concepts of single or multiple services have any special application to cooperative principles.

Selling at Market Prices

If a small, local cooperative such as the Rochdale pioneers of Toad Lane should wish to build net margins, it would have little choice but to operate efficiently and follow going prices. However, as business firms become larger, they sometimes become a significant force in their market—a force that by their own actions can appreciably influence market prices and practices. Under such circumstances, cooperative research may determine what they have to gain by assuming a position of price leader. The success of Migros, a highly integrated consumer cooperative in Switzerland, illustrates this point. It has consistently followed the policy of selling at the lowest prices possible. Experiences of consumer societies in Great Britain and Scandinavia are similar.

For some years, Swedish cooperatives have followed a so-called active price policy in which prices are reduced to where they provide only reasonable gross and net margins. Regional farm-supply cooperatives, by operating on or close to a cost basis in times of drought or floods, have prevented the exploitation of members who have emergency needs for such items as feed, seed, and fertilizer. The price policy of a firm, cooperative or otherwise, is a function of market position and business policy. It is strictly a business practice and does not justify classification as a cooperative principle.

Cash Trading

It is easy to see why the Rochdale pioneers would favor cash trading. They had observed many embryonic cooperatives that had crashed on the rocks of uncontrolled and ill-advised credit. Necessity demanded cash trading. Professor Bonner also made the pertinent point that cash trading was a technique developed to keep members from becoming debt-ridden. In the United States, many farm supply cooperatives attempted to operate on or near a cash basis to avoid financial difficulties, but they soon found it to their advantage to engage in noncash business.

Experience has demonstrated that a credit business may be good or bad for a firm, depending on the credit control policies it may have adopted and the competency of the personnel in charge of its credit program. It also may depend on the nature of the business. Chain stores in the United States have demonstrated the merits of a cash trading policy. Such a policy, however, has nothing to do with whether any given firm is a cooperative and does not justify considering it as a cooperative principle. It is strictly a business practice, the merits of which may or may not apply to all kinds of businesses.

Control of Facilities and Service Institutions

General economic conditions rather than special cooperative features seem to be the most important consideration in determining whether a cooperative should own facilities and service institutions. During periods of scarcity, such a policy obviously is desirable. This fact was brought home to cooperatives that experienced shortages of refining facilities and crude oil supplies during World War II. Cooperatives were faced with similar problems, in addition to shortages of fertilizer, transportation facilities, and many farm supplies, in 1973.

In periods of surpluses, in contrast, cooperatives may be able to operate more efficiently by holding the ownership of facilities and service institutions to a minimum. This is especially true when they cannot make full use of such facilities. Cooperatives, it is recognized, have obligations to see that they have the necessary facilities and service institutions to provide members with the services they need when they need them. This is an economic issue, however, that has a quite similar application to most kinds of businesses. It does not justify consideration as a basic cooperative principle.

Cooperation among Cooperatives

Cooperatives should work together for many reasons. Only through joint action and the combining of resources of all cooperatives, for example, can state cooperative councils, in their educational and lobbying efforts, demonstrate and achieve the strength necessary to be effective. The same holds for the ability of various national cooperative trade associations that seek to develop strong educational programs, effective lobbying efforts, and helpful service programs. The International Cooperative Alliance made a distinct contribution by focusing attention on this cooperative concept.

Likewise, in their business operations many noncompeting cooperatives can coordinate various activities. Examples of directions such an effort can take are the joint use of computers; sharing of office facilities; ownership of feed mills, fertilizer plants, and petroleum refineries; operation of sales organizations; ownership of transportation facilities; and the presentation of educational programs. Also, when a grain or a dairy cooperative buys its tires and petroleum supplies from a farm supply cooperative, it is helping to build a stronger cooperative system. It should be emphasized that cooperation among cooperatives should be justified on economic rather than emotional grounds.

In some instances, of course, cooperatives are in direct competition with one another. Farm supply and certain marketing cooperatives are prime examples. This competition is often of an even more vicious type than that which exists between cooperatives and other types of businesses. It is not always realized that where such competition exists, it is the members' own money that is used to finance duplicating facilities and competitive practices. Although some cooperative leaders will emphasize the stimulating benefits of competition, most cooperatives have all the motivating competition they need without competing with one another. Some regional supply cooperatives that actively compete with one another on a local level, however, own such facilities as petroleum refineries on a joint basis.

The idea of cooperation among cooperatives has much to recommend it. Benefits of joint action may be significant. Certainly the many rapid changes taking place in the business world—expansion of large conglomerates, fluctuations in market structure, and escalation of energy problems—are among the forces that place a premium on joint cooperative effort. Agreement is general, also, that cooperatives can go much farther in this direction than they have. It may even be that cooperatives' members may gain more through joint effort than is achieved through similar effort by other kinds of businesses. It is a sound business practice under most circumstances, but cooperatives do not always practice what they preach. However, as cooperatives gain a better understanding of business practices, they may recognize the advantages of cooperating with one another and be more willing to accept such cooperation as a distinct cooperative principle.

SUMMARY

The Rochdale principles were developed by trial and error. They reflected the conditions of their day and the efforts of laboring people to successfully operate their local cooperative society. In practice, the rules developed by the Rochdale pioneers included basic and distinct features that distinguished it from other forms of business. They also embodied pragmatic operating practices that met members' needs and applied to any type of business venture.

It is to the credit of the Rochdale pioneers that their principles contained the embryonic ideas that have come to be approved by cooperators over the years as generally accepted principles. These are service at cost, democratic control, and limited returns on equity capital.

A reexamination of cooperative principles, however, suggests that it is possible to improve the traditional terminology and to add basic ideas that seem to be gaining universal acceptance. The following five cooperative principles seem to be basic in distinguishing cooperatives from other types of businesses:

- Operation at cost
- Member control
- Member ownership
- Limited returns on equity capital
- Duty to educate

QUESTIONS

1. With respect to the Rochdale principles:
   a. List the principles.
   b. Identify those relating to basic cooperative concepts and those relating to business practices that also may apply to other types of businesses.
   c. Which principles did the Pioneers adopt from their predecessors?
   d. Are the Rochdale principles applicable today? Which ones and under what conditions?
   e. How have they been modified over time?
2. When cooperative leaders refer to basic principles today, which ones do they have in mind?
3. Are cooperative principles timeless, possessing universal validity and waiting to be discovered, or are they subject to change and modification as economic, social, and political forces influence them?
4. Are some cooperative principles applicable to different kinds of cooperatives? Discuss those that may be.
5. Classify cooperative principles according to the following categories:
   a. Those that relate to membership.
   b. Those that relate to income accumulation and income distribution.
   c. Those that relate to social advancement.
6. Is it reasonable to classify some cooperative principles as fringe or secondary principles? Which ones would you place in this classification?
7. What are the basic modifications and additions to cooperative principles that are suggested in this book?
8. Develop your own list of cooperative principles. Explain any suggested modifications in terminology, and any omissions or additions you would make to the three principles generally accepted as basic by cooperators.

REFERENCES

Bakken, Henry H.: *Basic Concepts, Principles and Practices of Cooperation,* Mimir Publications, Madison, Wis., 1963.

Bonner, Arnold: *British Cooperation,* Cooperative Union Ltd., Holyoake House, Hanover St., Manchester, England, 1970, pp. 41–58 and 305–330.

Fetrow, Ward W.: *Three Principles of Agricultural Cooperation,* FCS Educational Circular 13, U.S. Department of Agriculture, Farmer Cooperative Service, Washington, 1958, 9 pages.

Gardner, Kelsey B.: "Matching Cooperative Principles with Today's Operating Practices," *American Cooperation,* American Institute of Cooperation, Washington, D.C., 1971, pp. 160–166.

Lambert, Paul: *Cooperative Principles and the International Cooperative Alliance,* Annals of Public and Cooperative Economy, Liège, Belgium, 1971, 29 pages.

_____: *Studies in the Social Philosophy of Cooperation,* Cooperative League of the U.S.A., Washington, D.C., 1963, pp. 61–90.

Nourse, Edwin G.: "The Economic Philosophy of Cooperation," *American Economics Review,* December 1922, pp. 577–597. (Also in Abrahamsen and Scroggs, *Selected Readings in Agricultural Cooperation,* The University of Minnesota Press, Minneapolis, 1957, pp. 161–183.)

Schaars, Marvin A.: "Basic Principles of Cooperatives—Their Growth and Development," *American Cooperation,* American Institute of Cooperation, Washington, D.C., 1951, pp. 835–852. (Also in Abrahamsen and Scroggs, *Selected Readings in Agricultural Cooperation,* The University of Minnesota Press, Minneapolis, 1957, pp. 183–203.)

Voorhis, Jerry: *A New Look at the Principles and Practices of Cooperatives,* Cooperative League of the U.S.A., Washington, D.C., 1972, 16 pages.

Williams, Melville E.: "Capper Volstead—What It Means Today," *American Cooperation,* American Institute of Cooperation, Washington, D.C., 1971, pp. 154–159.

Chapter 4

The Evolution of Cooperative Thought

Dr. E. G. Nourse, who is considered by many to be the "Dean of Cooperative Scholars," states that "cooperatives are long on practice but short on theory." This observation is more valid for the United States than for countries such as England and Sweden, in which consumer cooperatives have gained much wider acceptance. It is well known, however, that many cooperative students differ sharply in the cooperative philosophies they espouse and the theories they have formulated.

The wide range of cooperative thinking that has evolved over the past 200 years is intertwined, to a rather considerable degree, with cooperative principles. It is, however, less formal and more inclusive than these principles. Important cooperative ideas, for example, have developed also in regard to concepts, objectives, practical operations, and legal aspects. We will here attempt to trace briefly the evolution of cooperative thinking, the basic concepts that have developed, and the individuals who have made substantial contributions to general cooperative thought. This review will cover cooperators in the pre-Rochdale and Rochdale eras, the views of some of the British and French socialists, and the ideas of selected early and more recent American researchers and writers.

The views of many leading American cooperators, both academicians and practical operators, are given in detail in *Great American Cooperators: Profiles of 101 Cooperative Pacemakers.*[1]

PRE-ROCHDALE

Robert Owen

Not all agree as to the extent of Robert Owen's contributions to cooperative thinking. Some refer to him as the "Father of Cooperation"; others contend, however, that only a few of his basic ideas have achieved lasting acceptance among cooperators and that those that have are applied to substantially different forms of cooperatives than the kind he envisaged.

Owen was credited with developing a "new view of society," which he described in four essays that received wide recognition. The first essay developed his belief that "Man's character is made *for* him and not *by* him." His second and third essays described in detail the economic system at his textile mills in New Lanark, Scotland, and the educational program he had developed there. It was his view that education is basic to the success of any program and can be relied upon to facilitate giant steps in eliminating poverty, misery, and crime. His fourth essay expounded his ideas for the reorganization of Britain's then-existing poor laws. Although Owen was a most persuasive speaker, his unorthodox views with respect to marriage and his denunciation of organized religion hindered his efforts to gain acceptance for his ideas.

Owen's experience at New Lanark encouraged him to advocate communal cooperative villages that would largely be self-sufficient in character to deal with the impact of the fast-developing industrial revolution. He continued throughout his life to emphasize the need for extensive educational programs and to seek contributions from the wealthy to get his schemes underway.

In this framework, Owen created the environment in which four basic cooperative ideas emerged in embryonic form. These were:

Associated effort. Owen's thinking centered on bringing people together in an effort to deal with the problems confronting them.

Voluntary approach. People were free to join or not, but Owen believed that through educational efforts many of them would come to understand the merits of his ideas.

Democratic control. After understanding the objectives of his cooperative ventures, Owen believed, the people could be relied upon to make the "right" decisions in governing themselves. Owen thought he should act as a benevolent ruler until they did.

Service to members emphasized. The communal society should identify member needs and should seek to satisfy them. Production would be for *use* and not for *profit.*[2]

---

[1]Joseph G. Knapp and Associates, American Institute of Cooperation, Washington, D.C., 1967, p. 450.

[2]Paul Lambert, *Studies in the Social Philosophy of Cooperation,* Cooperative League of the U.S.A., Washington, 1963, p. 39.

When evaluated in terms of their contribution to cooperative enterprise today, the ideas advocated by Owen differ in these basic respects:

- Society in Owen's self-sufficient communities would be based only on production of goods and services for personal use. Today's cooperatives, however, are highly specialized; they restrict operations to specific member needs and are very much a part of the exchange economy.
- Owen thought in terms of joint ownership of property, a community of interests, and joint sharing of benefits. Modern cooperative operations, in contrast, are oriented toward accumulation of private property and the sharing of benefits in proportion to participation in the business.
- Owen depended on philanthropists for capital. Today, the members are expected to provide a substantial share of the capital necessary to start and operate their cooperative.[3]

Some of Owen's contemporaries also contributed to cooperative thought, often by reinforcing or slightly modifying his ideas. Their thinking is summarized here:

Dr. William King

In 1827, Dr. King organized a consumer cooperative at Brighton, England, that was to serve as a model for hundreds of local societies in the 1830s. He emphasized that (1) cooperation is voluntary and not compulsory, and (2) cooperatives should be neutral as to political and religious convictions. He, like Owen, hoped to transform society completely.

Charles Fourier

A Frenchman, Fourier, is credited by Professor Lambert with being one of the original communal city planners. Fourier suggested cooperative phalanxes—groups of associated people living on land owned in common and in rationally constructed communities. He placed special emphasis on agricultural production and on reduction of distribution costs. Even more than Owen, he stressed democracy in governing the phalanxes, and voluntary association for participants. He emphasized "the right to work" principle that was designed to achieve "the common good" rather than to realize profits.

Saint Simon

The first evidence that socialistic thought was developing to influence cooperative thinking is found in the ideas of another Frenchman, Saint Simon, and his followers. In about 1830 they envisioned competition as the "exploitation of man by man," and coined the famous phase "To each according to his ability, to each according to his work."

---

[3]Frank Robtka, "Cooperative Theory," *Journal of Farm Economics,* February 1947, pp. 94–95.

Philippe Buckez

Buckez applied the ideas of associated enterprise, proportional returns, indivisible capital, and limitations on the employment of "nonaffiliated" labor to the regulations and operations of worker cooperatives in France in the 1830s.

Louis Blanc

Blanc was a French revolutionist who looked on the State as an active supporter of cooperative activity—an approach that has been evaluated pro and con by cooperators ever since he advanced the idea in the 1840s.

We conclude that the main contribution of Owen and his contemporaries was their recognition of the impacts of the industrial revolution on society and their attempts to seek solutions to the problems that emerged. In so doing, they advanced broad concepts that emphasized voluntary membership and control by participants—concepts that cooperative business ventures later adapted to their organization and operating procedures.

THE ROCHDALE PIONEERS

Many cooperators accept the Rochdale principles as the distinguishing trademark of cooperative business endeavor. Here we will only identify the Rochdale pioneers as occupying an important place in the stream of cooperative thinking. In Chapter 3 we listed the Rochdale principles and compared them with other cooperative principles that have developed over the years.

It is important to note, however, that while the Pioneers were followers of Owen and hoped eventually to establish an ideal cooperative communal society, they were also realists. Hence, they were willing to take only one step at a time, and their first objective was to obtain better-quality food and clothing at reasonable costs. The many aspects of running local stores, developing a federated wholesale, and operating manufacturing plants used up all their resources and energies, and the idea of a cooperative commonwealth was postponed. It never actually materialized.

EARLY EUROPEAN POST-ROCHDALE THINKERS

Beatrice and Sidney Webb

The Webbs were Fabian socialists who were attracted to the Rochdale system of cooperation because it did away with the "profit-making entrepreneur." Beatrice Webb, in her book *The Co-operative Movement in Great Britain* (S. Sonnenschein and Company, London, 1889, p. 254), concluded that the cooperative techniques of patronage refunds and democratic control are compatible with the universal interests of consumers.

Notwithstanding the orientation of the Webbs to the cause of labor, they held no brief for producer (labor) cooperatives. In their view, such cooperatives retained the wage system and, what was worse, they might make "profit makers" of laborers. Thus, they drew sharp lines of demarcation between producer and consumer cooperation. They sought to encourage the cooperative commonwealth through trade unionism and political action, including taxation of "unearned wealth and surplus income." In their belief, this approach would lead to public enterprises in some instances and might discourage the consumer supremacy that many persons expected cooperatives to provide.

Charles Gide

Charles Gide, in addition to being an internationally recognized economist (his *Principles of Political Economy,* 1883, reportedly was later translated into forty-nine languages and issued in twenty-seven editions), was also a noted cooperative practitioner and theoretician. He first became interested in cooperatives when he helped to reconcile conflicts between member associates of the French Cooperative Union. He believed that the goal of cooperation should be to work not only for oneself, but also for others. To achieve that goal, workers should join together to raise the capital and purchase the necessary tools, thereby eliminating the capitalistic system of production.

Gide saw in cooperation the opposite of competition, and he believed strongly in the supremacy of the consumer. He advocated that the social and economic structure should be transformed by peaceful evolution. This achievement, he thought, would lead to cooperative domination that would transform cooperatives into national and municipal public service institutions favored by public opinion and supported by legislation.

Schulze-Delitzsch and Friedrich Wilhelm Raiffeisen

Schulze-Delitzsch, who was the founder of a number of consumer and manufacturing cooperatives, is known chiefly for his contribution to mutual credit associations. He accepted the established Rochdale principles with the exception of the distribution of savings to members. He maintained a strong anti-State bias, and his complete self-help orientation opposed the acceptance of any assistance from philanthropic sources or the State. His cooperative ideas centered strictly on economic improvement, and he desired to make members more affluent.

In contrast, Raiffeisen, the son of a German Lutheran minister, brought a highly ethical orientation to his credit union philosophy. He believed in going slowly but surely, and he emphasized the need for educating prospective members before oganizing a society. Unlike Schulze-Delitzsch, he stressed charity, believing that members should be "their brothers' keepers." Both men accepted the idea of unlimited member liability for the operation of credit unions. Raiffeisen is generally credited with being the "Father of the Credit Union Movement," which, with some modifications, spread to all parts of Germany and many other countries.

Both men started their cooperative work in the late 1840s and continued their efforts into the next two decades.

EARLY AMERICAN THINKERS

Early American cooperative thinkers, with the exception of James Peter Warbasse, had a rural orientation. They observed the initial and mostly unsuccessful attempts of general farm organizations to encourage cooperative efforts. They knew that the Grange introduced the Rochdale principles in the United States as early as 1875, and, as students of cooperation, they became acquainted with the thinking of cooperative scholars in Europe. Many of them were products of the land-grant college system, and they developed close contacts with farm people and understood their problems. They were, therefore, practical and realistic people, and they generally emphasized that cooperatives were business firms. They believed that cooperatives should operate with greater efficiency than their competitors if they were to make substantial contributions to the well-being of their rural members. Their thinking led to no finespun theories in the realm of social and political philosophy. Rather, they were concerned with cooperative business efficiency and performance so as best to serve the practical needs of farmers.

Before considering the views of leading contemporary agricultural cooperators in the United States, let us consider the ideas of the recognized pioneer leader of consumer cooperation in this country.

James Peter Warbasse[4]

Dr. Warbasse, a noted physician and surgeon, established the Cooperative League of the U.S.A. in 1916. He served as its president from 1916 to 1941 and, through grants and gifts, was its main financial supporter. He was a staunch believer in the Rochdale philosophy of cooperation. His views are well expressed in the dedication of his book *Cooperative Democracy,*[5] which brought him recognition as the leading spokesman for consumer cooperation in the United States. It reads, "Dedicated to consumers who are everybody and who may yet learn to unite to supply their needs, and ultimately to create a cooperative democracy through which to control and administer for their mutual service the useful functions now performed by profit-business and the political state."

It is easy to understand the consternation caused by his statement, "The ultimate destiny of the Consumers' Cooperative movement is to obtain or produce in factory, shop, mine, sea, air, and land all that consumers require." Many agricultural leaders took strong issue with such an objective—some of them rather provincial physiocrats in their own thinking. They believed that the views of Warbasse, if put into effect, would leave little opportunity for agricultural cooperatives to represent effectively their members' needs. It was not until agricultural leaders were assured that such a statement was not the official policy of the Cooperative League of the U.S.A. that some of them were willing to join the League. Speaking of Dr. Warbasse, Wallace J. Campbell said:

---

[4]Other cooperators who have contributed to American thinking regarding consumer cooperatives are Florence E. Parker, Murray D. Lincoln, and Jerry Voorhis. (See Knapp and Associates, op. cit.)

[5]Harper, New York, 1936.

... the Cooperative League in 1947 was a substantially different organization from the one that Dr. Warbasse had led in its earlier years. ... He lived a full and active life, gave generously of it, and perhaps endured no more than most parents who live to see their offspring come to independent adulthood. Heroes and founders are a people of the past; the present often speaks with blunt reality.[6]

Carl C. Taylor

We have emphasized that cooperatives are associations of people. As such, social, psychological, and ethnic overtones are often associated with their business efforts and hence deserve recognition. Carl C. Taylor, noted sociologist, writing in the 1940s and 1950s, gave attention to the social objectives of cooperatives. To him people are interested primarily in personal, rather than impersonal, relationships in business dealings. Secondly, he stressed that individuals naturally desire to join with others in pursuit of social objectives. He believed that cooperatives can be important in helping members to achieve these objectives.

There is, however, no universal agreement on this matter. Many people support the idea that competition is a stronger motivating force than cooperative relationships. Regardless of whether people respond to the desire to join with others or to compete with one another, these two conflicting views raise social questions that have important implications in respect to cooperative associations.

An ethical consideration appears when we raise the question: What happens when cooperative members realize economic benefits from operations? It is generally agreed that they are free to use these benefits as they see fit. There are those who believe that it is of no concern to cooperatives whether this income is directed to the realization of what are generally considered socially acceptable goals or dissipated in debauchery and intemperance. In contrast, there are those who look upon cooperatives as Christianity applied to business activities. Cooperatives to them are not only a way of life but a highly ethical way of life. They believe that cooperative business leads to a higher type of ethics in commercial activities, and they place more emphasis on frugality and the Christian ethic.

In commenting on religion as related to business ethics, Prof. Frank Robotka, formerly of Iowa State University, suggested that, although it is generally recognized that cooperatives have the potential for correcting certain business abuses, such reform is not a special Christian virtue since such abuses might also be corrected through legal or corporate action. He states: "... the cooperative is not an end but a means to an end. It is a tool like a hammer or atomic energy. The tool itself has no ethics. Is there such a thing as a Christian hammer? A cooperative ... may be used for good or evil ends. How it may be used will depend on the *ethics of the user*."[7]

Many view the exhilarating experiences of participation in the organization and operation of a cooperative as something that can be carried over into other activities of

---

[6]Knapp and Associates, op. cit., p. 533.
[7]Frank Robotka, *American Cooperation,* American Institute of Cooperation, Washington, D.C., 1950, p. 157.

life. For example, if cooperative members have learned that they can achieve certain economic objectives by working together, isn't it likely that they will be inclined to use the cooperative technique in dealing with a wide range of day-to-day problems? Their experience in a cooperative business undertaking may make them better community citizens who are able to participate more effectively in school board activities and political events.

Belonging to a cooperative may also give members a better understanding of how the economy functions, how businesses operate, and what can reasonably be expected as far as business performance is concerned.

Aaron Sapiro

Aaron Sapiro sold matches and newspapers on the streets of Oakland, California, at the age of five to add to the meager income of a large family. Later he earned a Phi Beta Kappa key in college. His association with cooperatives stems from his career as a brilliant lawyer who was first introduced to this form of business enterprise when he served as a legal counsel for the first market director of California. In the 1920s he was active in promoting large-scale centralized cooperatives among tobacco, cotton, grain, fruit, and livestock producers. He sought to form cooperatives that would be strong enough to tell merchants with whom they dealt what the price would be rather than ask them what they would pay. He emphasized that farmers need to organize large-scale centralized cooperative organizations in order to achieve monopoly powers for themselves. These "Sapiro cooperatives" relied on ironclad contracts with members to assure orderly delivery of products. His approach gained support at the time. Politicians favored it, many U.S. Department of Agriculture officials looked on it with interest, and university professors discussed and debated its possibilities.

Sapiro, however, overlooked membership, and he overemphasized the legal aspects of his marketing associations.

Experience demonstrated that farmers and their leaders were not ready for such far-reaching cooperative efforts. They lacked basic information on what could and could not be expected of marketing associations and their members. The lack of a member educational program meant that nearly all large-scale cooperatives organized by Sapiro soon passed out of the picture.

With the disappearance of the Sapiro type of cooperative associations, emphasis turned toward effective business performance and the development of membership and director awareness through educational programs.

John D. Black

While a professor in the Department of Agricultural Economics, University of Minnesota, Dr. Black (with H. Bruce Price) prepared a bulletin, *Cooperative Central Marketing Organizations*, in 1924 that gained national recognition. Its main significance was in the emphasis it placed on the possible advantages that may result from the economic integration of cooperative operations. The ideas it presented on economic integration and market structure were innovative at the time. Black and Price proposed basic approaches that were extremely important in identifying practices that would increase the operating efficiency of cooperatives.

Black continued his emphasis on economic integration as related to cooperatives, and some twenty years later he wrote:

> The simplest way to accomplish this integration is to set up large farmer cooperatives that handle the products all the way from the farmer to the consumer; or, as an alternative, large consumer cooperatives that do the same thing for the consumer end; or middlemen's cooperatives that operate along the same line, but from somewhere in the middle. This will put the whole marketing process under one management, which is thus in a position to integrate all steps in it and make all of them efficient.[8]

Edwin G. Nourse

Dr. Edwin G. Nourse (a university professor, 1909–1923; director of the Institute of Economics and former vice president, Brookings Institution, 1927–1946; and the first chairman of the President's Council of Economic Advisors, 1946–1949) was interested in cooperatives throughout his illustrious professional career. In addition to being president of both the American Economic Association and the American Farm Economics Association, he was also one of the founders of the American Institute of Cooperation.

Dr. Nourse believed that the Rochdale principles ought to be reexamined in light of the changing conditions of agriculture. He placed special emphasis on the role of marketing cooperatives, and he accepted the central ideas of democratic control, limited returns on equity capital, and distribution of savings to members on the basis of their patronage.

His greatest contributions to cooperative thinking were his emphases on business efficiency, equitable distribution of control and benefits, and the relation of law to cooperative structure and operations. Nourse believed that efficient cooperative performance depends on avoiding unnecessary duplication of effort, identifying member needs with association performance, achieving sufficient size to bargain effectively, and adjusting production to market requirements. Nourse also stressed that cooperatives should be an effective tool for equitable distribution of wealth. His emphases on limited capital holdings, restricted voting privileges, and democratic control brought into focus the importance he attached to the individual member.

To round out his philosophy regarding cooperatives, Nourse feared political expediency in government, and he believed that the inherent conflict of self-help versus government assistance was unresolved. Nourse was a staunch foe of monopolies, and he looked on cooperatives as a counterbalancing force that could help farmers to achieve equality in the marketplace.

E. A. Stokdyk

E. A. Stokdyk, president of the Berkeley Bank for Cooperatives (1933–1945), Berkeley, California, in an article in the *Cooperative Digest* (August 1946, pp. 54–58), emphasized that cooperatives were in effect vehicles for resisting monopolies rather than monopolistic instruments in themselves. This role, he reasoned, resulted from the

---

[8]In *Journal of Farm Economics,* August 1947, p. 627.

important changes that were taking place in the agricultural economy—namely, the improvements in production techniques and the trend toward a large-scale distribution system, better transportation arrangements, and strong financial centers.

These forces motivated farmers to flex their economic muscles. How better could they advance economically than through their own cooperatives? He emphasized that while cooperatives were nonprofit in nature, members were motivated by the profit incentive. He pointed out that an effectively integrated marketing association can serve as the farmers' middleman by performing various marketing functions. In this way the middleman was not eliminated; instead, the farmers, through their cooperatives, performed the middleman function themselves. Thus, they were able to obtain for themselves the various margins that might be realized by performing the different marketing functions.

More specifically, Stokdyk listed the objectives of marketing cooperatives as follows: (1) introduction of improved techniques with respect to grading and standardization; (2) development of highly differentiated products which would make effective advertising possible (Land O' Lakes Butter, Sunkist Citrus Products, and Diamond Walnuts are examples of such efforts); (3) ability to feed the market by allocating products produced over short periods to meet the long-term needs of consumers; (4) improvement of the market environment; and (5) achievement of more effective bargaining power.

Joseph G. Knapp

Joseph G. Knapp, Administrator, Farmer Cooperative Service, U.S. Department of Agriculture, 1953–1965, identified the objectives of purchasing cooperatives as antimonopolistic in character. He emphasized that the first objective of these cooperatives is *to provide members with products of the quality they desire at no higher cost than other suppliers charge*. There are many examples of such an achievement. One is the cooperative innovation of manufacturing and distributing high-analysis fertilizers that no longer use sand as filler. Another is the introduction of open-formula feeds to enable farmers to know exactly the ingredients that go into the feed they are using. Similarly, many purchasing cooperatives emphasized the importance of quality seeds—seeds that were adapted by the local community and were free of obnoxious weeds and other impurities. Southern States Cooperative, Inc., Richmond, Virginia, was known, for example, as Virginia Seed Service during its early years of operation because it gave special attention to providing high-quality seeds for members.

Knapp emphasized that the second objective of purchasing cooperatives is *to provide members with just the types of supplies and services they desire*. This responsibility sometimes requires that they provide services for patrons that hitherto were unavailable. In other cases, special attention is given to helping members plan their production practices. For example, by implementing a soil-testing program and providing suitable fertilizers, these cooperatives have made substantial progress in enabling their members to improve production practices.

The third basic objective of farm supply cooperatives identified by Knapp is *to help members save money*. With an emphasis on efficiency, some cooperatives have eliminated unsound business practices and services that are no longer needed. Purchasing cooperatives generally have an enviable record when it comes to returning savings to members. Many have returned to members millions of dollars annually, and over the years these savings usually have averaged between 3 and 7 cents per dollar of purchases.

In addition, Knapp, in *Farmers in Business: Studies in Cooperative Enterprise,*[9] a book that reproduces some fifty of his articles and talks, presents his cooperative thinking under the following headings: "The Nature of Cooperative Business Enterprise," "Organization and Operation," "Lessons from Experience," "Challenges and Problems," and "The Road Ahead." Knapp also was a pioneer in studies of economic integration as applied to cooperatives (see *The Hard Winter Wheat Pools: An Experiment in Agricultural Market Integration*).[10]

Ivan V. Emelianoff, Frank Robotka,[11] and Richard Phillips

The observations on the ideas of these cooperative thinkers are largely limited to those of Emelianoff. With minor exceptions, Robotka and Phillips accepted his views wholeheartedly and served largely as enthusiastic endorsers of the ideas he expounded.

Ivan Emelianoff, a Russian exile, developed his ideas on the economic nature of cooperatives in his book *Economic Theory of Cooperation.*[12] His theme throughout is that a cooperative is an "aggregate of enterprises and households" and not an enterprise in itself. If one asks why, the explanation appears to be that Emelianoff says so; and say so he does with monotonous regularity, as well as with dogmatic and uncompromising assurance. In one breath, he emphasizes that cooperatives are exclusively economic in nature and have no vestiges of human relationships; in another, he would have us believe that "the cooperative problem is a many-sided one and can be interpreted by lawyers, sociologists, social philosophers, moralists, political scientists, as well as by economists."[13] He tells us that cooperation has a "bewitching power," and that "it hypnotizes those who approach it."[14] One cannot but wonder if this does not explain why some of his interpretations try to support what appear to be preconceived ends.

Emelianoff's ideas are quite effectively demolished by Savage and Davidovic. In evaluating Emelianoff's economic views, Davidovic states,

> Emelianoff's entire economic theory of cooperation is an artificial construction, a speculation, an endless argument to prove some preconceived ideas. All the information, all the

[9] American Institute of Cooperation, Washington, D.C., 1963.
[10] The University of Chicago Press, 1933, p. 176.
[11] It would not be fair to Frank Robotka to think of him only as a member of this triumvirate of theoretical cooperative dissenters. In his own right as a distinguished cooperative scholar, researcher, and teacher at Iowa State University over a period of some thirty-five years, his contributions were substantial. He had a leading role in revising the Iowa Cooperative Law in 1935, and he was instrumental in organizing the Iowa Institute of Cooperation. He was a critical student of cooperative theory and, through a coordinated research and extension program in Iowa, he influenced the operations of many of the state's cooperatives. In his writings he emphasized the need for a multidiscipline approach in analyzing the problems of cooperatives. He stressed the need for cooperative educational programs and the importance of research as a basis for making sound policy decisions.
[12] Edwards Brothers, Inc., Ann Arbor, Mich., 1942.
[13] Ivan V. Emelianoff, *Economic Theory of Cooperation*, Edwards Brothers, 1942, p. 246.
[14] Ibid., p. 245.

data he presents, all the quotations he uses tend to go toward the same end. His arguments are as contrary to cooperative principles and reasoning, as his tortuous economic demonstrations are superficial and incorrect.[15]

Peter Helmberger and Sidney Hoos follow Savage and others in taking issue with Emelianoff and Phillips in their article "Cooperative Enterprise and Organization Theory."[16]

Emelianoff would have us believe that cooperatives achieve no economic results: "Based on the patronage of their own members, the cooperatives obviously serve as clearing offices of their patrons and an absolute acquisitive sterility of the cooperative association under such conditions . . . is the only corollary of their economic structure."[17] If Emelianoff had observed cooperatives in operation, he would have noticed that many of them were able to achieve an increased price of milk for farmer members by several cents per 100 pounds, or a reduced feed price by several dollars per ton. Davidovic puts it another way when he says, "One of the fundamental characteristics of cooperative enterprise is precisely that it transforms profit for capital into earned income for people [patrons]."[18]

As for the relationships with members, Emelianoff advances the ideas that (1) cooperatives should deal only with members, and (2) cooperatives have no influence on members. The answer to the first assertion is: Actual experience has shown that such a practice often results in inefficient operation and even inability to serve members adequately. As for the second of Emelianoff's ideas, Savage states:

> In some ways a cooperative is like the state. It seeks no profit for itself but for its citizens. . . . The state is organized to enforce the common will concerning certain phases of human conduct; whereas cooperatives are organized to carry out the common will of select groups dealing with the economic phase of human conduct, and correct analysis of their composition and purpose will not deny them the power to exercise the will delegated to them by their individual members."[19]

There seems to be every reason to agree with Davidovic when he says: "A cooperative influences its membership economically, socially, and morally, not because it wants to, but because it cannot do otherwise, as long as it exists and deals."[20]

The question also might be asked: If a cooperative is made up of member firms, as Emelianoff believes, is there any reason why, when they join together, they might not be forming another firm? If there is any reason why off-farm business may not be organized and operated as a separate firm, Emelianoff does not explain it.

Emelianoff makes much of the principle of proportionality as applied to the distribution of savings. While this is a pre-Rochdale discovery, it does not necessarily

---

[15]George Davidovic, "The Character of Cooperative Enterprise," *C.I.R.I.E.C., Canadian Review,* vol. 3, no. 2, July–December, 1970, p. 32.
[16]*Journal of Farm Economics,* May 1962.
[17]Emelianoff, op. cit., pp. 75–76.
[18]Davidovic, op. cit., p. 61.
[19]Job K. Savage, "Economic Nature of the Cooperative Association," *Journal of Farm Economics,* August 1954, p. 532.
[20]Davidovic, op. cit., p. 63.

follow that all cooperatives should use it in the control of their operations. On this point Savage further says: "I think the decision by the cooperative group as to whether they will have voting on the basis of proportional production or on that of "one man-one vote" will depend on facts which the classical model (Phillips) is not equipped to deal with. This decision will be influenced by ethical and social reasons as much as by economic considerations."[21]

It may be asked: Why is so much consideration given to a system of cooperative thought that no longer seems to have realistic foundations or general acceptance? Moreover, Emelianoff's system has scarcely made a ripple in the thinking of practical cooperators in the United States. In contrast, however, many professional people believed that Emelianoff's ideas were new, and they seized upon them without very critical evaluation.

RECENT VIEWS REGARDING COOPERATIVES

During the past twenty-five years, American economists have directed little attention to the unique nature of cooperatives, their basic objectives, and the place they occupy in the nation's economy.[22] While a number of articles have appeared in professional journals and other publications, they have been concerned largely with problems of structure and selected aspects of operations.[23]

Many of these writings also have been characterized by what some consider to be a propensity to make unrelated, unsupported, and gratuitous observations relative to "special treatment" and "exceptional privileges" accorded cooperatives and their status as to tax treatment, application of antitrust laws, and bargaining operations. These observations are briefly examined here.

"Special Treatment" and "Exceptional Privileges"

Two things can be said about such observations: (1) When one considers recent actions of regulatory agencies and even legislators, it would be necessary to look hard and long to find special treatment or exceptional privileges that are favorable to cooperatives. And (2) one may ask whether writers are really objective when they do not at least balance such observations, for whatever they are worth, with recognition of the special treatment accorded such firms as the Pennsylvania Railroad, the Lockheed Corporation, and the major oil companies.

---

[21] Savage, op. cit., p. 533.

[22] Exceptions are: (1) Peter Helmberger and Sidney Hoos, "Cooperative Enterprise and Organization Theory," *Journal of Farm Economics,* May 1966; (2) Raphael Trafon, "The Economics of Cooperative Ventures," *Journal of Farm Economics,* May 1961; and (3) Ronald Knutson, "Cooperative Strategies in Imperfect Competitive Markets," *Journal of Agricultural Economics,* December 1974.

[23] See Eugene Clark, "Farmer Cooperatives and Economic Welfare," *Journal of Farm Economics,* February 1952; Peter G. Helmberger, "Cooperative Enterprise as a Structural Dimension of Farm Markets," *Journal of Farm Economics,* August 1964, and "The Future Role for Agricultural Cooperatives," *Journal of Farm Economics,* December 1966; James G. Youde and Peter G. Helmberger, "Marketing Cooperatives in the U.S.: Member Policies, Market Power, and Antitrust Policy," *Journal of Farm Economics,* August, 1966; Harold F. Breimyer, *Individual Freedom and Economic Organization of Agriculture,* The University of Illinois Press, Urbana, 1965, chap. 16; and James Rhodes, *Who Will Control Agriculture,* North Central Regional Extension Bulletin 32, Cooperative Extension Service, University of Illinois, Urbana-Champaign.

Income Tax Treatment

To speak of cooperatives maximizing profits or of cooperatives avoiding income taxes shows the need for what Breimyer calls "accuracy and impartiality" when objectively exploring the cooperative taxation issue. Cooperatives do not maximize profits as a firm nor do they avoid paying income taxes when they have no income to tax. (Chapter 11 examines the cooperative taxation issue in further detail.)

Application of Antitrust Laws

Much confusion exists among economists as well as regulatory agencies when they examine the question of monopoly as it relates to the application of antitrust laws to cooperatives. There seems to be too little awareness of the fact that distinct treatment of cooperatives has been recognized by the courts because of the unique nature of their operations. To the extent that cooperatives are treated differently from other corporations, the special approach may well be only a means of attempting to achieve equitable treatment *for* them rather than an attempt to bestow special favors *upon* them. Quite generally, too, economists and others have failed to recognize cooperatives as an antimonopoly force.

Another area that needs careful exploration in antitrust discussions is the common misuse of the word "exemption" when referring to cooperatives. Likewise, there is a tendency, when suggesting the elimination of section 2 of the Capper-Volstead Act, to ignore the fact that this section was developed specifically to protect consumers. The fact that there has been little occasion to enforce provisions of this section may well indicate the nonexploitative nature of cooperative business enterprise rather than failure to use the section. (The antitrust issue as it relates to cooperatives is discussed in more detail in Chapter 10.)

Bargaining

Bargaining is another area where considerable confusion exists among economists. There is often a tendency to view bargaining associations as unlike cooperatives—especially to contend that they are not involved in the marketing of farm products. This is to ignore that marketing need not necessarily require the physical handling of products. The important point is that as a result of bargaining efforts, title to products does change. Moreover, that bargaining is marketing was supported by the recent decision in *Treasure Valley Potato Bargaining Association v. Ore-Ida Foods, Inc.* In this case, the court held that bargaining, in effect, means marketing when an association negotiates a contract of sale for its members. (Bargaining is discussed more fully in Chapter 18.)

Obviously the issues we have identified are of basic importance to cooperatives. If they are to be examined, they cannot be disposed of through rather incidental observations growing out of general studies. They are fruitful fields for detailed and objective study that are a worthy challenge to the best efforts of economists.

Ronald D. Knutson, administrator (1973–1975) of Farmer Cooperative Service, did much to put into realistic perspective the nature of the economy in which cooperatives operate when he pointed out that "the pervasiveness of imperfect competition in agriculture is not generally recognized. If it is recognized it is seldom taken into consideration. More often than not our research is done in a vacuum of purely competitive explicit or implicit assumptions. . . ."[24]

He further emphasizes that cooperatives, notwithstanding the attention that has been directed to their size and operating practices, usually are in a weak market position. If they are to operate effectively in today's economy, he further contends, they have a need to integrate their operations "horizontally, vertically, and conglomerately." Such integration, he emphasizes, has special legal implications, particularly as it relates to the Capper-Volstead Act and to marketing with respect to nonmember problems, bargaining activities, and joint ventures—especially those with corporations other than cooperatives. To Knutson this means that cooperatives "should remain competitive, not-monopolistic . . . ," and that they should take steps to "remain pure and family-farmer oriented" in order to protect their legal status under the Capper-Volstead Act.

SUMMARY

A review of the more recent thinking regarding the unique nature of cooperatives suggests some of the questions of economists that need to be explored further. Foremost of these are:

- To what extent should membership be selective or voluntary?
- What are the inherent problems and conflicts in the concepts of equal versus equitable treatment of members?
- To what extent is control on the basis of volume of business compatible with the accepted principles of cooperation?
- Cooperatives have continually wrestled with the problems of their relationships with government. At issue is the question: Should cooperatives "go it alone," or is it reasonable and desirable for them to seek government assistance? Can such assistance be accepted while still maintaining the basic features of democratic control? Other aspects of government relations that are in need of further study are the relationships of cooperatives with regulatory agencies and an evaluation of present and prospective cooperative legislation.
- Do cooperatives from time to time attain a monopoly position in their business activities, or are they essentially an antimonopoly institution?
- Can cooperatives achieve desirable goals by serving as a measuring stick by which to judge business efficiency and operations?
- Does the emphasis that cooperatives place on service and benefits to members put them in a unique or distinct category with respect to taxation, application of antitrust laws, and bargaining?
- Is the cooperatives' emphasis on efficiency of their business operations compatible with the view that they also have social responsibilities?
- How far can and should cooperatives integrate their operations, and what are the implications of integration on their organizational structure and operating practices?

[24]Ronald Knutson, "Cooperative Strategies in Imperfect Competitive Market Structures—A Policy Perspective," *Journal of Agricultural Economics,* December 1974, pp. 905–907, 912.

• How far is it feasible for cooperatives to go in undertaking joint ventures with other cooperatives? With firms other than cooperatives?
• Given the unique nature of cooperatives, to what extent can their operations be accounted for by the economic theories of market structure or by public welfare analysis?

All these questions, the issues they raise, and the widely varying views that have been expressed about them suggest the need for economists to explore carefully and objectively these cooperative issues. It is hoped that a better understanding of the implications of these and related questions will unfold as we pursue our studies of cooperative business enterprise.

The importance of the cooperative institution to farmers and other rural people emphasizes the responsibilities of researchers and writers in this field. A realistic approach is needed to bring into proper focus the place of cooperatives in the imperfect economy in which they operate. These subjects are worthy of the most penetrating analysis, and they deserve impartial and objective research.

QUESTIONS

1. What is meant by the statement "Cooperatives are long on practice but short on theory"?
2. Are we justified in describing Robert Owen as the "Father of Cooperation"?
3. Contrast the views of early English and early French cooperative thinkers.
4. What are the basic contributions of the Rochdale pioneers to cooperative thought? How did they benefit from views of their predecessors?
5. Contrast the cooperative ideas of Schulze-Delitzsch and Friedrich Wilhelm Raiffeisen.
6. Compare the cooperative views of James Peter Warbasse and Edwin G. Nourse.
7. Who were the American thinkers who stressed the concept of cooperative business efficiency, and what were the forces that led them to do so?
8. Who was the first American to emphasize the desirability of economic integration by cooperatives, and what was the significance of this concept?
9. What are the basic tenets of the Emelianoff economic theory of cooperation? Evaluate the strengths and weaknesses of this theory.
10. Contrast the cooperative views of Aaron Sapiro and E. A. Stokdyk.
11. Is there a basis for promoting a social and ethical theory of cooperation? Who was the principal proponent of this theory in the United States?
12. What problems have economists encountered in applying the concepts of the firm, market structure, marginal analysis, and welfare economics to cooperatives?
13. Are the assertions of some present-day economists that cooperatives have tax advantages, have favorable antitrust status, and are granted special government assistance well founded?

REFERENCES

Abrahamsen, Martin A., and Claude L. Scroggs: *Agricultural Cooperation: Selected Readings,* The University of Minnesota Press, Minneapolis, 1957, pp. 57–203.

Aresvik, Oddvor: "Comments on the Economic Nature of the Cooperative Association," *Journal of Farm Economics,* vol. 37, no. 1, pp. 140–144.

Bonner, Arnold: *British Cooperation,* Cooperative Union Ltd., Manchester, England, chaps. 1–3, 17, 18, pp. 1–58, 429–491.

Davidovic, George: "The Character of Cooperative Enterprise," *C.I.R.I.E.C., Canadian Review,* July–December 1970, pp. 27–90.

Emelianoff, Ivan V.: *Economic Theory of Cooperation,* Edwards Brothers, Inc., Ann Arbor, Mich., 1942, p. 269.

Helmberger, Peter: "Cooperatives as a Structural Dimension of Markets," *Journal of Farm Economics,* vol. 46, no. 3, pp. 603–617.

——— and Sidney Hoos: "Cooperative Enterprise and Organization Theory," *Journal of Farm Economics,* vol. 44, no. 2, pp. 275–290.

Knapp, Joseph G., and Associates: *Great American Cooperators: Profiles of 101 Cooperative Pacemakers* (no. 17, J. D. Black; no. 70, Edwin Griswold Nourse; no. 82, Frank Robotka; no. 85, Aaron Sapiro; no. 90, E. A. Stokdyk; no. 93, Carl C. Taylor; and no. 98, James Peter Warbasse), American Institute of Cooperation, Washington, D.C., 1967.

Knutson, Donald D.: "Cooperatives and the Competitive Ideal," *Journal of Farm Economics,* vol. 48, no. 5, pp. 111–121.

Lambert, Paul: *Studies in the Social Philosophy of Cooperation,* Cooperative League of the U.S.A., Washington, D.C. pp. 37–158.

Youde, James A., and Peter Helmberger: "Marketing Cooperatives in the U.S.: Membership Policies, Market Power, and Antitrust Policy," *Journal of Farm Economics,* vol. 48, no. 3, part II, pp. 23–36.

Chapter 5

Historical Development of Cooperatives in the United States[1]

Many forces have contributed to the development of cooperatives in the United States during the past two and a half centuries. During that time, on a trial-and-error basis, various types of cooperative enterprises have come into being. They have ranged in scope from local enterprises to large-scale, national associations that serve farmer, consumer, and worker groups. The understanding, the dedication, and the competency of some government agencies—both state and federal—have made important contributions to cooperative development. Also, hundreds of cooperative leaders have provided a high degree of similar support.

Not all the cooperatives that came into being over the decades, however, succeeded. By learning from failures and successes, sound operating principles and practices have gradually evolved. American cooperatives also have benefited greatly from cooperative experiences in other lands—particularly Great Britain and the Scandinavian countries.

---

[1]Much of the material presented in this chapter is an adaptation and updating of information developed for FCS Bulletin Reprint 1, prepared by the author when he was associated with Farmer Cooperative Service, U.S. Department of Agriculture. In addition, Joseph G. Knapp, in *The Rise of American Cooperative Enterprise: 1620–1920,* provided much useful information.

EARLY COOPERATIVE EXPLORATIONS: UP TO 1870

Joseph G. Knapp, in tracing early cooperative developments in the United States, mentions that the Pilgrim Fathers, by terms of the Mayflower Compact in 1620, banded together in what was a mutual agreement on a cooperative basis. By so doing, they were able to deal more effectively with the problems that grew out of the dangers and tribulations of establishing homes in a new land. Their efforts were followed by numerous cooperative explorations on the part of agricultural, urban, and industrial groups.

In Agriculture

The following are examples of important early cooperative developments that occurred in the agricultural area:

- As early as the 1780s, farmers organized societies to import purebred cattle; later, they joined in community drives of livestock to the eastern coastal cities. Early agricultural developments were colorful. They included husking bees, threshing rings, bull and stallion rings, cheese rings, and other forms of group activity. They grew out of necessity and reflected the ingenuity of the participants.
- In 1810, associated groups of dairy farmers organized cooperatives to manufacture cheese in Goshen, Connecticut, and South Trenton, New York.
- In 1820, a group of Ohio farmers united to slaughter their hogs and transport them by boat to the Montreal markets.
- During the early 1800s, rural mutual fire insurance companies became common in New England. By 1860, about one hundred such companies were in operation. These organizations have been referred to as "the primary schools of American cooperation."
- In the 1840s, Mormon settlers in the West introduced cooperative irrigation ventures that were highly successful. Members paid for irrigation on a cost-of-service basis.
- In 1857, a cooperative grain elevator was organized at Madison, Wisconsin. It failed when the manager absconded with the money.
- Farmers' clubs were organized in both Wisconsin and Illinois in the 1850s to buy farm supplies, and farmers at Riverhead, New York, organized a cooperative in 1863 to buy fertilizers.
- A fruit and vegetable marketing cooperative was organized in New Jersey in 1867.

In Urban and Industrial Communities

The following examples illustrate early cooperative developments among urban and industrial groups:

- In 1735, Benjamin Franklin took the lead in organizing the Union Fire Company, a mutual association to fight fires. Later, his proposal for developing some form of mutual fire insurance led to the formation of the Philadelphia Contributionship for the Insurance of Houses from Loss by Fire in 1752. This idea proved so successful that by 1800, ten other insurance companies were operating in the Philadelphia area. By 1830, mutual insurance companies had expanded operations to include coverage of factories and life.

- In 1806, the Journeyman Cordwainers of Philadelphia decided to become their own employees. For a time, they marketed, on both a wholesale and a retail basis, shoes and boots manufactured by members.
- By 1830, much interest in cooperative workshops had risen among furniture makers, cabinetmakers, weavers, tailors, and saddlers.
- In the 1840s, with the support and encouragement of labor unions, a number of cooperative store ventures were tried. They were successful for a few years, but gradually failed, owing to incompetent management and irresponsible members.
- Building and loan associations were founded in the 1850s to combat the high cost of housing. They adopted as their motto, "Do Your Own Landlording."
- A unique development in cooperative living occurred in 1825 when the famous New Harmony Indiana Cooperative Colony was established under the direction and encouragement of Robert Owen—the well-known British cooperator and philanthropist. It was a poorly planned venture and most participants had little if any understanding of their responsibilities. As a result, the colony failed within three years.

THE AGE OF EXPERIMENTATION: 1870-1920

After the Civil War, farmers stepped up their search for self-help methods and techniques that would aid them in solving their intensifying economic problems. At this time, two general farm organizations, first the National Grange and then the Farmers' Alliance, made an important contribution by introducing cooperatives into the nation's agricultural areas.

The National Grange

The National Grange, known officially as The Order of Patrons of Husbandry, was founded in 1867. Oliver Hudson Kelley, of the U.S. Department of Agriculture, was active in its formation. Largely because its local granges urged it to deal with the economic problems of their members, the National Grange soon turned its attention to cooperatives. Cooperative marketing was emphasized in some states, cooperative buying in others, and both marketing and buying in still others.

Early local granges assembled farmer-members' orders and placed them with dealers who often shipped carloads of supplies directly to them or to their farmer-members. The local granges obtained price concessions from suppliers for quantity purchases in wholesale lots. One such supplier was Montgomery Ward and Company, organized in 1872 and known as "the original Grange supply house." Much of its business was with grange groups in Illinois and other Midwestern states. Between 1871 and 1876, more than 20,000 local granges, as well as some 26 state agency systems, were established. County granges in many cases served as business enterprises for members of the local units.

In its heyday, the National Grange organized many cooperative stores in Michigan, Maine, New York, Kansas, Texas, and California. They sold groceries, clothing, general farm supplies, hardware, and agricultural implements. In Iowa, a cooperative was organized to manufacture grain binders. Grangers in the South concentrated on marketing cotton. State organizations in Alabama and Mississippi put selected cotton firms under bond. The Alabama Grange had an agency in New York City to handle cotton on consignment, and the Mississippi Grange had its own cotton sales office in Liverpool, England.

In 1874, the National Grange sent a representative abroad to gather information about European cooperation. As a result of the representative's findings, the Grange began to sponsor the organization of business cooperatives. Although this venture was undertaken too late to save many grange organizations that were encountering operating difficulties, it did introduce the seeds of cooperation to fertile American soil. While the Grange never again achieved the dominant position in cooperative affairs it enjoyed in the 1870s and 1880s, it has continually encouraged and supported cooperative endeavors. Until the 1960s, a number of statewide associations in the Far West were still known as Grange cooperatives.

The Farmers' Alliance

Following the decline of the Grange in the late 1870s, the Farmers' Alliance sprang up in several areas, and later these local units united and spread over the whole South. Efforts of the Alliance in cooperative business enterprises were quite similar to those of the Grange. It became especially active in the later years of the 1880s.

While most of the Grange and Alliance cooperatives died young, those that survived provided a seedbed from which important pilot-plant operations developed. The results were these: (1) Many people came to understand the significance of cooperatives as a self-help tool. (2) The value and the effectiveness of the Rochdale principles were demonstrated. (3) The importance of sound principles of business operations as a requisite for success was recognized. (4) People gained an understanding of the possibilities and limitations of cooperative business ventures.

As we shall see, the experience gained in these early years made it possible for the Farmers Educational and Cooperative Union of America and the American Farm Bureau Federation—two additional general farm organizations—and several other unaffiliated independent groups to establish cooperatives on a firmer foundation at the turn of this century.

The Farmers Educational and Cooperative Union of America

The Farmers Union, the third general farm organization to advocate and sponsor cooperative business enterprises, was launched in Texas in 1902 as an outgrowth of the Farmers' Alliance movement. Although the Farmers Union dealt with educational and social problems, it emphasized mainly economic activities.

In its first years, it performed purchasing and marketing services through Farmers Union locals, but it soon began organizing local cooperatives and, in later years, federated and centralized regional associations. The Farmers Union was first active in Arkansas, Louisiana, Mississippi, and Texas. Later it became especially prominent in Colorado, Kansas, Minnesota, Missouri, Montana, Nebraska, North Dakota, Oklahoma, South Dakota, Washington, and Wisconsin.

In the South, the Farmers Union concentrated on storing and marketing cotton, on improving cotton prices, and on establishing a credit and mortgage system. It also used the business-agent system for buying supplies for members of Farmers Union locals. In the Midwestern states, it gave attention to organizing cooperative elevators, creameries, livestock shipping associations, stores, and oil and supply cooperatives.

The Farmers Union consistently advocated buying production supplies by the carlot. The secretary or purchasing agent of a local, sometimes jointly with a nearby local, made up carlot orders of supplies needed by members. State organizations, directly or through a subsidiary, developed contracts with supplying business firms. Eventually these activities led to the organization of cooperatives to distribute production supplies. The State Farmers Union in Nebraska established a wholesale supply purchasing department in 1914 to serve Farmers Union locals, other cooperatives, and some farmers directly. In 1919, a separate wholesale cooperative, the Farmers Union State Exchange, Omaha, Nebraska, was formed. The influence of the Farmers Union on cooperatives has continued to the present day.

In the early 1930s, Nebraska reported about 100 Farmers Union cooperative stores, 100 oil associations, 200 elevators and cream stations which also handled supplies, and about 50 Farmers Union locals buying supplies through secretaries or agents.

In 1965, the Farmers Union State Exchange merged with the Farmers' Elevator Service Company, Fort Dodge, Iowa, to form Felco (later known as Farmers' Regional Cooperative). Since 1970, Farmers' Regional Cooperative has been a part of the farm supply operations of Land O' Lakes, Inc.

The Farmers Union also exercised a great deal of influence in organizing cooperative livestock shipping associations, both local and regional, and commission associations at terminal points. The first of these commission associations was set up at South Omaha, Nebraska, in 1917, and it pioneered the way for several similar organizations. One was established at St. Joseph, Missouri, the same year. In 1918, the Farmers Union Livestock Commission opened at Sioux City, Iowa. At that time the Farmers Union Livestock Commission Association, Kansas City, Kansas, was organized. A year later, a Farmers Union Livestock Commission Association was formed at Denver, Colorado.

The Farmers Union helped organize many cooperative grain-marketing associations, particularly in Kansas, Nebraska, and the Dakotas. In 1914, the Kansas associations formed a regional grain-marketing agency (Farmers Union Jobbing Association, Kansas City, Missouri), to sell their members' grain on the terminal market.

Another successful enterprise was the Farmers Union Cooperative Creamery Company, Superior, Nebraska, which was organized in 1917 and began operating in 1920.

The Minnesota Farmers Union purchased the Equity Cooperative Exchange at St. Paul, Minnesota, in 1922. In 1925, the Farmers Union Terminal Association was formed at St. Paul. This was the forerunner of the present Farmers Union Grain Terminal Association (GTA), which began operations in 1938. The original terminal association set up a subsidiary in 1927 to market supplies. In 1931, this subsidiary was incorporated separately as the Farmers Union Central Exchange, St. Paul, Minnesota.

This organization, known as Cenex since 1972, has been listed in *Fortune* magazine's list of 500 leading industrial concerns for a number of years.

The American Farm Bureau Federation

Another major general farm organization that influenced and stimulated business cooperation among farmers was the American Farm Bureau Federation, with its various state and county affiliates. The Farm Bureau was unique among general farm organizations in that it grew out of the agricultural extension service movement. The various state Farm Bureau federations formed the national organization in 1919, but it was not until the 1920s that the Farm Bureau Federation became involved in cooperatives. It began by setting up special committees of thirteen to twenty-one members to prepare plans for cooperative marketing enterprises in the fields of livestock, grain, fruits and vegetables, and eggs.

As a result of the efforts of these committees, several national organizations were established, including the United States Grain Growers, Inc., Federated Fruit and Vegetable Growers, Inc., and the National Livestock Producers' Association, all of Chicago. The first two operated only a few years.

The American Farm Bureau Federation, in sponsoring the organization of cooperatives, frequently assumed the expenses incurred before organization and furnished initial capital. The cooperatives usually repaid the money advanced for these expenses.

Farm Bureaus in various states also were interested in the cooperative purchase of production supplies for farmers. In 1921–1923, those in Indiana, Ohio, and Mississippi pooled members' orders for carload shipments of items used in quantity.

Later in the mid-1920s, many countywide Farm Bureau supply associations became incorporated.

Within a short time, a number of statewide Farm Bureau wholesale cooperatives were organized to serve affiliated local supply associations. These cooperatives expanded operations, and many now provide marketing services as well as production supplies and related services. Included among large-scale regional associations having Farm Bureau ancestry are: Illinois Farm Supply Co. (now F. S. Services, Inc.), Bloomington, Illinois; Indiana Farm Bureau Cooperative Association, Indianapolis, Indiana; The Farm Bureau Cooperative Association (now Landmark, Inc.), Columbus, Ohio; Tennessee Farmers' Cooperative, La Vergne, Tennessee; and Farm Bureau Services, Inc., Lansing, Michigan.

During the 1920s the American Farm Bureau Federation became a major educational and business organization for the nation's farmers. As such, it acknowledged the importance of cooperatives and it sought to improve their purchasing and marketing activities.

Federal and State Government Encouragement

From 1900 to 1920, several government efforts stimulated the development of agricultural cooperatives. To be discussed in detail in Chapter 21, here they are only briefly identified:

- In 1908, President Theodore Roosevelt formed the Country Life Commission. It called attention to the success of cooperative credit associations in Europe and recognized the contributions and improvements that cooperatives could make to rural living by introducing better business practices.
- President Woodrow Wilson, in 1913, sent a commission to Europe to study and report on cooperative development there. As a result, the Federal Farm Loan Act was passed. It provided long-range mortgage credit for farmers and later proved to be the forerunner of the present cooperative Farm Credit System.
- Also in 1913, the U.S. Department of Agriculture established the Office of Markets, which initiated a comprehensive research and advisory service program for cooperatives.
- The Smith-Lever Act, passed in 1914, provided for the extension system of the U.S. Department of Agriculture and the state agricultural colleges. Thus, by bringing about new opportunities for study and education, it increased the importance of cooperatives.
- Another development that encouraged cooperatives at this time was the general support of state universities. For example, in 1908 Alexander E. Cance was hired by Massachusetts State College of Agriculture to teach the first course in agricultural cooperation in the United States. In rapid succession, the states of New York, Minnesota, Wisconsin, and Kentucky offered similar courses, conducted research on the problems of cooperatives, and took the results of their research to rural people in action-oriented extension programs.

Two other cooperative developments during this period were important:

- The first two national cooperative trade associations were organized in 1916. They were the Cooperative League of the U.S.A. and the National Milk Producers Federation, both now having headquarters in Washington, D.C.
- By 1920, in addition to local cooperatives, large-scale federated and centralized cooperatives were actively marketing the products of American farmers.

COOPERATIVE COMMODITY MARKETING GAINS: 1920–1933

Early in 1920, "orderly commodity marketing" became an accepted slogan of the American farmer. It focused on developments that were already underway and proposed the creation of regional associations to handle an entire crop in important producing areas.

The original impetus for this movement developed at a meeting in Montgomery, Alabama, in April 1920. The leader was a brilliant California lawyer, Aaron Sapiro, who presented ideas that were destined to influence the course of cooperative development among American farmers for the next decade. His main objective was to organize commodity associations that would operate on a state or an area basis. Up to this time, only local associations had received primary attention in the building of farmer cooperatives.

Sapiro proposed state or regional single-commodity cooperatives, each controlling enough of its respective crop to be a decisive factor in determining prices. Following the Montgomery meeting, cooperative leaders proceeded to form a number of state and regional marketing associations.

During this period, two additional national organizations were set up. They were the American Institute of Cooperation (AIC) and the National Council of Farmer Cooperatives, both with headquarters in Washington, D.C.

Legislative Benchmarks

Numerous contributions to the legal side of cooperatives that greatly influenced the direction and scope of their development were made during 1920–1929 (for further details see Chapter 9).

- Legislators in most states passed cooperative acts, many of them modeled after the Bingham Act of Kentucky.
- Three laws of national importance to cooperatives were enacted:

The Capper-Volstead Act (1922). It specifically sanctioned farmers' marketing cooperatives that meet certain requirements.

The Cooperative Marketing Act (1926). It provided for a division of cooperative marketing in the U.S. Department of Agriculture. This division later became the Farmer Cooperative Service.

The Agricultural Marketing Act (1929). This Act established the Federal Farm Board and authorized a revolving fund of $500 million to stabilize farm prices and to make loans to cooperatives.

During this period, a number of important associations were organized, some of them national in scope. They included the National Livestock Marketing Association, Chicago; the National Wool Marketing Corporation, Boston; the American Cotton Cooperative Association, Memphis; and the National Beet Growers Association, Denver—all federations of regional or terminal marketing cooperatives.

The termination of the Farm Board activities in 1933 marked the end of the rapid development of national commodity cooperatives. Some went out of business because they were unable to fulfill the high expectations they had generated. They could not control a sufficient share of any commodity to exert a strong and prolonged market influence.

BUSINESS PERFORMANCE IMPROVEMENT: 1933–1945

Various forces left their mark on farmer cooperatives between 1933 and 1945. Among them were economic depression, drought, new agricultural programs, and World War II. The overall results were a growing demand for agricultural commodities, frequent shortages of many production supplies, and pronounced shifts to mechanized, scientific, and commercialized farming.

This period was characterized by growth in the volume of cooperative business, by an increase in memberships, and by greater recognition of the importance of sound business practices. A trend developed toward more complex associations that provided broader services for members.

During these years, the number of large-scale organizations and bargaining associations increased, and cooperatives often began to combine their marketing and purchasing operations.

Many cooperatives improved their financial situation and increased their attention to processing farm products and manufacturing production supplies. Furthermore, they recognized the contributions that research and education could make to improve business operations. Frequently, cooperatives became the "pacesetters" in serving farmers.

A few illustrations and some important features of the developments during this period deserve mention here.

Increased Research and Educational Assistance

With the greater emphasis on sound business operations, the need for further research and educational assistance to farmer cooperatives was recognized. Such work, started by the U.S. Department of Agriculture in 1913, was strengthened and formalized in 1926 by the Cooperative Marketing Act. Beginning in 1933, the resulting program of research and assistance was carried on by what was to become the Cooperative Research and Service Division of the Farm Credit Administration and later the Farmer Cooperative Service.

The Division's assistance to farmers with cooperative problems was an additional step in helping farmers with marketing and farm-supply buying problems. It supplemented the longtime assistance program on crop and livestock production problems offered by other agencies of the U.S. Department of Agriculture.

Somewhat similar research was also being undertaken at a number of land-grant colleges. State extension services became increasingly active in the educational assistance necessary to implement research findings. Some cooperatives, too, were developing quality-control programs and establishing their own research departments to work on specific operating and general economic problems. (For further details, see Chapters 21 and 23.)

Processing Expansion

Farmer cooperatives began to increase the number of marketing services they provided members between 1933 and 1945. Much of the expansion involved further processing of fruit and vegetable, dairy, and poultry products.

Many supply cooperatives started to market farm products, and many local marketing cooperatives began to handle a wider line of supplies in addition to feed, seed, and fertilizer. Regional farm supply cooperatives started to explore for crude oil and to refine petroleum products. They also began to manufacture feed and fertilizer, and to handle such items as insecticides, veterinary supplies, and miscellaneous farm and home equipment.

Several local supply cooperatives offered such services as fertilizer and lime spreading, feed mixing, seed cleaning, and paint spraying. A number of both marketing and purchasing cooperatives also added frozen-food locker plants and local processing services.

Even before World War II, decentralization of livestock marketing resulted in more local slaughtering and processing. Six meat-packing cooperatives were launched between 1930 and 1938.

The first cooperative sugar mill in the United States was established in 1932, and several others soon followed. Rice cooperatives began acquiring milling and drying facilities during the same period.

Most of the cottonseed oil mills started after 1936, and all the soybean oil mills were established after 1940. They helped to meet the critical shortage of protein feeds that followed World War II, and they improved returns to producers. World War II greatly stimulated cooperative processing of dried milk and dehydrated fruits and vegetables. Cooperative canning of fruits and vegetables continued to grow. Freezing, dehydration, and prepackaging services were added by these cooperatives. Some of these dehydration and processing plants later ceased operations because of problems encountered in adjusting to changing market conditions. In 1940, the first cooperative to process and market broilers was organized, and in California, cooperative wineries began to assume even greater importance.

The first cooperative petroleum refinery was built in 1939, and several more were soon acquired to provide farmers with adequate fuel supplies during the war period. Feed mills, fertilizer and insecticide plants, and also box shook mills were added between 1933 and 1945.

Modern Business Techniques

Cooperatives gave increased attention to the selection and training of competent employees and directors during the same period. Manager and employee compensation and incentive plans were accepted as a part of modern business practices. Regional associations, especially, gave more attention to departmentalizing operations, improving membership and public relations, and increasing operating efficiency.

Two national cooperative trade associations—the National Federation of Grain Cooperatives and the National Rural Electric Cooperative Association (NRECA), both of Washington, D.C.—were organized during this period.

New Deal Assistance

The New Deal, under the leadership of President Franklin Roosevelt, introduced much social and economic innovation and experimentation. The cooperative form of business enterprise was often encouraged to achieve various desired ends. For example:

- The Cooperative Farm Credit Administration was established in 1933 to coordinate credit programs. One result was the organization of banks for cooperatives that provided long-term mortage credit and short-term production credit for farmers.
- The Tennessee Valley Authority began operations in 1933. It encouraged cooperative development in the TVA area and demonstrated the soundness of rural electric cooperatives.
- In 1935, drawing on TVA experience, the Rural Electrification Administration was established to finance local rural electric cooperatives. As both a direct and an indirect result, 99 percent of all rural homes have been electrified. In 1942 the REA program was expanded to finance rural telephone systems.

- The Farm Security Administration encouraged cooperatives as a means of rehabilitating depressed rural areas.

As Dr. Knapp has said, "The New Deal period was a time of ferment." New ideas were tried. Some of the resulting cooperatives succeeded; others failed. Desperate times, however, call for imaginative measures, and cooperatives were recognized as an effective type of business enterprise that could help members help themselves. (Further details are given in Chapter 21.)

ADJUSTMENTS TO CHANGE: 1945 TO DATE

An important period of cooperative development followed World War II. It was marked by tremendous shifts in agriculture, by technological impacts, by changes in corporate business structures, and by new developments in national and international relationships. All these changes caused far-reaching adjustments in cooperative operations.

It is true, of course, that many of these adjustments had begun in the previous period. World War II, however, stimulated and accelerated them and made them more significant. The most important developments were the following.

Integration Intensified

Economic integration was of course not a new concept among cooperatives. In fact, most of it started as a form of horizontal integration (bringing together associations that provided like services for members) when local cooperatives banded together into regional federations.

Integration also occurred when large numbers of similar types of farmers formed large-scale, centralized associations. As these cooperatives gained economic power, not unlike the federations, they were able to undertake various vertically integrated activities (providing additional marketing or production supply services for members). They also gave more emphasis to contractual agreements that, in varying ways, coordinated production, financing, processing, and marketing within the same management function. The results presented cooperative management with many completely new and expanded problems.

Many cooperatives have entered into a large number of contractual arrangements with farmer producers. Vertical integration by cooperatives has progressed rapidly. Most of the feed, seed, and petroleum products and two-thirds of the fertilizer that regional cooperatives furnish their locals are processed in cooperative plants.

Many combination marketing–farm supply cooperatives are providing a growing number of processing and distributing services that help to move farm products closer to final consumers. An example of such a cooperative is Gold Kist, Inc., Atlanta, Georgia. It serves some 153,000 farmers in Georgia, Alabama, southern South Carolina, southeastern Tennessee, and northern Florida. Gold Kist has developed marketing programs for broilers, peanuts, eggs, pecans, cotton, grain soybeans, fish, and livestock. In 1973, the value of products marketed by Gold Kist, Inc., amounted to about $430 million.

The 1973 wholesale value of Gold Kist's supplies, such as feed, fertilizer, seed, general farm supplies, pesticides, L. P. gas, and chicks, was $150 million. The firm's assets totaled about $240 million. Gold Kist operates feed mills, a seed plant, fertilizer plants, insecticide plants, hatcheries, poultry processing plants, peanut plants, pecan plants, grain elevators, and a soybean plant. Members have an equity of approximately $88 million. (For further details see Chapter 23.)

Consolidations and Mergers Increased

Consolidations and mergers of small cooperatives have occurred mainly among dairy, grain, fruit and vegetable, and production supply associations. Many merged to increase member income, to improve services, and to get the advantages of larger volume, modern equipment, and more capable and efficient management. Information obtained by the Farmer Cooperative Service indicates that 965 cooperatives consolidated or merged during the fourteen-year period from 1957 through 1970.

Marked progress is being made in coordinating the efforts of both local and regional cooperatives. Some ten or twelve area or national federations of regional supply cooperatives have been organized, mostly to manufacture such farm supplies as fertilizer and feed and to refine petroleum products.

Bargaining Activities Expanded

Another important development has been the organization of a number of bargaining cooperatives. This type of cooperative has been important in the dairy field for a number of years, and now accounts for about half the milk sold by cooperatives. About twenty-five of the thirty-five fruit-and-vegetable bargaining associations that are presently operating were organized since World War II.

Also, in the last decade, general farm organizations have given considerable support to national legislation to strengthen the position of bargaining cooperatives.

A recent development among sugar beet bargaining associations has been the acquisition of facilities from private sugar-refining firms or the building of their own facilities. In 1972, the Red River Valley Sugar Beet Growers Association, Fargo, North Dakota, acquired the American Crystal Sugar Company. In addition, three sugar beet processing cooperatives were organized. They were: Minnesota-Dakota Farmers Cooperative, Mooreton, North Dakota; Red River Valley Cooperative, Inc., Grafton, North Dakota; and Southern Minnesota Beet Sugar Cooperative, Olivia, Minnesota. (Bargaining is discussed at greater length in Chapter 18.)

Foreign Market Ventures

Marketing cooperatives have taken steps to develop international markets for farm products.

- In 1959, four Midwestern grain regionals formed Mid-States Terminals, Inc., with facilities at Toledo, Ohio, for exporting grain.
- Soy-Cot Sales, Inc., Des Plaines, Illinois, an association of twenty-two cooperative oilseed processors, was established in 1962 to market cottonseed and soybean products.

- Through AMCOT, Inc., the four largest cotton associations have joined to expand their cotton export marketing programs.
- California's two leading dried fruit marketing cooperatives—Sun-Maid Raisin Growers of California and Valley Fig Growers—merged their marketing facilities in 1971 into a new organization known as Sunland Marketing, Inc., to increase the emphasis on marketing dried fruits, including both domestic and foreign sales.
- Some of the larger cooperatives, for example, Sunkist Growers and Riceland Foods, have their own export programs.

Education and Research Emphasized

Farmer Cooperative Service, in the Department of Agriculture, was set up as a separate agency in 1953 to take over the work formerly conducted by the Cooperative Research and Service Division of the Farm Credit Administration. Through a program of problem-oriented research, advisory assistance, and educational activities, the Service assists cooperatives to improve services for members.

Cooperative research at land-grant and other universities, and state extension service activities, has continued over the years. Educational efforts of state cooperative councils, the American Institute of Cooperation, and the Cooperative League of the U.S.A. have expanded, and thus have contributed to a better understanding of the role of cooperatives in the nation's economy.

A growing number of regional supply and marketing cooperatives have added small staffs to conduct market and other economic research studies. These occasionally include studies on membership relations and operating problems of their affiliated local cooperatives (for further details, see Chapter 21).

Financial Structure Broadened

Expansion and further integration of operations, the need to modernize facilities to achieve greater efficiency, increased emphasis on manufacturing and processing, recognition of ecological, health, and safety requirements, and increased demands of members for credit have all substantially increased the capital requirements of cooperatives. As a result, many have enlarged their financial base and altered their financing patterns. They are relying less on members to provide their growing capital needs, and they are using more debt capital—both borrowed funds and general credit—than in the past. (Chapter 15 presents further details.)

Employee and Director Training Improved

With cooperatives growing larger, more integrated, and more complex, the importance of capable management, competent employees, and knowledgeable policy makers becomes increasingly evident. A variety of programs has been developed to deal with these needs. Cooperatives themselves, through various training efforts, spend millions of dollars annually in training employees and members and in developing member communication programs. Most state cooperative councils, through annual meetings and specialized workshops, likewise seek to improve the understanding of cooperative members, employees, and the general public regarding problems of cooperative organization and operation.

In addition, land-grant and other colleges are now providing specialized training for employees and directors. Other agencies, such as national cooperative associations, have lent a helping hand. They include the American Institute of Cooperation, the Cooperative League of the U.S.A., the National Council of Farmer Cooperatives, and various commodity trade organizations.

Facilities and Equipment Modernized

Farmer cooperatives have made progress in modernizing their facilities, especially since World War II. They have built new plants and warehouses better to handle an increased volume of business. They have added modern fertilizer plants, petroleum refineries, and feed mills. Some even own railroad cars and river barges. Consumer cooperatives have acquired warehouse facilities and modernized their retail units.

Additional Services Provided

Many cooperatives are handling a wider variety of supplies and are marketing more kinds of farm products. They also provide additional services, as mentioned previously. The rice, fruit-and-vegetable, and production supply cooperatives illustrate the shifts toward diversified, across-the-board services that meet producer needs.

The early rice cooperatives functioned only as bargaining associations in selling members' rough rice to millers. Several rice cooperatives, in addition to drying and storing, now have mills that husk, polish, enrich, package, and market the rice. These cooperatives maintain extensive sales organizations, conduct nationwide advertising and sales promotion campaigns, handle farm supplies for members, and cooperate in research programs designed to develop new varieties and discover new uses. Some even operate irrigation systems for members.

"Great Society" Motivations

The nature and scope of cooperative activity was further extended by the Kennedy-Johnson administrations in the 1960s. Increased concern for economically disadvantaged groups—particularly low-income whites in the Appalachians, black farmers in the South, Spanish-speaking Americans in the Southwest, and Indian tribes throughout the country—prompted further examination of the cooperatives' possible contributions to the economic welfare of such minorities.

Legislation authorizing the Office of Economic Opportunity (OEO) was enacted in 1964. Among other objectives, it provided for grants to cooperatives serving low-income people. Encouragement also was given to handicraft, recreation, and farm machinery cooperatives, in addition to traditional marketing and purchasing associations, as a part of the special effort to help low-income groups. (Further details are provided in Chapter 21.)

SUMMARY

This chapter has highlighted some of the most important events that have contributed to cooperative development in the United States during the past 200 years. It also has identified some of the forces that gave encouragement and support to the cooperative form of business enterprise. The first 100 years were largely a period of exploration and experimentation. Leaders were groping for acceptable ways of organizing their cooperatives and developing operating methods that would achieve basic objectives. During this period, failures were numerous and unqualified successes were few. The needs, however, were urgent; leaders were determined; and gradually, successful patterns of organization and operation emerged.

Cooperatives in the United States obtained considerable encouragement from general farm organizations and from federal and state governments. Starting with the National Grange in the 1870s and continuing with the Farmers' Alliance, the Farmers Educational and Cooperative Union, and the American Farm Bureau Federation, all general farm organizations supported and encouraged cooperatives. Later, the federal government began to take up the cause of cooperatives. Theodore Roosevelt and Woodrow Wilson were the first Presidents to recognize the contributions that cooperatives could make toward the improvement of the economic status of the American farmer. The government's interest gave rise to the land-grant college system which encouraged and supported cooperatives through teaching, research, and extension programs.

As a result, cooperatives have developed to the extent that they now provide a wide range of services and handle a large variety of products. They have grown from small, local associations to large-scale organizations that give members an effective voice in the functioning of their own businesses. They are also an educational tool for acquainting their members with the nature of modern business enterprise. Cooperatives have done this by effectively adjusting to change, responding to member needs, providing business leadership, integrating their operations, and adopting modern business methods and practices.

QUESTIONS

1. Trace early exploratory cooperative developments in agriculture and in urban and industrial communities.
2. How did general farm organizations contribute to cooperative development?
3. Compare the cooperative programs of the National Grange, the Farmers' Alliance, the Farmers Educational and Cooperative Union of America, and the American Farm Bureau Federation.
4. How do the cooperative programs of general farm organizations and national cooperative organizations compare?
5. What were the early contributions of federal and state governments to cooperative development?
6. In what ways did the New Deal and the Kennedy-Johnson administrations encourage cooperatives?
7. What were the basic objectives and accomplishments of the commodity marketing era (1920–1933)?
8. In what ways did cooperative business performance improve between 1933–1945?
9. How have cooperatives adjusted to change since 1945?

REFERENCES

Abrahamsen, Martin A.: *Development of Cooperatives*, FCS Bulletin Reprint 1, U.S. Department of Agriculture, Farmer Cooperative Service, Washington, 1976, p. 36.

—— and Claude L. Scroggs: *Agricultural Cooperation: Selected Readings*, The University of Minnesota Press, Minneapolis, 1957, pp. 3–56.

Hibbard, B. H.: *Marketing Agricultural Products*, D. Appleton and Company, New York, 1926. See especially pp. 183–282.

Knapp, Joseph G.: *The Advance of American Cooperative Enterprise*, The Interstate, Danville, Ill., 1973, p. 646.

—— and Associates: *Great American Cooperators*, American Institute of Cooperation, Washington, D.C. 1967, p. 607.

McKay, Andrew W., and Martin A. Abrahamsen: *Helping Farmers Build Cooperatives: The Evolution of Farmer Cooperative Services,* U.S. Department of Agriculture, Farmer Cooperative Service, 1962, p. 82.

Parker, Florence E.: *The First 125 Years: A History of Distributive and Service Cooperation in the United States, 1828–1954,* Cooperative League of the U.S.A., Washington, D.C., 1956, p. 462.

Chapter 6

Cooperative Growth

Cooperative leaders suggest many reasons for emphasizing economic growth. They include these facts:

- Most cooperative business enterprises are relatively small compared with other firms.
- Limited size restricts many cooperatives to providing only the most elementary marketing and purchasing functions and services.
- Growth enables cooperatives to integrate operations more fully.
- Growth provides an opportunity to increase efficiency, improve performance, enlarge operations, and offer an expanded range of services.
- Growth enables cooperatives to exercise increased market power to the degree that they may approach the market power of the firms with which they deal and compete.

It should be recognized that growth per se is not justified. Growth should not be used by directors or managers to build personal monuments that reflect their pride and personal ambition. Rather, growth should be employed to enhance the ability of cooperatives better to serve their patrons.

In a general way, cooperative growth relates to the ability of these associations to provide goods and services for their members. There are such basic questions as: Are cooperatives growing at a slower, comparable, or faster rate than their business counterparts? Is cooperative growth of such a nature and in such directions as to provide members efficiently with the goods and services needed to adjust their operations to changing economic conditions?

There are a number of sources of information that gives us clues about the nature and extent of cooperative growth. The Farmer Cooperative Service (FCS), for example, assembles yearly information on the numbers, memberships, and volume of business of farmer marketing, purchasing, and related service cooperatives classified according to principal commodities and states. (See *Statistics of Farmer Cooperatives*, published yearly.) The 1969–1970 edition also provides similar information for general service cooperatives. This information is supplemented in other publications that occasionally present additional information on the growth and market shares of various types of agricultural cooperatives. The Farm Credit Administration and the Rural Electrification Administration provide similar information for the respective types of cooperatives they finance. The Cooperative League of the U.S.A. publishes estimates of numbers, memberships, and volume of business of the principal types of consumer cooperatives. In addition, some of the cooperative trade associations assemble statistics on the types of organizations they represent.

Other important measures of cooperative growth are net savings, patrons' equity, demonstrated ability to meet established objectives and extent of integration. Important as these are, only limited information is available on the first two, and of course the extent of conformity with objectives is quite hard to determine. More information is available on the degree of cooperative integration than on any of the other measures of economic growth (see Chapter 23). The FCS also makes annual estimates of savings of farmer marketing, purchasing, and related service cooperatives. It assembles information on patrons' equity in these associations from time to time. Except for periodic trade association reports for other types of associations, the FCS materials are the basic sources of information available on cooperative savings and equity.

Limited as they are, these data give some indication as to the growth of cooperatives in this country. Growth comparisons are most meaningful, insofar as they provide both absolute and relative information on cooperatives and other comparable types of business firms. Because of changes in price levels, more information on physical volume of products handled by cooperatives would be extremely useful. Also, it would be helpful to have more information on the volume of products or supplies processed and manufactured and the extent of cooperative wholesaling and retailing services. Such data would help to bring into complete and proper perspective the nature and extent of cooperative growth.

FARMERS' MARKETING AND PURCHASING COOPERATIVES[1]

Growth Reflects Changes in Agriculture

Growth of farmers' cooperatives has occurred largely in response to the increasing and changing demands of modern commercial agriculture.

---

[1]This section is adapted from, and is an updating of, information presented in *Cooperative Growth: Trends, Comparisons, Strategy,* FCS Information 87, U.S. Department of Agriculture, March 1973. It was prepared by the author when he was associated with Farmer Cooperative Service.

Back of the available data, which give some measure of the growth of cooperatives, are the various forces to which cooperatives are responding and adjusting as they seek to serve members efficiently. The extent to which cooperatives have grown, therefore, indicates how successful farmers have been in getting their off-the-farm business to help them meet their needs and to adjust to the forces contributing to change. The most important of these forces consist of the following facts:

Agriculture Has Become Increasingly Mechanized When cooperatives were first organized, farmers' energy needs were provided by hand and horsepower. Homegrown hay and oats provided most of the "fuel" for horsepower. Now farmers expect their cooperatives to provide them with fuel to power their trucks, tractors, and other machinery. In most instances, electrical cooperatives supply the energy needed to run countless motors and appliances.

Technical and Economic Research Has Introduced Profound Changes in Production, Processing, and Marketing Research has contributed to continual and marked changes in plant varieties, animal breeding, production practices, and cultural methods. It also has initiated improvements in farm management and marketing methods that in turn have greatly influenced the whole agribusiness structure.

Modern Agriculture Requires New and Improved Services Improved management practices and marketing methods have necessitated new services. These include bulk delivery of feed, fertilizer, and petroleum products and bulk handling of milk, grain, and fruit and vegetable products. To meet farmers' needs, fertilizer cooperatives often mine and manufacture plant foods, and apply them directly to the fields. To meet expanding marketing requirements, cooperatives operate modern storage and processing facilities and provide transportation and credit services.

Changes in Other Business Sectors Necessitate Larger Cooperatives Studies by the Federal Trade Commission and other government agencies have called attention to substantial concentration of business enterprises in most segments of the economy. Mergers have occurred by the thousands; horizontal and vertical integration have become common; and huge conglomerate business enterprises are engaged in highly diversified business operations. These firms have marshaled the financial resources necessary to achieve substantial market penetration. The cooperative is the major economic tool of farmers for dealing, even to a limited extent, with the economic power of these firms.

Farmers and Cooperative Leaders Are Becoming More Sophisticated Today's farmer has a better appreciation not only of production and cultural practices needed to succeed, but also of the economic tools, including cooperatives, that can be put into use to help meet the challenges of change and adjustment. Cooperative directors and managers are now better selected and trained than they were twenty years ago. As a result, they have a more realistic appreciation of how cooperatives can help their members to meet the growing and changing needs of agriculture.

How farmers' cooperatives have responded to these changes is shown in information on trends for number of associations, memberships, net volume of business, cooperative share of total business, size of business firms, and relative growth as compared with businesses similar to cooperatives.

Trends in Numbers, Memberships, and Net Volume

Figure 6-1 and Table 6-1 present basic farm cooperative information on numbers, memberships, and net volume of business over the past two decades—from 1950–1951 through 1971–1972.

Number of Cooperatives The number of agricultural cooperatives has generally followed the same trends as other types of business firms and reflects the decline in the number of farms. From 1950–1951 through 1971–1972 the number of marketing, farm supply, and related service cooperatives fell from 10,064 to 7,786. This decline was slightly under 1 percent a year, or 21 percent for the entire period.

The decline was greater for marketing cooperatives than for farm supply cooperatives—66 percent as compared with 16 percent. In 1971–1972, marketing cooperatives accounted for 62 percent of all cooperatives, and supply cooperatives for 34 percent. Related service cooperatives, which include trucking, storage, drying, and similar services affecting the form, quality, or location of farm products and supplies handled by cooperatives, accounted for only 2 percent of all farm cooperatives.

Memberships Total farm memberships increased from a little more than 7 million in 1950–1951 to a high of 7.7 million in 1955–1956. Since then they have

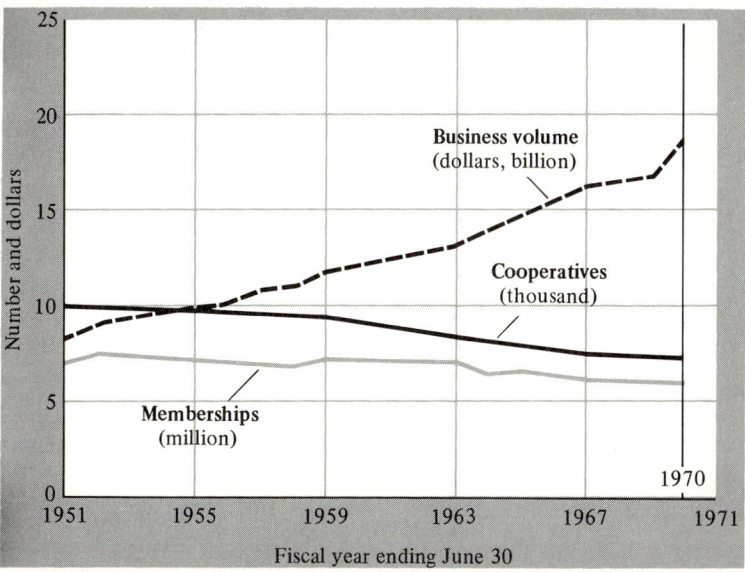

Figure 6-1 Cooperative numbers, memberships, and volume of business, 1951 through 1970.

Table 6-1 Number, Memberships, and Net Volume of Business Reported for Farmers' Marketing, Purchasing, and Related Service Cooperatives, 1950–1951 to 1970–1971

Period	Cooperatives	Memberships (in thousands)	Net volume (in millions)
1950–51	10,064	7,091	$ 8,147
1951–52	10,179	7,364	9,410
1952–53	10,128	7,475	9,521
1953–54	10,072	7,608	9,475
1954–55	9,903	7,604	9,642
1955–56	9,894	7,732	9,756
1956–57	9,891	7,673	10,379
1957–58	9,735	7,486	10,753
1958–59	9,658	7,559	11,747
1959–60	9,345	7,273	12,036
1960–61	9,163	7,203	12,409
1961–62	9,039	7,099	13,024
1962–63	8,907	7,219	13,842
1963–64	8,847	7,080	14,354
1964–65	8,583	7,082	14,742
1965–66	8,329	6,826	15,608
1966–67	8,125	6,502	16,557
1967–68	7,940	6,445	17,050
1968–69	7,747	6,364	17,387
1969–70	7,790	6,355	19,026
1970–71	7,994	6,158	20,180
1971–72	7,786	6,147	21,665

declined quite consistently until, in 1971–1972, they numbered 6.1 million. We should be careful to distinguish between membership and the actual number of members. Membership figures are much higher because members belong, on the average, to between two and three cooperatives. The decline in memberships reflects the decline in number of farms, but it has been less pronounced. Between 1950–1951 and 1971–1972 the number of memberships dropped 24 percent for marketing cooperatives, but it increased 4 percent for farm supply cooperatives.

During the twenty-two-year period, the average net volume of cooperative business increased from about $1,150 to $3,524 per cooperative membership, or 306 percent. For the same period, the percentage of farm supply memberships rose from 41 to 49 percent and that of marketing memberships declined from 58 to 51 percent (general service cooperatives accounted for 0.4 percent of membership numbers).

Net Volume Net farm cooperative business, unadjusted for change in the price level, increased from $8.1 billion in 1950–1951 to $21.7 billion in 1971–1972. Net volume is that remaining after eliminating intercooperative business, such as that between local and regional associations.

By type of business, the value of products marketed through farm cooperatives (1950–1951 through 1971–1972) increased from $6.4 billion to $16.5 billion, and

COOPERATIVE GROWTH

supplies purchased, from $1.7 billion to $4.7 billion. In 1971–1972, products marketed accounted for 77 percent of total cooperative volume, supplies purchased for about 21 percent, and general service cooperatives for 2 percent.

The Cooperatives' Market Share

Figure 6-2 shows the growth trends of cooperative marketings and cash receipts of all farmers for 1950–1951 and 1971–1972.

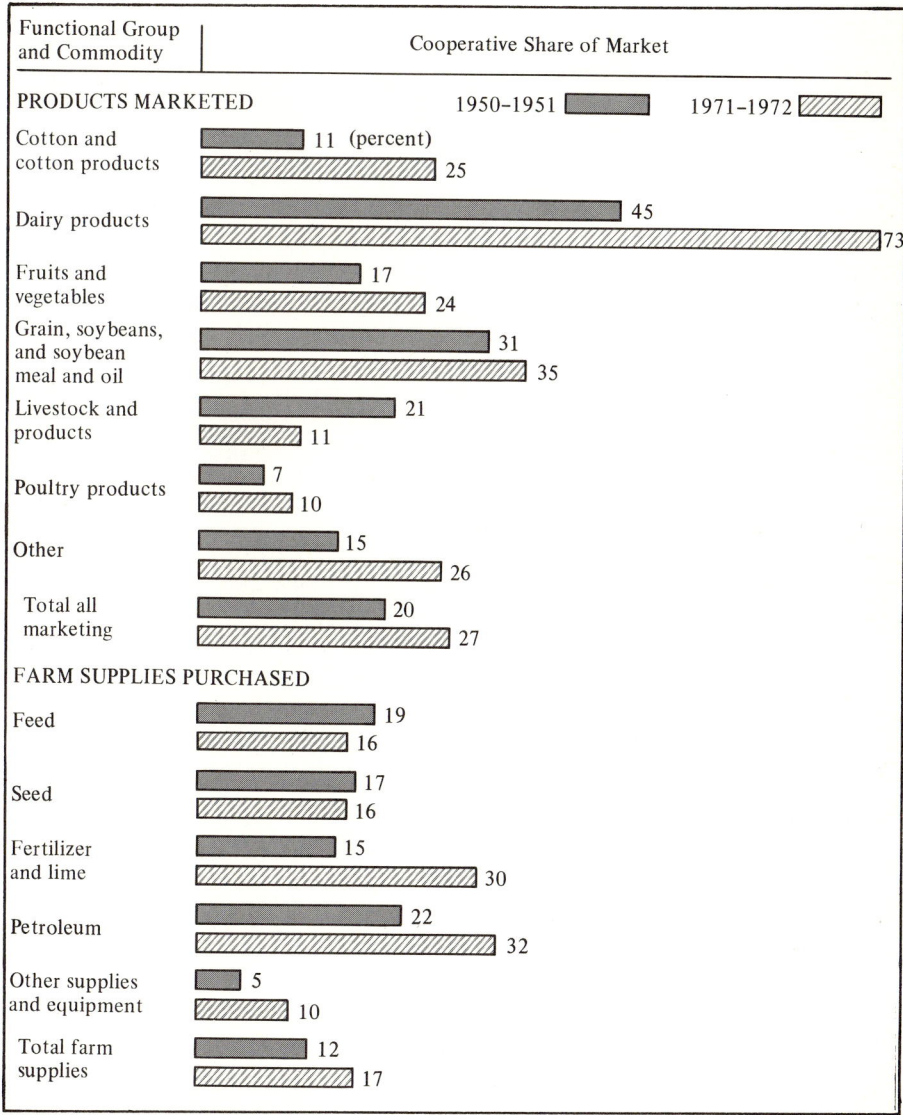

Figure 6-2 Estimated share of the market obtained by farmer cooperatives, by selected commodities.

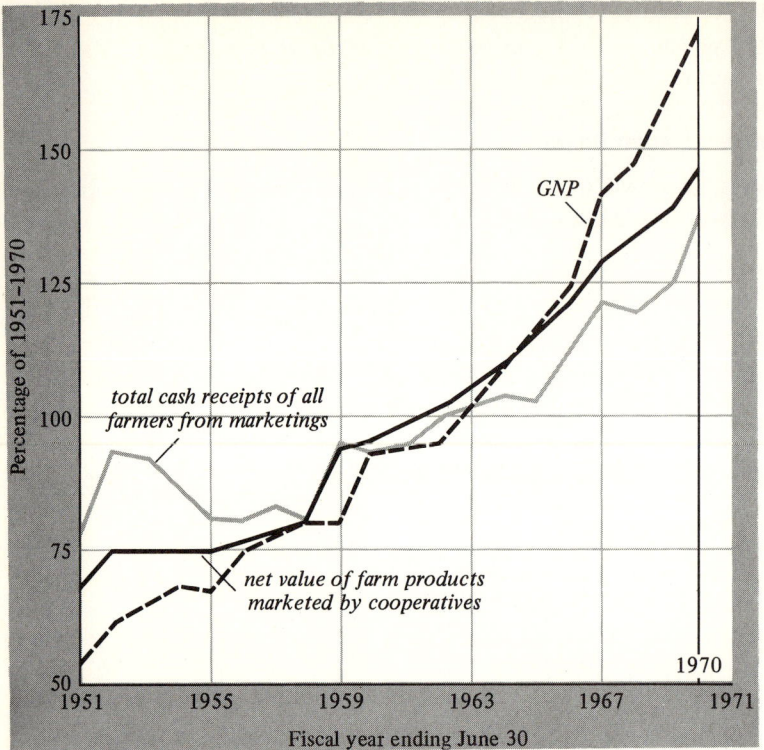

Figure 6-3 Growth trends of cooperative marketings, cash receipts of all farmers, and GNP, 1951 through 1970.

Over the twenty-two-year period, the cooperative proportion of all products marketed increased from 20 to 27 percent. The cooperative increases were especially significant in dairy products, fruits and vegetables, and cotton and cotton products. Livestock and livestock products declined from 21 percent to 11 percent during the period. The cooperative share of farm supplies purchased increased from 12 to 17 percent. The most significant increases occurred in fertilizer and lime and petroleum products.

However, a word of caution: Statistics on the net sales of cooperatives and their share of the farm market often are misinterpreted. For marketing cooperatives, the data shown in Figure 6-2 refer only to the amount of cooperative business at one stage or the other in the marketing process. For example, most marketing cooperatives do comparatively little processing, integrate operations only to a small extent, and achieve only limited market penetration. Major exceptions are the dairy cooperatives that manufacture butter, cheese, and related products, and fruit-and-vegetable processing cooperatives.

Among farm supply cooperatives, a greater degree of integration exists. The evidence of this is the ownership by regional associations of feed mills, fertilizer manufacturing facilities, and petroleum refineries. Little progress, however, has been

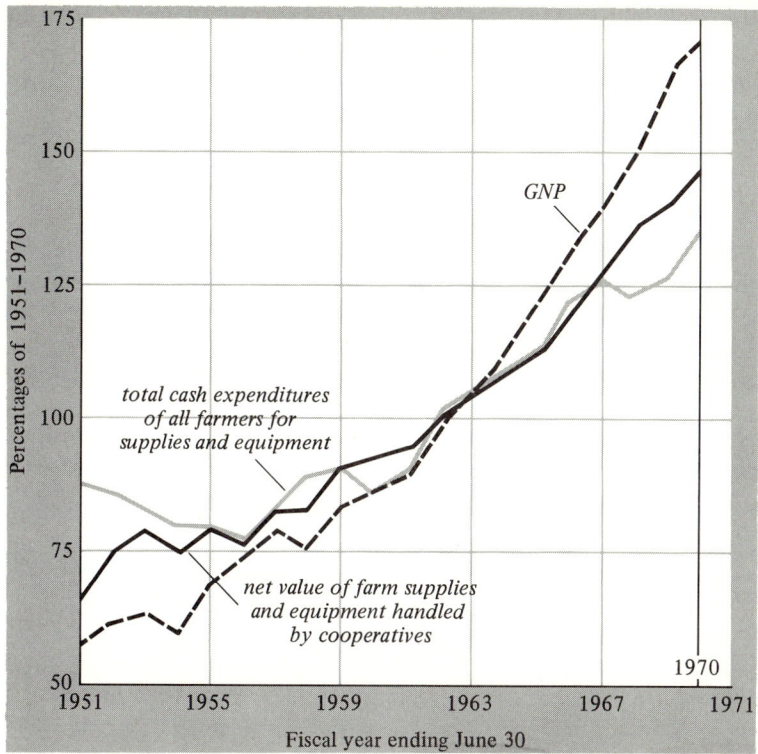

Figure 6-4 Growth trends of supplies and equipment handled cooperatively, cash expenditures of all farmers, and GNP, 1951 through 1970.

made in the manufacture and distribution of farm machinery and appliances and in the provision of related services.

A comparison of index numbers between cooperative marketings, cash receipts for marketings of all farmers, and the gross national product (GNP) is shown in Figure 6-3. The indexes for each year are determined by the ratio of yearly volumes to the average volumes of the twenty-one year period, which are assigned an index of 100. A similar comparison of expenditures for supplies and equipment handled by cooperatives with cash expenditures of all farmers and with the GNP shows the same general relationships (Figure 6-4). Both comparisons indicate that cooperatives have made significant progress in their marketing and purchasing activities when compared with other segments of agriculture.

For example, the index for products marketed by cooperatives increased from 64 in 1951 to 146 in 1970, or 82 points. During the same period, indexes for cash receipts from marketings and for the GNP rose 55 points and 120 points, respectively.

The index for farm supplies provided by the cooperatives increased from 65 in 1951 to 149 in 1970, or 84 points. During the same period, the index of total cash expenditures for farm supplies and equipment increased 47 points and the GNP index rose 113 points.

Since 1965, however, growth of cooperative marketings has been slower than the overall economic growth. Farmers' purchases of supplies and equipment through cooperatives also rose more slowly between 1963 and 1970 than the overall economy. But again, the cooperative sector grew faster than the entire agricultural sector for farm supplies and equipment.

SELECTED INDUSTRIAL COMPARISONS

The FCS growth study also compared growth trends of the four largest cooperatives with the four largest comparable business firms. These comparisons were made for such commodities as dairy, livestock, poultry, cotton, grain, fruits and vegetables, and tobacco. Among farm supplies, comparisons were made for feed, fertilizer, petroleum, pesticides, and seed. Here we will briefly review the findings of the study in two representative commodities—dairy products and petroleum.

Dairy Products

Industry Comparisons The dairy industry has changed greatly during the past two decades. The trend has been toward large-scale operations by both plants and producers. The number of farmers selling whole milk has declined from 1.1 million to 330,000. Following the record-high milk production of 127 billion pounds in 1964, the annual volume has declined by 10 billion pounds to about the same production level as in 1950.

A total of 824 farmer cooperatives had net dairy sales, after eliminating intercooperative business, of about $5.4 billion in 1970–1971. This is an increase of 177 percent from 1950–1951 when net sales totaled $1.9 billion.

Cooperatives increased the volume of raw whole milk they marketed from 58 billion pounds in 1957 to 76 billion pounds in 1964. In terms of market share, they marketed 59 percent of all milk sold to plants and dealers in 1957 and 67 percent in 1964. Cooperatives marketed about 70 percent of the nation's total milk supply in 1970. They accounted for about 85 percent of grade A milk but for only about 40 percent of the manufactured grade milk.

The Largest Dairy Cooperatives Compared with the Largest Other Dairy Firms Comparisons can be made between the sales, assets, and net worth of the four largest dairy cooperatives and those of the four largest other dairy firms.

Sales While dairy cooperative sales increased 251 percent from 1960 through 1970, compared with a 107 percent increase for noncooperative dairy firms, the absolute increases were about $1.5 billion by the four cooperatives and $3.7 billion by the four other dairy firms. The cooperatives' volume of sales equaled 28 percent of the volume of the other business corporations in 1970, compared with 17 percent in 1960.

Although the other largest dairy business firms have expanded their sales largely in nondairy industries, the cooperatives have concentrated on a restructuring of their dairy operations. In both 1960 and 1965, the four large dairy cooperatives accounted for 15 to 20 percent of the total sales of all dairy cooperatives; this percentage increased, however, to between 35 and 40 percent by 1970.

Assets From 1960 through 1965, the four other dairy business firms increased their assets by 51 percent, compared with 19 percent for the four large dairy cooperatives. During the next five years, the four other dairy business firms further increased their assets by 65 percent. At the same time, a restructuring of the dairy cooperatives created four large organizations whose assets were 229 percent greater than those of the four largest in 1965. Even so, their 1970 assets were only one-seventh of those of the four business firms having the largest dairy volume.

Net Worth Trends in net worth of the four dairy business firms and the four dairy cooperatives are similar to trends in assets. During the 1960–1965 period, the other dairy firms outgrew the cooperatives by increasing 52 percent, compared with 18 percent. During the next five years, the net worth of the other dairy firms grew by 46 percent, while the four largest dairy cooperatives increased their net worth by 157 percent.

It is important to bring growth trends in the dairy industry into proper perspective. Data reported by the Federal Trade Commission indicate that 7,838 acquisitions and mergers have occurred since 1921. Of these, the eight largest noncooperative firms accounted for 2,319, other noncooperatives for 4,420, and farmer cooperatives for 1,099.[2]

It seems that recent acquisition and merging efforts of dairy cooperatives reflect, to a considerable degree, the efforts of these associations to catch up in their expansion and modernization programs so as to serve members more effectively. Data from the Federal Trade Commission may reflect some of the decline in acquisitions and mergers by noncooperatives that has occurred in recent years. It is notable that only 42 percent of the acquisitions and mergers by the eight largest noncooperative firms occurred in the last half of the forty-four-year period, compared with 40 percent rate for all other dairy businesses. In contrast, 64 percent of the cooperative acquisitions and mergers occurred during this period.

Petroleum

Industry Comparisons The petroleum industry supplies three-fourths of the nation's energy needs. It consists of many highly integrated corporations which have diverse domestic and foreign operations. Reports on twenty-seven of the largest petroleum corporations show that their sales and service income totaled $92 billion in 1970. This was almost 6 times the total income of the thirty major oil companies in 1950, and 1.8 times that of the largest thirty-two companies in 1960.

A total of 2,774 farmer cooperatives had gross petroleum sales of about $1.2 billion and net sales (after eliminating intercooperative business) of $862 million in 1969–1970. Net sales of cooperatives have increased 129 percent from 1950–1951, when they totaled $377 million. Estimates indicate that cooperatives now supply about 32 percent of all petroleum products used in farming operations, compared with 22 percent in 1950.

Cooperatives, along with other companies, have further integrated their petroleum operations in the past two decades. Although the number of cooperative refineries has declined from twenty in 1950 to eight by 1969, capacity increased about 50 percent and

---

[2]Federal Trade Commission, Bureau of Economics, *Economic Papers 1966–69*, 1970, p. 133.

output about 75 percent. However, cooperative refinery capacity and runs were still less than 2 percent of the industry total in 1969. Cooperatives also have acquired crude oil–producing properties during the same period, but their wells and production were less than 2 percent of the United States total.

The Largest Cooperatives Handling Petroleum Compared with the Largest Oil Companies The four largest cooperatives in 1970, in terms of their petroleum operations, were engaged in refining operations and three had considerable crude oil production and pipeline operations. Two sold their products at the wholesale level; one sold part at wholesale and part at retail; and one sold only at the refinery level.

Sales Sales of the top four cooperatives increased 297 percent from 1960 to 1970, compared with 120 percent for the four largest oil companies, but the amount of increase was $901 million for the cooperatives and $20.2 billion for the oil companies. Cooperatives' sales amounted to only 3.2 percent of the sales of the four other oil companies in 1970. These four noncooperative companies ranked second, seventh, eighth, and ninth in sales volume among the nation's 500 largest business corporations in 1970.

Net Margins Net margins on all sales of the four cooperatives increased 117 percent from 1960 to 1970, compared with 100 percent for the four largest oil companies. Amounts of increases, however, were $27 million for the cooperatives versus $1.6 billion for the four oil companies. Net margins of the cooperatives were 1.7 percent of the total net income of the four oil companies in 1970, compared with 1.4 percent in 1960.

Total Assets Cooperatives showed a greater percentage increase in total assets from 1960 through 1970 than did the largest oil companies. But the amount of increase for the cooperatives was only $581 million, compared with about $28 billion for the largest other oil companies. Assets of the four cooperatives were only 2.1 percent of those of the four oil companies in 1970. They were 1.5 percent in 1960.

Refinery Output The four cooperatives processed or refined 161,000 barrels per day, or 1.4 percent of total refinery runs of the four largest oil companies and 4.7 percent of total United States runs in 1970. Gross crude oil production of the cooperatives was 1.2 percent of the total production of the four oil companies, and their net production was only 0.2 percent of the total.

Largest Cooperatives Compared with Largest Similar Businesses

The FCS growth study also briefly compared the growth of the ten largest cooperatives with the growth of the ten largest firms in similar businesses. Cooperatives generally tend to diversify into marketing farm products and providing farm supplies. The trend among large industrial conglomerates is to diversify operations into unrelated enterprises.

The ten largest cooperatives were selected on the basis of volume of sales, provided they had more than $5 million of assets. Cooperatives with larger volumes of business that operated on a bargaining or a commission basis, thus with little investment in fixed facilities, were not included.

While the ten largest firms had total sales of almost $34 billion in 1970, the ten largest cooperatives had total sales of almost $4.3 billion. All ten cooperatives marketed one or more farm products. Seven of the ten cooperatives also handled farm supplies, and another purchased feeder livestock for patrons. Nine of the ten cooperatives processed farm products. Five of the ten manufactured substantial quantities of feed, fertilizer, and petroleum; and two formulated considerable quantities of pesticides.

Some indication of the operations of the ten large conglomerates can be obtained by briefly examining the operations of one. It has some 155 subsidiaries that include large meat-packing, poultry processing, and transportation operations. Its sales and service revenue in 1970 consisted of: food, 61 percent; transportation, 18 percent; grocery and pharmaceuticals, 8 percent; industrial and construction equipment, 7 percent; and financial and other services, 6 percent.

Total sales, financial data, number of employees, and number of stockholders for the ten largest cooperatives and the ten largest similar other business firms in 1970 may be tabulated thus:

Item	Ten largest other business firms	Ten largest cooperatives	
		Amount	Percentage of other business firms
Total sales	$33,927,000	$4,259,000	13
Net margins	$1,718,000	$79,000	5
Total assets	$25,233,000	$1,444,000	6
Net worth	$14,137,000	$610,000	4
Employees	435,000	39,000	9
Stockholders or members	1,305,000	844,000	65

Relative and Absolute Growth Compared

The following summary shows the relative growth from 1960 to 1970 of the four largest cooperatives and the four largest other business firms, as indicated by the financial comparisons of sales, total assets, and net worth in dairy, livestock, grain, fruit and vegetable, tobacco, feed, fertilizer, petroleum, pesticides, and seed products:

Financial comparison	Percentage increase in growth, 1960 through 1970	
	Cooperatives	Other firms
Sales	134	116
Total assets	175	164
Net worth	88	99

These data show that sales and total assets increased at a slightly greater relative rate for cooperatives than for the other firms. At the same time, net worth of cooperatives rose at a somewhat slower rate than that of the other firms.

In general, great caution should be observed in the interpretation of relative growth trends. While such trends suggest the rate of growth that has occurred in a given period, they do not indicate the size of the base from which such changes occurred or the actual volume of the change, the type of growth, or the level at which it occurred.

It is more meaningful to report the absolute financial changes that occurred. Figure 6-5 shows these for the four largest of the types of cooperatives and their counterparts in the same areas of the agribusiness economy from 1960 to 1970.

The absolute increases in the various financial indicators for cooperatives and their counterparts from 1960 through 1970 are as follows:

Types of operation	Sales (dollars, billion)		Total assets (dollars, billion)		Net worth (dollars, billion)		Net margins (dollars, billion)	
	Coops.	Others	Coops.	Others	Coops.	Others	Coops.	Others
Marketing	2.2	11.7	0.6	6.1	0.2	2.0	n.a.	0.2
Farm supply	3.3	33.6	2.2	44.1	0.7	19.9	0.12	2.2
Total	5.5	45.3	2.8	50.2	0.9	21.9	0.12	2.4

These growth trends also may be expressed in terms of the number of times absolute growth of other business firms was greater than that of cooperatives. From 1960 through 1970, these were: sales, 8; total assets, 18; net worth, 25; and net margins, 18.

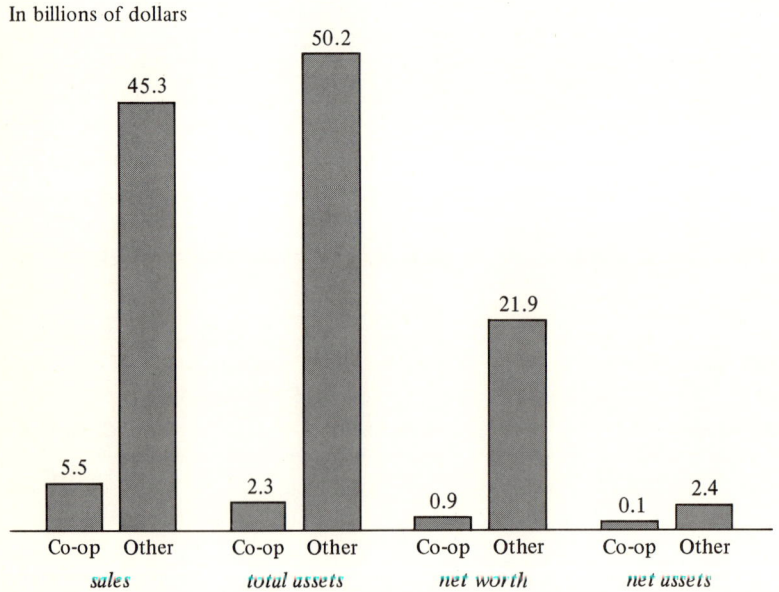

Figure 6-5 Absolute increases in selected financial comparisons for cooperatives and other business firms, 1960–1970.

The general conclusion undoubtedly is that, by any measurement, the absolute growth of agricultural cooperatives has been extremely modest in comparison with the noncooperative sector, and that it has occurred in response to the growing and changing needs of American farmers.

GENERAL SERVICE COOPERATIVES

Among the general service cooperatives serving rural communities, the most complete growth information is available for the Cooperative Farm Credit System and the rural electric cooperatives.

The Cooperative Farm Credit System

Growth trends of the Cooperative Farm Credit System are shown in Table 6-2.

Banks for Cooperatives Highlights in growth trends of the thirteen Banks for Cooperatives are these:

- A substantial increase in the number of cooperative-member borrowers, indicated by a tripling of the number of loans outstanding from 1935 to 1960. Since then, a slower but continual increase in cooperative memberships has occurred in spite of the decline in the number of farmer marketing, purchasing, and related service cooperatives during the period.
- A constant and very marked increase in the annual volume of loans made.
- An increase from 46 percent to 64 percent between 1954 and 1970 in the percentage of total capital borrowed by farmer cooperatives from the Banks for Cooperatives.

Federal Land Banks Important growth trends in the Cooperative Federal Land Bank System have been these:

- The number of local Federal Land Bank associations declined from over 5,000 in 1935 to 553 in 1974, primarily because of emphasis on consolidation to increase efficiency and eliminate duplication of services.
- Memberships, which reached a high in the emergency refinancing program during the Depression years of the 1930s, declined until the 1950s, and since then have increased considerably.
- Loan volume was high during the Depression of the 1930s. It increased steadily during the 1950s and has tripled since 1960.
- The proportion of total farm mortgage debt provided by Federal Land Banks was about 30 percent in 1940. It declined to 15 percent in 1955, then increased to 26 percent as of January 1, 1974.

Production Credit Associations Important trends among production credit associations have been the following:

Table 6-2 Numbers, Participants, and Volume of Business as Reported by Various Units of the Farm Credit Administration, Selected Years 1920–1975

Year-end	Banks for Cooperatives				Federal Land Banks				Production Credit Associations			
	Banks	Members with loans outstanding*		Loans made (in millions)	Associations*	Members†		Loans made (in millions)	Associations*		Stockholders†	Loans made (in millions)
1920	—	—		—	3,966	122,707		$ 119	—		—	—
1925	—	—		—	4,657	331,049		136	—		—	—
1930	—	—		—	4,656	410,054		47	—		—	—
1935	13	979		$ 51	5,034	631,713		450	559		218,814	$ 164
1940	13	1,689		90	3,846	616,308		56	529		230,857	328
1945	13	1,247		380	1,884	391,721		80	514		214,096	500
1950	13	1,754		373	1,211	308,798		199	500		288,068	968
1955	13	2,129		500	1,090	350,888		403	498		270,534	1,329
1960	13	2,754		672	809	376,371		517	494		520,534	2,568
1965	13	2,890		1,277	724	384,330		1,193	477		547,997	3,850
1970	13	2,897		2,105	616	404,908		959	446		529,442	7,742
1972	13	3,021		2,912	584	406,473		1,771	439		522,376	10,021
1973	13	3,113		4,900	578	413,763		2,953	435		519,558	11,400
1974	13	3,057		6,759	553	431,460		3,600	433		520,888	14,000
1975	13	3,173		8,898	552	460,378		4,603	433		n.a.	16,185

*Cooperatives.
†Individual members or stockholders of member cooperatives.

- Emphasis on consolidation and elimination of duplication of efforts led to the merging of a large number of local PCAs, with the result that, in 1974, there were 433 in operation.
- Membership remained relatively constant between 1935 and 1955, but since then has doubled, notwithstanding the substantial decline in the number of farms.
- The proportion of short-term farm debt provided by production credit associations has increased rather steadily from a low of 5 percent in 1940 to a high of 19 percent as of January 1, 1974.

Rural Electric Cooperatives

Highlights in the growth of the Rural Electric Cooperative System, as shown in Table 6-3, are:

- A stabilization in the number of systems after 1950 at just under a thousand.
- A stabilization in the percentage of farms served at over 96 percent of the total number after 1960.
- Substantial increases in the number of customers, miles of line, assets, net worth, annual revenue, monthly average use in kilowatthours and loans approved in practically every decade since 1940.

Member Investment in Rural Cooperatives

Equity capital provides some measure of cooperative growth. The total investments of all rural cooperatives as reported in the Balance Sheet of Agriculture (*Agricultural Statistics*), and the percentages of these investments in relation to the total farm assets for selected years are shown here:

Year	Investment in all rural cooperatives (in billions)	Investment in all rural cooperatives as a percentage of total assets
1940	$0.8	1.5
1950	2.1	1.6
1955	3.1	1.9
1960	4.2	2.1
1965	5.6	2.4
1970	7.2	2.4
1971	7.6	3.4
1972	8.0	2.4
1973	8.5	2.2
1974	9.2	1.9

Two observations are in order: (1) Cooperative investments in absolute terms increased almost 12 times between 1940 and 1974; and (2) as a percentage of total assets, investment increased until 1972 and, since then, declined substantially. Many will agree that, in view of the savings farmers realize on their equity in cooperatives, they should be willing to increase their investment in these associations. This view, however, does not

Table 6-3 Operating Trends as Reported for Rural Electrification Systems, Selected Years, 1940-1974*

Year	Systems	Consumers (thousands)	Miles of line (thousands)	Farms served (percentage)	Assets (dollars, million)	Net worth (dollars, million)	Annual revenue (dollars, million)	Average monthly use in KWH by residential consumer	REA loans approved (dollars, million)
1974	984	7,800	1,800	98.6	$9,229	$2,407	$2,905	793	$730
1970	983	6,292	1,649	98.4	6,182	1,670	1,309	687	344
1960	981	4,754	1,450	96.5	3,509	691	615	357	211
1950	977	3,389	1,083	77.2	n.a.	119	241	146	375
1940	684	674	368	30.4	n.a.	n.a.	35†	n.a.	42

*About 95 percent of borrowers from the Rural Electrification Administration are member-owned cooperatives, but separate statistics were tabulated only for recent years. Statistics in this tabulation include 915 cooperatives, 46 public power districts, 19 municipal systems, and 4 investor-owned power companies (1974).
†In 1941; no figure available for 1940.

consider the alternative investment opportunities that farmers must take into account when investing capital.

The Farmer Cooperative Service reported the net equity capital in farmers' marketing, purchasing, and related service cooperatives to be $1.6 billion, $2.6 billion, and $3.2 billion respectively for 1954, 1962, and 1970. Although these figures represent a doubling of equity capital for the period, the proportion of total net equity capital in total cooperative investments actually declined—from 57 percent in 1962 to 43 percent in 1970.

CONSUMER COOPERATIVES

Data compiled by the Cooperative League of the U.S.A. provide growth estimates of consumer cooperatives. Except for credit unions, data on other types of consumer cooperatives are rather limited in scope, although they give some indication of trends among this type of cooperative (see Table 6-4). Available data suggest that:

- Consumer goods cooperatives have experienced considerable fluctuations in numbers, memberships, and volume of business.
- Credit unions and group health, housing, and memorial associations have shown a rather sustained growth in terms of numbers, memberships, and volume of business.
- Nursery and student cooperatives, except for student housing organizations, have maintained a constant rate of growth for the period.
- Except for credit unions and group health cooperatives, consumer associations generally have not reached many people. Until they grow substantially, their impact on most segments of the economy will be limited. Encouraging growth was achieved, however, in the past decade by housing and memorial associations.

Table 6-4 Trends in Estimated Numbers, Memberships, and Volume of Business for Selected Types of Consumer Cooperatives, 1954, 1964, and 1974

Type of cooperative	Cooperatives			Memberships (in thousands)			Volume of business (in millions)		
	1954	1964	1974	1954	1964	1974	1954	1964	1973
Consumer goods	1,050*	60	223	600*	200	577	$ 110	$ 118	$ 570
Credit unions	14,500	21,944	22,879	7,300	15,623	29,900	1,454†	7,046†	24,600†
Group health	28	180	183	800	4,600	8,000	250	260	n.a.
Housing	150	525	800	30	150	800	10	160	5,000
Memorial	50	110	125	50	120	500	0.6	0.8	63
Nursery	—	1,200	1,700	—	60	60	—	6	14
Student	500	500	270	50	55	375‡	11	30	n.a.

*Includes some petroleum cooperatives.
†Savings.
‡Includes twenty-five student housing cooperatives.

GROWTH STRATEGY

Growth does not just happen. It is the result of careful planning and effective implementation of plans. It involves determining what a cooperative wants to achieve (its objectives), and how it can best reach these objectives (by selecting and facilitating methods of growth). The following outline, adapted from FCS Information 87, *Cooperative Growth: Trends, Comparisons, Strategy*, identifies important considerations in developing a strategy for cooperative growth. Although developed especially for farmers' marketing and purchasing cooperatives, this strategy has general application to all types of cooperatives.

Identifying Elements of Growth

Setting Objectives and Goals by Giving Attention to:

1. Areas served: Should emphasis be placed on intensifying service within the existing area or in adjacent areas?
2. Types of farmers or farm enterprises served: Should attention be directed to meeting the needs of certain specialized producers, or should the cooperative seek to serve all farmers?
3. Size of farms served: Are there advantages in serving only large, commercial farms, or should all farms be served?
4. Types of members or patrons served: Should the cooperative serve only agricultural producers, or should it seek to serve all people in a rural community?
5. Services provided: Should service be on a cost basis only, or, in the case of new and experimental services, on a subsidized basis?
6. As for percentage increase in volume over previous year or base year: Is a 5, 10, or 15 percent annual increase reasonable?
7. Market share: Should emphasis be placed on service as a measuring stick of performance, or should the cooperative seek to dominate the business in a community?
8. Most effective ways of increasing members' net income: Should emphasis be placed on volume and expansion or on efficiency and cost reduction?
9. Desirable degree of integration: To what extent should a cooperative process products or manufacture supplies?
10. Source of capital: What percent of assets should a cooperative finance with member equity capital or with loan capital?

Developing Growth Plans that Cover:

1. Short-range periods of one, two, or three years
2. Long-range periods of five to ten years
3. Operating and capital budgets
4. Necessary control techniques

Selecting Methods of Growth

Achieving Internal Growth by:

1. Providing existing services more effectively
2. Enlarging operations by:
    a. Adding member or branch facilities (horizontal integration), and/or
    b. Adding processing, manufacturing, and related services (vertical integration)

COOPERATIVE GROWTH

3 Franchising private dealer-agents
4 Providing only marketing, supply, or related services, or providing all services that farmers needs to run their farm enterprises
5 Selecting proper volume-building techniques by using sales campaigns, modern merchandising methods, prospective patron visits, and meetings
6 Pricing—granting volume discounts for supplies purchased and volume premiums for products marketed
7 Providing field or management services

Accomplishing External Growth through Acquisition and Merger by:

1 Enabling cooperatives to integrate horizontally
2 Enabling cooperatives to integrate vertically
3 Merging with several small cooperatives or with one or more of equal size
4 Merging to add new services and products or to expand existing lines

Encouraging Growth by Joint Ventures—with One or More Firms (Cooperative or Otherwise) on a Partnership Basis—by:

1 Developing national brands for marketing of farm products or providing farm supplies
2 Building programs to encourage export sales
3 Providing wholesale, purchasing, warehousing, and transportation services
4 Manufacturing supplies or processing farm products
5 Performing specialized services such as farm accounting, farm management, and ownership and operation of transportation equipment

Facilitating Growth

Growth Financing by:

1 Retaining net margins
2 Revolving capital
3 Encouraging investments in stock, noncash patronage refunds, per unit capital contributions, and sale of debentures
4 Developing nonmember or public sources of capital
5 Borrowing funds
6 Determining the extent of equities of current members that should be used to expand services to other groups or other members
7 Exploring the feasibility of using subsidiaries or setting up separate cooperatives under the same management and board

Utilizing Research and Technical Assistance by:

1 Product or technical research designed to
   a Improve varieties of livestock and crops
   b Better cultural practices
   c Develop new foods
   d Develop new supplies
2 Business or economic research relating to
   a Items discussed earlier under Setting Objectives and Goals

      b Information needed for planning
      c Operations, including methods of internal and external growth and the feasibility of joint ventures and growth of federations
      d All aspects of cooperative finance, transportation, storage, and management
      e All aspects of cooperative communication programs, including member, information, and training programs and effective use of educational techniques
      f Broad economic questions concerning impacts of national economic, political, and social policies on cooperatives
3 Determining sources of research and technical assistance through
      a Cooperatives, including regional cooperatives, state cooperative councils, cooperative trade organizations, and national cooperative associations
      b Land-grant and other universities, particularly agricultural experiment stations and state extension services
      c Federal agencies, especially the Farmer Cooperative Service, other agencies of the Department of Agriculture, and the Bureau of the Census and other departments
      d Private research firms

Developing a Supporting Educational Program by:

1 Identifying publics to reach (see Chapter 14):
      a Cooperative members
      b Potential members, such as farmers, other rural people, and suburban dwellers
      c The general public, including business people, educators, legislators, and clergy
2 Determination of educational techniques to be used:
      a Annual meetings, conferences, workshops, and regional and national meetings
      b Radio and TV programs and/or commercials
      c Newsletters, house organs, exhibits, magazine articles, video and cassette tapes, and other audiovisuals
      d Training programs for employees and directors
      e Special programs for youths, young farmers, and farm women
      f Sources of assistance (much the same as those for research and technical assistance)

SUMMARY

There is much support for the view that continued and expanded cooperative growth is needed if cooperatives are to improve their service to patrons. Growth requires increased emphasis on processing and manufacturing, greater integration of services, adequate financial resources, and competent management. It also requires a growth strategy that considers the limiting and strategic factors and the available resources of each individual cooperative.

    Cooperative growth in the United States has been most pronounced among farmers' marketing and purchasing, credit, mutual insurance, rural electric and telephone, and credit union cooperatives. Most American consumer cooperatives are still hovering at the "take off" stage, and only time will tell whether they will achieve the size and market share necessary to make a significant impact in segments of the economy in which they operate.

QUESTIONS

1. Why is economic growth important to cooperatives?
2. What are the best ways to measure cooperative growth?
3. What precautions are necessary in interpreting statistics on cooperative growth?
4. Compare the relative growth of farmers' marketing and purchasing cooperatives, service cooperatives, and consumer cooperatives in the United States. What factors account for the variations in the growth of each type?
5. How would you explain the differences in the cooperative market share for the various products marketed and supplies purchased by cooperatives?
6. How does growth of farmers' marketing and purchasing cooperatives compare with the noncooperative segments of farm marketing and production supply industries?
7. What conclusions do you draw from the comparison between the four largest cooperatives in selected industries and the four largest other business firms in the same industries?
8. How do the ten largest cooperatives compare with the ten largest other business firms in the same or related industries as to volume of business, assets, and net margins?
9. How do you account for the relatively rapid rate of growth of credit and rural electric cooperatives?
10. Why did consumer cooperatives experience considerable difficulty in gaining a foothold in the United States?
11. What are the growth prospects for credit unions and fishing, group health, housing, nursery school, and student cooperatives?
12. Why should cooperatives develop a strategy for growth? What factors do you consider important in developing this strategy?
13. Evaluate the following statement: "Cooperatives operating in response to the economic needs of members make their greatest progress during periods of economic recession."

REFERENCES

Abrahamsen, Martin A.: *Cooperative Growth: Trends, Comparisons, Strategy,* FCS Information 87, U.S. Department of Agriculture, Farmer Cooperative Service, Washington, 1973, p. 107.

————: *Cooperative Growth,* ARE Mimeo Series No. 4, University of Maryland, Department of Agricultural and Resource Economics, College Park, 1973, p. 14.

Avidor, Abraham, and Martin A. Abrahamsen: *Cooperative Growth in Maryland,* University of Maryland, Department of Agricultural and Resource Economics, College Park, 1974, p. 22.

Cooperative League of the U.S.A.: *Cooperatives, USA: Facts and Figures* (a yearly publication), Washington, D.C.

Farmer Cooperative Service: *Statistics of Farmer Cooperatives* (a yearly publication), U.S. Department of Agriculture, Washington.

Mather, J. Warren: *Major Regional Cooperative Supply Associations,* FCS Research Report 29, U.S. Department of Agriculture, Farmer Cooperative Service, Washington, 1971, p. 57.

Samuelson, Paul A.: *Economics,* 9th ed., McGraw-Hill, New York, 1973, pp. 732–786.

————: "The Statistical Story," in *American Cooperation,* American Institute of Cooperation, Washington, D.C., 1973, pp. 336–360.

Chapter 7

Cooperatives in Other Selected Countries

Business cooperatives, ever since their beginning in England and Scotland in the early nineteenth century, have gained universal recognition. As a result, various types of cooperative ventures have been undertaken in many countries, often on a trial-and-error basis. The emerging cooperatives have generally demonstrated great flexibility in adjusting to different and changing economic, political, and social conditions throughout the world. We in the United States are indebted to cooperatives of many other nations for the contributions they have made to our own cooperative development.

EARLY COOPERATIVE EFFORTS

As civilizations emerged, families and clans, either by necessity or by inclination, found it to their advantage to cooperate in order to meet the pressing needs of the day. Indications are that, invariably, such efforts were first directed to assure safety, procure food, or obtain shelter. We are told that in China, for example, cooperation initially took the form of crop watching to discourage plundering and thievery by roving bands.

When people gained experience in joint efforts of various kinds, they undertook new and more complicated cooperative activities. This was a natural outcome as human beings gave up nomadic wandering for a permanent type of agriculture.

In many arid areas, the need for irrigation led to community effort to develop crude cooperative irrigation systems, particularly in China, Egypt, and among the Incas and certain other Indian tribes in both South and North America. Gradually, additional business efforts along cooperative lines were developed. In ancient Egypt, artisans and craftworkers developed trade associations, and in the Babylonian era, cooperative tenant farming was mentioned in the Code of Hammurabi as an accepted practice. The early burial societies of Greece and Rome were forerunners of the medieval trade associations of craftworkers. Communal societies are also reported to have flourished in Crete. In China, cooperative credit and savings societies became instruments to finance weddings, funerals, and certain religious festivals.

During the seventeenth century, various guilds and crafts formed such social groups as the Freemasons, Odd Fellows, Druids, and Foresters. These groups, with their mystic rites and observances, held to certain religious and spiritual beliefs that also brought people together.

In England, the idea of self-help became established when its people, as early as 1793, gained parliamentary sanction to form associations to aid one another in times of need and sickness.

COOPERATIVE BUSINESS EFFORTS

As the benefits of informal cooperation became more and more apparent, people in many countries started to introduce the idea of cooperation into their business ventures. With the gradual emergence of a market economy, many people came to recognize the advantages of joining together in cooperative business enterprises to buy the necessities of life and to sell the products and services they produced. Some of the highlights in the development of cooperatives in selected countries deserve mention here.

Great Britain

For the early appearance of significant cooperative business efforts, we turn to Great Britain. The prevailing views of the times are indicated by a pamphlet published in 1766 entitled "Proposals Humbly Offered to the Public for an Association against the Inquisition Practices of Engrossers, Forestallers, Jobbers, etc., and for Reducing the Price of Provisions, Especially Butchers' Meat." Although there is no indication that any association was actually formed, the idea of setting up societies (cooperative business ventures) to procure the basic necessities of life was evidently gaining momentum.

One of the first attempts to conduct business on a cooperative basis was that of weavers in the village of Fenwick in Ayrshire, Scotland. In 1769 the weavers formed an association to purchase such items as oatmeal and other household staples, as well as weaver supplies. This society was financed from its members' own meager capital, and as a result they came to be called penny capitalists.

In 1795, people in Hull, England, set up their own flour mill and organized a society to handle production of some basic necessities and supplies. In about 1800, the Good Intent Society of Brentford, England, was organized "to erect a corn mill to make flour for members, and if necessary, bake the flour into bread." How the cooperative institutions developed from the experience of various groups is indicated by the association set up at Lennoxtown, Scotland, in 1812, and incorporated as a friendly society fourteen years later. It continued operations until about 1919. We have previously mentioned that this association was credited with introducing the idea of patronage refunds when it provided for the distribution of yearly surpluses among its patrons according to the amount of business they did with it.

Developing along somewhat different lines was a cooperative set up in Brighton, England, in 1828. In addition to operating a store for the sale of household staples, this association acquired land on which its members grew products for sale through the store.

Like shooting stars, these ventures cast but brief light on the economic problems of participants, and they were soon extinguished because of a combination of such unfavorable circumstances as mismanagement, inadequate financing, and undisciplined membership.

Robert Owen We previously have referred to Robert Owen as the social philosopher who revolted against the exploitive conditions of the English factory system. Here we will examine how he responded to the economic and social conditions that prevailed. His initial approach was to organize along communal lines the textile mills he owned at New Lanark, Scotland. He visualized a "perfect society" of some 3,000 people who would operate their own mills and factories, work their own land, and be as self-sufficing as possible. Under Owen's dynamic leadership, these early efforts were quite successful.

Owen's idea of communal societies led to less successful, grandiose experiments by others. A community was founded at Orbiston by Abram Combe in 1825. He organized a company financed with a capital fund of 50,000 English pounds divided into shares of 250 pounds each. Combe served as a trustee for an estate of 291 acres, which was to serve as the base of operations.[1]

Many of the people selected as members of Combe's community had little understanding of the venture. Except for the foundry, which was operated by skilled workers, most activities achieved but little success. The original plans could not be carried through to completion, and the estate was sold in 1827.

Another venture was the agricultural community organized at Ralahine, Ireland, which included a homogeneous group that operated in a highly successful manner for a few years. It was forced to discontinue operations, however, when the owner of the land gambled away all his property and fled the country.

Rochdale Pioneers The Rochdale pioneers, while far from establishing the first cooperative society in Great Britain, deserve recognition for forming the first permanent cooperative business venture. They provided a model that achieved worldwide

---

[1]F. Hall and W. P. Watkins, *Cooperation*, Cooperative Union, Ltd., Hanover Street, Manchester, England, 1937, pp. 62–66. The book describes these cooperative communities in considerable detail.

acceptance by introducing unique cooperative principles and sound business practices that were meaningful to their members.

The legendary Rochdale pioneers knew what failure was. As early as 1830, some of them had established a friendly society to operate a mill and buy household necessities. It soon failed. In 1843, some of the people of Rochdale started discussing the merits of organizing a society to provide basic necessities. By August 15, 1844, such a society had been organized.

Some of the deliberations that went into the preparations to launch the business operations are described by Hall and Watkins.[2]

> After examining several shops that were available the board, on November 25th, agreed to take the warehouse of Mr. Dunlop in Toad Lane at a rent of £10 per year for three years, the society to do the necessary repairs. The board on December 16th appointed William Cooper as cashier and Samuel Ashworth as salesman; four days earlier the board had decided that David Brooks and John Holt should purchase the necessary stock for the society which was to consist of flour, butter, sugar, and oatmeal. On November 28th, James Tweedale, Miles Ashworth, and James Daly were appointed to see to the repairing of the premises; George Ashworth and Thomas Holt were appointed to purchase the necessary furniture for commencing business; and George Ashworth was appointed to purchase three forms for five shillings. We are informed from another source that the shop was first opened on December 21st, 1844.

The Rochdale pioneers started business by saving some £28 to provide the necessary capital for their business venture. At first the store was open only a few hours on certain days, but business gradually improved and before long the example of Rochdale led to the establishment of other cooperatives in various parts of Great Britain.

From modest beginnings, the initial society grew and new departments and branches were organized. In 1850 the Rochdale Cooperative Corn Mill was organized. In 1851 the original store remained open all day. In 1852 the Industrial and Provident Societies Act provided for an allocation of 2.5 percent of savings for an educational fund, and the Rochdale cooperative took full advantage of this provision to start an aggressive educational program. In 1854 the pioneers entered into the manufacture of cotton cloth. As Rochdale grew, new ventures were undertaken which often served as models for other groups interested in organizing a cooperative. For a while it provided wholesale services for nearly all British cooperatives, and later it supported the organization of the Cooperative Wholesale Society.

The question may well be asked: Why did the Rochdale cooperative succeed where others failed? A few observations seem in order. First of all, Rochdale benefited from the experiences of others. Next, it was among the first to do some planning. It developed a set of objectives which included:

- Operation of a store to sell food and clothing
- Manufacture of basic necessities

[2]Ibid., p. 84.

- Building and purchasing of houses for members
- As soon as practicable, establishing a self-supporting colony
- Promoting sobriety through the opening of a temperance hotel as soon as possible[3]

Cooperative Wholesale Society (CWS)   Not unlike the Rochdale pioneers, the Cooperative Wholesale Society owed much to those who had gone before it. Despite the handicaps of limited capital, poor transportation, and the distrust of strangers, the idea of a wholesale service was a frequent subject of discussion by cooperative officials.

In 1830, John Finch suggested in the *Birmingham Cooperative Herald* that the first Liverpool Cooperative Society act as agent for other retail societies. Later in the year, he reported that seven societies were buying "at the lowest rate articles of genuine quality." By 1831, after much discussion, the Federal Wholesale Company was organized in Manchester, England. How long the society operated is not known, but reportedly some thirty-one transitory societies dealt with the society in the early 1830s.

Throughout the 1840s and 1850s, support of the Christian Socialists, meetings of innumerable groups of delegates of local societies, and the passage of the Industrial and Provident Societies Act all stimulated interest in a wholesale cooperative. Starting in 1860, a new cooperative magazine, *The Cooperator,* also became an important vehicle for supporting the idea of such a cooperative.

Much discussion took place, and plans were drawn up to delineate the services a wholesale cooperative would perform. By late 1863, the Cooperative Wholesale Society had been formally organized and had announced a slate of officers. The Society encountered the usual conventional problems of limited loyalty, credit losses, and boycotts from suppliers. During the first year, there even were those who desired to divide the remainder of the initial capital of £1,000 "before it was all lost." Nevertheless, the CWS survived and, owing to astute leadership, business began to expand dramatically.

Later, the Cooperative Wholesale Society reported that it was handling a quite complete line of groceries. Then it "had to turn to boots and shoes, to draperies, and to furniture. There was no stopping. Boots somehow led to blankets and blankets to bedsteads and brushes." There was much discussion as to whether the CWS should expand beyond serving as a purchasing agent and go into processing and manufacturing.

By 1873, the Society had entered into manufacturing, which at first included only boots and shoes, biscuits and sweets, and possibly blankets. Then, in rapid succession, the march of business activity included establishing banking services which developed into the present Cooperative Bank, building factories for the manufacture of just about every type of product consumers used in quantity, owning of ships, and purchasing tea plantations in Ceylon (now Sri Lanka) and India.

The CWS, with a program of "unity, service, and quality," continued to grow at a dramatic rate during the first half of the twentieth century. It developed a social

---

[3]Arnold J. Bonner, *British Cooperation,* Cooperative Union, Ltd., Hanover Street, Manchester, England, 1970 (rev. ed.), p. 46.

consciousness that resulted in its providing food for striking workers in Ireland, making facilities available for wartime production in World Wars I and II, and pioneering in emphasizing recreational, insurance, and medical services for members.

The Cooperative Wholesale Society has shown remarkable growth during the past 100 years. In 1870 net sales were reported at £507,000 (English). Sales increased to £16 million in 1900; £105 million in 1920; £182 million in 1945; and £903 million in 1974. Approximately 70 percent of sales now consist of food, principally groceries, milk, provisions, meat, soft drinks, and bakery and milling products. The most important nonfood items handled are "housewares and optical, coal, drapery, men's wear, and footwear." Either on its own or through joint arrangements with other cooperatives or private firms, CWS operates about 100 factories that account for about 25 percent of the Society's trade. The principal items manufactured or produced include bacon, margarine, tea, flour (milling and baking), clothing, and household goods. CWS also farms about 35,000 acres, provides insurance and banking services, and collaborates with other cooperatives in international trading ventures.

Interest in forming a wholesale society also developed in Scotland. Some early Scottish societies joined the English CWS and interest was expressed in having it establish a branch in Scotland. Although limited resources did not permit this development, CWS's officials offered the Scottish retail societies extensive assistance in setting up their own wholesale operations. As a result, the Scottish Cooperative Wholesale Society was formed in 1868. Both wholesale societies have worked closely together. In fact, since the turn of the century, they have joined in efforts to procure tea, cocoa, and chocolate and to provide insurance through jointly owned companies.

After World War II, the Cooperative Wholesale Society incurred substantial competition from chain stores and other private businesses. As a result, it has not realized the same dramatic increases in business activity that it did prior to World War II. To meet these problems, the Society has placed special emphasis on increasing the efficiency of distribution and manufacturing, and on working with local associations to modernize and merge facilities.

CWS's educational and training program is primarily conducted through the Cooperative Union, Ltd. Strong emphasis is put on public relations, legal and technical advice, assembling of statistics, and general policy. As early as 1919 it established a cooperative college at Stanford Hall on a 300-acre estate located near Loughborough. This college has facilities for 120 students and provides a wide range of special cooperative and more general managerial training courses. The college also conducts correspondence courses and runs an international cooperative training center for students from overseas.

Agricultural Cooperation in Britain To round out the discussion of cooperative development in the United Kingdom, let us briefly review the development of its agricultural cooperatives. Margaret Digby reports that these cooperatives began in 1867.[4] Observers of the success of consumer and industrial cooperatives established

---

[4]Margaret Digby, *Agricultural Cooperatives in the United Kingdom,* The Plunkett Foundation for Cooperative Studies, Oxford, England, 1968, p. 9.

the Agricultural and Horticultural Association, Ltd., of Manchester, to provide farmers with production supplies. Emphasis was on "quality and purity of products handled." This development was followed in 1869 by the action of Cumberland farmers who, concerned with fraudulent practices in the sale of fertilizer, set up a cooperative to provide themselves with fertilizers and related items.

In Ireland, Sir Horace Plunkett, after an unsuccessful venture in the organization of cooperatives which attracted maximum opposition from the private trade, turned his attention to agricultural marketing and processing associations with the help of George Russell, R. A. Anderson, and Father Finlay, a Jesuit priest. They established the Irish Agricultural Organization Society. Emphasis primarily was on providing a trained staff ready to assist in the formation and organization of new societies and on being ready to provide them with legal, technical, and business advice. It also represented these societies in their dealing with the "government and other bodies."

The development of agricultural cooperatives in England continued, and Digby further reported that, by 1908,

> the number of such societies had risen to 114. By 1914, it stood at 200, by 1920, it had increased to 381 exclusive of small holdings and allotment societies which were very numerous. Membership totaled nearly 85,000, perhaps one-third of the farmers of England, and trading turnover stood at 17.5 million pounds of which 10 million pounds were made up of agricultural requirements and the remainder of agricultural produce—milk and milk products, eggs, poultry, meat and bacon, fruit and vegetables.[5]

Following World War I, there was a marked drop in the number of agricultural cooperatives and a lesser decline in their volume of business in Great Britain. The milk cooperatives, for example, in the 1930s came under the regulations of the newly established Milk Marketing Board. Lacking necessary capital and failing to get the desired support from the marketing board, these cooperatives were unable to build the facilities required to process fluid milk. As a result, they had to discontinue operations.

In 1971, cooperative officials estimated that the proportions of farm products marketed through cooperatives in the United Kingdom were: cereals, 14 percent; livestock, 12 percent; fruit, 11 percent; vegetables, 10 percent; potatoes, 6 percent; eggs, 21 percent; wool, 40 percent; and poultry, 7 percent.

The tabulation on page 133, prepared by Dr. A. Herlitzke, Secretary General of COPA/COGECA (The EEC General Committee for Farmers Cooperative Organizations), which represents, respectively, farmers and cooperative interests in ECH (Farmers Professional Organization), gives the proportion of principal farm products marketed through cooperatives in selected European countries in 1971.

This comparative tabulation shows that the proportion of agricultural products marketed in the United Kingdom was substantially less than that of the other Common Market countries.

A number of new services are being provided by agricultural cooperatives in Great Britain, however. They include credit and special services, such as grain and grass

---

[5]Ibid. p. 11.

	Percentage						
Item	West Germany	Belgium	France	Italy	Luxemburg	Netherlands	United Kingdom
Cereals	45	20	82	15	70	55	14
Milk	83	50	52	29	91	84	—
Meat	25	5	10	—	26	20	—
Fruit	22	60	25	10	100	95	11
Vegetables	32	40	20	15	—	99	10
Potatoes	22	—	15	32	50	14	6
Eggs	20	2	—	—	—	21	21
Poultry	—	4	25	—	—	20	1

drying, sale of pedigree seeds, artificial insemination of livestock, marketing of forest products, and production syndicates.[6]

Agricultural cooperatives in Great Britain have moved in the direction of merger and consolidation and are characterized by the tendency to provide both marketing and purchasing services by the same cooperatives. Progress has not been marked, however, in the organization of large-scale wholesale cooperatives that entail coordination and large manufacturing and processing operations. The Farmer Trading Central Board was organized as early as 1912 to provide central buying services. Operations expanded, and it became an agricultural wholesale society in 1918. Because of problems in the selection of management and the impact of the postwar slump, failure was foreordained, and it discontinued operations in 1924.

Since then, the agricultural cooperative leadership in England has encountered serious problems in its attempts to assume an effective role in the development of a national organization and in establishing harmonious working relations with various agricultural organizations. Inability to agree as to just what should be the role of the National Farmers Union (NFU) in regard to cooperatives led to an invitation to Dr. Joseph G. Knapp, then Administrator of Farmer Cooperative Service, U.S. Department of Agriculture, to study the British cooperative system.

His report, *Analysis of Agricultural Cooperation in England*,[7] recommended, among other things, that an agricultural central cooperative association be established as a totally independent organization of cooperatives, with increased financial support from both its members and the government. This suggestion led, in 1966, to the reestablishment of the Agricultural Cooperative Association, now the Agricultural Cooperative Marketing Service (ACMS). The National Farmers Union, however, has also continued some business operations, and an effective coordination of national cooperative effort awaits further development.

[6]Production syndicates are primarily organizations of two to twenty farmers who jointly own one or more machines and provide necessary farm services. More recently, these practices have been expanded to include hop-poles (poles used in the cultivation of hops), preservation units, and farm accounting practices.

[7]Joseph G. Knapp, *An Analysis of Agricultural Cooperation in England,* Agricultural Central Cooperative Association, Ltd., Knightsbridge, London, England, 1964, p. 242.

The leadership of agricultural cooperatives in Wales, Scotland, and Northern Ireland is in the hands of the agricultural organization societies of these countries. These societies, together with ACMS, are united in a federated body, Federated Agricultural Cooperatives, an organization which represents British agricultural cooperatives at meetings of COGECA, which is responsible for putting the cooperative case before the European Economic Community (EEC).

Switzerland

Cooperatives of all types have made very substantial progress in Switzerland. Local agricultural and consumer associations, many of them federated with national cooperatives providing wholesale services and engaging in manufacturing, are commonplace. In some instances, national cooperatives operate their own branches. Often large local cooperatives in the major cities also operate a number of branches. Many of the agricultural cooperatives are multipurpose organizations handling a wide range of agricultural products as well as supplying consumer goods for members.

Agricultural Cooperatives Among the first agricultural cooperatives in Switzerland were small Alpine dairy associations. These organizations flourished, and a 1924 report of the Federal Trade Commission stated that there were some 5,500 farmer cooperatives in the country. Included in this number were 3,500 dairy associations engaged in supplying fresh milk for the city market and in manufacturing the famous Emmenthaler and Gruyère cheeses. The report also identified some 800 agricultural societies ("syndicates") that provided machinery, implements, fertilizers, and seeds for about 80,000 members at wholesale prices. In 1907, these cooperatives formed a national federation which placed special emphasis on stabilizing prices and on influencing national agricultural policy in the interests of dairy farmers.

In 1971, about 4,500 dairy cooperatives, grouped into sixteen federations, were serving some 93,000 farmers. These cooperatives handled over 99 percent of the total dairy production of the country. Five poultry and egg associations served 80,000 farmers, reported a net volume of business of 16 million Swiss francs, and accounted for about 40 percent of the country's poultry and egg business. About 100 cooperatives were engaged in the marketing of food grains. They had about 35,000 members and a net volume of 37 million francs, and they handled between 50 and 60 percent of the country's total grain production in 1971. A total of 1,088 fruit and vegetable cooperatives, grouped into nine federations, were serving 116,000 members, had a net volume of 75 million Swiss francs, and accounted for about 40 percent of the national fruit and vegetable production. Livestock breeding syndicates for cattle, horses, and small animals also were numerous.

Most of the fruit and vegetable marketing cooperatives also handle farm supplies. The farm supply business amounts to approximately 240 million Swiss francs, and available information suggests that the Swiss cooperatives now provide 40 to 50 percent of the feed, 70 percent of the seed, 50 to 55 percent of the fertilizer, and 10 percent of the machinery. Nearly all Swiss cooperatives are affiliated with the Federal Union of Cooperative Associations, which provides technical assistance and coordination. They also coordinate with agricultural societies and associations that are set up on a language and commodity basis and emphasize technical improvement in agriculture as well as the social and cultural development of members.

For a country in which cooperatives are such an integral part of the farm picture, the absence of livestock cooperatives is unusual. Swiss farmers sell their livestock to local dealers, butchers, and meat packers.

Consumer Cooperatives Consumer cooperatives are well established in Switzerland. The 1924 report of the Federal Trade Commission stated that the Union of Swiss Consumer Societies had been organized by 1890, and that it included some 500 societies that operated 1,900 retail stores. These retail societies served some 370,000 individual members and reported an annual volume of approximately 340 million Swiss francs. In 1920, about 270 credit societies of the Raiffeisen type reported some 70,000 savings accounts. About 1,100 mutual loan banks of the Raiffeisen type (see Chapter 4, page 75), serving about 150,000 members including many from agricultural communities, were in operation in the early 1970s.

By 1893, the Union of Swiss Consumer Societies had become active in wholesaling and had entered into shoe manufacturing, coffee roasting, preparation of spices, book printing and binding, and furniture manufacture. It is also reported to have entered the agricultural production field, operating corn mills and dairy and truck farms. In addition, the Union provided insurance and emphasized selling under the "Co-op" trademark. This organization is presently known as Co-op Switzerland, and in 1974 it reported 229 affiliated cooperatives. Through them it served 900,000 families through 148 member cooperatives. Its annual volume of business was 2.5 billion Swiss francs.

Migros, a federated consumer cooperative that was founded by Gottlieb Duttweiler in 1925, is an example of how these cooperatives have developed in Switzerland. To quote Mr. Duttweiler:

> For a short time, I was a planter in Brazil. When I came back to Europe, I was amazed to discover that retailers in Switzerland took as much for selling goods over the counter as the coffee planter received for his harvested coffee, after tending the coffee bush carefully for five years before any berries could be picked.

His response was the organization of Migros, which means "half-wholesale" and which was responsible for introducing a revolutionary form of distribution. The program was initiated when five Migros "mobile shops" took to the streets of Zurich and sold such specialty items as granulated and cube sugar, noodles, coffee, rice, soap, and related articles. The first store was opened in Zurich in 1927. At all times, emphasis was on selling at the lowest possible price consistent with quality and service.

The growth of Migros has been dramatic. As of 1974, it reported 444 retail stores with 988,000 members. In addition, Migros served 78 specialty stores and 119 "stores on wheels." Retail sales of affiliates totaled 5.4 billion Swiss francs, and wholesale sales of Migros amounted to 2.1 billion Swiss francs. Sales of Migros cooperatives approximated 10 percent of the retail sales of Switzerland. For such items as food, however, the figure, estimated at about 25 percent, was substantially higher.

Migros now provides a complete line of consumer goods. For example, it handles all types of clothing and operates a number of factories that manufacture and process a high proportion of its clothing items. As a federation, it emphasizes quantity purchasing of imports, production, financing, coordination, research consultation, development, and press relations.

Though Migros began as a private business venture, arrangements were made to convert it to a consumer cooperative in 1935. It moved outside the traditional consumer field by using funds accumulated as "social capital" for such programs as the establishment of a hotel plan to promote the foreign tourist trade and holiday rates at reasonable prices for lower-income classes.

In each of its principal locations, Migros has also developed school clubs with language courses for members. It maintains a book and record club, a complete insurance service, and a handicraft program. And in this and in other ways, it provides an active education and research program for members. To support its cultural program, Migros has entered into an agreement with cooperative affiliates to use 1 percent of its net margins for these activities.

The direction in which Migros has further developed is indicated by its operating principles. These can be summarized as follows:

- Direct wholesale purchasing from the producer whenever possible, thus eliminating any intermediary agent's profit
- Markup just low enough to cover the costs of efficient distribution and a modest profit
- Medium-sized packages
- Refusal to accept retail prices fixed by manufacturers (retail price maintenance)
- Advertising of high quality and low prices, which engenders mouth-to-mouth recommendation—the best of all publicity
- Careful testing of goods in laboratories and by taste panels
- Hygienic prepackaging of merchandise in the central warehouse
- Freshness guaranteed by quick turnover, the first in/first out system, date stamping, and the use of refrigerated warehouse space and display cases
- Limited assortment (mobile shops carry approximately 500 items; self-service stores, 1,000 to 1,200; Migros-Markets, 3,000 to 5,000)
- Introduction of the round-price system (with odd weights), for quicker addition and easier checking by the purchaser; also, the price per weight-unit printed on each package for the customer's easy comparison
- Special promotion of nutritionally valuable foods (fruit juices, fruits and vegetables, yoghurt, pasteurized milk)
- Refusal to sell alcohol and tobacco, in spite of their high profitability
- Net prices without rebates or patronage dividends
- Cash payment
- No home delivery

As to scope of operations, services provided, and organizational and operating practices, Co-operative Switzerland and Migros show much similarity.

Scandinavia

Because of the extensive, and in some respects unique, cooperative development in the Scandinavian countries, we will review this development in Denmark, Sweden, Norway, Finland, and Iceland. (Although, technically, Finland is not a Scandinavian country, its cooperatives are typically Scandinavian.) These five countries, representing no more than 25 million people, have pioneered successfully in adapting the cooperative technique to changing economic, social, and political conditions.

Denmark The agriculture of Denmark is highly developed, as are its cooperatives. In fact, the many accomplishments of Danish cooperatives are recognized internationally. A number of conditioning forces no doubt have contributed to their success. As early as 1844, Bishop N. F. S. Grundtvig started folk high schools for adult farm men and women. These schools taught such subjects as history, political science, civics, and geography. They aimed to encourage a broad, all-round education and provided a fertile ground for the introduction of cooperatives. Denmark also had the advantage of being near England. The Danes' close communication with that country soon acquainted them with the cooperative efforts underway there.

As a nation, Denmark is no larger than the state of Maryland, and the homogeneity of its people and agriculture, coupled with a high level of education, provided a sound basis for the introduction of cooperatives. Moreover, economic conditions encouraged cooperative development. The traditional grain and livestock farm economy was influenced by imports of cheap grain from the United States in the 1870s. Consequently, farmers expanded their dairy and hog economy. Many of them, having extremely small units, soon recognized the importance of joint efforts if they were to market their products effectively.

Denmark is unique among the Scandinavian countries in that its consumer cooperatives, except for a few large societies in Copenhagen, are primarily oriented toward serving the rural areas.

The first consumer cooperative in Denmark was founded in 1866 by Hans Christian Sonne, an agricultural statesman from North Jutland. Others were soon established, and by 1896 the Danish Cooperative Wholesale Society was organized to purchase consumer goods, provide accounting assistance, and furnish advisory services. As of 1972, about 1,600 consumer societies served substantially all urban and rural communities in Denmark.

In response to the varying needs of rural people, a large number of agricultural cooperatives were organized. It was reported that in 1880, for example, some 120 were in operation. Although attempts were made to establish a cooperative dairy in the 1860s, the first successful cooperative dairy was not established until 1882 in Hjeddie, West Jutland. No doubt, P. C. Neilsen's invention of the cream separator in 1879 gave much impetus to the dairy industry. The first cooperative bacon factory was established in 1887. Local egg cooperatives followed in 1889, and by 1895 these cooperatives had developed export outlets for eggs.

As Danish cooperatives developed spontaneously in response to people's needs, a number of distinct characteristics appeared. Various commodity groups, for example, established national cooperative federations that assumed responsibility for educational work and technical programs. These federations in turn have coordinated the efforts of farmers' organizations and export agencies to speak for agriculture in negotiations with government.

Danish cooperatives have developed a high degree of flexibility, and some have become multipurpose in operation. Consumer cooperatives, for example, have served as assembly points for eggs, and they have established feed and fertilizer plants that are local distributing points for these products.

As of 1972, pertinent data on Danish agricultural cooperatives were as follows:

Type of cooperative	Number of		Turnover	Percentage of market share
	Societies	Members		
Dairies	274	63,000	3,100*	86
Bacon factories	26	91,000	6,500*	92
Cattle	39	60,000	247,000†	38
Poultry	1	4,000	31‡	39
Eggs (integrated)	0	6,500	25‡	49
Farm supplies	840	100,000	2,300*	45

*Millions of Danish crowns.
†Number of head.
‡Millions of kilograms.

Consolidation and coordination have become the order of the day among most types of Danish cooperatives, but especially among dairy cooperatives. For example, the number of local associations engaged in marketing farm products declined from 4,481 in 1960 to 537 in 1972. During the same time, however, volume of business nearly doubled, increasing from 983 million Danish crowns to 1,673 million Danish crowns. The situation is similar among farm supply cooperatives. The number declined from about 1,800 to 940 during the same period, while volume increased from 121 million to 330 million Danish crowns. In 1972 the 1,616 consumer societies reported an annual volume of business of 5.2 billion Danish crowns.

Sweden While there is considerable similarity in the development of cooperatives in Denmark and Sweden, there are also differences. Sweden's consumer cooperatives have been more closely oriented to laborers and other urban dwellers than their Danish counterparts, although they developed close operating relations with farm cooperatives. Swedish cooperatives are of somewhat more recent origin—following those of Denmark by a decade or two. They are also larger and more systematically integrated than those in Denmark. This is true especially for consumer cooperatives, which have pursued aggressive economic policies. They have never hesitated to follow a "cartel-busting" policy when they found that consumers were being exploited.

Agricultural Cooperatives Mortgage societies are the oldest form of cooperative known in Sweden, tracing their origin to the 1830s. By 1860, many mortgage societies had been formed, and the General Mortgage Bank of Sweden was organized. Dairy, egg, and purchasing cooperatives were organized in the 1890s, and meat-marketing cooperatives were formed at the turn of the century.

Substantially all local cooperatives are coordinated through county and district federations into national federations which, in turn, are members of the Federation of Swedish Farmers (LRF). The numbers of farmer members, local societies, county and district federations, and the names of the national federations are given in Figure 7-1.

In the mid-1970s, Sweden reported that 80 percent of all farm products are marketed wholesale through cooperatives. The proportion ranges from 99 percent of its dairy products to 73 percent of its poultry and eggs. About 70 percent of the feed and fertilizer used by Swedish farmers is also provided by cooperatives. While the number of county and district associations has declined from 262 to about 100 since 1960, the net volume of business has increased from 4.7 billion crowns to over 10 billion crowns by 1974.

Prior to 1970, policy matters relating to Swedish agriculture were handled by the National Farmers Union (RLF) of which all national cooperatives were members, and by the Federation of Swedish Farmers Associations (SL). In 1970, the two organizations merged into the Federation of Swedish Farmers (LRF), which came to represent all farmer interests—political and economic.

Consumer Cooperatives Consumer cooperation in Sweden has achieved international recognition because of the accomplishments of Kooperativa Forbundet (KF). This organization started as a service organization in 1899. Its stated purpose was: "To promote the development and success of the cooperative movement and, for that purpose, to furnish advice and disseminate appropriate literature. . . ." In response to requests of member associations, however, it went into the procurement of necessary supplies in 1904. G. H. von Kock, who drew on the experiences of British consumer cooperatives, provided the early leadership for this effort. In 1908, KF opened a savings bank, and in the next year it entered into the production of basic consumer goods. A large proportion of the insurance business in Sweden also is conducted through cooperative associations under a complex organizational structure known as Folksam.

As KF developed, rather strict membership provisions that followed the Rochdale principles were formulated. Local associations could be members only if they subscribed to the principles of unlimited membership, democratic control, cash trading, refund of surpluses according to purchases, limited interest on shares, and allocation of at least 2.5 percent of savings to an educational fund.

Over the years, KF has carried on an aggressive, and sometimes militant, role in fighting national and international cartels. When the margarine cartel refused to give KF the usual wholesale rebate, KF started to produce its own margarine in 1908. In 1922, it entered the milling business, capturing 25 percent of Sweden's production of milling products and destroying the milling cartel that had greatly increased its profits (which were reported to have risen from 8 percent to 33 percent from 1914 to 1919). In 1926, KF started to manufacture overshoes, with the result that some prices were reduced as much as 50 percent. In 1931, it defied the international light-bulb cartel by joining with cooperatives in other Scandinavian countries to operate a light-bulb factory. As a result, the average price of bulbs dropped considerably.

KF has also from time to time worked with farmer cooperatives. When some

Figure 7-1 The Federation of Swedish Farmers (LRF)

Swedish dairies' association	Swedish farmers' meat marketing association	Swedish farmers' purchasing and market association	Swedish egg and poultry marketing association	Swedish forest owners' association	Association for Swedish livestock breeding and production	Association of Swedish rural credit societies	General mortgage bank of Sweden	Swedish distillers' association	Swedish fur breeders' association	Swedish starch producers' association	Swedish oilseed growers' association	Swedish seed growers' association	Swedish sugarbeet growers' association
SMR	SS	SLR	SÄ	SSR	SHS	SJF	SAH	SBI	SPR	SSF	SOC	SFF	SBC
8 Dairy associations 13 Co-operative societies	19 Meat marketing cooperative societies	19 Purchasing and marketing societies	14 Egg marketing societies	11 Forest owners societies	20 Artificial insemination societies and milk recording societies 6 cattle breeding societies Swedish Pig Breeding Association	12 Central agricultural credit societies	10 Mortgage societies	22 Distilleries	22 Local societies 1 special society	8 Starch societies	16 Seed and oilseed growers' societies		8 Local societies

26 COUNTY AND DISTRICT FEDERATIONS FOR REGIONAL CO-OPERATION

		Local societies	Local societies			477 Society banks 760 offices							
150 dairies													
120,000 members SMR	180,000 members SS	124,000 members SLR	20,000 members SÄ	131,000 members SSR	104,000 members SHS	204,000 members SJF	45,000 members SAH	1,500 members SBI	1,300 members SPR	3,000 members SSF	7,900 members SOC	1,500 members SFF	14,000 members SBC

Source: *Facts on Farmers' Organizations in Sweden*, published by Federation of Swedish Farmers, Stockholm.

slaughter cooperatives encountered economic difficulties in the 1920s, KF stepped in, reorganized them, and handed them back to the farmers. In 1928, KF bought a superphosphate plant and operated it together with the Farmers Central Supply Cooperative. During World War II, KF built a nitrogen fertilizer plant which was operated jointly with the Federation of Farmers Cooperatives.

KF reported that from 1960 to 1971 the number of affiliated societies declined from 592 to 216. During this period, however, their memberships increased from 1.2 million to 1.7 million, and KF's sales increased from 2.3 billion to 6.7 million crowns. Aggregate retail sales to members also rose from 3.4 billion to 8.7 billion crowns during the same period. As of 1971, 55 percent of all Swedish households were members of KF affiliates.

Like LRF, KF has an active educational and research program. The two organizations have their own training seminars, study circles, and schools. In addition, they publish several cooperative magazines and books through their publication departments. They also maintain an auditing service which provides consulting, advisory, and many other services. KF's international activities include membership in the International Cooperative Petroleum Association, the International Cooperative Alliance, and joint business ventures with cooperatives of other nations. LRF is also a member of the International Cooperative Alliance (ICA) and of the International Federation of Agricultural Producers (IFAP). KF, the National Cooperative Petroleum Association (OK), and LRF together administer the Swedish Cooperative Centers (SCC) for cooperative assistance to the developing countries.

Norway Cooperatives in Norway have demonstrated the ability to develop in response to member needs. This propensity explains why agricultural, consumers', fishery, and housing cooperatives are of almost equal significance in the nation's economy.

The first consumer society in Norway was established in 1851, and the first cooperative dairy plant in 1856. Fishery cooperatives, however, did not start until 1915, and housing cooperatives were first organized in 1929.

Norway has no separate cooperative law, and, in contrast to Denmark, most cooperatives are incorporated and operate on the principle of limited liability. These and other operating provisions are covered by general business legislation, leaving cooperatives free to establish their own operating rules and regulations. Exceptions are the Agricultural Marketing Act (1930), the main objective of which was "to promote through cooperation the marketing of agriculture and gardening products" and the Fresh Fish Act, which provides the basis for the operation of the country's fishery cooperatives.

Norway's agricultural cooperatives have developed along the same general lines as those in Sweden. A large proportion of the country's farmers are members of local associations which, in turn, are affiliated in a limited number of district or regional cooperatives. The regional cooperatives are associated with national associations in the fields of dairy, meat, eggs, fruits and vegetables, potatoes, furs, distillery operations, forest ownership, farm supply, rural credit, and banking services.

Consumer cooperatives have pioneered in the development of self-service facilities, in addition to handling a wide range of food items and limited amounts of clothing and furniture. Considerable emphasis is placed on providing cultural opportunities for employees and members.

Conditions of poverty among Norwegian fishing families, coupled with insecurity as to market outlets, led the Norwegian government to encourage the organization of fishery cooperatives. Favorable legislation has been enacted over the past thirty years, and now some 800 fishery associations, representing 30,000 members and accounting for about 95 percent of the catch, own boats and process, package, and store processed fish. Fishery supply associations have also been established to provide boats, equipment, and insurance.

The most recent cooperative development in Norway is in the housing field. Currently, between 15 and 20 percent of all housing starts in Norway are evidently made by cooperatives.

Norway's cooperatives account for a large market share. In 1973, the following proportions of total agricultural production were marketed through cooperatives: milk, 100 percent; wool, 80 percent; livestock, 71 percent; eggs, 57 percent; fruits and vegetables, 40 to 45 percent; furs, 98 percent; forest products, 65 to 70 percent; and farm supplies, 65 percent. At the same time, consumer cooperatives accounted for about 30 percent of the nation's retail business, and cooperative credit institutions handled 10 percent of all credit needs.

In contrast to other Scandinavian countries, Norway has experienced fewer cooperative consolidations. This fact is due in part to the deliberate policy of the Norwegian government in encouraging rural settlement and development, especially in the north. Another contributing factor is the country's geographic character, which limits, to some degree, consolidation of cooperatives if they are effectively to serve members residing in the fjords and other widely scattered communities. The national coordinating associations service all agricultural, forestry, and consumer societies.

Finland Finnish cooperative development is somewhat unique for two reasons: (1) The country is still relatively rural, with 20 percent of the people in 1970 working in agriculture, forestry, and hunting; and (2) sharp cleavage in ideology has resulted in highly competitive situations among the principal national associations.

Finnish cooperatives usually operate on a multipurpose basis, and they place considerable emphasis on financial services. The ideological differences that have developed in Finland do not seem to have diminished the extent of cooperative activity. As of 1970, approximately 27 percent of national retail sales and over 75 percent of the farmers' income, including 96 percent of the dairy products and 86 percent of the livestock received at slaughterhouses, were handled through cooperatives. In addition, cooperatives provided over 50 percent of the supplies used by farmers.

Although it was not until Finland gained its independence, in 1918, that cooperative development made significant progress, early cooperative efforts can be traced to the leadership of Prof. Hannes Gebhard, who in 1899 helped organize the Pellervo Society. The Society is unique in that it was founded from the top down. In fact, its board of directors was made up of university professors. The organization drew on the experience of consumer cooperatives in Germany and Great Britain, and it encouraged the establishment of a number of local societies. Although Pellervo started as an educational and advisory organization called the Advisory Cooperative Union, later known as YOL,[8] it soon entered the wholesale business. It did this through the organization of the Finnish Cooperative Wholesale Society (SOK) in 1904. The SOK effectively provides such services as banking, wholesale procurement of consumer goods and production supplies, and marketing services for dairy products, livestock, and eggs.

Approximately 7 percent of Finland's population are Swedish-speaking people. In 1919, they set up a separate wholesale cooperative (FSA) to serve their dairy, egg, and fish producers, and to provide them with necessary production supplies. The consumer affiliates of FSA are members of SOK. Emphasis is on providing supplies for producers of milk, eggs, and fish.

Following World War I, sharp ideological differences developed within Pellervo. The emphasis on the one-association, one-vote principle led many of the larger associations serving working-class members to believe that this provision did not give them adequate representation. As a result, they formed a separate organization (OTK) which, in contrast to the so-called neutral emphasis of Pellervo, was known as the E Movement or the progressive cooperative group. OTK is largely consumer-oriented, in contrast to SOK, which has an agricultural orientation. The educational and auditing services of OTK are provided by the Cooperative Union (KK). The OTK cooperatives closely follow a socialistic orientation, and they put greater emphasis on matters of political philosophy than does Pellervo. In practice, however, its member cooperatives and their wholesale organization provide substantially the same services as does Pellervo.

As cooperative organizations have developed in Finland, they have covered a wide range of agricultural and consumer services, including housing, water supply, telephone, electricity, and artificial breeding of livestock. These national organizations are active in providing many different services for member affiliates. They include architectural, manufacturing, advertising, publishing, legal services, and related educational programs.

Not unlike cooperatives in Denmark and Sweden, Finnish cooperatives have been going through a period of consolidation and integration. As a result, the number of associations has decreased while volume of business has shown substantial growth.

Iceland. The oldest cooperative society in Iceland, a combination of farmers' and consumer associations, was established in 1892. Cooperative development has primarily emphasized multipurpose associations, and by 1919 some twenty-four were operating. The growing need for supporting services led to the formation of the Federation of Iceland Cooperative Societies (Samband, or SIS) in 1902. It represents substantially all the fifty or so cooperatives in Iceland. As of 1974, Samband reported a volume of business of 15.4 billion Icelandic kronur and the employment of some 1,600 people.

The Agricultural Products Division of Samband reports that it handles all the meat

---

[8]Although cooperative names are given with their English translations, abbreviations are given by the native language initial letters.

and dairy products, and approximately 70 percent of the wool and lamb skins, sold by Icelandic farmers. Its volume of business in 1974 was 3.5 billion Icelandic kronur, and exports accounted for about 54 percent of that total.

In response to the demand for increased services, Samband marketed from 25 to 50 percent of the various fish and seafood products sold in Iceland in 1974. Turnover totaled 4 billion kronur. That same year, Samband reported operating thirty fish-freezing plants.

In rounding out its cooperative services, Samband operates eight factories engaged in producing such consumer items as textiles, shoes, soaps, detergents, paints, electrical appliances, and roasted and packaged coffee. In addition, it owns seven ships on which it carries its export trade. Its import division is the country's largest importer. It handles groceries and household utensils, and its machinery division focuses on farm machinery, electrical appliances, and automobiles.

Israel

Cooperatives in Israel are unique and complex. They are unique because they reflect the pragmatic and revolutionary way in which their members, with the encouragement of government, have adjusted and modified their cooperatives to meet changing conditions in a rapidly growing young nation. They are complex because they reflect a national policy which is dedicated to the rehabilitation of the country, the resettlement of thousands of immigrants, and the establishment of a system of national defense.

Israel's agriculture is largely cooperative in character. Of its nearly 800 agricultural settlements, about 600 are organized as cooperatives. The two principal types are the moshav (a settlement of small individual farms) and the kibbutz (a collective settlement). There are about 360 of the former, and they account for around 40 percent of Israel's agricultural output. The some 240 kibbutzim (the plural of kibbutz) provide about 33 percent of this output.

Cooperative emergence in Israel dates back to the preindependence times when, in 1909, the first kibbutz was established. The kibbutz is a voluntary collective settlement of individuals. The input allocation method of the kibbutz has been described as "from each according to his abilities," and distribution follows the principle "to each according to his needs." When directed toward agricultural efforts, the kibbutz represents a type of cooperative farming. Since kibbutzim have achieved a substantial success, we are justified in taking a brief look at their organization and operation. The kibbutz, in its earlier periods, was quite largely self-sufficing. To quote a Jewish writer, Moshokerem, "The Kibbutz assumes complete responsibility for all the needs of its members from razor blades to housing, from window curtains to concert tickets, from full medical care to honeymoons, from education to financial aids to dependents outside the Kibbutz, from plants for the garden to trips abroad." Now, however, the kibbutzim have become closely integrated with the surrounding market economy. Members presently buy many of the personal items they desire directly with their own "disposable money."[9]

---

[9]As a kibbutz shifts toward a money economy, the individual members have some money they can spend as they wish.

The operation of a kibbutz is conducted through an elected committee system. The individual committees concern themselves with such matters as farm management, education, medical needs, recreation and culture, clothing, food, and, in fact, all other basic requirements. As an element of national policy, encouragement was often given to the formation of kibbutzim for the purpose of establishing and maintaining defensive outposts. They were frequently settled by youth groups and members who joined the army and spent all, or a part of, their military service in these settlements. Early efforts were characterized by "frontier existence." But, as members gain experience and as lands are improved, many kibbutzim now represent highly affluent communities.

At the same time, cooperatives known as the moshavim (the plural of moshav) have become well established. They are organized along somewhat more traditional agricultural cooperative lines. Like the kibbutzim, however, they rent land from the government. They operate largely as multipurpose organizations, providing marketing, farm supply, and consumer services. Each member, after complying with general stipulations as to planting, leasing, and employment of labor, is free to operate the leased land in accordance with his or her own interests. Moreover, in contrast to the members of the kibbutz who receive little money and whose work contributes largely to the overall economic improvement of their community, the member of the moshav benefits according to the individual's diligence and effectiveness.

Both forms of cooperatives are members of Tnuva, a wholesale society which sells fresh and processed agricultural products in the principal cities. They also are members of Hamashbir, a supply wholesale operation that provides both consumer goods and necessary farm supplies for each type of cooperative. Tnuva is reported to handle about 70 percent of the agricultural products sold domestically, and a substantial part of this trade is done through consumer cooperatives.

There are also a number of service cooperatives in Israel. They include irrigation, insurance, and credit associations. In addition, all cooperative effort is coordinated by the national labor organization (Histadrut) through its section (Hevrat Ovdim) which runs its various economic enterprises. In some instances it provides credit, is instrumental in training cooperative officials, and is engaged in business ventures in support of local cooperative associations. Through the office of the Registrar of Cooperative Societies, operations are inspected, advice is provided, and unsuccessful cooperatives are liquidated.

Cooperatives are also important in the industrial economy of Israel. Although the kibbutz at first was almost entirely an agricultural venture, many kibbutzim have expanded their operations to include industrial enterprises. This move has turned out to be desirable for several reasons. In some instances, cyclical patterns of agricultural production had been causing unemployment during certain times of the year. Again, in some instances, the growing population of the kibbutzim justified entrance into enterprises that included both light and heavy industry. Indeed, cooperatives such as these have been more successful in Israel than in most other countries. It should be added, finally, that consumer cooperatives in Israel have risen to importance in transportation, housing, banking, credit, and other consumer needs.

Some indication of the scope and nature of cooperative activity in Israel is shown in the following tabulation, which gives the number of memberships and cooperatives according to type, as of January 1, 1972.

Type of cooperative	Cooperatives	Membership
Agriculture (kibbutzim, moshavim, irrigation, marketing, and others)	1,144	100,000
Production and transport	213	12,000
Housing	273	69,000
Consumer	34	200,000
Credit and savings	102	680,000
Provident and pension funds	111	275,000
Other	28	
Total	1,905	1,336,000

An appraisal of cooperative development in Israel would be incomplete without a consideration of the future of kibbutzim. Labor problems are recognized, particularly those concerning many younger members who leave the kibbutz. With a growing and maturing economy, some members believe they can do better by striking out on their own. The proportion of children leaving the kibbutz is small, however, and the total population in the kibbutzim continues to grow, although not at the rate of the other segments of the economy. The kibbutz remains a distinct way of life and an important segment of Israel's cooperative community.

Much of the success achieved by Israeli cooperatives no doubt can be traced to their ability to meet basic needs of a young and growing nation. The cooperative institution has served as an effective vehicle for helping people to adjust to the unique political, social, and economic conditions in Israel.

Another factor contributing to the success of Israeli cooperatives is the active support that they have received from government agencies. Cooperatives are recognized as an important vehicle for achieving national objectives, and accordingly they are encouraged and supported by these agencies.

Finally, in its agricultural economy, Israel is fortunate in being able to draw on a large number of extremely well-trained individuals. Although not always intimately conversant with the operation of cooperatives, they nevertheless recognize the important contributions that cooperatives can make to their own individual well-being and to the nation's economy.

Japan

Cooperative development in Japan started before the turn of the present century. It was largely centered on agriculture, and emphasis was placed on credit, marketing, and purchasing societies. Marketing cooperatives, through the handling of tea and silk cocoons, gave impetus to the development of foreign markets as Japan moved into large-scale commercial production. Cooperatives were further encouraged in 1900 with the passage of cooperative legislation that gave legal sanction to these associations and also to processing cooperatives. As a result, a substantial number of local cooperatives and federations were formed.

As in many other countries, Japanese cooperatives had to cope with the ravages of the Depression of the 1930s and the impact of World War II. Modern cooperative development primarily stems from the postwar enactment of the Agricultural Cooperative Society Law of 1947. This, together with the Land Reform Act of 1945, which provided for the abolition of the traditional Japanese landlord system, set the stage for the establishment of cooperatives on a voluntary and democratic basis.

Cooperative legislation further emphasized the autonomy of farmers, with the aim of preventing domination by nonfarm interests. Emphasis was on the improvement of agricultural production and on avoiding, to the extent possible, supervision by the government. As a result, many local associations were established. They were supported by a number of prefectural and national cooperatives.

Agricultural Cooperatives While some 12,000 specialty cooperatives were formed, covering such activities as sericulture, dairying, livestock and poultry raising, horticulture, and land reclamation, about 6,200 local associations operate as multipurpose cooperatives. They account for about 90 percent of the business volume of all agricultural cooperatives. Both the multipurpose and the specialty cooperatives operate at the local, prefectural, and national levels.

As of 1971, 99 percent of Japan's nearly 5.3 million farmers were members of cooperatives. The net volume of business of these associations amounted in American dollars, to about $9 billion, of which $6.4 billion came from marketing products and $2.5 billion from purchasing supplies. In the same year, about 60 percent of all farm products were marketed through cooperatives, the proportion varying from a high of 94 percent for rice to a low of 20 percent for potatoes.

The proportion of principal agricultural products marketed through cooperatives in 1971 was:

Commodity	*Percentage*
Rice	94
Wheat and barley	34
Dairy	75
Fruits	56
Silk cocoons	55
Eggs and meat	33

Feeds, fertilizer, agricultural chemicals, and machinery are important items in Japan's cooperative farm-supply business. They accounted, respectively, for 48 percent, 80 percent, 85 percent, and 39 percent of the production supply needs of the country's farmers in 1971.

The cooperative system in Japan is highly integrated. All local and prefectural associations are members of such national associations as the National Federation of Agricultural Cooperatives (Zen-Noh), the Central Bank for Agriculture, and the National Insurance Federation of Cooperatives. These business cooperatives, in turn, are members of the Central Union of Agricultural Cooperatives. The Central Union functions chiefly as a service organization and reports that it engages in such activities as:

• Giving guidance in the organization and business management of agricultural cooperatives
• Auditing agricultural cooperatives
• Providing education and information services
• Functioning in a liaison capacity with, and mediating disputes among, agricultural cooperatives
• Representing opinions of the movement on relevant matters before administrative authorities

Japanese agricultural cooperatives have two classes of members, regular and associate. Regular members are farmers who are encouraged to vote at business meetings. Associate members are nonfarm people who, at the discretion of the cooperatives, are permitted to use cooperative services but are not entitled to vote at business meetings. Cooperatives have an active program of service for members. The program includes the employment of over 14,000 farm management advisors at 5,000 local multipurpose associations, youth and women's organizations, and a wide range of "better living" activities. In the field of cooperative education, a central cooperative college is maintained, as are a technical center and a cooperative management research institute.

The high degree of coordination among Japan's cooperatives is indicated by the operations of Zen-Noh. This organization was formed in 1972 as a result of the merger of the National Purchasing Federation (ZENKOREN) and the National Marketing Federation (ZENHANREN). It provides local multipurpose and specialized associations with manufactured or processed production supplies and it sells products handled by local associations in the Japanese market.

Zen-Noh is perhaps the largest cooperative in the world. It reported an annual volume of business of approximately $7 billion in 1971. This volume is equal to the net volume of business of the twenty-three largest regional associations in the United States as reported for 1970.

Zen-Noh, together with the National Federation of Forestry Cooperatives and the National Federation of Fishery Cooperatives, has organized UNICOOP-JAPAN. Through prefectorial federations, UNICOOP-JAPAN represents 6,200 local agricultural cooperatives, 4,500 fishery cooperatives, and 3,600 forestry cooperatives. Primarily, it carries on the foreign trade of Japanese cooperatives, including selling farm products in export markets and obtaining raw materials and finished products for its member affiliates. The volume of business of UNICOOP-JAPAN has increased from $2 million in 1961 to $165 million in 1971. In the latter year, approximately 55 percent of this business was with the United States, and it consisted largely of corn, milo, soybeans, and alfalfa. UNICOOP-JAPAN's business is 80 percent agricultural, with the rest accounted for by the national fishery and forestry associations.

Consumer and Service Cooperatives While relatively less important than agricultural cooperatives, consumer cooperatives are receiving increased attention in Japan. Their programs now cover a wide range of activity, including the purchase and sale of consumer goods, recreational and cultural pursuits, and community services such as fire and disaster relief. These associations are classified into two types—those organized on a geographic basis, and those organized on an occupational basis.

A consumer cooperative law enacted in 1948 emphasized government support through the granting of subsidies and protection against the anticooperative efforts of retail merchants and insurance companies. In 1970, some 1,200 consumer associations were operating in Japan, with a reported membership of approximately 12 million. Included are some 500 cooperatives operating such facilities as barbershops and beauty parlors, laundries, public bars, restaurants and cafeterias, pawnshops, medical systems, and housing. Nearly 1,000 associations are engaged in providing retail services. They handle such items as groceries, clothing, hardware, land, and building materials. The consumer and service cooperatives in Japan are oriented mainly toward serving the laboring class.

Reasons for Success   An appraisal of Japanese cooperatives suggests that their remarkable success can be attributed to the following factors:

• Close ethnic ties, with emphasis on thrift, education, and business competence.
• A comprehensive educational system, with emphasis on employee training, member communication, and business efficiency.
• A highly integrated cooperative system that emphasizes three levels of cooperative development, local, prefectural, and national. Moreover, the marketing and production supply activities are supported by effective credit, insurance, and service activities.
• Extensive government assistance and support from the legislative and financial standpoints.

Brazil

Cooperatives are becoming increasingly important in Brazil. Because that nation is as large as the continental United States, there are noticeable differences in the performance and operation of its various cooperatives. The differences are probably as great as those that exist among cooperatives of all the other Latin American countries combined. Brazil and Argentina account for about 80 percent of all Latin American cooperatives. Cooperative development in Brazil is most pronounced in its southern states—the states that have the most advanced agricultural development.

Cooperatives were first reported in Brazil at the beginning of the twentieth century. By 1903, they were recognized in the government's Decree No. 979. Not unlike the United States, Brazil can trace its early cooperative growth to the influence of immigrants. Father Teodoro Amstadt, a German immigrant, was instrumental in introducing the Raiffeisen type of credit union in the state of Rio Grande de Sul. Since then, membership in such cooperatives has grown to include some 60,000 farmers. Immigrants from Italy also introduced credit unions and wine-marketing cooperatives. Japanese immigrants, some twenty years later, took the first steps in organizing what is now called the Agricultural Cooperative of Cotia-Central Cooperative (CAC-CC), generally known as Cotia.

Mixed feed, fertilizer equipment, and transportation facilities of Cooperative Cotia at São Paulo, Brazil. This highly integrated regional cooperative provides a wide range of marketing, production supply, and consumer services for its members.

A supermarket operated by Cooperative Cotia.

Cotia is an example of what can be accomplished when dedicated members embark on a program of carefully planned cooperative development. It began operations in 1927 as a potato-marketing cooperative. When organized, it was oriented chiefly toward serving Japanese immigrants who had settled in the state of São Paulo. Presently, Japanese descendants make up about half the membership.

Experiencing all the difficulties of newly organized cooperatives as well as boycotts from the established wholesale trade, Cotia, reflecting the tenacity of its members, prevailed. Today, it is recognized as one of the most influential and innovative associations in Brazil, if not in the world. It presently serves over 10,000 producer-members and markets over 100 commodities. The principal ones are eggs, broilers, peanuts and peanut products, cotton and cotton products, soybeans and soybean products, coffee, and tea. It also handles fertilizer and mixed feeds, in addition to such other basic production supplies as seeds, agricultural chemicals, pesticides, veterinary products, packing materials, construction materials, petroleum products, farm implements and hardware, and a variety of consumer goods. Furthermore, the association provides not only extensive technical advice and assistance to members, but also such services as production credit, engineering advice, assistance in construction of buildings, and machinery repair.

Cotia directs special emphasis to member relations. Through local groups of producers, Cotia also obtains the advice and assistance of members as to major production practices and marketing and purchasing services it should perform.

The cooperative has demonstrated flexibility in adjusting to various institutional changes. Because of restrictive legislation, Cotia recently shifted from a centralized to a federated system of operation by converting branches into member associations. Moreover, it shifted its credit services to a separate corporation in response to legislation aimed at prohibiting marketing and supply cooperatives from providing credit.

Cotia also carries on an extensive educational program. In this connection, it employs a number of field specialists who, in effect, serve as county agents for farmer members of regional affiliates. Through publications, seminars, and institutes, it has an extensive program for training employees and informing members. Moreover, it maintains a progressive program with respect to medical services, youth training programs, and retirement provisions for employees.

Cotia stands as a monument to the ingenuity and dedication of its members and as an example of what can be done, even under adverse circumstances, in building a cooperative dedicated to improving the economic and social well-being of its members.

Cotia is unique because many cooperatives in Brazil and other South American countries are characterized by insufficiently trained management and technical personnel, limited planning, inadequate financial resources, and an absence of research and technical assistance. Failure to adopt realistic legislation has also been a restrictive factor.

Agricultural cooperatives are especially important in handling dairy products, cotton, soybeans, wine, wheat, and rice. Consumer cooperatives, the first type historically, are today weakened by "inflation-caused decapitalization." They are therefore locked in a struggle for survival with supermarket chain operations. Cooperatives are also active in other areas, particularly rural electricity, medical clinics, and school supplies.

Other recent developments that have contributed to cooperative growth in Brazil are:

- Establishment of the National Cooperative Council as the policy-making body for cooperatives. It is composed of four representatives of the government agencies responsible for cooperatives and three representatives of the Organization of Brazilian Cooperatives. It has final jurisdiction on legal matters as well as on issues arising from organizational and operational problems.
- The establishment of the Organization of Brazilian Cooperatives (OBC), together with affiliated state organizations, as the representative for cooperatives. All cooperatives are required to register with OBC.
- The establishment of a national cooperative college to train employees on all levels from vocational and technical courses to postgraduate work in economics, business administration, and related subjects.

India

Initial efforts to encourage cooperative development in India began in 1904 with the passage of the Cooperative Credit Societies Act. This act provided only for the organization of local (primary) urban and rural credit societies. The Cooperative Societies Act of 1912 provided, however, for the organization of other types of cooperatives. In 1915, new legislation made provision for the decentralization of cooperatives to the provincial level.

It was not until India won independence in 1948 that substantial cooperative development got underway. This development was largely the result of deliberate national policy that supported all types of cooperative organizations—credit, large-scale processing, marketing enterprises, farm supply organizations, consumer cooperatives, and artisan activities.

As a result of a credit survey conducted in 1954 by the Reserve Bank of India, government support for cooperatives was extended even further. It took the form of state partnership in which individual states provided cooperatives with large amounts of grant and loan capital and participated to a substantial degree in the management of associations. In addition, state business, whenever possible, was conducted through cooperatives. As would be expected, such intensive government programs caused a number of problems. Some associations, for example, were organized without competent leadership.

Nevertheless, cooperatives have experienced considerable growth. Reports of the Department of Cooperation of the Ministry of Agriculture indicate that from 1950–1951 to 1968–1969 the number of cooperatives increased from 180,000 to 330,000. During the same period, membership rose from 13.7 million to 57 million; share capital, from 450 million to 6,630 million (rupees); and working capital, from 2,700 million Rs. to 40,890 million Rs.

Agricultural credit has continued to play a key role in cooperative development in India. From 1950–1951 to 1968–1969, local credit societies increased in number from

A training meeting for field representatives of Indian Farmers Fertilizer Cooperative, Ltd.
Cooperation among cooperatives on an international level together with assistance from government and cooperative service agencies helped in the organization of this large-scale regional association.
Courtesy of Cooperative League of the U.S.A.

105,000 to 162,000. These societies cover one or more villages, and in 1970–1971 they represented some 32 million members and accounted for approximately 39 percent of the rural credit granted to Indian farmers. They are supported by a number of district and state cooperative banks. Membership has grown substantially, and since 1950–1951 loan volume has increased 12 to 15 times.

A cooperative credit system also exists for long- and short-term loans for villagers. The Cooperative Department reports that since 1950–1951, the proportion of such credit provided through the cooperative credit system has increased from 3 percent to 43 percent.

Cooperatives have also become important in meeting the marketing and farm supply needs of members. Since 1950–1951, volume of marketing business has increased nearly 15 times, and in 1970–1971 it was reported at 6 billion Rs. Principal commodities marketed are dairy products, food grains, sugarcane, cotton, and oilseeds. In the 1970–1971 period, 3,261 local marketing associations were in operation. They were affiliated with 159 district societies, which in turn were members of 24 state federations.

Cooperatives have also become important in the manufacture and distribution of fertilizer (see pages 36–37 for recent developments). In 1970–1971, eighteen granulated fertilizer manufacturing plants were in operation. In addition, cooperatives are active in the handling of seeds and pesticides; and recently, they established twenty-nine pilot agroservice centers to service and repair tractors and other agricultural implements. Cooperative processing has become especially significant for sugar, rice, cotton ginning, oilseed plants, and tea and coffee. Some 11,000 local cooperative dairy plants are now in operation, many of which are affiliated with 32 large-scale dairy processing plants.

Consumer cooperatives, too, are becoming increasingly important in India. A system of local consumer stores is in existence; many of them are affiliated with state-operated department stores, 107 of which were active in 1971. The Department of Cooperation reports that these stores deal in a wide assortment of consumer goods and services, which include:

> . . . basic necessities such as groceries and provisions, cosmetics, and toilet goods, textiles, household goods, and utensils . . . a number of them are also selling fruits and vegetables, eggs, fish and meat, and are running cafeterias. A few of them sell such articles as furniture, footwear, radios, graphophone records, scooter and motor parts, opticals, etc. The Super Bazar also runs a dental clinic. Some of the stores provide a variety of service to consumers such as dry cleaning, tailoring, repair of radio and electrical equipment and watches, distribution of cooking gas, and etc. Four department stores provide banking facilities. . . .[10]

Recently, the government has established a policy to provide support and encouragement for cooperatives in "weaker sections" of the country, and to expand the number of overall types of services provided. Special encouragement is given to fishing, farming, forestry, labor (industrial), and various transportation groups (including rickshaw pullers and other transport workers); to insurance for laundry workers, printers, and military personnel; and to housing cooperatives. In certain specialized areas, support is also given to cooperative weaving and spinning mills which are important in rural development. In some states, special attention is being directed to developing cooperatives that serve tribal groups.

India has recognized the value of cooperative training and education to support its cooperative programs. Training programs are developed to meet the needs of specific groups. Senior cooperative officials are trained at thirteen cooperative training colleges that are run by the National Cooperative Union of India. These schools are supported in part by government grants, and courses are set up to train government officials and national cooperative leaders. Training for those classified as junior personnel is conducted at the state level. Specialized fourteen-week courses are offered for employees who work in various types of cooperatives. In addition, short courses in accounting and sales management are provided, as are postgraduate courses for cooperative officials at various levels. The Cooperative Department of the Central Government of India reports that, in 1971, some 1,845 senior personnel, 2,350 intermediate personnel, and nearly 100,000 junior officials had completed their training.

The National Institute of Cooperative Management also conducts some research that covers, among other subjects, management and human resources development, as well as evaluation of operating efficiencies for various types of cooperative endeavor.

[10]Government of India, Ministry of Agriculture, Department of Cooperation, *Report 1971–72*, p. 61.

In addition, a far-reaching publicity and information program is underway. It includes publication of cooperative journals, development of basic literature on specialized cooperative subjects, preparation of photographic and film material, and arrangements for numerous visits and study tours.

A report of the All-India Rural Credit Committee in 1954 set in motion the forces that established the predecessor of the National Cooperative Development Corporation (NCDC) in 1956. The report advocated an integrated approach to cooperative development that would supplement credit cooperatives with associations that would provide the marketing, processing, and other services needed by Indian farmers. To this end, NCDC was established "to promote planned development of marketing, processing, and storage of agricultural produce and distribution of essential requirements of farmers . . . and to provide financial assistance for these activities through state governments by way of loans and subsidies." NCDC serves as a coordinating agency in planning cooperative development with public-sector organizations. Considerable emphasis is also being directed to management development and to working with cooperatives in the most disadvantaged rural areas.

An evaluation of cooperative development in India suggests that substantial progress has been made, notwithstanding the wide range of cooperative activities undertaken. To be most effective, far-reaching programs are needed to counteract illiteracy among Indian villagers. Such education, perhaps, is the most effective way to minimize the power of private moneylenders. To strengthen cooperative efforts, the Indian Department of Cooperation emphasizes the need:

- To develop modern and necessary facilities
- To work out effective operating standards
- To increase the financial support of members
- To emphasize personnel training and development
- To achieve greater coordination of effort

As Indian cooperatives demonstrate progress in these directions, they will be in a better position to divest themselves of government control. This point is well made by Dr. O. R. Krishnaswami, who recently stated: "Non-official leadership should be developed through education and training and the movement should be gradually deofficialized by transferring the work of supervision, audit, and other functions to cooperative federal organizations and unions. The management efficiency should be improved by appointing trained personnel for managerial posts."[11]

FACTORS INFLUENCING COOPERATIVE DEVELOPMENT IN OTHER COUNTRIES

A comprehensive evaluation of the many economic, social, and political forces that influence the direction of cooperative development in individual countries would require a more detailed analysis than we can offer here. The section "Factors Influencing

---

[11]O. R. Krishnaswami, *The Cooperator,* National Cooperative Union of India, New Delhi, August, 1972, p. 32.

Types of Cooperatives Established'' in Chapter 2 (pages 42–44) may give some clues on why cooperatives developed the way they did where they did. It is obvious, too, that government policy has had considerable influence in shaping the direction of cooperative development in various countries.

Another important consideration is the situation that may or may not prevail with respect to available leadership. The emergence of a national cooperative leader at the right time, in the right place, and under the right combination of circumstances may have far-reaching implications for cooperative development in any given country. We have only to recall Raiffeisen in Germany, Robert Owen and Horace Plunkett in England, N. F. S. Grundtvig in Denmark, Reverend M. M. Coady in Canada, Murry Lincoln in Ohio, G. Harold Powell in California, and Howard Cowden in Missouri to appreciate the influence of individuals in shaping cooperative development. We can merely speculate as to where cooperatives in many countries would have been had not such leaders appeared on the scene at the time they did. Likewise, the availability or absence of local leaders is important in determining the direction that cooperative development may take.

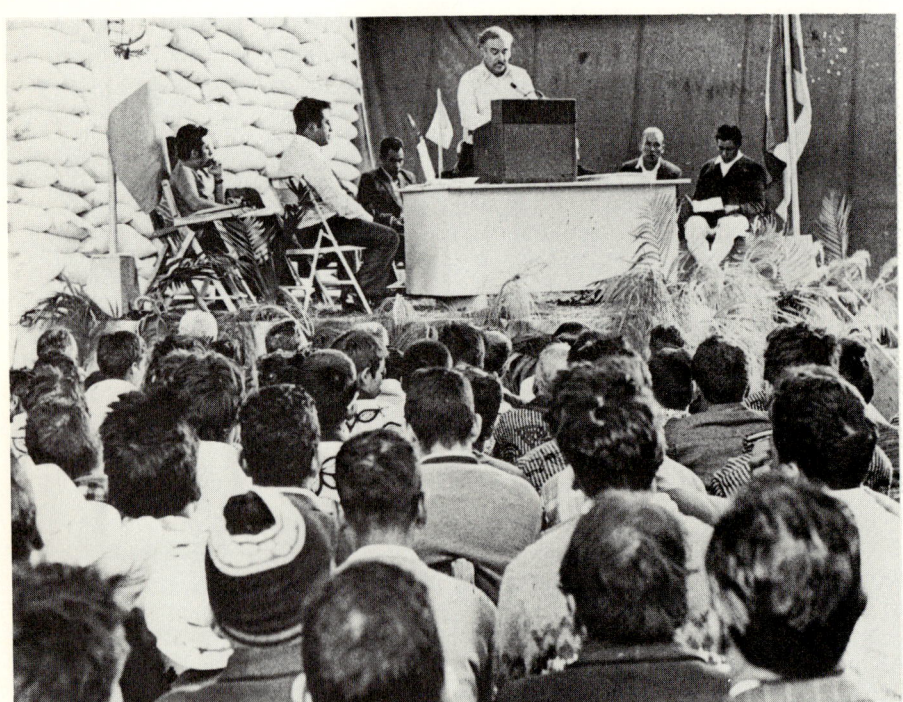

Directors of a cooperative in Guatemala, C.A., in session. Cooperatives are a worldwide development that seeks to further the economic interest of members. *Courtesy Agricultural Cooperative Development International.*

QUESTIONS

1. What were some of the first developments of cooperation in antiquity? Give examples of early cooperation in business enterprise.
2. Discuss the principal characteristics of, and trends in, the cooperative development of:

    Great Britain
    Switzerland
    Scandinavia—Denmark, Sweden, Norway, Finland, Iceland
    Israel
    Japan
    Brazil
    India

3. Why has agricultural cooperation lagged in England?
4. Contrast the principal features of Israel's kibbutzim and moshavim.
5. Compare the operations of the following cooperative wholesale societies: CWS, OTK, Zen-Noh, and Cotia.
6. What factors were important in determining the direction of cooperative development in other countries?

REFERENCES

Anschel, Kurt R., Russell H. Brannon, and Eldon D. Smith (eds.): *Agricultural Cooperatives and Markets in Developing Countries,* Praeger, Washington, D.C., 1969, p. 373.

―――. *American Cooperation,* American Institute of Cooperation, Washington, D.C. Annual issues generally contain a section on international cooperation.

―――. *Yearbook of Agricultural Cooperation,* Blackwell, Oxford, England. Annual issues contain information of cooperative development and operations of cooperatives in many countries.

The following publications contain many articles relating to cooperatives in other lands.

1. *Canadian Journal of Public and Cooperative Economy,* CIREC, 1455 Blvd. de Masson Luve, Montreal, Canada 107.
2. *Journal of Rural Cooperation,* Jerusalem Academic Press, CIRCOM, 24 Ha' Arba'a St., P.O. Box 7020, Tel Aviv, Israel.
3. The "Occasional Paper" series of The Plunkett Foundation for Cooperative Studies 31, St. Giles, Oxford, England OX13LF. The series contains individual publications on the cooperatives of most countries having significant cooperative development.

The United States embassies of foreign countries usually can provide information on the local cooperatives.

National cooperative organizations and international cooperative associations frequently have English publications that describe cooperative development and operations in the various countries they serve.

Chapter 8

Organizations That Serve Cooperatives

Alert cooperative leaders gradually came to realize that many of the problems they faced extended beyond the spheres of activity of their associations. Just as individual members found advantages in group action, so cooperative officials concluded that they should work together to advance or protect their common interests. They learned that not only cooperative members, but also such widely divergent groups as legislators, educators, religious leaders, and business executives, had little or no knowledge about cooperative aims and objectives.

Today's cooperative leaders generally believe that the responsibility to protect cooperative interests and to inform the general public—beyond general information provided by state and local agencies—largely rests with cooperatives themselves. To this end, they have organized various educational, research, technical assistance, public relations, and trade-lobbying organizations. Some of these organizations are regional or national in scope, whereas others are international. Some engage in many activities, and others restrict their operations to specific functions. Some serve agricultural cooperatives; others are oriented toward consumer or service cooperatives. These organizations can be classified as:

- National cooperative organizations which deal with broad aspects of endeavor that apply to all or most types of associations

ORGANIZATIONS THAT SERVE COOPERATIVES

- Cooperative commodity or trade organizations whose basic objectives are directed toward furthering the interests of specific types of commodity or service cooperatives on a national level
- State cooperative councils that conduct a wide range of educational and service programs for members
- General farm organizations that actively support and encourage cooperatives
- International trade and service organizations that share cooperative information intercountry

A brief description of the operations of the main organizations in each group follows.

NATIONAL COOPERATIVE ORGANIZATIONS[1]

Starting in 1916, three new and dynamic national cooperative associations appeared on the American scene. They established headquarters in the nation's capital and devoted their efforts to improving the economic situation of their members.

American Institute of Cooperation (AIC)

The American Institute of Cooperation was incorporated on January 22, 1925, under the laws of the District of Columbia. It is a national educational organization supported by agricultural cooperatives and endorsed by cooperative leaders, educators, and research workers.

AIC concentrates on educational activities in the economic and public-interest aspects of cooperatives, and it makes special efforts to stimulate sound and constructive thought on cooperative principles, practices, and operations. AIC functions as a nonpolitical, informational, and fact-providing organization.

AIC held its first session in Philadelphia on July 20, 1925, in cooperation with the University of Pennsylvania. This four-week session concentrated on courses in cooperative philosophy and operation. These courses, with outstanding educators and agricultural leaders as instructors, were a unique educational venture. People who completed the courses were given credits acceptable toward a college or university degree.

Succeeding summer sessions have been held annually on land-grant university campuses throughout the country, with the one exception being the 1973 session held on the campuses of Tulane and Loyola Universities in New Orleans. AIC sessions were gradually shortened after the first few years, and since 1950 they have each been three days long.

These shorter sessions, called "National Institutes on Cooperative Education" (and now drawing about 2,500 people), include a university conference, a state cooperative council secretaries' meeting, and a seminar for graduate students and new

---

[1]This section is an adaptation of material that appears in FCS Bulletin I, Reprint 1, to be issued by Farmer Cooperative Service. The material was prepared by the author when he was associated with Farmer Cooperative Service, U.S. Department of Agriculture.

Training session for youth and young farmers at the annual conference of the American Institute of Cooperation. This national cooperative organization, in addition to giving attention to current problems of interest to cooperatives, places special emphasis on educational programs for youth and young farmers.

employees. The National Institutes also have special educational events for young farm couples who are sponsored by cooperatives; youth scholars, many of them members of Future Farmers of America and 4-H clubs and also sponsored by cooperatives; and farm women.

General and smaller sectional special sessions provide an opportunity to hear about problems of interest and to discuss them with scores of national cooperative leaders, educators, and business and professional authorities. Through these efforts, AIC seeks to improve awareness and to develop greater understanding of cooperatives among members, cooperative employees, and the general public.

Presentations at the annual sessions are published in AIC yearbooks entitled *American Cooperation*. Beginning with the 1972–1973 edition, each yearbook has carried additional articles and material to give a broader and more comprehensive picture of cooperatives. The monthly *AIC Newsletter* provides members and leaders with educational information and news about developments that affect them. AIC also issues publications, slides, and movies for educators and cooperatives.

AIC promotes educational programs by cooperatives and others, stimulates research through an awards program and other means, and distributes materials and information especially designed for the use of local and regional cooperatives, associations of cooperatives, educational institutions, farm organizations, and other public and private agencies. It also provides services to help member cooperatives develop special educational programs for youths, young farm couples, and women's groups.

AIC maintains a continuing representation in national organizations, thereby contributing to a better understanding of the place of cooperatives in today's social, political, and economic environment. Moreover, it serves as a coordinator and central clearinghouse to stimulate maximum use of those educational programs, materials, ideas, and concepts that are available through cooperatives and educational institutions everywhere in the country.

Sponsorship of regional member educational conferences with Farmer Cooperative Service began in 1958. Other conferences sponsored by AIC include those centered on the responsibilities of cooperative directors, chief executive officers, and board chairpersons; on cooperative relations; on personnel; on training directors of regional cooperatives; on planning and research; and on legal problems.

National Council of Farmer Cooperatives

Although the National Council of Farmer Cooperatives was not organized until 1929, the idea of some type of cooperative council had long been attractive to cooperative leaders. As early as 1903, representatives of farmer cooperatives formed a state association to promote the interests of farmers' elevators at Springfield, Illinois. This action was followed by the formation of similar associations in other grain-producing states. Six of these state associations, meeting at Minneapolis in June 1912, organized the National Council of Farmer Cooperative Associations.

One of the early presidents of the Council described its activities as follows:

> All matters of interstate or national importance are handled by the National Council. Its officers have made several trips to Washington, D.C., to urge, and assist as far as possible, in securing the enactment of legislation, and preventing the enactment of unfavorable legislation; to appear before the Interstate Commerce Commission on behalf of the elevator companies, when necessary; and on several occasions we have carried our troubles to the Secretary of Agriculture. We opposed, to the very extent of our power, the efforts of the railroads to advance rates on grain. Our efforts were successful and this alone has saved the farmers millions of dollars.

This early National Council was primarily interested in the efficiency of farmers' elevators because associations of grain elevators were one of the important segments of cooperative development at that time. At the annual convention of the National Council at Chicago in March 1920, the name of the association was changed to the Farmers National Grain Dealers Association. It was replaced by an entirely new organization, the National Federation of Grain Cooperatives, in February 1939 (see page 168 for details).

In response to interest in establishing a council that would represent the principal types of cooperatives, a three-day conference was held in Washington in December 1922. It drew delegates and visitors from thirty states and also from Canada and Denmark.

Active at the conference were representatives of cooperatives marketing such products as cotton, fruits and vegetables, tobacco, dairy products, grain, rice, livestock, and nuts. Delegates from the American Farm Bureau Federation and the Farmers Educational and Cooperative Union of America were also present.

By unanimous vote on the last day of this national gathering of cooperating farmers, the National Council of Farmer Cooperative Marketing Associations was

CHAPTER EIGHT

Vice President Gerald R. Ford addressing the 1974 annual meeting of the National Council of Farm Cooperatives. National issues are discussed at the annual meeting of this organization and other organizations serving cooperatives. *Courtesy Farmer Cooperative Service.*

created. The conference delegates elected an executive committee of fifteen and charged it to set up the new organization. It selected a secretary and opened an office in Washington.

The executive committee worked out and signed an organizational agreement. The Council's purposes were: (1) to strengthen contacts between farmer cooperatives, (2) to supply crop information, (3) to develop national publicity, (4) to establish contact with federal agencies for members, (5) to assist in legislative problems, and (6) to supply reliable commodity and market information to farm groups.

This organization held annual conferences in Washington in 1924, 1925, and 1926. Strong differences of opinion marked the 1926 conference. Progress had been made during that year, even though some member cooperatives had not fared well. They had expected cooperative commodity marketing to bring them prosperity despite the prevailing unfavorable economic conditions. But, as experience proved, cooperation was unable to accomplish the impossible, and financial support for the Council's program dwindled.

At a meeting of the executive committee, held in Chicago, suspension of the National Council of Farmer Cooperative Marketing Associations as of July 20, 1926, was reported.

At the 1929 midsummer meeting of the American Institute of Cooperation, held at the University of Louisiana, Baton Rouge, cooperative leaders created a new organization known as the National Chamber of Agricultural Cooperatives.

In December 1929, at a meeting of the organizing board of directors in Chicago, the name was changed to National Cooperative Council. This name was retained until the annual meeting in 1940, when it was changed to National Council of Farmer Cooperatives.

The organization in 1929 decided to establish a Washington office. In its first year, the Council listed as members eighteen well-known cooperatives.

Objectives of the National Council of Farmer Cooperatives were stated as follows:

- To promote actively and persistently the interests of farmer cooperatives
- To impress on government and other agencies the importance, value, and potentialities of cooperatives in agriculture
- To provide an avenue through which cooperatives may be quickly advised of current developments significant to them
- To serve as a forum or conference body through which better understanding and bonds of friendship may develop among cooperatives

Since the National Council was organized in 1929, the number of direct members has increased from 18 to 147 in 1975. Most of these member organizations are federated associations that serve as central agencies for smaller local cooperatives. Thus, through its affiliates, the National Council represents some 5,800 farmer cooperatives, or about 75 percent of the United States total.

The main goal of the National Council of Farmer Cooperatives is to represent farmer cooperatives before the Congress and Executive and administrative agencies of the government that are involved in matters affecting cooperative businesses and agriculture. A related goal is the maintenance and improvement of relationships of farmer cooperatives with business, labor, and the general public. The Council also seeks to join with other agricultural, business, and commodity groups in developing favorable agricultural policies.

Officials frequently participate as members of United States delegations during international negotiations and conferences relating to economic and trade matters. Council representatives also serve as members of numerous advisory commissions and boards established by government or private agencies to develop policy recommendations. The Council is also an active member of the International Federation of Agricultural Producers.

The extensive programs of the Council promote and protect diversified interests of farmer cooperatives in the areas of bargaining; marketing and foreign trade; research and education; legal issues; rural development; tax and accounting; transportation; application of antitrust laws to cooperatives; farm supplies and services; energy; finance and credit; management and personnel; price controls; public relations; and public affairs.

State councils of farmer cooperatives are members of the National Council, and they contribute to the solidarity cooperatives seek in legislative and public affairs.

Annual membership meetings of the Council are held each January and are attended by farm and cooperative leaders from all parts of the nation. At these meetings, members formulate Council policy on a wide range of developments and matters that are significant to farmer cooperatives and their members. The areas covered include reviews of the economic situation, modification of existing policies, and formulation of policies. The Council's position on top-priority subjects and the framework within which the Council will operate are established through resolutions approved at its annual meetings. Between annual meetings, the Council's activities are conducted largely by the staff of the Washington headquarters.

The National Council issues to members and the general public a mimeographed monthly letter entitled *Washington Situation*, which constitutes a general information service. From time to time, the Council issues special publications and news releases on matters of current importance.

The Cooperative League of the U.S.A. (CLUSA)

The Cooperative League of the U.S.A. is a national federation of all types of cooperatives—including farmers' purchasing associations, credit unions, consumer societies, and organizations providing electricity, telephone, health, housing, and insurance services. CLUSA, established in 1916, is the oldest of the national cooperative organizations. It moved its headquarters from Chicago to Washington in 1972.

The League has six major functions: (1) to advance public knowledge of cooperatives, (2) to improve the skills of cooperative directors and employees, (3) to encourage wise cooperative financing and operative policies, (4) to help cooperatives strengthen their member relations, (5) to seek federal laws and administrative decisions consistent with cooperative aims and purposes, and (6) to promote development in the world's less-developed areas, both at home and abroad, through cooperatives.

To help its members develop and maintain professional competency, the League has taken a leading part in founding such organizations as:

- Cooperative Management Development (CMD)
- Cooperative Editorial Association (CEA)
- Association for Cooperative Educators (ACE)
- Consumers Cooperative Management Association (CCMA)
- Insurance–Finance Conference

The Cooperative League also has had an active program for providing assistance to cooperatives in developing countries since the early 1950s. Partially funded by the U.S. Agency for International Development, this program assists cooperatives chiefly in Asia and Latin America. CLUSA also is the United States member of the International Cooperative Alliance and is represented on its executive committee.

In India, where League assistance began in 1954, United States cooperatives have helped Indian cooperatives to establish a $125-million fertilizer-production complex in Gujarat state. Also in India, the League has assisted fifteen oilseed cooperatives to begin operations, and the CLUSA representative continues to advise the Indian National Cooperative Development Corporation. With Ford Foundation financing, CLUSA is supplying seven consultants to assist in detailed planning of various aspects of Operation Flood, a quarter-billion-dollar dairy project which will help to supply milk to India's four largest cities.

Other examples of CLUSA's support of cooperative programs in developing countries are:

- Assistance in establishing the Organization of Cooperatives of America and the Inter-American Cooperative Finance Development Society (SIDEFCOOP) and in maintaining membership on the executive committees of their boards.

- Assistance in analyzing the technical assistance and training needs of Guneydogu Cooperative Union, Gaziantep, Turkey, a marketing federation composed of seventy-seven small farmer cooperatives.
- Under an agreement with the World Bank, provision of a CLUSA specialist to perform an analysis of the labor power training needs of agricultural cooperatives and the Cooperative Bank of Iran.
- Assistance in organizing FENACOOPARR, a regional rice-marketing federation in Ecuador, which provides farm supplies and accounting and auditing services to thirty member cooperatives.
- Assistance in establishing the National Agricultural Cooperative Federation of Panama (COAGRO), which provides farm supplies and management assistance to sixteen member rural cooperatives.
- Assistance in the establishment of eight cooperative insurance companies and four cooperative banks in Latin America; help to other cooperative banks in strengthening their lending operations; completion of a CLUSA study on rural cooperatives in Latin America under a contract with the Inter-American Development Bank.

CLUSA has trained Peace Corps volunteers who have organized cooperatives in Colombia, Panama, and Peru. It has prepared photographic exhibits and radio tapes for the U.S. Information Agency for use overseas, and its movies and publications have been translated into many languages.

The League produces the weekly Cooperative News Service for 140 cooperative publications across the country, and *What's New*, a bimonthly publication tracing developments in the cooperative information-education field, sent free to those who request it. Other publications issued regularly include *CLUSAgram*, a biweekly newsletter distributed to members; *Washington/A Cooperative Slant*, also a biweekly, featuring comment on legislative and federal agency developments concerning co-ops; *The Calendar*, a monthly listing of national and regional events of interest to cooperatives; *Legislative Summary from the Hill*, a monthly report on the status of congressional legislation affecting cooperatives; and *KONSUM*, a bimonthly newsletter dealing with consumer cooperation. The League publishes a magazine, *Co-Op Report*, ten times a year to help cooperative leaders improve their skills.

The League also distributes *This Is a Cooperative*, a thirty-minute sound-and-color film showing several important ways people are using the cooperative form to meet basic needs.

Located in the League's Washington headquarters are a historical film library, the Jerry Voorhis Memorial Library, and the recently established Cooperative Hall of Fame.

COOPERATIVE TRADE ORGANIZATIONS

In addition to the national organizations that represent all types of cooperatives, many cooperatives handling one particular product or providing one special service have joined together into trade organizations. Some of these organizations serve farm cooperatives and others serve consumer organizations. Let us discuss them briefly.

Credit Union National Association, Inc. (CUNA)

The Credit Union National Association, Inc., with headquarters in Madison, Wisconsin, was organized in 1934. It grew out of the philanthropic support of Edward A. Filene and the promotional genius of Roy F. Bergengren. A forerunner organization was the Credit Union National Extension Bureau that was established in 1921 with the objectives of (1) promoting favorable credit union legislation, (2) carrying on active experimentation in the organization of credit unions, (3) establishing state credit union associations ("leagues"), and (4) achieving national status through the membership of the state credit union leagues.

CUNA, Inc., adopted the slogan, "Promote, perfect, and protect." To this end, it formulated the following objectives:

- To spread the understanding of credit union principles throughout the world, to create an atmosphere of acceptance of these principles, and to foster the organization of credit unions through which these principles can be put to work
- To promote the organization of credit union leagues, associations, and other agencies whose function it is to serve individual credit unions and the credit union movement as a whole
- To encourage thrift, wise use of credit, and prudent management of personal and family financial resources
- To encourage participation in the democratic processes of credit union control at all levels and in the exercise of officer responsibility
- To offer information and guidance to credit union board members, officers, and committee members, so that the credit unions they represent will offer a maximum of thrift and credit service consistent with the ideals of the credit union movement
- To establish and maintain good working relationships with chartering and supervising agencies of credit unions, with the intention that these agencies will reduce liquidations to a minimum, and to assure the freedom of action of credit unions
- To foster legislation helpful to the achievement of credit union goals, and to combat legislation hostile to them

As membership expanded, CUNA, Inc., established divisions to facilitate its wide-ranging programs. Currently, they are Communications, Education and Development, Financial Support, Governmental Affairs, Public Relations and Advertising, Corporate Affiliates, and Research. In addition, many supporting administrative staff functions were set up.

CUNA also has several affiliated and related organizations. CUNA Supply Corporation is the central production unit and mail-order house of the credit union movement. Approved forms for credit union operations and a wide range of supplementary and promotional materials are offered at advantageous prices. CUNADATA Corporation provides credit unions with electronic data processing for efficient handling of information and accounting records. ICU Services Corporation provides special financial programs and services. They include government securities investment programs, credit union interlending programs, traveler's checks, and money orders.

In May 1973, ICU Services Corporation, CUNA Supply Corporation, and CUNA-DATA became part of a single unit, CUNA Service Group, Inc., a holding company designed to generate capital and to determine and coordinate overall policy for these national service organizations.

In addition, CUNA Mutual Insurance Society provides loan protection and life savings insurance for credit unions and their members. As a mutual company, it returns all income, after operating expenses and reserves, to its policyowners in the form of dividends. CUMIS Insurance Society, Inc., a stock insurance company, is the property, casualty, and fidelity insurance arm of the credit union movement. Ownership is vested in credit union members, credit unions, chapters, leagues, and CUNA Mutual. In addition to providing the non-life insurance needs of credit unions and their organizations, CUMIS offers homeowner and tenant insurance plans and automobile insurance to credit union members.

CUNA is the United States confederation member of the World Council of Credit Unions. Since the Agency for International Development (AID or USAID) assists credit unions, CUNA serves with AID as the contracting agency for technical assistance to credit unions in Latin America, Asia, and Africa.

Foundation for Cooperative Housing (FCH)

The Foundation for Cooperative Housing, with headquarters in Washington, is a nonprofit organization that provides research and educational assistance to low- and middle-income housing cooperatives. It was organized in response to provisions of the Housing Act of 1950, which directed the Federal Housing Administration (FHA) to provide blanket mortgage coverage on cooperative housing projects.

The Foundation created FCH Services in 1952 to help meet the needs of members for:

- Guidance in architecture, engineering, and site-planning
- Assistance in locating sources of finance and conducting member education and training
- Aid in managing cooperative housing projects

The Foundation also created Technicoop (TCI) in the late 1960s to explore new technical, financial, and organizational structures for cooperative housing. Another subsidiary, National Service for Housing Cooperatives (NSHC), was organized to provide insurance protection and other services for members.

Progress and growth of the Foundation's program has been substantial. After twenty years of operation, the Foundation reports that it had provided assistance for the building of 51,000 homes in more than 500 cooperatives. The mortgage loans on these homes amounted to $722 million.

National Association of Housing Cooperatives

The National Association of Housing Cooperatives, organized in 1960, is a federation of local, state, and regional housing associations. It serves largely as a clearinghouse for information on housing. Emphasis is placed on the development of new housing associations and the strengthening of existing ones. To this end, its basic objectives are the provision of technical services, assistance on management problems, and educational guidance to members.

National Federation of Grain Cooperatives

On February 21, 1939, the regional grain cooperatives organized the National Federation of Grain Cooperatives, with executive offices in Washington. The Federation provided the medium through which members:

- Were advised on federal and state legislation affecting them or their producer members
- Exchanged information among their organizations
- Obtained aid in their dealings and relations with state and federal governments and their departments
- Could develop ideas and initiate action to improve cooperative marketing and embark on joint enterprises
- Were informed on other matters of interest to them and their producer-members

The original membership consisted of seven large regional grain-marketing associations. In 1972, the Federation's membership included nineteen regionals, with three of these being joint terminal-elevator organizations operated by two or more regional cooperatives. Several of these regionals also handled farm supplies. As of January 1, 1973, the National Federation of Grain Cooperatives became a division of the National Council of Farmer Cooperatives.

National Livestock Producers Association

About 1920, the livestock producers and their organizations requested the American Farm Bureau Federation to study the desirability of establishing a national organization of livestock producers. The Farm Bureau's Committee of Fifteen made the study and reported: "Such an association properly financed and directed should be able to represent wisely and with authority the livestock producers' interest whenever and wherever they are concerned."

As a result, the National Livestock Producers Association was organized in 1921. Headquarters were in Chicago until June 1, 1975, when the Association relocated in Denver. Membership now consists of 15 state or area livestock cooperatives that operate in nearly 200 markets and represent 295,000 livestock producers.

The Association provides members and patrons of its member associations with a wide variety of services, such as credit, research, market information, and legal assistance. It does no marketing, but its articles of incorporation permit it to perform marketing functions if it so desires. It also publishes a monthly livestock magazine, carries on educational work, represents its members in legislative matters, trains personnel, and performs public relations services.

Livestock producers and feeders have developed, and now own, financial institutions that provide them with the credit necessary to carry on operations. They make loans to farmers and feeders from funds obtained by discounting borrowers' notes with the Federal Intermediate Credit Bank of the Farm Credit System.

Six of these dozen or so credit companies are affiliated with the National Feeder and Finance Corporation, a subsidiary of the National Livestock Producers Association. Other livestock credit companies are affiliated with their regional marketing agencies.

National Milk Producers Federation (NMPF)

The National Milk Producers Federation was incorporated in December 1916, with headquarters in Washington. Membership includes virtually all the farmer-owned dairy-marketing cooperatives in the country.

The Federation provides the organizational basis for the development of current policies and long-range objectives of dairy farmers and their cooperatives. It performs this role by working with Congress and executive agencies of government on policies and programs that are in the interest of its members. By serving as a liaison between Congress, government agencies, news media, consumers, and member associations, the Federation seeks to create and maintain a favorable governmental environment (regulatory and legal).

The Federation also provides numerous informational services for its members. It interprets the findings of government as they relate to dairy cooperatives, and it accumulates and disseminates dairy industry information and statistics to members.

The National Milk Producers Federation reports that its major responsibility is to make certain that American dairy cooperatives have a unified, decisive, and qualified representation that is powerful enough to be heard and considered by the legislative and administrative bodies of the nation.

National Rural Electric Cooperative Association (NRECA)

The rural electric systems have organized statewide associations and a national association to represent them on legislative and policy matters and to carry out educational activities. The National Rural Electric Cooperative Association, organized in 1942, is located in Washington. It has nearly 1,000 member-systems. NRECA provides legislative and management services, as well as employee benefit and insurance programs. The Association maintains the George W. Norris Memorial Library. It also offers technical assistance to less-developed countries under a special arrangement with the United States Agency for International Development.

NRECA's managerial program includes a series of institutes, technical workshops, and consultation services carried out at varied locations so that managers and directors of member systems can enroll at the most convenient time and place. NRECA operates through its General Manager's Office and five departments: Government Relations; Energy and Environmental Policy; Public and Association Affairs; Management Services; and Retirement, Safety and Insurance.

NRECA has developed employee group insurance and pension programs, and a fire and casualty insurance pooling plan for the benefit of its member systems. The Association publishes the monthly *RE Magazine,* which reaches 25,000 rural electric leaders, federal and local government officials, and interested organizations. It also prepares a legislative news weekly, the *Rural Electric Newsletter,* and distributes other educational material.

National Telephone Cooperative Association (NTCA)

NTCA is the national organization of the country's independent cooperative rural telephone companies, with headquarters in Washington. It was organized in 1954 to provide legislative liaison with federal agencies and to establish and maintain industry relations with the Bell System, the Federal Communications Commission, and other groups in the telephone industry. The Association also offers members a complete program of insurance coverage and employees retirement compensation and a program of management development and employee training.

NTCA publishes a monthly magazine, *Phone Call;* a biweekly Washington newsletter, *NTCA Report;* and a bimonthly newsletter, *Management Notebook.* It also sponsors regional and national meetings at which system managers and directors discuss how to solve mutual problems and how to operate more effectively.

Agricultural Cooperative Development International (ACDI)

ACDI is a unique organization unlike any of the service organizations discussed previously. It is a nonprofit, educational, consulting, and technical assistance organization located in Washington. Membership consists of thirty regional cooperatives, five cooperative farm credit districts, and joint national cooperative and farm organizations. Its program is geared toward providing assistance to cooperatives and governments in developing countries on problems of organization, planning, operations, management information, and member involvement. Special emphasis is placed on assistance in matters of agricultural credit and banking, facilities, marketing, processing, farm supplies, training, and policy planning.

ACDI is primarily financed through AID, although member associations pay a fee upon joining and contribute annually to a voluntary fund that is used to instigate special projects and to finance activities not covered by AID programming. Preliminary consultations with cooperatives and AID missions in host countries determine the type of assistance that will be provided. This assistance takes the form of feasibility studies, special and long-term technical assistance, consulting liaison arrangements, and observational and on-the-job training. Assistance has been, or is being, provided to some sixty countries in Central and South America, Africa, and Asia.

While ACDI is the only organization in the United States that works exclusively on cooperative programs in developing countries, specialized assistance is also provided by such organizations as CLUSA, CUNA, ILO (International Labor Organization), NRECA, and, on occasion, other trade associations and general farm organizations.

STATE COOPERATIVE COUNCILS

Cooperatives, by setting up overall statewide service organizations, are able to solve common problems and increase cooperative benefits for members. These organizations also provide a medium for official, public, and private agencies that have an interest in the problems of cooperatives.

The first steps toward organizing state councils of cooperatives were taken a little more than a half-century ago. Among the earliest councils were those in California, Oregon, and Wisconsin. The Agricultural Legislative Committee of California was formed in 1919, and in 1933 it became the Agricultural Council of California. The Agricultural Cooperative Council of Oregon was organized in 1921, and the one in Wisconsin in 1926. By 1972, cooperatives in forty states had some type of overall statewide organization. Most of these organizations carry the term "council," "association," "federation," "committee," or "institute" in their titles.

Early state cooperative councils were concerned largely with legislative problems. But as cooperatives increased in number and importance, leaders saw the need for developing better working relationships among themselves, other national cooperatives, educational institutions, general farm organizations, consumer groups, and legislative and political bodies. The state councils have therefore enlarged their memberships, obtained larger budgets, and expanded their programs. The main objectives of state councils and associations of cooperatives are:

• To promote and foster the welfare of cooperatives by bringing directors, key employees, and agricultural and urban community leaders together for study, discussion, and solution of mutual problems.
• To assist and encourage the organization of cooperatives of every type.
• To gather and disseminate information pertaining to the development of cooperatives, their functions, their obligations, and their contribution to the welfare of the American people.
• To sponsor and support constructive legislation that will be helpful to cooperatives, and to oppose potentially unfavorable measures.
• To assist cooperatives, federal and state agencies, extension and vocational groups, colleges, state departments of agriculture, consumer groups, and other agencies in promoting appropriate cooperative educational programs. These usually include (1) youth programs with considerable emphasis directed toward the FFA, 4-H clubs, young farmers, and college students; and (2) adult programs, giving attention to director-manager training, employee training, women's programs, and public education. State cooperative councils sometimes maintain loan, grant, and scholarship programs.

Some state councils limit their membership to farmer cooperative business associations. Others include general farm organizations and consumer cooperatives. The cooperative councils in Wisconsin, Minnesota, and South Dakota, for example, work with health, housing, consumer goods, and cable TV cooperatives. Still others limit their membership to statewide or federated cooperatives, while some have only direct members. The majority have provisions for associate or advisory members.

State councils differ considerably in methods of financing their activities. Some carry on broad programs, have large budgets, conduct manager and director training conferences, issue periodic house organs and other publications, and maintain year-round staffs. Others have limited budgets but maintain close working relationships with state extension services, educational institutions, and farm and urban organizations, and depend on all of them for assistance. Sometimes specialists of the state extension services function as part-time council secretaries.

To keep in touch with one another on matters of national scope, most councils have become associate members of the National Council of Farmer Cooperatives and the Cooperative League of the U.S.A. and direct members of the American Institute of Cooperation. In a few states, county councils have been established to promote various interests of cooperatives.

The state secretaries have formed an informal organization called the National Conference of State Council Secretaries. The purpose of the Conference is to serve as an exchange place for ideas and to provide up-to-date, relevant information for their personnel.

GENERAL FARM ORGANIZATIONS

The early contributions of general farm organizations to cooperative development, described in Chapter 5, have been significant. The extent of involvement has varied widely, but all the major general farm organizations are united in their support and encouragement of cooperatives irrespective of any philosophical or political differences.

The National Grange supports all cooperative activity and operates a number of statewide cooperative insurance companies. Both the Farm Bureau Federation and the National Farmers Union, through statewide or multistate regional associations as well as locally affiliated units of these regionals, are active in cooperative marketing of livestock and grain, the distribution of farm supplies, and the provision of insurance.

The direct control of general farm organizations over the operations of cooperatives varies from the payment of patronage refunds to only those patrons who are also members of the general farm organization to the requirement that all officers either be members or administrators of the general farm organization or its insurance affiliates. Other general farm organizations exercise no such control. Their affiliated cooperatives return patronage refunds to all patrons. The patrons also participate in the election of officers, who need not be members of the general farm organization that sponsored the cooperative.

The Midcontinent Farmers Association and the National Farmers Organization also engage in cooperative business activities, and each limits financial benefits to its affiliated members.

INTERNATIONAL COOPERATIVE ORGANIZATIONS

Like national organizations that serve cooperatives, international cooperative organizations may be oriented toward specialized functions and broad aspects of endeavor. They may also serve individual commodity trade associations.

Food and Agriculture Organization (FAO)

Ever since its organization in 1946, the Food and Agriculture Organization, with headquarters in Rome, Italy, has recognized the importance of cooperatives in solving the world's basic food problems. FAO believes that cooperatives, when efficiently operated, can contribute to the general welfare of poor communities as well as to their production and distribution of food. Through a small staff, it has encouraged research on practical problems confronting cooperatives. Often this encouragement has taken the form of coordinated efforts with government officials and university researchers. Occasionally, grants are given for initiating technical assistance, paying the costs of consultants' contractual services, and publishing cooperative studies and reports. FAO closely coordinates its cooperative program with the Joint Committee for the Promotion of Aid to Agricultural Co-operatives (COPAC).

FAO's cooperative activities are often carried out by the General Farmers Organization, the cooperative unit of the Human Resources Institutions, and the Agrarian Reforms Division. General assistance is also obtained from FAO's Agricultural Banking and Credit and Agricultural Marketing program and its Farm Supply programs. The FAO cooperative program is unique in that it gives special attention to educational and social, rather than commercial, efforts.

Inter-American Cooperative Finance Development Society (SIDEFCOOP)

The Inter-American Cooperative Finance Development Society was organized in 1966, with headquarter offices in Washington. USAID, in cooperation with the Fund for International Cooperative Development, studied the feasibility of such a financial institution and recommended its establishment. Membership in SIDEFCOOP consists of cooperative banks and finance institutions, cooperative societies, associations and federations, and nonprofit organizations dedicated to promotion of cooperatives.

The basic objective of SIDEFCOOP is to help Latin American countries strengthen the financial structure of their cooperatives by assisting them in organization, capital formation, and the operation of cooperative banks.

More specifically, the Society reports its objectives as follows:

- Promoting the establishment of cooperative finance institutes and cooperative banks throughout Latin America
- Assisting the cooperative finance institutes in the procurement of loans and guarantees, underwriting or direct placement of equity shares of debt, and procurement of other financial assistance from private sources; and acting as fiscal agent to perform these services more effectively
- Strengthening and promoting cooperative finance systems to achieve a greater integration of the Inter-American Cooperative Movement
- Establishing the Inter-American Cooperative Finance Institute (IIFCOOP) in order to provide:

    1 Technical assistance in the organization and operation of banks for cooperatives
    2 Consultation in the preparation of standards and procedures
    3 Auditing services
    4 Financing, including discounting of securities, acting as guarantor, and serving as fiduciary

- Studying laws related to cooperatives in the Latin American countries
- Fostering economic integration in general and, specifically, establishing contacts and negotiating contracts between interested parties

International Cooperative Housing Development Association (ICHDA)

The International Cooperative Housing Development Association, located in Washington and one of the most recent international cooperative associations, was organized in 1966. It was established because of the increased interest in cooperative housing that became evident at meetings of the housing committee of the International Cooperative Alliance.

The basic idea behind the organization of ICHDA was that national housing organizations, by pooling their varied experience and expertise, could be extremely effective in providing technical assistance to housing cooperatives in developing countries. Special emphasis is also given to assistance to low-income groups.

To achieve these goals, ICHDA has formulated four fundamental objectives:

- To establish pilot programs in selected countries by drawing on the combined experiences of member organizations
- To collaborate with the United Nations in its program of aid to developing countries
- To serve as a facilitating agency in finding sources of seed capital for initiating cooperative housing programs
- To establish a "talent bank" of individuals qualified to provide technical assistance on problems of cooperative housing

International Labor Organization (ILO)

The International Labor Organization was founded under the Treaty of Versailles in 1919. It is unique in that workers and employee representatives, along with national governments, have an equal voice in formulating its policies. ILO's headquarters are in Geneva, Switzerland, and in 1972 its membership consisted of 120 nations. Its major objective is to help develop programs on national and international levels in order "to provide productive embursement for the world's rapidly growing population."

From its beginning, ILO recognized that cooperatives could be an important instrument of economic and social progress for workers. To this end, the Cooperative, Rural and Related Institutions Branch was established. Early emphasis was placed on conducting research and providing information. Large amounts of information and data were collected, analyzed, and evaluated with the help of a panel of some thirty cooperative experts.

Following World War II, increased attention was directed toward providing assistance to cooperatives in developing countries. Member countries were encouraged to provide their cooperatives with ". . .economic, financial, and administrative aid and encouragement without effect on their independence." The role of government with respect to legislation, education and training, and financial responsibilities was also examined.

ILO's cooperative efforts have included the organization of schools, seminars, and regional and international cooperative conferences, often in cooperation with other international agencies. Between 1950 and 1969, some 200 grants and fellowships for relevant study were given to cooperative leaders and potential leaders in developing countries for feasibility studies of prospective cooperative ventures. Supervisory assistance was also provided for initiating cooperative programs.

International Research Center on Rural Cooperative Communities (CIRCOM)

The International Research Center on Rural Cooperative Communities, as its name implies, is a research organization designed to study the problems of agricultural cooperatives. Organized in 1965, its headquarters is in Tel Aviv, Israel. Its membership consists primarily of international cooperative organizations, government officials interested in cooperatives, and university research workers. In 1973, twenty-five countries were represented on its membership rolls.

The purposes of CIRCOM are:

- To provide a framework for investigations and research on problems concerning rural cooperative communities and publication of the results
- To coordinate the exchange of information on current research projects and published works
- To encourage organization of symposia on the problems of cooperative rural communities, as well as the exchange of experts between different countries

CIRCOM maintains close relationships with such groups as the Food and Agriculture Organization, International Labor Organization, International Cooperative Alliance, and the United Nations Research Institute for Social Development. Contacts are also maintained with researchers in Asia, Africa, Europe, Latin America, and North America. CIRCOM holds periodic conferences, publishes proceedings, and in 1974 it inaugurated the publication of *The Journal of Rural Cooperation*.

Joint Committee for the Promotion of Aid to Agricultural Co-operatives (COPAC)

Between 1968 and 1970, initiative was taken by the International Labor Organization and the Food and Agriculture Organization, together with the International Cooperative Alliance and the International Federation of Agricultural Producers, to set up the Joint Committee for the Promotion of Aid to Agricultural Co-operatives. COPAC was established in January 1971 as an informal mechanism linking the United Nations agencies and nongovernmental organizations to improve consultation and coordination, and to encourage initiative in the field of cooperative development. At that time the International Federation of Plantation and Agricultural and Allied Workers (IFPAAW) also joined. In its Resolution 1668 of June 12, 1972, ECOSOC (Economic and Social Council of the United Nations) included a recommendation that the membership of COPAC should be broadened. To that end, the United Nations, through its Social Development Division, and subsequently through the World Council of Credit Unions, became a member.

Special emphasis is placed on developing liaison arrangements among these organizations and on coordinating efforts among aid-giving and aid-receiving countries. Attempts are made to develop suitable techniques for the promotion of cooperatives in developing countries.

COPAC organized the international group called INTER-COOP primarily to encourage and coordinate the distributive efforts of consumer cooperatives. Membership comprises thrity organizations from twenty countries. The main emphasis is on providing technical assistance to help member organizations deal with such pressing problems as increased competition from multinational firms.

In furthering this major objective, attention is also directed toward developing intercooperative trade among countries, training cooperative personnel in developing countries, improving cooperative legislation, and appraising the role of women in cooperative work.

Organization of Cooperatives of America (OCA)

Established in 1963, the Organization of Cooperatives of America is designed to provide educational and technical assistance to cooperatives in the developing countries of Latin America. As of December 1970, OCA reported 144 cooperative members in twenty-three countries. Headquarters are in Lima, Peru.

The OCA's basic objectives are reported to be:

- To improve cooperative education techniques and coordinate technical training
- To provide assistance to cooperative development projects with national impact
- To promote cooperative trade
- To seek financial resources for cooperative development
- To encourage the creation of "high-level" cooperatives, and to try out new cooperative integration techniques
- To improve cooperative legislation
- To urge individual governments to include cooperatives in their national development plans

Training activities emphasize courses in cooperative management. In 1970, for example, a total of 314 participants were trained in eleven courses. A function of the education department has been to translate basic cooperative publications from English into Spanish. Technical assistance is concentrated on coordination of cooperative efforts, feasibility studies, and improvement of cooperative legislation.

International Cooperative Bank Company, Ltd. (INGEBA)

The International Cooperative Bank Company, Ltd., has its headquarters in Basel, Switzerland. It reports its main activities to be:

- Receiving interest-bearing deposits
- Granting loans and current account credits
- Discounting, collecting, and buying and selling of bills
- Purchasing and selling securities
- Administering property

- Safekeeping of securities and valuables
- Negotiating loans

Membership consists of approximately sixty national and international cooperative associations, including banks and other financial institutions, insurance associations, and wholesale distribution cooperatives. Among its members are the Nationwide Mutual Fire Insurance Company, Columbus, Ohio; Kooperativa Forbundet and Folksam International Insurance, both in Stockholm, Sweden; and Bank Hapoalim B. M., Tel Aviv, Israel.

International Cooperative Alliance (ICA)

The International Cooperative Alliance is the answer to Robert Owen's dream of an international cooperative organization. Since his day, many cooperative leaders have attempted to put together some form of international organization. It was not until 1895, however, that E. O. Greening, the managing director of the first agricultural cooperative in Britain, was successful in bringing together cooperatives from several nations. Although membership at first was made up mainly of European cooperatives, it later expanded to include a large number of Latin American, African, and Asian organizations. As of 1974, membership consisted of about 165 national or regional federations of cooperative business and service, and trade associations from 65 countries. The International Cooperative Petroleum Association, New York City, is a member. Regional offices are maintained in New Delhi, India, and Moshi, Tanzania. In 1974 its professional staff numbered thirty-three.

As the Alliance gained momentum, it, like many of its member associations, became engaged in heated discussions on such essential questions as the role of government in cooperative development and the capitalistic nature of cooperatives. The conclusions reached were (1) that cooperatives are anticapitalistic, since they seek to eliminate profit; and (2) in many countries, the knowledge and understanding of cooperative enterprise were so limited that state support and protection were necessary. The Alliance at all times has emphasized the need for bringing together all types of cooperatives—agricultural, consumer, and various sorts of service associations.

The Alliance has set up as criteria for membership what it considers to be basic: the Rochdale principles. While the principles were subject to somewhat continuous reinterpretation, members were required to adopt and practice (1) voluntary membership; (2) democratic control; (3) limited interest, if any, on equity capital; and (4) savings distribution in such a way that no member gains at the expense of another.

The International Cooperative Alliance has established the following objectives as the basis for its operations:

- To be a universal representative of cooperative organizations of all types
- To promulgate cooperative principles and methods throughout the world
- To promote cooperation in all countries
- To safeguard the interests of the cooperative movement in all its forms
- To maintain good relations among its affiliated organizations

- To promote friendly and economic relations among cooperative organizations of all types, national and international
- To work for the establishment of lasting peace and security

Strong emphasis is given to preparing and distributing publications and educational material, supporting and conducting research, assembling cooperative statistics, and providing educational materials for programs that include annual seminars for women and youth.

The biennial congresses convened by ICA consider a wide range of cooperative subjects. The Alliance serves its members through a number of auxiliary committees that are set up to deal with specific cooperative problems. The most important of these committees are: Agriculture (whose members include thirty-eight organizations from thirty countries, and which has a fisheries subcommittee), Banking, Housing, Insurance, Inter-coop, Workers Protective, and Artisan Societies.

International Federation of Agricultural Producers (IFAP)

The International Federation of Agricultural Producers, with headquarters located in Paris, carries out its cooperative program through its Standing Committee on Agricultural Cooperation. The Committee was organized because of the substantial contributions cooperatives could make to the economic welfare of members. Its stated purpose is to "identify and put into practice those kinds of internal business-operating and member-relation practices that will enable farmers to make better use of cooperatives to improve the quality of rural living."¹

The Standing Committee meets every eighteen months, during the IFAP conferences and usually once in between these conferences. The conferences are quite similar to those of the American Institute of Cooperation or the National Council of Farmer Cooperatives. The Committee, representing members from many countries, attempts to bring into focus the diverse approaches used by cooperatives to solve problems of farm cooperatives. It develops no legislative policies but discusses nonpartisan political action programs.

Some indication of the scope of its interests is illustrated by the fourteenth session, held in Rome in 1973. Subjects covered were: (1) the social, economic, and political environment affecting cooperatives; (2) the role and functions of directors; (3) cooperation between cooperatives, with emphasis on ability to compete with international firms; (4) the extent of public approval and support; (5) information and education; and (6) structural problems of cooperatives.

The Committee also functions in a liaison capacity with groups and organizations that have an interest in problems of cooperatives, especially the organizations that make up COPAC. IFAP reports important problems for future consideration, such as the relation of marketing boards to cooperatives, new developments in management, mergers, cooperation in developing countries, and international cooperation to meet the competition of large multinational firms.

The Plunkett Foundation for Cooperative Studies

The Plunkett Foundation for Cooperative Studies was established in 1919 by Sir Horace Plunkett, a noted Irish cooperator and statesman. Plunkett believed that cooperatives could be an important factor in helping farm people. He summed up his belief in his noted slogan, "Better farming, better business, and better living." In 1974, membership consisted of eighty-four institutions and forty-three individuals. Of the 127 total membership, 58 were in the United Kingdom and 69 were overseas.

The Plunkett Foundation, with offices in Oxford, England, describes itself as a research and educational foundation. To this end it conducts a wide range of training courses for both British and overseas students. These courses cover such subjects as business communications, cooperative law, cooperative practice, bookkeeping, cooperative management and administration, and general economics. Correspondence courses and seminars are also offered with the assistance of the Overseas Development Administration of the British government.

Over the years, the Foundation has conducted a number of studies relevant to cooperatives. These studies have featured detailed analyses of cooperative development trends in certain countries and investigations of cooperatives as related to selected commodities and enterprises. The Foundation has also undertaken a number of studies of functions and services provided by cooperatives. It publishes a yearbook, *Agricultural Cooperation*, which provides general information on subjects of current interest, as well as reports on cooperative development in both developed and developing countries. Liaison arrangements are maintained with many national and international organizations interested in cooperatives. The Foundation also sponsors international conferences on topics of current concern.

World Council of Credit Unions, Inc. (WOCCU)

The World Council of Credit Unions, Inc., was organized in 1971. Its main office is located in Madison, Wisconsin. Membership consists of the national credit unions and associations of Australia, Canada, the United States, and four regional confederations—the Asian Confederation of Credit Unions, the Africa Cooperative Savings and Credit Association, the Caribbean Confederation of Credit Unions, and the Latin American Confederation of Credit Unions. Through these memberships WOCCU serves about 48 million members in some seventy nations.

WOCCU was formed when CUNA International, which for a number of years had maintained an active international program, reorganized and concentrated its efforts on serving credit unions only in the United States, except for functioning as the contract agency, with USAID for technical assistance to credit unions in developing countries.

The program of WOCCU is directed largely toward developing countries. Emphasis is on maintaining and strengthening international ties of the credit union movement by coordinating the efforts of national and regional confederations in providing technical assistance and conducting educational programs.

QUESTIONS

1 Identify the national cooperative organizations serving cooperatives in the United States, and contrast their objectives and methods of operation.
2 Distinguish between national cooperative organizations and cooperative trade associations.
3 What similarities and differences exist in the objectives and functions of the various cooperative trade associations?

4 How do functions of the state cooperative councils and the National Council of Farmer Cooperatives differ?
5 Distinguish between general farm organizations and national cooperative associations.
6 To what degree do you believe general farm organizations should control cooperative associations?
7 Identify the international organizations serving cooperatives. Contrast their objectives and methods of operation.
8 To what extent can national associations serving cooperatives in the United States coordinate their programs with their international counterparts?

REFERENCES

There are no comprehensive references on the national and international organizations that serve cooperatives. The most up-to-date and most accurate information may be obtained by writing directly to the following:

National Cooperative Organizations

American Institute of Cooperation
1129 20th Street, N.W.
Washington, D.C. 20036

Cooperative League of the U.S.A.
1828 L Street, N.W.
Washington, D.C. 20036

National Council of Farmer Cooperatives
1129 20th Street, N.W.
Washington, D.C. 20036

Cooperative Trade Organizations

Agricultural Cooperative Development International
1430 K Street, N.W.
Washington, D.C. 20036

Credit Union National Association, Inc.
1617 Sherman Avenue
P.O. Box 431
Madison, Wisconsin 53701

Foundation for Cooperative Housing
1012 14th Street, N.W.
Washington, D.C. 20005

Group Health Association of America
1717 Massachusetts Avenue, N.W.
Washington, D.C. 20036

National Association of Housing Cooperatives
1828 L Street, N.W., Suite 1100
Washington, D.C. 20036

National Livestock Producers Association
307 Livestock Exchange
Livestock Exchange Building
Denver, Colorado 80216

National Milk Producers Federation
30 F Street, N.W.
Washington, D.C. 20001

National Rural Electric Cooperative Association
2000 Florida Avenue, N.W.
Washington, D.C. 20009

National Telephone Cooperative Association
2100 M Street, N.W.
Washington, D.C. 20037

General Farm Organizations

American Farm Bureau Federation
225 Touhy Avenue
Park Ridge, Illinois 60068

National Farmers Organization
Corning, Iowa 50841

National Farmers Union
12025 E. 45th Avenue
P.O. Box 2251
Denver, Colorado 80201

National Grange
1616 H Street, N.W.
Washington, D.C. 20002

International Organizations

Food and Agriculture Organization
Via delle Terme di Caracalla
Rome, Italy 00100

Inter-American Cooperative Finance and Development Society
c/o Cooperative League of the U.S.A.
1828 L Street, N.W.
Washington, D.C. 20036

International Cooperative Alliance
11 Upper Grosvenor Street
London, England, WIX9PA

International Cooperative Bank
Dufourstrasse 54
4002 Basel, Switzerland

International Federation of Agricultural Producers
1 Rue d'Hauteville
75010 Paris, France

International Labor Organization
CH 1211
Geneva 22, Switzerland
(ILO also publishes a regularly updated directory of cooperatives that can be useful)

International Research Center on Rural Cooperative Communities
24 H'a Arba'a Street
P.O. Box 7020
Tel Aviv, Israel

Organization of Cooperatives of America
Calle Baltazar La Torre #1056
Lima, Peru

The Plunkett Foundation for Cooperative Studies
31 St. Giles
Oxford, England OX13LF

World Council of Credit Unions
P.O. Box 431
Madison, Wisconsin 53701

Chapter 9

Benchmarks in Cooperative Legislation

This chapter will identify and describe important state and federal laws relating primarily to agricultural cooperatives. Subsequent chapters will cover (1) the implications of major cooperative legislation, court decisions, and administrative regulations; and (2) income tax issue and other aspects of tax laws as related to cooperatives.

To understand how cooperative legislation evolved in the United States, it will be helpful to review briefly how these organizations developed. Early American cooperatives, urban and agricultural, were small and informally organized and operated. They were typically grass roots in character and "just grew" in response to member needs. Often they were unincorporated, or incorporated under the general corporation laws that existed at the time when there was no cooperative legislation under which to incorporate. From the legal standpoint, it was often difficult to determine if a so-called cooperative was actually functioning and whether those who used it were really members.

This situation posed difficult problems for American legislators. Except for the Industrial and Provident Societies Act of 1852 in England, there was no body of law anywhere to guide them. As legal problems arose, the local character of cooperatives resulted in these problems being called to the attention of state legislators rather than of the federal Congress.

STATE LEGISLATION[1]

Except for Canada, which has separate provincial cooperative acts, and to some degree for India,[2] the United States stands alone among major countries in its system of state cooperative legislation. The United States is unique in that each of the fifty states has its own cooperative law or laws. Likewise, these states deal with problems of cooperative taxation, consolidation and liquidation, antitrust provisions, and various operating regulations in their own particular way. Notwithstanding the considerable differences that may exist from state to state, there is a substantial degree of similarity in their basic legislative provisions.

In general, early state legislators were ill-prepared to develop effective cooperative legislation. First efforts at the end of the nineteenth century largely involved experimentation and modification of state corporation laws. Such legislation usually included a limited number of features that reflected an attempt to graft the unique character of cooperatives into general corporation laws. Then some of the states, by special legislation, authorized the formation of nonstock cooperatives which were organized "on a non-profit basis for the mutual benefit of members." These early state legislative efforts were followed by a more sophisticated approach as cooperatives were confronted with the implication of other state and federal antitrust, taxation, and related legislation. Many states at that stage took legislative cognizance of the provisions of the Sherman, Clayton, and Capper-Volstead Acts. The last two were the first federal legislative acts, other than tax legislation, that specifically recognized the unique nature of cooperatives.

The question might well be asked: Why establish special cooperative legislation? It has been pointed out that Sweden, for example, has no such legislation. In the United States, cooperative leaders emphasized these reasons:

- Cooperatives should be identified by restricting the use of the term *cooperative* to only those associations that are organized under cooperative law.
- Although some cooperatives were organized under general corporation laws, this practice often resulted in problems relating to voting and the distribution of net margins. Some states, for example, required voting on the basis of shares of stock owned.
- In some states, there was a desire to provide special assistance to cooperatives, such as auditing services or help from state departments of agriculture or colleges of agriculture. This desire could best be achieved under special cooperative legislation.

States therefore began to move on cooperative legislation. For example, while the provisions applied to only one type of cooperative, the New York State legislature in 1857 passed a law covering the organization of mutual fire insurance companies. For at least twenty years prior to that time, they could be chartered only by a special act of the legislature.

[1]E. G. Nourse, in *The Legal Status of Agricultural Cooperation* (MacMillan, New York, 1927) particularly chaps. 2, 3, 4, and 5, provided valuable information for the development of this section.

[2]Constitutional reform in 1919 authorized India's states to develop their own cooperative legislation. In practice, however, all states have substantially identical cooperative legislation.

As would be expected, early cooperative legislation was in a highly formative stage. It was quite general in nature, and often it did not enable cooperatives to organize and operate in accordance with their stated objectives.

Early Legislation Authorizing Stock Cooperatives

Some of the principal features of early state cooperative legislation in the states that pioneered in the enactment of these laws as they related to stock cooperatives are here described:

Michigan (1865) The Michigan act is generally recognized as the first state cooperative law. It briefly modified the state's general corporation law and was titled, "An Act to Authorize the Formation of Mechanics' and Laboring Men's Cooperative Associations." Originally authorized to permit the organization of cooperative stores, it was amended in 1875 to cover "agricultural and horticultural associations." Shares of stock could range in value from $5 to $10 each, and cooperatives, in their articles of incorporation, were permitted to (1) control the number of shares, (2) specify how members would vote these shares, and (3) indicate methods of determining and "paying dividends."

Massachusetts (1866) The second cooperative law in the United States was enacted in Massachusetts. It was more comprehensive than the Michigan act. It spelled out, in some detail, (1) the number of persons necessary to form a cooperative (seven or more); (2) the nature and amount of authorized capital stock (not to exceed $50,000); (3) voting arrangements (one vote per member); and (4) the kinds of business that the association could engage in ("for the purpose of trade, or for carrying on any lawful mechanical, manufacturing, or agricultural business within the state . . ."). This law also provided that no member should have a claim on, or interest in, the cooperative in excess of $1,000, and that profits "might be distributed after setting aside a sinking fund equal to at least 10 percent of 'profits' until this fund should equal 30 percent of the stock outstanding."

Wisconsin (1887) Gradually, legislation became more inclusive. In 1887 Wisconsin passed an act for carrying on any trade or business on the "mutual, reciprocal, or cooperative plan." Among its provisions were: shares of stock not to cost more than $5, limited liability of members, sales to nonmembers only on a cash basis, ownership by one cooperative of shares in another (holdings to be limited to not over one-third interest in that cooperative), debt never to exceed two-thirds of the paid-up capital, and prohibition of proxy voting.

The Wisconsin law was rewritten in 1911 in response to the interests of the American Society of Equity and the Right Relationship League. It recognized three basic cooperative principles—limited capital holdings, democratic voting, and dividends on patronage. It specified how cooperatives should operate to comply with these principles. The law also permitted voting by mail, and it made mandatory the distribution of patronage refunds by directors after provisions for setting up educational and reserve funds. The law was widely accepted, being copied in whole or in part by sixteen states within seven years.

Nebraska (1911)   The Nebraska law made one additional contribution. It was the first to attempt to define a cooperative—a term widely used but not described in other state laws. It also authorized "the distribution of earnings in proportion to the property bought and sold to members, the labor performed, or other services rendered to the corporation." This law was copied by three states.

Other States   The Massachusetts law served as a guide for early cooperative laws in other states—Pennsylvania in 1868, Minnesota in 1870, Connecticut and New Jersey in 1875, California in 1878, and Ohio in 1884. The California law authorized the formation of "cooperative business corporations for doing any lawful business, and dividing a portion of 'profits' among persons other than their stockholders." This law also provided that a cooperative could regulate "the number of votes to which each stockholder is entitled." The Ohio law was among the first to provide for one member, one vote. It also limited stock holdings to $1,000 per individual and specified that the bylaws might provide for "the distribution of earnings to patrons and others."

In 1887, Kansas passed a law that permitted "any industrial pursuit" and contained the one-member, one-vote provision. Also in 1887, a revised Pennsylvania law provided for "permanent" and "ordinary" stock, limited voting, cash trading, and patronage refunds. Revisions in the Minnesota law provided (1) that stockholders might petition for the dissolution of their cooperative if it failed for five years to pay dividends on its stock, and (2) that cooperative federations should be recognized.

The Early Nonstock Cooperative Legislation

Prior to 1895, all cooperative legislation in the states had been drafted on the assumption that cooperatives were stock corporations. In other words, this legislation attempted to deal with the legal problems of cooperatives by recognizing them as modifications of the corporate form of business enterprise. This was in accord with the Rochdale tradition of building members' responsibility for financing their associations, but questions began to arise. Many believed that too much emphasis was placed on the concepts of "profits" and "capital."

The response was state legislation that in one way or another attempted to achieve three objectives:

• *The elimination of capital stock by having members provide capital on a loan basis.* To achieve this objective, levies on members were made on the basis of the amount of business they did through their cooperative.

• *The elimination of the competitive-price relationship with members.* This was achieved by the "net-returns" settlement practice (returning to members all proceeds after deduction of expenses). Emphasis was on the cooperative's functioning as the members' sales representative, rather than on its merely trading with them.

• *The elimination of nonmember business.* This provision did two things: (1) It tended to remove the profit incentive, and (2) it introduced the fraternal idea of "common interests and participation."

The legal formulation of these ideas developed in quite unrelated ways in California, Alabama, and Texas. Let us briefly trace their legislation.

California (1895)   California was the first state to enact nonstock cooperative legislation. Its provisions aimed at achieving the three objectives previously outlined. There are indications that the Farmers' Alliance encouraged the formulation of this law. It contained an interesting fraternal idea: "... the rights and interests of all members are equal, and no member shall acquire a greater interest therein than any other member has." The law also emphasized the personal nature of cooperative membership, and, according to Nourse, "... instead of a 'company' of stockholders the idea became that of an association of persons engaged in a like undertaking, specifically qualifying for membership and accepting the discipline of the association."

The law was permissive in its provisions regarding nonmember business, methods of financing, formation of federations, and the use of contracts. A 1909 amendment authorized equal or unequal voting and in general allowed cooperatives to govern themselves in any way they saw fit. Although it was not until 1916 that the first large cooperative in California was incorporated under this law, it was copied in whole or in part by five other states.

Alabama (1909)   In some respects the nonstock cooperative law of Alabama goes back to 1893, when "single-tax" followers of Henry George settled in Balwin County. To achieve "the common welfare" of members, they secured the passage of "an act to provide for the organization and regulation of corporations not for the pecuniary profit in the sense of paying interest or dividends on stock, but for the benefit of its members through their mutual cooperation and association." This idea appealed to nearby fruit producers as a means of achieving mutual objectives. Therefore, making some slight changes in title and purpose, they obtained passage of "an act for the incorporation of mutual cooperative societies or associations for farming or trucking purposes, and for exemption of the same from all corporate taxation and licenses." As one feature, this legislation required members to pay 3 percent of the gross selling price for products sold outside the association—a provision upheld in the Alabama courts in 1919.

Texas (1917)   The fraternal idea of membership in nonstock types of cooperatives was drafted into legislation in Texas by Walton Peteet, who later served as Secretary of the National Council of Farmers' Cooperative Marketing Associations. During his experience as an extension worker in the state, he was impressed by the frequency with which farmers lost control of their cooperatives because stock was sold to outsiders. To him, the solution was the organization of a nonstock type of business organization with nontransferable membership that would not permit such a situation to develop. The act also provided that: (1) "only those engaged in agricultural pursuits can become incorporators" (persons not farmers, however, were allowed to contribute up to one-third of the working capital of the association); (2) each corporation chartered shall contain as part of its name these words, "Farmers Cooperative Society"; and (3) membership could be obtained only through election by members.

The Standard Marketing Act   During the first fifty years of the states' cooperative legislative effort, there was much groping among legislators and uncertainty among cooperative leaders as to just what type of legislation they wanted. During this time, however, a trial-and-error approach resulted in the testing of many approaches and the development of a better understanding as to the type of legislation needed. Another factor that contributed to the increased interest in cooperative legislation was the battering experienced by many associations in the courts as a result of federal and state antitrust legislation.

Developments in California helped to initiate far-reaching changes in legislation. The establishment of the California State Marketing Commission, with the ambitious Colonel Harris Weinstock as director and with the brilliant Aaron Sapiro as legal advisor, did much to get new legislation under way. Weinstock and Sapiro favored "commodity marketing" rather than "community marketing." To be effective, this approach called for large-scale cooperatives adequately financed and supported by strong marketing contracts that would provide for liquidating damages should members sell outside their cooperative.

This proposal resulted in more comprehensive suggested state legislation, which Sapiro was instrumental in drafting. It became known as the Standard Marketing Act. It is of interest that California never adopted this act but that Sapiro was able to incorporate many of his ideas in an amendment to the Oregon Cooperative Law in 1921 while working with the Oregon Growers Cooperative Association. By this time, Sapiro was achieving national recognition as a lawyer. In rapid succession during the next two years, his drafts of cooperative laws were adopted in whole or in part in Texas, Arizona, Kansas, Montana, North Carolina, North Dakota, Washington, Georgia, and Alabama.

In addition, the Bingham Act of 1922 included a number of revisions based on experience in the drafting of legislation in the aforementioned states. It became known as "the Sapiro law," and with modifications it was adopted by over twenty states in the next three years. It was by far the most comprehensive cooperative legislation to date. Specific provisions often replaced permissive practices, particularly with respect to (1) member qualifications and voting power, (2) requirements of the articles of incorporation and bylaws, and (3) membership contracts and their enforcement.[3]

Two other things should be said about the Standard Marketing Act: (1) It drew on the previously developed "Department Bill" (see page 193) for suggestions, and (2) it dealt with the antitrust problem of cooperatives by specifically stating that cooperatives organized under provisions of this act were not to be considered in restraint of trade. For example, section 28 of the Bingham Act stated:

> Any association organized hereunder shall be deemed not to be a conspiracy nor a combination in restraint of trade nor an illegal monopoly; nor an attempt to lessen competition or to fix prices arbitrarily or to create a combination or pool in violation of any law of this State; and the marketing contracts and agreements between the association and its members and any agreements authorized in this act shall be considered not to be illegal nor in restraint of trade nor contrary to the provisions of any statute enacted against pooling or combinations.

[3]For details, see Nourse, op. cit., pp. 100–114.

The Bingham Act had a very substantial impact on cooperative legislation over the years. Although some state cooperative laws have been completely rewritten since their enactment (as was the Bingham Act in 1966), much of the emphasis in the new legislation has been on refinements and form rather than on substance. In one way or another, many of the ideas that were included in the Bingham Act are still part and parcel of state cooperative legislation.

State Legislation Applicable to Consumer Cooperatives

Consumer cooperatives and farmer or rural cooperative stores with many nonfarm members may be incorporated under broad nonprofit, mutual, or cooperative state statutes in all but eleven states. These statutes frequently are referred to as cooperative society or mutual association acts. Generally, they have not been updated to the extent that agricultural cooperative acts have been.

Perhaps half these state statutes are quite inadequate. Consumer cooperatives in states with inadequate laws and in states without specific laws for incorporation often incorporate under general corporation statutes. When they do so, they attempt to embody cooperative features in their bylaws.

When consumer cooperatives incorporate under general corporation statutes, they may encounter problems in eliminating proxy voting and in effectively maintaining basic cooperative features. Many consumer cooperatives solve this problem by incorporating as "foreign corporations" in the District of Columbia or in such states as California, Minnesota, or Wisconsin—all of which have comprehensive consumer cooperative statutes.

Special State Assistance to Cooperatives

A study by Raymond J. Mischler and John H. Donoghue, *State Statutes Authorizing Assistance to Farmer Cooperatives,*[4] provides information on state agencies and the types of assistance they are authorized to provide cooperatives, as reported by thirty-nine states. The state legislation relates to the following issues:

• *Departments of agriculture or comparable agencies—twenty-four states.* This form of state legislation authorizes such forms of assistance as feasibility studies, collection of statistics, supervision of operations, promotion and advisory assistance, development of accounting systems, grants in aid, and protection for bargaining associations from unfair trade practices. The New York law, for example, "Authorizes its Department of Agriculture, among other things, to co-operate with agricultural associations, investigate and recommend useful methods of co-operative production, marketing and distribution of foods, aid in the organization and operation of cooperative associations, call conferences of cooperative associations organized under chapter seventy-seven for discussion of cost of production, transportation and marketing, etc., to facilitate marketing operations for such cooperative associations." Some laws require that a division or section be established within the state's Department of Agriculture to carry out the cooperative responsibilities assigned to it.

[4]FCS Information 22, U.S. Department of Agriculture, Farmer Cooperative Service, Washington, 1961, p. 22.

- *Appointment of public directors—twenty-four states*. Most state laws with this provision *permit* cooperatives to specify in their bylaws that they may request "any public official" to appoint one or more public directors to their board of directors. Other states specifically designate that such officials as the dean of the College of Agriculture, the State Director of Extension, the Commissioner or Director of Agriculture, or the Governor may make these appointments. A few states make such appointments by specific individuals mandatory. The Georgia law is an example of legislation authorizing the appointment of public directors. It provides that: "one or more directors of an association organized under the Cooperative Marketing Act may be appointed by the State Commissioner of Agriculture, the dean of the College of Agriculture or any other public official or commission."
- *Colleges of agriculture—nine states*. Some state laws authorize, encourage, or suggest that agricultural experiment stations or the state extension services conduct feasibility studies, provide advisory and technical assistance, and otherwise help cooperatives. The Kentucky law, for example, provides that: "The Dean of the College of Agriculture of the University of Kentucky shall, upon request, inform any group of persons contemplating the organization of a cooperative marketing association what the results of a survey of the marketing conditions affecting the commodities proposed to be handled indicate regarding probable success."

Other states also have special provisions with respect to cooperatives. The Minnesota law authorizes the Governor to remove any association official or director under certain circumstances, and to refer the winding up of the affairs of a cooperative to the Attorney General. The Wisconsin law requires the University of Wisconsin to provide that "adequate and essential instruction in cooperative marketing, consumers cooperatives, and conservation shall be taught in the University, county teachers colleges, high schools, and schools of vocational, technical, and adult education." The law also directs the dean of the College of Agriculture and the state superintendent of public instruction to prepare outlines for teaching cooperation in the public schools.

Federal Legislation

We have already pointed out that cooperative legislation in the United States has developed on both state and federal levels, in contrast to legislation in most other nations which have only national cooperative laws. Except for the Capper-Volstead Act, which relates entirely to farmer cooperatives (associations of producers), most other federal legislation relates to cooperatives only in part and often does so in indirect, albeit in very important, ways. Let us consider the principal federal laws that have significant implications for cooperatives.

Common Law Background

As large-scale business enterprise started to develop in the United States during the latter part of the nineteenth century, strong antimonopoly feelings were beginning to surface. These feelings were deeply rooted in English common law, which attempted to deal with market abuses. For example, English common law prohibited:

- *Forestalling:* buying from traders who were on the way to market
- *Engrossing:* buying to resell at higher prices
- *Regrating:* buying at markets or fairs to resell at higher prices in the same area

It is of interest that these provisions were repealed in 1844, the year the Rochdale Society was formed. There was no direct connection, however. By that time, prohibition of these practices, rather than being viewed as restraining trade, was considered favorable to its development.

Farmers felt especially exploited by the large scale business firms with which they were forced to deal. What is more, no state legislation had been developed to deal with the problem within state borders. As a result, through the National Grange, farmers joined with other groups in seeking corrective action on a national level, since the monopoly problem was extending beyond state lines.

The Sherman Antitrust Act (1890)

The Sherman antitrust law was approved on July 2, 1890. Its eight sections were brief and general. Sections 1 and 2 were to prove to be of special concern to cooperatives. To quote them:

> *Section 1.* Every contract, combination in the form of trust or otherwise, or conspiracy, in restraint of trade or commerce among the several states, or with foreign nations, is hereby declared to be illegal.

The Miller-Tydings Act of 1937 which sanctioned "retail price maintenance" agreements, in effect, amended and further extended the scope of section 1 of the Sherman Antitrust Act.

> *Section 2.* Every person who shall monopolize, or attempt to monopolize, or combine or conspire with any other person or persons to monopolize any part of the trade or commerce among the several states, or with foreign nations, shall be deemed guilty of a misdemeanor and, on conviction thereof, shall be punished by fine not exceeding five thousand dollars [raised to $50,000 in 1955] or by imprisonment not exceeding one year, or by both said punishments in the discretion of the court.

By amendment in 1974, a "misdemeanor" became a "felony" and fines upon conviction were increased to $1 million for corporations and $100,000 for others, and the prison term was increased to three years.

While the Sherman Act did not mention cooperatives directly, they were the subject of much discussion by the framers of the law. In debate on the bill, Senator Teller stated: "Is it possible that we are putting it [a general farm organization known as the National League and similar to the Farmers' Alliance in objectives] in the power of some men to coerce and force farmers to abandon these organizations?" Senator Sherman, who viewed farm organizations as educational and advisory rather than as business firms, gave assurance that the bill "does not interfere in the slightest degree with voluntary associations. . . . They are not business combinations."

As the debate continued, however, Senator Stewart expressed his concern: "This measure strikes . . . at the very root of cooperation. . . . When capital is combined and strong, it will for a time produce evils, but if you take away the right of cooperation you take away the power to redress those evils: it gives rise to monopolies that are protected by law, against which the people cannot combine."

Senator Sherman came to accept this view, and he agreed to an amendment which read:

> . . . this act shall not be construed to apply to any arrangements, agreements, or combinations between laborers made with a view of lessening the number of hours of their labor or of increasing their wages; nor to any arrangements, agreements, associations, or combinations among persons engaged in horticulture or agriculture made with the view of enhancing the price of their own agricultural or horticultural products.

This proposed amendment, was lost, however, when the bill went back to committee, where it was largely rewritten. In its enthusiasm for checking monopolies, Congress was not inclined to make exceptions.

Notwithstanding the mood of the times, the Sherman Act appeared to do little to control the monopoly practices of the era. What is more, in 1911 the U.S. Supreme Court held, under the "rule of reason," that large business combinations would be restricted only if their methods were "unreasonable." As we shall see in the next chapter, the farmers high hopes that the Sherman Act would correct injustices soon turned to ashes as they found themselves prosecuted under the act. Moreover, many states passed antitrust legislation modeled after the Sherman Act, and cooperatives often found themselves in double jeopardy.

The Clayton Act (1914)

Cooperatives had made substantial growth during the twenty-four years that elapsed between the passage of the Sherman Antitrust Act and the Clayton Act. This growth was made notwithstanding the impediments that the Sherman Act and state antitrust acts had put in their way. Cooperatives were first able to get a small degree of national recognition only in the Clayton Act, which was formulated in an attempt to correct the weaknesses and abuses of the Sherman Act. Section 6 of this act provided that:

> The labor of a human being is not a commodity or article of commerce. Nothing contained in the antitrust laws shall be construed to forbid the existence and operation of labor, agricultural, or horticultural organizations, instituted for the purposes of mutual help, and not having capital stock or conducted for profit, or to forbid or restrain individual members of such organizations from lawfully carrying out the legitimate objects thereof, nor shall such organizations or the members thereof be held or construed to be illegal combinations or conspiracies in restraint of trade under the antitrust laws.

Two other provisions of the Clayton Act, while not mentioning cooperatives specifically, have had important implications for these associations. Section 7 forbids any corporation to acquire the stock of another corporation and forbids any corporation subject to the jurisdiction of the Federal Trade Commission to acquire the assets of another corporation if the effect of such stock and asset acquisitions "may be substantially to lessen competition or tend to create a monopoly." Section 15 provides that a person injured "in his business or property by reason of anything forbidden in the antitrust laws may sue" and "shall recover threefold the damages by him sustained and the cost of suit including a reasonable attorney's fee."

No one seems to have ever explained why the Clayton Act recognized only nonstock associations. Even in 1914 they were relatively unimportant when compared with stock cooperatives. Perhaps the most significant contribution of the Clayton Act was the recognition it gave to certain types of business organizations established for mutual benefit on a nonprofit basis. It opened the door, if only a crack, to the consideration of cooperatives as a special and distinct form of business enterprise.

Some legal scholars and court statements take a somewhat different view of the Clayton Act. They contend that the fundamental recognition of special cooperative statutes came with provisions of section 6 of the Clayton Act. They view the Capper-Volstead Act as a mere extension of this recognition to stock cooperatives. In actual practice, most legal pleadings rely jointly upon both section 6 of the Clayton Act and section 1 of the Capper-Volstead Act.

The obvious weakness of the Clayton Act, however, led to an attempt to develop uniform state cooperative legislation that would recognize the many changes occurring among cooperatives. While only limited formal legislation resulted from these efforts, the impact was considerable. The impetus for obtaining uniform state legislation was furnished by Senator Robert M. La Follette, who believed that farmers and laborers should be exempt from laws that were enacted to correct the abuses of industrial firms. To this end, he sought the help of the Chief of the Office of Markets of the U.S. Department of Agriculture. Technicians there drafted and circulated a recommendation titled, "Suggestions for a State Cooperative Law Designed to Conform to Section 6 of the Clayton Act."

The model bill was based to a considerable extent on the California nonstock law. In all, it contained twenty-five sections which recognized the basic features and unique nature of cooperative business enterprise. (The thinking in the Department of Agriculture was that it would draft a separate model bill for stock cooperatives.) The bill gave special consideration to achieving rather specific "mutual help," "nonstock," and "nonprofit features"—terms used in the Clayton Act. Nourse, in *The Legal Status of Agricultural Cooperation*,[5] reports that the bill influenced the development of cooperative legislation in New York, Louisiana, Pennsylvania, New Jersey, Ohio, and Iowa.

The Capper-Volstead Act (1922)[6]

Legislative History Continued problems with the Sherman Act and shortcomings of the Clayton Act set in motion forces for more comprehensive cooperative legislation. Especially, dairy bargaining cooperatives were being charged by milk dealers with restraining trade. To deal with this situation, the National Cooperative

---

[5] Nourse, op. cit., p. 88.

[6] For a good discussion of the development and impacts of the Capper-Volstead Act, see Joseph G. Knapp, *Capper-Volstead Impact on Cooperative Structure*, FCS Information 97, U.S. Department of Agriculture, Farmer Cooperative Service, Washington, 1975, p. 42.

Milk Producers Federation joined with the National Farmers Union, the National Grange, and other farm groups to organize the National Board of Farm Organizations in order to seek legislation that would enable farmers to operate cooperatives without being in conflict with antitrust laws. A resolution asking Congress to amend the existing antitrust laws was passed at a meeting of this organization. In response, John D. Miller, chairman of the legislative committee of the Dairymen's League, drafted the initial bill in 1917. It was first sponsored by Senator Capper and Congressman Hersman as an amendment to section 6 of the Clayton Act. Opposition was strong and no congressional action took place in 1919. With a Republican administration controlling Congress, it was agreed, as a matter of strategy, to have the Republican Volstead replace the Democrat Hersman as the House sponsor, and to develop the legislation as a separate bill rather than as an amendment to the Clayton Act.

Strong Senate opposition was overcome only after the Secretary of Agriculture called a National Agricultural Conference at which President Warren G. Harding gave firm support to the Capper-Volstead bill. He said: "American farmers are asking for, and it should be possible to afford them, ample provision of law under which they may carry on in cooperative fashion those business operations which lend themselves to that method, and which, thus handled, would bring advantage to both the farmer and his consuming public."

At the same meeting, Thomas Wilson, of the Wilson Packing Company, spoke out in support of the Capper-Volstead bill when he said: "I believe the time has been reached when associations of producers, under proper supervision, should systematize the orderly marketing of their products." With such support the bill was enacted into law on February 18, 1922.

President Warren G. Harding signing the Capper-Volstead Cooperative Marketing Act. This basic legislation authorized the association of producers of agricultural products and spelled out in detail the requirements necessary to maintain the protection it afforded. *Courtesy of National Council of Farmer Cooperatives.*

The bill consisted of only two sections. The first reads:

Section 1. . . . That persons engaged in the production of agricultural products as farmers, planters, ranchmen, dairymen, nut or fruit growers may act together in associations, corporate or otherwise, with or without capital stock, in collectively processing, preparing for market, handling, and marketing in interstate and foreign commerce such products of persons so engaged. Such associations may have marketing agencies in common and such associations and their members may make the necessary contracts and agreements to effect such purposes: *Provided, however,* that such associations are operated for the mutual benefit of the members thereof as such producers and conform to one or both of the following requirements:
    First: That no member of the association is allowed more than one vote because of the amount of stock or membership capital he may own therein, or
    Second: That the association does not pay dividends on stock or membership capital in excess of 8 per centum per annum.
    And in any case to the following:
    Third: That the association shall not deal in the products of non-members to an amount greater in value than such as are handled by it for members.

The second section authorized the Secretary of Agriculture, if and when there was reason to believe that farm cooperatives had monopolized or restrained trade in interstate and foreign commerce so as to unduly enhance prices, to order them to cease and desist from enforcing such prices. If they neglected to obey such an order, he was empowered to request the court to enforce the order. This section also spelled out in detail the administrative procedures for hearings and the court action in an event of noncompliance by a cooperative.

Basic Provisions of the Capper-Volstead Act   The act gave agricultural producers permission to act together. It was entitled, "An Act to Authorize Association of Producers of Agricultural Products." It said nothing about antitrust exclusion, and in no way supported the commonly expressed myth that cooperatives are exempt from antitrust legislation. The act merely spelled out in considerable detail the requirements a cooperative must meet to maintain the protection afforded by it. To reemphasize the major provisions specified by the act:

- The cooperative must operate for the mutual benefit of members.
- Members can only be farmers, planters, ranchmen, dairymen, nut or fruit growers.
- A cooperative, to obtain the protection of the act, must operate so that non-member business does not exceed member business, and either (1) no member shall be allowed more than one vote because of amount of stock or membership capital he owns, or (2) dividends on stock and member capital cannot be in excess of 8 percent.
- A cooperative may be incorporated or nonincorporated.
- A cooperative may be organized on a stock or a membership basis.
- A cooperative may have marketing agencies in common.
- The cooperative may engage in processing.
- Only marketing cooperatives are covered by the act.

- Consumers are protected from unreasonable price enhancement by cooperatives under provisions of section 2.

What the Capper-Volstead Act Does Not Do A careful examination of the provisions of the Capper-Volstead Act makes it obvious that there are also many things that the act does not do. These are succinctly identified by Marvin A. Schaars in *Cooperatives, Principles and Practices.*[7] He points out that:

- It does not regulate agricultural production nor establish marketing quotas.
- It does not prevent cooperatives from monopolizing the marketing of an entire crop through internal growth. (The Clayton Act may prevent such monopolization if done via merger or through external growth.)
- It does not give cooperatives special immunity from antitrust or other laws which would not apply to other business firms under similar situations.
- It does not apply to purchasing or service associations, but is exclusively restricted to farmers' marketing cooperatives.
- It does not prevent price increases, but undue price rises might invite prohibitory action by the Secretary of Agriculture and/or the Justice Department.
- It does not enable cooperatives to incorporate under it.
- It does not permit members to buy products and then sell them through the association as dealers or speculators—it is restricted to members as producers of the products marketed.
- It does not automatically grant eligibility to borrow from Banks for Cooperatives. These have their own criteria for making loans.
- It does not require cooperatives to incorporate to qualify under the Act.
- It does not grant exemption from payment of federal or state income taxes.
- It does not prevent pooling of products, expenses, sales receipts, and net earnings.

Benefits of the Capper-Volstead Act The benefits of compliance with the Capper-Volstead Act may be summarized as follows:

- Producers have the right to organize marketing cooperatives with the certainty that they do not violate any antitrust laws.
- Marketing cooperatives can attain a strong economic position as long as it is achieved through voluntary attraction of members and natural growth.
- Marketing cooperatives may join with other marketing cooperatives in collectively marketing farmers' products, providing that they comply with provisions of the Capper-Volstead Act.
- Marketing cooperatives have a right to do what any other business may do in carrying out their legitimate objectives. They may, for example, enter into contracts and agreements so long as this is done in a legal manner.
- The public is protected in that the Secretary of Agriculture may, if there is reason to believe that a cooperative is "unduly enhancing" prices as a result of monopolization or restraint of trade, bring administrative proceedings against it.

The impacts of the Capper-Volstead Act were far-reaching. Joseph G. Knapp

---

[7]University of Wisconsin—Extension, Madison, 1971, p. 99.

states: "It opened the throttle for cooperative marketing advancement."[8] He further points out that the meaning of the act was explained by Lyman S. Hulbert, of the Agriculture Department's legal staff, in a bulletin, "Legal Phases of Cooperative Associations."[9] It was Hulbert who described the act as the "Magna Carta of cooperation." Congressional recognition of cooperatives was noted by the courts, and the act also served as the steppingstone for the passage of the Cooperative Marketing Act of 1926 and other cooperative legislation that followed.

Other Federal Legislation

In addition to the legislation just described, a number of other laws relating in whole or in part to cooperatives have been enacted. They cover one or more aspects of such cooperative items as organization, taxation, antitrust, financing and credit, and regulatory measurers.

Organization In addition to the Clayton Act and the Capper-Volstead Act, the following federal legislation having application to cooperatives has been enacted:

- *Cooperative Marketing Act (1926).* This act established the Division of Cooperative Marketing in the Bureau of Agricultural Economics, U.S. Department of Agriculture, to conduct research, to provide advisory assistance, and to engage in educational work with cooperatives. This division and its successors were predecessors of Farmer Cooperative Service, established in 1953, and legal authorization for the FCS program is found in the act (see Chapter 21).
- *The Agricultural Act (1929).* In addition to establishing the Federal Farm Board and providing for loans to cooperatives, the framers of this legislation drew on the provisions of the Capper-Volstead Act to define the essential features of a cooperative. The guidelines set forth were used to determine eligibility for loans from the banks for cooperatives when the Farm Credit Administration was established.
- *The Fishery Cooperative Marketing Act (1934).* The act, administered by the Secretary of the Interior, legalized fishery cooperatives engaged in marketing fish and aquatic products. It was patterned after the Capper-Volstead Act.
- *Rural Electrification Act (1936).* This legislation established the Rural Electrification Administration to make loans to rural electric cooperatives and other rurally based utilities. This loan program was extended to rural telephone companies by amendment in 1949.
- *The District of Columbia Consumers' Cooperative Act (1940).* This law authorized the incorporation of consumer cooperatives in the District of Columbia and elsewhere.
- *Federal Legislation Authorizing the Chartering of Cooperatives.* Only federally chartered credit unions and the federal land-bank associations, production credit associations, and banks for cooperatives among all cooperatives, are chartered under federal laws.

[8]Knapp, op. cit., p. 12.
[9]Lyman S. Hulbert, *Legal Phases of Cooperative Associations,* Department Bulletin No. 1106, U.S. Department of Agriculture, Washington, 1929, p. 126.

Taxation The following acts have special reference to cooperative taxation:

- *The War Revenue Act (1898).* This was the first act that specifically referred to cooperative taxation. It precluded farmers' cooperatives from the payment of stamp taxes.
- *Income Tax Statute (1913).* This act granted "labor, agricultural, or horticultural associations" "exemption" from federal income tax payments.
- The Revenue Acts of:

1916 and 1918: Provided that when marketing cooperatives served as sales agents for members, they were "exempt" from the payment of income taxes.

1921: Applied tax "exemption" provisions to cooperatives acting as purchasing agents for members.

1926: Eliminated the application of tax provisions to only those cooperatives that served as agents for members.

1951: Eliminated the "exemption provisions" and introduced in their place the concept of "exclusion" from gross income of patronage refunds which cooperatives made to patrons under "prior mandatory obligations."

1962: Assured that a single tax will be paid currently at either the cooperative or patron level on earnings generated by the cooperative. Farmer cooperatives that comply with section 521 of the 1954 Internal Revenue Code are allowed deductions on amounts paid as dividends on stock and income derived from nonpatronage sources that is distributed on a patronage basis. A basic amendment in 1966 required that members treat "per unit capital retains" (investments) in the same manner as patronage refunds for tax purposes.

Antitrust

- In addition to the Clayton Act and the Capper-Volstead Act, the Robinson-Patman Act (1936) related to antitrust. It provided that patronage refunds to members were not a form of price discrimination—a practice which this act prohibited.

Finance and Credit In addition to the Federal Farm Loan Act (1916), the War Finance Corporation Acts (1918 and 1921), the Federal Intermediate Credit Act (1923), the Farm Credit Act (1933) with later amendments (all discussed in Chapter 16), the Agricultural Marketing Act (1929), and the Rural Electrification Act (1936), the following legislation related specifically to cooperative finance and credit:

- *The Federal Credit Union Act (1934).* This act provides for the federal chartering of credit unions that until that time could only be chartered under state law
- *The Federal Housing Acts* (1948, 1950, and 1961). These acts provided that the Federal Housing Administration could insure long-term loans to nonprofit housing cooperatives

Regulatory Measures

- *Packers and Stockyards Act (1921).* This act did not permit rebates but ruled that patronage refunds were not rebates.
- *Future Trading Act (1920).* This act was known as the Commodity Exchange Act after 1936 and the Commodity Future Trading Commission Act after early 1975. It

provides that grain exchanges can not deny membership because a firm is a cooperative, and that patronage refunds are not rebates.

• *Motor Carrier Act (1935).* Provisions of this act do not apply to vehicles operated and owned by cooperatives.

• *Agricultural Marketing Agreements Act (1937).* This act contains provisions as to voting, pooling of returns, and serving members under marketing agreements and orders.

• *Civil Rights Act (1964).* This act stated that membership in cooperatives cannot be denied for reasons of color, race, religion, or political views. Compliance with these provisions is also required by cooperatives receiving financial assistance or services from the federal government.

• *Agricultural Fair Practices Act (1967).* This act attempted to prohibit unfair trading practices by handlers in their dealings with cooperatives and their members. It is administered by the Agricultural Marketing Service, U.S. Department of Agriculture.

SUMMARY

Cooperative law in the United States has developed on both state and federal levels. State legislation has largely been enabling legislation under which all but certain types of credit cooperatives can be organized. Federal legislation covers cooperative organization, taxation, antitrust, financing, and regulatory measures.

State laws developed first, dating back to 1857 when the first act was passed in New York. First legislative efforts were modifications of general corporation laws. Most laws were rather permissive in nature, and they allowed cooperatives to operate much as they saw fit. Later, both stock and nonstock state laws were gradually enacted. As cooperatives encountered problems with state and federal antitrust legislation, the state cooperative laws became more specific and took into account the increased services cooperatives were providing members. The Bingham Act of Kentucky, passed in 1922, became a model for much of the state cooperative legislation. Since then, state legislation has grown more mandatory in nature and has been broadened to reflect the changing nature of cooperative operations. A number of states also provide for educational, research, and advisory assistance for cooperatives.

The first federal laws to affect cooperatives substantially reflected the growing concern about the way in which large-scale business firms were engaging in monopolistic practices and the restriction of trade. To cope with these problems, the Sherman Act was passed in 1890. It did not mention cooperatives as such, but interpretation of its provisions and the provisions of state laws patterned after this act contributed to uncertainty regarding the rights of farmers to join together to organize cooperatives.

The Clayton Act was passed to correct the abuses and to strengthen the provisions of the Sherman Act. It recognized the organization of nonstock agricultural marketing cooperatives as not being in conflict with any existing antitrust legislation. The Capper-Volstead Act, referred to as the "Magna Carta of cooperation," attempted to remedy the shortcomings of the Clayton Act. It was "an act to authorize the association of producers of agricultural products" and not, as many have held, an act giving immunity from the provisions of antitrust legislation. The act spelled out the rights of producers and served as a benchmark for guiding much of the federal legislation that in one way or another applied to cooperatives. This legislation had far-reaching implications on how marketing cooperatives may organize, on how they are taxed, on how they can operate, and on the various forms of financial and credit assistance that are made available to them.

QUESTIONS

1. It has been said that supporting legislation often lags twenty years behind the development and operations of various economic institutions. Does this statement apply to cooperatives, and if so, why?
2. Characterize the development of early cooperative legislation in the various states.
3. Contrast the development of state and federal legislation authorizing stock and nonstock cooperatives.
4. What was the basic thrust of the Sherman Antitrust Act and what were the implications for cooperatives?
5. Was the Clayton Act "an empty shell" for cooperatives, as some have charged, or did it have real significance for them?
6. What are the implications to cooperatives of provisions in the Clayton Act relating to restraint of trade, mergers, and treble damages?
7. Does the Capper-Volstead Act give substantial antitrust exemptions as far as the operations of cooperatives are concerned?
8. What inference can we draw from the title of the Capper-Volstead Act: "An Act to Authorize Association of Producers of Agricultural Products"?
9. How does the Capper-Volstead Act seek to protect consumers of products that cooperatives may handle?
10. On what basis does Lyman S. Hulbert refer to "cooperative exemption" from antitrust laws as a myth or a fallacy?
11. What requirements must a cooperative fulfill to qualify under the provisions of the Capper-Volstead Act?
12. On what basis do many legislative acts of interest to cooperatives distinguish between ordinary business rebates and patronage refunds?
13. Identify other legislative acts that are important to cooperatives.

REFERENCES

Knapp, Joseph G.: *Capper-Volstead Impact on Cooperative Structure,* FCS Information 97, U.S. Department of Agriculture, Farmer Cooperative Service, Washington, 1975, p. 42.

Mischler, Raymond J.: "Agricultural Cooperative Law," *Rocky Mountain Law Review,* vol. 30, 1958, pp. 381–401.

―――: "Agricultural Cooperatives Have Legal Foundations," and "Federal Income Tax Status Is Defined," in *Farmer Cooperatives in the United States,* FCS Bulletin 1, U.S. Department of Agriculture, Farmer Cooperative Service, Washington, 1965, pp. 14–22.

Neely, Morrison D.: *Legal Phases of Farmer Cooperatives,* FCS Information 100, U.S. Department of Agriculture, Farmer Cooperative Service, Washington, 1976, p. 743.

Nourse, Edwin G.: *The Legal Status of Agricultural Cooperation*, Macmillan, New York, 1927, p. 555.

Packel, Israel: *The Organization and Operation of Cooperatives,* Joint Committee on Continuing Legal Education of the American Law Institute and the American Bar Association, Philadelphia, 1970, p. 372.

Schaars, Marvin A.: *Cooperatives, Principles and Practices,* University of Wisconsin—Extension, Madison, 1971, pp. 57–64.

Shereff, Henry D.: *Agricultural Cooperatives* (Corporate Law and Practice Course Handbook Series No. 151), Practicing Law Institute, New York, 1974, p. 616.

Volkin, David: "Keys to Understanding Capper Volstead," *News for Farmer Cooperatives,* July 1974, pp. 4–5.

Chapter 10

Special Legal Problems

Legal issues have arisen in practically all areas relating to the organization and operation of cooperatives. Hulbert and Mischler, in *Legal Phases of Farmer Cooperatives*,[1] refer to nearly 1,500 cases that either directly or indirectly apply to cooperatives. These and other cases in which cooperatives have been involved cover, among other areas, organization; incorporation; duties and responsibilities of directors, officers, and employees; meetings; marketing contracts; monopoly and restraint of trade; taxes; and federal statutes that mention cooperatives.

In this chapter three areas—antitrust legislation, contracts, and marketing orders and agreements—will be singled out for special attention. Before considering these areas as they relate to cooperatives, however, it will be helpful to examine briefly the legislative and regulatory environment in which cooperatives find themselves.

LEGISLATIVE AND REGULATORY ENVIRONMENT

In various sections of this book, we have mentioned the unique nature of cooperatives. The early history of cooperative legislation, however, did not adequately recognize

---

[1]Lyman S. Hulbert and Raymond J. Mischler, FCS Bulletin 10, U.S. Department of Agriculture, Farmer Cooperative Service, Washington, 1958, pp. 272–300.

how cooperatives differed from other business firms. The result was misunderstanding and confusion. As we shall see, the courts early took the stand that two or more farmers acting together were comparable to two or more giant firms taking similar action. Gradually, however, the unique nature of agriculture and the cooperatives that served farmers became recognized. In *Frost v. Corporation Commissioner*, 278 US 515 (1928), Justice Louis Brandeis in a dissenting opinion stated: "It is settled that to provide for the peculiar needs of farmers or producers is a reasonable basis for classification." In 1927 Justice James McReynolds, after saying "cooperative marketing statutes promote the common interest," stated: "We take judicial knowledge of the country and from current events we know that . . . the agricultural producer was at the mercy of speculators and others who fixed the price of the selling producer and the purchasing price of the final consumer through combinations and other arrangements whether valid or invalid and that by reason thereof the farmer obtained a grossly inadequate price for his products."

There is reason to believe, too, that much of the talk, even by such persons as justices, government administrators, and even some Secretaries of Agriculture, about cooperative "exemptions" and special treatment in antitrust laws is often misleading and beside the point. It fails to come to grips with the basic problem, which is equitable treatment of individual cooperative members, taking into account the inherent differences of relatively small-scale agricultural cooperatives when compared with their industrial counterparts (for details, see Chapter 6).

As we examine the implications of antitrust and other legislation, we will see that it is only when legislative recognition is given to the disadvantaged and weak position of farmers in the economy that they can hope to achieve some degree of countervailing power in the marketplace. Rather than emphasize exemptions and preferential treatment for cooperatives, a more realistic approach seems to be to emphasize the legal steps necessary for cooperatives to achieve or maintain equality in an economy of giant conglomerates. This view was well stated by the U.S. Supreme Court in the *United States v. Maryland and Virginia Milk Producers Association, Inc.,* when it concluded that the general philosophy of the Clayton and Capper-Volstead Acts was "simply that individual farmers should be given, through agricultural cooperatives acting as entities, the same unified competitive advantage—and responsibility—available to businessmen acting through corporations." It should be emphasized that in the absence of cooperatives, farmers were one segment of the economy that approached atomistic competition.

Rather than express unwarranted fears about cooperative monopolies, recognition needs to be given to the antimonopoly role that unshackled cooperatives can play if they are permitted to compete effectively. Instead of accusing cooperatives of contributing to high food prices, it would be highly desirable to consider carefully the economic forces that have influenced food production during recent years.

The issue is put into perspective by Assistant Secretary of Agriculture Clayton Yeutter when replying to a letter from Congressman Peter Rodino to Secretary of Agriculture Earl Butz. The letter inquired about actions taken under section 2 of the Capper-Volstead Act to make certain that cooperatives were not permitted to achieve monopoly power. Assistant Secretary Yeutter stated: "The testimony received by your committee to the effect that monopoly power on the part of Section 1 Capper-Volstead cooperatives may be a major source of rising food prices is not supportable in fact. The tight supply-demand conditions which existed this past year were caused by vagaries of weather and a sharp but unpredictable increase in world demand for food. Cooperatives had nothing to do with these conditions.''

As legislators and courts gained a better understanding of cooperatives, the need for different treatment for these associations, if they were to receive equitable consideration, became increasingly apparent. For example, the following facts are beginning to be recognized:

- Both marketing and purchasing cooperatives usually are providing much-needed competition in the marketplace rather than being contributors to monopoly.
- Cooperatives make it possible for their members to negotiate with large multibillion-dollar corporations on a more nearly equal basis rather than perpetuate a situation where individual farmers continue to compete against one another in selling their products or purchasing supplies and services. Obviously, the individual farmer cannot possibly compete with chain stores, implement dealers, or large oil companies on anything approaching an equal basis. To put this another way, cooperatives may be the effective way for members to achieve the economic power they need to prevent their exploitation by a limited number of dominant firms that characterize the oligopolistic situation that has developed in many industries. In fact, cooperatives still have a long way to go to fully achieve this objective.
- Many cooperatives are in the forefront in introducing improved market stability, increased operating efficiency, and innovative distribution practices—all developments that benefit consumers as well as producers.
- Without cooperatives, farmers, because they produce bulky and perishable products, are often confronted with a "take-it-or-leave-it" offer from firms in the marketplace. By using their cooperative to process, store, and transport products to prevent the need for immediate sale, farmers are only trying to achieve equality in the marketplace rather than overt market power.

There are other inherent legal problems with which cooperatives have to contend. For example:

- Many judges and most people in charge of state and federal regulatory agencies are political appointees. As a consequence, (1) for better or worse, they tend to reflect the varying legal, political, and philosophical views of those who appoint them; and (2) some use their positions to promote political objectives and their own ambitions rather than deal objectively with the various issues they encounter.
- Under all circumstances, judges and agency administrators reflect their training and experience. Unfortunately, many know little about cooperatives. On this point Donald E. Graham, Vice President and General Counsel of the National Council of Farmer Cooperatives, speaking about the knowledge and understanding that regulatory officials have of cooperatives, stated: "Our problem exists due to a lack of comprehension and understanding of the unique nature of farmer cooperatives by the career civil servants of the Department of Justice." He emphasized his point by saying that these people ". . . have a very incomplete and distorted picture of what cooperatives are all about."

SPECIAL LEGAL PROBLEMS

- Opinions handed down by the courts relate only to the specific points of law presented to them and necessary to decide the case at hand. As a result, there are many holes and unsettled issues in legal areas of concern to cooperatives.[2]
- While the number of qualified cooperative attorneys is increasing, sometimes cooperatives have suffered from poor legal advice and poor presentation of their cases. Cooperatives have also suffered from a misunderstanding of their place as members of the business community requiring legal advice to guide them through the many problems all businesses face.
- Agriculture is a dynamic industry and the cooperatives that serve it are constantly changing, with the consequence that new problems that require new legal and regulatory solutions are continually arising.

ANTITRUST DECISIONS

In the preceding chapter, we indicated that federal antitrust legislation was centered in the Sherman Antitrust Act and in the Clayton Act. The former took no formal recognition of cooperatives, and the latter sanctioned the existence and operation of labor, agricultural and horticultural organizations, organized for mutual benefit and not having capital stock. The Capper-Volstead Act related specifically to marketing cooperatives and authorized associations of producers of agricultural products. Many states also enacted antitrust legislation to supplement federal legislation. Over the years, these laws had a significant impact on the organization and operation of cooperatives.

Early state antitrust action, as it related to cooperatives, was decided in both state and federal courts. Let us look briefly at some of the significant cases and their implications.

State Court Decisions

- *Reeves v. Decorah Farmers Cooperative Society* (1913). This cooperative had a provision in its bylaws to the effect that its members would have to forfeit 5 cents per 100 pounds of livestock they sold to any competitor of their cooperative. Reeves, a livestock buyer in the trade territory of the cooperative, brought suit against the cooperative to prevent it from enforcing this provision. The Supreme Court of Iowa held that the cooperative was acting in restraint of trade because Reeves was placed at a disadvantage in purchasing hogs from the association. He would forfeit his profits, pay too much for hogs, or members would be penalized for dealing with him.

Two observations should be made: (1) Viewed in hindsight, if the cooperative had emphasized the maintenance and upkeep of the association, which it might well have done, rather than "doing in" its competition, it might have been on stronger legal

---

[2]Gaps and unresolved issues do exist in cooperative antitrust law. However, the way these are filled through court proceedings is for a cooperative to sue or get sued. Lawsuits, then, are a means of defining issues. At present several areas of law are being defined. For example, the Central California Lettuce Cooperative case brought by the Federal Trade Commission is defining issues of bargaining and the permissible functions of a cooperative. The National Broiler Marketing Association case is defining issues of the definition of "producer" in the Capper-Volstead Act. Defining issues is expensive.

ground; and (2) when the state of Iowa later included in its cooperative legislation the provision that an association might provide for liquidated damages in its contracts or bylaws, the State Supreme Court declared the validity of a provision requiring members to pay their cooperative 25 cents per 100 pounds on all livestock sold outside the association.

• *Burns v. Wray Farmers Grain Company* (1913). The bylaws of the Farmers Grain Company (a cooperative) provided that stockholders might sell grain to competitors if they paid the cooperative 1 cent per bushel for grain sold in this way. Burns, a member who agreed to this bylaw, sold 3,500 bushels of grain to a competitor. The association brought suit against him to recover $35, but the Colorado State Supreme Court held the bylaw invalid and in restraint of trade.

Other state courts followed the lead of Iowa and Colorado. In all instances, however, when states enacted cooperative laws that included provisions for liquidated damages, such laws were upheld. The Colorado State Supreme Court, for example, at a later date held that the public policy of the state was changed with the passage of the Cooperative Act of 1923. Hulbert and Mischler, in *Legal Phases of Farmer Cooperatives*,[3] also mention that not all early state decisions were against cooperatives. In Illinois, Indiana, New York, and Alabama, for example, liquidated damage provisions in cooperative bylaws were upheld on common law principles.

Federal Court Decisions

A number of state antitrust cases also found their way to federal courts. Some of the more significant decisions involved the following cases:

• *Connolly v. Union Sewer Pipe Company* (1893). Connolly purchased pipe from the Union Sewer Company and was indebted to that firm on two notes. When sued for payment, he claimed that Union Sewer Company was a trust and, since the Illinois Antitrust Act provided that purchasers of articles from a trust were not liable for the purchase price, he consequently contended that he had no obligation. The Sewer Company claimed that the State Antitrust Act violated the equal protection clause of the Fourteenth Amendment by exempting "agricultural products or livestock while in the hands of producer or raiser." This view was supported by both the Federal District Court and the United States Supreme Court.

Essentially similar provisions in state antitrust legislation in Texas, Colorado, California, and Kentucky were held invalid over the next thirty years. The results of these decisions were twofold: (1) Variations in the application of state antitrust legislation based on special classifications (agricultural or otherwise) were frowned upon; and (2) these decisions invalidated the entire state antitrust laws in the states in which they were handed down.

• *Liberty Warehouse Company v. Burley Tobacco Growers' Cooperative Association* (1928). In this case, the Supreme Court of the United States upheld the right

---

[3]Hulbert and Mischler, op. cit., p. 158.

SPECIAL LEGAL PROBLEMS

of the tobacco cooperative to provide in its bylaws for recovery of damages from third parties who purchased tobacco from a cooperative member when they knew that the member was committed to market only through the cooperative. This decision came after passage of the Bingham Act in Kentucky. It reflected both (1) the state legislature's willingness, as a matter of public policy, to recognize the unique nature of agriculture and the cooperatives farmers organized to provide the services they desired; and (2) a changed attitude on the part of courts as to the rights of the state to specify how cooperatives could be organized and operated.

The State Supreme Court in Florida, for example, held that state's antitrust statute constitutional even though it excluded agricultural, horticultural, and nonprofit associations from terms of the statute. The court stated: "Orderly, systematized cooperative marketing associations have no analogy to financial combinations in restraint of trade and by a parity of reason no analogy to combinations of skill and labor in the same enterprises to accomplish the same lawful purposes."

- *Tigner v. Texas* (1940). This case examined further the issue of whether farmers should be treated differently from persons engaged in other business activities. The case for such a classification was made by Justice Felix Frankfurter who, in giving the Supreme Court's decision, said: "Farmers are widely scattered and inured to habits of individualism: their economic fate was, in large measure, dependent upon the contingencies beyond their control. In these circumstances, legislators may well have thought combinations of farmers and stockmen presented no threat to the community or, at least, the threat was of a different order from that arising through combinations of industrialists and middlemen." The effect of this decision was to overrule the Connolly case.
- *Cape Cod Food Products v. National Cranberry Association* (1954). The significance of this case is found in the Federal District Court's charge to the jury which stated: "It is not unlawful under antitrust acts for a Capper-Volstead cooperative, such as the National Cranberry Association admittedly is, to try to acquire even 100 percent of the market if it does so exclusively through marketing agreements approved under the Capper-Volstead Act. . . ."

Court Decisions Relating to Federal Legislation

Among the hundreds of cases relating to federal legislation that have been tried in the courts, seven will be reviewed briefly because of their special significance:

- *United States v. Borden Company* (1939). This case was important because it started to establish perimeters on the application of antitrust legislation to cooperatives. Prior to this case, the idea was rather widely held that antitrust action could be brought against a cooperative only by the Secretary of Agriculture. In fact, in 1930 an opinion by the Attorney General held that cooperatives had complete immunity from the antitrust laws. This was changed, however, by the decision written by Chief Justice Charles Hughes in *United States v. Borden Company*.

This case was brought by the Antitrust Division of the Justice Department, which charged a cooperative with conspiring with the Borden Company and others to fix the retail price of the milk it provided for its dealers. The cooperative contended that the provisions of the Capper-Volstead Act gave it immunity from prosecution. The Court held that when a cooperative enters into an agreement with third persons, it has no special immunity and it should be treated under antitrust legislation on the same basis as any other corporation.

The Supreme Court, after reviewing the provisions of the Clayton Act and the Capper-Volstead Act, stated that "we cannot find in the Capper-Volstead Act . . . an intention to declare immunity for the combinations and conspiracies charged in the present indictment."

In other words, the rights of producers to unite to market their products did not authorize conspiracies with others to restrain trade by maintaining artificial and noncompetitive prices for fluid milk.

- *United States v. Maryland Cooperative Milk Producers and Maryland and Virginia Milk Producers Association, Inc.* (1956). In this case the two cooperatives were indicted for conducting an unlawful combination and conspiracy to fix prices at which milk was sold to distributors. The cooperatives agreed that they combined to form a common marketing agency, but contended that this was permissible under provisions of the Capper-Volstead Act. In handing down its decision, the Court held that "a combination between two or more agricultural cooperatives to fix prices of their products is exempt from provisions of antitrust laws providing no other person that is not of such an organization or a member of such a group is part of the combination."

This decision gave legal approval to the establishment of sales agencies in common by cooperatives as authorized by the Capper-Volstead Act, provided they functioned in a legal manner. It also distinguished between illegal combinations that involved third parties and legal combinations involving only cooperatives. The theory was that the effect of such agreements between cooperatives is the same as the effect of members' forming one cooperative rather than two.

- *United States v. Maryland and Virginia Milk Producers Association, Inc.* (1960). This case examined further the provisions of antitrust legislation as it related to the rights of cooperatives to merge or acquire other commercial firms. The facts of the case were, briefly:

    1. The Maryland and Virginia Association controlled about 86 percent of the milk marketed in the Washington metropolitan area.
    2. The Maryland and Virginia Association acquired Embassy Dairy, Inc., which represented an additional 10 percent of the milk sold in the area. Since Embassy was able to purchase local milk on a different price basis from that available to Maryland and Virginia, and since it also purchased some less expensive milk outside the Washington area, it was able to compete aggressively with Maryland and Virginia for the business of government installations in the Washington area.
    3. The Antitrust Division of the Justice Department contended that the Maryland Virginia Association had purchased Embassy Dairy in order to eliminate that firm as an outlet for the milk of producers who were not cooperative members and thus to monopolize the market.
    4. The cooperative was also charged with predatory trade practices, which included interference with shipments of nonmember milk, trying to induce a distributor to

switch market outlets from the cooperative's territory, encouraging its members to boycott a business to force it to deal with the cooperative, using economic power to compel a firm to deal with the cooperative, and buying out a competitor at an excessive price to eliminate competition.

Maryland and Virginia Milk Producers Association built its defense on the fact that it was a cooperative composed exclusively of dairy farmers and that, as such, it was exempt and immunized by section 6 of the Clayton Act and sections 1 and 2 of the Capper-Volstead Act.

The United States District Court, which first heard the case, held that "an agricultural cooperative is entirely exempt from provisions of the antitrust laws, both as to its very existence as well as to all its activities, provided it does not enter into conspiracies or combinations with persons who are not producers of agricultural products." It therefore dismissed the monopolization charge which was based on paragraph 2 of the Sherman Act. The District Court, however, upheld the right of the government to go to trial under other provisions of the Sherman Act and section 7 of the Clayton Act, because in dealing with Embassy Dairy the cooperative was dealing with third persons. The Court ordered the Association to divest itself of Embassy Dairy and to cancel all contracts ancillary to the acquisition. Both parties to the trial appealed.

Justice Hugo Black, in writing the decision of the United States Supreme Court, stated that it "unequivocally rejected" the cooperatives' argument that section 2 of the Capper-Volstead Act excluded prosecutions under the Sherman Act. He held further that the reasoning of the Borden case applied, and stated: "We do not believe that Congress intended to immunize cooperatives engaged in competition-stifling practices from prosecution under the anti-monopolization provisions of paragraph 2 of the Sherman Act while making them responsible for such practices as violations of the anti-trade restraint provisions of paragraphs 1 and 3 of this act." The U.S. Supreme Court reversed the dismissal of monopoly charges under paragraph 2 of the Sherman Act with the statement: "It was an error of the District Court to dismiss the paragraph 2 charge." At the same time it upheld the judgment of the District Court relative to its ruling requiring that the cooperative divest itself of Embassy Dairy, on the grounds that neither section 7 of the Clayton Act nor the Capper-Volstead Act condoned predatory practices.

- *Sunkist v. Winckler and Smith Citrus Products* (1962). This suit, which involved treble damages, was brought against Sunkist Growers, Inc., and the Exchange Orange Products Company, a wholly owned subsidiary and part of the Sunkist system. It was charged that Sunkist had conspired with the Exchange Lemon Products Company by refusing to sell oranges to the plaintiff. Both the trial court and the Ninth Circuit Court held that the plaintiff had been damaged. The trial court placed the damages at about $500,000; the Ninth Circuit Court placed them at a lower amount.

Sunkist Growers appealed and contended that ". . . under the exemptions from antitrust laws granted agricultural associations, . . . Sunkist, Exchange Orange and Exchange Lemon being made up of the same growers and associations, cannot be charged with conspiracy among themselves." This argument was accepted by the U.S.

Supreme Court, which held erroneous the previous theories of liability upon which the case rested. In effect, the Court said, the various wholly owned subsidiaries of the Sunkist system should be treated as one and therefore the cooperative could not conspire with itself.

- *Case-Swayne Co. v. Sunkist Grower, Inc.* (1967). The Case-Swayne Company, a manufacturer of single-strength orange juice and other blended orange juices, charged Sunkist Growers with conspiracy in restraint of trade, in violation of section 1 of the Sherman Act. Accordingly, it filed for treble damages on the grounds that the cooperative had limited the supply of citrus fruit available to the company.

The Court of Appeals for the Ninth Circuit Court dismissed the case on the grounds that, irrespective of monopoly considerations, Sunkist Growers qualified as a cooperative under the Capper-Volstead Act. The case subsequently came before the U.S. Supreme Court, which said: "The issue is whether Sunkist is an association of persons engaged in the production of agricultural products as . . . fruit growers within the meaning of the Capper-Volstead Act, notwithstanding that some of its members are not actually growers. We hold that it is not."

The facts which led to this conclusion were:

1 The 12,000 members of Sunkist were organized into local associations. Of the associations, 80 percent by number and 82 percent by volume represented local fruit growers who marketed through the Sunkist system.

2 Substantially all the other members were nonproducers who purchased fruit that they marketed through the Sunkist system.

3 The nonproducers participated in the control of Sunkist on the same basis as member producers.

The issue was not the extent of nonmember business, but rather, that nonproducers participated as members in the control of Sunkist. Since they did, the association could not qualify for the protection of the Capper-Volstead Act and could not use it as a defense in the suit, which was centered on section 1 of the Sherman Act.[4]

- *Treasure Valley Potato Bargaining Association v. Ore-Ida Foods, Inc.* This case was especially important because the U.S. Supreme Court affirmed that the protection of the Capper-Volstead Act applied to bargaining cooperatives. In doing this, the Court decided that the activities of bargaining associations came within the meaning of the word "marketing" in that they negotiated contract sales for members of potato cooperatives. To the Court, marketing was "the aggregate of functions involved

---

[4]The producer issue is currently in litigation in the National Broiler Marketing Association case in the U.S. District Court in Atlanta. The members of the cooperative are using contract growers as a source of broilers, and the Department of Justice contends that the members are not true producers since the risk of production falls on the contract grower. On August 26, 1975, Judge Henderson, of the U.S. District Court for the Northern District of Georgia, ruled that members of the National Broiler Marketing Association were producers and "therefore qualify for the antitrust exemption provided by the Act." This ruling will probably be appealed by the Department of Justice.

in transferring title and in moving goods from the producer to the consumer. . . ." The Court also recognized the right of cooperatives to have marketing agents in common as provided by the Capper-Volstead Act.

- *United States v. Associated Milk Producers, Inc.*[5] In this case the government alleged that the association (AMPI) engaged in an illegal conspiracy to attempt to monopolize. More specifically, the complaint alleged that AMPI:

1. Depressed the price that competing producers could receive for their milk under the applicable federal milk-marketing order in various geographic areas by loading the pool, while insulating AMPI members from economic loss.
2. Agreed that processors who purchase milk from AMPI should not purchase milk from AMPI's competitors, or should pay a substantially higher price for milk than do their competitors who do not deal with AMPI's competitors.
3. Agreed that some processors should not sell or deliver milk acquired from AMPI to other processors except as directed by AMPI.
4. Agreed that haulers who haul milk produced by AMPI members should not haul milk produced by competitors of AMPI.
5. Acquired the business and assets of the processors of milk produced by competitors of AMPI and terminated that processing.
6. Acquired the business and assets of the haulers of milk produced by competitors of AMPI and terminated that transportation.
7. Compelled producer-members of AMPI to sign membership agreements which unreasonably restrained their right to withdraw from AMPI and to market milk in competition with AMPI.

While receiving wide attention, the charges brought against AMPI contained little that was new. They centered on points already shown to be illegal in the Borden and Maryland and Virginia cases.

The case was settled without trial in the District Court of western Missouri. The court recognized the legality of the cooperative's participation in common marketing agencies, of over-order pricing, and of the standby pool. At the same time, the consent decree signed by Judge John W. Oliver covered, among other things, (1) restrictions on cooperative actions concerning haulers, processors, and relations with members; and (2) enjoinment, for specified periods, on cooperatives' refusing to receive and market milk of producers, on their voting on behalf of members relative to termination of existing federal milk-marketing orders, and on their purchasing or consolidating with, or acquiring control of, other plants without prior approval of the Department of Justice or the court. The final judgment also prohibited Associated Milk Producers from making any contribution to regulatory agencies, required the amendation of bylaws to comply with provisions of the judgment, and specified that a copy of the decree be mailed to members and employees, to haulers transporting AMPI milk, and to handlers and purchasers with whom AMPI had marketing agreements.

---

[5] In addition to rulings on the antitrust issue, the Internal Revenue Service is claiming $16 million from AMPI for fraud and unpaid income tax items, some of which is disallowed and some which it reduced. In 1974, AMPI had pleaded guilty to making political donations to the Nixon reelection campaign and to Democratic presidential hopefuls. The cooperative is appealing the tax and fraud charges.

STATUS OF COOPERATIVES UNDER ANTITRUST LEGISLATION

Much uncertainty exists as to the status of cooperatives under antitrust legislation. What is more, this status is subject to change with new court decisions and rulings of regulatory agencies, some of which are not known to be friendly to cooperatives. In general, however, it appears that:

- There is no question about the right of cooperatives to organize. Their existence is not evidence of restraint in trade.
- When marketing cooperatives are dealing with third parties, their dealings will have the same status as if two firms other than cooperatives were engaging in similar deals.
- Marketing cooperatives that comply with provisions of the Capper-Volstead Act in all likelihood can merge, irrespective of the volume of business that results.
- Other cooperatives may also merge, but the merger apparently will be viewed according to the same standards that apply to the merger of firms other than cooperatives.
- The Capper-Volstead type of cooperatives may meet and agree on prices. The theory is that such meetings in reality are no different from those of producers who have organized one cooperative.
- Although there has been no legal decision on the subject, Antitrust Division statements suggest that cooperatives may not enter into agreements with their members to restrict production. On this issue, the Cooperative Marketing Act of 1926 provides that farmers "may acquire, exchange, interpret, and disseminate part, present, and prospective crop, market, statistical, and economic and other similar information by direct exchange between such persons, and/or such associations or federations thereof and/or through a common agent created or selected by them." It is obvious, however, that cooperatives may carry on aggressive programs to acquaint members with production-price relationships.
- Under antitrust legislation, cooperatives may actively seek to improve operating efficiency, to expand services provided through internal growth resulting from further horizontal and vertical integration, and to form federations and achieve more voluntary cooperation between cooperatives.

Capper-Volstead Modification Considered

We have mentioned that the Capper-Volstead Act has never been amended. Both cooperative supporters and opponents, however, have explored the possibility of amending this legislation.

Raymond J. Mischler,[6] formerly cooperative attorney in the Office of the General

---

[6]Notwithstanding statements by Hulbert, Mischler, and others that the Capper-Volstead Act basically is an act authorizing the existence of cooperatives rather than legislation granting them immunity and exemption from antitrust legislation, we have noted previously that many cooperative leaders, the courts, and government officials have continued to disabuse themselves of the idea that the Capper-Volstead Act grants substantial antitrust exemption to cooperatives. What the act originally did was to sanction the organization of cooperatives and thus to attempt to give cooperatives equality with other firms, while at the same time seeking to protect consumers from enhancement of prices by cooperatives. It was not widely accepted that organized cooperatives were subject to antitrust legislation on substantially the same basis as their counterparts in the business arena.

Counsel, U.S. Department of Agriculture, identified the basic issue confronting cooperatives in his question: "What are the limits within which a cooperative can acquire the stock or assets of another corporation by purchase, merger, or consolidation?" In an attempt to dispel these and other uncertainties as to the scope of the Capper-Volstead Act, cooperatives were the first to attempt to modify the act. They were prompted to strengthen the legislation by the concern that arose over the government's case against the Maryland and Virginia Milk Producers Association.

In support of cooperative interests, in 1959 Senator Russell Long introduced a bill to clarify and amend the Capper-Volstead Act. He stated that the basic objective of the bill was "to make clear that farmers and farmers' cooperatives should be able to acquire processing and marketing facilities." He further stated: "Monopolistic giants (large dairy corporations) continue their strangle hold on the American economy while the Justice Department seems to be very little concerned about that which is happening." There was considerable cooperative support for the bill, but the Department of Agriculture's recommendation to defer action until the Maryland and Virginia case was decided prevailed.

The Supreme Court decision on the Maryland and Virginia case prompted further efforts by cooperatives to amend the Capper-Volstead Act. In 1960, President-elect Kennedy said that "early next year" legislation would be recommended to Congress to "clarify the Capper-Volstead Act so that farmers would have adequate legal protection to act together effectively and efficiently in processing and marketing their products." To this end, the Senate Agricultural Committee approved a provision in the farm bill to amend the Capper-Volstead Act to permit cooperatives to purchase, merge, or consolidate with other companies. Many cooperative leaders, however, believed that such an amendment would be unwise. Moreover, Senator Estes Kefauver strongly opposed all provisions relating to cooperatives, and in the Senate-House conference on the bill, it was deleted as "unnecessary and a mere restatement of existing law."

In 1963, legislation was proposed that provided for premerger review by the Secretary of Agriculture. This legislation, however, was never enacted.

During the 1950s and early 1960s, the views expressed by high officials in the Justice Department and the Federal Trade Commission were quite favorable to cooperatives. For example:

• In a talk made in 1953, Stanley H. Barnes, then assistant chief of the Antitrust Division, U.S. Department of Justice, recognized the increasing importance of cooperatives. He closed his talk by saying that the strengthening and advancement of agricultural cooperatives "does not depend on license to act outside the antitrust laws—it depends rather on ability to live in 'cooperation' with them." He looked on the cooperatives' ability to do so, however, as one of the simpler tasks confronting them.

• Even more favorable were comments by Everett MacIntyre, a member of the Federal Trade Commission. In a talk before the American Institute of Cooperation, in 1965 he expressed the view that any hard-core violations of antitrust laws by cooperatives could be prosecuted as in the past. He also stated his belief that cooperatives were antimonopoly in effect and that "strengthening farmer cooperatives may play an important complementary role supplementing the enforcement of antitrust statutes."

He further said:

It is not a violation of the Sherman Act or any other antitrust act for a Capper-Volstead cooperative to acquire a large, even a 100 percent, position in a market if it does it solely through those steps which involve cooperative purchasing and cooperative selling. On the other hand, it would be a violation of the law, and it would be a prohibited monopolization for a person or group of persons to seek to secure a dominant share of the market through a restraint of trade which was prohibited, or through a predatory practice, or through the bad faith use of otherwise legitimate devices.

The backwash of the Watergate scandals, which involved several dairy cooperatives in illegal campaign contributions, ushered in a changed environment for cooperatives with respect to antitrust problems. Following this exposure the U.S. Department of Justice charged AMPI and Mid-American Dairymen, Inc., with violations of the Sherman Act. Furthermore, Thomas E. Kauper, assistant attorney general, Antitrust Division of the Justice Department, in the Hearings on Monopolistic Practices and Concentration in the Food Industry before the Antitrust Subcommittee of the House Judiciary Committee in 1973, expressed concern about what he referred to as the immunity conferred on marketing cooperatives by the Clayton Act and the Capper-Volstead Act. He also mentioned the possibility of "super co-ops" raising food prices and the need for "congressional reevaluation of antitrust immunity by cooperatives," and he even spoke of imposing size limitations on cooperatives.[7]

An unusual development in 1974 was the establishment of a Republican task force on antitrust and monopoly. This committee, interestingly enough, was headed by H. J. Heinz III, scion of the founder of the H. J. Heinz Company, famous for its "57 varieties." The investigation was a political venture designed to enhance the GOP image by attempting to examine rising food prices. Much of the testimony was slanted. Kauper again used it as a sounding board to express anticooperative views.

Secretary of Agriculture Earl Butz was quoted in committee minutes as saying, "Some cooperatives may have outgrown the need for some of the special privileges to which they are entitled under current law." He further said, "These privileges are derived not only from Capper-Volstead but also from tax laws.[8]

---

[7]In answering these assertions, Kenneth D. Naden, executive vice president of the National Council of Farmer Cooperatives, in a letter to Peter W. Rodino, Jr., chairman of the House Committee on the Judiciary, stated:

The statement of Thomas E. Kauper, . . . before your Subcommittee . . . raised by direct implication an accusation that cooperatives are enhancing food prices to the detriment of the public interest. Such a statement is alarming since it indicates an appalling lack of sound economic analysis and judgment. Indeed, farmers and their cooperatives should be the last area to be considered as a possible cause of unduly high food prices.

Justice made a gigantic and unjustified leap from its experience with a few alleged unfair trade practices to a broad generalization about the market power of all large cooperatives. . . .

The Department doesn't recognize there is a fundamental difference between concentration which increases competition in the interest of consumers and that which decreases competition to the detriment of consumers.

[8]It would be commendable to encourage an objective study to determine the merits of such assertions. It would also be commendable if U.S. Department of Agriculture officials would encourage an objective study of the extent to which cooperatives may serve as a competitive force that supplements antitrust laws.

As the committee members gained an appreciation of the political implications of the testimony of special-interest groups, they recognized the impact of inflation on food prices and reported: "We have seen that farmers and their cooperatives are essential to the nation's production and distribution of agricultural products."

In 1975, the Justice Department continued its attack on cooperatives. Keith I. Clearwaters, deputy assistant attorney general for Antitrust, suggested the following as possible modifications of the Capper-Volstead Act.:

- Requiring the Secretary of Agriculture to "clear" the expansion of a cooperative, with provisions that every farmer cooperative be licensed and that the license be renewed every five years.
- Removing section 2 of the Capper-Volstead Act. It states that the Secretary of Agriculture is the authority to determine when and if a cooperative causes "undue enhancement of prices."
- Adding a specific provision that the Capper-Volstead Act doesn't protect cooperatives from challenges to their mergers under section 7 of the Clayton Act.
- Amending the Capper-Volstead Act so that long-term membership clauses, and other conditions of cooperative participation that appear to limit the freedom of farmers to move in or out of a cooperative, would be prohibited.

Such proposed restrictive requirements raise several questions. If it is increased competition that is desired, the Justice Department might well listen to the recommendations of the National Commission on Food Marketing, which suggested that stronger cooperatives, instead of contributing to a monopoly situation, actually would be a force for increased competition.

Does the Justice Department mean to imply that cooperatives are immune from unlawful conduct? Certainly facts do not support any such contention. Obviously, the real problem is the domination of the food industry by giant food-processing and retailing corporations rather than cooperatives. It should be rememberd that, in the mid-1970s, the Federal Trade Commission has even questioned its own ability to investigate the concentration of monopoly power such as that developed by ITT and some of the other giant conglomerates in the business world.

Students of antitrust issues have emphasized that if the Justice Department were really interested in tackling the problem, it would look into the operation of the mammoth conglomerates—those handling cereals, soups, baby foods, soft drinks, and dessert mixes, to mention a few—that are in a position really to monopolize markets.[9]

Cooperatives have a minimum of monopoly power because (1) they cannot curtail output, (2) they cannot permanently withhold production from the market, (3) they cannot prevent substitution of most products, (4) they cannot exclude others from entering a market, and (5) they cannot, as a rule, influence prices to wholesalers and retail distributors substantially or prevent prices from going up or down in response to

---

[9] On this point Willard Mueller (in *Economic Issues,* June 1975) expresses general agreement with Prof. John Kenneth Galbraith's view that antitrust laws are a mere charade because of their failure to challenge the big corporations. Mueller states: "Galbraith is correct that the trust-busters have not laid siege to the many existing citadels of market power, have not indeed even kept their siege guns free from rust."

changing supply and demand conditions. (Data presented in Chapter 6, Cooperative Growth in the United States, emphasize the very modest economic position of cooperatives when compared with other segments of the economy.)

MARKETING CONTRACTS AND MARKETING AGREEMENTS AND ORDERS

Marketing Contracts

The unique nature of cooperative operations has resulted in the use of marketing contracts by many cooperatives. To be effective, the use of contracts must result in mutual advantages for both the member and the cooperative. When members agree to market products through their cooperative, the cooperative assumes responsibility to sell these products.

Marketing contracts are beneficial in that they assure members of an outlet for their products and reward their loyalty to the cooperative by preventing disruptive influences by minority or outside groups. The cooperative also benefits from well-executed marketing contracts. They provide reasonable assurance of a given volume of business, eliminate the need for patronage solicitation, and give the association a better business image among members, the trade, and agencies providing credit.

The marketing contract has specific provisions as to the rights and duties of the signers, the obligations of the cooperative, and measures that may be taken if contracts are broken. Contracts may be separate legal documents or they may be a part of an association's bylaws. Marvin A. Schaars, in *Cooperatives, Principles and Practices*,[10] states: "The prevailing practice now is to use the contract during the early years of the association, but to discontinue its use as the organization becomes established."

Types of Contracts Cooperative marketing contracts may be classified in different ways, not all of them mutually exclusive. The specific types merit brief discussion here.

- *Agency.* In this type of contract, the cooperative acts as an agent for members who maintain the ownership and identity of their individual products.
- *Outright purchase and sale.* This contract specifies a definite price or a basis by which price is determined for the producer's products. The cooperative buys the members' products outright, thereby taking title to them. As a general rule, credit agencies and the trade look with more favor on purchase and sales contracts because the cooperative has greater control over the product it owns. As a consequence, they can deal with the cooperative on a more secure basis than if they use agency contracts with its members.
- *Maintenance or output.* The primary feature of this type of marketing contract is that the seller agrees to sell to the cooperative all the products specified in the contract, and the cooperative agrees to purchase all these products. The result of such a contract is that the seller has a market for his or her product and the cooperative has a more realistic basis for ascertaining the volume it will handle. To enforce these provi-

[10]University of Wisconsin—Extension, Madison, 1971, p. 63.

sions, cooperatives, going back to the *Reeves v. Decorah* case, provide for liquidated damages in the event of noncompliance by the seller. This penalty usually takes the form of a specified payment of so much per unit of produce sold outside of the cooperative. The chief purpose is to counter the problem of vacillating member support and to build association stability. As indicated previously, the courts have overruled *Reeves v. Decorah* and this contract provision has enjoyed long-standing legal acceptance.

• *Full supply*. As cooperatives have become a more important market factor, they have developed contractual arrangements with firms to which they sell products. For example, the cooperative will sell a milk distributor all the milk it requires and the distributor will agree to purchase all the milk it needs from the cooperative. Professor Willard F. Mueller, in "The Economics and Law of Full Supply Contracts as Used by Agricultural Cooperatives," *Proceedings of the National Symposium on Cooperatives and the Law,*[11] states: "Full supply contracts are not illegal *per se*, that is, the so-called rule of reason is applied in judging the legality of such conduct." He suggests that such contracts have "anticompetitive potential" because of their "capacity to foreclose markets." The prevailing view of the courts was well expressed in *United States v. Maryland and Virginia Milk Producers*. While the court in this case stated that the government's case was "barren of proof that the full supply contracts were made for illegal purposes" and was "merely economic hypothesis," it stated that "full supply contracts are illegal when made for the purpose of elimination and suppressing competition. . . ." In other words, cooperatives must not engage in boycotts, acquisitions, predatory practices, or coercion to get purchasers of their products to agree to full supply contracts. This general view has been supported by numerous legal decisions.

On the other hand, Mueller further suggests that "relative strength of the parties" may be used as a criterion to determine the reasonableness of full supply contracts. He points out that unless cooperatives have the protection of such contracts with firms, "There are four ways oligopolists can destroy cooperatives: (1) offering higher prices to non-members than to members, (2) refusing to buy from cooperative members, (3) employing partial integration into farm production, and (4) engaging in order-of-buying discrimination . . . forcing the cooperative to carry the surplus."

• *Tie-in*. In a tie-in contract, a buyer or seller of milk, for example, agrees to do business with the supplier or purchaser of the milk only if there is an agreement to handle another product, say farm supplies. Although the courts on occasion have approved tie-in contracts when they were necessary to the adequate operation of the market for the product involved, the courts have usually disapproved of such contracts on the ground that they tend to limit competition.

General Provisions of Contracts   Contracts usually contain special provisions, supported by legal sanction with respect to:

1 *Time of becoming effective:* The general practice is to specify that contracts do not become effective until a specified acreage or volume has been obtained.

2 *Duration:* Most state laws specify the maximum time which a marketing contract may run—usually five to ten years but sometimes as long as fifteen or twenty years. Many contracts also have provisions for yearly self-renewal unless a member wishes to cancel the contract during certain specified periods.

[11]University of Wisconsin—Extension, Madison, 1974.

3 *Force and fraud:* Contracts obtained by force and fraud have been declared illegal.

4 *Third-party notice:* Some state laws provide that filing of contracts with proper agencies is a notice to all interested persons of rights of the association and its members. For example, the Wisconsin cooperative law provides that such a contract be filed with the Register of Deeds of the County in which signers live. The law also prohibits anyone from interfering with compliance of contract provisions.

5 *Transfer of title:* Considerable confusion often exists as to the time when title passes in a contract. If the contract participants wish to pass title prior to the time of delivery of the product, it is important that the contract be "a contract of sale rather than a contract to sell." A contract of sale, for example, may be signed January 1 and provide for the transfer of title any time between January 1 and July 1, the date specified for delivery of the product.

A word of caution is in order as to what may be expected of marketing contracts. It is generally recognized that they strengthen the bargaining position of cooperatives and that they contribute to market stability. Some cooperative representatives see the need for member discipline and suggest that the use of contracts will go a long way in solving cooperative problems. The experience that cooperatives had with the "ironclad" contracts of Aaron Sapiro, however, indicates that nothing could be farther from the truth. For contracts to be effective, member education and communication and efficient business performance are the building blocks which cooperatives can use to help achieve their desired objectives. (Chapter 18 considers the relationship of contracts to bargaining associations, and *Legal Phases of Farmer Cooperatives*[12] covers important legal cases relating to marketing contracts.)

Marketing Agreements and Orders

Agricultural cooperatives, particularly bargaining associations, have an interest in marketing orders and agreements. Although the Agricultural Adjustment Act of 1933 provided federal authority to regulate the handling of milk, the Agricultural Marketing Agreements Act of 1937, as amended, is the enabling legislation authorizing marketing orders and agreements. This legislation was enacted in response to the low farm prices and chaotic marketing conditions for agricultural products that prevailed in the 1930s.

The basic objectives of the act are (1) to promote steady and dependable markets and assure reasonable prices in certain commodity markets, and (2) to provide consumers with adequate supplies of wholesome food. Thus, increased agricultural purchasing power and protection of consumer interests are criteria for guiding the administration of the act. The act also has provisions covering cooperative voting, pooling of returns, and services provided producers.

Although the 1937 act authorized both marketing orders and agreements, marketing orders are the principal ones that have been used. The reason is that they are mandatory on all handlers of a product in a given market. Marketing agreements, in contrast, are merely voluntary arrangements between handlers and the Secretary of

---

[12]FCS Bulletin 10, U.S. Department of Agriculture, Farmer Cooperative Service, Washington, 1958, pp. 89–120.

Agriculture. They involve only those who sign the agreement. Depending on how the agreement works out, those who do not sign may be benefited or harmed accordingly.

Three steps are involved in the development of marketing orders: (1) Interested producers petition the Secretary of Agriculture to hold a hearing; (2) under the jurisdiction of the Secretary of Agriculture, a public hearing is held if preliminary investigations appear to justify such action; and (3) this hearing is followed by a referendum to the producers.

Generally, approval of either two-thirds of the producers in a given market or producers handling two-thirds of volume sold in a market is required to make a marketing order effective. In addition, 50 percent of handlers must approve the order unless the Secretary of Agriculture, with the approval of the President, decides to, in the interest of market stability, approve the order even though less than 50 percent of the handlers sign the agreement. If approval is obtained, the provisions of the order apply to all producers in the market. The marketing order then becomes a legal instrument that imposes certain requirements on the handlers of the commodity involved. The 1937 act also specifically declared that marketing orders and agreements are not to be considered a violation of antitrust laws.

Federal orders and agreements were formulated to supplement similar state legislation by covering markets operating on an interstate basis. They have been developed primarily for fluid milk, fruits and vegetables, and tree nuts. Of these, milk marketing orders are the most important. In 1973, there were sixty-two milk marketing orders in effect; they accounted for 78 percent of all fluid milk sold. A number of other agricultural products are eligible for inclusion under marketing orders, but wheat, soybeans, feed grains, cotton, rice, livestock, and poultry and eggs are excluded in market-order programs.

Milk marketing orders are the only ones that have provisions for setting minimum prices to be paid producers by handlers for a specified volume of fluid milk. These orders are under supervision of a market administrator who is appointed by the Secretary of Agriculture. Fruit and vegetable marketing orders, in contrast, are operated by an industry administrative committee. Marketing orders for fruits and vegetables and tree nuts control the volume marketed through specific provisions as to quality and size of produce authorized for fresh markets.

Experience has demonstrated that marketing orders are more likely to be successful when certain conditions exist. The most important of these are:

- *Limited opportunities for substitution.* For example, it is more difficult to substitute for fluid milk than for butter or cheese, or for meats or feed grains.
- *Multimarket outlets for a product with different price elasticities.* Milk may be sold as fluid milk or as an ingredient for the manufacture of cheese, butter, or ice cream. The manufactured dairy items have greater price elasticity than has fluid milk. There also are quite distinct markets for most fresh and processed fruits and vegetables. The price is invariably less elastic for the fresh produce that for the processed produce.
- *Adequate volume control.* Limitations on the volume of milk that handlers must market as fluid milk, the establishment of a minimum price for this milk, and the establishment of quality and size provisions for fresh fruits and vegetables—these are the conditions that influence the volume of products moving to a given market, at least

in the short run. They help to explain why prices for most market-order produce are relatively inelastic when viewed on a short-run basis. They also help to explain why concentration of production in homogeneous areas may contribute to successful marketing-order administration.

- *Perishability.* There is general recognition in the trade that some kind of market regulation is essential if anything approaching orderly marketing is to prevail for perishable products.
- *Effective leadership.* The U.S. Department of Agriculture does not promote market orders. A knowledgeable leadership that understands the various economic, political, and social forces involved, and that is attuned to the legal implications that exist, appears to be essential for the effective establishment of marketing orders.

Relationship to Cooperatives Marketing orders and agreements create an environment that is conducive to bargaining by cooperatives. They do so for these reasons:

- Marketing orders, although they provide the mechanism for stabilizing markets, do not perform marketing functions, which is logically a responsibility of the bargaining cooperative.
- Marketing orders are flexible, and provisions take into account the special conditions that exist in the various markets where market orders are in force.
- The provisions of market orders add stability and regulate the volume of produce going to different types of markets.
- Marketing orders provide basic industry information for handler assessments, methods of covering expenses, reports required to administer the order, and specific provisions as to the duration of the program.
- The products for which marketing orders and agreements have been developed are also the ones that most successful bargaining cooperatives handle.

All these factors give security of expectation to bargaining cooperatives. They also provide an environment in which bargaining cooperatives can operate. These facts explain why a high degree of parallelism exists between marketing orders and bargaining associations. In effect, in most instances after the marketing orders and agreements establish a favorable institutional setting and provide the necessary control and regulatory tools, cooperatives become the implementing agency of producers. Thus, the tie-in between market-order programs and bargaining cooperatives is very close.

In the dairy industry, since farmers' production costs have increased, bargaining cooperatives in many markets have been able to treat the minimum prices established for fluid milk in milk marketing orders as minimum prices to which are added "over-order" prices for members who attempt to take into account their increased production costs. While it reflects little real understanding of the complexities of dairy marketing by the U.S. Department of Justice, over-order pricing is one of the reasons advanced by the Department for suggesting a reexamination of the marketing-orders and agreements program.

SUMMARY

Many legal problems confront cooperatives in all phases of their operations. Areas of special significance to them, however, are antitrust, contracts, and marketing orders

SPECIAL LEGAL PROBLEMS

and agreements. Cooperatives operate in a legislative and regulatory environment that is not always favorable to them. This in part is because legislators and regulatory agencies do not always recognize that if cooperatives are to achieve equal consideration, they may, because of their unique characteristics, have to receive different, if not sometimes special, treatment.

Important antitrust decisions have been handed down by both state and federal courts (see pp. 205–211). While much uncertainty prevails as to the antitrust status of cooperatives, it appears that (1) they can organize without being subject to antitrust legislation; (2) when dealing with third parties, they have the same antitrust status as do firms other than cooperatives; (3) marketing cooperatives can merge with other cooperatives; (4) marketing cooperatives can form a marketing agency in common, permitting them to meet and agree on prices; (5) although there is no legislation on the subject, statements by the U.S. Department of Justice officials suggest that they would look with disfavor on agreements by cooperatives to restrict production (a special limitation on cooperatives); (6) under antitrust legislation, cooperatives may actively seek to improve operating efficiency, expand services, and organize federations to achieve more voluntary cooperation between cooperatives; and (7) cooperatives other than marketing cooperatives have the same antitrust status as noncooperative business firms.

While the Capper-Volstead Act has never been amended, amendments were attempted unsuccessfully by cooperatives in the 1960s and have been suggested by the U.S. Department of Justice, an agency not known in the 1970s for its sympathetic views relative to cooperatives.

Contracts have become an important tool of cooperatives. When realistically developed, they have proven beneficial to cooperative members, cooperatives, and firms with which cooperatives trade. They are not a cure-all for all cooperative problems, however. To be most effective, they need to be supplemented with well-planned member information and communication programs as well as good business performance.

Marketing orders are tools to stabilize markets, assure reasonable prices, and protect consumers. In practice, bargaining cooperatives perform the marketing functions needed to implement the provisions of these orders. They are able to do so because the market environment created by marketing orders supplements and provides the basis upon which sound bargaining associations can operate.

QUESTIONS

1. How would you evaluate the legislative and regulatory environment confronting cooperatives?
2. What were the implications for cooperatives of such early state antitrust decisions as *Reeves v. Decorah Farmers Cooperative Society* and *Burns v. Wray Farmers Grain Company*?
3. Identify five important federal antitrust cases and briefly explain their implications for cooperatives.
4. What is the basis for contending that cooperatives are entitled to a different antitrust treatment from other firms? Is the result favoritism or an attempt to achieve equality for cooperatives?

5   What is the status of cooperatives under antitrust legislation? Are cooperatives exempt from antitrust laws?
6   Trace efforts to modify the Capper-Volstead Act.
7   Are the U.S. Department of Justice and the Federal Trade Commission justified in their recent observations and recommendations concerning modification of antitrust legislation as it relates to cooperatives?
8   What are the benefits of marketing contracts to cooperative members, cooperatives, and firms with which cooperatives deal?
9   What kinds of contracts are used by cooperatives?
10 What general provisions are covered in cooperative contracts?
11 Distinguish between marketing orders and marketing agreements.
12 In what ways are marketing orders and agreements helpful to farmers' bargaining associations?

REFERENCES

American Institute of Cooperation, *American Cooperation,* Washington. These yearly proceedings reports contain a number of articles on antitrust and related legal subjects. See especially the issues of 1974–75, pp. 182–193; 1968, pp. 136–146; 1966, pp. 38–44; 1965, pp. 179–191; and 1950, pp. 393–412.

Hulbert, Lyman S.: *Legal Phases of Farmer Cooperatives: Part III, Antitrust Laws,* FCS Information 70, U.S. Department of Agriculture, Farmer Cooperative Service, Washington, 1970, p. 57.

Jacobson, Robert: "Marketing Orders: Bargaining Aid on Vehicles," in *Bargaining in Agriculture: Potentials and Pitfalls in Collective Action,* North Central Regional Extension Publication 30, University of Missouri—Extension Division—C911, Columbia, 1971, pp. 34–39.

Knapp, Joseph G.: *Capper-Volstead Impact on Cooperative Structure,* FCS Information 70, U.S. Department of Agriculture, Farmer Cooperative Service, Washington, 1975, p. 42.

Mueller, Willard F.: "The Economics and Law of Full Supply Contracts as Used by Agricultural Cooperatives," in *Proceedings of the National Symposium on Cooperatives and the Law,* University of Wisconsin—Extension, Madison, 1974, pp. 99–131.

———: "Antitrust in a Planned Economy: An Anachronism or an Essential Component," *Journal of Economic Issues*, June 1975.

Rubel, Donald M., and Budd A. Holt: "Marketing Agreements," in *Marketing, Yearbook,* U.S. Department of Agriculture, 1954, pp. 357–365.

U.S. Department of Agriculture, "Questions and Answers on Federal Milk Marketing Orders," AMS 529, Washington, 1975.

Chapter 11

Cooperative Taxation

Cooperative taxation is a topic about which there is much confusion and misunderstanding. Cooperatives are subject to taxation by many of the over 2,000 tax entities existing in the United States. These entities have widely differing laws that result in much uncertainty with respect to property, franchise, sales, and income taxes.

Legal terminology, court decisions, and various rulings of the Internal Revenue Service and the Federal Trade Commission have also contributed to some of the confusion and misunderstanding that exist. In addition, there are indications that the distorted propaganda campaigns of opponents who seek to discredit the cooperative form of business enterprise have compounded the taxation issue. Moreover, cooperatives themselves have often intensified the problem by using incorrect terminology in their financial reports and in the statements of cooperative officials. This is so because they often use ordinary corporate terminology to describe operations, and such language can be quite misleading.

Some of the terms that have deepened misunderstanding of the tax issue are:

- *Exemption:* The term *exemption* is an example of the lack of precision when the income tax status of cooperatives is described. Legal and regulatory terminology has been saturated with this term even though provisions of the Revenue Act of 1951, as amended in 1954, show that the "exemption" label is erroneous. As we shall see, cooperatives in actual practice often operate in such a way as to have no income to tax.

• *Profits:* Another area of misunderstanding is found in the use of the term *profits*. If an organization operates in line with fundamental cooperative principles, it has a contractual obligation to allocate and return to patrons all funds remaining after the payment of expenses. Therefore, its net margins or savings belong to its patrons and constitute additional income upon which they are subject to income taxes. Such income belongs to the patrons, not the cooperative as an independent entity. Also misleading is the use of the term *earnings,* which is frequently used as a synonym for profits.

Cooperatives, however, may do some business with nonmember patrons on the same basis as ordinary business corporations. In other words, these nonmember patrons receive no patronage refunds. Cooperatives have profits on such business and should, and do, pay an income tax on these profits. This obligation emphasizes the need to understand just how cooperatives operate when describing their tax status and deciding on the terminology that best describes their actual situations.

• *Patronage dividends:* The term *patronage dividend* is also confusing when applied to the distribution of net margins or savings. Dividends are returns on capital investments and have no relation to returns made to patrons in proportion to the business they do with their cooperative. Although cooperatives may pay true dividends for the use of capital, the term *patronage refunds,* which describes how cooperatives distribute their net margins or savings, is an entirely different concept. The two should not be confused.

In this chapter we shall give attention to all types of taxation relating to cooperatives. While this issue primarily involves income taxes, attention also will be directed to property taxes and franchise and sales taxes.

PROPERTY TAXES

Buildings, office equipment, and other physical property owned by cooperatives are taxed in each state on the same basis as the property of other business firms. In all instances, these taxes are imposed in accordance with the rather broad powers of state or municipal subdivisions. There appears to be little support for the idea that the property of a cooperative, because it operates on a nonprofit basis, has a value different from what it would have if it were owned by a profit-oriented business.

In general, the tax liability on products a cooperative receives from its members is determined by its method of operation. For example, if the cooperative takes title to the products it handles, in all likelihood it will be subject to taxes on such products. Should the cooperative operate on an agency basis, it is not the owner of these products, and consequently it is not subject to a tax on them. By the same reasoning, bargaining cooperatives that do not take title to their members' products are not subject to a property tax on these products.

It is well established, however, that states may classify property and set such varying tax rates as they wish on different kinds of property. For example, the Kentucky General Assembly is authorized "to determine what class or classes of property shall be subject to local taxation." When the assembly of that state enacted legislation providing that "agricultural products in the hands of the producers or in the hands of any agent or agency of the producer" were exempt from the liability of local taxes, such classification was upheld by the courts. Likewise, an Arizona case held that the wholesaler who provides a cooperative with goods on consignment, rather than the cooperative, was subject to tax on these goods. In Montana, a cooperative irrigation company was held not liable for property tax on its lands on the theory that the value of all its property was reflected in the increased value of the land of its members and was taxed there.[1]

FRANCHISE, SALES, AND OTHER RELATED TAXES

The special status of cooperatives was first recognized in the War Revenue Act of 1898, which did not require local cooperatives to pay stamp taxes. In some instances, franchise taxes for cooperatives are smaller than those levied on other types of business. Often, the state laws under which they are incorporated provide that they pay an annual fee in lieu of various franchise, license, or corporation taxes. Depending on the provisions of state constitutions and tax legislation, courts usually have held that if specific exclusions of franchise taxes are spelled out, the unique and distinct nature of a cooperative will be recognized. For example, courts frequently have viewed a cooperative as an extension of its members' operations for franchise, sales, and other related tax purposes, and as such, they have recognized it as a nonprofit organization.

Usually, cooperatives are required to pay sales taxes on the same basis as other firms. The Pennsylvania State Supreme Court has held that if a tax is levied on business activities "related to profits realized," such a tax does not apply to a corporation operating as a cooperative because of its nonprofit character. Since cooperative stocks are not traded, stock transfer taxes do not apply to these associations.

On the federal level, cooperatives are treated the same as other businesses on social security taxes. Among the states and local jurisdictions, cooperatives and other businesses have substantially the same treatment for occupational, other licenses, and unemployment compensation taxes.

FEDERAL INCOME TAXES

This section deals primarily with farmers' marketing and purchasing cooperatives. Special legislation covers the taxation of farm credit, rural electric, and other cooperatives.

Early Income Tax Legislation

Starting in 1909 and continuing to the present day, the tax status of agricultural cooperatives has been subject to frequent legislative review. In addition, a continuous stream of tax rulings by the Internal Revenue Service (IRS) has given further interpretation to the legislation that has been enacted. As a result, the income tax position of cooperatives is constantly evolving. It will help us to understand the present tax status

---

[1]For important legal decisions on general taxes and income taxes as related to cooperatives, see D. Morrison Neely, *Legal Phases of Farmer Cooperatives, Part II: Federal Income Taxes*, FCS Information 69, U.S. Department of Agriculture, Farmer Cooperative Service, Washington, p. 101.

of cooperatives if we trace the early development of federal income tax legislation and examine in more detail the income status of cooperatives under the Revenue Act of 1951 as amended in 1954. Then we shall consider the present federal income tax position of cooperatives as covered in subchapter T, added to the Internal Revenue Code of 1954 by the 1962 Revenue Act and the modifications that have been made since then.

Some of the important early legislative acts that have contributed to the tax status of cooperatives are these:

- *The Revenue Act of 1913*. This act was the first tax measure after the adoption of the Sixteenth (income tax) Amendment to the Constitution in the same year. It did not mention cooperatives as such, but it exempted "certain types of non-profit concerns, including agricultural and horticultural associations." In practice, it was first interpreted by the IRS to include nonstock dairy cooperatives making "patronage dividends based on the percentage of butterfat in milk furnished the cooperatives." This ruling was soon modified to include dairy cooperatives organized with or without capital stock. The ruling also provided that cooperatives must file returns of annual net income; their reports could exclude amounts actually paid to members but could not exclude funds retained at the end of the year. The latter funds were taxable.
- *The Revenue Act of 1916*. This act gave federal income tax "exemptions" to those agricultural marketing cooperatives that dealt only with members.
- *The Revenue Act of 1921*. This act contained provisions that gave "tax exemptions" to farmer cooperatives acting as purchasing agents for "the purpose of purchasing supplies and equipment for the use of members in turning over special supplies and equipment at actual costs" and operating with capital stock. In 1922, IRS regulations under this act also authorized the accumulation of reasonable reserves.
- *The Revenue Act of 1924*. Regulations under this act used the word "producer" rather than "member." The regulations also provided that cooperatives might do a limited amount of dealing with nonmembers.
- *The Revenue Act of 1926*. This legislation provided that purchasing cooperatives might deal with nonmembers who were nonproducers to the extent of 15 percent of their business.
- *The Revenue Act of 1934*. This act provided that business done with the U.S. government should not be included in determining a cooperative's taxable income.

By 1934, thus, it was well established that farmers' marketing and purchasing cooperatives were not required to pay income taxes on net margins that they distributed as patronage refunds. No legal consideration, however, had been given to the income tax responsibilities of members or patrons for money received as patronage refunds.

The Revenue Act of 1951 as Amended in 1954

No significant change occurred in cooperative tax legislation between 1934 and 1951. Although it was recognized that farmer cooperatives, if they operated on a strictly cooperative basis, had no income to tax, it also was seen that not all patronage refunds were being taxed at the point where they represented taxable income.

The 1951 act, as far as farmers' marketing and farm supply cooperatives were concerned, therefore attempted to make certain that patronage refunds and dividends on stock would be taxed. The stated legislative objective of this act was to collect a single tax on these items at the patron's level.

Although the Internal Revenue Code of 1954 was completely revised, it made no change in the act of 1951 as it related to farmers' marketing and supply cooperatives except that section 101 (12)(A) of the 1939 Code was designated section 521, and section 101 (12)(B) became section 522. Because of their significance to cooperatives, these sections are reproduced here. Section 522 was repealed by the Revenue Act of 1962, but substantially the same deductions it authorized are also authorized in the more recently enacted section 1382(c) of subchapter T.

SEC. 521. EXEMPTION OF FARMERS' COOPERATIVES FROM TAX
(a) Exemption from Tax.—A farmers' cooperative organization described in subsection (b) (1) shall be exempt from taxation under this subtitle except as otherwise provided in section 522. Notwithstanding section 522, such an organization shall be considered an organization exempt from income taxes for purposes of any law which refers to organizations exempt from income taxes.

(b) Applicable Rules.—

    1 Exempt Farmers' Cooperatives.—The farmers' cooperatives exempt from taxation to the extent provided in subsection (a) are farmers', fruit growers', or like associations organized and operated on a cooperative basis (A) for the purpose of marketing the products of members or other producers, and turning back to them the proceeds of sales, less the necessary marketing expenses, on the basis of either the quantity or the value of the products furnished by them, or (B) for the purpose of purchasing supplies and equipment for the use of members or other persons, and turning over such supplies and equipment to them at actual cost, plus necessary expenses.

    2 Organizations Having Capital Stock.—Exemption shall not be denied any such association because it has capital stock, if the dividend rate of such stock is fixed at not to exceed the legal rate of interest in the State of incorporation or 8 percent per annum, whichever is greater, on the value of the consideration for which the stock was issued, and if substantially all such stock (other than nonvoting preferred stock, the owners of which are not entitled or permitted to participate directly or indirectly, in the profits of the association, upon dissolution or otherwise, beyond the fixed dividends) is owned by producers who market their products or purchase their supplies and equipment through the association.

    3 Organizations Maintaining Reserve.—Exemption shall not be denied any such association because there is accumulated and maintained by it a reserve required by State law or a reasonable reserve for any necessary purpose.

    4 Transactions with Nonmembers.—Exemption shall not be denied any such association which markets the products of nonmembers in an amount the value of which does not exceed the value of the products marketed for members, or which purchases supplies and equipment for nonmembers in an amount the value of which does not exceed the value of the supplies and equipment purchased for members, provided the value of the purchases made for persons who are neither members nor producers does not exceed 15 percent of the value of all its purchases.

    5 Business for the United States.—Business done for the United States or any of its agencies shall be disregarded in determining the right to exemption under this section.

Specific Requirements for Section 521 Status

To qualify for the tax treatment provided in section 521 of the Revenue Code of 1954, agricultural cooperatives must meet certain specific requirements.[2] These requirements are outlined in *Farmer Cooperatives in the United States*[3] as follows:

   1   It must be a farmer, fruit grower, or like association organized and operated on a cooperative basis to (a) market the products of members and other producers, or (b) purchase supplies and equipment for the use of members or other persons.
   2   If organized on a capital stock basis, substantially all its stock (other than preferred nonvoting stock) must be owned by producers marketing products or purchasing supplies through it.
   3   The dividend rate on capital shares must not exceed the legal rate of interest in the State of incorporation, or 8 percent a year, whichever is the greater, based upon the value of the consideration for which the capital shares were issued.
   4   Financial reserves are restricted to those required by State laws or those that are reasonable and necessary, and must be allocated to patrons unless the cooperative includes them in computing taxable income.
   5   Business with nonmembers may not exceed 50 percent of the cooperative's total business, and purchasing for persons who are neither members nor producers may not exceed 15 percent of the cooperative's total purchasing.
   6   Nonmembers are to be treated the same as members in such business transactions as pricing, pooling, or payment of sales proceeds, in prices of supplies and equipment, in fees charged for services, or in the allocation of patronage refunds to the accounts of patrons.
   7   Permanent records of the patronage and equity interest of all members and nonmembers must be maintained.
   8   The legal structure of the organization must be cooperative in character and contain no provisions inconsistent with these requirements, and the association must be actually operated in the manner and for the purposes outlined in the requirements.

SEC. 522. TAX ON FARMERS' COOPERATIVES
(a) Imposition of Tax.—An organization exempt from taxation under Section 521 shall be subject to the taxes imposed by section 11 or section 1201.

(b) Computation of Taxable Income.—
   1   General Rule.—In computing the taxable income of such an organization there shall be allowed as deductions from gross income (in addition to other deductions allowable under this chapter)—

   (A)   amounts paid as dividends during the taxable year on its capital stock, and
   (B)   amounts allocated during the taxable year to patrons with respect to its income not derived from patronage (whether or not such income was derived during such taxable year) whether paid in cash, merchandise, capital stock, revolving fund certificates, retain certificates, certificates of indebtedness, letters of advice, or in some other manner that discloses to

---

[2]D. Morrison Neely, ibid., pp. 36–63, covers important cases and regulations that apply to each of these requirements.
[3]FCS Bulletin 1, U.S. Department of Agriculture, Farmer Cooperative Service, Washington, 1965, pp. 19 and 20.

each patron the dollar amount allocated to him. Allocations made after the close of the taxable year and on or before the 15th day of the 9th month following the close of such year shall be considered as made on the last day of such taxable year to the extent the allocations are attributable to income derived before the close of such year.

2 Patronage Dividends, etc.—Patronage dividends, refunds, and rebates to patrons with respect to their patronage in the same or preceding years (whether paid in cash, merchandise, capital stock, revolving fund certificates, retain certificates, certificates of indebtedness, letters of advice, or in some other manner that discloses to each patron the dollar amount of such dividend, refund, or rebate) shall be taken into account in computing taxable income in the same manner as in the case of a cooperative organization not exempt under section 521. Such dividends, refunds, and rebates made after the close of the taxable year and on or before the 15th day of the 9th month following the close of such year shall be considered as made on the last day of such taxable year to the extent the dividends, refunds, or rebates, are attributable to patronage occurring before the close of such year.

The essential features of section 522 for cooperatives that qualified under section 521 were that they could exclude from gross income:

- All payments of dividends during the taxable year
- Nonpatronage income allocated to patrons during the taxable year derived from business with government agencies, rent, investments, and similar items
- Patronage dividends (refunds) to patrons, to be made in accordance with preexisting agreement and returned or allocated before the fifteenth day of the ninth month following the close of the fiscal year

Thus, cooperatives, in practice, no longer had "exemption" from income tax under section 521. What developed was a recognition of conditions under which a cooperative had no income to tax. Basically, a cooperative has no taxable income when it distributes net margins remaining after paying all expenses to patrons in accordance with prior mandatory obligations to do so.

Under section 522, farmers' marketing and purchasing cooperatives—those qualified under section 521 and others—were subject to normal, surtax, and capital gains taxes the same as other corporations. Section 314 of the 1951 Revenue Act authorized these cooperatives to make certain deductions and other adjustments in computing their statutory net income. Complying associations could exclude from gross income the patronage refunds made under prior mandatory obligations.

Status of Patronage Refunds

The basic feature of the 1951 Revenue Act related to conditions under which cooperatives might exclude patronage refunds from gross income. In 1951 the Treasury Department developed a memorandum on this subject. Since this is a basic position document on the subject and applies to all cooperatives, its essential features are reproduced here.[4]

[4]Neely, op. cit., part I, p. 11.

A taxable cooperative is a cooperative other than a farm cooperative specifically exempt from income tax under section 101 (12) (now section 521) of the Internal Revenue Code. It is subject to the corporate tax. However, if a cooperative has agreed at the time of any sale to or purchase from its patrons to allocate or return to them any net proceeds of the current year in proportion to patronage, it can compute its tax only on the amount of its net proceeds which have not been so allocated or returned as "patronage dividends." It should be noted that, if only members of the cooperative may receive patronage dividends, the cooperative may not omit from gross income the portion of any distributions to members which represents profits from dealings with nonmembers.

This treatment of patronage dividends has been a long-established practice of the Bureau of Internal Revenue. Such treatment, at the time of its adoption, was based on the theory that amounts allocated or returned as patronage dividends represented a reduction in cost to the patron of goods purchased by him through the cooperative or an additional consideration due the patron for goods sold by him through the cooperative.

Innumerable legal cases have supported and elaborated on the basic provisions of this memorandum as they apply to "521" cooperatives (those that qualified under section 521), other cooperatives, and other corporations operating on a cooperative basis.[5] The distinguishing feature of 521 cooperatives is that only they are permitted to deduct as business expenses: (1) dividends paid on stock or other equity interests during the taxable year, and (2) amounts allocated patrons on nonpatronage business, such as business done with the U.S. government, rents, investment revenues, and sale of depreciated property.

The Revenue Act of 1962 as Amended in 1966 and 1969

The belief that the Revenue Act of 1954 assured that a single tax on patronage refunds would be paid by patrons of a cooperative was shattered by two legal decisions in the 1950s.

In *Commissioner v. B. A. Carpenter* (1955), the court took the position that patronage refunds paid on a cash tax basis to members were reportable when made or allocated by their cooperative, but only at "the fair market value" if made in a noncash form.

In *Long Poultry Farms, Inc., v. Commissioner* (1957), the court held that for patrons reporting on an accrual basis, noncash patronage refunds allocated to them were not an accrued item in the year in which the allocation was made.

These decisions and subsequent IRS rulings had the effect of undermining the single-tax theory that presumably had been well established by the Revenue Act of 1951. As a result of these decisions, the 1951 act no longer achieved the congressional intent desired, and corrective action was attempted through the Revenue Act of 1962. This act, in effect, was designed to assure that amounts distributed to patrons by their cooperatives would be taken into account by either the patrons or the cooperatives for income tax purposes. In other words, the main focus was not on cooperatives but on their patrons.

[5]See, for example, *Appeal of Paducah and Illinois Railroad Co.*, 2 B.T.A. 1001 (1925).

The 1962 act applies to "any corporation operating on a cooperative basis" which includes organizations qualifying under section 521 of the 1951 Revenue Act. As indicated previously, it repealed section 522, and most of the significant provisions of section 522 were included in section 1382(c) of subchapter T.

Taxation of Patronage Refunds

To assure that patronage refunds are taxed at the patron level, subchapter T provides either that the written notice of allocation must be redeemable within ninety days of its issuance or that patrons must agree to include these amounts as a part of their income for tax purposes. If they do not agree to do this, the cooperative is required to consider these amounts as income for its own tax purposes, even though it may meet all provisions of section 521. Thus, either the patron or the cooperative is taxed.

Patron Consent The act provides that the patron's consent to include the full value of all allocations from the cooperative in his or her tax returns may be given in three ways.

- The patron may send an individually written consent to the cooperative before the end of the year in which the patronage occurs. This statement remains in effect unless revoked in writing.
- The patron may consent by becoming, or continuing as, a member following the adoption (after October 16, 1962) of a bylaw provision by the cooperative that states that membership constitutes such consent. This is known as *bylaw consent* and is effective only after the patron individually receives a copy of the cooperative's bylaws, together with a written statement that explains the significance of this provision.
- The patron may consent by endorsing and cashing a qualified check that represents at least 20 percent of the patronage refund not later than ninety days after the close of the payment period of the cooperative's taxable year and that bears the printed statement that such endorsement constitutes patron consent.

The act also has provisions covering methods of giving notice of cooperative *allocations* to members. Allocations mean capital stock, revolving fund certificates, certificates of indebtedness, letters of advice, or other written notices which disclose the amount allocated to the patron.

A *qualified written notice of allocation* must be provided for patrons who report such allocations as a part of their taxable income. Such a notice (1) must be in writing, (2) must provide that the patron has the option to redeem his or her allocation at face value within ninety days of issue or include it in taxable income, and (3) must be distributed together with the patronage refund, at least 20 percent of which must be in money or in a qualified check. Patronage refunds must be paid patrons by the cooperative within eight months and fifteen days following the close of the taxable year.

If the provisions for qualifying allocations are not met, these allocations must be included in the cooperative's taxable income rather than in the taxable income of the patron. When the cooperative returns a nonqualified allocation to the patron in cash at a later date, it can claim this allocation as a deduction for income tax purposes. At the same time, the patron who receives this nonqualified allocation must take it into account when reporting taxable income.

The implications of these provisions are to let the patron, in effect, determine who pays the tax—the patron or the cooperative. The law and related regulations determine how a patron makes this decision and then how the individual and the cooperative are taxed.

Section 1388(a) defines a *patronage dividend* (patronage refund) ". . . to mean an amount paid to a patron by a cooperative (1) on the basis of quantity or value of business done with or for such patron, (2) under an obligation of the cooperative to pay such amount which obligation existed before the cooperative received the amount so paid, and (3) which is determined by reference to the 'net earnings' of the cooperative from business done with or for its patrons.''

Taxation of Section 521 Cooperatives

Except for greater leeway given patrons in determining how and when allocations are paid, the tax status of section 521 cooperatives under the 1962 Revenue Act is substantially the same as under the 1951 Revenue Act.

To summarize again, specific tax provisions are:

- Amounts paid to members as dividends on capital stock or other equities may be deducted by the cooperative in determining its taxable income.
- Income allocated to patrons from nonpatronage business, such as business with the United States government, rents, or returns on invested capital, may also be deducted by the cooperative in determining its taxable income.
- Cooperatives seeking to qualify as section 521 cooperatives must request and receive a "letter of exemption" from the District Director of the Internal Revenue Service. This is done by filing Form 1028, which provides basic information on how the cooperative is organized and operated. Once a letter of exemption is obtained, the cooperative need only refile Form 1028 if it substantially changes its method of organization and ways of operation.
- Cooperatives that qualify as section 521 cooperatives file income tax return Form 990C, even though they may have no taxable income. They must do this within the fifteen-day limit after the eighth month following the close of the fiscal year.
- While section 521 cooperatives are usually thought of as operating in such a way as to have no income to tax, this is not always the situation. If it decides to make patronage refunds in unallocated form, the cooperative, rather than its patrons, is subject to income tax on such allocations.
- Section 521 makes no specific reference to federated cooperatives. Revenue Ruling 69-651, however, established the "look through" principle. This means looking through to the ultimate member of a local member cooperative. In the case of a federated cooperative, if a local member association does not qualify under section 521, it appears that neither would the federated cooperative of which it is a member.

Taxation of Non–Section 521 Marketing and Purchasing Cooperatives

Some farmers' marketing and purchasing cooperatives may not be able to, or may choose not to operate in accordance with the provisions of section 521. They may act thus, for example, because they wish to restrict patronage refunds to members only.

They also may want to build their capital structure by increasing their unallocated reserves by adding the funds remaining after paying taxes on savings resulting from nonmember business.

Others may not find it possible to comply with the strict provisions as to membership, types of business, or operations that are required if they are to qualify as section 521 cooperatives. Some cooperatives, especially purchasing associations, often find that they cannot operate under the rather confining restrictions of section 521 because they are doing more than 15 percent of their business with nonproducers who are nonmembers. Other purchasing cooperatives find IRS regulations on "look through" provisions and determination of patronage refunds by departments ("netting") too restrictive for efficient operations.

A comparison of section 521 cooperatives with non–521 cooperatives shows many differences. The non–521 cooperatives have greater flexibility of operations. For example:

- Although they may operate as farmers' marketing or purchasing cooperatives, they need not do so. Consequently, they are not necessarily agriculturally oriented, and their members need not be producers.
- All patrons need not be treated alike. Therefore, non–521 cooperatives may choose to pay income taxes on the savings derived from nonmember business and may add the funds remaining as unallocated reserves or use the remaining funds to increase returns to members.
- The provision that not over 15 percent of the business of a purchasing cooperative can be with nonmember, nonproducer patrons does not apply to non–521 purchasing cooperatives. They are required, however, to do 50 percent of their business with members if they are to be recognized as "operating on a cooperative basis."
- Non–521 cooperatives are not subject to Internal Revenue restrictions as to rate of interest paid on capital stock or profit business with nonmembers, although other legislative provisions may cover this practice if the cooperative is a farmers' cooperative.
- These cooperatives must allocate net margins to patrons on the basis of business they do with their cooperative if such distributions are to comply with the statute's definition of a patronage refund. They cannot, however, deduct (1) dividends paid on capital stock, or (2) allocations to patrons on savings resulting from business done with the U.S. government or other nonpatronage sources in computing their income tax obligations.

Both cooperatives that qualify under section 521 and those that do not may deduct patronage refunds when determining their income for tax purposes if they comply with pertinent legal provisions. Both are required to make patronage refund allocations within 8½ months after closing their fiscal year. Moreover, both types of cooperatives are required to report to IRS the names of individuals to whom they pay $10 or more in patronage refunds, dividends, or interest. Also, both classes of cooperatives may deduct per unit capital investments if members so agree.

We have indicated that the relative advantages and disadvantages for a cooperative operating under provisions of section 521 depend on many factors. An important factor is the greater flexibility in operating as a nonqualifying association as balanced against the extra costs that may be involved. These costs include paying income taxes on dividends on stock and savings resulting from business with other than patrons. Also important in reaching a decision are relevance of other federal and state statutes, specific charter and bylaw provisions, capital structures developed, and the type of business activities members wish to carry on.

Tax Alternatives for Farmers' Marketing and Purchasing Cooperatives Illustrated

We shall get a better idea of how cooperatives may be taxed if we examine a hypothetical case showing the tax position of a cooperative when it serves both members and nonmembers and when it serves members only. If it serves members and nonmembers, it may either (1) pay patronage refunds to members and nonmembers alike, or (2) pay patronage refunds to members only. Stock dividends are paid to members only.

How net margins may be distributed under these two methods of operation is also illustrated in Table 11-1.

When the cooperative serves both members and nonmembers, two possibilities are open to it in returning patronage refunds. In the illustration used, the nonmember business amounts to approximately 30 percent of the total business, and therefore the association may qualify as a section 521 cooperative, provided that net margins are distributed in the same way for both member and nonmember patrons and that the association adheres to other legal requirements. In this case, the nonmember business is treated in the same way as member business as far as patronage refunds are concerned. The members will receive their dividends on stock, and patronage refunds will be distributed in proportion to the business done with both member and nonmember patrons. In other words, $82,945 goes to member patrons and $37,055 to nonmember patrons. Thus, the association fulfills its obligation to treat patrons alike and it continues to qualify under provisions of section 521.

It is possible, however, for the cooperative to have both member and nonmember patrons and to distribute patronage refunds to members only. If it does so, the cooperative, as previously, would make a distribution of $15,000 as dividends on stock and $82,945 to members as a patronage refund. Savings of $41,680 on nonmember business as well as the $10,375 dividends on stock attributable to member business, or a total of $52,055, would be taxable because, in all respects, this becomes a profit operation, and the cooperative is subject to income tax on that part of its business at the rate of 22 percent for the first $25,000 and 48 percent on the remainder. The cooperative, therefore, pays an income tax of $18,569 on this part of the business. Of the $39,069 remaining, $15,000 is paid out as dividends on stock and the remainder might be allocated to patrons in proportion to the business they have done with the cooperative association or, as a more general practice, added as retained margins to the capital of the cooperative as unallocated funds.

If an association only serves members, its patronage refund position is shown in part 2 of Table 11-1. In this case, its total volume of business is $1.5 million and its net margins are $93,320. These net margins are the same as for the member business reported in part 1 of Table 11-1, and they are distributed in the same way. If this distribution is made in accordance with the provisions of section 521, the cooperative

COOPERATIVE TAXATION

will distribute all net margins, and it will have no taxable income, since dividends on stock and patronage refunds may be deducted in computing its taxable income.

One of the considerations a cooperative and a patron must use in making the tax decision is that of the differential tax rate between the cooperative and the patron. For

Table 11-1 Payment of Patronage Refunds under Different Methods of Operation

Item	Total	Patrons Member business	Patrons Nonmember business
1. Serving both members and nonmembers			
Sales	$2,170,000	$1,500,000	$670,000
All expenses	2,035,000	1,406,680	628,320
Net margins	$ 135,000	$ 93,320	$ 41,680
A. Paying patronage refunds to members and nonmembers (qualifying as a 521 cooperative)			
Net margins	$135,000	$93,320	$41,680
Source of funds for dividends on stock	15,000	10,375*	4,625*
Distributed as patronage refunds	$120,000	$82,945	$37,055
Dividends on stock	15,000	15,000	—
Distributed to patrons	$135,000	$97,945	$37,055
B. Paying patronage refunds to members only (not qualifying as a 521 cooperative)			
Total net margins	$135,000	$93,320	$41,680
Less patronage refunds	82,945	82,945	
Taxable income	$ 52,055	$10,375	$41,680
Federal income taxes†	18,486		
Dividends on stock†	15,000‡		
Retained as unallocated revenues†	18,569		
2. Serving members only§ (qualifying as a 521 cooperative)			
Net sales	$1,500,000	$1,500,000	
All expenses	1,406,680	1,406,680	
Net margins	$ 93,320	$ 93,320	
Distribution of net margins			
Dividends on stock	$15,000	$15,000	
Patronage refunds	78,320	78,320	
Total	$93,320	$93,320	

*When an association operates as a 521 cooperative, net margins from both member and nonmember business are a source of funds for dividends on stock even though such dividends are only paid to members.

†When an association is not operating as a 521 cooperative, sources of these funds are derived from the net margins on nonmember business and that portion of net margins on member business that would be allocated to pay dividends on stock.

‡When an association is not operating as a 521 cooperative, funds for payment of dividends on stock are available only after income taxes are paid on net margins after distribution of patronage refunds.

§Assumes no change in volume, expenses, or net margins when only members are served.

example, if a refund of $100 is due a patron, the tax, if nonqualified and retained, is $48 (if taxed at the cooperative level and if the marginal rate of tax is 48 percent) for the cooperative but only $20 for the patron (if income is within the 20 percent tax bracket).

Per Unit Capital Investments (Retains) and Federal Income Taxes

The term *per unit capital retains* is another instance of confusing terminology. Retains imply an arbitrary withholding of funds on the part of the cooperative. *Capital contributions* also may be a misleading term. The real situation, however, is that members make a capital investment in their cooperative on an agreed-upon basis. Therefore, we shall use the term *per unit capital investments* in this discussion.

Per unit capital investments by members should be distinguished from "per unit deductions" to cover current operating costs. Per unit deductions are, in effect, the primary income of the cooperative, and any remainder after paying all operating expenses is returned to patrons as a patronage refund. Per unit capital investments, in contrast, provide a means by which patrons of a marketing cooperative can provide funds for acquiring current, fixed, or other assets. They become a part of the net worth of the cooperative. These distinctions should be recognized for tax purposes, even though they both may be expressed in marketing contracts or agreements in not clearly distinguishable terms. (How per unit capital investment plans operate are described in detail in Chapter 17.)

In 1965, an IRS ruling held that per unit capital investments are subject to income taxes. This ruling was supported by an amendment to subchapter T in 1966. It provided that cooperatives pay a federal income tax on these investments unless patrons agree to include them in their current income at their face value. Each member is furnished a qualified certificate by the cooperative which indicates the dollar amount of the per unit investment or "allocation." These certificates are fixed, and bear no relationship to the net margins realized by the cooperative.

The situation is not unlike that of patronage refund allocations. The member agrees to include his or her per unit capital investments as income for tax purposes by (1) agreeing to do so in writing, or (2) joining a cooperative that has adopted bylaws after November 13, 1966, which provide that membership constitutes such an agreement, after the member has received a written copy of the bylaws. Written consent may be revoked by a patron at any time by filing a written statement to that effect with the cooperative. Should the cooperative not comply with qualifying provisions, it will incur a tax liability. However, when a nonqualifying certificate of per unit capital investment is redeemed in cash by the cooperative, it may deduct the amount redeemed for tax purposes.

To qualify for this tax treatment, the nonqualifying certificate must be issued within 8½ months after the cooperative closes the tax year "during which the marketing occurred." The law provides that if the qualifying certificate has no fair market value at the time it is issued, the cooperative need not report it. When the certificate is redeemed, however, it must report the amount received.

Income Tax Status of Certain Cooperatives and Other Organizations

A number of other types of organizations and corporations, and other organizations operating on a mutual basis, were organized after 1900. Although they do not qualify under section 521, most of them were recognized under section 501 of the Internal Revenue Code of 1954 as exempt from the payment of income taxes provided they conformed with the specified conditions outlined. The rationale of taxation of these organizations is different in that, technically, cooperatives have no income tax exemption.

Organizations Covered by Section 501 Section 501 lists several types of organizations that are reported to be "exempt" from the payment of federal income taxes. These organizations are: corporations organized under acts of Congress; corporations holding title to property and collecting income which is turned over to organizations now exempt from income taxes; community chests, foundations, and religious and charitable organizations; civic leagues or organizations not organized for profit; agricultural fairs and festivals; business leagues and chambers of commerce; clubs organized for pleasure and recreation; fraternal beneficiary societies; voluntary employees' beneficiary associations; teachers' retirement funds; benevolent life insurance associations; cemetery companies owned and operated for the benefit of members; credit unions and corporations without capital stock, operated for mutual purposes without profits; mutual insurance companies or associations with annual premiums not exceeding $150,000; corporations financing ordinary crop operations; and religious or apostolic associations or corporations.

The tax status of ordinary business corporations also differs widely in the United States because state and federal legislators have the right to incorporate certain exclusions in tax legislation. In 1958, for example, Congress enacted legislation permitting corporations having not over ten shareholders (all of whom are individuals), no nonresident shareholders, and only one class of stock to exclude from their taxable income profits distributed to their individual stockholders. In other words, they are taxed essentially the same as partnerships.

Specific Income Tax Provisions for Other Cooperatives

The specific income tax provisions that relate to other selected types of cooperatives are here identified briefly:

Farm Credit Administration Units The federal land banks, federal land-bank associations, and federal intermediate credit banks are exempt from federal income tax under the provisions of section 501. A bank for cooperatives or production credit association has a statutory exemption from federal income tax whenever the Governor of the Farm Credit Administration holds stock in it. Since December 31, 1968, no such stock has been held by the Governor; therefore, all banks for cooperatives and production credit associations currently are subject to federal income taxes. The banks for cooperatives allocate their earnings to borrowers on the basis of interest paid and qualify such allocations for deduction from taxable income in accordance with the provisions of subchapter T. Production credit associations are authorized to operate on a cooperative basis and pay patronage refunds; to the extent they do, they are entitled to the tax treatment provided by subchapter T.

Rural Electric and Telephone Companies Section 501 is generally held applicable to electric and telephone cooperatives. This act (c) (12) provides exemption for: "Benevolent life insurance associations of a purely local character, mutual ditch or irrigation companies, mutual or cooperative telephone companies, or like organizations; but only if 85 percent or more of the income consists of amounts collected from members for the sole purpose of meeting losses and expenses." Electric cooperatives are considered "like organizations" within the meaning of this provision. Tax exemption is not automatic in that it is granted only after appropriate application papers are filed with the IRS.

Consumer Cooperatives There are special income tax provisions that relate to the various types of consumer cooperatives.

• Consumer cooperatives selling retail goods, such as foods, clothing, and other consumer items, and providing services pay taxes on the same or substantially the same basis as other non–section 521 cooperatives. Their patrons do not pay taxes on patronage income from these associations because such refunds are considered not to be additions to income but, rather, a reduction in costs of goods and services provided by their cooperative.
• Mutual insurance companies insuring casualty risks and owned and controlled by policyholders are recognized as differing in capital structure from ordinary stock insurance companies. Mutual companies may deduct underwriting losses from underwriting gains and then set aside a part of their underwriting gain as a protection against future losses. Special provisions permit deferring tax payment for five years on the undeferred portion of underwriting gains.
• Credit unions are required to provide IRS with information on member shares. They, as nonstock cooperatives operated for the interest of members and without profit, are exempt from the payment of income taxes. In this respect, they are in the same category as building and loan associations.

It is obvious that the income tax laws and regulations applying to these types of cooperatives differ in many respects. Anyone working with them, therefore, should carefully study the specific provisions of the tax laws and regulations that apply to them.

STATE INCOME TAXES

When applied to cooperatives, state income taxes generally follow the same basic provisions as federal law and regulations. They permit deductions of patronage refunds from taxable income, provided there is a preexisting obligation to distribute these refunds to patrons. States, of course, vary as to how they handle such items as income from nonpatron business and dividend payments on member equities. Also, states differ on when and how cooperatives may qualify to exclude obligations to patrons and also on the rate of taxation.

BASIC INCOME TAX ISSUES

Of the many income tax issues that confront cooperatives, three should be examined here in further detail. They are: (1) taxation of patronage refunds, (2) elimination of section 521, and (3) the need for better understanding of the nature of cooperative enterprise by the legislators and regulatory agencies.

Taxation of Patronage Refunds

This is the key taxation issue concerning cooperatives. The main argument for taxing the patronage refunds of cooperatives centers on the way in which present taxing methods differ from the double tax imposed on the profits of ordinary business corporations. It is well known that these profits are taxed at both the corporate level and the individual stockholder level.

To counter the single-tax status of cooperatives or their members, critics favor a tax on the patronage refunds of these associations. Without going into the arguments for or against a double tax, we know there is much opposition to this form of taxation. In their opposition to taxing patronage refunds, cooperatives can and do contend that "two wrongs don't make a right" in tax policy. Moreover, they also maintain that cooperatives should not be penalized by being taxed at separate production, processing, or distribution stages in the marketing process, whereas most business firms have highly integrated operations and are taxed only after they have completed the final stages of their operations. Cooperatives also emphasize that they have no profits to tax when they operate on a strictly cooperative basis. They further call attention to many special restrictions that present tax laws already impose on their organization structure, operating methods, and financial practices. These, they contend, may more than offset the advantages some of them may realize through the use of patronage refund and per unit capital investments (with the consent of members) in their capital structure, sometimes on an interest-free basis.

Elimination of Section 521

The Treasury Department and others argue for the elimination of section 521. This elimination, in the opinion of those favoring it, would do three things: (1) It would do away with the recognized tax status of cooperatives that meet certain specific and restrictive requirements of section 521 as to type of cooperatives, methods of organization, and operating practices; (2) it would eliminate provisions with respect to exclusion for tax purposes of dividends paid patrons on equity capital and net returns on nonpatron business distributed to patrons; and (3) it would strengthen the public relations position of cooperatives in their community because of their present single-tax status.

The views of cooperatives on the issues, of course, are conditioned by the amount of dividends on stock they are committed to pay or could eliminate paying, as well as the extent of their nonpatron business. It is recognized, too, that substantial extra bookkeeping and accounting costs may be involved when records are kept on the business of all patrons. In practice, however, about half the farmers' marketing and purchasing associations have found it desirable to operate in accordance with section 521 provisions. Moreover, 521 status is the key to cooperative status as to securities registration requirements of the Securities Exchange Commission. This provision has implications beyond tax law.

Cooperatives can also realistically argue that their equity capital differs from other capital in that it has "loan capital" status. As such, dividends paid on these equities should be considered a business expense of the cooperative and should not be paid out of net margins in the way dividends of ordinary corporations are. As for opposition to the single-tax status of cooperatives, it may have little support as long as our present legislation recognizes that under certain conditions, net margins belong to members or patrons and not to the cooperative. If opponents of cooperatives should want to attack cooperatives, they would shift the basis of such an attack if the single-tax issue were foreclosed to them.

Better Understanding of Cooperatives by Legislators and Regulatory Agencies

We have already referred to the lack of understanding of antitrust issues by legislators and many government agencies. It is charitable to say that the same situation exists as to the taxation of cooperatives. Some would assert that both groups contain elements that are conducting an anticooperative crusade.

A case in point was the proposed income tax treatment of cooperatives in the Tax Reform Act of 1969. This proposed legislation would have denied to cooperatives the right to deduct patronage refunds in determining taxable income unless they increased cash patronage refunds from 20 percent to 50 percent over a ten-year period and retired the balance within a period of fifteen years.

Melvin E. Sims, President of the National Council of Farmer Cooperatives, in 1970 at the annual meeting of that organization, characterized this effort thus:

> A very punitive and discriminatory restriction was proposed for cooperatives after the House Ways and Means Committee moved into executive session. This proposal was not on the announced agenda, and none of those who would have been adversely affected were given an opportunity to testify. I believe that we must conclude that we had few friends on the Committee or that they failed to comprehend the devastating effect that the proposal would have had on cooperative activity.

While legislative action on this proposal has been held in abeyance pending completion of a study of the so-called nonrelated business of cooperatives, the situation illustrates the diverse views that prevail with respect to cooperatives.

When the IRS contends, as it does, that member investments in the form of per unit capital investments are, in effect, member income for tax purposes, and when it initiates a "look through" regulation with respect to the application of section 521 to a federated cooperative, and when it suggests that voting on a basis of other than one member, one vote is not in compliance with cooperative objectives, some people wonder how objective and impartial the IRS is. While no one objects to tax reform, there again may be a justifiable reason for asking why legislators and regulatory agencies "don't go where the action is" when considering tax reform.

SUMMARY

There is much misunderstanding and confusion about the taxation of cooperatives. Legislators, court decisions, Internal Revenue Service and Federal Trade Commission rulings and interpretations, distorted propaganda campaigns, and cooperatives themselves have contributed to this misunderstanding and confusion. Misuse of such terms as *exemption, profits,* and *dividends* illustrates the problem.

In general, cooperatives are subject to the same property, franchise and sales, and income taxes as other corporations. If cooperatives pay no income taxes, they are free from taxation because their unique nature of operation results in no income to tax. This is the situation when prior contractual obligations of cooperatives require them to return net savings or margins as patronage refunds to patrons in proportion to the business these patrons do with their cooperatives.

The income tax position of cooperatives has evolved through the passage of numerous revenue acts, starting as early as 1913, and the establishment of interpretative IRS tax rulings. Thus, by 1934 the patronage refund tax position of cooperatives was reasonably well established. It was not until passage of the Revenue Act of 1951, however, that the income tax status of cooperative patrons was considered. The Revenue Act of 1951 brought into perspective the fact that no income tax exemption was involved when there was no income to tax in any corporation that operated on "a cooperative basis." It also provided "tax exemptions" (section 501) for organizations, cooperative or otherwise, that operated in such a way as to have little or no income to tax.

Because of court decisions, the objective of achieving a single tax on patronage refunds was not realized in the Revenue Act of 1951. The Revenue Act of 1962, as amended in 1966 and 1969, sought to remedy this situation. To make certain that patronage refunds would be taken into account by patrons in determining their taxable income, the act specified ways in which patrons could consent to comply with provisions designed to realize this objective. If such consent was not obtained, or if the cooperative operated in such a way as to have taxable income, the cooperative was obligated to consider allocations to members and taxable income in determining its income tax obligations.[6] In 1966 the Revenue Code of 1962 was amended to also tax per unit capital investments of cooperative patrons on substantially the same basis as allocated patronage refunds.

Significant income tax issues that confront cooperatives are these: Should patronage refunds be taxed as corporation profits? Should section 521 be eliminated? And

---

[6]For a detailed summary of the tax alternatives available to cooperatives and their patrons, see Neely, op. cit., pp. 88–91.

how can the understanding of the nature of cooperative enterprise among legislators and regulatory agencies be improved so as to assure that they will approach the tax treatment of these associations more realistically?

QUESTIONS

1. Trace the important developments in income tax legislation as they relate to cooperatives.
2. What deficiency in tax legislation did the 1951 Revenue Act seek to remedy? Why did it fail in its objective?
3. What are the advantages to farmers' marketing and purchasing cooperatives of qualifying as a section 521 cooperative? What are the requirements?
4. What shortcomings of the 1951 Revenue Act did the 1962 Revenue Act attempt to correct? How did it do this?
5. How do per unit capital investments compare with patronage refunds from the standpoint of income tax obligations of cooperatives and their members?
6. Why are patronage refunds referred to as "the cornerstone of the cooperative tax issue"?
7. Would you favor eliminating section 521 from the 1962 Revenue Code as amended?
8. Is it correct to characterize some legislators and regulatory agencies as being on an "anti-cooperative crusade"?
9. What is the significance of section 501 of the Revenue Act of 1951?
10. How do federal income tax laws for cooperatives differ from the income tax laws for cooperatives in your state?

REFERENCES

Agricultural Cooperatives, Cooperative Law and Practice Course Handbook Series Number 151, Practicing Law Institute, New York, 1974, secs. 3, 8, 9, and 18.

American Cooperation, the yearly proceedings report of the American Institute of Cooperation, Washington, D.C., contains a number of articles on cooperative taxation. See especially the following issues: 1974–75, pp. 193–198; 1973–74, pp. 256–262 and pp. 267–270; 1970, pp. 63–89; 1969, pp. 107–112; 1968, pp. 147–166; and 1962, pp. 347–352.

Davidovic, G.: *The Tax Position of Cooperatives in Various Countries,* The Cooperative Union of Canada, Ottawa, 1963.

Neely, D. Morrison: *Legal Phases of Farmer Cooperatives: Part II: Federal Income Taxes,* FCS Information 69, U.S. Department of Agriculture, Farmer Cooperative Service, Washington, 1970, p. 101.

Packel, Israel: *The Organization and Operation of Cooperatives,* The American Law Institute and the American Bar Association, Philadelphia, 1970, pp. 209–262.

Schneider, Vernon: *Facts about Cooperatives and Taxation*, American Institute of Cooperation, Washington, D.C., undated, p. 12.

Schrader, Lee L., and Ray A. Goldberg: *Farmers Cooperatives and Federal Income Taxes,* Ballinger Publishing, Cambridge, Mass., 1975, p. 116.

Chapter 12

Organizing a Cooperative

Our discussion on organizing a cooperative will center upon the problems encountered in getting a local association underway. This approach is advisable because many of the people interested in cooperatives have only a limited knowledge of how a cooperative should be organized and how it actually works. In many instances, such people can contribute little more than an evangelistic fervor that envisages cooperatives as the solution to their economic ills. Much of the material in this chapter, however, will also apply to the organization of large-scale cooperatives, since their organizers face many of the same problems that confront those starting a local association.

THE PROBLEM IDENTIFIED: SOLUTIONS EXPLORED

The forces that contribute to the organization of a cooperative arise when the would-be organizers encounter problems that they cannot effectively deal with alone. As they speculate on what to do about this predicament, they are likely to discuss these problems with others in their community, particularly those who are facing the same or similar circumstances. If the would-be organizers find other people with similar interests, they will have a basis for starting to explore some joint course of action. And these people may, in turn, seek to determine whether there are still others who are confronted by the same problems. If so, what have they done about them? Have their efforts succeeded or failed, and why? Finally, are there any knowledgeable people or pertinent government or educational agencies to whom they can turn for sound advice and guidance?

If and when the cooperative approach is suggested, those interested may want to explore its potential under the prevailing conditions. Such exploration usually brings people together and leaders are likely to emerge. At the exploratory stage, people should ask themselves some discerning questions. Answers to these questions will give an indication of the feasibility of going farther along cooperative lines. Some of the questions that might be asked are:

- Are many persons in the community interested in organizing the proposed cooperative?
- What kinds of services should the proposed cooperative perform?
- What are the problems with respect to the desired services? Are the services already available? If they are, can they be improved? If they do not exist, can a cooperative provide them?
- What has been the community's experience with any other kind of cooperative?
- What are the available community assets in terms of potential members, leaders, financial resources, facilities, and potential productive capacity?
- Who wants a cooperative? Is it needed and will the people really use it, or is it being forced upon them by outside promoters?

Caution is desirable at this stage. Although, in the past, high-pressure promoters, stimulated by the prospect of signing up cooperative members and reaping commissions on the cooperative stock they could sell, were more likely to exploit the unwary and the uninformed, they still stand ready to do so today. In a Midwestern state, for example, a railroad station agent tried to organize a potato marketing cooperative in an effort to move sufficient carloads of potatoes through the depot to maintain its established size classification. In another state, an unsuccessful vegetable-processing firm tried to organize a cooperative to take over its operations.

A critical look at the feasibility of organizing a cooperative should include an evaluation not only of possible problems but also of potential benefits. Sound prior investigation would do much to discourage unsound proposals and would prevent the premature launching of a cooperative enterprise.

Holding Exploratory Meetings

If the preliminary answers to the six discerning questions suggested are encouraging, the prospective organizers may wish to hold exploratory meetings to investigate more fully the feasibility of organizing a cooperative. The procedures that will be followed in conducting such a meeting will be determined to a large extent by the group's knowledge of cooperatives.

It is well known that people plan their course of action on the basis of their knowledge and past experiences. If their experience with cooperatives is limited, it may well be premature to ask them to pass judgment on the desirability of organizing a cooperative at the first communitywide meeting. Therefore, a better approach may be to hold a series of "preorganizational" meetings that will enable interested people to become acquainted with the nature of cooperative business enterprise, its possibilities, and its limitations. They will then be much better prepared to evaluate the merits of seeking a solution to the problems confronting them through a cooperative business venture.

On the other hand, if the people of a community have already had considerable experience with local cooperatives, they may be able to pass immediate judgment on the desirability of further exploring the pros and cons of organizing a new cooperative at the initial community meeting. In any event, the meetings should be carefully planned. They should provide basic information on local and relevant economic, social, and political factors, and they should explain how cooperatives operate and what benefits prospective members may reasonably expect.

Economic and Social Factors

Cooperatives do not operate in isolation. They are a part of the economic and social fabric of their community. Therefore, an evaluation of the general local economic and social conditions that have a bearing on the desirability of organizing a community cooperative should be the starting point for exploring cooperative opportunities. It is important to find out, for example, whether similarities or differences in economic status have a significant bearing on community relations, and whether people in the community have demonstrated, in other ventures, the necessary business capability.

People considering the organization of a medical cooperative, for example, would want information on the present status of available medical services in the community, on what additional services are needed, and on the most realistic way to obtain such services. As to the last point, it might well be asked: Is a cooperative the answer?

Since cooperatives are organizations of people, the human equation must be taken into account. The people considering organizing a cooperative should have the ability to work together regardless of racial differences, national origins, or varying religious beliefs. Support, or at least understanding of the nature of cooperative business enterprise, by educators, religious groups, and the general business community, also contributes much to creating a favorable environment for organizing a cooperative.

Political Considerations

Prevailing political institutions have an important bearing on the possibility of successfully initiating a cooperative business venture. Account must be taken of the provisions of state cooperative laws in general, as well as specific provisions relating to the type of cooperative association being contemplated. The views of influential political leaders—both local and state—may also be significant in getting the necessary support. Likewise, the attitudes of pertinent local, state, and federal agencies can do much to encourage or discourage a proposed cooperative. Regulatory agencies, for example, are in a position to take actions that are favorable or unfavorable to the formation of cooperatives or other types of business firms.

Is a Cooperative the Answer?

After evaluating the general economic, social, and political environment in which the proposed cooperative would operate, the people interested in its formation should now explore in detail the more specific problems that are related to its organization. More detailed information will provide better answers to the discerning questions already mentioned. In addition, the prospective organizers must now give greater attention than ever to the economic feasibility of the proposed venture. Among other things, such attention involves:

- *Evaluating the performance of local and other firms already providing the desired services*. The evaluation can be made by considering the local market impact, procurement practices, product quality, and service effectiveness. Evidently something has been lacking in this regard, or a new cooperative would not have been proposed. The investigation involves identifying the nature and extent of the desirable improvements that may be possible through cooperative action. For example, if present market costs are too high, farm services inadequate, and agricultural products of inferior quality, the need for a cooperative becomes increasingly apparent.
- *Projecting operating costs*. This step requires careful determination of potential fixed and operating costs, possible economics of scale, and realistic considerations of growth potentials.
- *Determining possibilities for providing new and additional services*. Will a new farmers' cooperative, for example, be able to integrate marketing and purchasing operations effectively? Can the new medical cooperative add dental services or operate its own hospital? Is there an opportunity for the proposed grocery cooperative also to handle furniture, drugs, a service station, or other services for the advantage of members?
- *Considering the possible short-term and long-term future opportunities*. What new and expanding services will the cooperative be able to provide within one, three, five, or ten years from now?
- *Determining how a successful cooperative may enable members to improve their business operations and their patterns of living*. What will better business performance and improved services mean to prospective members?
- *Ascertaining the necessary human, financial, and physical resources available in the community to organize and effectively operate a cooperative*. Can the cooperative obtain the managerial talent, potential employees, adequate capital, assurance of adequate volume, and necessary legal and technical guidance?
- *Evaluating alternatives*. A key question is whether or not the prospective benefits outweigh the time, the costs, and the headaches and exhausting work of organizing and operating a cooperative. Finally, the possibility of other and more effective ways to provide the services a community needs and desires should be explored.

The Committee Approach

Discussion of these and related questions by those attending exploratory meetings will provide them with a better foundation for deciding whether the possibilities of organizing a cooperative should be considered in greater detail. When interested people have background information on the economic, social, and political factors bearing on their situation, and when they understand what a cooperative can and cannot do, they are better equipped to determine whether they wish to go further in examining the opportunities for organizing a cooperative.

If the people attending exploratory meetings decide that it is desirable to continue their deliberations, they can best do so by establishing a number of working committees to obtain and evaluate basic information related to their particular situation.

Although the kinds of committees set up may vary, experience has shown that at least five are generally needed. They are those on general survey, membership, facilities, finance, and legal documents. Under some conditions, combining some of these committees may be advisable.

Groups may differ as to how they would like committees to function. We have indicated that the usual practice is first to make a general survey that would consider the need for a cooperative, and then to report back to the potential membership. On the other hand, if prospects look especially encouraging, and the group decides to go ahead and organize a cooperative, all committees may be set up at the first organizational meeting. Such action, however, is only justified when there is assurance of adequate volume of business, strong member interest and support, and sufficient financial resources. If all committees are established at the same time, the best sequence for coordinating findings as a basis for committee deliberations should be determined. Firm yet realistic schedules need to be worked out, so that committee activities are kept moving and on schedule.

Nature and Responsibilities of Committees

General Survey Committee The first responsibility of the general survey committee is to determine whether a need exists for corrective action upon a local economic problem, and whether a cooperative offers promise of being able to meet this need. The many questions that previously have been raised will provide guidelines in reaching conclusions. However, it is important to emphasize that the matter must now move beyond the speculative stage. Firm information and data as to services desired and estimated costs of providing these services must be obtained by the committee. This information will indicate whether the cooperative can provide such services at reduced cost; therefore it is the basis for developing specific recommendations on whether the group should proceed to organize a cooperative. To avoid possible duplication of effort, this committee should also determine whether the prospective cooperative is the only way to provide the services needed. Possibly, a nearby, already-established cooperative may be providing the services wanted, or could readily expand its operations to do so.

Membership Committee The principal function of the membership committee is to make an evaluation of the size of potential membership and the volume of business. Experts in such determinations add a note of caution when estimating membership and volume. It is only when prospective members are willing to sign a membership application form and indicate some measure of financial support that there is a firm base for determining just how sincere their interests are. On the strength of its findings, the membership committee should make definite recommendations as to whether or not sufficient volume and financial support exist to justify a cooperative business venture.

We have previously suggested that usually the general survey and membership committees should prepare their reports before other committees start to function. It is only when they recommend organizing a cooperative, and when the interested people in the community concur, that the other committees are ready to go ahead with their deliberations. Then next in order is the need for considering facility and equipment requirements. Obviously, such findings necessarily have a bearing on financial requirements.

Facilities Committee Armed with information on the feasibility of organizing a cooperative and having guidelines as to the type of services desired, the facilities committee is in a position to start its deliberations. Obviously, the facilities needed will be influenced by the prospective volume, the type of services provided, and the number and location of members. The committee has to consider, for example, the size and kind of facilities, the type of equipment required, and whether or not branch units are needed.

The committee should also explore the new cooperative's present and future needs for land. It should carefully consider whether the cooperative should rent or own its facilities. This decision has a special application to land, buildings, and certain types of equipment.

If the type of cooperative venture proposed is one that involves considerable investment in buildings and equipment of various types, the evaluation of competent engineers should be obtained. Caution in regard to facility deliberations is always desirable because, in many instances, unscrupulous owners have sought to unload antiquated, poorly located, and ill-suited facilities and equipment on unsuspecting organizers who felt strongly pressed to get their cooperative under way.

Finance Committee Once preliminary facts have been determined regarding the type of cooperative to organize, and once facility needs have been ascertained, the finance committeee is ready to go into action. The new cooperative will need financial resources for fixed facilities, operating capital, and perhaps for financing commodities or inventories. Fixed facilities relate primarily to land, buildings, and equipment. Operating capital is used for such expenses as salaries and wages, rent, supplies, interest, taxes, and utilities. Commodity and inventory financing for farm marketing cooperatives may involve farm products that are to be stored or processed. For farm-supply purchasing cooperatives, such financing may be necessary to maintain inventories of fertilizer, feed, seed, petroleum products, and other production supplies and funds for extending credit (accounts receivable). Consumer cooperatives have similar financial needs to cover their inventory costs for the products they sell.

Sources of capital vary considerably. Experience has demonstrated that it is desirable for members to provide a substantial proportion of the capital needs of their cooperatives. The proportion may vary from 10 percent to 50 percent or more, depending on the economic status of the members and on the kind of cooperative they organize. By digging into their own pockets for funds, members are making a stronger financial commitment to the success of their cooperative than they might otherwise do.

Experience has also shown that it is advisable for members and patrons to finance cooperatives in proportion to the use that they make of them. They often do this through retained patronage refunds or per unit capital investment.

Among lending agencies, the most important source of capital is the banks for cooperatives of the Cooperative Farm Credit System. Other lending agencies include insurance companies, private banks, and the general public. (Lending agencies and sources of capital are discussed in Chapters 15, 16, and 17.)

Legal Documents Committee Cooperatives are organized under the provisions of state enabling legislation. Although the provisions of such legislation vary from state to state, they generally cover, among other things, the following:

- Number of members necessary to incorporate
- Capital structure—nonstock or stock
- Terms of membership and voting rights of members
- Powers, obligations, and rights of the cooperative
- Methods of distributing savings or net margins
- Provisions to be included in articles of incorporation and bylaws and method of filing

In addition, those forming a cooperative should carefully consider the provisions of federal and state laws as they relate to income tax and antitrust requirements (see Chapters 10 and 11).

A number of legal documents need to be drawn up to organize a cooperative. They include articles of incorporation, bylaws, organization agreements, membership application forms, marketing agreements, and waiver notices of first meetings of members and directors.[1]

Articles of Incorporation The articles of incorporation indicate the relationship that exists between the cooperative and the laws under which it is incorporated. It is important, therefore, that these articles be drawn up in accordance with state cooperative laws. They describe the nature and kind of business the cooperative proposes to conduct. The articles include such items as the name of the cooperative, its purposes, powers and limitations, place of business, period of duration, incorporators, provisions as to the number of directors and their periods of service, membership qualifications, and capital structure, among other things.

Bylaws Bylaws describe more detailed provisions than do the articles of incorporation as to how the cooperative will operate. They are, in effect, additional laws that relate to a specific cooperative. They also generally state the requirements for membership, how business is to be conducted, and whether or not marketing agreements are to be used. They, however, must be in conformity with state laws. Therefore, the committee is well advised to secure the services of a competent lawyer in their preparation.

Bylaws also have to do with directors and officers, giving attention to provisions

---

[1] D. Morrison Neely, *Legal Phases of Farmer Cooperatives: Sample Legal Documents,* FCS Information 66, U.S. Department of Agriculture, Farmer Cooperative Service, Washington, 1970, p. 45. This publication provides sample documents that identify various legal considerations that should receive attention when organizing a cooperative.

as to the method of their election, filling of vacancies, compensation, and general powers. Moreover, they should cover duties of such officers as the president, vice president, secretary, treasurer, and manager. The bylaws generally provide for the establishment of committees; they include a section on operations; and they spell out methods of distributing net savings. Provisions relating to the dissolution of the association and the interest of members in such cases should also be included, as well as identification of the fiscal year and ways of changing membership. Finally, bylaws should provide for a calendar of meetings, arrangements for annual and special meetings, quorum requirements and voting regulations, and the general order of business.

Organization Agreement and Membership Application Forms The organization agreement form essentially states the obligations of the cooperative, specific provisions that make it a going concern, and concurrent obligations of members. Membership application forms are sometimes a part of a marketing contract. At other times, they are separate. In general, they provide for a statement of application together with general provisions relating to the duration of membership and acceptance of the provisions of the articles of incorporation, the bylaws, and other legal documents.

PRECAUTIONARY ORGANIZATIONAL MEASURES

Members may wish to take special action to ensure that their cooperative will operate in their interests. They can, for example, often avoid misunderstanding and dissatisfaction if precautionary steps are taken in drafting or modifying their bylaws. Such care can do much to assure a good start once the cooperative gets organized, and good progress once it is underway. The following precautionary measures are among the areas that ought to receive attention.

Board Makeup and Qualifications

The size of the board of directors should generally vary with the size of the cooperative. As a cooperative grows larger, it may well wish its board to operate on a committee basis, selecting directors to serve on such committees as those responsible for financing, facilities, membership, and transportation.

Another question that has received considerable attention centers upon the selection of "outside" directors for the board. There are some distinct advantages and disadvantages in selecting such directors. One argument is, for example, that bankers, lawyers, and college professors, owing to their professional experience, can add substantially to the capability of a board of directors. The desirability of such a policy depends, no doubt, on how capable and conscientious such individuals are, as well as on the care and diligence that are used in selecting them.

Sometimes outside directors pay scant attention to their cooperative responsibilities, have little understanding of cooperative principles, objectives, and operations, and accordingly make ill-considered decisions and suggestions. At times, too, their suggestions and decisions are given undue weight in deference to their position in the community, and not because of their knowledge of business practices and cooperative objectives and principles. In other instances, conflicts of interest may occur as such directors, unwittingly or otherwise, use the cooperative to the advantage of the outside agencies or organizations to which they belong.

In contrast, such individuals can perhaps introduce innovative ideas, broaden the horizons of regular board members, be convincing spokespersons for cooperatives in the community, and, in general, make substantial contributions to operations. It should be kept in mind, however, that if they are relied on too heavily, they may inhibit the development of other board members. The best solution appears to be to increase the competency of member directors by initiating thoughtfully planned director training and development programs.

The primary question in arriving at a sound decision on this matter is: What are the alternatives? One solution may be to bring in specialists as advisors to the board if and when it encounters specific problems with which it cannot deal effectively because it lacks the necessary expertise.

Some state cooperative laws provide for public directors, especially for regional associations. These laws specify that such directors should include the dean of the state College of Agriculture, the State Extension Director, or representatives of general farm organizations. The advantages and disadvantages previously mentioned also apply to their appointment as directors.

Election of Directors

There are many ways in which members can make certain that they will be well represented by their directors. For example, rather than the members' relying on nominations from the floor, characterized by the all-too-frequent statement, "I move that the present directors succeed themselves," bylaws may provide for a nominating committee. Such a committee will be elected by the membership or appointed by the chairman of the board with the approval of the directors. Such a committee should be instructed on the criteria for nominating and selecting directors, and then it should propose at least two candidates for each position. Cooperatives are also realizing that they can strengthen the democratic process by providing for secret ballots in electing directors and conducting other business affairs. A curriculum vitae should be provided for each candidate, and additional nominations from the floor should be permitted.

Careful thought should also be given to the structure of the board of directors. Such structure is usually specified in the cooperative's bylaws. Directors may be selected, for example, according to geographic districts or to the different functions that the cooperative performs. A combination grain–farm supply cooperative, for example, might specify that three of its directors represent grain producers, that three of them be dairy farmers who are primarily interested in feeds and related farm supplies, and that one represent general agricultural interests in the community.

Manager Directors

Cooperatives, particularly regional associations, should also decide whether they wish to permit managers of affiliated member local cooperatives to serve on their board of directors. More and more, it is recognized that the viewpoints and desires of local managers often differ from those of the members that the cooperative is organized to serve. This is not to say, however, that the capabilities of managers should not be acknowledged. Some associations handle this matter by providing that managers constitute only a specified minority of the full board of directors. Others stipulate that one or two managers may serve on the board in a consultative or advisory capacity.

Employment of Directors

On occasion, directors have simultaneously served as cooperative managers or in other positions with the cooperative. Although experience has shown that this practice sometimes works satisfactorily, it is generally not a sound policy for a cooperative to establish. The basic problem is that directors, as policy-making individuals, should continually check the performance of the manager and the staff. The directors who also function as managers are, in effect, charged with the unreasonable responsibility of checking and evaluating their own performance. Moreover, as directors, they participate in determining their own salaries—an untenable situation. This practice should be avoided by cooperatives, as should also the employment of directors in any other position.

Avoiding Conflicts of Interest

Great care needs to be taken by the cooperative to make certain that neither directors nor the manager engage in activities that result in conflicts of interest. For example, managing a cooperative is generally a full-time job and should be the first priority of the individual hired to do it. Except in very small cooperatives, or in cooperatives operating on a seasonal basis, no other responsibilities should compete with the manager's duties. Moreover, he or she should not have any interest, financial or otherwise, in a competing business. The same restrictions should apply to directors who may have an interest in a business that competes with the cooperative or that engages in a substantial amount of business with it. It might happen, for example, that a marketing cooperative buys its gasoline from a service station in which a manager or a director has an interest, when, actually, the cooperative should develop its own petroleum operations. Similarly, it may be using banks and insurance companies in which its managers or directors have direct or indirect interests, whereas better banking or insurance services can be obtained from other firms, sometimes cooperative firms. Conflict of interest is a sensitive area, and cooperatives have a special obligation to be above suspicion in this matter.

Rotation of Directors

The association may wish to decide whether or not it wants to rotate directors automatically. Arguments can be advanced pro and con on this decision. It can be argued that if a cooperative has good directors who have demonstrated their capability, they should not be removed at perhaps the very time when they are able to provide the greatest service. On the other hand, rotation of directors may provide new blood, fresh ideas, and a broader base of understanding and support of cooperative contributions to the community. Many associations solve this problem by rotating directors off the board for at least one year, after they have served two or three terms, usually of three years each. They then may be renominated as vacancies occur, if their previous performance as directors so justifies. This is a painless way of avoiding retaining directors who no longer actively and beneficially participate in association affairs.

Provisions as to Maximum Age

In deference to the "founding fathers," cooperative directors have too often continued to serve long beyond their productive age. Many cooperatives deal with this problem by limiting the age at which they can be nominated. Setting a firm retirement age for managers is also becoming accepted business practice. This age is usually sixty-five, and it seldom exceeds seventy.

Youth Directors

Cooperatives may wish to provide for supplementary boards of directors made up of young persons, often under twenty-one years of age. These directors are encouraged to participate in business discussions, but they have no voting privileges. Arrangements for youth directors can help to develop a broader base of interest and train potential board members for more effective future service.

Prevention of Nepotism

At times, managers and directors are inclined to look upon the cooperative as a source of employment for relatives. This unhealthy situation can be avoided by taking precautionary measures. One association, for example, states in its bylaws: "No member of the immediate family of an officer or director shall be eligible for employment by or be employed by the association."

Bonding, Accounting, and Auditing

By specifying provisions with respect to bonding and accounting arrangements, cooperatives can assure that control measures that are in the members' interest are adopted.

More new and small cooperatives founder because of poor accounting practices than is generally realized. For this reason, not only should special precautions be taken to ensure that a sound accounting system is installed, but provisions should be made for auditing by disinterested parties. Auditing is really a check on operating performance and, since it is the manager whose performance is being checked, the auditing firm should be chosen by no one but the directors. This is an important but sometimes overlooked consideration in developing sound operating practices.

GETTING THE COOPERATIVE UNDERWAY

The cooperative is brought into being by filing incorporation papers, or a charter, with the proper state agency (usually the Secretary of State) or one of its divisions. Generally the organizing committee does the filing and, depending on provisions of the state law, its members may serve as the charter members of the association. As soon as the association is incorporated, the board of directors should hold its first meeting. The items of business at this board meeting usually include:[2]

- Electing the first officers of the association
- Adopting a form of membership application or stock subscription
- Adopting the form of marketing agreement, if one is to be used
- Selecting a bank with which to do business
- Designating officers or employees to be authorized to handle funds and issue checks
- Arranging for bookkeeping and auditing
- Arranging for printing and distribution to all members of copies of the articles of incorporation and the bylaws
- Arranging for obtaining a location and facilities for doing business
- Transacting other business, such as insuring and bonding the manager and other key employees
- Selecting the manager

Final steps in getting the cooperative underway are signing up potential members, securing financial commitments and selling capital stock or other equities, obtaining necessary loans and lines of credit, and recording all necessary organizational papers.

Precautionary measures concerning the enthusiasm with which a new cooperative is started are now in order. Experience has demonstrated that it is well for cooperatives to learn to "walk before they run." In other words, a conservative response with respect to facilities, business services provided, and territories to be served helps to set the stage for effective and sound business operations that are in the best interest of members.

Where to Go for Assistance[3]

Those interested in exploring the possibilities of organizing a cooperative are fortunate in that they do not need to rely entirely on their own resources. Assistance can be obtained from such sources as state and federal government agencies, banks for cooperatives, regional cooperatives, state and national cooperative organizations, and cooperative trade associations.

State Agencies State land-grant universities can provide assistance to groups interested in exploring the opportunities for organizing a cooperative. They can do this through their state cooperative extension service, with their county agent staffs, and often with the help of state specialists knowledgeable in problems of cooperative organization. If they do not have such specialists on their staffs, they can suggest where to turn for guidance. Also, if a group interested in organizing a cooperative is faced with questions relating to an evaluation of alternatives for various types of agricultural enterprises, it may call on its state experiment station to conduct research on these and other basic problems. Schools of economics and business administration at land-grant

---

[2]Irwin W. Rust, *How to Start a Cooperative,* FCS Educational Circular 18, U.S. Department of Agriculture, Farmer Cooperative Service, Washington, April 1965.

[3]For further information on any of the agencies identified here, see Chapter 8.

colleges and at other universities may also be able to provide special assistance to groups interested in organizing the consumer and service types of cooperatives as well as agricultural associations. State departments of agriculture may also be able to provide aid to people interested in starting cooperatives.

The Federal Government The Farmer Cooperative Service of the U.S. Department of Agriculture has special responsibility to provide technical assistance to groups interested in organizing cooperatives. Many staff members have wide experience and can advise groups on matters of organization. Depending on the direction that cooperative enterprise takes, the Economic Research Service (ERS), as well as commodity specialists and other agencies in the U.S. Department of Agriculture, may be able to provide organizational assistance. In addition, the Small Business Administration, the Department of Commerce, and the Bureau of the Census can often supply information useful to organizing groups.

State Cooperative Councils Cooperatives in most states have organized cooperative councils that serve in effect as trade organizations. They function as representatives for cooperatives in their states. Many of these councils have a wide range of members and are in a position to provide guidance and assistance to various groups interested in organizing a cooperative.

The Banks for Cooperatives The Banks for Cooperatives, a part of the Cooperative Farm Credit System, can provide financial assistance and legal guidance for groups interested in organizing farmers', marketing, purchasing, and related service cooperatives.

Regional Cooperatives These organizations often provide organizational, legal, engineering, and accounting services, and in this way they are able to assist many groups who wish to organize a cooperative.

National Cooperative Associations Two national cooperative associations—the National Council of Farmer Cooperatives and the American Institute of Cooperation—assist groups that want to form agricultural cooperatives. The Cooperative League of the U.S.A. offers organizational assistance for both agricultural purchasing and consumer types of cooperatives. The cooperative trade organizations are also usually able to supply helpful organizational information for the specific types of cooperatives they represent.

ORGANIZATIONAL STRUCTURES COMPARED[4]

Cooperative leaders have given much consideration to the relative merits of centralized and federated structures when organizing a large cooperative (see Chapter 2). The subject also has been widely discussed by cooperative spokespersons. Both successful

---

[4]Information in this section is adapted from unpublished material developed in 1970 by J. Warren Mather, Senior Agricultural Economist, Farmer Cooperative Service, U.S. Department of Agriculture.

and unsuccessful cooperatives, as well as other types of associations, use each type of structure. The strong and weak features of federated and centralized cooperatives merit identification here.

Centralized Cooperatives

Advantages

1 The centralized cooperative has complete control of local retail employees, including their selection, training, placement, pay, and supervision. This can be an advantage in building volume and attaining efficient operations.

2 Important decisions affecting wholesaling and manufacturing can be made more quickly and action can be taken faster.

3 Capital and personnel can more readily be allocated to the most critically needed activities.

4 Member capital may be raised more easily because the regional cooperative is more integrated, and there is not the competition for member capital that may exist between a federated regional and its local cooperatives.

5 Borrowing power is usually greater because of size, pooling of risks, and greater access to money markets.

6 Purchasing, manufacturing, and distributing functions can be better coordinated and made more efficient, because all the volume at retail outlets is channeled through their regional cooperatives. More effective long-range plans can also be developed.

7 Manufacturing and processing and other vertically integrated operations can be launched more easily because the cooperative has control of margins at all levels of operation.

8 Accounting is centralized, uniform, and is likely to be more efficiently performed. Internal auditing and efficiency analysis can result in better controls.

9 A large proportion of nonmember business can be conducted by some outlets, where advantageous, without greatly affecting the overall percentage handled by the association.

Limitations

1 Members may have less feeling of ownership, control, responsibility, and loyalty because the center of operations is further removed from the member than in local cooperatives and because they have less direct voice in policy determination.

2 Members may have less contact and communication with management and, therefore, less understanding and participation in cooperative affairs.

3 Control of the entire system sometimes tends to be more officer-dominated, or run from the top down.

4 Operating departments may be less sensitive to members' needs and slower in adjusting or adding local services.

5 Experiences with different operating policies and methods at the local level are not so readily available as in the federated system with independent locals.

6 Good public relations in local communities may be more difficult to maintain.

7 Members of branches with high net savings may have to absorb losses of other branches, or share their savings with them.

8 Losses or liabilities are borne by the entire cooperative instead of being divided between the federated regional and its affiliated locals.

Federated Cooperatives

Advantages

1 Members may have a greater feeling of ownership, control, responsibility, and loyalty because of investment in, and direct control of, local cooperatives. More local leadership is developed in such associations.

2 Contact and communication with members may be easier and better, and members have a better understanding of cooperatives and participate more in cooperative affairs.

3 Control of the entire system is to a greater extent maintained from the grass roots up, rather than from the top down.

4 Local cooperatives may be more sensitive to farmers' needs, and may make quicker local decisions in their direct interests.

5 Stronger and better public relations can often be maintained in the local community.

6 Capital for local facilities can be raised more easily.

7 Net savings realized by each local cooperative are distributed to its own members rather than pooled with all other locals in the system.

8 Instead of being incurred by the entire system, losses or liabilities are usually limited either to the regional or to its affiliated member locals.

Limitations

1 The regional has no direct control over the employees of its member locals. It can only encourage and recommend sound local policies and assist in training local employees.

2 Important decisions affecting regional cooperatives may at times be too slow.

3 Capital and personnel throughout the local retail cooperatives cannot be as readily allocated or shifted to areas where most needed. Raising member capital for the regional may be more difficult because of the needs of its locals.

5 Borrowing power may be less, because the system is made up of a regional and many locals, and risks are not pooled in one integrated cooperative.

6 Purchasing, manufacturing, and distributing functions are not as well coordinated, because the regional may not know the proportion of the local associations' volume that will be acquired through it. Long-range plans then are more difficult to develop.

7 Manufacturing or other vertically integrated operations cannot be launched as easily by the regional, because it does not have control of margins at all levels.

8 Accounting and auditing are not uniform and adequate in all locals, thus making comparative analysis of operating efficiency more difficult.

Methods Used to Strengthen Organization Structures

Centralized

1 The setting up of an informal council or association at each branch outlet or subsidiary, and providing for the election of advisory committee persons.

2   Formation of a subsidiary association at each branch. Voting common stock of each subsidiary is owned or controlled then by the regional cooperative, and the preferred stock of each is owned by local farmer members.

3   The conduct of an annual meeting of members at each branch outlet or subsidiary.

Federated

1   The use of financing and/or management contracts between regional and local cooperatives that indicate the services the regional will provide and what it will charge for them.

2   The encouragement of members to make financial commitments and to assume a responsibility to patronize their cooperative.

3   The development of effective member, director, and employee education and communication programs.

SPECIAL ORGANIZATIONAL PROBLEMS OF LIMITED-RESOURCE COOPERATIVES

Limited-resource cooperatives present special organizational problems. Often potential members have little or no understanding of what a cooperative can accomplish. Not only are potential members generally short of capital, but uncertain prospects for success generally discourage conventional lenders. The problem is further complicated by the political orientation of programs to assist these groups. The special agencies established to promote these cooperatives unfortunately often have "danced to political tunes," and their employees as a rule lack the training and experience necessary to give constructive guidance to them.

There are fundamental, even though unspectacular, guidelines that can be advanced to guide these groups in their cooperative organizational efforts. Namely:

- The organization should deal with basic considerations. If the group consists of farmers, they need thorough training in agricultural and production practices if they are to produce farm products that justify forming a marketing cooperative. Likewise, groups interested in forming credit unions need training in thrift and in the productive use of money. Consumers, too, need training in business practices and "buyership" if they are adequately to understand what consumer cooperatives can and cannot do for them.
- Member involvement and commitment are essential. Even for people of limited financial resources, such involvement means a willingness to make some financial commitments and to assume responsibility to patronize their cooperative. Until members understand the need for involvement and commitment, it might be better to develop precooperative arrangements as a testing ground for determining eventual possibilities for organizing a cooperative.
- Once a limited-resource cooperative is started, a number of fundamentals must be constantly kept in mind. They include:

1   A realistic training program for directors and employees
2   The establishment of effective communication techniques

3   Installation of an adequate accounting system, independent auditing, use of effective control techniques, and the building of a sound financial program

The constant challenge is to keep cooperative objectives and principles in mind and to do "common things uncommonly well."

SUMMARY

People become interested in organizing a cooperative when they encounter economic problems that are difficult if not impossible to solve alone. If they know other persons with similar problems, they may start to consider a cooperative as a possible way of dealing with these problems. As they explore cooperative possibilities, they should ask themselves discerning questions about their community, the nature and extent of their needs, the resources at their disposal, and the prevailing local economic, social, and political situation.

Should the answers to these questions be favorable, prospective members may wish to hold exploratory meetings. If interest still prevails, they usually form committees to examine the diverse problems involved in organizing a cooperative. These committees may include a general survey committee, a membership committee, a facilities committee, a finance committee, and a legal documents committee.

Once a cooperative is decided upon, it is important for the initiators to be conversant with the many legal and operational requirements necessary to get a cooperative underway. If the cooperative is to be a large-scale association, the initiators may want especially to consider whether they wish to adopt a centralized or federated organizational structure. Cooperative organizers, through precautionary and preventive provisions in their bylaws, can assure that their associations will operate as they desire with respect to such matters as methods of electing directors, establishment of an efficient record-keeping system, avoidance of nepotism, prohibition of the employment of directors, and avoidance of conflicts of interest. If it is to be a limited-resource cooperative, its leaders need to understand the implications of the special and unique problems that have a bearing on its organization.

QUESTIONS

1   What are the discerning questions any group contemplating the organization of a cooperative should ask itself?
2   What precautions are desirable when considering the organization of a cooperative?
3   What is a preorganization meeting, and what can it reasonably be expected to accomplish?
4   Identify important economic, social, and political factors that should be taken into account in organizing a cooperative.
5   What should a cooperative be able to accomplish for its organization to be justified?
6   In exploring opportunities for organizing a cooperative, what use can be made of the committee approach? What committees should be established, and how should each function?
7   What legal documents need to be developed in organizing a cooperative?

8   What is the difference between articles of incorporation and bylaws? What are the essential provisions of each?
9   What precautionary measures can be incorporated to improve the articles of incorporation?
10 What are the arguments against having directors serve as cooperative managers?
11 Do you favor adding outsiders, such as bankers or lawyers, to the board of directors of a cooperative?
12 How can cooperatives avoid nepotism? Conflicts of interest?
13 What are the strong and weak features of centralized cooperatives? Of federated cooperatives?
14 Enumerate the essential steps in getting a cooperative underway.
15 Where can people go for assistance in organizing a cooperative?
16 Can a cooperative be organized most easily during periods of favorable, or of unfavorable, economic conditions?
17 What aspects of organization need special attention when a limited-resource group is considering forming a cooperative?

REFERENCES

Derrick, B. B.: "A Pre-Organization Survey for Farmers Cooperative Associations," *Journal of Farm Economics,* October 1933, pp. 691–697.

Huddleston, Norman F.: *Considerations for Organization and Operation of Limited Resource Cooperatives,* Federal Extension Service and Auburn University, Auburn, Ala., 1970, p. 120.

Hulbert, Lyman S.: "Organizing and Incorporating a Cooperative," in *American Cooperation,* American Institute of Cooperation, Washington, D.C., 1946.

Markeson, Clyde B.: *Identifying the Need for Forestry Associations,* FCS Educational Circular 20, U.S. Department of Agriculture, Farmer Cooperative Service, Washington, 1969.

Neely, D. Morrison: *Legal Phases of Farmer Cooperatives: Sample Legal Documents,* FCS Information 66, U.S. Department of Agriculture, Farmer Cooperative Service, Washington, 1973.

Rust, Irwin W.: *How to Start a Cooperative,* FCS Educational Circular 18, U.S. Department of Agriculture, Farmer Cooperative Service, Washington, 1965.

Salter, L. C.: *Organizing and Incorporating Fishery Marketing Associations,* Fish and Wildlife Leaflet 277, Department of the Interior, Washington, 1948.

U.S. Department of Agriculture, Farmer Cooperative Service: *Forming Farmer Cooperatives,* FCS Educational Circular 10, Washington, 1956.

———: *Organizing a Farmer Cooperative,* FCS Circular 18, Washington, 1956.

Volkin, David: "Any Corporation Can Achieve a Tax Status Comparable to Cooperatives," *FCS News for Farmer Cooperatives,* U.S. Department of Agriculture, Farmer Cooperative Service, Washington, October 1966.

Chapter 13

Cooperative Management

The members of cooperatives, the directors who represent them, and the employees who work for them frequently do not well understand the true nature of cooperative management. In particular, they are all too often unaware that successful cooperative management calls for a team approach that involves their best coordinated efforts. In this respect, cooperatives differ significantly from ordinary business enterprises, which are controlled only by directors and a managerial staff. Emphasis in this chapter is on these unique features of cooperative management.

In a broad sense, cooperative management, like the management of any firm, involves the use and control of physical, financial, and human resources. It involves handling commodities or products and providing services. Cooperative management, then, coordinates and controls all aspects of operations.

Moreover, cooperative management embraces financing, pooling, bargaining, processing, purchasing, merchandising, transportation, accounting, personnel management, and communications, including member and employee education. In performing these functions, cooperative management, if it is to serve members effectively, must give special consideration to how the techniques of operating as a cooperative should influence the way management does the job.

Successful cooperative management must embody conceptual, human, and technical skills. To be effective, managers should, for example, have the capacity to deal with the idiosyncrasies of human nature. They also must be conversant with cooperative objectives and principles, and they must have the ability to analyze trends and situations and make sound and realistic decisions. And, at the same time, they should have the technical knowledge necessary to handle products and provide services.

Kelsey B. Gardner, former Director of the Management Services Division, Farmer Cooperative Service, emphasized the distinctive nature of cooperative management when he stated that "management responsibilities include ability to achieve success (1) as a cooperative and (2) as a business organization." This is a very important and basic observation. It brings into focus the special responsibilities and uniqueness of cooperative management. Often managers and staff personnel tend to take the easy way out and blink at their responsibilities as cooperative leaders. At times they even seem to believe that operating as a cooperative prevents their moving with dispatch and making sound business decisions.

Managers must never forget that cooperatives essentially are "people organizations" that are owned and controlled by member-users for their benefit. It is the members who contribute time, financial resources, and patronage to their associations. Paid management at all times should be attuned to serve their needs. Students of cooperatives frequently have expressed the view that not more than 25 percent of these associations operate at what might be termed a high level of performance. The implications of this statement are far-reaching when considered in terms of the opportunities that exist for improving cooperative managerial performance.

SUCCESS AS A COOPERATIVE

We have suggested that one of the basic responsibilities of cooperative management is to function as a team in making important decisions. Let us now examine the responsibilities of each of these groups.

Members' Role

We have mentioned that a unique feature of the cooperative business enterprise is the role of member-users in management. The members are the people who own the cooperative, use its services, and are interested in seeing it perform with the greatest possible efficiency. They benefit from effective performance, just as they are bound to lose when management performs its responsibilities poorly. Cooperative members have a more direct interest and influence in major decisions than do stockholders in an ordinary business firm who usually control only a small fraction of the total votes in these corporations. Therefore, the usually accepted idea that management includes only paid managers and division heads and the board of directors does not apply to cooperatives.

The contributions individual members can make to assure successful management of the cooperative are here adapted from those identified by Farmer Cooperative Service. Specifically, members can:

- Select the most able and best qualified members to serve on the board of directors. Check and analyze the attitudes and performance of the board and remove incompetent directors. (See the qualifications of a good director given on p. 264.)

- Adopt and amend bylaws.
- Approve changes in the capital structure.
- Increase or decrease the capitalization; approve loans under special circumstances; adopt marketing contracts and other contractual arrangements between themselves and the cooperative.
- Require officers, directors, and other agents to comply with the laws under which the association was set up, and with its articles of incorporation, bylaws, and membership contracts. Hold directors and officers who fail to do so liable for any losses caused.
- Make a special effort to understand business operations.
- Recognize cooperative possibilities and limitations, and do not expect more of the association than it can deliver.
- When in doubt about any phase of operations, discuss the question promptly with a director, a responsible officer, or the employees. If outsiders criticize operations, obtain the facts from proper association sources.
- Give the association complete loyalty and support, based on good performance and an effective communications program. Keep up membership interest and active participation. Avoid an apathetic attitude which could lead to the selection of an indifferent or inactive board. Such a result could lead to one-person control by the manager.
- Attend meetings regularly to discuss business matters and to approve or disapprove proposed actions.
- Avoid interference with employees' administrative duties. If there are any questions or suggestions regarding the manner in which these duties are performed, they should be directed to the proper officials.
- Support a policy of adequate wages for employees.
- Assist the board of directors in formulating policies by making members' views and wishes known.
- By electing new directors from time to time, make certain that the board does not develop a sense of owning the association. "New blood" will bring new ideas to the board.
- Do everything practicable to increase the business volume through improved services for members.
- Through directors, allow the manager adequate latitude in performing duties and in using judgment and experience.

To these member responsibilities the following should be added: (1) acceptance of decisions reached by majority action; and (2) discontinuance of membership when dissatisfied with policies and performance.

For the member to meet these responsibilities fully and completely, communications programs by the entire management team are required. Directors must report to members on basic policy decisions, and the manager and the staff must report to them on current operations and the business outlook. This responsibility includes regular presentation of comparative balance sheets and operating statements, division or departmental reports, and future financial and economic projections. The annual meeting provides an opportunity to furnish such information to members. It is only when members have this information that they can make intelligent managerial decisions. At times, special meetings may be called, in accordance with bylaw provisions, to consider matters of special interest to membership.

Directors' Duties and Responsibilities

The board of directors is the elected representative of the membership. Authority for determining general policy and checking on performance is delegated to it by members, generally in accordance with provisions of state enabling legislation. As a rule, this authority involves formulating general business policies, selecting managerial personnel, delegating operational authority, and evaluating results. It should be emphasized that directors can act legally only as board members; no director can act as an individual unless authorized to do so by the board. Board members should also avoid seeking or accepting special favors or taking over the manager's function by giving directions to employees.

Often one of the pronounced weaknesses in cooperative management results from a lack of members' attention to the selection of directors. The qualifications for such selection generally are the same as those of any other successful business. They may be determined, according to the Farmer Cooperative Service by use of the following questions:

- What are the prospective directors' business records? Do they manage their own affairs well? Do they possess sound business judgment?
- Are they willing to work at the job of being a director or are they more apt to be inactive? Have they shown a capacity for working with others or are they "individualists"?
- Do their neighbors regard them as leaders? Do they enjoy others' confidence for honesty and integrity? What capacity have they shown as leaders?
- Do they possess a high degree of loyalty to the association and to cooperative principles? At the same time, do they properly understand the limitations as well as the possibilities of what can be accomplished through cooperative effort?
- Is it clear that they will help their fellow members to obtain a complete understanding of the association and its various activities and problems? Will they conscientiously make information available to members?

Directors generally have a twofold responsibility. One relates to the business operations of the cooperative and, among other things, includes such duties as:

- Developing basic objectives and establishing guidelines to control the business activities of the association
- Appointing, supervising, and removing officers; determining their pay; and describing their responsibilities
- Setting up necessary committees to explore operational problems
- Calling special meetings whenever necessary or upon the request of members, as provided by the bylaws
- Approving such general business arrangements as entering into contracts with distributors or suppliers
- Selecting the bank in which to make deposits, and designating the people who may sign association checks
- Borrowing funds for any legal and approved purpose
- Insisting that an adequate bookkeeping system be maintained, that regular financial reports and audits be made, and that a complete record of board meetings be kept

The business responsibilities of the board of directors are further emphasized by Wilson and Smith.[1] They state:

> It is essential that a board understand the key elements that add up to the success of the enterprise and be closely acquainted with the current and forecast progress of the business in respect to each of these elements. Board members should be familiar with the company's purpose, its history, the market in which it is entered and the share of this market it enjoys, the strength of competition, the degree of obsolescence of physical assets, the sales volume of each product or service, the current value of financial assets, and the long-term objectives of the business. The board should also have an opportunity to review periodically the company's earnings, the soundness of its organization, and the ability of the employees to meet current and future challenges.

Directors also have responsibilities to members. These have been identified by Farmer Cooperative Service as the following:

- Serving to the best of one's ability and capacity
- Representing members' interests on an impartial basis
- Selecting a capable manager
- Adopting policies and procedures along sound business lines, based on study and analysis of available facts and compatible with the association's objectives
- Using adequate checks to make certain that the manager is conforming to the board policies adopted by the association and its board of directors
- Studying operating results in order to determine whether policies should be continued, changed, or dropped
- Taking active and energetic steps to keep the membership fully informed as to association activities and problems
- Providing high-quality, reliable service and making members' interests of first importance regardless of any other interests they may have

To these might be added, developing long-range plans to meet members' needs.

Manager and Key Staff Duties and Responsibilities

We have said that the duties and responsibilities of the manager and the key staff center upon the execution of the policies established by the board of directors. They are responsible to the board of directors for the cooperative's performance, which involves all aspects of day-to-day operations.

The manager has responsibility for planning, directing, and controlling the use of personnel, capital, facilities, and equipment. Managers are also responsible for the commodities or materials handled and the services provided. In addition, they must establish guidelines for the organization and coordination of general business operations.

The managers must never forget that, as hired employees of the cooperative, they are responsible to members for running their business and serving them effectively.

---

[1]Robert A. Wilson and Frank J. Smith, Jr., *Managing the Agribusiness Firm*, Special Report 16, University of Minnesota, Agricultural Extension Service, St. Paul, 1967, p. 16.

Their distinct and unique responsibilities bring into special focus the need for conducting business along the lines desired by members and authorized by board action.

Since managers are working with other people's money, they have the duty of operating the cooperative in the most economical way possible. Their main responsibilities, stated more explicitly, are:

- Serving the cooperative, either directly or through assistants, in accordance with the policies determined by the board
- Being cognizant of cooperative objectives and complying with all policies designed to achieve them
- Providing the board with basic information and suggestions for developing new objectives, changing established ones, and controlling operations
- Selecting, training, supervising, and developing assistants and other personnel
- Establishing realistic compensation schedules
- Operating the association on a sound business basis by giving attention to:
    1. Developing an effective business structure
    2. Using operating and financial budgets
    3. Developing and maintaining an adequate accounting and record system
    4. Developing sound union relationships
    5. Initiating sound purchasing, marketing, and pricing practices
    6. Achieving technical proficiency with respect to the products handled and the physical facilities operated
    7. Studying, planning, and conducting research on problems of interest to the cooperative
    8. Identifying and using external sources of assistance on problems affecting the cooperative

- Building confidence, understanding, and loyalty among members by effective operating performance, business integrity, and an alert response to the changes and adjustments needed to serve members more constructively (member relations)
- Developing confidence among business associates and bringing about, within the community, an understanding of association goals and objectives (public relations)
- Recognizing that management of a cooperative is usually a full-time job, and understanding that engaging in other activities might lead to a conflict of interests

Since employees "are the association," so far as the members who have most frequent contact with them are concerned, it is important that great care be given to selecting only those who are eminently qualified for their jobs. Not only should they know the technical aspects of the products they handle and the services they provide, but they must also be able to build a favorable image by their ability to meet people well and dedicate themselves to the service of members. In his publication *Cooperatives, Principles and Practices*,[2] Prof. Marvin A. Schaars identifies another aspect of cooperative employment when he says: "Although for many employees work at a cooperative is just like any other job, for others it is an opportunity for dedicated service and for community welfare."

[2]University of Wisconsin—Extension, Madison, 1971.

Manager—Board of Director Relationships

Effective relationships between the manager and the board of directors are a key factor in the success of a cooperative. Depending on how these relationships develop, the board of directors may be a source of additional ideas, serve as a guiding force in emphasizing basic goals and objectives, and function in an advisory capacity. It can support the manager in her or his relations with employees and the general public.

It has become a cliché of cooperative management that the board of directors formulates policies and the manager and staff execute them. This statement calls attention to the special nature of board of directors–member relationships in cooperatives. For example, a board of directors, in response to member interests, ought to establish fundamental policies with respect to such questions as: Should a grain cooperative begin distributing farm supplies? Should a livestock cooperative start processing operations? Should a consumer cooperative add a service station, develop a furniture department, or provide insurance? Definite policies also ought to cover such areas as quality of products handled, services provided, and community responsibilities assumed.

Policies should suggest a planned course of action for a cooperative. They might start with the current financial position and provide guidance in planning where the cooperative should be in this regard in one, two, or five years. They should also indicate how the cooperative is to get there. Policies are not developed in a vacuum. The competent board, in its planning, should request all available facts and information about operations from the manager and the staff, and when necessary, it should also use other sources of assistance.

Manager–board of director relationships also can be a source of discord in the cooperative. Failure to understand the policy-development and policy-execution responsibilities of the respective parties in their relationships with one another often is at the heart of such discord. When managers attempt to direct and directors seek to manage, the result often is unreconciled tensions. Failure to recognize where responsibilities for basic policy decisions are centered can cause difficulties for cooperatives. For example, as Watergate investigations ascertained, problems arose when managers of a limited number of dairy cooperatives took it upon themselves to make illegal contributions to political parties.

SUCCESS AS A BUSINESS

Quite obviously, many of the managerial responsibilities involved in achieving success as a cooperative also contribute to success as a business. Likewise, in varying degrees, responsibilities for managing a successful business also have special implications for cooperatives. Owing to the emphasis that cooperatives place on people and services to member-users, such responsibilities, when fully met, are distinctly oriented toward maintaining the cooperative nature of their business. At the same time, fully meeting these responsibilities helps to develop a successful business that serves the economic interests of members.

A number of general management functions contribute to the success of every business enterprise. They apply to all types of business, cooperative or otherwise. Many schools of business administration, departments of agricultural economics, state extension services, cooperatives, banks for cooperatives, and state cooperative councils provide management schools for directors and management staffs. Thus they assist cooperatives in improving business operations. Briefly identified, the principal management functions are usually considered to be the following.

Planning

Planning involves establishing cooperative objectives, recognizing alternative courses of action, and selecting the most feasible one. It is a thinking, a judging, and a deciding process. The main concern, as stated earlier, is: Where, from the standpoint of successful business operations, do cooperatives want to be at the end of any given period of time? Planning may be short-range (a season, a year, or even two or three years) or long-range (five years, ten years, or even longer).

Organizing

Organizing has to do with assembling the necessary resources to carry out plans. It involves determining the type of organizational structure and human relationships that will be most effective in getting the job done. It includes identifying the various available resources that can be used in business operations—human resources, financial resources, and physical facilities and equipment—and deciding how they will be used.

Directing

Directing is the assignment of respective duties to employees so as to make the best use of resources. The objective is to get things done well. In fact, it involves the establishment of guidelines for projects to be undertaken, decisions on when and how to do them, and supervision to see that the job is done. It should be added that, important as assigning duties are, those doing the directing must delegate adequate authority to assure completion of the necessary work.

Coordinating

Coordinating is the integrating of the various resources of a cooperative into a going concern. Emphasis is placed on integration to achieve established objectives.

Controlling

Controlling is actually a check on the use of resources. It involves techniques to determine whether plans are being carried out effectively and as intended. Controls are designed to prevent unauthorized actions, to identify danger signals, to predict trends or forecast changes, and to help all parts of the management team evaluate results. Included, also, are techniques for remedial action when certain operating aspects prove unsatisfactory.

Identification and study of the various management functions are important for the

COOPERATIVE MANAGEMENT

training of cooperative directors and managers. Knowledge of management functions enables these groups to have a better understanding of important managerial considerations that bear on successful operation. A word of caution, however, is in order. Frequently, training sessions in management functions are conducted by people whose background, experience, and thinking are oriented toward other than cooperative business enterprises. Therefore, they do not fully appreciate the distinct personal relationships that exist within cooperatives. Neither are they fully aware of the special emphasis that these associations place on services to members. To express this another way, the final test of cooperative success does not rest entirely on favorable balance sheets, operating statements, and business ratios. Rather, the final test is: What do cooperatives contribute to the net income of their members? In other words, when management stresses favorable operating statements and balance sheets, it is important to ascertain whether they were really achieved because of efficient operations, high gross margins, or inadequate services to members. Proper attention should be given to members' interests and to making certain that business success is not achieved at the expense of success as a cooperative, which centers on service to members.

SPECIAL CONSIDERATIONS IN COOPERATIVE MANAGEMENT

The unique features of cooperatives suggest special considerations for the attention of their management.

Adequate Association Records

In addition to the accounting system, there are important association records that need to be kept. Some cooperatives have experienced great difficulties because accurate records of board meetings and official actions were not maintained. In the absence of such records, the board may not know, for example, whether the association really has established a credit policy and what its provisions are. As a consequence, much of the board's time may be wasted in dealing with recurring problems that have already been covered in prior policy decisions.

Effective Tripartite Communications

We have emphasized the unique nature of the cooperative management team—a team that includes members, directors, and the manager and the key staff. For management to be effective, quite obviously, good communications must exist among the members of the team. If directors are to establish sound policies, they should know how the members wish their association to operate. Members, in turn, not only need to know how and what their cooperative is doing, but they also ought to inform the directors about the services they wish it to provide. For members to judge how well their cooperative is serving them, directors must shoulder the responsibility to inform them as to policy decisions and operating performance.

In addition to their responsibility to report to directors on operations, managers, because of the key positions they and their staffs occupy, can identify important policy matters for the consideration of the board of directors. They are also especially equipped to advise directors on where they may turn for counsel and assistance in formulating association policy.

Another communication responsibility of managers and their staffs is to report to members on the cooperative's operations at annual meetings. These communications are often supplemented by additional reports to members and to members' house organs and other information media. Managers, especially in the larger regional cooperatives, also rely on research to strengthen member communications. Such research centers upon member attitudes, the services they desire, and the ways in which the cooperative should adjust operations in order to keep abreast of economic and social change. (Cooperative communications are discussed in detail in Chapter 14.)

Legal Responsibilities

Cooperative directors frequently do not appreciate their legal responsibilities. Recognition of these responsibilities and the personal liability involved can be a sobering experience for them. For example, many directors are not aware that they have all the legal powers, and are subject to all the legal provisions, that have to do with the operation of a cooperative. There is a substantial body of statutory legislation that relates to such matters as board meetings, conflicts of interest, and obligations and liabilities. Courts have ruled, for example, that directors are legally responsible if they permit a cooperative to exceed its legal debt limit, if negligence or fraud can be established, and if the board takes action on matters that, under state law, should be referred to the membership. State laws, too, impose a number of specific liabilities and responsibilities on cooperative directors, as do charter and bylaw provisions. If directors are to effectively discharge their duties, and if they are to avoid legal pitfalls of both a personal nature and a cooperative concern, they need a full understanding of bylaw and statutory provisions.

There are, of course, legal responsibilities that apply to members and the manager and other employees also. Although large regional cooperatives may have their own full-time lawyers or legal departments, local associations usually do not. Since they cannot be their own lawyers, they need to arrange for competent legal advice when necessity arises.

Title of the Chief Executive Officer

A recent development of some interest concerns the best title for the chief executive officer of a cooperative. A number of cooperatives have changed the title of "general manager" to that of "president." In some cases, such action appears to be motivated by little more than a desire to "keep up with the Joneses," or at least to follow the same practice used by other business concerns. The argument for using the title of president often is that this title is better known and understood by officials of firms other than cooperatives, especially overseas firms, than is the title of manager. Officials of large cooperatives also say that many legal documents require the signature of the president. To meet this requirement expeditiously the manager may carry such a title. Then the title "chairman of the board" comes into common usage and division or department heads often become vice presidents.

Other cooperative officials argue, however, that they want to be accepted only for what they are and what they do. To them, performance and integrity, rather than a title, are the most important considerations in developing and maintaining the business relationships involved in cooperative management.

Reasons for Cooperative Failure

As in any other type of business undertaking, the reasons for cooperative failure are legion. Here, we identify only the major areas that contribute to cooperative failure. Among others, they are:

- *Premature start.* Often, the many factors that have a bearing on the feasibility of organizing a cooperative are not determined (see Chapter 12).
- *Inadequate member support.* This may stem from poor communications on the part of the cooperative, poor business performance, and/or lack of members' appreciation of what they can or cannot expect their cooperative to accomplish.
- *Failure of management (members, directors, and the manager and key employees).* These participants on the management team do not assume responsibility for the successful operation of the cooperative.
- *Inadequate financial support and poor financial management.* Members often fail to give the necessary financial support, and in other instances, the directors and the manager mismanage the financial resources available.

Listing some specific danger spots may help:

1 Poorly planned annual meetings
2 Ineffective communications techniques
3 Failure to recognize the need for effective member and public relations programs
4 Selection of incompetent board members, including board members who fail to attend meetings and who do not patronize their cooperative
5 False economy in hiring management
6 Poor accounting and auditing practices
7 Failure to give members a full and accurate report on association performance
8 Failure to build protective features into the operation of the cooperative (see pp. 250–253)
9 Poor business sense with respect to such things as facility location, methods of handling products, handling of inventories
10 Cliques or special-interest groups that may develop among members, directors, or employees
11 Unfair competition coupled with a misinformed public and unfriendly regulatory and governmental agencies
12 Failure to recognize the contributions that sound research can provide for the decision-making process

SUMMARY

We have stated in this chapter that cooperative management in a broad sense relates to all aspects of the business operations of a cooperative. It encompasses decisions concerning such specialized areas as financing, membership, communications, transportation, and law, as well as the whole gamut of operating practices.

We have shown also that cooperative management is unique in that it is concerned with achieving success not only as a business firm but also as a cooperative. This means that members should have a say in the operations of their own business and a responsibility for its success beyond and above the benefits that accrue to them.

Cooperative management, in contrast to other business management, involves a coordinated team effort by members, directors, and the manager and the key staff. Though each has distinct duties and responsibilities in this scheme of management, they must—as a team—pay special attention to those measures that will enable the organization to start and progress according to members' needs and desires. Careful attention must therefore be given to such matters as annual meetings, makeup and qualifications of the board of directors, adequate records, provisions for training, and an awareness of legal responsibilities.

QUESTIONS

1. What are the basic differences in management between a cooperative and other types of business?
2. What are the roles and responsibilities of members in cooperative management?
3. What is the role of directors in cooperative management? What are their responsibilities to members? To the cooperative?
4. Identify the duties and responsibilities of the manager.
5. What is meant by the statement: To the member the employee *is* the cooperative?
6. What are the basic functions of cooperative management?
7. What protective provisions can be built into cooperative bylaws to protect the members and to ensure that operations are in their best interests?
8. What types of training are needed to develop directors? Managers?
9. What is meant by saying that the annual meeting is an important management tool?
10. How far should employees, including labor unions, be permitted to go in determining cooperative operating policies?

REFERENCES

Abshier, George S., Robert D. Dahle, and Paul O. Mohn: *Management for Agricultural Marketing Firms,* Federal Extension Service and North Carolina State University, Raleigh, 1966, p. 63.

Gardner, Kelsey B.: *Managing Farmer Cooperatives,* Educational Circular 17, rev., Farmer Cooperative Service, U.S. Department of Agriculture, Washington, 1972.

Garoian, Leon, and Arnold F. Hasely: *The Board of Directors in Agricultural Policy Businesses,* Oregon State University Cooperative Extension Service, Corvallis, 1964, p. 141.

Kirkman, C. H.: *Managers Hold an Important Key to Cooperative Success,* FCS Information 74, Farmer Cooperative Service, U.S. Department of Agriculture, Washington, 1970.

Manuel, Milton L.: *Improving Management of Farmer Cooperatives,* General Report 120, Farmer Cooperative Service, U.S. Department of Agriculture, Washington, 1964.

Rust, Irwin W.: *Assuring Democratic Election of Cooperative Directors,* Educational Circular 21, Farmer Cooperative Service, U.S. Department of Agriculture, Washington, 1965.

————: *Using Cooperative Directors to Strengthen Member Relations,* Educational Circular 23, Farmer Cooperative Service, U.S. Department of Agriculture, Washington, 1965.

Sims, Melvin: *Director and Management Teamwork Means Cooperative Progress,* Farmer Cooperative Service, U.S. Department of Agriculture, Washington, 1963.

Smith, Frank J., Jr., and Ken Cooper: *The Financial Management of Agribusiness Firms,* Special Report 26, University of Minnesota Extension Service, St. Paul, 1967, p. 211.

Volkin, David: *What Directors Expect of Management,* Reprint 337, Farmer Cooperative Service, U.S. Department of Agriculture, Washington, 1967.

————, Nelda Griffen, and Helin H. Hulbert: *Directors of Regional Cooperatives—Selection, Qualifications, Duties, Performance,* Farmer Cooperative Service, U.S. Department of Agriculture, Washington, 1960, p. 40.

Wilson, Robert A., and Frank J. Smith, Jr.: *Managing the Agribusiness Firm: 10 Areas,* Special Report 16, University of Minnesota Extension Service, St. Paul, 1967, p. 100.

Chapter 14

Cooperative Communications

Cooperatives are confronted by a passing parade of many different publics. Most of these publics have either a direct or an indirect interest in how cooperatives operate. The people who make up the various publics are constantly changing, and their importance may shift considerably over time. To understand cooperative issues, they must know how and why cooperatives are organized. Moreover, they also need such information to draw valid conclusions and make sound decisions concerning cooperatives whenever they have occasion to do so.

Cooperatives have long recognized the importance of educating their members. In our study of the Rochdale principles, we found one principle stipulating that "a definite percentage of profits should be allocated to education," and another providing that "frequent statements and balance sheets should be presented to members." As early as the 1920s, American cooperatives gradually began to explore member relations, and later some began to recognize the need for public relations programs.

The International Cooperative Alliance reformulated its statement on cooperative principles in 1966. Included among the six principles it identified was the following on education: "All co-operative societies should make provision for the education of their members, officers, and employees and of the general public, in the principles and techniques of Co-operation, both economic and democratic."

American cooperatives, especially regional associations, now emphasize the importance of providing many of their publics with technical and economic information as well as basic facts on their operating performance. The term *communication* has become the most suitable one to describe the messages cooperatives convey to, and receive from, members, potential members, directors, employees, and the general public.

Communication may be described, then, as a process of conveying an idea or a message from one person or group of persons to another person or group. It includes the idea or message that is conveyed, the way it is expressed, how and when it is delivered, and the person or persons it is intended to reach. It is a what, a how, a who, and a when process. It must be emphasized, also, that successful communication is a two-way process that depends to a large extent upon the response of those to whom the messages are initially directed. For the cooperative, the main object is to provide information through the various media channels, and in many instances to motivate the receivers—once they have heard, read, or seen the communication—to take a course of action favorable to both themselves and their cooperatives. Quite obviously, communication has become a very specialized and complex process. It requires the coordination of psychological, educational, and economic disciplines.

WHY IS COOPERATIVE COMMUNICATION NEEDED?

Communication is not something that is done once and for all, nor can it be turned on or off at the whim of management. Neither is it a process to be dusted off and used only when a cooperative is encountering stormy times, whether of an economic nature or pertaining to a wide gamut of human relationships. Rather, it may be regarded as a type of insurance that represents a built-up reserve that a cooperative may draw upon to achieve its basic objectives. Indeed, communication can serve as a countermeasure to put problems in proper perspective and to dispel rumors, innuendos, and false statements. More important, however, communications can be a positive force for better recognition of good cooperative performance. This idea has been succinctly stated by J. H. Heckman, former head of the Member Relations Section, Farmer Cooperative Service, as "Doing a good job and getting credit for it."

A number of specific factors contribute to the growing need for cooperative communications. They are:

The Unique Nature of the Cooperative Cooperatives are unique business organizations in that the people who patronize them are also the ones who own and control them. For patrons to evaluate properly how well their cooperative serves them, they must know its basic objectives, its operating policies and practices, and its record of performance.

Growth We have indicated that cooperatives are still relatively small businesses when compared with other types of businesses. Many, however, have experienced substantial growth. As a result of this growth, not only are physical facilities often far removed from members, but also the manager and other employees who make decisions affecting patrons may be located hundreds of miles away from those they serve. Unless informative two-way communication constantly flows between the members and the management, personal contacts will be increasingly hard to maintain. The cooperative, therefore, has to appear not so big and so far removed as no longer to care about its patrons. Aptly stated, the cooperative has a responsibility to "be big, and yet . . . seem small."

New People in Various Publics Not only does the membership of a cooperative constantly change, but so do its employees, directors, and the makeup of the general publics with whom it has contact. The cooperative therefore deals with ever-changing groups of people, and the need for constant communication is imperative if the unique nature of the cooperative system is to be known.

New Developments Of special interest to cooperative patrons are the manifold new technical developments that concern their cooperatives as well as themselves. Among other things, these developments, as they affect agricultural cooperatives, may reflect the impact of new research and technology on such matters as cultural practices, processing and manufacturing methods, market requirements, and procurement methods. All types of cooperatives have frequent need to inform members about changes in government regulations and controls that influence their policies and practices.

Creation of a Favorable Cooperative Image The cooperative is a citizen of the community in which it operates. Therefore, through communication, it has a responsibility to inform all publics about its performance. Communication also is a powerful force in dispelling rumors and misunderstandings that arise because of a lack of information. It does not, however, exist in isolation. Under all circumstances, communication, no matter what kind, creates some sort of image. Effective communications can help a cooperative to get full credit for any favorable performance it has achieved and thus to avoid "hiding its light under a bushel basket."

Communications with Dollar Value On this point, Prof. Frank Groves, of the University of Wisconsin, is quoted in *Cooperatives, Principles and Practices,*[1] by Prof. Marvin A. Schaars of the University of Wisconsin, as follows:

> A well-informed member who understands the organization, its policies and actions, generally will remain more loyal, have fewer complaints, and take a greater interest. He will patronize the cooperative when given a choice, stay with the organization when the going is rough, and offer more constructive criticism and suggestions. He will inform his neighbors about the organization in terms they understand, serve as an effective salesman for the organization, help promote new products and services, and be easier to do business with. He will meet his obligations and pay his bills to the cooperative. An educated member will help stop rumors; defend the cooperative; and develop a favorable climate of understanding

[1] University of Wisconsin—Extension, Madison, 1971.

between members, employees, and directors. He will promote a progressive attitude and build member confidence in the cooperative and its management. A knowledgeable member will develop a pride among members and within the community in the cooperative as a business organization—and he will inform the community of the cooperative's contribution to the local economy.

While it is hard to measure the dollar value of communicating with members, there is every reason to believe that the dollar value of communications with directors, employees, top management, and the general public is equally important. The role of communication may be illustrated by asking: What is, or what would be, the situation if no formal communication programs were undertaken by cooperatives.

Well-informed directors can do much to create a favorable image by demonstrating a knowledge of how their cooperative functions and operates. The director who can ask searching questions, who knows his or her responsibility and those of the members and the manager, and who is technically competent is an invaluable asset to the cooperative. A well-planned communications program can help develop such a director.

Often employees, in effect, *are* the cooperative as far as the patrons and the general public are concerned, because they are the persons with whom these publics most frequently have direct contact. Likewise, a well-informed and knowledgeable manager can do much to develop favorable cooperative communications. In the same way, knowledge based on sound information and facts can create a favorable image for the cooperative among such publics as educators, the clergy, business people, and legislators.

WHO SHOULD COMMUNICATE FOR COOPERATIVES?

Cooperatives are actually communicating at all times and in a number of ways. They do this directly or indirectly. The member who is knowledgeable or ignorant about the operations of the cooperative creates accordingly a favorable or an unfavorable image among the general public. The cooperative's telephone operator and the truck driver, by their very actions, are also communicating for better or for worse with those with whom they are in contact. The way the manager behaves at annual meetings, answers questions, and serves as spokesperson for the cooperative help to create an appealing or an unattractive image for the organization.

Most cooperatives now have formally organized techniques for communicating with their publics. The larger regionals, for example, have established communication or information departments. These departments are designed to give attention to a wide range of programs. Their programs may include one or more such activities as member relations, public relations, publications, training, advertising, and special activities including communications with women, young adult members, and youth. Communication departments commonly report to the general manager. They have their own budgets and established objectives, and they carry on comprehensive planning programs.

Local cooperatives usually have much more modest communication programs. Often one individual may have responsibility for all association communications and will direct attention to those particular areas that, in the opinion of management, have the highest priority. In other areas, the responsibility for various areas of communication may be divided on a part-time basis among employees. The manager, for example, may handle public relations, while other employees may be assigned to such activities as member relations (education), publications, training, and special programs.

Communication functions in large cooperatives are not limited to personnel in communication departments. Many cooperatives have member advisory committees for each major program area, for example. Other program areas may consist of communication programs that include personal, printed, and audiovisual techniques that are outside, though perhaps coordinated with, corporate communication departments.

WITH WHOM SHOULD COOPERATIVES COMMUNICATE?

We have already mentioned the various publics with whom cooperatives communicate. These publics are found both within and outside the cooperatives.

Within the Cooperatives

Members, directors, and employees are the principal groups within a cooperative that a communications program seeks to reach.

Members Members are the cooperative's reason for being. They have every right to know how their business is being run and what the results of its operations are. It is generally agreed that the basic purpose of a member information program is to improve the members' understanding of their cooperative. The program should, among other things, acquaint them with cooperative objectives, policies, and operating results, and present future problems that may confront their association. It should involve their participation in the communications process. The primary objective of such a program is to provide members with the information they need to make them understanding and responsive participants in the affairs of their cooperative.

Incomplete information and half-truths do not build desirable long-time member support. Cooperatives are also increasingly recognizing that nothing is gained by passing over bad news and difficult problems. When members are informed in a straightforward way about their association's problems, they are much more likely to support their cooperative. A lack of information results in rumors and misunderstanding.

Cooperatives, more and more, are thinking of their membership as a family decision-making unit. To act intelligently, all the members need fundamental information about their cooperative. In addition, many cooperatives maintain special programs for women and youth. Such programs are considered part and parcel of member-information activities.

Directors Directors are delegated responsibility by members for determining the general operating policies of their association. A carefully thought-out communications program is necessary if they are to fulfill their responsibilities effectively. For example, the directors need operating information in order to formulate sound business policies. As spokespeople for their cooperative, it is important that they be well informed not only about its operations, but also about the many general economic, political, and social forces that have an impact on its activities. The training aspects of a cooperative's communications frequently involve directors. To function at a maximum level, most of them would benefit from a carefully planned training program. Some regional associations have special training programs for new directors and for the presidents of their member affiliates.

Employee and Key Management Staff Employees also need information about the real nature of cooperative enterprise if they are to be helpful in building a favorable image. In addition, they should be among the best informed people in the community as to their specific responsibilities in order to build respect and confidence for the cooperative form of business enterprise. Similarly, the manager and staff ought to be informed about their own responsibilities, their relationships with other employees, directors, and members, and their general training in business administration.

Outside the Cooperatives

Outside the cooperatives are potential members and patrons and various segments of the general public that cooperative communications programs are often geared to reach.

Potential Patrons and Members Some cooperatives may wish to direct special communications to potential patrons and potential members. The importance of these communications depends upon an association's appraisal of the possible benefits of such efforts. In agricultural communities, this group may include 4-H club members, members of Future Farmers of America, and young farmer groups. It is only when potential patrons and members have complete and accurate information about a cooperative that they can hope to determine the real advantages of patronizing it.

The General Public There are many general publics with whom the cooperative needs to communicate. Some of the most important ones that directly influence cooperatives are schools (elementary schools, high schools, vocational schools, colleges and universities), the news media, government agencies, and legislators.

Civic clubs, chambers of commerce, churches, and almost all other groups have an indirect influence on cooperatives. If reached with convincing cooperative communications programs, these groups can produce substantial changes in the prevailing attitudes toward cooperatives. Cooperative communicators often classify the general public into such categories as local, regional, national, and international. Only when these various publics have accurate information about cooperative performance are they able to evaluate intelligently the contributions of cooperatives to their communities.

HOW DO COOPERATIVES COMMUNICATE?

Cooperatives have three basic ways of communicating: by personal contact; by the use of printed material; and by audiovisual aids.

Personal Contact

Personal contact, if well handled, is generally recognized as the most effective means of cooperative communication. The most important forms of personal contact include annual and special meetings, field days and open-house tours; member committees; and manager, employee, director, and member meetings—formal or informal. Personal contacts, however, are slow and costly and in practice must be supplemented by other techniques.

Printed Material

Printed material may take a number of forms, including personal and special letters, member magazines, direct mail, annual reports, and newspaper accounts.

Audiovisual Aids

Audiovisual communication techniques are a more recent development. They include a wide variety of techniques such as special telephone calls, computer systems, cartridge films, closed-circuit television, and radio and television.

The ways in which communication channels can be used in face-to-face and mass media techniques are summarized by Profs. Dick Vilstrup and Frank Groves in their publication *Communications Techniques*[2] (see Figure 14-1).

WHAT MAKES AN EFFECTIVE COMMUNICATIONS PROGRAM?

A number of factors need to be taken into account in building an effective communications program. First of all, it is important that the program be tailored to each audience. It is highly desirable, for example, to recognize the specific characteristics of the publics with whom the cooperative wishes to communicate. Some publics may have special concern for status, recognition, or job security. Some may have a wide span of biases that influence personal relationships. A careful consideration of whom it wishes to reach will determine to a large extent the approach and effectiveness of any cooperative's communications program. In addition, to be successful, any communications program needs the support of management. In other words, management must be willing to provide an adequate budget and to employ qualified people to develop the communications program. It also means that the communicators must be part of the

[2]University of Wisconsin—Extension, Madison, 1972.

COOPERATIVE COMMUNICATIONS

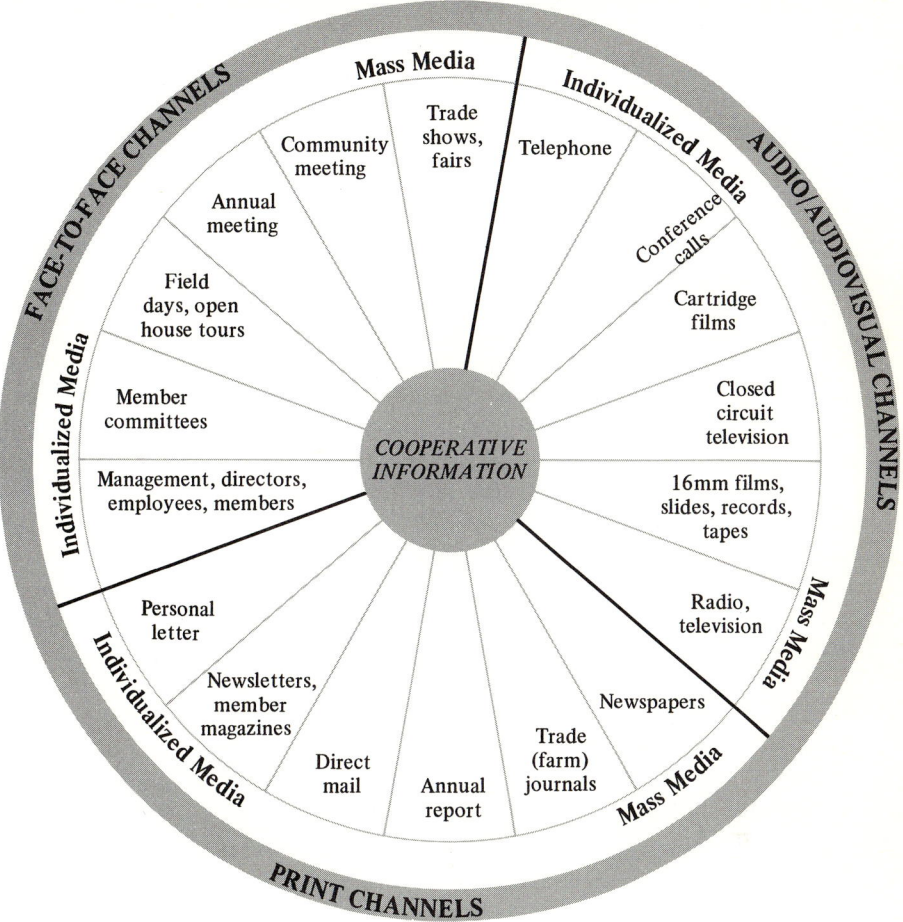

Figure 14-1 Media channels used in cooperative communications. (*Source:* Dick Wilstrup and Frank Groves, Communications Techniques, *University of Wisconsin—Extension, Madison.*)

management team to the extent that they are conversant with association objectives, plans, problems, and projections.

We have emphasized that effective communication must be based on creditable business performance and on readily accepted approaches. People generally tend to fear the unknown, the untried, and the uncertain. Only a limited amount of what is new, different, or unique can be successfully introduced at any one time. Attempting to communicate too much of such information will lead to the withdrawal of the person communicated with and a tendency to discredit or run down the communicator.

Experience has demonstrated that it is usually well to arrange for a preparatory communication when introducing new material so that the people the communicator wishes to reach are not caught by surprise. Another strategy is to involve a wide range of people in the communications process. This approach helps to build support and understanding for what is to be communicated. When these major considerations are taken into account, it is possible to use motivating forces to make communication successful. These forces may include appeals to status, income, prestige, and, in any event, identification with areas of mutual interest.

Helpful in building an effective communications program are: (1) reliance on research, (2) careful consideration of information that cooperatives should communicate, and (3) measurement of results. Let us examine these factors further.

Reliance on Research

It is not always recognized that communications are closely related to research. For a communications program to contribute to successful member and public relations, basic information about the cooperative is needed. Such information might include the income level of members, their average age, member and public attitudes toward the cooperative, member needs, and important trends or changes in the community. The last consideration may relate to changes in agricultural production, the degree of urbanization in the community, and trends in movement to the suburbs, with its possible effects on consumer and service cooperatives.

Cooperatives also need basic information on the nature of their competition. Information on these and related topics helps them to establish the benchmarks necessary for measuring the effect of their communications programs.

What Information Should Cooperatives Communicate?

Each individual cooperative is confronted with specific problems in determining what its communications program should communicate. In planning a communications program, attention should be given to identifying the places where it will do the most good and to taking steps necessary to put it into effect. A careful look at operations and results, knowledge of problem areas, and information about new services can help in planning an effective program.

Specific areas of communication that generally are important include:

Economic Information Members, directors, and employees stand to benefit from information on major trends affecting their cooperative's business operations. This information may relate to factors all the way from foreign trade, domestic trade, and competition with other products to the impact of research on production, marketing, and business structure and organization. Specific industrywide information on the type of business the cooperative is engaged in, as well as information about consumers of the products or services the cooperative provides, is also extremely useful to cooperative decision makers.

Technical Information New developments in industrial technology have an important bearing on the adjustments which both members and their cooperative must make if they are to operate with maximum efficiency. From the standpoint of the cooperative, such developments may relate to processing techniques, changes in feed and fertilizer manufacturing, the impact of the computer, and any number of other technical developments. The agricultural cooperative member has particular interest in the latest information concerning production practices and marketing methods. Members of consumer cooperatives are greatly interested in unit pricing, quality-price relationships, information on nutrition, and techniques for providing the services they require.

Cooperative Information There is much information specifically relating to cooperatives that should be a part of any cooperative communications program. Every so often, for example, a cooperative needs to reemphasize the unique nature of cooperative enterprise and to review its background and history, its basic principles, its objectives, and its general operating policies and practices. This information should be communicated to all patrons, as should information about the cooperative's operating and financial condition. This also applies to presentation and interpretation of operating statements and balance sheets. Members could also benefit from information about, among other things, the cooperative's organizational structure, pricing practices, competitive position, tax status, and available services.

Questions may arise as to how far cooperatives should go in providing information. Is there any limit to the kind and amount of information that should be made available to members and employees? Generally, it is recognized that cooperatives should not provide information that would be helpful to competitors. While operating statements should be specific as to total salaries, the salaries of individual employees ought not to be revealed. Neither should cooperatives report initial merger explorations to members or the general public, since such information might cause unnecessary concern among members and employees or become helpful to competitors. If, however, the board of directors reaches the point where it recommends a merger, this decision should be taken to members and carefully and completely explained before they are asked to vote on such a measure.

It should be reemphasized, also, that fundamental to any effective cooperative communications program is the degree of the cooperative's success. Under no circumstances can a slick, Madison Avenue–type communications program be used to gloss over an explainable bad year or inefficient performance. The first and most essential requirement of any cooperative communications program is the highest possible level of operating performance. Only when the program achieves the peak level is the cooperative in a strong position to appeal for member and general public support. Only then is it equipped to start building a desirable image. Business success is the foundation upon which any sound, successful long-range communications program must be developed.

COORDINATING COMMUNICATIONS AND MEMBER RELATIONS

Most major cooperatives have well-developed communication and member relations and public relations programs. When well planned and coordinated, the programs are closely related and complementary. The communications programs place emphasis on techniques for developing and using various media channels. The member and public relations programs stress education of members and the general public. To this end, they use the communications techniques that they have developed as tools to achieve this purpose. How such a coordinated program operates in practice is illustrated in selected highlights of the program developed by Farmland Industries, Inc.[3]

Farmland Industries, Inc., with headquarters in Kansas City, Missouri, is a regional farm-supply cooperative that, through more than 2,000 local, member retail cooperatives, serves some 500,000 farm and ranch families in 15 Midwestern states.

Communications Techniques

Selected communications techniques used by Farmland Industries, Inc., are here briefly described.

- *A membership newspaper.* A membership newspaper, *Farmland News*, has been published continually since 1933, and reaches approximately 400,000 farms and ranches. It is published twice monthly and subscriptions are sponsored by member cooperatives. *Farmland News* reports new programs, new facilities, and general programs of Farmland and its members, and it carries features of general interest throughout the Midwest.
- *A monthly magazine for board members and managers.* The monthly magazine *Leadership* informs board members and managers of member cooperatives on such subjects as available assistance from their regional on a wide range of problems, including supply distribution, marketing, finance, management, and member relations. A related feature of this technique is the Annual Leadership Award which recognizes the outstanding contributions to their cooperative by a board of directors of a member association.
- *A manager's newsletter.* This newsletter is published biweekly to acquaint managers of member associations in brief, concise statements with Farmland's operations and policies, community information, general cooperative and business news, and government regulations.
- *An annual newsletter seminar.* This seminar is conducted to assist local member cooperatives develop and improve newsletters for their farmer and rancher members.
- *The annual report.* Farmland looks upon its annual report as a major member and public relations tool. The report provides a detailed account of the cooperative's financial position and summarizes important events and developments. It is distributed at each annual meeting and by mail to all member associations as well as to many others interested in the operation of the cooperative.
- *An audiovisual department.* This department maintains an extensive file of photographs of the cooperative's facilities, products, and personnel. These pictures are used in publications, slide presentations, sales promotions, special events programs, and member and public relations projects. The department occasionally makes movies about association activities, which are extensively used by personnel for sales and information services.

---

[3]Information on this program was provided by Mr. Bill Matteson, Director of Communication Services of Farmland Industries, Inc.

- *Corporate citizenship*. As the representative for hundreds of thousands of farmers and ranchers, Farmland, in recent years, has conducted a "speaking out for farmers" campaign to tell the farmers' story to urban audiences through major daily urban newspapers. Along closely related lines is the cooperative's policy to support community projects through ads in local newspapers and through dissemination of news releases on cooperative developments that are of interest to the general public and local communities.

Member Relations

Farmland reports that its member relations program is designed to develop the pride of local cooperative's members in the ownership of their cooperative. Special emphasis is on (1) the relationship of Farmland with its local member associations, and (2) the relationship of its local member cooperatives with their member-patrons. Important techniques used to strengthen the member relations program are:

- *The annual meeting*. This meeting is geared to providing delegates of member associations with a firsthand understanding of the operations of Farmland Industries, Inc. For those who are unable to attend annual meetings, the cooperative has a "keep in touch" policy which involves a series of some thirty to forty district meetings throughout its fifteen-state operating area. At these meetings, yearly operations and future plans are reviewed and information is sought from local members as to their changing needs and the new services they require.
- *Assistance on local meetings*. Farmland has an active program of assistance to local members on how to conduct successful annual meetings.
- *Tours for groups of cooperators*. Farmland and member cooperatives conduct a series of two- or three-day bus tours which enable representatives and members of member cooperatives to visit specific Farmland facilities, such as a refinery, a steel plant, a fertilizer plant, a research and demonstration farm, or the central research department. This "see what you own" program is designed to acquaint newly affiliated cooperatives with the services the regional provides and to assist established member cooperatives in expanding their services by adding new commodity lines. A new members' tour program also has been developed in order to acquaint these cooperative members with available facilities and services.
- *Scholarship programs*. The scholarship program at land-grant universities and postsecondary schools supports the education of students majoring in agribusiness. One of the objectives of this program is to encourage students to seek employment in Midwestern cooperatives.
- *Family conferences*. Three week-long family conferences are conducted yearly at Estes Park, Colorado. Some 500 to 800 people participate in each of these conferences, which includes an "eye opener" session for exchange of cooperative information and activities as well as recreational and sightseeing programs. Similar week-long youth conferences are held for high school students active in vocational education, Future Farmers, Future Homemakers, 4-H club members, and similar groups. Participation usually is based on competitive selection by demonstrated ability in essay and speaking contests. Also, twice a year a four-day young-farmer-and-rancher conference is conducted that accommodates forty couples. Emphasis is on how cooperatives can meet young farmers needs in modern-day agriculture.

Annual meeting of the Maryland and Virginia Milk Producers Association. Annual meetings provide an excellent opportunity for cooperatives to inform members about business operations and current matters of interest to them. *Courtesy Maryland and Virginia Milk Producers Association (Adams' Studio, Inc.)*

- *Wives' luncheon meetings.* Recognizing that women are becoming more important as partners in the farm operation, Farmland assists member cooperatives in conducting a series of free luncheon meetings specifically for wives of farmer members. The objective is to acquaint women with local cooperative personnel and to inform them as to the purpose and background of their cooperative with the hope of getting them more involved in its operations.

Measuring Results

Some measure of the effectiveness and success of cooperative communication programs can be obtained from the following criteria:

- *Changes in share of the market*. Is the cooperative share of the market increasing or decreasing, and by how much?
- *Changes in member and patron attitudes*. How well are the cooperative and its services accepted by members and patrons?
- *Changes in public attitudes*. What image has the cooperative succeeded in building in its community? Should this image be maintained or improved?
- *Membership turnover*. It is important to know this trend and to have information on why changes have occurred.
- *The extent of complaints and compliments*. While a cooperative generally tries to operate in such a way as to hold complaints to a minimum, cooperative leaders recognize the importance of giving constructive complaints a chance to be heard. Perhaps the key issue is not so much the number of complaints, as how those that are received are handled. The same can be said for compliments.
- *The number and effectiveness of contacts made*. Cooperative communicators are well aware that effective communications involve more than just making contacts. When its contacts have a favorable impact, the cooperative is provided with an excellent opportunity to tell its story, provide information as to its operations, and work on strengthening its image.

SUMMARY

Communications can be an effective management tool in building strong member and public relations programs and in establishing a desirable cooperative image. Cooperatives have a special need for such a program because of the unique nature of cooperative business enterprise, the growth of these organizations, the constant change in the makeup of the various interested publics, the impacts of new developments on members and on their cooperatives, and the practical dollar-and-cents value of a favorable image.

A strong cooperative communications program must be built on careful planning, competent research, and knowledge of objectives, problems, operations, and accomplishments. The program planners should give careful attention to such considerations as who should do the communicating, what they should communicate and with whom, and how they should carry on the communications. If cooperatives are to have a successful communications program, they also need the wholehearted support of management. Cooperative communicators should recognize the distinguishing features of each public with whom they communicate and the motivating forces that condition the response of these publics to communications. Two further items are key factors in effective communications: (1) credibility of the message communicated, and (2) a foundation of high-level performance upon which the communications program can be initiated and carried on.

QUESTIONS

1. Why are member relations, public relations, and cooperative education an integral part of cooperative communications?
2. What factors have contributed to the increased need for cooperative communications?

3   Why does the unique nature of cooperatives require that they give special attention to communications?
4   Does cooperative communication have a dollar value? Can it be determined?
5   With whom should cooperatives communicate?
6   What should cooperatives communicate? How are the significant areas determined?
7   Why is cooperative performance considered an important prerequisite for effective communication?
8   Indicate the different means by which cooperatives can communicate.
9   Who should communicate for cooperatives?
10 How can the effectiveness of a cooperative communications program be measured?
11 What are the basic considerations in building an effective communications program?
12 How important is member involvement for successful communication?

REFERENCES

Copp, James H., and Irwin W. Rust: *Exploring Communication Processes in a Farmer Cooperative*, General Report 97, Farmer Cooperative Service, U.S. Department of Agriculture, Washington, 1961, p. 24.

Groves, Frank, Dick Vilstrup, Gerald Dryer, and Paul Mohn: *Cooperative Communications—Ideas That Work*, University of Wisconsin—Extension, Madison, 1972.

————, and Dick Vilstrup (project leaders); *Cooperative Communications–Instructor's Guide*, University of Wisconsin—Extension, Madison, 1972, p. 243.

Hyre, French M., and Irwin W. Rust: *Organizing and Conducting Cooperatives' Annual Meetings*, Educational Circular 32, Farmer Cooperative Service, U.S. Department of Agriculture, Washington, 1967, p. 60.

Raper, Luther E.: *Stepping Stones to Good Member Relations*, Information 29, Farmer Cooperative Service, U.S. Department of Agriculture, Washington, 1969, p. 28.

Rust, Irwin W.: *Creating Training Programs for Cooperative Directors*, Educational Circular 22, Farmer Cooperative Service, U.S. Department of Agriculture, Washington, 1964, p. 14.

————: *Effective Information Devices for Cooperatives*, Educational Circular 29, Farmer Cooperative Service, U.S. Department of Agriculture, Washington, 1966, p. 14.

————: *Making Member Relations Succeed*, Information Circular 32, Farmer Cooperative Service, U.S. Department of Agriculture, Washington, 1963, p. 16.

————: *Recruiting, Training, and Developing Workers for Farmer Cooperatives*, Information 77, Farmer Cooperative Service, U.S. Department of Agriculture, Washington, 1971, p. 44.

————: *Using Cooperative Directors to Strengthen Member Relations*, Educational Circular 23, Farmer Cooperative Service, U.S. Department of Agriculture, Washington, 1965, p. 8.

————: *What Cooperative Members Should Know*, Educational Circular 24, Farmer Cooperative Service, U.S. Department of Agriculture, Washington, 1965, p. 10.

Schaars, Marvin A.: *Cooperatives, Principles and Practices*, University of Wisconsin—Extension, Madison, 1971, pp. 43–48.

Vilstrup, Dick, and Frank Groves: *Cooperative Communications—Techniques*, University of Wisconsin—Extension, Madison, 1972.

————: *Cooperative Communications—Bibliography*, University of Wisconsin—Extension, Madison, 1972.

Chapter 15

Cooperative Finance

Unique features are reflected in the financial structure of cooperatives. These features are found in two of the five basic cooperative principles that were developed in Chapter 3. They are member ownership and limited returns on equity capital.

Member Ownership Ownership and control in cooperatives go hand in hand. It follows that members who benefit from the use of a cooperative should have major responsibility for financing it. Only in this way, unless there is a subsidy from the government or from private foundations, can sufficient capital be obtained to organize and start operations.

We have emphasized that a unique feature of cooperatives is the application of the concept of proportionality. This concept has special application to financing because, under ideal conditions, members have a responsibility for providing capital in proportion to the business they do with their cooperative.

Control in a cooperative (i.e., voting rights) is frequently tied to the ownership of at least one share of stock or to the payment of a membership fee. Another feature of cooperatives is that their stock, unlike stock in an ordinary business corporation, cannot appreciate in value. Members therefore carry the additional responsibility to continually help to finance their cooperative if it is to obtain needed funds.

Limited Returns on Equity Capital In our discussion of this principle, we emphasized that members organize cooperatives primarily to obtain services at cost. Insofar as they have this goal, they do not look upon their capital contributions to the cooperative as a profitable investment that results in high dividends on capital or capital gains. As in any business operation, capital is an essential ingredient, but in the cooperative it is only a means to an end and not an end in itself.

The distinct nature of cooperative finance is further emphasized by two additional features: (1) Cooperative capital is redeemed on a face-value basis; and (2) in most instances, the cooperative exercises the option to be the first purchaser of members' stock whenever members wish to sell. The idea is to have members furnish capital to provide needed services, rather than to serve as an investment upon which a dividend is earned irrespective of whether the members patronize their cooperative. This arrangement also helps to keep voting control in the hands of active members.

COOPERATIVES' NEED FOR CAPITAL

Economists have long recognized capital, along with land, labor, and management, as one of the essential factors of production. With the rapid mechanization of American industry, the importance of capital came into sharper focus because of the great extent to which it was substituted for labor. On the farm, in the factory, and at the warehouse and retail store, modern, automatic machinery—which requires large capital outlays—has gone a long way in replacing labor.

Like any other business establishment, the cooperative also needs capital to carry on its day-to-day operations. Capital is required, for example, for:

- Providing necessary offices and facilities
- Building or leasing plants
- Purchasing necessary equipment
- Paying for the products handled or the services provided
- Meeting all operating expenses—salaries and wages, travel costs, taxes, utilities, insurance, legal and auditing fees, directors fees—and establishing necessary depreciation reserves
- Establishing reserves for contingencies

Cooperatives also need increasing amounts of capital to assure necessary growth. New or expanded operations usually require additional capital for enlarging physical facilities, building new plants, replacing old machinery, modernizing equipment, engaging in new business enterprises, and joining with other cooperatives to provide additional services.

The Nature of Cooperative Capital

Inadequate capital and poor capital management have led to the demise of many hundreds, if not thousands, of cooperatives.

The extent of the capital invested in agricultural cooperatives was discussed in

Chapter 6. We indicated that in 1974 these investments totaled $9 billion and represented 1.9 percent of total farm assets.

The study *A Financial Profile of Farmer Cooperatives in the United States*[1] indicates that, as of 1970, farmers had invested $3.2 billion in net equity capital in farmers' marketing, purchasing, and related service cooperatives. This figure equals about 40 percent of the total net assets in these cooperatives. In addition, farmer cooperatives borrowed $2.8 billion during the same year. Other types of cooperatives also use large amounts of capital, particularly housing associations, consumer cooperatives, and credit unions.

Equity Capital and Its Sources

Equity capital in a cooperative is the portion of assets that is owned by members. It is also described as the risk capital, in that all other obligations must be met in case of liquidation before any equity capital can be returned to members. Equity capital is important in the financial structure of cooperatives for three basic reasons.

- It serves as a measure of members' interest in their cooperative and their desire to support it. If such interest and support exists, it answers the question: Are they really serious about the organization and operation of their cooperative? We know from experience that when members are willing to dig down into their own pockets and make necessary capital contributions, they are more likely to have an interest in their cooperative and to support its business ventures.
- It is used by creditors as an indicator to determine the feasibility of lending cooperatives the capital they request. A cooperative that has a substantial amount of equity capital is in a better position to negotiate with lenders in obtaining additional funds.
- Equity capital also functions as a shock absorber for cooperatives. Depending upon the nature of the business, abnormal years are not at all uncommon in cooperative enterprise. When prices decline sharply, when droughts occur, or when unemployment becomes high, cooperatives need a financial cushion to fall back on if they are to weather the resulting economic storms.

In general, equity capital may be divided into two classes: (1) initial capital investments consisting of common stock, preferred stock, and membership fees; and (2) capital obtained through operations that result in member or patron investments. These investments consist of patronage refunds and per unit capital investments that are invested by members in their cooperative, and of stock or other types of equity certificates that are sold to members and patrons.

About 85 percent of the equity capital of farmers' marketing and purchasing cooperatives is obtained from operations. Also, in some instances, reserves, allocated and unallocated, are built up from operations. We should keep in mind that these classifications are at best quite arbitrary. Initial capital is only relatively permanent and

---

[1] Nelda Griffin, FCS Research Report 23, Farmer Cooperative Service, U.S. Department of Agriculture, 1972.

generally represents a very small percentage of total equity capital. Capital from operations may sometimes take the form of common or preferred stock.

Initial Capital

Initial capital may take several forms:

- *Common stock.* When large amounts of capital are needed, the most usual way of raising such funds is through investments of actual or prospective members in common stock. Quite generally, common stock is tied to voting rights. The association may issue several kinds of common stock. They may be identified, for example, as classes A, B, and C. Class A common stock, for example, may be voting stock, and may be limited to one share per member or to the number of shares that reflect additional votes if voting is based on volume or patronage. In any event, the number of shares of stock that may be voted should be clearly indicated. Class B stock may well represent other initial capital investments of members. This may be nonvoting stock that members may own in proportion to the use they will make or are making of their cooperative. In some instances, per unit capital investments and deferred patronage refunds are identified as some such class of common stock as C stock. When members retire, their voting stock may be retired or converted to another form of common or preferred stock.

Dividends up to 8 percent per year or the legal limit in the state in which the cooperative is incorporated may be paid on all three classes of capital stock, but often no dividends are paid on that stock originating from patronage refunds.

- *Preferred stock.* Preferred stock, as its name implies, is preferred over common stock because of fewer risks and assurance of paying dividends. Usually it is nonvoting, and it may be dividend- or interest-bearing and either cumulative or noncumulative. Cumulative means that, should the cooperative become unable to meet its dividend payment obligations in one year, these obligations are carried over and must be paid when operations become successful. Preferred stock is more in the nature of an investment than other types of equity capital issued by cooperatives, and in many instances it may even represent capital raised from the general public or other nonpatron groups. When it does, such stock actually does not represent financial contributions of members and technically should not be classified as member equity capital. The amount of nonmember preferred stock in the capital structure of cooperatives, however, is not significant.

- *Membership fees.* The use of membership fees as a form of equity capital is most common when cooperatives are organized on a nonstock basis, with payment of a membership fee being equivalent to the purchase of a share of voting stock. Because of provisions in some early state cooperative laws, membership fees have been most often used among marketing cooperatives in Western states. They are also quite generally used by service cooperatives. Membership fees often range from $1 to $5 or $10 per member and carry with them provisions for voting control. A few associations provide for fees to be paid yearly and for the amount of fees collected to be in proportion to the business the member does or will do with the association. In practically all instances, cooperatives operating on a membership-fee basis make provisions for division of property rights in proportion to the equity capital held by their members, which was, or will be, acquired on a patronage basis. (See Table 15-2 for an illustration of member equity accounts.)

Capital Obtained from Operations

This capital is primarily represented by funds raised either through the investment of noncash patronage refunds or through per unit capital investments. Such capital, when formally identified, is usually evidenced by some form of certificates of equity. These may be described as revolving fund certificates, certificates of interest, "debt" certificates, patronage refund certificates, or capital stock certificates.

Certificates of equity may or may not be interest-bearing. Quite generally, they are not. Also, they may not technically have a due date. When certificates issued as a result of patronage have a due date, they in effect become loan capital rather than member equity. The reason is that the obligation of the cooperative to redeem such certificates at a specific date changes their status and therefore puts such funds in a loan category. Often such capital is described by the term *certificates of indebtedness*, and it is listed on balance sheets with other liabilities as "debt" capital. Because of their loan status and growing capital needs, cooperatives are not inclined to issue certificates with due dates to members.

Many cooperatives are less formal in their identification of equity capital resulting from operations. They may merely issue a statement or a letter advising members of their share of accumulated equity capital. Such equity capital may be referred to as capital credits, book credits, or allocated equities.

Other forms of operating capital relate to allocated and unallocated reserves. Allocated reserves, while not covering depreciation and obsolescence, may be an important part of an association's capital structure. Unallocated reserves or "surplus" accounts accumulate in a number of ways. In some cases, cooperatives that carry on substantial nonmember business and make no refunds on such business pay income taxes on the net margins that result, and the remaining capital becomes a part of the unallocated reserves or surplus of the association. (See Table 15-3 on how net margins may be distributed to various equity accounts.)

Building More Permanent Equity Capital Cooperatives are discovering that the patronage refund and per unit capital investment plan does not always enable them to build the equity capital necessary to maintain a sound and stable financial structure. This condition exists because the yearly amounts of capital that these techniques provide vary substantially owing to vagaries of weather, economic conditions, and other factors. Many cooperatives, therefore, are paying more attention to the building of a financial structure based on larger amounts of so-called permanent capital. They can do so through careful financial planning and management. By projecting capital needs, for example, the cooperative can determine and allocate to individual members the contributions they each need to make in order to discharge their financial responsibilities. This type of financing—variously called an adjustable revolving capital plan, a permanent capital plan, or a base capital plan—is now used by a number of cooperatives.

The chief features of such a base capital plan are: (1) Having made a determination of capital needs, the cooperative can then adjust the capital contributions of individual members on a yearly or periodic basis so as to reflect their use and financial responsibilities to the association over a base period; and (2) it provides greater stability and reliability of capital resources. In practice, this plan may require that member equities be temporarily frozen at a given time and then, on the basis of projection, may make necessary adjustments by (a) requiring additional contributions from those who will be increasing the use of their cooperative, and (b) returning capital to those making but limited use of their cooperative. There would not be a separate "revolvement" of the entire amount of member capital, but only a revolvement of the "net balances" depending upon the extent to which each member's existing capital measured up to the capital requirement allocated.

How the base capital plan works is illustrated in Table 15-1. To change to this plan, it is necessary for the cooperative to:

1 Ascertain the capital requirements of the cooperative
2 Determine each member's share of the revolving fund yearly
3 Balance each member's account in the revolving fund yearly
4 Ascertain each member's balance in the revolving fund, using an annual moving average
5 Balance each member's revolving fund account

Borrowed Capital and Its Sources

Borrowed capital is becoming an increasingly important source of funds for cooperative associations. Studies by Farmer Cooperative Service show, for example, that from 1954 to 1970 the proportion of borrowed funds has risen from approximately one-fourth to one-third of all cooperative liabilities and member equity.[2] As cooperatives demonstrated the ability to manage their financial resources more effectively, they also increased their use of borrowed capital in order to undertake new and more complex business ventures.

These studies further show that, in 1970, banks for cooperatives provided 65 percent of all borrowed funds; individuals, through purchase of bonds, promissory notes, debentures, and other forms of debt obligations, provided 19 percent; commercial banks provided 8 percent; and all other sources provided the final 8 percent. The last two sources of credit have remained approximately the same since 1954. At that time, banks for cooperatives provided only 46 percent of the funds borrowed by cooperatives, while individuals provided 37 percent.

Banks for Cooperatives The banks for cooperatives are the farmers' own cooperative credit institutions. It is sufficient to indicate here that these banks provide all necessary types of credit for cooperatives—facility, operating, and commodity loans for farmers' marketing, purchasing, and related service cooperatives. In general, loans by the banks for cooperatives will vary with the financial condition of the cooperative receiving the loan; and the extent to which loans are for term (facility),

---

[2]While borrowing totaled $2.8 billion in 1970, this is the total at the end of the cooperatives' fiscal year and does not include peak borrowings for seasonal credit.

Table 15-1 Base Capital (Adjusted) Revolving Plan as Applied to Individual Members

Five-Year Average Patronage Basis

Members	Revolving credits outstanding	Average deductions (5-year basis)	Members' average deductions as a percentage of total deductions	Each member's adjusted capital obligations	Capital adjustment for each member*
Siljan	$ 1,050	$ 60	3.00	$ 329	+$ 721
Brown	975	295	14.75	1,619	− 644
Kovac	2,250	375	18.75	2,058	+ 192
Agronski	4,250	810	40.50	4,445	− 195
Pederson	1,950	460	23.00	2,524	− 574
Harden†	500				
Total	$10,975	$2,000	100.00	$10,975	+$ 913
					−$1,413

* + = capital to be repaid to members. − = additional capital to be furnished members.
†Inactive member.

operating, or commodity purposes. The banks for cooperatives emphasize that their operations are geared to meet the credit needs of their borrowers, and that they provide a wide range of supplementary credit services (see Chapter 17 for details).

The National Rural Utilities Cooperative Finance Corporation. This cooperative finance institution was established in 1970 to meet the critical financial needs of rural electric cooperatives. It makes both long-time secured loans and short-time operating loans to Rural Electrification Administration distribution systems, power systems, and statewide rural electric associations (see Chapter 17 for details).

Rural Telephone Bank This bank was established in 1971 to meet the increasing needs of rural telephone systems for more capital (see Chapter 17).

Government Agencies A number of government agencies make loans to cooperative associations. The effectiveness of their programs depends on such factors as the competence of the individuals administrating these programs, the amount of funds available, the philosophy of the federal administration in power as to support of cooperatives, and the prevailing business conditions influencing the competitive situation in which the cooperatives find themselves. Government funds have provided seed money for new and urgently needed cooperative ventures. It is commendable, too, that such efforts often have been undertaken with the primary objective of making the cooperatives financed and full-fledged independent organizations as soon as they demonstrate the ability to build capital resources and operate on their own. When government-financed ventures have not achieved this goal, the failure can usually be traced to such factors as failure to determine program feasibility, changes introduced by new administrations, vacillation and uncertainty in program objectives, lack of support and understanding of programs, incompetency in the execution of public affairs, and political interference in selection of personnel and in operations.

The most important of the government agencies financing cooperatives are:

- *Rural Electrification Administration.* The Rural Electrification Administration has operated since 1935, and in 1974 it lent about $6 billion for facilities and operations to local REAs as well as to a limited number of generating plants. Since 1949 it has also made such loans to telephone cooperatives. Practically all the nation's nearly 1,000 rural electric cooperatives and 239 telephone cooperatives have borrowed funds from the REA. The electric cooperatives now serve 8 percent of the consumers in 3,100 of the nation's nearly 3,500 counties and 98 percent of the nation's rural families; but they generate only 1 percent of the power supply.
- Prior to 1973, all loans were at the fixed rate of 2 percent interest, the theory being that the rate was justified because of scattered rural settlements which resulted in only 4.1 customers and gross revenue of $1,000 per mile. In 1973, the REA started operating under legislation that provided for insured loans on a revolving fund basis. All funds came from private sources rather than directly from the U.S. Treasury. Except for about 200 systems that qualify for 2 percent on their loans owing to low customer density, all the systems now pay 5 percent on their loan funds.
- *National Marine Fisheries Service (NMFS), U.S. Department of Commerce.* This agency has two fishing-vessel financial assistance loan programs for which cooperatives or individual members of cooperatives may qualify. One program provides a federal guarantee of private financing for up to 75 percent of costs for constructing or reconditioning fishing vessels. The other permits lessors of fishing vessels to defer payment of federal income tax on income derived from the operation of these vessels to use the deferred funds for constructing or acquiring fishing vessels.
- *Bureau of Indian Affairs.* This agency is authorized to make loans to Indian tribes and other Indian groups to carry on certain business enterprises. Particular emphasis has been placed on the development of handicraft programs.
- *Bureau of Reclamation.* The Bureau makes loans to facilitate the development of land resources through irrigation, particularly in irrigated sections of the West. Mutual irrigation companies can borrow from this agency.
- *Commodity Credit Loans.* The Commodity Credit Corporation (CCC) provides nonrecourse loans for qualified agricultural cooperatives that market cotton, dry edible beans, honey, rice, and soybeans. The commodity serves as security, and it may be redeemed by the cooperative during the course of the marketing season if prices advance above loan levels. Three peanut cooperatives also operate under a loan and handling agreement with CCC. They contract with warehouse personnel to receive, handle, and store loan-collateral peanuts and to issue warehouse receipts to the CCC and drafts to growers. These associations may withdraw from the loan, for unrestricted use, any part of, or all, the peanuts offered for sale under policies approved by CCC. The cooperatives assist in this program by receiving and accepting offers, preparing lot lists, collecting for and arranging delivery of the peanuts, and supervising their disposition.

The Commodity Credit Corporation has similar arrangements with eleven tobacco marketing cooperatives. These cooperatives provide the services associated with carrying out the CCC price support efforts through a loan program for various grades of tobacco.

• *Federal Housing Administration.* While not making loans as such, the Federal Housing Administration has helped to finance cooperative housing units by providing guarantees on loans from banks, other credit agencies, or approved lenders.

• *Office of Economic Opportunity.* The OEO made credit available to limited-resource types of cooperative organizations from 1965 to 1971. Sometimes these loans were administered by other agencies. For example, in the late 1960s funds were made available to the Farmers Home Administration for loans to limited-resource cooperatives.

• *Small Business Administration.* This agency has made a limited number of loans to cooperative associations. For some years cooperatives did not qualify for loans because of administrative rulings that loans should be made only to profit-making firms. Recently, however, a more realistic interpretation has resulted in a few loans, especially to groups of limited-resource cooperatives such as those in the Appalachian mountains, in the South, and in the Far West.

Individuals We have already said that some member certificates carry due dates having the status of borrowed capital. In prior years, the amount of such certificates was substantial and represented a larger share of the debt capital of farmer cooperatives than they now do. Members and nonmembers both have provided funds for cooperatives through promissory notes, debenture bonds, and other credit instruments.

Commercial Banks and Insurance Companies Commercial banks and insurance companies have over the years been active in providing loan funds to cooperatives. The extent to which they make loans to businesses largely depends on these firms' interest in, and support and understanding of, cooperatives as well as on the inclination of cooperative officials to use such sources of credit.

Other Sources of Borrowed Funds There are a number of other sources that provide loan funds for cooperative associations. They include:

• *Regional cooperatives.* A majority of local associations are members of regional associations which, in many instances, directly or indirectly through finance cooperation subsidiaries, have provided substantial amounts of credit to support the operations of their local affiliated members. In so doing, they of course also are helping build their own business volume. Regional cooperatives are also making some loans directly to farmers.

• *Municipal bonds.* In some instances, municipalities interested in stimulating business and industrial development raise money from the general public through the sale of tax-free industrial revenue bonds to build facilities and purchase necessary operating equipment. The facilities initially are leased at relatively low rates to cooperatives, which over a period of time usually exercise an option to purchase them. An example of such financing was the $750,000 BAWI (Balanced Agriculture with Industry) bonds voted by the residents of Yazoo County, Mississippi, to help construct a modern fertilizer-manufacturing facility to be used by a farmer-owned fertilizer cooperative.

- *Foundations and private grants.* Individuals and private foundations from time to time make funds available to cooperatives. These grants primarily have been for limited-resource cooperatives that provide opportunities for special groups or promise to furnish new and needed services.

LEASING AND LEVERAGED LEASING FINANCING

In recent years cooperatives have made increased use of leasing and leveraged leasing to finance their operations. The employment of these techniques has special appeal to cooperatives whose members have limited financial resources and are in need of substantial amounts of capital to finance high-cost facilities or equipment. Such financing enables them to strengthen their equity position while gaining the use of facilities made available by funds provided by investors.

In practice, the cooperative (the lessee that is the user of facilities) employing this technique has lower financing costs because the amount of capital it needs to provide is reduced. Moreover, cooperatives, because of the limited benefits they usually can realize from tax credits and accelerated depreciation, use the leasing technique to transfer these benefits to the financial institutions and business firms (the owners or investors) with which they have worked out leasing or leveraged leasing arrangements, because such organizations can make better use of them.

The Single Investor Lease

Leasing is the renting of facilities and/or equipment instead of buying it. This technique, which has been used by cooperatives for the past twenty-five years or so, is most generally used to finance relatively small and short-term asset requirements. After the cooperative, as the lessee, has determined the assets it needs, it negotiates: (1) the prices for these assets with a manufacturer or owner, and (2) the terms of lease with the lessor. When these arrangements are made, the lessor buys the asset at the price previously determined, and the lessee starts making rental payments in accord with prior agreements. Generally, the lessee has the option to renew the lease or to purchase the assets at fair market value at the end of the lease period. In some cases, the cooperative may sell all or part of its fixed assets to another firm that will then lease these facilities back to the cooperative.

The Leveraged Lease

The leveraged lease has many of the same general features as the single investor lease. It is more complicated, however, in that the assets leased are larger, more parties usually participate, and legal arrangements are more complex. Several parties, rather than one, may participate as lessors and as investors. Frequently, the lessors achieve ownership by providing a limited portion of the capital needed (20 percent to 40 percent). In addition to the lenders, who supply the remaining capital, other parties in the leveraged lease arrangement include: (1) *the owner trustee,* who holds title to the leased asset for the lessors and issues trust certificates to them as evidence of ownership; (2) *the indenture trustee,* who holds security interest in the leased property for the benefit of debt lenders; and (3) *the agent* (usually an investment banker, a leasing company, or a bank), who arranges the leverage lease but is not involved in the transaction. These relationships are illustrated in Figure 15-1.

Some of the banks for cooperatives have started participating as institutional lenders for cooperative leveraged leases. When they do so, as the lenders, they establish relationships with the cooperative lessee which involve making a mortgage loan to the cooperative, which then assigns the loan to the owner trustee. When arrangements are completed, the cooperative pays rent to the indenture trustee, who pays the bank for cooperatives interest and principal due.

An example of cooperative bank involvement in leveraged financing is the financing of interim construction funds and mortgage funds by the New Orleans Bank for Cooperatives for a $10 million fertilizer plant that will be leased by the Mississippi Chemical Corporation (a farmers' fertilizer cooperative).

The advantages of using the leveraged lease technique for cooperatives are:

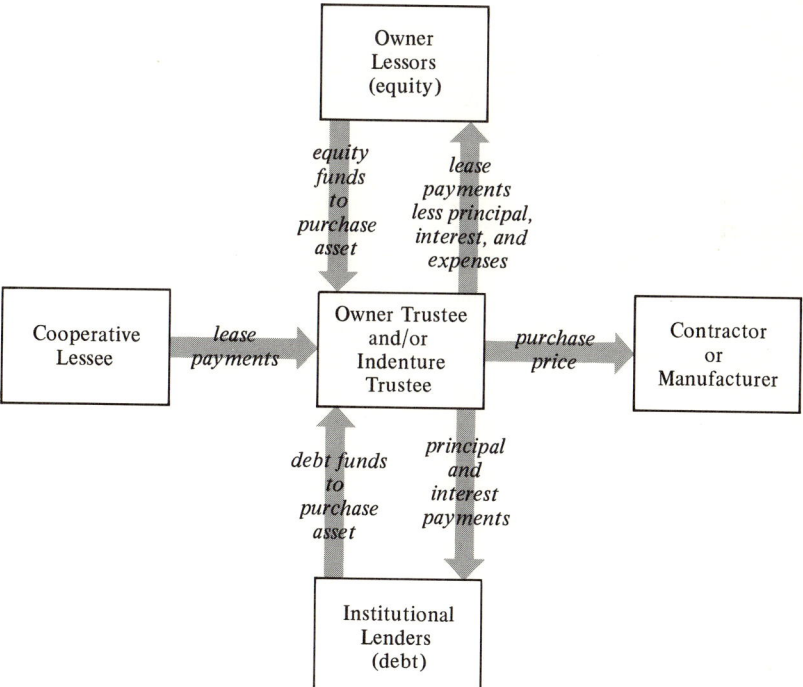

Figure 15-1 Leveraged financing relationships. (*Source:* News for Farmer Cooperatives, December 1974, p. 12.)

- Improved and stabilized cash flow.
- Lower capital costs and lease rates resulting from the transfer of tax benefits to investors who have high tax rates and can use accelerated depreciation methods. Part of these benefits can be passed on to the cooperative in the form of lower loan rates.
- An opportunity to strengthen the capital structure.

FINANCIAL PLANNING AND MANAGEMENT

Since the process of financial planning and management has much the same application for cooperatives as for other types of business, it is well covered in many general texts on the subject. Therefore, this section is limited to a brief identification of the need for such efforts. Two publications by the Agricultural Extension Service, University of Minnesota, in cooperation with the Federal Extension Service, are especially helpful since they relate to the financial analysis of agribusiness firms. These are Special Report 17 (1965), *Financial Analysis and Control of the Farm Supply Business,* by Robert J. Moeller and Frank J. Smith, Jr., and Special Report 26 (1967), *Financial Management of Agribusiness Firms,* by Frank J. Smith, Jr., and Ken Cooper.[3]

Financial planning and management essentially involve looking ahead and answering some key questions. Foremost of them are: What are the objectives of the cooperative? How does it propose to achieve them? From the standpoint of financial resources, what is required? How much capital is needed? Which kind of capital is needed, and where can it be obtained? Obviously, too, answers to these questions require capital budgeting, by departments, so as to determine their capital needs according to the services provided and the seasonal needs for each.

Financial Planning

Most financial planning starts with profit analysis and profit forecasting. In a cooperative, these activities mean net margin analysis and net margin forecasting. Net margins or savings are a necessity if the cooperative is to accumulate funds for expanding or modernizing facilities, building reserves, and distributing patronage refunds to members. Net savings per dollar of sales or per unit of commodity has been the major measure in analyzing operations and prospects for payouts of loans on new facilities. In recent years as cooperatives have become more diversified and invested large amounts in plants and warehouses, management also has been looking at return on investment in fixed assets as another factor in planning and determining priorities for use of resources.

Since cooperatives are expected to provide services which will help farmers increase their net profits, some services, such as custom feed grinding, may not realize much net margin for the cooperative as a business entity. Likewise, some supplies that farmers need may carry low margins but will provide a reasonable return on capital invested for handling them.

Cooperatives, since their emphasis is on economic benefits for members, are interested in determining where savings can and should be realized and in making

---

[3]Both reports are published by The University of Minnesota—Agricultural Extension, St. Paul.

projections as to likely trends in such savings. This determination involves, among other things, giving attention to possible savings by departments, to potential volume of business, and to the specific factors that influence these considerations. These factors are:

- *Volume of business.* This item and the factors that determine it may include the geographic area served, the share of the market in respect to areas served and products handled, and the general trends in the economy that influence the agriculture in the territory served.
- *Costs.* Cost figures should be analyzed from both a long-term and a short-term viewpoint. Recognition should be given to fixed and variable costs in order to determine how they are likely to be influenced by changes in volume of business. Financial analysis also emphasizes the concept of *opportunity costs*. This factor involves the comparison of the net margins that may or may not be realized because an association does or does not enter a certain line of business. To the extent that capital is the limiting factor, any engagement in one type of business will require a sacrifice of another. The basic question then is: What type of business undertaking results in the greatest returns for members?
- *Product mix.* This item relates closely to the services that are available and the resources that the cooperative may or may not be able to provide. A critical analysis needs to be made of the impact on capital requirements of (a) different products, (b) the use of personnel, and (c) necessary physical facilities.
- *Cash flow.* This figure provides an estimate of the income and expenses for certain periods of time. It serves as a guide in determining how much capital is needed on a seasonal basis, and it identifies the extent to which borrowed capital will be needed to supplement equity funds.

Implementing Financial Plans

Having obtained information on volume, costs, product mix, and cash flow, the cooperative is in a position to start implementing financial plans. This procedure usually begins with a consideration of its net worth position. Knowing this, the cooperative then can determine how much capital it needs to generate or borrow in its efforts to realize basic objectives. Generally, it has been recommended that borrowed funds should not exceed the net worth of the cooperative, but obviously circumstances and conditions will modify this general guideline.

Some of the factors that have a bearing on a cooperative's ability to implement a financial program are the stability of the industry, its line of business, its realized savings, and its repayment ability or payout period. Any financial plan must also carefully evaluate economic trends and their impact on the ability of the association to grow. A final consideration, and perhaps the most important of them all, is the competency of management. To what extent has it demonstrated ability to operate efficiently, to achieve member support, and to manage capital and other resources effectively?

FINANCIAL CONTROLS

The information provided in the balance sheets and operating statements give much useful information for analyzing how well cooperatives are performing. They provide, for example, essential information as to volume of business, operating costs, gross and net margins, assets, liabilities, net worth, and debt obligations.

With this information, cooperative management is able to devise meaningful ratios that can be useful in implementing financial controls. These ratios, in effect, show relationships and most frequently are determined for monthly and yearly operations. It should be kept in mind, however, that they serve only to pinpoint symptoms and do not indicate the basic forces that contribute to these symptoms. They are not unlike a medical thermometer that registers a fever and indicates illness but does not diagnose the cause of the fever and does not prescribe a remedy. It is necessary to look back of the ratios to determine whether, for example, a decline in net margins is due to "acts of God," to drought which has reduced the volume of business, or to high expenses stemming from such factors as inability to control costs of operations, inadequate and inefficient facilities, excess shrinkages, possible fraud, or general mismanagement. Similar questions need to be explored for explanations of trends shown for each of the ratios used to establish financial controls.

Ratios are particularly useful when analyzed over a period of time. They also may be helpful in comparing one business with another. When such a comparison is made, however, it is especially important that differences in accounting practices as well as possible differences in types of cooperatives and methods of operation be recognized. Unless they are, many ratio comparisons can become quite meaningless. Also, the time factor should be taken into account. A business tends to "tidy up" its financial statements when making its annual report. Accounts receivable, for example, may be much greater then than at other times. Seasonal factors also may have an important bearing on trends in the use of capital.

Selected Ratios

Cooperative management should identify and develop ratios that are especially important and meaningful for its specific operations. We will here identify three types of ratios which cover the areas of financial liquidity, operational efficiency, and solvency. Using data presented in the sample balance sheet and operating statement of the Soldal Cooperative (Tables 15-2 and 15-3), the following ratios are calculated:

Liquidity Ratios Liquidity ratios indicate the ability of the cooperative to meet its current obligations.

- *Current ratio*. Current assets divided by current liabilities gives the current ratio ($699,250 ÷ $371,817 = $1.88). In other words, the Soldal Cooperative has $1.88 of current assets for each $1 of current liabilities. This is often expressed as: 1.88:1. It is a measure of the ability of the association to meet its yearly current obligations.
- *Acid ratio*. Current assets less inventory and accounts receivable over 60 days old, divided by current liabilities, gives the acid ratio [$699,250 − ($265,100 + $210,130) ÷ $371,817 = $0.60]. This ratio is a more demanding one than the current ratio in that it takes into account two practical conditions: (1) Inventories cannot always readily be converted into cash, and (2) accounts receivable vary in collectibility, becoming less collectible with age. To develop the acid ratio, therefore, inventories are deducted, as are all accounts receivable over sixty days of age. The acid ratio, in our

Table 15-2
Soldal Farmers Cooperative
Balance Sheet
December 31, 1975

Assets (what the cooperative owns)
Current assets
Cash	$125,000	
Accounts receivable	210,150	
Merchandise Inventory	265,100	
Notes receivable and prepaid items	99,000	
Total		$ 699,250
Fixed assets		
Land	$126,000	
Buildings (after depreciation)	280,438	
Equipment (after depreciation)	120,200	
Total		$ 526,638
Other		
Investments in other cooperatives	$149,340	
Miscellaneous	90,502	
Total		$ 239,842
Total assets		$1,465,730

Liabilities and Patrons' Equity (what the cooperative owes)
Current liabilities		
Accounts and notes payable	$253,017	
Patrons' refunds payable	82,300	
Accrued expenses	36,500	
Total		$ 371,817
Long-term liabilities		
Mortgages	$300,000	
Certificates of indebtedness	109,875	
Total		$ 409,875
Total liabilities		$ 781,692
Patrons' equity		
Common stock	$147,220	
Preferred stock	237,500	
Allocated reserves	190,303	
Unallocated reserves	109,015	
Total		$ 684,038
Total liabilities and net worth		$1,465,730

example, shows that after these adjustments are made, the Soldal Cooperative still has $0.60 available in current assets to meet each $1 of current liability obligations. The ratio is 0.60:1.

Efficiency (Operations) Efficiency ratios show the effectiveness with which the Soldal Cooperative is operating.

Table 15-3
Soldal Farmers Cooperative,
Operating Statement
December 31, 1975

Net purchases by patrons	$1,921,400	
Cost of patrons' purchases	1,498,200	
Gross margins		$423,200
Operating Costs		
Salaries and wages	$ 225,032	
Taxes	14,978	
Utilities	8,851	
Insurance	12,652	
Depreciation	32,168	
Legal and auditing	15,273	
Miscellaneous	48,578	
Total		$357,532
Net operating margin		65,668
Other Income and Expenses		
Patronage refunds received	$ 47,375	
Other revenue received	9,663	
Other expenses	25,451	
Total		$ 31,587
Net margins		$ 97,255

- *Inventory turnover.* Cost of purchases by patrons divided by the closing inventory gives the inventory turnover ratio ($1,498,200 ÷ $265,100 = $5.65). This ratio shows that the cooperative, over the year, has realized $5.65 in sales for each $1 of inventory it had at the end of the year. The rapidity of inventory turnover, of course, varies with commodities, seasons, and the competency of management. The average monthly inventory for the year will give a more accurate turnover rate.
- *Days' sales in accounts receivable.* This ratio is obtained by multiplying by 360 (the days in the year) the quantity of accounts receivable divided by purchases for patrons ($210,150 ÷ $1,921,400 × 360 = 39.4 days). This ratio means that, on the average, 39.4 days of sales were tied up in accounts receivable. Another method is to divide annual sales by 360 and then divide the answer into accounts receivable. Since many cooperatives operate on a thirty-day cash basis, this ratio shows that some portion of the association's accounts exceeded this period. The days of credit sales in accounts receivable also should be calculated to determine the length of time that credit or accounts receivable was extended. In the above example, if 50 percent of sales were on credit, then 78.8 days of credit sales were actually in accounts receivable.

It is not always realized how accounts receivable adversely affect the financial structure of a cooperative. For example, they represent money that is not available for operations. Moreover, as accounts receivable become older, the costs of collection and the amounts written off as bad debts become increasingly great.
- *Salaries and wages in proportion to patrons' purchases (sales).* This ratio is

obtained by dividing yearly expenditures for salaries and wages [by net sales] (sales), and then multiplying by 100 to get the percentage ($2[...] ÷ [...] × 100 = 11.7 percent). This ratio indicates the proportion of exp[enses that] go to pay salaries and wages. In this case, their expenditures a[re ... of] their total purchases. Similar ratios can be developed to show [the] costs of various items that go to make up administration, [and] overhead expenditures.

• *Gross margins.* Net purchases or sales for patron[s less pur-]chases (cost of sales) gives gross margins. To express th[is as a percentage of] patrons' purchases (sales), it is divided by net purchases b[y patrons times] 100 ($1,921,400 − $1,498,200 = $423,200 ÷ $1,921,400 [× 100 = 22%). This] ratio shows that the cooperative had $423,200 left after p[urchases] (cost of sales). This figure equals 22 percent of net purch[ases and is indica-]tive of the ability of the cooperative to meet operating costs and to realize sa[vings f]or members. Thus, it is a measure of how effectively management is able to adjust operations to annual changes.

• *Net margins.* Net margins (savings) is what remains after all operating costs are paid and other income and expenses are taken into account. To express it as a percentage of patrons' purchases (sales), net margins are divided by purchases for patrons and multiplied by 100 ($97,255 ÷ $1,921,400 × 100 = 5.1 percent). This ratio shows that the Soldal Cooperative realized a net margin of 5.1 percent of net purchases or sales by patrons. It reveals the ability of the cooperative to realize savings on its operations for patrons.

Solvency Solvency ratios relate to the ability of the cooperative to meet long-term obligations.

• *Total liabilities to patrons' equity (net worth).* This ratio is obtained by dividing total liabilities by patrons' equity ($781,692 ÷ $684,038 = $1.14). It shows that for $1 of patrons' equity, the association has liabilities of $1.14, a ratio of over 1.1:1 and just over the ratio of 1:1 that is generally accepted as a desirable objective. This ratio indicates the relative proportion of capital provided by members and by creditors. In reality, it shows the extent to which members or creditors own the cooperative. Often patrons' equity as a percentage of total assets is used to measure member ownership.

• *Long-term liabilities to patrons' equity.* This ratio is obtained by dividing long-term liabilities by patrons' equity ($409,875 ÷ $684,038 = $0.59). It shows that for every $1 of patrons' equity the association has $0.59 in long-term debt.

• *Fixed assets to patrons' equity.* This ratio is obtained by dividing fixed assets by patrons' equity ($526,638 ÷ $684,038 = $0.77). It shows that for every $1 in patrons' equity, the association has $0.77 in fixed assets. This is a measure of the extent to which member capital supports long-term investments.

Financial Controls

We have said that financial ratios provide tools that are useful to cooperatives in controlling their operations. To develop this idea somewhat further, it is generally emphasized that an efficacious financial control system provides for:

• *Identifying control points*. Control points frequently used by cooperatives are departmental performance, costs, margins, and equity and debt relationships.
• *Setting up acceptable standards of performance*. Each association, taking into account its particular situation, should establish a range of acceptable standards. This range can be determined by an evaluation of such factors as objectives, operating history, and prevailing economic conditions.
• *Taking corrective action*. Corrective action may well include developing departmental budgets and using the technique of management by exception. This means that as deviations from accepted standards occur, a necessary corrective action is taken to bring performance back into line. Providing monthly and comparative balance sheets and operating statements is a means of obtaining fundamental information for developing financial controls. Equipped with such information, management can spot undesirable trends and take corrective action before excessive damage results.

It should be emphasized, too, that a control system for a cooperative not only needs to deal with the business aspect of operation, but it should also direct attention to maintaining essential cooperative characteristics. Through financial controls, it is possible to take the steps necessary to achieve this goal. For example, the cooperative should develop a policy of retiring equity capital of inactive members within a reasonable time. Moreover, the cooperative can develop a policy to assure that active members are, or will become, the owners of the cooperative. Finally, the cooperative can provide that owners meet financial responsibility, preferably in proportion to the use they make of the cooperative and the benefits they realize from belonging to it. By taking such precautions, it is possible to maintain the cooperative as a sound business organization and also to assure that it keeps its unique form of business organization.

SUMMARY

Sound financing and competent financial management are basic to the successful operation of cooperatives. Sound financing relates to the need for equity or ownership capital and debt or creditor funds for operations and growth. It is concerned with the sources of such funds and the relative merits of using each. It also involves the analysis of financial data in order to develop financial controls. It recognizes the importance of identifying control points, establishing standards, and developing techniques for determining when and how to take corrective action.

QUESTIONS

1. Identify the basic cooperative principles that relate to finance, and indicate how each one is related.
2. What are the important capital needs of cooperatives?
3. What are the principal sources of equity capital? Identify the important features of each.
4. Are accountants justified in classifying as loan capital certificates of indebtedness having a due date?
5. What are the principal sources of loan capital? Identify the important features of each.
6. What are the principal government agencies that provide capital for cooperatives?

to as *retains*. Since they represent a procedure agreed upon by members to finance their cooperative, however, the term *investment* seems more accurately to describe this arrangement. Such investments are made by deducting an agreed-upon amount from member proceeds or returns on each unit of product marketed. For example, it may be 10 cents per 100 pounds of milk, 8 cents per bushel of grain, or 15 cents per box of fruit.

Member investments from either patronage refunds or per unit capital contributions may take many forms (see Chapter 15). As a general rule, these investments are redeemed (revolved out) at the discretion of the board of directors after they have given due consideration to the financial needs of the cooperatives.

PATRONAGE REFUNDS

We have previously stated that cooperatives are obligated to return to their members or to all patrons the savings that result after deducting operating expenses and such specified expenditures as reserves, dividends on capital stock and other equities, and any additional authorized items. They discharge this responsibility by declaring patronage refunds which are in proportion to the business that members or all patrons do with their cooperative. It is well known that this is the way cooperatives achieve operation at cost—a basic cooperative principle.

Patronage refunds may be classified as *cash* and *noncash*. Cash patronage refunds are those refunds that are returned to patrons following the close of each year's operations. For all cooperatives, they average about 40 percent of all refunds. Amendments to the federal income tax law in 1966 require that 20 percent of all allocated patronage refunds must be distributed in cash. Noncash patronage refunds are that portion of patronage refunds that members invest in their cooperative to meet their financial obligations to it. In common usage, the terms *deferred* or *retained* are often used to describe the contributions to capital that members make by leaving their patronage refunds with their cooperative. Noncash, however, seems to be a more realistic description of these patronage refund investments.

It should be emphasized that, although there is nothing to prevent other types of business from paying patronage refunds, the technique is a characteristic feature of most types of cooperatives. We have mentioned that several railroad companies that jointly own and operate a railroad bridge at Paducah, Kentucky, on a cooperative basis use the patronage refund technique.

Legal Status

To review, patronage refund is described in subchapter T of the Revenue Act of 1962 as the amount distributed to a patron (1) on the basis of the quantity or value of the business done with or for that patron, (2) in accordance with a preexisting written obligation between the patron and the cooperative, and (3) based on the patron's share of the net savings realized by cooperatives from business done with or for that person.

This legislation further set up these basic requirements for patronage refunds: (1) At least 20 percent of the refund must be paid in cash. The remainder may be in property or written notices of allocation. And (2) all refunds shall be allocated within 8½ months after the close of the cooperative's fiscal year and paid within 90 days after allocation (see Chapter 11 for additional details).

Distinction between Patronage Refunds and Dividends

One of the areas in which cooperatives have experienced problems in terminology is in distinguishing patronage refunds from dividends. We have said that cooperative legislation, Internal Revenue Service rulings, and common usage all contribute to this misunderstanding. The reason is that they often use the term *patronage dividend* instead of *patronage refund* when describing savings returned to patrons. As previously noted, *patronage refund* is the correct term to use in describing such returns. Dividends on stock or on other equity, in contrast, differ from patronage refunds in that they may be paid out of funds that have accumulated over one or more years, or that have, for that matter, been borrowed to meet dividend obligations. Boards of directors of ordinary business corporations are empowered to determine their firm's dividend policy. This stipulation is in contrast with that of the cooperative, where bylaws or other legal documents require that savings resulting from business operations shall be returned or allocated to members or to all patrons. Boards of directors of cooperatives, unless otherwise specifically stated in bylaw or other provisions, have jurisdiction as to the form in which refunds may be returned and whether interest will be paid on invested patronage refunds.

Proportion of Net Margins Distributed as Patronage Refunds

A study by Farmer Cooperative Service (Research Report 23) shows that cooperatives have been very effective in operating on a cost basis. Moreover, they have been able to increase the proportion of patronage refunds returned in cash. Distributions of total net margins of all farmers' cooperatives in 1954 and 1970 and the distribution of net margins ($506 million) as reported by 7,289 marketing and marketing/farm supply, and farm supply cooperatives in 1970 are shown on page 311.

These data show that a very large proportion of all net margins, ranging from 77 percent for farm supply cooperatives to 89 percent for marketing cooperatives, are accounted for by patronage refunds. When dividends on capital stock and retained earnings are included, these items, together with savings, account for 93 percent or more of all net margins. Since 1954, the proportion of patronage refunds distributed in cash has increased from 31 percent to 41 percent.

Distinction between Patronage Refunds and Final Pooling Settlements

It is important to distinguish between patronage refunds and final pooling settlements or payments. The final pooling settlement is based on returns attributable to prices received for the delivered products. When only such returns are made, the cooperative is conducting a strictly pooling operation. Should the cooperative also have savings above the market value of the products, however, these savings may be recognized as patronage refunds. Thus the cooperative that pools its products may return final pooling settlements and patronage refunds to members at the same time or separately.

	Percentage of savings for				
	Marketing cooperatives 1970	Marketing-farm supply cooperatives* 1970	Purchasing cooperatives 1970	All cooperatives	
Item				1954	1970
Patronage refunds					
Cash	58.5	26.1	40.2	30.9	41.4
Noncash†	30.3	50.8	37.2	55.6	39.7
Total	88.8	76.9	77.4	86.5	81.1
Unallocated reserves‡	4.2	8.1	9.5	3.6	7.1
Dividends and interest on equity capital	5.9	8.7	6.0	5.7	7.0
Federal and state income tax	1.1	6.3	7.1	4.2	4.8
Total	100.0	100.0	100.0	100.0	100.0
Savings (millions)**	$174	$150	$182	—	$506

*Neither marketing nor farm supply operations accounted for two-thirds of the total volume of cooperatives in this classifcation.
†Includes allocated capital reserves.
‡Unallocated reserves are accounted for largely by those cooperatives that follow the policy of paying patronage refunds only to members rather than to all patrons. When this practice is followed, the cooperative must pay income taxes on savings retained as a result of nonmember business. It then may add the remainder of these savings as unallocated reserves to its permanent capital structure or as further distributions to members.
**Only those cooperatives with net savings are included in this tabulation. This excludes those cooperatives having losses and those of the bargaining and pooling associations that operate in such a way as to have no net savings to report. Also, intercooperative distributions have not been eliminated.

How to Determine and Return Patronage Refunds

It is not possible or feasible to determine the amount of refunds for each transaction or for each day or month of operations. Nearly all cooperatives therefore distribute their refunds on the basis of their annual operations.

    Cooperatives have developed a variety of methods for calculating patronage refunds. We have indicated that usually they are determined on the basis of dollar sales, purchases, or value of services provided, and that all savings are allocated to patrons on the basis of their business with their cooperative. The patrons' share of the total savings is in the same proportion that their business is to the total business of the cooperative.

    In some associations, especially agricultural marketing associations, the return of savings is based on units handled—cents per bushels of grain sold, boxes of fruit handled, or pounds of milk delivered.

    Cooperatives are also confronted with the problem of devising equitable means of distributing patronage refunds. This is a relatively simple procedure in a local cooperative that markets milk, distributes petroleum products, or provides groceries.

    The problem becomes more complicated, however, when dairy cooperatives distribute feed, when petroleum cooperatives sell feed or manufacture insecticides, and when grocery cooperatives enter the furniture, hardware, or drug business. The practical question is: How much of the cooperative's savings are due to the specific products handled or services provided? The problem becomes even more complex for large regional associations handling a wide range of products and performing many far-flung services.

If a cooperative is to operate strictly on a cost basis and to treat all members equitably, it must strive to determine both the amount and source of savings and the most equitable way of distributing them. This responsibility becomes especially important when patron business is with a department whose savings differ from the savings, or even the losses, that prevail for other departments. It is quite obvious that under these circumstances, the principle of operation at cost may be in jeopardy when all expenses and returns are pooled in one final figure.

To distribute their patronage refunds in a way that assures the most equitable treatment possible, most cooperatives determine and return patronage refunds by divisions and/or departments. This especially is the practice when they market farm products and handle farm supplies. A cooperative in a grain-producing area usually declares separate patronage refunds for its marketing and farm supply divisions. If it is a large regional, the various divisions may be departmentalized for patronage refund purposes. For example, the grain division may have separate refunds for its wheat, corn, and sorghum departments. Likewise, a consumer association may make special refunds for grocery, dry goods, hardware, and furniture departments. Some cooperatives distribute separate patronage refunds for wholesale and retail divisions.

It seems important that the concept of "reasonableness" prevails when dealing with patronage refunds. The cooperative must arrive as accurately as possible at various costs and sources of savings or losses. Having this determination as a general goal, cooperative officials and members should then decide how far they can and should practically go in seeking to attain this objective. Consideration should also be given to the income tax implications of a policy of "netting" losses of one part of the business against gains in another. (For details, see Chapter 11.)

Many members have found that when they invest their patronage refunds with their cooperative, it can conveniently finance new ventures and expand business operations. How members use their patronage refunds to finance their cooperative internally is explained later in this chapter when we examine how the revolving capital-financing plan works.

PER UNIT CAPITAL INVESTMENTS

In actual practice, the per unit capital investment plan of financing involves the investment of members' money for certain periods of time and the return of this money to them in accordance with mutually agreed-upon arrangements.

For example, cooperative members may decide that they wish to finance the construction of a new dairy plant by the deduction of 10 or 20 cents per 100 pounds of the milk they deliver.

To do this, the cooperative:

• Must have provisions in its bylaws or marketing agreements with patrons that authorize it to make such deductions from returns on the sale of their milk.

- Must issue patrons some form of equity or a letter of evidence of the amount of capital they have provided. There should also be agreement as to whether or not these certificates are interest-bearing and under what conditions they should be revolved.
- Must comply with Treasury Department regulations issued in 1965. These, in effect, provide for the collection of an income tax, at either the patron or the cooperative level, on capital invested in proportion to dollar value or the physical volume of products marketed through the cooperative.

HOW REVOLVING CAPITAL FINANCING WORKS

Both the patronage refund investment and the per unit capital investment techniques lend themselves to the use of revolving capital financing. Let us now consider how these techniques work when applied to noncash patronage refund investment and to the per unit capital investment plans.

The Noncash Patronage Refund Investment Plan

Let us assume that the Bountiful Ridge Producers Cooperative started operations at the beginning of 1968 with member investments amounting to $100,000 (Table 16-1). For the purpose of this illustration, we will assume that no other factors influence the association's capital structure. The cooperative has obtained a $75,000 loan from a bank for cooperatives upon which it is obligated to repay $15,000 yearly. It proposes to use some of its patronage refunds to liquidate this loan. Its ability to do so, of course, will depend upon the size of the annual patronage refund. The extent to which the Bountiful Ridge Producers Cooperative can meet its loan obligations to the bank for cooperatives from deferred patronage refunds is indicated by the net yearly balance that exists after each year's operations.

In 1969, for example, Bountiful Ridge determined that its 1968 operations resulted in noncash patronage refunds of $10,000. This refund failed by $5,000 to meet the cooperative's obligation to the bank for cooperatives. This deficit had to be made up from existing capital unless other arrangements could be made. As a result, the total capital of Bountiful Ridge Producers Cooperative in 1969 was depleted by $5,000. Larger noncash patronage refunds in 1970, however, made it possible for the association to exceed that year's loan obligations by $10,000 from these patronage refunds. Thus, after replacing the $5,000 of depleted capital that occurred in 1969, the cooperative could still add $5,000 to its total capital (see net yearly balance of noncash patronage refunds). It will be noted, too, that as noncash patronage refunds accumulate, member investments increase in the same amount. Likewise, the obligations to the bank for cooperatives decrease with each annual payment of $15,000.

In 1973 the cooperative reaches the stage when the last loan obligations can be paid. On the assumption that no additional capital is needed for expansion of operations or some other activity, Bountiful Ridge is now in a position to plan for revolving its noncash patronage refunds out to its members. Some of the problems involved in the revolving fund financing plan will be considered subsequently. It is necessary now only to point out that, at the discretion of the board, it was decided to wait until 1975

Table 16-1 Operations of the Revolving Fund as Reported by Bountiful Ridge Producers Cooperative

			Capital status at end of the year (in thousands)				
				Noncash patronage refunds			
Year	Cumulative member investment	Bank for cooperatives' loan	Invested (noncash)*	Revolved	Net yearly balance	Cumulative yearly balance†	Total capital in use
1968	$ 100	$ 75	—	—	—	—	$ 175
1969	110	60	$ 10	—	$− 5	$− 5	170
1970	135	45	25	—	+10	+ 5	180
1971	153	30	18	—	+ 3	+ 8	183
1972	156	15	3	—	−12	− 4	171
1973	176	—	20‡	—	+20	+16	176
1974	186	—	10	—	+10	+26	186
1975	193	—	22	$ 15	+ 7	+33	193
Net change, 1968–1975	$+ 93	$−75	$+108	$+15	—	$+33	$+ 18

*The cooperative is required by law to distribute 20 percent of its refunds in cash to members. Like many other cooperatives, it makes an additional cash distribution (in this case, 20 percent). Therefore, only 60 percent of the patronage refunds allocated to members are in the noncash or invested category.

†The total reported here is the balance of the noncash revolving fund account after $15,000 is used yearly for five years to pay off the facility debt and $15,000 is revolved in 1975.

‡The last $15,000 on the loan was paid in 1973, leaving a $5,000 increase in total capital in use.

before revolving the noncash patronage refunds. This delay was desirable because of year-to-year variations in the size of these refunds. Since the noncash refunds for 1969 were comparatively small in relation to those for other years, the cooperative—once it had accumulated capital to revolve funds—had the choice in 1975 of revolving only the $10,000 invested in 1969 (from 1969 operations), or of revolving at least a part of the 1970 patronage refunds ($25,000) invested in 1970. The cooperative chose to revolve 20 percent of these 1970 patronage refunds, and hence in 1975 it revolved $15,000. This was a logical action, since the funds were available and since it seemed desirable to start revolving the exceptionally large noncash refunds that were invested in 1970.

How the revolving fund financing plan works when applied to the noncash patronage refunds of a single patron is shown in Table 16-2. Patron Carlsen was allocated $200 in patronage refunds in 1969. Since the cooperative has followed the practice of refunding 40 percent of its refunds in cash, he received a cash refund of $80 and a noncash refund of $120. When the association started revolving its noncash patronage refunds in 1975, Patron Carlsen received all of his 1969 noncash refund and 20 percent of his 1970 noncash refund. This amounted to $150 ($120 for 1969 and 20 percent of $150, or $30, for 1970). Since Patron Carlsen's investment in 1975 was only $135, his total investment in the cooperative declined $15—the difference between the $150 "revolved out" to him and the $135 he invested that year.

Table 16-2 Operation of the Revolving Fund as Applied to Patron Carlsen of the Bountiful Ridge Producers Cooperative

	Capital status at the end of the year			
		Patronage refunds		
Year	Cumulative member investment	Invested (noncash)	Distributed in cash*	Revolved
1968	$1,000	—	—	—
1969	1,120	$120	$ 80	—
1970	1,270	150	100	—
1971	1,330	60	40	—
1972	1,540	210	140	—
1973	1,720	180	120	—
1974	1,870	150	100	—
1975	1,855	135	90	$150

*See Table 16-1, footnote *

The Per Unit Capital Investment Plan

Revolving fund financing, when applied to the per unit capital investment plan, operates in much the same way as the deferred patronage refund plan. It differs only in that all the transactions that occur are, in effect, completed during the current operating year. Patron investments are then available within the marketing year for the purposes agreed upon. It is important, too, to keep in mind that such an investment on the part of members is distinctly different from per unit or per dollar deductions from member business (with their cooperative) to cover day-to-day operating costs.

To illustrate how the plan works, let us assume that the Sunny Valley Cooperative Association found it necessary to construct a $200,000 fruit-storage facility (see Table 16-3). The cooperative decided to use the per unit investment plan to raise capital necessary to pay off this mortgage. If the Association had been operating for a number of years, of course, it might have put the per unit capital investment plan in operation previously in anticipation of building the storage facility, thereby accumulating a large share of the necessary funds. Because of its satisfactory business performance to date, however, Sunny Valley was able to obtain a loan from its bank for cooperatives for construction of the storage facility, which was completed in 1969.

Each member of the Association agreed to invest 5 cents per box of fruit to raise the money necessary to pay off the loan. On this basis, it was expected that the loan would be paid off by five annual payments averaging $40,000, starting in 1970. The amount of capital invested naturally varied with production, amounting to a high of $62,000 in 1972 and lower amounts for the other years. The extent to which per unit investments were more than sufficient to meet mortgage obligations is indicated by the increase in the yearly balance (the amount of per unit investment remaining after meeting mortgage payments) reported for each year's operations. The last payment on the mortgage was made in 1974, and the next year the association was in a position to

Table 16-3 Operation of the Per Unit Capital Investment Plan as Reported by Sunny Valley Cooperative Association

	Capital status at the end of the year (in thousands of dollars)						
			Capital invested				
Year	Cumulative member investment	Mortgage on new storage	Yearly amount	Revolved	Net yearly balance*	Cumulative yearly balance	Total capital in use
1969	—	200	—	—	—	—	200
1970	50	160	50	—	+10	+10	210
1971	88	120	38	—	− 2	+ 8	208
1972	150	80	62	—	+22	+30	230
1973	175	40	25	—	−15	+15	215
1974	230	—	55†	—	+55	+30	230
1975	232	—	52	+50	+ 2	+52	232
Net change, 1969–1975	+232	−200	+282‡	+50	—	+32	+32

*The net yearly balance of capital invested is the amount left at the end of each year's operation after deducting the $40,000 payable each year to satisfy the mortgage on the storage facility and the capital revolved in 1975.
†The last $40,000 on the loan was paid in 1974, leaving a $15,000 increase in total capital in use for that year.
‡The $50,000 invested in 1970 was revolved to investors in 1975.

start revolving the per unit capital investments made in previous years. The capital investment of $55,000 in 1974 was sufficient to meet the $50,000 revolved in 1975.

How the per unit capital investment plan works when applied to the orchard business of Patron Boyd is shown in Table 16-4. His investments (at 5 cents per box) are in proportion to the volume of apples he delivered, and in 1970 they amounted to $550. In 1975 his 1970 investment of $550 was "revolved out," and since he invested

Table 16-4 Operation of the Capital Investment Plan as Applied to Patron Boyd of the Sunny Valley Cooperative Association

				Capital invested			
Year	Cumulative member investment	Production (in boxes)		Per box	Yearly amount	Cumulative yearly balance	Capital revolved
1970	$ 550	11,000	x	5¢	$550	$ 550	—
1971	1,085	10,700	x	5	535	1,085	—
1972	1,225	2,800	x	5	140	1,225	—
1973	1,505	5,600	x	5	280	1,505	—
1974	1,630	13,500	x	5	675	2,380	—
1975	1,560*	9,300	x	5	465	2,295	$550

*After deducting the capital revolved.

$465 in his cooperative in that year, his total cumulative investment decreased by $85 and at the end of that year was $2,295.

Advantages of the Revolving Fund Financing Plan

An evaluation of the revolving fund method of financing as it relates to the operation of the noncash patronage refunds and per unit capital investment plans is now in order.

- The plan enables patrons to invest capital in proportion to the amount of business they do with their cooperative. This is important in maintaining an interest in, and in developing a responsibility to finance, their cooperative.
- The plan provides a comparatively easy way to build ownership and raise capital among participating patrons.
- The plan can involve nonmember patrons as well as member patrons, so that no one will get a free ride in the financing of the cooperative. Patron-users can become members.
- The plan provides a substantial degree of flexibility. Interest rates may be optional and paid at the discretion of the board of directors, as is the amount of funds to be revolved each year.
- The plan provides a systematic way for obtaining capital contributions for the cooperative and for returning investments to members.
- The plan helps patrons increase their financial resources by contributing capital to their cooperative.

Problem Areas

The revolving fund method of financing as applied to both noncash patronage refunds and per unit capital investments is not without problems. Although these problems are not insurmountable, they do suggest the need for careful planning in the development and operation of such a revolving financing plan. They also emphasize the need for effective educational programs to acquaint patrons with just how the plan operates. Principal problem areas are:

- Funds raised by the revolving financing plan (when noncash allocated patronage refunds are the basis for financing) may vary widely from year to year, depending on market conditions and on the operating efficiency of the cooperative. In fact, losses may occur in some years. Unless cooperative volume and margins continue to grow, revolving noncash patronage refunds may be difficult in later years. Likewise, a poor crop may drastically reduce member investments in some years. During these same years, however, capital requirements may be constant or growing. Consequently, noncash patronage refunds may not be a dependable source of capital for meeting specific obligations of the cooperative.
- The revolving period of financing often covers a long span of time, in a few instances ten to fifteen years or more. This is especially true if new ventures are undertaken or if the cooperative is expanding. Under such circumstances, inflation may mean that the dollars involved are comparatively cheap when returned to members, as compared with their value at the time they were invested.
- Financing is not necessarily in relation to the financial ability of the patrons. Often rather severe financial obligations are placed on young farmers, whereas the

well-established ones are in a better position to meet cooperative obligations. This problem can be solved to a certain degree if all member investments are not placed in the revolving fund. Members could make additional investments, for which they would receive interest payments.

- The funds available to pay off noncash patronage refunds or per unit capital investments may be relatively low when compared with the funds that members may expect to be revolved in any given year. In other words, the element of uncertainty must be recognized and dealt with. Members, in any event, must be prepared to assume responsibility to finance their cooperative.
- An effective capital-revolving program requires good communications between the cooperatives and its members. Members need to be aware of the inherent problems of this method of financing. They should understand, for example, why directors may have to change or eliminate interest payments on various forms of equity as well as to lengthen or shorten the period of revolving capital investments. Likewise, it is important that patrons understand the inherent problems caused by large and small yearly noncash patronage refunds and per unit capital investments. Patrons should not expect the revolving-fund method of financing always to revolve invested capital after the same number of years. Not only is it desirable to introduce flexibility as financial obligations vary, but flexibility may also be necessary if the cooperative should decide to further expand facilities and operations.
- Because of uncertainties as to the amount of money that may be available for capital purposes through the use of revolving-fund plans, many cooperatives are seeking to raise capital through a modification of these plans, sometimes referred to as the adjustable revolving fund plan (see Chapter 15).

A special problem area relates to the mechanics of such programs in diversified cooperative operations. Equitable treatment of members is substantially more complicated for the marketing cooperative which enters the farm supply business, or for the farm supply cooperative that decides to engage in livestock or poultry marketing. It is not reasonable, for example, to expect members to approve of diverting capital raised to improve grain marketing facilities to initiate a poultry-and-egg operation. The same problem may confront a consumer that enters into the furniture business.

To treat patrons equitably under such circumstances requires detailed and accurate accounting practices as well as realistic judgment as to the extent to which patronage refunds should be made by divisions, by departments, and by specific commodities. Problems of equitable treatment arise because expanding cooperatives are often involved in business operations that relate only to some of their members. Unless adequate records are kept, the cooperative may not know the costs of various operations and the extent to which they may or may not contribute to funds available for patronage refunds.

For example, who should finance the entrance of Bountiful Ridge into the livestock marketing business? How should the revolving-fund method of noncash patronage refunds be worked out when the livestock marketing service is provided? Furthermore, in many cases cooperatives are allocating patronage refunds only to members. The problem then arises of how the cooperative should handle additions to capital that accrue from savings resulting from nonmember business. Should these funds be distributed to members in proportion to their business with the cooperative, or should they be added to capital as "tax paid" surplus?

SUMMARY

Patronage refunds and per unit capital investments are distinct cooperative techniques. They provide a means for internal financing and for strengthening the financial structure of cooperatives. In using the patronage refund financing plan, it is important for cooperatives to consider their legal status carefully, in order to recognize how allocated patronage refunds differ from dividends, and to understand the relationship of these refunds to net margins or savings.

Cooperatives have developed a variety of methods for calculating patronage refunds. They usually are calculated on a dollar-volume-of-business basis or according to units marketed or purchased by members through their cooperative. Per unit capital investments are made by deducting a specified amount per unit of product—for example, 10 or 20 cents per 100 pounds of milk, or 5 or 10 cents per bushel of fruit.

The revolving fund financing plan is distinctly cooperative and has many advantages. In the first place, it involves all members, and they assume financial responsibility in proportion to the use they make of their cooperative. It is a time-tested and effective way of building needed capital resources. Finally, the plan is relatively easy to administer.

Although revolving fund financing has proved to be a relatively successful and easy way of raising capital, it also involves a certain degree of instability. Patronage refunds will vary from year to year with business conditions and the operating efficiency of the cooperative. Likewise, variations in yields will influence the amount of money that may be raised on a per unit basis.

Another problem arises in that cooperatives often find it necessary to provide new and expanded services. Consequently, the pressure for financial resources may make it difficult to revolve invested capital as originally planned and as the members expect. To help solve this problem, many cooperatives are developing a modified or adjusted revolving fund program that provides for the building and maintenance of a more permanent supply of member capital.

QUESTIONS

1. Distinguish between patronage refunds and per unit capital investment.
2. How do these two techniques for acquiring equity capital relate to cooperative principles? Why are they sometimes referred to as unique cooperative features?
3. Explain how the revolving-fund financing plan works when applied to noncash patronage refunds; to per unit capital investments.
4. What forms of cooperative investment may noncash patronage refunds and per unit capital investments take? What are the essential features of each?
5. What are the advantages of the revolving fund method of financing?
6. What problems may be encountered when using the revolving fund method of financing?

7 What is the legal status of patronage refunds and per unit capital investments?
8 What provisions should be included in a cooperative's bylaws when using the noncash patronage refund and the per unit capital investment techniques?

REFERENCES

Davidson, Donald R.: *Methods and Policies Used in Making Patronage Refunds by Selected Farmer Cooperatives*, FCS General Report 137, Farmer Cooperative Service, U.S. Department of Agriculture, Washington, October 1966, p. 22.

―――: *How Farm Marketing Cooperatives Return Savings to Patrons*, FCS Research Report 7, Farmer Cooperative Service, U.S. Department of Agriculture, Washington, 1969, p. 81.

Erdman, Henry E., and Grace H. Larson: *Revolving Finance in Agricultural Cooperatives*, Mimir Publishers, Madison, Wisc., 1965, p. 117.

Griffin, Nelda: *Financial Structure of Cooperatives*, FCS Research Report 10, Farmer Cooperative Service, U.S. Department of Agriculture, Washington, 1970, pp. 34–46, 73–90.

―――: *How Adjustable Revolving Fund Capital Plan Works*, FCS General Report III, Farmer Cooperative Service, U.S. Department of Agriculture, Washington, 1963, p. 8.

Neely, D. Morrison: *Legal Phases of Farmer Cooperatives*, FCS Information 100, Farmer Cooperative Service, U.S. Department of Agriculture, Washington, 1976, p. 743.

Packel, Israel: *The Organization and Operation of Cooperatives*, American Law Institute and the American Bar Association, Philadelphia, Pa., 1970, pp. 186–196.

Schaars, Marvin A.: *Cooperatives, Principles and Practices*, University of Wisconsin—Extension, Madison, 1971, pp. 32–37.

Volkin, David, and D. Morrison Neely: *Tax Laws Changed on Capital Retains*, FCS Reprint 382, Farmer Cooperative Service, U.S. Department of Agriculture, Washington, 1967, p. 4.

Chapter 17

Cooperative Finance Associations

Cooperatives and their members know from experience that limited financial resources often have restricted their opportunities to succeed. Consequently, cooperatives have given much thought and effort to setting up their own financial institutions so as to marshal the financial resources necessary to provide the many services that modern cooperative business requires.

Most of the early cooperative credit problems that have attracted public attention have been in agriculture. Although consumer cooperatives have also encountered the need for more credit, it was largely the credit problems of farmer cooperatives that aroused major public concern and caused the first widespread cooperative finance associations to be formed in the farm sector.[1] In the past forty years, however, credit unions have become increasingly important.

BACKGROUND DEVELOPMENTS

Ever since the beginning of the twentieth century, agriculture in the United States has been highly commercialized. Large sums of money were needed to buy land, equip-

---

[1] In 1975 a bill was introduced to establish a national bank for consumer cooperatives which would be patterned after the cooperative Farm Credit Administration.

ment, and production supplies. We have mentioned that the nature and scope of these problems first drew the public eye when President Theodore Roosevelt established the Country Life Commission in 1908. The Commission's encouragement and support of cooperatives set in motion a number of pioneering cooperative credit studies. As a result, a series of steps was taken to improve the credit position of American agriculture. To review, the most important of these steps were:

- A study of European cooperatives with special emphasis on cooperative credit systems (see Chapter 7).
- The passage of the Federal Reserve Act of 1913, which was the first step in providing limited financial assistance for cooperatives.
- Largely as a result of European credit studies, the Federal Farm Loan Act of 1916 was passed. The first step in what was eventually to become a farmer-owned cooperative finance institution, it initially provided long-term farm mortgage credit through the federal land banks and the national farm loan associations—now the federal land bank associations.
- Organization of the War Finance Corporation in 1918 to finance wartime industries, and its reactivation in 1921 to make loans to banks and other agencies which were financing agricultural and other cooperative associations.
- The Federal Trade Commission report, following a study of the credit needs of farmers, indicating the illegal interference of certain bankers in the organization and operation of cooperatives.
- The passage of the Agricultural Credits Act of 1923, which provided for Federal Intermediate Credit banks as wholesalers of credit. In addition to providing short-term and intermediate credit for farmers by discounting notes of agricultural credit corporations, livestock loan companies, and state banks, these banks were authorized to make loans to cooperatives to the extent of 75 percent of the "market value of products stored or in the marketing stage." These federal banks were capitalized at $5 million, and they were authorized to obtain loan funds by selling short-term debentures in the investment market.
- The enactment of the Agricultural Marketing Act of 1929, which authorized the establishment of the Federal Farm Board. In addition to its price stabilization function, the Board was authorized to make loans to cooperatives for constructing or acquiring facilities, merchandizing farm products, conducting educational programs with producers, and extending credit to cooperatives to enable them to make larger advances to members. The Board promoted the organization of several national commodity marketing cooperatives for grain, wool, livestock, and cotton.

These steps were sporadic attempts to provide new credit services for farmers and their cooperatives. They were mostly uncoordinated and highly centralized. Except for the Federal Farm Loan Act which led to the establishment of local farm loan associations and several agricultural credit corporations, the efforts were largely developed by marketing cooperatives. Few other cooperative credit agencies were established. Such loans as cooperatives could obtain were generally inadequate and interest rates were high.

Quite obviously, these piecemeal efforts to meet the credit needs of farmers and their cooperatives were ill-suited to deal with the growing credit problems of agriculture. As the lengthening shadows of the agricultural depression of the 1920s and the catastrophic general depression of the early 1930s were appearing, the need for a coordinated credit system became ever more apparent.

THE COOPERATIVE FARM CREDIT SYSTEM

Formation

The Farm Credit Administration (FCA) was created by an Executive order of President Franklin Roosevelt on March 27, 1933. When he signed the Farm Credit Act of 1933 on June 16, providing for the establishment of banks for cooperatives and production credit corporations, he gave permanence to FCA. The primary objective of the Farm Credit Administration was to coordinate all credit needs of farm people. It came into being after President-elect Roosevelt immediately assigned the responsibility for developing a farm credit program to Henry Morganthau, his agricultural advisor in the fall of 1932. Morganthau, in turn, recruited William I. Myers, professor of finance and marketing at Cornell University, to assist him in designing a program to deal with the

Farm Credit Banks of the Louisville District, Louisville, Kentucky. Offices of the Louisville Bank for Cooperatives, Federal Land Bank of Louisville, and the Federal Intermediate Credit Bank of Louisville. *Courtesy Louisville Farm Credit Banks.*

credit problems of agriculture. Professor Myers was an ideal choice for the assignment. Not only was he acquainted with the credit needs of farm people, but also he had the ability to work effectively with farm leaders and congressional committees. The proposed program that was developed by Myers and other agricultural and congressional leaders was accepted by Roosevelt.[2]

Structure

The Farm Credit Administration from its beginning was charged with designing and building a farmer-owned and-controlled cooperative finance system. It coordinated all government credit programs for agriculture in one agency made up of four major units:

The Federal Land Bank System, which has been in operation since 1917

The Federal Intermediate Credit Banks, organized in 1923 and consolidated with the Production Credit System in 1956

The Production Credit System, authorized by Congress in 1933 and developed as a part of the Cooperative Farm Credit System

Banks for Cooperatives, also initially developed as part of the Cooperative Farm Credit System

The Farm Credit Administration (FCA) adopted the idea of operating through districts (twelve), as developed by the Federal Farm Loan and Intermediate Credit Bank systems. The units in each district were supervised and serviced by the central staff of the Farm Credit Administration in Washington.

Control

While the cooperatively oriented Farm Credit Administration set out to build a farmer-owned and -controlled cooperative credit system, the government had provided the initial seed capital for each of the banks that financed the various FCA units. Therefore, Congress naturally was interested in maintaining sufficient supervision through the Farm Credit Administration to protect the government's financial investment in capital stock. However, it was expected that farmer control would be increased and supervision lessened as government capital was replaced by farmer-owned stock and reserves built from earnings or savings, and as farmer participants demonstrated capacity to take over managerial responsibilities. All the local cooperatives using the services of the units in the Farm Credit Administration districts have retained their independence by electing their own boards of directors and selecting their own managers, without FCA dictation. In the early stages, top district bank officers, however, had to be approved by the Governor of FCA and the district banks had to approve the local board-of-director appointments of managers of national farm loan associations and production credit associations.

Each of the twelve Farm Credit districts has its own board of directors. The Farm

---

[2]For an informative discussion of the development of the Farm Credit System, see Joseph G. Knapp, *The Advance of American Cooperative Enterprise*, 1920–1945, Interstate, Danville, Ill. 1973, chap. 14.

Credit Act of 1933 provided that three board directors were to be chosen by member-borrowers—one each by boards of directors of the national farm loan associations (now federal land bank associations), the production credit associations, and the boards of directors of cooperatives borrowing from the Banks for Cooperatives. The Governor of the Farm Credit Administration selected the remaining four directors—three being district directors, with two of them representing the general public, and one representing the national farm loan associations and also required to be a borrower from a federal land bank, as a director-at-large.

The Farm Credit Act of 1937 provided that the Governor of the Farm Credit Administration make one of his four appointments from three nominees of the national farm loan association boards of directors.

The Farm Credit Act of 1953 moved much farther in the direction of increased user control. It provided that the national farm loan associations and the production credit associations could elect two directors each. The cooperative borrowers were permitted to elect one director, with the provision that they would elect two directors as soon as they met certain bank ownership requirements. As the case might be, the other one or two directors were appointed by the Governor of the FCA.

The 1971 Farm Credit Act retained this provision with respect to directors. Since the district banks for cooperatives were all member-owned at this time, they were qualified to elect two members to each Farm Credit district board.

The Central Bank for Cooperatives is governed by a board of directors made up of one director elected by each of the twelve Farm Credit district boards and a thirteenth member appointed by the Governor with advice and consent of the Federal Farm Credit Board.

When the Farm Credit Administration again became an independent agency in 1953, after being in the Department of Agriculture since 1939, Congress established a policy-making board of thirteen members to direct its operation. Twelve directors, one from each Farm Credit district, are appointed by the President of the United States "with the advice and consent of the Senate." The President is required by law to consider the three nominations made by the board of directors of federal land bank associations, production credit associations, and cooperatives borrowing from the banks for cooperatives in each Farm Credit district. The thirteenth member is appointed by the Secretary of Agriculture and serves as his or her representative.

After the passage of the 1971 Farm Credit Act, the Federal Farm Credit Board approved the Governor's recommendations for important organizational changes in Farm Credit Administration supervision. It established the Credit Service and the Operations and Finance Service, each headed by a deputy governor who is also its director. These divisions, replaced the former Land Bank Service, Production Credit Service, and Cooperative Bank Service, which were headed by deputy governors who were also the Service directors. In late 1974 after appointment of a new governor, the Farm Credit Board approved another change. The present deputy governors each head one of three services—Credit and Operations; Finance and Research; and Administration. Figure 17-1 summarizes control arrangements for the Farm Credit Administration.

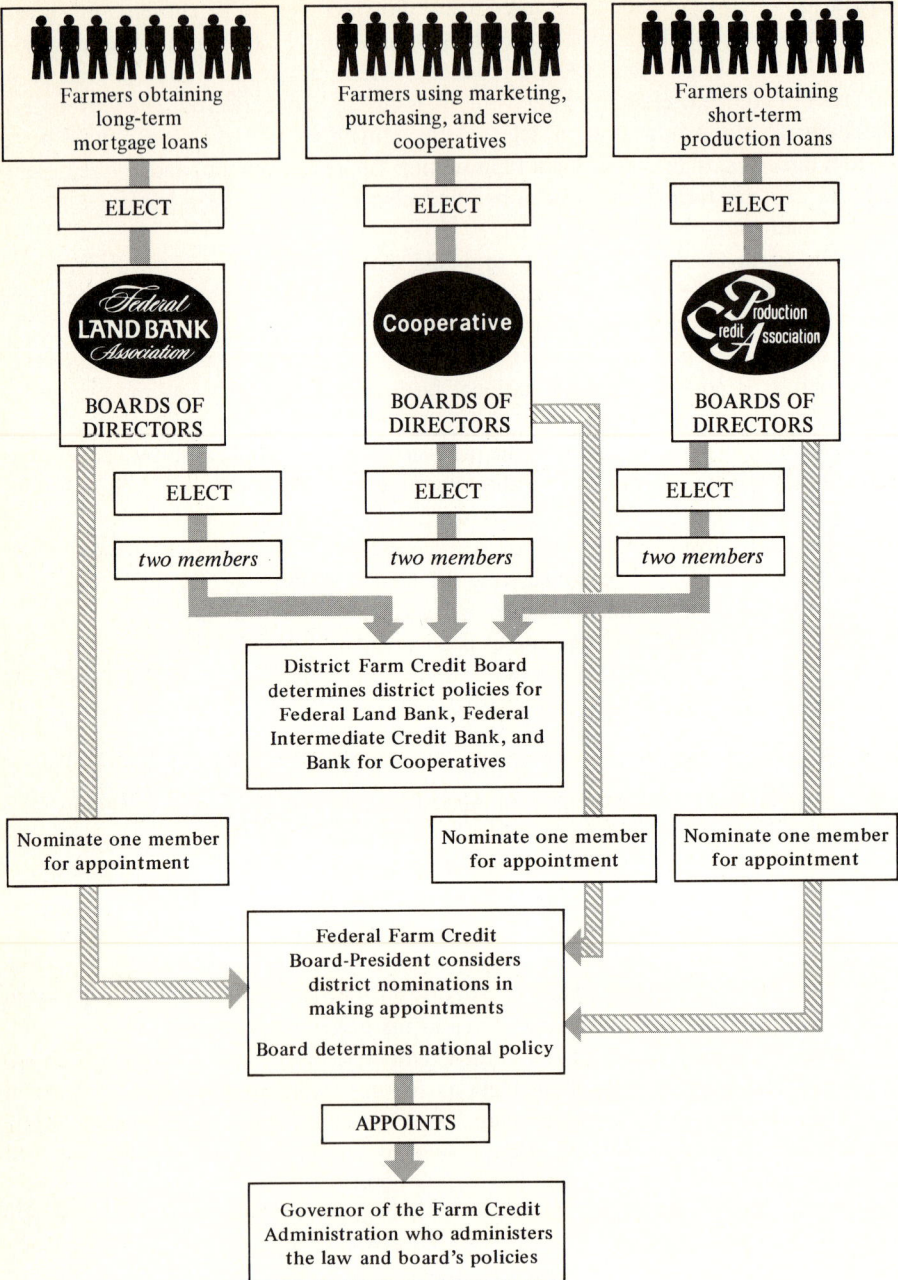

Figure 17-1 Control arrangements for the various units of the Farm Credit Administration. (*Source: 1971–72 Annual Report of the Farm Credit Administration.*)

Operations

Normal Value The Farm Credit Administration pioneered in developing the "normal value" concept in appraising farm land. The concept was based on the earning power of a farm operated by a typical farmer and subject to base-period prices rather than current market prices. The original base period (1909–1914) was moved forward owing to increases in the price level. On the basis of FCA studies, Congress raised the maximum long-term mortgage loan from 50 to 65 percent of the farm property's normal valuation. The Farm Credit Administration conducted many schools to train loan appraisers in all operating systems. In the Farm Credit Act of 1971, Congress raised the maximum for farm mortgage loans to 85 percent of the appraised market value. With this liberalization, the federal land banks are putting much more emphasis on other credit factors, such as the borrower's financial condition and repayment capacity and management's ability in determining how much to loan.

Decentralization The many problems of initiating a national agricultural credit program required a substantial degree of centralized supervisory authority. FCA, however, has always had, as its chief objective, movement toward decentralization of operations just as soon as realistic guidelines were met and competent district and local officials and directors were trained. Drawing on the experience of the federal farm loan associations (now federal land bank associations), FCA has consistently placed emphasis on bringing credit services as close to the farmer as economically feasible. To this end, over 600 production credit associations (PCAs) were established. There are now about 430 PCAs with 1,500 branch offices.

Although the banks for cooperatives operate out of their district offices except for the Baltimore and Berkeley banks, which have long had branches at San Juan, Puerto Rico, and Los Angeles respectively, this arrangement was still a big improvement over the cooperative loan program of the Federal Farm Board which required all prospective borrowers to come to Washington to arrange a loan.

A number of specific decentralization actions have been taken over the years:

- Many of the supervisory responsibilities that were formerly carried by the FCA in Washington were delegated to district banks. These included the approval of dividends and salary ranges of association employees.
- The responsibility for making appraisals for loans was transferred from the Farm Credit Administration to the Federal Land Banks System.
- The responsibility for policies relating to employment, compensation, leave, retirement, and other conditions of employment was transferred to the district Farm Credit Boards.
- The Farm Credit Administration has also encouraged and urged the district banks to transfer more and more authority and responsibility to local association boards and managers under proper regulations and guidelines and a continuing training program.

Expanded Activities The Farm Credit Act of 1955 expanded the loan program by permitting recognition of dependable sources of nonfarm income. The act also provided that loans could be made for such off-the-farm requirements as family homes (production credit associations made such loans almost from the beginning) and facilities for handling farm products and equipment and supplies. Operations were further expanded by providing for the making of loans to corporations engaged in farming. Over the years, the original $10,000 loan limit was increased to $200,000 on farm mortgage loans.

The Farm Credit Act of 1971 further substantially enlarged the scope of operations of the Cooperative Farm Credit System. It provided for new and expanded credit services. These included eliminating the $200,000 limitation on farm mortgage loans and limiting them only to their relationship to the federal land bank's net worth. Production credit associations and banks for cooperatives were authorized to make loans to harvesters of aquatic products in uncontrolled waters. Federal land banks and production credit associations were authorized to make rural housing loans to nonfarmers and to farm-related businesses. Federal land banks and Farm Credit boards were authorized to participate jointly on large loans. Farm Credit boards can do likewise with production credit associations. Production credit associations and banks for cooperatives can participate in loans of commercial banks. Moreover, the entire Cooperative Farm Credit System was authorized to provide farm-related financial services.

Problems in Maintaining a Nonpartisan Status

From the very beginning, Governor Morganthau of the Farm Credit Administration emphasized the need for staffing FCA with the best personnel available irrespective of political considerations. He believed that the complex nature of operations required an especially resourceful, honest, and efficient staff. This stipulation called for generous salaries and freedom from political interference. During their careers as governors, W. I. Myers and F. F. Hill placed the same high premium on maintaining a nonpartisan status. They said that one could not expect to collect loans that were made on a political basis. It was not always easily accomplished, however. C. R. Arnold, in *Farmers Build Their Own Production Credit System—Organization and First 25 Years*,[3] stated: "Some political influences were in evidence during the organization period but, in most cases they were a minor factor in the location of association headquarters and the selection of the secretary-treasurers."

Political considerations, however, led to a change in the status of the Farm Credit Administration from an independent government agency to an agency of the Department of Agriculture in 1939. Prior to that time, the Resettlement Administration, the Commodity Credit Corporation, and the Rural Electrification Administration had been transferred to the Department of Agriculture. A power-hungry and politically ambitious Secretary of Agriculture, Henry A. Wallace, with the help of his assistant, Paul H. Appleby, tried to redirect the operations of the FCA by increasing the role of government and reversing the trend toward farmer control. Only the opposition of cooperative groups and general farm organizations, which was reflected in Congress, together with

[3]Circular E 45, Farm Credit Administration, 1958, p. 89.

the intervention of World War II, kept Wallace from making much headway. The threat to FCA independence was sufficient to cause Governor F. F. Hill to resign in 1940 with the statement, "I do not believe it possible to maintain such a system on a sound basis if it becomes an integral part of a department of government." The mobilization of cooperative and general farm organization leaders to get the FCA out of the Department of Agriculture was accomplished with the passage of the Farm Credit Act of 1953.

The 1959 Farm Credit Act, which took district bank employees out of the federal civil service retirement system, provided that all appointments, promotions, and separations are to be based on merit and efficiency. No political tests or qualifications are permitted or given consideration. This left the major possibility for political influence in the appointments with the Farm Credit Board (p. 325). Should the President fail to give adequate consideration to the suggested nominees of the district banks when making appointments for Senate confirmation, and should a Secretary of Agriculture be swayed by political considerations in making his or her nomination to the Federal Farm Credit Board, the door would still be open for some political interference. Every President from 1953, when the 1953 act set up this board, through 1975—Eisenhower, Kennedy, Johnson, Nixon, and Ford—have made all their appointments, however, from those nominated by farmers through their elected local boards of directors. Therefore, a firm precedent has been set over a twenty-year period.[4]

Emphasis on Member Ownership and Control

We have mentioned that from its beginning, the Cooperative Farm Credit System was planned as a farmer-owned and -controlled credit institution. The following discussion of the structure, organization, and operation of the units of the System shows how this goal has been achieved. Gradually, member capital in each unit has replaced government capital. Similarly, as members have demonstrated the capacity to determine policies, they have been given more and more control through the selection of their own directors. At the same time, there has been a strong tendency toward decentralization of operations by placing decision making as close to the farmer and cooperative member-borrowers as possible. Emphasis has been put on intensive training followed by delegation of authority and responsibility.

THE BANKS FOR COOPERATIVES

When the Farm Credit Administration came into being, cooperatives were expanding operations and services. A number of large-scale or regional associations had been, or were being, organized, and their financial requirements were expanding greatly. Except for the highly centralized lending operations of the Federal Farm Board, little progress had been made in developing a credit system that had the resources and ability to provide the credit cooperatives needed. Even the Federal Farm Board was interested chiefly in serving large cooperatives.

[4]For further details on problems in maintaining a nonpartisan status, see Knapp, op. cit., pp. 273–286.

Structure

Like other units of the Farm Credit System, banks for cooperatives were organized on established FCA District bases. They all carried the name of the city in which the districts maintained their headquarters. The cooperative bank system differed from other FCA units in that it also included the Central Bank for Cooperatives. This bank was authorized to make loans to the district banks and to large cooperatives—especially those operating in more than one district; to buy and sell commercial paper; and to borrow from, and rediscount with, intermediate credit banks. For many years, however, it has not made any loans directly to cooperatives. It has limited its financing to participating in loans to larger cooperatives and loans to district banks. It also channels surplus funds from any bank in the system to those needing them on a daily basis. Control features of the district banks and central banks are discussed on pages 324–325.

The first district bank was organized in the St. Louis district on August 9, 1933. The Central Bank was established on September 12 in Washington, D.C., but is now located in Denver, Colorado. All the other district banks were organized before the end of the same year.

Capitalization

Money salvaged from the $500 million Agricultural Marketing Act Revolving Fund provided the basis for originally capitalizing the cooperative bank program. While these funds totaled $186 million, the cooperative Farm Credit System initially invested $110 million in stock from these funds—$5 million for each district bank and $50 million for the central bank. The investment grew until it reached $178.5 million in 1954. Limited amounts of capital were also raised by the provision that each cooperative must purchase stock in the amount of $100 for each $2,000 it borrowed from its district bank. This stock could be redeemed, however, when the cooperative repaid its loan. As of June 30, 1955, farmers owned $18.3 million of stock in the banks for cooperatives and the federal government owned capital stock amounting to $150 million.

The Farm Credit Act of 1953 gave renewed emphasis to the building of a farmer-owned and -controlled cooperative credit system. To this end the Farm Credit Act of 1955 further provided a plan for building cooperative capital and gradually retiring government capital. This plan called for three classes of capital stock. Existing government stock was transferred to so-called A stock. Cooperatives in addition could invest in B stock, which paid dividends ranging from 2 to 4 percent. The C stock had to be purchased in an amount ranging from 10 to 15 percent of the amount of interest cooperatives paid on their loans. In addition, cooperatives began to receive patronage refunds in C stock and allocated surplus. All government capital was paid off in 1968; as of June 30, 1974, net worth approximated $392 million.

When a cooperative receives its first loan from the district bank, it purchases one or more shares of voting stock, which has a par value of $100. Savings of district banks are distributed to borrowers as patronage refunds in class C stock and allocated surplus.

The majority of the operating funds of the banks are obtained by the sale of bonds on the nation's central security markets. These bonds are backed by the notes of borrowers. The practice of selling bonds, then called debentures, was initiated in 1950 after careful study.

The 1971 act also raised the maximum debt to capital ratio of the banks for cooperatives from 8:1 to 20:1. This is in line with the maximum ratios allowed for other banks in the system.

Other Services

The banks for cooperatives have been "partners in progress" with the borrowing local farmer cooperatives. Over the years they have emphasized sound financial and operating policies. John Eidam, retired president of the Omaha Bank for Cooperatives, identified some of the early efforts of the banks in helping borrowing cooperatives build a stronger financial structure as: (1) maintaining good accounting records; (2) presenting monthly reports by managers to boards, committees, and members; (3) maintaining adequate margins; (4) striving to strengthen the financial structure; and (5) improving member and public relations. The district banks have encouraged the revolving method of financing, pooling, and financing planning. They have worked closely with the Farmer Cooperative Service, the state experiment stations and extension services, the National Council of Farmer Cooperatives, national cooperative associations, and general farm organizations in maintaining and developing new and expanded services for members.

Operations

To be eligible to borrow from a bank for cooperatives, a cooperative must (1) operate so that at least 80 percent of its voting control is held by farmers, ranchers, or producers and harvesters of aquatic products;[5] (2) do at least 50 percent of its business with members, except for business done with the government and services or supplies furnished by the cooperative as a public utility; and (3) restrict any member of the cooperative to one vote, regardless of the amount of stock or membership capital the member owns, *or* restrict capital stock dividends to either 10 percent or the maximum allowed by state law, whichever is less.

The banks for cooperatives can make loans for the following purposes:

- Storing, packing, processing, or marketing farm or aquatic products
- Purchasing, testing, grading, processing, furnishing, or distributing farm or aquatic products
- Furnishing business services to farmers, producers, or harvesters of aquatic products

The banks also make "term loans" to finance long-term obligations of up to forty years, or working capital and "seasonal loans" to finance current operations that mature within eighteen months. Loans may be either secured or unsecured.

[5]There is considerable interest in some cooperative circles in reducing their percentage, and from time to time, legislation is proposed to achieve this result.

Factors considered by banks for cooperatives before making a loan are:

- The reputation of the cooperative as a business organization
- Financial position and demonstrated financial responsibility
- Repayment ability
- Competency of management
- Purpose of the loan
- Collateral offered as security
- Membership support

FEDERAL LAND BANKS

In the early 1900s, the growing need for long-term farm credit became apparent. Often farmers were unable to obtain credit suited to their needs. In the search for a solution, the following were among the early steps taken to deal with the critical credit needs of the day:

- As previously mentioned, the Country Life Commission revealed a lack of adequate credit for farmers, and drawing on European experience, it suggested exploring the potential of cooperative credit.
- In 1912 President Taft requested our ambassadors in the principal European countries to look into the rural credit systems operating in these countries.
- In 1913 two commissions—the American commission appointed by the Southern Commercial Congress and the United States commission appointed by the President of the United States—went to Europe to study the credit systems in European countries and make recommendations for a credit system for the United States. They later published joint and separate reports.
- As a result of the commissions' recommendations, some thirty bills were introduced in Congress. In general, three approaches were suggested: (1) direct government loans, (2) organization of private land banks, and (3) establishment of a system of cooperative land-bank associations.
- After much deliberation and the recognition "that no foreign system would be entirely suitable to the United States," the Federal Farm Loan Act of 1916 was passed. It was a compromise in that it provided for both private and cooperative land banks. The private banks were called Joint Stock Land Banks. Over eighty were organized. Many of them competed with one another. When they fell into serious financial trouble, they were placed in liquidation by the Emergency Farm Mortgage Act of 1933. The Federal Farm Loan Act, therefore, became in effect the basis for developing the first comprehensive cooperative farm credit system in the United States.

The Federal Farm Loan Act

President Wilson signed the Federal Farm Loan Act into law on July 17, 1916. It provided for a five-member Federal Farm Loan Board appointed by the President with the advice and consent of the Senate. The Secretary of the Treasury was designated as chairman of the board.

The Board took very seriously its responsibility to establish federal land bank districts. In all, fifty-three hearings were held in over forty states. Some 30,000 people, largely farmers, attended. The hearings not only provided invaluable information for determining boundaries of Farm Loan districts and the location of federal land banks, but also helped to focus on the expressed credit needs of farmers. In deciding on district boundaries, the Board gave attention to such factors as total land area, farm land area, improved farm land area, number of farms mortgaged, amount of mortgage indebtedness, value of farm land and buildings, gross value of farm products, total population, and rural population.

The Board also decided that the federal land banks should not be located in the largest urban cities. The first federal land bank was chartered in Wichita, Kansas, on March 1, 1917, and all other banks were chartered by April 3, 1917. The banks were capitalized with a sum of $750,000 each. In 1932, the Federal Farm Loan Act was amended to provide an additional $125 million of capital for the twelve federal land banks.

Aware of the desirability of bringing credit directly to rural people, the district land banks immediately set about organizing local farm loan associations. The first one organized was the Pawnee County Farm Loan Association at Larned, Kansas, chartered on March 27, 1917. By the end of that year, some 2,100 local farm loan associations were in operation and by the 1930s the number had increased to more than 5,000. As means of communication improved and as the local associations' leadership gained experience, a great deal of attention was given to eliminating overlapping territories and reducing the number of local associations in order to have economically sized cooperatives; by July 30, 1974, their number had decreased to 553. Many of these associations, however, maintain branches in certain parts of their territory and other contact points that are open on specified days of the week.

To finance the federal land banks, securities are sold in the open money markets. In 1921 the legality of issuing these securities was questioned because they were exempt from federal and state taxes, and the program was suspended for ten months until a favorable decision was handed down by the United States Supreme Court. For many years, however, these securities have no longer been exempt from federal income taxes.

An important development for the Federal Land Bank System was the passage of the Agricultural Credits Act of 1923. It authorized the Federal Farm Loan Board to charter twelve federal intermediate credit banks. These banks were placed under the supervision of the federal land banks. They were empowered to discount short-term agricultural notes and make loans to agricultural marketing cooperatives.

The 1923 act also authorized other changes, foremost of which were:

- Raising the limit on individual mortgage loans from $10,000 to $25,000.
- Assessing various operating costs to the federal land banks which previously had been covered by congressional appropriations.
- Providing for issuance of consolidated bonds.
- Providing for two additional members on the Farm Loan Board and for a seven-member board of directors for the district land banks—three selected by national farm loan associations, three appointed by the Federal Farm Loan Board to represent the public, and one appointed from the three names highest on a list submitted by national farm loan associations.

Early Farm Credit Operations

The Federal Land Bank System was the only going cooperative credit system in existence when the Cooperative Farm Credit Administration was established on March 27, 1933. The Emergency Farm Credit Act was passed by Congress in response to the critical credit situation resulting from mounting farm foreclosures during the Depression years. It provided for refinancing at reduced interest rates and gave the land banks authority to grant extensions. Land bank commissioners' loans, made from a $200-million government appropriation and with first and second mortgages as security, were made up to 75 percent of the appraised normal value of farms. The Federal Land Bank System was used to handle these loans. This program remained in effect until 1944. The $200 million was used in 1934 to capitalize the Federal Farm Mortgage Corporation so it could sell government-guaranteed bonds to raise more loan funds. The government got the entire $200 million back, plus $150 million in dividends.

Many important developments occurred during the first years of the Farm Credit Administration. Government funds invested in the Depression years—$125 million of land-bank capital stock plus $189 million in paid-in surplus—were paid off by 1947 to make the Land Bank System 100 percent farmer-owned. The System also placed considerable emphasis on consolidation and reorganization of many small, weak, local farm loan associations, a program which started in the late 1930s and reached its peak in the 1940s. Like other units of the Cooperative Farm Credit System, the Federal Land Bank System emphasized decentralization of operations, expansion of services, and movement in the direction of complete farm ownership and control.

Operations

Loans made by the Federal Land Bank System run from five to forty years, with security usually being a first lien on real estate. Those eligible to borrow are:

- Farmers and ranchers
- Legal entities—partnerships, trusts, and corporations that qualify as farmers, growers, or ranchers
- Rural residents—for loans on conventional, modular, or mobile homes in the open country but not in towns or villages with a population of over 2,500
- Farm-related businesses
- Combined operations

The Federal Land Bank System uses the same general criteria that the Production Credit System and the Banks for Cooperatives use in determining loan decisions, membership financing, and savings distribution.

The Farm Credit Act of 1971 authorized the following modifications in the operation of the federal land banks: (1) making loans on nonfarm homes; (2) increasing the percentage of the value that can be loaned on farm real estate from 65 percent of the "normal value" to 85 percent of the appraised (market) value of the property, (3) financing businesses providing on-farm services; (4) providing members with financially related services; and (5) continuing decentralization of operations.

PRODUCTION CREDIT ASSOCIATIONS

Background

Many of the forces that were contributing to the need for long-term farm mortgage credit were also contributing to the need for short-term production credit. In addition, the demand for such production supplies as feed, fertilizer, and seeds was increasing. Changes in agriculture, particularly increased specialization and larger-scale operations, were common throughout all farming regions. Contributing to the farmers' credit woes were high interest rates, a frequent lack of understanding, and an absence of local loan funds on the part of commercial banks, merchant creditors, and small loan companies.

In response to these problems, the government attempted to lend a hand.

- As early as 1918, Congress appropriated $2 million for the purchase of seed by farmers in designated drought-stricken areas.

Modern farm operations in Wisconsin. Farmers, through their production credit and federal land bank associations, obtain the capital needed to carry on modern farm operations. *Courtesy Farm Credit Administration.*

- The War Finance Corporation and the Agricultural Credits Act played roles in providing agricultural credit, as mentioned earlier in the chapter.
- In an attempt to reach agricultural lenders, regional agricultural credit corporations were set up by the Reconstruction Finance Corporation in each of the twelve land bank districts in 1932. These corporations in turn operated twenty-two branch offices.

The critical situation with respect to season agricultural credit for production purposes was brought into sharp focus by the impact of the Depression which had existed in rural areas since the early 1920s and which became nationwide ten years later. As a consequence, general farm organizations took the lead in demanding that something be done to alleviate the credit shortage in agriculture.

The Farm Credit Act of 1933 provided for the establishment of production credit corporations in each of the twelve Farm Credit districts. These were originally capitalized at $7.5 million each and were authorized to capitalize and supervise local production credit associations. There was considerable discussion as to whether production credit should be provided by Federal Land Bank Associations. The belief prevailed, however, that the program might tend to be subordinated to the critical long-term farm mortgage financing and refinancing programs that were being initiated by the Federal Land Banks at this time if the associations were also required to make such loans. Consequently, separate district production credit corporations were established, the first one for the St. Louis district on August 9, 1933. All twelve credit corporations were chartered by the end of the same year. The production credit corporations' job was to organize, capitalize, and supervise a nationwide system of local production credit associations.

Steps were immediately taken to set up local production credit associations, and the first one was incorporated at Champaign, Illinois, on September 11, 1933. Conscious of the need to bring the credit program directly to farmers, 663 local production credit associations were in operation by mid-April, 1934. Their assigned territories included all the forty-eight states and Puerto Rico. C. R. Arnold, former Production Credit Commissioner of the Farm Credit Administration, in a report on the first twenty-five years of the Production Credit System, pointed out some of the problems that developed. First of all, it was necessary to get the program underway in a hurry to meet the critical credit needs of farmers. Since there was only limited experience to draw on, a considerable amount of red tape and bureaucracy had to be overcome. Then, there was the problem of selecting district Production Credit Association officials and secretary-treasurers (managers) of local Production Credit Associations. An urgent need soon appeared for a comprehensive educational program to train employees and directors of these Associations. This goal was aggressively pursued, thereby contributing much to the sound basis on which these associations were established.

During the next two decades, a number of developments helped to convert the Production Credit System into a truly cooperative system. As of June 30, 1974, the combined net worth of the production credit associations was $1.4 billion, and that of the twelve federal intermediate credit banks about $524 million. In 1956, the twelve production credit associations were merged into the twelve federal intermediate credit banks, and those banks assumed the responsibility of supervising the local production credit associations for which they had been providing the loan funds from their beginning. This act also provided a means by which the Production Credit Associations started to pay off the government capital stock in the Federal Intermediate Credit Banks. This repayment was completed in 1968. As pointed out previously, these banks served essentially as wholesalers of credit, making no loans of their own. Their principal function was to sell debentures (now bonds) and discount farmers' notes for the Production Credit Associations and other lenders.

Operations

Like other units of the Cooperative Farm Credit System, the Production Credit unit has undergone an evolutionary and maturing process in achieving complete farmer ownership. Production credit is generally available to the same type of borrowers and with the same criteria as those established for the Federal Land Bank Associations except that they lend to farm tenants as well as to farm owners and to producers and harvesters of aquatic products.

Each borrower from a production credit association has to invest in that association and has to purchase class B voting stock in proportion to the amount of the loan. The borrower may, however, also purchase larger amounts of class A nonvoting stock to help finance the association. When loans are repaid, members frequently keep their class B stock for use when they obtain future loans. If no loans are made, class B stock is converted to class A nonvoting stock after two years.

The local production credit associations perform an important educational function as far as their members are concerned. They assist members in financial planning, thereby helping them gain sophistication in money management and in the effective and efficient utilization of capital.

The 1971 Farm Credit Act permitted production credit associations to expand operations by:

- Financing the purchase, repair, or modernization of rural homes
- Providing financially related services to meet needs of farmers
- Financing certain farm-related businesses providing on-farm services
- Participating with commercial banks on loans
- Financing producers or harvesters of aquatic products

NATIONAL RURAL UTILITIES COOPERATIVE FINANCE CORPORATION (CFC)

The CFC came into being as a result of the financial gap between the inadequate appropriated funds for the Rural Electrification Administration (REA), an agency of the Department of Agriculture, and the large financial needs of rural electric systems. When it became increasingly evident that REA was unable fully to meet the growing credit needs of rural electric associations, the National Rural Electric Credit Association (NRECA) initiated a study of the long-term credit needs of rural electric cooperatives. While recognizing that REA should continue as a primary source of credit for rural electric systems, the study recommended that a credit corporation be established to supplement credit for these associations. Acting on this recommendation, local electric cooperatives incorporated the Cooperative Finance Corporation in 1969. It is wholly owned and controlled by member systems.

Structure

CFC's board of directors consists of twenty-two persons—two from each of the eleven districts into which the nation is divided for the purpose of electing directors. The directors from each of ten districts must be from different states within the district, and two of them must be, respectively, a manager and a director of a member system. The two directors from the eleventh district are designated by the board of the NRECA.

Staffing

The chief administrative officer of CFC, known as the Governor, is appointed by the board of directors. This officer directs day-to-day operations and employs a staff to head the corporation's seven basic departments. These are: Loan, Finance, Legal, Engineering, Information and Member Relations, Borrowers' Operations, and Administration.

Source of Funds

CFC has two principal sources of capital: capital term certificates (CTCs), which are sold to rural electric cooperatives; and loan funds obtained in the private money markets by the issuance of long-term debt securities known as collateral trust bonds. CTCs mature in forty-six to fifty years and earn interest at the rate of 3 percent per year. Another source of capital is that subscribed by borrowing members in the amount equal to 5 percent of the long-term loans.

Types of Loans

CFC makes four types of loans: (1) short-term unsecured loans that do not exceed twelve months; (2) intermediate-term loans (generally on a secured basis and for periods up to five years); (3) long-term secured loans made often concurrently with the loans from REA; and (4) power-supply loans, in which both the CFC and the REA participate, made in accordance with predetermined arrangements.

Loans were first made in 1971; as of May 31, 1975, CFC reported a cumulative total of 1,877 loans amounting to over $1 billion. In fiscal 1974–1975, approved loans consisted of 395 long-term loans totaling $146 million, 13 intermediate-term loans totaling $113 million, and 587 line of credit commitments totaling $642 million.

Membership

Over 80 percent of all rural electric cooperatives were members of CFC in 1975. The number included 792 local REA distribution cooperatives, 41 power-supply associations, 40 regional and statewide associations, and NRECA, giving a total of 874 members.

RURAL TELEPHONE BANK

The Rural Telephone Bank, a credit institution organized and operated by the United States government, was created on May 7, 1971, in response to the growing needs of rural telephone systems for additional credit to supplement that available through the REA telephone lending program. In establishing the Rural Telephone Bank, Congress declared that its purpose was to supplement the financing of the REA program, and that the basic objective was to develop a bank that eventually would become a privately owned and operated corporation. Thus, the Rural Telephone Bank started in much the same way as the Farm Credit Administration.

Structure

The board of directors is made up of thirteen members. It includes the Administrator of the REA (in the Department of Agriculture) and the Governor of the Farm Credit Administration as provided by the law establishing the bank, and, in addition, three Department of Agriculture employees, two members of the general public, and six from the rural telephone industry. They all were initially appointed by the President of the United States subject to congressional approval.

At the end of the first year of operation, however, the six directors representing borrowing members were duly elected by them—three from among the directors, managers, and employees of cooperative telephone systems and three from among the directors, members, and employees of commercial-type telephone systems. The Rural Telephone Bank, therefore, is, in effect, a joint venture of cooperatives, with borrowers of the commercial type. It is anticipated that as the Bank gains experience, more and more policy-making decisions will be turned over to it and more of the directors will be elected by borrowers, so that its objective of becoming an entirely user-owned and -operated bank will be achieved.

Types of Stock

The Telephone Bank is financed by three types of stock. Class A stock is purchased by the United States government, and the law provides that $30 million will be purchased each year until government capital totals $300 million. Class B stock is purchased by borrowers in amounts equal to 5 percent of their loans. Class C stock is available for purchase by telephone systems eligible to borrow from the bank. All loans are made for the same purpose as that of the REA telephone loans.

Operation

The Governor of the bank is the Administrator of REA and, together with one employee, constitutes the present staff.

On June 30, 1972, the 251 stockholders consisted of 147 commercial firms, 100 cooperatives, and 4 borrowers' organizations. Of the systems eligible to borrow, 42 percent of the cooperative telephone systems and 22 percent of the commerical telephone systems held C stock. This stock was held by 847 borrowers, of which 236 were cooperatives and 611 were commercial firms.

The loan program started in January 1972 when five loans were made to telephone systems. During the 1973 fiscal year, 132 loans, totaling approximately $150 million, were made. Of this amount, 116, amounting to $132 million, were made by commercial systems and the rest by cooperative systems.

COOPERATIVE CREDIT CORPORATIONS

The idea of an agricultural credit corporation was first advanced in the Agricultural Credits Act of 1923. Only three credit corporations were established, however, and two of these handled commodity loans for a short period. More recently, regional marketing and supply cooperatives, both confronted with substantial credit requirements by their member affiliates, have organized cooperative credit corporations as subsidiaries to help meet these needs.

In 1973, nine regional cooperatives operated eleven credit corporation subsidiaries. They were Ag-Way, Inc., Midland Cooperatives, Inc., Land O'Lakes, Inc., Gold Kist, Inc., Farmland Industries, Inc., F S Services, Inc., Pacific Supply Cooperative, Tennessee Farmers Cooperative, and Missouri Farmers Association, Inc. Most of the credit corporations are organized to make direct loans to patrons of member cooperatives and specialty loans to large turkey and livestock producers. In other instances, they help member cooperatives finance their inventories and other working needs.

In addition to these cooperative credit corporations, there are a number of cooperative credit corporations that serve livestock cooperatives and have close working relationships with the affiliates of the National Livestock Producers Association. Others serve fruit growers in the West, cotton producers in the South, and local farm supply cooperatives in the Midwest.

That some of the credit corporations are of substantial size is shown by the fact that the Cooperative Finance Association, Inc., which is a subsidiary of Farmland Industries, Inc., reported loans of $222 million in 1973. These loans were primarily made to help member cooperatives with their budget and capital needs and to develop financial programs to obtain funds from other sources. Most cooperative credit corporations use the Federal Intermediate Credit Banks for discount purposes.

An FCS study, *How Cooperatives Use Credit Agencies to Meet Patrons' Needs* (General Report 52)[6] by Bailey, Pursell, and Engberg, reported that favorable factors in the operation of cooperative finance corporations were their adaptability (1) to meet specialized needs, and (2) to operate so as to qualify many of them for direct loans from Federal Intermediate Credit Banks.

Factors limiting their effectiveness in some instances, reported in the same study, include: (1) restrictive organization and operations that limit meeting growing and changing agricultural credit needs, (2) frequently insufficient capital to meet credit needs, and (3) a too-close relationship with sales departments, which sometimes results in relaxed credit standards in order to promote sales.

---

[6]John Bailey, Arthur Pursell, and Russell Engberg, FCS General Report 52, Farmer Cooperative Service, U.S. Department of Agriculture, Washington, 1958, p. 6.

CREDIT UNIONS

Credit unions are cooperative finance institutions that provide low-cost savings and loan services for members. Their broad base of operations is found in nearly 23,000 associations that have over 29 million accounts and that operate throughout the United States. In 1974, credit unions accounted for 2.3 percent of the total savings in the United States. The holders of credit union accounts, as a percentage of total population, increased from 11.1 percent in 1964 to 13.9 percent in 1974. During the same period, savings in credit unions increased from $15 billion to $28 billion. Credit unions are becoming especially important in the installment field; they account for over 14 percent of installment loans made by major lenders in 1974. This was just over half the installment credit of finance companies and nearly one-third that reported by commercial banks. It was about one-seventh more than that reported by retail outlets.

Some 600 credit unions operate in rural communities. Many of them are closely associated with supply cooperatives and some of the larger ones hire field representatives to service their loans. They make producer loans to finance feed, supplies, and equipment purchases for members.

Bailey, Pursell, and Engberg reported in their FCS 1958 study[7] that factors favorable to the operations of rural credit unions were (1) flexibility in operations and adaptability to various patron needs; (2) close working relationships with sponsoring cooperatives; and (3) the use of local funds which are thus retained in the community. Limiting factors were (1) problems in development and maintenance of active membership programs, and (2) problems in raising capital adequate to meet highly seasonal demands. Although credit unions have established no regional or national banks to provide credit for their operations, many state credit union leagues serve as sources of funds for local credit unions, especially during initial periods of operation. Emphasis is on building capital through the savings of members.

The Farm Credit Administration was given the job of organizing and supervising the Federal Credit Unions authorized by Congress in 1934 because Congress decided FCA was the only organization that understood cooperative credit. Supervision of these unions was transferred to the Federal Deposit Insurance Corporation in 1942.

SAVINGS AND LOAN ASSOCIATIONS AND MUTUAL SAVINGS BANKS

The importance of savings and loan associations and mutual savings banks as cooperative financial organizations frequently is not recognized by the general public. These associations, numbering in the thousands, provide essential credit and saving services at cost for members. For example, in the decade from 1964 to 1974, memberships in savings and loan associations increased 154 percent. Savings accounts in mutual savings banks increased 100 percent during the same period. As of 1974, savings and loan associations accounted for 20 percent of the savings in major savings institutions, and mutual savings banks accounted for 8 percent.

[7]Ibid., pp. 7–8.

SUMMARY

The trend toward a highly specialized and commercial agriculture ever since the beginning of the twentieth century illustrates the changing and growing credit needs of rural America. Since established credit sources proved ill-suited to meet these needs, farm leaders, with the help of government, groped for possible solutions along cooperative lines. The first step in this direction was the Federal Farm Loan Act of 1916 which set the groundwork for what was eventually to become a farmer-owned and -controlled, cooperative, long-term mortgage credit system. In 1933 it was expanded into the Cooperative Farm Credit System, which constituted for the first time a coordinated cooperative credit system. The Farm Credit System is now composed of three units—the federal land banks and federal land bank associations, which provide long-term credit; the federal intermediate credit banks and production credit associations, which extend short-term credit; and the banks for cooperatives, which provide commodity, facility, and operating loans for member cooperatives.

The success of the Cooperative Farm Credit System has achieved international recognition. It is cited as an excellent example of the practicality of building a highly effective user-owned and -controlled cooperative credit system with initial government assistance combined with a plan for disengagement. The Farm Credit System has also served as a model for the organization and operations of the National Rural Utilities Cooperative Finance Corporation and the Rural Telephone Bank, which had as their goal the same objective of eventually achieving complete user-ownership and -control.

The many other government agencies that are providing financial assistance to various types of cooperatives, within the legal limits of their authorizing legislation, also have as their goal the eventual user-ownership of the cooperatives they serve. Cooperative credit corporations have developed to a limited extent to provide credit for certain specialized groups and regional cooperative associations.

Except for credit unions, cooperative credit has made less headway among consumer groups. In mid-1975, a bill was introduced to form a national bank for consumer cooperatives patterned after the agricultural banks for cooperatives. Credit unions, together with savings and loan associations and mutual savings banks, however, are becoming increasingly important credit institutions for consumer groups.

QUESTIONS

1 What were the principal forces that contributed to the credit problems of farmers in the early 1900s? The interest in cooperative credit institutions?
2 What were the factors that resulted in the passage of the Federal Farm Loan Act?
3 Which farm credit activities were coordinated with the establishment of the Farm Credit Administration?
4 What provisions and modifications made it possible for farmers to achieve ownership and control of the Cooperative Farm Credit System?
5 What important supplementary services are provided by the various units of the Cooperative Farm Credit System?
6 Why were the concepts of "normal value" and "decentralization" important in the success of FCA?

7   Compare the Cooperative Farm Credit System, the National Rural Utilities Cooperative Finance Corporation, and the Rural Telephone Bank as to basic objectives and initial operating practices.
8   What are the principal objectives of cooperative credit corporations?
9   What functions do credit unions perform and what factors have contributed to their success?
10 What is the justification for including savings and loan associations and mutual savings banks in the cooperative category?

REFERENCES

Arnold, C. R.: *1933–1958, Farmers Build Their Own Production Credit System–Organization and First 25 Years,* Circular E 45, Farm Credit Administration, Washington, 1958, p. 89.

Dublin, Jack: *Credit Unions: Theory and Practice,* Wayne State University Press, Detroit, Mich., 1971, p. 186.

Engberg, Russell C.: *Financing Farmer Cooperatives,* Farm Credit Administration, Bank for Cooperatives, Washington, 1965, p. 168.

Farm Credit Administration: *Banks for Cooperatives: How They Operate,* Washington, undated.

————: *Federal Land Banks: How They Operate,* Washington, undated.

————: *The Federal Land Bank System: 1917–1967,* Washington, 1967, p. 32.

————: *Production Credit Associations: How They Operate,* Washington, undated.

Hoag, Gifford, B. B. Sunbury, and Marie Puhr: *Banks for Cooperatives: A Quarter Century of Progress,* Circular E 47, Farm Credit Administration, Washington, 1960, p. 87.

Janke, E. A.: *39th Annual Report 1971–72 Farm Credit Administration,* Farm Credit Administration, Washington, 1973, p. 114.

Knapp, Joseph G.: *The Advance of American Cooperative Enterprise, 1920–1945,* Interstate, Danville, Ill., 1973. See chap. 10, Cooperative Progress in Credit and Insurance, pp. 192–205; and Building the Cooperative Farm Credit System, 1933–1940, pp. 246–287.

Puhr, Marie: *A Half a Century of Progress with the Cooperative Land Bank System,* Circular E 43, Farm Credit Administration, Washington, 1957, p. 54.

Chapter 18

Cooperative Bargaining

Bargaining is a process in which participating parties seek to reach an agreement on terms of a business transaction. The agreement usually states the price of products exchanged, the terms of sale as they relate to a transaction that occurs in the absence of fixed or established prices, and the obligations agreed to by each party. Specific points covered, in addition to price, may include credit or financial arrangements, production assistance, the quality and quantity of the products to be delivered, the time of delivery, transportation arrangements, product promotion, sharing of research findings, and the services to be provided and conditions under which they are made available. The main objective of bargaining is to exert sufficient market power to influence directly the terms of trade for the products involved.

THE NATURE OF BARGAINING

Before examining bargaining as it relates to the unique and distinct operations of specialized bargaining cooperatives, it will be helpful to identify briefly how, in a broad sense, the concept of bargaining applies to, and can be used by, various groups in the economy under many diverse conditions. The groups participating may have a substantial degree of equality in their bargaining efforts, or they may be strong bargainers or weak bargainers. They usually maintain little or no formal structure for bargaining, and as a rule, their bargaining applies to individual buying and selling activities and is greatly influenced by the special conditions that exist when a particular transaction is being negotiated.

General Bargaining

Individuals Individuals, consciously or unconsciously, bargain when they are looking for a job. They also bargain when they purchase a car, contract for the building of a home, or engage in any one of many transactions relating to products produced or services provided.

Firms Firms, even more often than individuals, bargain or haggle about the products they handle and the services they seek or provide. Manufacturing firms, for example, bargain with other firms for raw materials or processed or manufactured products. In a general way, retailers, even though they have determined their prices, are bargaining with consumers through the prices they charge and the services they provide. Discount stores emphasize price and minimize service in their bargaining. Other retailers place special emphasis on service and terms of sale. An exception to the more-or-less informal bargaining of retailers and other firms is the *formal* bargaining they do with labor unions for wages and conditions of employment.

Nations Nations often bargain for economic and political considerations. Russia, for example, while buying wheat from individual grain firms in the United States, engaged in nation-to-nation bargaining for credit, transportation arrangements, and other terms of scale in the notorious wheat deals of 1972 and 1975. The Arab nations bargained for price and political concessions when they withheld petroleum products from oil-hungry nations in 1973 and 1974.

Labor Unions On a trial-and-error basis, organized labor has bargained more-or-less successfully with employers in the United States for well over 100 years. First, local craft unions fought an uphill battle for recognition. Through the Knights of Labor and the American Federation of Labor, the labor movement slowly gained national recognition. Then the organization of industrial unions, coupled with increasingly favorable legislation after the early 1930s, culminated in the National Labor Relations (Wagner) Act of 1935. This act served to strengthen the hand of labor unions in bargaining. It provided that "Employees shall have the right to self-organization, to form, join, or assist labor organizations to bargain collectively through representatives of their own choosing. . . ." This legislation was followed by the Taft-Hartley Act of 1947, which prescribed rules of conduct for both labor and employers.

Strong industrial unions, such as the Teamsters, United Auto Workers, and United Steel Workers, came into being and total union membership approached 24 million, or about 27 percent of all nonfarm workers in the early 1970s. Using the strike as their principal weapon, labor unions bargained not only for wages but also for other conditions of labor, such as fringe benefits and job security. Other important provisions bargained for included dues checkoff, the union shop, seniority, pensions, and health and insurance plans. Unions also exercise substantial political influence through their stand on national issues and their support, or lack of it, for political candidates. Local and national unions usually maintain a federated organizational structure (e.g., AFL-CIO).

Operating Cooperatives To help us distinguish the nature of the bargaining function, it will be useful first to review briefly the essential features of operating cooperatives. Operating cooperatives either take title to, or market on a commission basis, the products grown by their farmer members. They usually handle physically, and at times may process or store, these products. They then bargain in a general way with purchasers. Land O' Lakes, Inc., Minneapolis, Minnesota, for example, uses this approach in negotiating with chain stores for the price of its butter and other dairy products. Sunkist Growers, Inc., Van Nuys, California, negotiates with domestic buyers and with representatives of foreign nations for the price and terms of sale for fresh citrus fruits and processed products. Farm supply cooperatives negotiate with domestic and foreign suppliers for such items as barbed wire, feed grains, fertilizer ingredients, and crude petroleum products. In this way, operating cooperatives provide a means by which members may enhance their income when dealing with large firms. They are able to do this when they have the quality and quantity of products the trade desires. This enhanced market power is sometimes referred to as bargaining power.

Operating cooperatives, functioning as they do on a buy-or-sell basis, may at times be confronted with a bargaining cooperative that will try to bargain with them to improve prices for its members.

Bargaining Cooperatives (Associations)

In contrast with the general bargaining activities of operating cooperatives, specialized bargaining cooperatives operate in a distinct and different way. It is the special features of the bargaining transactions of these associations, particularly as they influence the price-making process, that we shall explore in this chapter.[1]

In carrying on the bargaining function, bargaining cooperatives generally do not handle the products of members. For such products as fruits, vegetables, and sugar beets, they usually reach agreements as to price and terms of sale that cover a given season. In the case of livestock and poultry, established prices stay in effect until the time agreed upon for renegotiation. The price for milk or the method of determining it may be for an undefined period.

One example of a bargaining cooperative is the Maryland and Virginia Milk Producers Association, Arlington, Virginia, which bargains for the price of grade A milk marketed for members. Another example is the California Canning Peach Association, San Francisco, California, which, having been organized in 1921, is one of the first bargaining cooperatives established in the United States. It bargains for members with processors as to the price and conditions of sale for canning peaches.

[1]The closely related subjects of marketing contracts and marketing agreements and orders were discussed in Chapter 10.

Areas of Confusion

The Distinction between Bargaining Function and Bargaining Cooperatives Many people are confused when it comes to distinguishing between the bargaining function and a bargaining cooperative. The reason is that bargaining cooperatives, while obviously carrying on the formalized bargaining function for at least some products, in practice often perform other marketing functions. They may also handle products and function as operating cooperatives. For example, many dairy cooperatives will bargain for the price of grade A milk for fluid use, but will process surplus quantities into butter, milk powder, cheese, ice cream, or other dairy products. Similarly, fruit and vegetable producers may bargain with processors for certain grades and amounts of products, and then divert or process lower grades or surplus volume into various types of by-products.

Some students of bargaining believe that bringing producers together helps to integrate the marketing system. Others maintain that bargaining, even when successful, tends to fragment the marketing process. Their reason is that the performance of marketing functions is divided between producer and processor. This idea suggests that, if cooperatives are to be an effective force in helping the producer maintain control over operations, there will be a greater tendency in the future for them to combine bargaining with their other marketing functions. This trend would lead to a more completely integrated marketing operation over which producers would gain greater control.

The bargaining function, in contrast to the other functions, relates only to the completion of transactions with agreement as to price and terms of sale. The basic aspect of such transactions is that arrangements are made for title to change from the member to the purchaser and that prices are established. In itself, this is an important marketing function, and it is one that can be carried on in an office far removed from the producing area. It often functions most effectively when both parties to the bargaining transaction have ready access to financial resources, market information, and legal services. Since products need not be handled by the bargaining cooperative, it often has no need for the facilities commonly owned by an operating cooperative. With a perishable commodity like milk, however, ownership of processing facilities may strengthen a cooperative's bargaining position by providing alternative market outlets for its members' output.

Cooperative Bargaining Is Cooperative Marketing There is considerable misunderstanding as to the nature of bargaining cooperatives and whether they are actually engaged in marketing. In general practice, the term *bargaining association*, rather than *bargaining cooperative*, has had wide acceptance. This is no basis for a distinction, however, since *association* and *cooperative* are used interchangeably in cooperative terminology.

While there are those who question whether cooperative bargaining is cooperative marketing (see Chapter 2), serious students of cooperation will ask, "Is representing producers and negotiating contracts not marketing?" In their view, a bargaining association is a cooperative just as certainly as an operating association. Moreover, they will point out that as a result of negotiations, the members' products are sold, the title to these products changes, and produce moves on to processors or manufacturers for whatever use they wish to make of it. This is in contrast with the limited marketing functions performed by some operating cooperatives in which members even reserve the right to sell their products and thus determine the time and place of sale.

The benefits of a bargaining association's operations go to its members. The risks are assumed by them. They control its business affairs, and they provide such financing as is necessary. Members' products are marketed with the same degree of finality that would prevail if they had actually been handled by an operating cooperative.

That we are justified in classifying bargaining cooperatives as marketing associations is further substantiated by the decision handed down in the case of *Treasure Valley Potato Bargaining Association v. Ore-Ida Foods, Inc. and J. R. Simplot and Company.* In this case the court held that the bargaining function is, in effect, marketing which involves transferring title and moving goods from producers to consumers (for details, see Chapter 10).

WHY BARGAINING HAS BECOME IMPORTANT

The potential role of bargaining associations has received increased attention during recent years, largely because of appreciable changes in the marketing of farm products. The most important of these changes are the following:

Improvements in Technology and Market Structure

With the development of new technology, the market structure for farm production has undergone substantial change. Farming has become more specialized, requires increased managerial skill, and necessitates more dependable market outlets.

Avoidance of Traditional Markets

Processors and retailers, to assure themselves of available products, often bypass traditional terminal market sources in favor of direct buying and contracting. Some have partially or completely integrated their business operations. As markets have become decentralized, special arrangements, discounts and premiums, and wide variations in grades have come to be commonplace. Consequently, the traditional pricing structure for farm products has broken down in some instances or, at best, often functions very badly.

Greater Specialization in Market Functions

Processors and retailers are more specialized in the operations they perform. Their demands are concentrated on specific grades and qualities of products, on a definite volume, and on designated delivery schedules. To have dependable sources of supply, many processors contract in advance for as far ahead as a year. The results are more complex market relationships.

Disadvantages to Individual Farmers

As markets become more integrated and specialized, individual farmers find themselves at a disadvantage by being faced with fewer and larger market outlets for their products. Competition from producers in other regions is often more intense. Farmers are painfully aware of a weakened market position because, as individuals, they lack what is commonly described as market power or "muscle in the marketplace." Consequently, they seek some form of countervailing power. To achieve this end, some individual farmers have turned to bargaining associations, believing that they offer hope of achieving some degree of balance as far as market strength is concerned. In this way they seek to meet power with power.

Increased Importance of Institutional Changes and Consumer Preferences

Sanitation regulations and environmental problems are becoming more important. Nutritional research is influencing eating habits. The living habits of large segments of the population are changing.

A Plague of Surpluses (until the 1970s)

For the past century, with the exception of World Wars I and II and the years immediately following, American agriculture has been weighted down by depressing, chronic agricultural surpluses. Under these conditions farmers have found themselves in intense competition with one another. This situation no doubt has contributed substantially to their interest in achieving greater bargaining power. Such was the economic environment in which bargaining cooperatives developed and operated following World War II.

In especially critical situations, the federal government instituted programs, some designed to limit or control production. Examples include marketing orders and agreements. In Canada and many other countries, marketing boards came into existence. The European Common Market (1959) developed far-reaching price support measures for farm products.

In the early 1970s, however, this situation changed. Demand increased for the time being and deficits rather than surpluses became commonplace. This condition raises unique and distinctly different questions for bargaining associations to deal with. Will this development strengthen their hand, or will members, satisfied with temporary gains from being in a relatively favorable economic position, continue a fragmented approach and fail to take full advantage of a changed situation to strengthen their economic position in the marketplace? It can be argued that a shift from a surplus to a deficit situation would provide incentives for farmers to further strengthen their bargaining position. It remains to be seen, however, whether or not farmers will fully appreciate the opportunities they now have to do so.

THE EXTENT OF BARGAINING

The bargaining transaction is here examined as it relates to agricultural products. It has special application to those products that lend themselves to further manufacturing and processing. As of 1971, there were some 250 cooperative associations that primarily engaged in bargaining for such products as milk, fruits and vegetables, and, to a limited extent, poultry products and livestock. In that year they accounted for a net volume of business of nearly $4 billion, or about 20 percent of the net business volume reported by farmers' marketing, purchasing, and related service cooperatives.

In addition, there are a few small, informally organized, farm-supply buying groups that engage in bargaining primarily for feed. In these associations, a limited number of producers, often no more than ten to twenty, come together to determine specifications for the feed they desire, and then bargain with feed manufacturers for these products. Most of these associations are in California. Also, some in Illinois bargain for feed ingredients, chemicals, and other supplies.

There are two principal types of bargaining cooperatives—commodity and multicommodity associations. Most commodity associations bargain for only one product or at most one class of products, such as fruits. Except for those bargaining for milk and sugar beets, the others are largely in the Western states and Florida.

A recent study, *Bargaining Cooperatives: Selected Agri-Industries*, by Gilbert W. Biggs and J. Kenneth Samuels,[2] reports on bargaining by fruit and vegetable cooperatives in the United States. When this study is supplemented with data for dairy bargaining cooperatives, we have a reasonably good indication of the nature of the business of all bargaining cooperatives. Types of bargaining transactions, the number of bargaining cooperatives for which information was available, and their volume of business for 1971 are shown in Table 18-1.

Peaches accounted for approximately one-third of the dollar volume reported by fruit bargaining cooperatives. Other products, in the order of importance, were grapes, citrus fruits, pears, and plums. Potatoes composed approximately 85 percent of the bargaining volume reported by vegetable bargaining cooperatives. Asparagus, peas, sweet corn, and beans made up the other 15 percent.

Sugar beet bargaining is somewhat unusual in that it has been subject to the provisions of federal sugar legislation. This legislation authorized the Secretary of Agriculture to establish quotas for sugar-producing areas in the United States, and to set acreage limitations for individual growers. It was discontinued on December 31, 1974. Price bargaining is carried on through participation plans (see p. 353). Associations also bargain for such services as furnishing seed, arranging sampling procedures, providing weighing and testing practices, harvesting services, and developing methods of payment.

A recent development has been the tendency for some sugar-processing firms to sell their facilities to the bargaining associations. Since 1972, two associations have become operating cooperatives by purchasing sugar-processing facilities from firms with which they formerly bargained.

Multicommodity Bargaining

Two groups are characterized as multicommodity bargaining associations. They are the American Agricultural Marketing Association (AAMA), an affiliate of the American

[2] *FCS Information* 90, Farmer Cooperative Service, U.S. Department of Agriculture, 1973.

Table 18-1   Types of Bargaining Transactions, Number of Bargaining Cooperatives, and Volume of Bargaining Business, 1971

Type of bargaining transaction	Bargaining cooperatives		
	Associations	Members	Net volume of business (in millions)
Commodity:			
Fruits	11	6,599	$ 91
Vegetables	8	4,870	105
Sugar beets	5	28,515	416
Dairy products	141	234,000	3,200*
Total	155	273,984	$3,812
Multicommodity (American Agricultural Marketing Association):	29		
Fruits	†	—	24
Vegetables	†	—	26
Livestock	†	—	27
Poultry	†	—	32
Grain and soybeans	†	‡	5
Total	29	—	$ 114
National Farmers Organization§	1	§	§
	185	—	$3,926

*It is estimated that about 60 percent of the milk that cooperatives handle is sold as raw whole milk, and that substantially all of it is sold through bargaining cooperatives.

†Not reported separately.

‡AAMA reported forty-five state affiliates, of which twenty-nine provided information. No information is available on the number of their producer-members.

§NFO does not report information as to membership or volume of business.

Farm Bureau Federation, and the National Farmers Organization (NFO). AAMA, organized in 1960, reported forty-five state affiliates in 1971. The National Farmers Organization operates largely on a state basis. It reported some 50 area offices and over 400 dispatch points in 1971.

The state affiliates of AAMA differ widely in the nature and extent of their operations. Some are largely paper associations, while others actively engage in bargaining for several types of products, such as fruits and vegetables, poultry, and livestock.

Data provided by twenty-one of the state affiliates of AAMA show that about 30 percent of their bargaining volume was in poultry, chiefly broilers, and that between 20 and 25 percent was reported for each of such classes of farm products as livestock, vegetables, and fruit. AAMA emphasizes voluntary membership-control practices. No attempt is made to exercise area or industry supply management. The goal is to sign up a sufficient number of members to achieve recognition by processors and other buyers.

The National Farmers Organization was organized in 1955 for the purpose of collective bargaining. According to its representatives, it seeks prices that yield "cost of production plus a reasonable profit." NFO uses an industrywide approach to bargaining that covers the major farm commodities—livestock and meat, milk, grain, and special commodities. To demonstrate its economic power, from time to time it has called for withholding members' products from markets (holding actions). It bargains with processors and other users through its market-area offices. NFO emphasizes flexibility in operations geared to meeting the specific needs of given market situations.

OPERATING PRACTICES
Contract Relationships

Fruits and Vegetables Fruit and vegetable bargaining cooperatives usually have contracts with their members and also, quite generally, with processors. As a rule, they participate in the drafting of contracts between their members and processors. The contractual relations with members generally are referred to as agreements and cover such points as the obligations of members to deliver their products, the amount and quality of the product that will be delivered, and other items relating to control and operating practices. The obligations of bargaining associations to members are also set forth. These may cover production services such as the employment of field staff, record keeping, the purchase of supplies, arrangements for providing labor, and financial assistance. The most important marketing services provided by bargaining associations are collection and dissemination of market information, monitoring of processing operations, trade promotion, grading, and transporting. The bargaining association also frequently serves as legislative representative for its growers.

The contractual relations with processors cover such items as price negotiations, grades and quality of products to be delivered, arrangements for product delivery, and other services that may be provided by cooperatives and processors. They also cover penalties should the parties involved fail to comply with contract provisions. Most associations participate in contract negotiations between members and processors. When contracts provide for members to retain title to products until they are delivered to the bargaining cooperative, some managers believe the cooperative is not in as strong a market position as if it took title to the products before delivery, arranged for delivery to the contracting party, and then made final settlement with its members.

Milk Contract arrangements are different for milk bargaining cooperatives. These cooperatives primarily market grade A milk. They generally have contracts with members that designate the association as marketing agent. Agreements with handlers (processors) generally are not in writing. Changes in milk marketing conditions usually lead to price discussions with each handler served. Where the discussions do not lead to agreements with handlers on a uniform price, cooperatives often find it necessary to announce a price that all handlers must pay.

During recent years, prices have been negotiated largely by big regional bargaining federations. Also, member bargaining cooperatives have made increased efforts to develop contracts with processors covering prices to be paid and specific terms of sale, especially obligations to supply milk, make transportation arrangements, and provide services.

Price Negotiations

Fruits and Vegetables Fruit and vegetable bargaining associations have developed two methods of price negotiation. One calls for the establishment of a firm price at the time of executing the contract. The other provides for establishing "reasonable prices" at a later date. This practice requires, in effect, further negotiations as the product moves to market. When difficulties arise in reaching agreement, provisions generally are made for arbitration by third parties.

Sugar Beets Negotiating prices through participation contracts is commonly used by sugar beet bargaining associations. When these plans are used, the producer's net returns are determined by the sugar content of the beets produced, the cost of production, and the cost of processing. While contract provisions vary, Biggs and Samuels report one plan that provides that "(1) Growers stand all costs of producing and delivering sugarbeets to the processor, (2) the processor stands all processing costs, (3) warehousing costs are shared fifty-fifty by the growers and processor, and (4) net margins are shared 51 percent by growers and 49 percent by the processor."[3] Participation plans also are used in the Florida citrus industry.

Milk Price negotiations are substantially different for grade A milk. Most grade A milk is marketed under federal and state marketing-order regulations that provide for the establishment of minimum prices. The price of milk used in producing manufactured dairy products has also been supported under provisions of the Agricultural Marketing Act.

Besides bargaining for desired federal milk marketing-order prices and price support levels, dairy cooperatives bargain with handlers for prices higher than federal marketing-order prices that include costs to the cooperative for providing certain producer-related services formerly performed by handlers. These services include supply management and procurement, disposition of surplus grade A milk, field service, quality maintenance assistance, milk assembly arrangements, and producer payment calculations.

During recent years, most bargaining with handlers has been for premiums above minimum federal marketing-order prices. The negotiating process in milk bargaining is also quite different from that used by associations bargaining for fruit and vegetable prices for members. For example, there is little "across-the-table" bargaining. Rather, the negotiations committee decides on an asking price and then notifies the processing firms what the price will be for a designated period. The success of bargaining cooperatives in negotiating for milk prices is attributed to the special characteristics of the product, the ability to achieve satisfactory price alignment for most competing markets, and the price-supporting measures that the federal marketing orders provide for grade A milk.

---

[3]Gilbert W. Biggs and J. Kenneth Samuels, *Bargaining Cooperatives, Selected Agri-Industries*, FCS Information 90, op. cit., p. 60.

Negotiation Representatives

Bargaining cooperatives are represented in various ways in negotiating with other parties. Negotiating may be done by the managers and/or their staffs, by committees usually consisting of some staff members and selected producers, and by the boards of directors. The forty-two fruit and vegetable bargaining associations providing information on this subject in 1971 reported that in twenty instances, bargaining was done by committees, that in sixteen instances, the manager or the staff did the bargaining, and that in six instances it was done by boards of directors. Most dairy bargaining associations are represented by the management staff, which often includes research economists and consultants. A high degree of sophistication, a knowledge of the wide range of economic forces bearing on the industry, and the ability to interpret the impact of social and political developments are all required for bargaining cooperatives to negotiate effectively. Boards of directors are not always able to meet these and other criteria for successful bargaining.

For negotiations to develop effective bargaining strategies, it is important that they recognize these factors:

- Importance of volume control, taking into account such factors as the ability to maintain long-range volume control, the need for marketing agreements with members, possible restrictions on market entry, the possibility of product substitution, elasticity of supply, and control of alternative outlets
- Need to achieve recognition as the bargaining agent
- Necessity to develop a high degree of member discipline
- Importance of market knowledge, giving attention to basic characteristics of the industry, relative bargaining strengths of the parties concerned, and the range of price concessions and trade terms that each party can and will accept
- Status of the social and political climate in which bargaining is taking place
- Role of government in effective bargaining, including possible coordination with market orders and reasonable supportive legislative action

Ownership of the Product

The party that retains title to the product bargained for may give a clue as to the comparative strength of the participants involved. Bargaining cooperatives that take title to products may not only be better able to carry out obligations to the party with whom they deal, but also, should necessity arise, they may be in a stronger position to negotiate with processors and to speak for producers. Biggs and Samuels reported that six out of eleven fruit and vegetable associations took title to the products; two out of the eight vegetable associations took title; and none of the sugar beet associations followed this practice. Of fifty-three fruit and vegetable associations reporting, twelve took title to members' products and forty-one did not. As a rule, dairy bargaining cooperatives do not take title to milk. Milk is delivered on a regular basis, and the important consideration seems to be the willingness of the patron to perform according to contract provisions rather than to the type of contract.

Methods of Payment

Methods of payment have an important bearing on the status of the bargaining association and on the strength of the ties it is able to develop with members. Obviously, the cooperative that makes returns to its members is in a stronger position than the one that leaves payment to the firm bargained with. Biggs and Samuels found that in twenty-four instances the processor or buyer paid the association, and in thirty-six instances payments were made directly to growers. In some cases, both types of arrangements were used. Most of the dairy bargaining associations received payments from processors and assumed responsibility for paying their members.

PROBLEM AREAS

A number of factors have a bearing on the effectiveness with which bargaining associations are able to operate. They are here identified.

Gaining Recognition

A bargaining association can be effective only if it gains recognition by the firm or firms with which it hopes to bargain. It can best do this when it can demonstrate a substantial amount of market power, can identify the parties for whom it speaks, and can indicate in what way it speaks for them. In the rough and tumble business world, these capabilities require demonstration that the bargaining association has a substantial degree of control over a large portion of the crop in the area in which it operates. Only in this way is it likely to convince others that it is the agency to be reckoned with in the marketplace.

Both parties to a bargaining transaction should be aware that, in addition to the actual bargainers, there are also likely to be potential bargainers—both sellers and buyers. This suggests that for bargaining producers, the possibility exists that other producers already in production or capable of entering into production on short notice may enter the market—especially if profits look inviting. The opportunity for gain could even encourage processors to integrate operations and enter into production themselves. Likewise, if processing promises to be profitable, other firms might look with favor on moving into the territory. Producers, too, might be tempted, for example, to operate their own processing plants.

Cooperative bargainers, therefore, are most effective when they can avoid entering into negotiations in a spirit of confrontation. Identification of mutual interests can be an even more important factor in helping an association gain recognition as a bargaining agent. For example, a bargaining cooperative may be in a strategic position to work effectively with growers to assure the production of the quality and quantity of a product that buyers desire, to provide transportation, and to support favorable legislation—all matters of interest to the bargaining association and firms bargaining with it. These services may become more important if agricultural deficits become common.

Achieving Member Discipline

If cooperatives are to bargain successfully, it is important that their members be disciplined producers. For example, they must produce, in the amounts specified, the kind and quality of products processors require. They also must follow approved agricultural practices and be prepared to deliver their produce at the time and in the manner agreed upon.

To achieve such discipline among their members, bargaining cooperatives need to carry on extensive educational programs. Members will need specific information as to their responsibilities to their cooperative. Only when they recognize their obligations can their cooperative bargain with processors from a position of strength and with assurance that members will honor their commitments.

Members of bargaining cooperatives will also need to understand, among other things, the basic changes that are occurring both in agricultural production and in the marketplace, in order to support their association intelligently. Their bargaining cooperative must be as well informed as the firms with whom it is negotiating if it is to make sound policy decisions relating to the bargaining process. Consequently, it must have accurate market information and the ability to know how to use this information in price negotiations.

It should be emphasized, too, that achieving member discipline is often the result of demonstrated performance on the part of the bargaining association. Once a cooperative has proven to members that it has the market power to bargain effectively, it has come a long way in building member confidence. When the bargaining cooperative has reached this stage of development, it is usually in a position to represent, and to speak for, producers.

Understanding the Extent of Potential Gains

Much misunderstanding exists as to the potential gains that bargaining cooperatives can achieve. A look at the net profit margins of firms with which bargaining cooperatives deal can be discouraging. These net margins often are quite limited. The National Commission on Food Marketing reported, for example, that fruit and vegetable processors averaged a net margin of 2.4 percent for the five-year period from 1960 through 1964. This raises the question: To what extent can a bargaining association hope to share in the net profit margins of processors? Obviously, there are limits as to how far bargaining associations can go. What are the alternatives for the processors? Do they have other sources of supply, or are there other products that they might start to process to advantage? The processors have to decide whether or not they can bargain on a basis that will enable them to stay in business. It should also be recognized that the producer is faced with identical questions.

A look at existing net margins, however, does not tell the complete story as far as potential gains are concerned. To what extent, for example, might bargainers introduce institutional changes that would have a bearing on operations of both producers and processors and other buyers? It may be possible to bring about changes in marketing practices that will contribute to increased efficiency. Market stability to a degree previously unknown in the industry might result. Better market performance, too, may be achieved by the elimination of cutthroat pricing and high procurement costs.

The consumption patterns for agricultural products need to be taken into account in evaluating prospects for effective bargaining. It is generally recognized that the demand for some food products is relatively inelastic. When this situation prevails, some price increases can be passed on to consumers unless other products can be readily substituted. This possibility has special applications to dairy bargaining cooperatives, since the demand for grade A fluid milk is more inelastic than the demand for manufactured milk.

The human stomach is known to be just so large. While dietary shifts resulting from growing knowledge about health and from increased or decreased income do occur, the overall demand for farm products is very likely to reflect increases in population and expanded foreign trade. Other important considerations are the alternative sources of various products, particularly fruits and vegetables, that may be available to processors and other buyers.

Identifying Areas of Mutual Interest

Experience has demonstrated that mutuality of interest on the part of producers and processors may be the major factor in determining the possibilities of success of a bargaining cooperative. An effective bargaining association, for example, can do much to assure processors of a reliable source of supply—uniform produce of an agreed-upon quality at a specified time—even under such unusual conditions as inclement weather, increased competition, and inducements to shift production patterns. Likewise, producers reduce their price risks, have an assured market, and may well be able to develop new market outlets for their products and expand existing ones. Under such circumstances, bargaining associations can contribute to security of expectations, both for members and for processors and other buyers. Moreover, bargaining can increase market efficiency, particularly if emphasis is placed on improved production and procurement practices, and on the development and exchange of market information.

When bargaining is approached with an open mind, bargaining associations and processors may both find a mutuality of interest in the introduction of institutional and structural changes. This step has special application to grades and quality of products. In addition, an area of considerable importance to both producers and processors is that of negotiating with government agencies on matters of mutual interest to both groups. If both processors and producers can demonstrate a united stand, they are likely to increase their effectiveness greatly in getting government support for their industry recommendations.

Production Control

Agricultural producers often have been somewhat naive in their views on whether or not production should be controlled. Over the years, many agricultural leaders have expressed reservations, often more emotional than logical, on this issue. While conditions admittedly vary, industry in general has had no scruples about restricting production to anticipated demand. The manufacturers of automobiles or the builders of furniture have not hesitated to control output when economic conditions warranted. In most instances, their emphasis is on an attempt to produce what the market will take or can be persuaded to take at prescribed price levels.

When bargaining cooperatives are successful in their basic objective of increasing members' net income, they are confronted with the prospect of increased production that might result in lower prices. In the long run, the result could well be self-defeating as far as members are concerned. This dilemma brings into sharp focus the critical need for introducing some method of avoiding surpluses at negotiated prices, in order to keep such surpluses from building up and thus reducing prices. Production-control provisions are often supplemented with rules or criteria for sharing an established market among existing producers.

Should production control seem necessary, producers are confronted with the question of deciding whether such controls should be voluntary or compulsory. Quite obviously, producers would prefer voluntary controls to the heavy hand of some government agency that would tell them just what they could and could not produce and how they should operate. The extent to which voluntary controls are likely to be successful, however, will depend first of all on the nature of the product. If it is a highly specialized item with a limited production area, such as certain specialized fruits or vegetables, the possibilities of achieving voluntary control are much greater than if the product could be produced regionally or nationally.

Dairy cooperatives are in a unique bargaining position because of their ability to control the flow of products going to various markets. Having merged a number of local cooperatives into large multimarket organizations, they are in a strategic position to direct the flow of milk to these markets and align prices among producing areas.

The success of any voluntary scheme depends also on the willingness of growers to commit themselves permanently to controls. Before doing so, it is important that growers understand the many economic implications having a bearing on the production of their product or products, and that they be willing to submit to the discipline required. In some instances, producers have agreed to supplement their bargaining activities with government market orders and agreements, thus bringing in government support to influence production patterns.

It may well be that, in the short run, some voluntary control methods can be successful. However, if the long-run view is taken, there seems to be little indication that producers as yet are willing to make the firm, voluntary commitments to achieve the necessary degree of production control necessary to bargain effectively.

On the matter of production controls for basic farm products, Prof. George E. Brandow of Pennsylvania State University, in his article "Will Bargaining Really Work,"[4] states: "Lacking ability to control production and with no power over foreign trade, voluntary associations operating without government aid cannot have substantial and lasting effects on the prices of such crops as feed grains, wheat, and cotton. Some sort of government authority to enforce market-wide compliance by all producers and buyers seems essential to substantial farm bargaining power over prices." The success achieved by dairy bargaining cooperatives supports this observation.

We have referred to the changing situation confronting agriculture as it shifts from a surplus to a deficit situation. The implications to bargaining associations are far-reaching. The extent that deficit production might occur, agriculture will not be a

[4]In *Bargaining Power for Farmers,* The Iowa State University Press, Ames, 1968, p. 132.

source of market surpluses. Successful bargaining no longer will depend on production-control techniques for success. This fact emphasizes the need of bargaining associations for the best market information possible when they evaluate short- and long-time impacts of changes in their industry, and when they seek to develop effective bargaining strategies to deal with them.

Relationship with Operating Cooperatives

There are possibilities for built-in conflicts of interest between operating cooperatives and bargaining cooperatives. A commodity bargaining association, for example, may look upon a fruit- or vegetable-processing cooperative in much the same way that it views any other processor. The result could be an attempt to bargain with such a cooperative. Since the operating cooperative already is committed to returning to patrons all proceeds above operating costs, obviously confrontation with such a bargaining group could be a very disruptive experience. It is reported, in one instance, that a bargaining association "infiltrated" the board of directors of an operating cooperative in an effort to achieve its price objectives.

Likewise, the relations of the multicommodity bargaining associations with operating cooperatives often have been far from cordial. Their attitudes have varied all the way from soliciting the support of some cooperative processing organizations to actively competing with others. Conflicts and antagonisms have perhaps been most pronounced in the livestock and broiler fields.

Sometimes multicommodity bargaining associations have ignored operating cooperatives and proceeded to function in such a way as to superimpose their activities upon the operating territories of established cooperatives. This move has led to direct conflict and antagonism—especially with the dairy cooperatives—as multicommodity associations have, in effect, implied that these organizations have failed to achieve their basic objectives.

The Role of Government

Opinion differs considerably on what the actual and potential role of government should be in the bargaining process. We have suggested previously that, in some areas, federal and state marketing orders and agreements have been developed to assist in the diversion or disposal of surplus production. In some instances, these efforts have been supplemented with strong bargaining associations, which in effect have served as facilitating agencies for carrying out provisions of federal and state marketing regulations.

In the dairy industry, for example, state and federal marketing orders have also been developed at the instigation of bargaining cooperatives. These orders complement the programs of these associations. They establish a classified system of pricing milk based on use and on the minimum prices that handlers must pay for grade A milk. Milk used in fluid-milk products is included in the high-priced class. Surplus grade A milk not needed for the fluid-milk market is priced at levels paid by manufacturing-milk outlets. Thus, the price-depressing effect of seasonal surplus grade A milk is largely isolated from the high-priced class. Pooling arrangements are then used so that all producers receive a uniform, blended price without regard to the actual utilization of their milk.

Marketing orders, both federal and state, have also been developed for the fruit and vegetable industry. These orders, except when growers have marketing quotas, do not regulate the price or production. They do, however, cover such things as grade, quality, size, maturity, and surplus disposal. California, going farther than other states in the use of marketing orders, reports that most of its major fruits and vegetables were covered by the some twenty orders that were in effect in 1973.

Legal Status

Substantially all bargaining cooperatives are organized under state cooperative laws and are subject to the same restraints and freedoms as other cooperatives. As such, they may operate under the general provisions of the Capper-Volstead Act.

Producers have exerted considerable effort to achieve legislation strengthening their bargaining hand. To date, the basic federal legislation enacted has been the Agricultural Fair Practices Act of 1967. Its essential provisions state that it is unlawful:

To coerce any agricultural producer in the exercise of the right to join an association of producers

To coerce any producer in the exercise of the right to refrain from joining such an association

To refuse to deal with any producer because he or she has exercised the right to join such an association

To discriminate against any producer with respect to price, quantity, quality, or other terms of purchase because of that producer's membership in such an association or contract with it

To coerce or intimidate any producer to enter into, maintain, breach, cancel, or terminate a membership agreement or marketing contract with an association of producers or a contract with a handler

To pay or lend money, give anything of value, or offer any other inducement or reward to a producer for refusing to or ceasing to belong to an association of producers

To conspire, combine, agree, or arrange with any other person to do, or to aid or abet the doing of, any of these acts

While this legislation has been described as a short and slow step on the road toward bargaining strength, it has helped to make processors conscious of legal restraints and discriminatory practices.

The act has the major weakness of not enabling bargaining associations to correct the inequalities in market power that exist between them and processors. Moreover, at times, bargaining associations have registered complaints against operating cooperatives. Some cooperative leaders also believe that the act tends to prevent desirable changes in the market structure of cooperatives. Dairy cooperatives, for example, are undergoing changes in structure and some complaints have been lodged against them.

Of twenty-one complaints investigated under this act, four had been taken to court as of January 1, 1975. The legislation would be strengthened if it contained specific provisions covering: (1) the rights of producers to belong to bargaining associations, with penalties for interference with these rights; (2) requirements for recognizing these associations; (3) identification of unfair practices as they apply to producers, processors, and other buyers; and (4) bargaining in good faith by both producers and processors.

Some producers, however, have long believed that stronger legislation is necessary. The National Farmers Union desires more active governmental support of bargaining associations and the participation of the government in establishing rules with regard to bargaining practices. The American Farm Bureau Federation, in contrast, emphasizes the need for recognition of the right of producers to bargain with processors.

The extent of governmental support for bargaining legislation varies from administration to administration. For example, in 1974 a Department of Agriculture representative stated: "I believe farm bargaining should remain outside the realm of government as much as possible. . . . Much of the tampering with our free enterprise system has been counterproductive." This statement of course is not realistic as far as dairy bargaining cooperatives are concerned.

Some leaders of bargaining cooperatives have held that what is needed is legislation with provisions similar to those of the Wagner Act. Such legislation would provide for:

- Requiring recognition of the bargaining association by processors or buyers whenever it is determined that a majority of the growers are members of the association
- Requiring both producers and processors or other buyers to bargain in good faith
- Prohibiting discrimination against growers by processors or buyers, and against processors and buyers by growers

SUMMARY

Cooperative bargaining associations can be an effective instrument in strengthening the economic position of producers. It should be recognized, however, that the mere formation of a bargaining association does not automatically give members market power. Nor can bargaining associations be expected to achieve substantial accomplishments for nationally produced products (milk, because of special legislation, is an exception) or for products that move in large quantities into export markets. Where members have attained increased market power, they report such benefits as higher prices, market solidarity and security, increased market information and stability, supervised grading and inspection, standardized contracts, and legislative assistance. There also may be benefits to processors, including an assured volume, relief from the job of procuring tonnage, a reliable organization to represent growers, more stable prices, lower procurement costs, and improved communications with growers.

The extent of accomplishments depends on a number of factors, the most important of which are gaining recognition as a bargaining agent, effective member discipline, and skillful negotiations. These conditions involve the members' understanding of basic changes occurring in agriculture and in the market structure for farm products. To be effective, bargaining associations must have at least as much market information as the firm with which they desire to bargain, and they must know how to use this information in negotiating bargaining contracts. Effective bargaining also requires a knowledge of the extent of potential gains that can be achieved, identification of areas of mutual interest, the place of product and production-control techniques, and an understanding of the ways in which government agencies can be used to further the bargaining efforts of producers.

To invigorate bargaining efforts, officials of these associations view the following as especially important: more effective bargaining legislation; better producer-education programs; adequately financed associations; strengthened marketing contracts; and an effective means of preventing overproduction.

QUESTIONS

1. What do you understand the term *bargaining* to mean? For what commodities is it especially important?
2. What types of transactions may be included in the term *bargaining?*
3. Is there a basis for distinguishing between bargaining as a marketing function or technique and bargaining as a special type of cooperative activity?
4. How would you distinguish between a bargaining cooperative and an operating cooperative?
5. Why is bargaining especially important to agricultural producers?
6. What effect would it have on the position of bargaining cooperatives if, as a nation, we experienced a change from a position of surplus production to a position of deficit production?
7. What are the principal operating practices that should be considered in bargaining transactions?
8. What factors determine the ability of a cooperative to gain recognition as a bargaining agent for members?
9. Why is achieving member discipline important if bargaining is to be effective?
10. Why is production control considered an essential for effective bargaining? Should it be voluntary or compulsory?
11. Is it possible for parties to the bargaining transaction to develop areas of mutual interest? If so, what are they?
12. What should be the role of government in helping members achieve effective bargaining?

REFERENCES

Biggs, Gilbert W., and J. Kenneth Samuels: *Bargaining Cooperatives, Selected Agri-Industries,* FCS Information 90, Farmer Cooperative Service, U.S. Department of Agriculture, Washington, 1973, p. 23.

Farmer Cooperative Service: *Cooperative Bargaining: Selections from the Proceedings of the National Conferences of Agricultural Bargaining Cooperatives,* FCS Service Report 113, U.S. Department of Agriculture, Washington, 1970, p. 154. FCS also has published yearly proceedings of these conferences.

Ingalsbe, Gene: "Bargaining: How Are We Doing?" *News for Farmer Cooperatives,* Farmer Cooperative Service, U.S. Department of Agriculture, Washington, March 1973.

Knutson, Ronald D.: *Cooperative Bargaining Developments in the Dairy Industry, 1960–70, with Emphasis on the Central States,* FCS Research Report 19, Farmer Cooperative Service, U.S. Department of Agriculture, Washington, 1971, p. 36.

Ladd, George W.: *Agricultural Bargaining Power,* The Iowa State University Press, Ames, 1964, p. 163.

McMillan, Wendell M.: *Cooperative Bargaining by Farmers: A Selected Bibliography,* General Report 123, Farmer Cooperative Service, U.S. Department of Agriculture, Washington, 1964, p. 18.

National Farm Institute: *Bargaining Power for Farmers* (a series of seventeen articles), The Iowa State University Press, Ames, 1968, p. 132.

Roy, Ewell Paul: *Collective Bargaining in Agriculture,* Interstate, Danville, Ill., 1970, p. 282.

Torgerson, Randall E.: *Farm Bargaining,* Landbruksforlaget, Oslo, Norway, 1971, p. 146.

Volkin, David: *Legal Implications in Coordinating Activities of Bargaining Associations,* FCS Information 63, Farmer Cooperative Service, U.S. Department of Agriculture, Washington, 1969, p. 13.

Chapter 19

Pooling

Pooling is a technique that has special application to cooperatives. In actual practice, it facilitates operation at cost. Complete pooling encompasses the products handled and the averaging of the expenses incurred and the proceeds distributed. Most generally, pooling involves marketing cooperatives and results in the commingling of products.[1] Thus, the identification of the products of individual members usually is not maintained.

In some instances, however, product identity may be maintained if buyers desire products from certain areas or producers. Some cooperatives do not grade products but put them in one pool and pay all members the average price received. This is the practice followed by most dairy cooperatives, although these associations maintain established quality standards before milk is pooled. Other cooperatives may grade the products they receive, place all grades in one pool, but pay members on the basis of established grade differentials.

While pooling in the United States most generally is associated with the marketing of milk and fruits and vegetables, it also has come into recent use by cooperatives marketing other types of products. For example: rice, by American Rice Growers Cooperative Association, Lake Charles, Louisiana; and Riceland Foods, Inc.,

---

[1]Members of farm supply cooperatives may pool orders for fertilizers and some kinds of seeds, and a few informal buying groups even pool orders for feed and bargain with firms for its manufacture.

Stuttgart, Arkansas; cotton, by the American Cotton Growers, Lubbock, Texas; and grain by Far-Mar-Co, Inc., Hutchinson, Kansas.

EARLY POOLING EFFORTS

In one form or another, pooling has been practiced by cooperatives for close to one hundred years. Knapp, in *The Rise of American Cooperative Enterprise, 1620–1920*,[2] identified the pooling of fruit by the Pachappa Orange Growers Association of California as early as the 1880s. In *The Hard Winter Wheat Pools*,[3] he traced the organization and operation of wheat pooling efforts by state and regional grain-marketing cooperatives in the United States in the 1920s. Some people refer to Aaron Sapiro as the "Father of the Grain Pooling Movement." In any event, he had significant influence in its development. In the mid-twenties, too, it was common to speak of cooperative tobacco pools and cotton pools. Cooperatives in Canada and Australia also used the pooling techniques for the marketing of their members' wheat.

The 1920s were a period of trial and error among pooling cooperatives in the United States. Many kinds of pooling practices were tried out experimentally. Most of the early pooling efforts were discontinued after a few years. They were abandoned not because of any inherent shortcoming in the pooling process, but rather, that pooling was a type of operation whose time had not yet come. In many instances, members were unwilling to make the commitments necessary to achieve success. Often, bickering and internal dissension weakened the efforts of well-intentioned but ill-informed leaders. Frequently, managers were poor merchandizers and often lacked the necessary administrative ability to operate a large-scale marketing association of any type. On many occasions, the need for marketing agreements with members was not fully appreciated by the cooperatives. Also, most cooperatives failed to recognize the need for the kind of education program necessary to build their members' support and understanding of their responsibilities.

THE NATURE OF POOLING

Cooperatives quite generally pool their expenses, particularly such overhead items as taxes, utilities, insurance, and administrative costs. Various direct expenses, such as storage, transportation, and financing, usually are charged to the individual pools to which they specifically relate rather than to all operations. Under all circumstances, pooling, to be effective, is dependent upon a realistic allocation of expenses to the various pools established for the different grades of products handled or services performed.

Cooperatives often advance a substantial percentage of the estimated value of the product at the time it is received from members. Some make additional advances during the season. For example, the Arkansas Grain Corporation, in reporting on its 1961 soybean pooling operations, stated:

[2]Joseph G. Knapp, Interstate, Danville, Illinois, 1969.
[3]Knapp, The University of Chicago Press, 1933.

A "First Advance" of "$2.06 per bushel" was issued to each producer at the drier where delivery was completed. Additional advances at the rate of 10¢ per bushel each were issued during January, March, and June. The total amount advanced to date is $2.36 per bushel. A "Final Settlement" will be issued after the books have been closed on July 31 and the audit has been completed. The "Final Settlement" will be the actual "Net Proceeds" due on a quantity and quality basis less the amounts previously advanced.

A few cooperatives make no advances. When all the products of a pool are sold, the cooperative makes final settlement with each participating member on the basis of the volume and grade each has contributed.

Pooled receipts result in the cooperative's returning an average price for the same grades of products delivered by members for the respective pools maintained. In practice, some lots of products sell at higher prices than other lots, so that price risks are borne jointly by all participating members.

A modification of the pooling procedure is that of establishing a fixed differential for various classes or grades of products in a given pool before products are delivered or sold. For example, the cooperative may determine that fancy apples will sell at a premium of $1 a box over the U.S. No. 1 grade. This technique is often used to place a premium on quality production. It has the disadvantage, however, of necessitating very accurate price forecasting at the beginning of a growing season—a difficult thing to do. It also requires very accurate information about potential production of the various grades handled. Under these conditions, therefore, the final payments may not truly reflect the actual value of members' pooled products. As would be expected, pooling procedures vary with the products pooled, the objectives of members, and the operating practices of the cooperative doing the pooling.

For pooling to be successful, two things are necessary: (1) Producers must be willing to make longtime commitments as to quality production and to sell the products so produced through their cooperative; and (2) cooperative managers must have improved sales capability, resulting in increased market stability.

To achieve these two requirements, cooperatives engaged in pooling have generally found it necessary to use marketing agreements. Through their use, cooperatives can assure production of quality products and have reasonable expectations that such products will be delivered to them. This assurance gives the cooperative substantially greater bargaining power in the marketplace.

For example, the marketing agreement that Riceland Foods, Stuttgart, Arkansas, has with its members provides, among other things, that:

> The Grower appoints the Association his agent to sell, market, pool and deal with rice delivered by him to the Association in the manner and form provided herein; and Association accepts said appointment and agrees to act accordingly.
>
> The Association agrees to make an advance or advances to Grower on the rice delivered by Grower to the Association as soon as possible after the rice is delivered. . . .
>
> The rice delivered by Grower may be pooled, mixed and mingled either before or after milling with other rice of like class, variety, grade and quality delivered by other growers. There may be as many pools as there are different grades, classes and qualities of rice. Each pool shall be for a full season and all rice of the same variety, grade and quality

shall constitute one pool. . . . Notwithstanding the foregoing, the Board of Directors may establish such pools as are deemed advisable to conform with any Government program for rice; and may settle with growers on the basis of such pools. Whether Grower's rice is sold in the rough or milled and sold in the clean, it may be sold at any time in the sole discretion of the Association at the best price obtainable. Settlement for the rice shall be made at the end of the season and on the basis of the average price obtained for rice of like variety, grade, milling yield and quality in the same pool.

While pooling is not specifically mentioned in cooperative legislation, neither is it prohibited by statute. The general authorization to engage in marketing activities and to provide various marketing services gives implicit sanction to this method of operation. For an association to engage in pooling, however, it must specifically account for such operations through provisions in its bylaws or marketing contracts. Only such authorized pooling practices, and no others, may be undertaken by the cooperative.

THE POOLING OPERATION ILLUSTRATED

In general, a number of considerations must receive attention by any cooperative contemplating the pooling process. They are:

- The kinds of products and varieties or grades to be pooled
- The number of grades established
- The proposed length and number of pools
- The areas to be served

To bring into focus a number of basic problems associated with pooling, let us assume that next year a number of growers will be using Bountiful Ridge Producers Cooperative to market strawberries. Being a successful cooperative, it also handles orchard supplies and equipment. This program will involve setting up a supply department to handle such items as fertilizer, spray materials, box shook, and other related orchard supplies and equipment. Owing to its successful operations to date, the livestock and poultry marketing cooperative in the area has approached Bountiful Ridge Producers with a merger proposal. A committee is presently studying this possibility.

The pooling operations of the Bountiful Ridge Producers Cooperative (Table 19-1) show how a simple pooling operation works. This cooperative restricts its operations to marketing apples that it pools under three grades—Mountain Pride, Snow Drop, and processing apples. To simplify this illustration, let us examine operations as they relate to three farmers—Messrs. Bentsen and Buts and Ms. Freman.

Mountain Pride is the top grade of apples packed by the association. Standards are zealously guarded, and only apples of uniform size, color, quality, and free from blemish merit this grade, which has come to stand for a fancy, choice-quality apple. This policy has enabled Bountiful Ridge Producers to differentiate this grade effectively and to develop special outlets for it at premium prices for the Christmas trade. Snow Drop, in turn, includes all other apples that would still qualify as U.S. No. 1. These are sold in the highly competitive fresh fruit market. Processing grade apples, however, are sold to a local processing plant for the manufacture of apple butter, juice, and cider. While not reported separately, price variations for this grade reflects the proportion of apples that goes into each of these uses.

The apples delivered by members Bentsen, Buts, and Freman are graded as indicated. Bountiful Ridge Producers operates on the basis of an estimated 5 percent of gross returns to cover all operating costs. After these costs are deducted from gross returns, net returns are determined for each grade, as is also the average price per box. With this information, Bountiful Ridge Producers is in a position to determine the returns to each member (see Table 19-1). For example, for the Red Delicious crop, average prices per box for the Mountain Pride, Snow Drop, and processing grades were $6.65, $5.43, and $1.65, respectively. Net returns for Bentsen, Buts, and Freman, were, respectively, $298,360, $222,370, and $330,520.

We are now ready to consider some of the practical aspects of pooling as they relate to the operations of Bountiful Ridge Producers. The points discussed, however, have general application to all types of cooperatives that engage in pooling.

Should a Separate Pool Be Maintained for the Red Delicious and Golden Delicious Varieties?

The price differentials that prevail suggest the desirability of separate pools for these varieties. Year-to-year price changes for varieties may be even more pronounced. From all indications, the separate pool is the most equitable way of paying members, since production of certain varieties by members will differ widely from year to year. Moreover, it is the most equitable way for them to share such risks as may result from the production and marketing of individual varieties. As a general rule, a cooperative pooling apples or any other product will limit its pooling operations to grades and products that have recognized consumer acceptance.

Are the Grades Established Reasonable?

Bountiful Ridge Producers seems to have been able effectively to differentiate the quality of apples its members produce. Under such circumstances, it is justified in establishing the Mountain Pride brand and in carefully guarding its reputation. The price differentials for apples merit selling the remainder as U.S. No. 1 under the Snow Drop brand.

Obviously, fruit for processing sells at a substantially lower price. Judging from the wide variations in quality of fruit produced by different members, there is a sound basis for maintaining the pools set up by the cooperative to reflect these price differences.

The cooperative, however, is under no obligation to keep the established grades for an indefinite period of time. If new markets develop or established markets disappear, it should maintain sufficient flexibility to establish realistic pools that reflect a changed situation. The basic requirement is that the different grades should reflect actual differences in product quality, market preferences, and result in prices that consumers are willing to pay.

Table 19-1 Apple Pooling Operations of Bountiful Ridge Producers Cooperative

Item	Red Delicious			Golden Delicious		
	Mountain Pride	Snow Drop	Processing	Mountain Pride	Snow Drop	Processing
Boxes produced						
Bentson, Orville	10,000	15,000	15,000	8,000	10,000	7,000
Buts, Ezra	15,000	12,000	8,000	4,000	2,000	3,000
Freman, Mary	20,000	8,000	2,000	18,000	3,000	5,000
Total	45,000	35,000	25,000	30,000	15,000	15,000
Cooperative sales	45,000 @ $7.00	10,000 @ $6.00 10,000 @ $5.75 15,000 @ $5.50	15,000 @ $2.00 10,000 @ $1.35	20,000 @ $7.50 10,000 @ $7.00	5,000 @ $6.25 8,000 @ $6.50 2,000 @ $5.25	10,000 @ $1.75 5,000 @ $1.25
Gross returns	$315,000	$200,000	$43,500	$220,000	$93,750	$23,750
Operating costs (5 percent)	$15,750	$10,000	$2,175	$11,000	$4,687	$1,187
Net returns	$299,250	$190,000	$41,325	$209,000	$89,063	$22,563
Average price per box	$6.65	$5.43	$1.65	$6.97	$5.94	$1.50

	Bountiful Ridge Producers Cooperative	Bentsen	Buts	Freman
Receipts	$896,000	10,000 × $6.65 = $66,500 15,000 × $5.43 = 81,450 15,000 × $1.65 = 24,750 8,000 × $6.97 = 55,760 10,000 × $5.94 = 59,400 7,000 × $1.50 = 10,500 65,000 $298,360	15,000 × $6.65 = $99,750 12,000 × $5.43 = 65,160 8,000 × $1.65 = 13,200 4,000 × $6.97 = 27,880 2,000 × $5.94 = 11,880 3,000 × $1.50 = 4,500 44,000 $222,370	20,000 × $6.65 = $133,000 8,000 × $5.43 = 43,440 2,000 × $1.65 = 3,300 18,000 × $6.97 = 125,460 3,000 × $5.94 = 17,820 5,000 × $1.50 = 7,500 56,000 $330,520
Operating costs	$44,800			
Total	$851,200			

Duration and Number of Pools

Apples are a seasonally produced crop, and consequently, pools exist only for the marketing season. Bountiful Ridge Producers, however, will face some more complex pooling problems as expansion occurs. Strawberry pools, for example, are of very short duration, usually varying from one lot to a day or week, because of wide fluctuations in prices. Consequently, those producers who have the greatest production during the high-price periods would not be satisfied with a seasonal pool. Thus, such factors as perishability, seasonal price trends, and wishes of members also influence the length of the pooling period. Such nonperishable crops as rice and cotton, for example, may find themselves in pools that extend into the next crop season before final sales are made. The longer the pooling period, the greater is the tendency to make one or more financial advances to members.

In the case of Bountiful Ridge Producers, the committee exploring merger with the livestock association has quite different pooling problems to consider. To illustrate, should livestock pools be geared to each shipment of livesotck? Should orders for feeder livestock be pooled? And if the cooperative pools poultry, should special turkey pools be set up for the Thanksgiving and Christmas seasons?

Determination and Allocation of Costs

The proposed farm supply operation mentioned earlier introduces additional problems for Bountiful Ridge Producers. When a department is set up to conduct this business, it will require the development of an accounting system that accurately allocates overhead costs between marketing and farm supply operations. As far as operations are concerned, it may well be that the cooperative will also wish to pool orders for such products as seed, fertilizer, and feed. This pooling will enable the cooperative more accurately to determine what its yearly volume will be and thus to better adjust production, financial, and other operating requirements to meet member needs.

Bountiful Ridge Producers Cooperative also is confronted with a basic problem in deciding how costs should be allocated. It might, for example, make a flat charge per box or develop charges in proportion to the price received for the products marketed. While sound arguments can be developed for both approaches, some additional expense might perhaps be involved in selling its Mountain Pride brand. Consequently, there seems to be justification for allocating costs according to receipts. If costs are to reflect operations truly, it is essential to develop and maintain an adequate accounting system. From a practical standpoint, the question confronting the cooperative is: How far should we allocate direct costs to various grades as compared with an across-the-board allocation of these costs?

ADVANTAGES OF POOLING

Having examined the pooling operations of the Bountiful Ridge Producers, we are now in a position to look at some of the advantages of pooling operations.

Spreads Risks

Pooling enables both the member and the cooperative to spread risks. These risks may include such items as problems in producing the quantity and quality of products the market desires, wide fluctuations in price, and uncertain market outlets. The cooperative can largely avoid risks if it makes certain that market conditions will justify the advances it makes.

Builds a Stronger Merchandising Program

Pooling enables members to turn over marketing operations to specialists who presumably are more knowledgeable in this area than they are. As a result, the cooperative has an opportunity to develop a stronger and more efficient merchandising program than individual producers can hope to do. The quantity and quality of products are known and, as the marketing season gets underway, cooperative management can develop its merchandising program accordingly. The pooling process, therefore, helps to smooth out price fluctuations for the members and volume fluctuations for the cooperative. Pooling usually involves storage and, therefore, commodity financing can be obtained more easily than is otherwise possible because the quality and quantity of the commodity are easily known. Such knowledge enables the cooperative better to enter into long-term marketing arrangements with buyers that require an assured supply, particularly foreign customers. By feeding the market regularly, the cooperative is also better able to help avoid gluts. Thus, to some extent, it can achieve a leveling of prices.

Recognizes Quality Production

When quality is standardized, most consumers develop a high degree of acceptance for uniformly graded products. This fact holds irrespective of whether quality is high or low because consumers have assurance as to the uniformity of the products they are buying.

Improves Association Performance

Pooling can contribute to improved association performance by (1) enabling the cooperative to do a better job of long-term planning, since member commitments give greater assurance that the cooperative will have the quality and quantity needed to develop a dependable merchandising program; (2) providing a firmer basis for determining operating costs; (3) moving the decision-making process up to a more knowledgeable level; and (4) facilitating the introduction of the per unit capital investment plan of financing.

DISADVANTAGES OF POOLING

There are also disadvantages in pooling. Although there can be many disadvantages, here we only cover some of the more important ones.

Final Settlements Delayed

Unless the cooperative can develop a strong financing position and make one or more advances, members often have to wait until sales have been completed before settlements are possible. This delay may place a difficult financial burden on some of them because of their need for the full market price at the time they deliver products.

Special Abilities of Members Ignored

Those producers who believe that they are especially shrewd and can market their products independently to special advantage see no benefit in pooling their products. Neither do those producers who believe they have produced premium products have much enthusiasm for a pooling operation. Receiving average prices will not appeal to them. While experience usually demonstrates that such an evaluation of one's ability is often ill-founded, pooling indeed does not permit independent action.

Possible Misunderstanding of Technical Aspects

Another disadvantage is the possibility of ineffective and inefficient pooling operations. For example, too many or too few grades may be established for a given product. In other instances, cooperatives may not establish sufficient grades to take advantage of unequal production areas or special qualities in the products that members produce. On other occasions, management may be a poor merchandiser and inclined to speculate on prices to the detriment of members.

Quality/Price Imbalance

It should be kept in mind, too, that pooling involves grading and the prospect of establishing favorable price differentials for quality. Obviously, it generally costs growers more to produce a quality product. This expense must be balanced against the willingness of consumers to pay premium prices for quality products. Consumers' willingnesss to do so will depend to a large degree upon their disposable income and will reflect general economic conditions.

Complex Operations

Pooling can be a complicated and complex operation. Its success requires a complete marketing program—an assured product of a known quality, necessary facilities, established market outlets, and sales expertise. The complexity of the operation is further illustrated by the problem of making equitable cost and return allocations among pool and nonpool members when the cooperative also operates on a buy-and-sell basis. Depending on production and market conditions, the cooperative also may have to determine if any given pool should be open to nonmember patrons as well as member patrons. In any event, the cooperative that shifts to pooling operation makes a complete change in its marketing program, which calls for a substantial change in its market strategy. Unless these factors are taken into account, there is no assurance that pooling will result in better returns for producers.

COMPARING POOLING WITH OTHER METHODS OF SALE

Since cooperatives may use or compete with other sales practices, it will be well to identify briefly these practices, which include bargaining (covered in Chapter 18), outright purchase and sale, member accounts, and commission sales.

Outright Purchase and Sale

Many products, for example, grain and potatoes, are generally sold by cooperatives on an outright purchase-and-sale basis. In this arrangement, the cooperative takes title to the products and pays cash for them. This type of operation may be closely attuned to member needs. It appeals to those members who wish to discount future prices and settle for assured and immediate returns. Moreover, under such circumstances a cooperative is often better able to meet and deal with the competitive forces found in the marketplace.

There are, however, many disadvantages in this method of operation, particularly from the standpoint of the cooperative. It must assume additional risks, especially as they relate to price changes. Such a practice also places increased demands for working capital upon the association. The possibility also exists that cooperatives may be tempted to make overpayments to secure volume of business. Furthermore, some people may argue that this practice is contrary to the basic cooperative approach to marketing, which provides for the joint sharing of risks, responsibilities, and benefits.

Member Accounts

Another sales method used in some cooperatives is for the members to maintain the identity of their products and to have several options available as to the method of their sale. Under these circumstances, the cooperative does not take title to the products, and no highly organized system of merchandising can be developed. Members, in effect, are competing with one another in the sale of goods. They may, for example, reserve the right to determine specifically when their packed fruit or cotton is to be sold and to whom. In other instances, they may place a standing order to sell their products when prices reach a given level, or at certain times during the marketing season. In any event, the identity of the individual's products is maintained. The member makes the marketing decisions and bears the risk, while the association in effect acts only in the role of agent. From the standpoint of members, they may realize special premiums for special quality, and are not weighted down by average prices. From the standpoint of the cooperatives, less expert sales ability is needed and less cash is required. There are, however, the disadvantages of considerable bookkeeping and increased costs. Besides, this method of operation does not enable the cooperative to build an effective merchandising program.

Commission Sales

Arrangements closely related to the individual member-account sales system are the commission form of sales. In this arrangement, members retain title to the product, and the cooperative, charging a set commission for selling and providing other related services, functions strictly in an agency capacity. This method of operation is most frequently used by regional livestock and fruit and vegetable cooperatives at terminal markets.

SUMMARY

Pooling is uniquely adapted to the cooperative way of doing business. It relates primarily to the marketing of farm products, and it may include the pooling of receipts, expenses, and risks. To be successful, pooling requires long-term commitments on the part of producers and a high degree of sales capability on the part of cooperative managers. To assure long-term commitments, most pooling cooperatives require members to sign marketing agreements. The products handled are commingled, and receipts and expenses are averaged. The cooperative contemplating pooling operations needs to consider the kinds of products that lend themselves to pooling, the number of grades to establish, the time length of pooling periods to operate, the area to serve, and the accounting practices to use in order equitably to allocate costs and returns.

The advantages of pooling include spreading risks; building a strong merchandising program; recognizing quality production; and improving association performance. Among the possible disadvantages of pooling are delays in final settlement; no opportunity to take advantage of the special marketing abilities an individual may have; the existence of ineffective, inefficient operations; failure of quality production to command premium prices; and the chance that operations may prove too complex for management.

QUESTIONS

1. Distinguish between pooling and other methods of sale.
2. What functions does the pooling process involve?
3. What is meant by the statement: Pooling is an averaging process. Explain how it works.
4. What are the important factors to consider in deciding whether a cooperative should operate on a pooling basis?
5. What considerations would you take into account in determining the number of pools to establish?
6. Why is an effective accounting system important in achieving a sound pooling operation?
7. What factors influence the time length of pools?
8. What are the advantages of pooling?
9. What are the disadvantages of pooling?
10. What types of cooperatives are most likely to use pooling? What types of product are most likely to be pooled? Why?
11. What special problems confront a cooperative in conducting a pooling operation?
12. Explain why cooperatives pool all or part of their operating expenses.

REFERENCES

There are few recent pooling studies. However, information relative to specific aspects of pooling is found in the following references.

Bakken, Henry H., and Marvin A. Schaars: *The Economics of Cooperative Marketing,* McGraw-Hill, New York, 1937, chaps 16, 17, pp. 430–473.

Carle, W. F.: "Cooperative Pooling of Soybeans under New Price Support Regulations," in *American Cooperation,* American Institute of Cooperation, Washington, 1961, pp. 326–330.

Christiansen, C. L.: *Pooling as Practiced by Cooperative Marketing Associations,* U.S. Department of Agriculture, Misc. Pub. 14, 1929. See also *American Cooperation,* American Institute of Cooperation, Washington, 1928, pp. 122–134.

Erdman, H. E., and H. R. Wellman: *Some Economic Problems Involved in the Pooling of Fruit,* California Agricultural Experiment Station Bulletin 432, 1927.

Knapp, Joseph G.: *The Hard Winter Wheat Pools,* The University of Chicago Press, Chicago, 1933, p. 180.

Markeson, Clyde: *Pooling and Other Grower Payment Methods as Used by Local Fruit, Vegetables, and Tree Nut Cooperatives,* FCS General Report 67, Farmer Cooperative Service, U.S. Department of Agriculture, Washington, 1959, p. 44.

Stevens, I. M., and J. T. Haas: *Feeder Cattle Pooling,* FCS Report 565, Farmer Cooperative Service, U.S. Department of Agriculture, Washington, 1962, p. 39.

———: *Livestock Pooling,* FCS Report 510, Farmer Cooperative Service, U.S. Department of Agriculture, Washington, 1961, p. 52.

Chapter 20

Cooperative Mergers and Liquidations

There was a lawyer named Berger,
Who planned a conglomerate merger,
Said he:
If I had my desire, I'd rather acquire,
A company about to submerger.
John E. Noakes

Many of the economic forces that have led to cooperative growth have also contributed to mergers and even liquidations of these associations. Mergers and liquidations are usually undertaken to improve the use of scarce financial, physical, and human resources. This objective is generally reflected in the trend toward fewer but larger and highly integrated associations that operate more efficiently and provide members with greater benefits.

Cooperative combination or unification may take the form of merger, consolidation, or acquisition. These terms are briefly discussed here.

Merger Merger means the absorption of one or more businesses by another business. Generally, but not always, it involves a stronger business taking over a weaker one. In the course of a merger, the surviving firm maintains its identity and many of its organizational features. It operates, however, on a greatly expanded basis.

Consolidation The term *consolidation* is used to describe the bringing together of two or more business firms into a new corporation. As a result, the parent firms cease to exist and one entirely new business is created.

Acquisition Acquisition involves the outright purchase of all or part of one firm's assets by another firm. In most cases, this is a comparatively simple action in that only the approval of the directors of the acquired firm is needed to complete action. Directors, in contemplating the sale of all or a substantial amount of a cooperative's fixed assets, however, may wish to give members and preferred stockholders the final word in approving or disapproving such action. Moreover, the acquiring firm is not liable for the debts of the firm acquired, nor does it get involved in its capital structure.

These distinctions apply to cooperatives as well as to all other types of business firms. In this discussion, because of common usage and brevity, the term *merger* will be used to cover all these forms of business combination. This usage is justified because many of the problems and relationships that develop are much the same irrespective of the forms of combination that have occurred.

The primary purposes of a merger from the standpoint of cooperatives are to: realize additional benefits, such as improved income and services for members; reduce costs; expand services; build markets and realize greater growth potential; make better use of financial resources; improve management; and use personnel and facilities to greater advantage. To achieve these purposes, the people involved must support the idea of a merger. Consideration should be given to potential barriers they might put in the way of such efforts if they should not favor the merger.

The key question in evaluating any merger, however, is: What will it do for members and how successful will it be in achieving projected objectives? People other than members, such as employees, competitors, legislators, and regulators, also have considerable influence on whether mergers actually take place, because they are in a key position to encourage or discourage such efforts.

EXTERNAL MERGER CONSIDERATIONS

Cooperatives operate as part of the general business environment. They are influenced, to a considerable extent, by the same economic, social, and political forces that have a bearing on how the entire economy operates. This fact suggests that in considering the feasibility of mergers, cooperatives should evaluate the external conditions as well as the internal and local ones that especially relate to their particular situation.

General Economic Factors

All business firms, cooperative or otherwise, need to take into account the impact of broad economic forces because they may influence both the desirability and the feasibility of a merger. Such forces, among others, relate to: (1) prospects for world peace; (2) health of the economy as indicated by the effects of recession, inflation, and the energy crisis; (3) special problems affecting the products or services the cooperatives concerned plan to provide; and (4) any of a number of national and international problems that are important at the time a merger is under consideration. Important, too, is the influence of general economic conditions on such factors as the prevailing market structure, the relative market power of cooperatives and other firms, and the extent of competition or the degree of monopoly that may exist in the industry at the time a merger is being considered.

In the economic environment in which cooperatives operate, the formation of huge conglomerates and the concentration of industry have become commonplace. One of the large conglomerates with which cooperatives compete, for example, reported some 115 subsidiaries in the early 1970s. It had large meat-packing, poultry-processing, and transportation activities. Sales and services consisted of food, 60 percent; transportation, 20 percent; groceries and pharmaceutical products, 8 percent; industrial and farm production, 7 percent; and financial and other services, 5 percent. We have previously pointed out (Chapter 6) that very large conglomerates also characterize the petroleum, feed, and fertilizer industries, as well as the grocery, financial, and insurance businesses. Since 1950, for example, the number of retail grocery stores has been reduced 50 percent. The Federal Trade Commission reports that since 1921, approximately 8,000 acquisitions have taken place in the dairy industry, most of them involving firms other than cooperatives.

It is obvious, therefore, that mergers in other industries have had a profound impact upon the operations of cooperatives that are constantly confronted with the necessity to adjust to these developments. This impact is especially important because many cooperatives are relatively small compared with other types of business enterprises.

Studies by the Farmer Cooperative Service, for example, show that:

- Forty percent of all farmers' marketing, purchasing, and related service cooperatives in 1970 reported an annual volume of under $500,000. Another 22 percent had an annual volume of $500,000 to $1 million, and 31 percent reported annual sales of $1 million to $5 million. Less than 7 percent did over $5 million of business annually.
- When the ten largest cooperatives were compared with the ten largest comparable types of business firms, the cooperatives' proportion of business as a percentage of the business of the ten largest comparable firms for selected comparisons was: sales, 13 percent; net margins, 5 percent; total assets, 6 percent; and net worth, 4 percent.
- In step with the consolidation trend among other business firms, cooperatives, too, have merged in increasing numbers. During the period from 1957 through 1970, approximately 1,000 farmers' marketing, purchasing, and related service cooperatives have discontinued operations, the great majority of them to merge with other associations. Marketing and purchasing cooperatives have, for example, averaged some seventy mergers a year during the period. Two-thirds of these mergers were among dairy marketing and farm supply associations. During the last seven years of this period, mergers were 50 percent more numerous than during the first seven years, notwithstanding the fact that the number of these cooperatives had declined from 9,400 to 8,200.

The preceding information on size and mergers suggests that the very survival of cooperatives in the economy in which they operate will depend fairly heavily upon their ability to achieve increased market power. It is evident that cooperatives, in their efforts to obtain an increasing degree of market power, are giving greater attention to mergers. To date, however, they have not gone as far down the merger trail as most other business firms have. If they are even to approach the economic strength of their competitors (large, highly integrated conglomerates), they will need to improve their operating efficiency. This objective will involve, among other things: a larger volume of business, greater integration of marketing and distribution functions, provision of new and needed services, and increased competency of management. Mergers offer one of the most effective ways of achieving these results.

Human Relations

Although many of the problems of merging are much the same irrespective of whether a firm is a cooperative or some other type of business, cooperatives have a greater concern with the human relationships that are involved in merger undertakings because of their special orientation to people. This characteristic brings into focus the nature of these relationships as they influence mergers. We have suggested previously that, although most economists find it convenient to think of people as rational human beings who seek facts as a basis for arriving at economic decisions, think objectively, observe relationships, draw sound conclusions, and act accordingly, there is considerable evidence that people often are not so logical. They may, instead, act in a thoroughly irrational way, guided by intuitive feelings, personal opinions, and hunches.

Because of human differences, students of cooperation emphasize the importance of diplomacy and understanding on the part of individuals—employees, members, directors, persons in regulatory agencies, legislators, competitors, and the general public—involved in cooperative merger negotiations. To help interested groups to make rational decisions on the merits of merging, basic facts should be assembled and used for educational programs among all concerned groups.

Legal and Regulatory Considerations

In general, cooperatives find themselves in a relatively weak position when they become involved in legal and regulatory matters. First of all, they are often plagued by the conflicting views and interests that are reflected in the different ideologies of general farm organizations. Moreover, cooperatives themselves are far from being in agreement as to how far they should go in seeking changes in antitrust and other cooperative legislation. They also often are at a disadvantage when dealing with government agencies and regulatory bodies because the individuals in charge of these agencies, as previously indicated, often lack understanding and appreciation of the unique nature of cooperatives and how they operate.

The legal status of cooperatives interested in merger is complex and at best uncertain. Regional and local cooperatives, for example, are confronted with quite different legal situations. Regional cooperatives have special concern with the impact of federal legislation (the Clayton Act and the Capper-Volstead Act) and various regulations of the Internal Revenue Service and the Federal Trade Commission on their proposed merger actions. Both regional and local cooperatives are subject to state statutes and the specific provisions of their own charters and bylaws as they relate to merger.

In Chapters 9 and 10 we stated that, starting with the Sherman Act in 1890, any merger that was in restraint of trade and that monopolized or attempted to monopolize any of the trade among the states was considered illegal. We also identified the nature and the extent of the legal modifications introduced by the Clayton Act and the Capper-Volstead Act. In general, we emphasized that mergers between cooperatives are precluded only when there is a reasonable doubt that the result would be to eliminate competition. Of special significance was the recognition of the unique nature of agricultural producers by the Capper-Volstead Act, which sanctioned marketing agencies in common. This sanction led many students of cooperation to conclude that marketing cooperatives could merge without violating any existing legislation; however, it does not apply to the merger of purchasing cooperatives or to a cooperative's acquisition of a firm other than a cooperative. (Legal developments relating to mergers were discussed further in Chapter 10.)

Cooperatives contemplating merger may submit their merger proposal to the Department of Justice or to the Federal Trade Commission for "conditional rulings" as to whether such merger would be in conflict with antitrust laws. It should be emphasized, however, that any ruling made is, as the term states, "conditional" and that it in no way protects a cooperative from subsequent action by other parties who claim to be damaged. Neither does it give any assurance that, in actual legal action, the preliminary judgments will be supported by the agencies making them.

A recent conditional ruling did not give approval to the proposed merger of a combination marketing and farm supply regional with two other farm supply regionals. It is not clear whether this ruling reverses, in effect, the previously held view that there is no substantial legal difference between a single cooperative's adding members and one cooperative merging with another. One factor may be that farm supply cooperatives do not come under the provisions of the Capper-Volstead Act.

Cooperatives considering merger should also give attention to federal income tax laws so as to obtain all possible benefits provided by them. If cooperatives contemplating merger qualify as "521 cooperatives" as defined by the Internal Revenue Code, they will want to determine the effect of a proposed merger on their tax status.

When mergers involve regional associations operating in two or more states, the associations also should study the merger statutes of the specific states in which they operate. Merger under the laws of one state may be much more advantageous than merger under the laws of another.

Both regional and local cooperatives must comply with provisions of state law when considering merger. State laws usually specify all conditions covering mergers. Many states govern cooperative mergers through general corporation statutes; others have special laws that apply to cooperative mergers.

LOCAL AND INTERNAL CONSIDERATIONS

Local Economic Factors

If cooperatives are to make sound merger decisions, it is essential that they consider the local economic factors that will have a bearing on their opportunities for achieving a successful merger in the territory in which they operate. A first requirement is to know the number and kind of cooperatives already operating in the territory. It is also desirable to determine trends in the total volume of business, the proportional share of business accounted for by all cooperatives, and the proportional share of business credited to those cooperatives that are planning to merge.

It is important, also, to evaluate economic trends in the territory from the standpoint of the future. For example, is the area rapidly becoming urbanized, or is it an area that seems destined to be permanently agricultural and to have an opportunity to expand into newly developing farming enterprises? Likewise, consumer cooperatives contemplating merger need to consider whether they are located in communities that have the potential for population growth or in communities that are likely to experience pronounced exodus to the suburbs.

Other economic considerations relate to (1) existing facilities and possible duplication that might be eliminated through merger, (2) the number of members who belong to all the associations considering merger, and (3) the extent to which services provided and trade territories overlap or supplement each other.

Personnel Implications

Exploration of what merger may mean in terms of the use of personnel is also advisable. Obviously, only one general manager is needed when cooperatives merge. Similarly, one set of bookkeepers or one office manager may be able to discharge all the new cooperative's responsibilities. It should be emphasized, however, that cooperatives ought to take a dynamic view when looking at employment implications of a merger. The ability of a cooperative to grow may well mean increased responsibilities and new opportunities for many employees, and the need to retain others for new positions. The new, unified association, for example, may need personnel to staff a new or expanded field force, a public relations or a communications division, and enlarged personnel functions. Merged regional cooperatives may also be able to add planning, research, product control, and accounting services for their members.

IMPACT ON PRACTICES, RESOURCES, AND FUNCTIONS

Merger, too, may open the door for reexamination of general operating practices, such as bargaining and pooling. The impact of a merger on the opportunities to exercise increased market power, and on circumstances favorable to integrate operations so as to provide members with new and expanded services, should also be examined. Likewise, mergers may facilitate the introduction of important improvements in pricing, inventory, accounting, and processing practices.

Also, merger may have a synergistic effect on the operations of a cooperative. In other words, the combined effect of unifying the various resources and functions that merger makes possible may be greater than the sum of the independent effects. This result may apply in varying degrees to such cooperative matters as the use of personnel, financial resources, and facilities, as well as to such functions as communications, market development, procurement practices, and administrative actions. Especially important are the financial and management adjustments made possible as a result of mergers.

Financial Considerations

There are a number of important financial considerations to which cooperatives contemplating merger may need to direct attention. Mergers, for example, will result in expanded assets and the necessity for realigning liabilities. Cooperatives planning to merge may become involved in evaluation of assets, methods of paying for assets, and the need for planning to build a stronger financial structure.

As cooperatives examine the value of the assets that may be involved in a merger, the following questions arise: What kind of accounting practices should be used to evaluate these assets? What adjustments may be needed between the financial statements of the associations concerned, and, if appraisal is necessary, who is to make it?

Experience has shown that, whenever possible, it is to the advantage of cooperatives to accept the balance sheets and operating statements of the merging associations. In the long run, this practice has generally proved to be better than insisting on "getting the last pound of flesh" in working out merger arrangements. It is important, however, to have assurances that such matters as inventory, investments, and fixed asset values are reported accurately. Payment for assets also involves a number of problems, such as the form of payment. For example, it may be in cash, stock, notes, debentures, or book credit. Likewise, cash payments may be made in a lump sum or made over a period of years. Arrangements for financial settlement with equity holders who object to the merger is another issue that must be faced.

Often a most crucial problem is that of making financial budgets or plans for expanded operations. This task gives rise to the critical question: What changes can and should be made in operations as a result of a merger? The answer requires recognition of the importance of knowing the financial resources available and the setting of realistic priorities in the development of new programs and operations.

The Role of Management

The democratic nature of the cooperative form of business enterprise means that members, directors, and managers all have more influence on merger undertakings in cooperatives than is common in most other types of business ventures. Experience has shown that, generally, the prevailing economic situations may be significantly weighted in favor of cooperative mergers. Economies of scale may be introduced, better facilities can be constructed, better and expanded services may be provided, and more effective use can be made of human, financial, and physical resources.

Notwithstanding these obvious benefits, we must remember that it is the members who have the final say when it comes to determining whether merger should be consummated. Much depends on whether their attitude is provincial and whether they fully understand the nature of the economic forces that may be moving them in the direction of business merger. Such matters as the major objectives of the projected cooperative, essential operating features, the name of the proposed organization, facilities that will be used, sold, or abandoned, brands that will be used, and how directors will be elected, are among the many difficult issues that members are likely to face.

The elected directors are also instrumental in determining whether a merger proposal will be considered. They should assume the role of cooperative leaders and objectively evaluate the feasibility of mergers in the interest of members. On the other hand, if prestige and personal status are their motivating forces, they may put self-interest before their responsibilities as directors. In other instances, because of their lack of information or interest, they may forget that they have policy-making obligations in arriving at decisions, and that they should not serve as rubber stamps for the interests of the manager and the key staff.

The role of the cooperative manager and the staff is also basic in cooperative merger considerations. Theoretically, as both a policy executor and a hired hand, the manager should not pass final judgment on the desirability of a merger. This executive's recommendations to the board, however, may have a substantial bearing on whether mergers are considered, and if they are, how carefully they are explored. The inclination to make or not to make a recommendation in the best interest of members again may reflect either possible conflicts of interest or cooperative leadership.

DETERMINING MERGER FEASIBILITY

Merger is not something that can be achieved overnight. To determine the feasibility of such action will require hard and dedicated effort on the part of cooperative directors and officials and outside agencies. The first question they are confronted with is: Is merger feasible? If it is, they then need to consider how it is to be accomplished and the steps involved in its implementation.

Often it is desirable to call in outside agencies, such as state extension services, Farmer Cooperative Service, and consulting firms, to determine the feasibility of merger or to give advice and guidance. These agencies have had experience in evaluating merger possibilities under widely varying conditions. They can objectively apply their experience to the specific problems confronting cooperatives considering merger. They can also be particularly helpful in presenting facts, interpreting information, and working with officials to keep merger considerations moving.

Cooperatives have learned from experience that there is no substitute for participation of directors and key cooperative personnel in merger deliberations. They can make substantial contributions through careful consideration of such matters as organizational structure, operating policies, use of facilities and personnel, and financial structure.

MERGER PROCEDURE

The usual merger procedure is to draw up plans and agreements for approval by the cooperatives involved. If this approval is obtained, members of these cooperatives then vote on the agreements in accordance with the provisions of their charter and bylaws. Frequently, these agreements include provisions that become a part of the articles of incorporation of the new or surviving cooperative. In any event, these new articles should cover such things as the necessity for marketing contracts, pooling practices, and the introduction of management-control features, in addition to the regular provisions that are generally a part of a cooperative's papers of incorporation.

One final observation: Cooperatives exploring merger possibilities need the guidance of a competent cooperative lawyer. The attorney's knowledge of legislative provisions and counsel in developing charters, bylaws, and other association papers can mean the difference between acceptance or rejection of merger proposals by members.

POSTMERGER CONSIDERATIONS

Even when efforts in achieving merger are successful, key questions still remain: What happens after merger? Are basic objectives being realized? To what extent do members really benefit?

One of the common failings after the completion of a merger is not to plan ongoing operations and, even when plans are made, to neglect to implement them. It is one thing to make the plans, to develop the framework, and even to launch the new organization on its way. It is something else to achieve a smoothly functioning organization that, after two or three years, has improved operating performance in the interest of members. Involved is the complex, intricate, and delicate task of implementing plans that require consolidating the operations of two or more cooperatives that formerly operated in many different ways. The parent associations have developed certain traditions and values which are reflected in operating methods, status, and leadership that have emerged over the years. The people in each organization, even though they participated in planning, will tend to resist change, especially when it is imposed from above and when it appears to offer some threat to their security and status.

Studies by the Farmer Cooperative Service show that a cooperative usually takes three or more years to achieve the contemplated advantages of merger. We have said that advantages may include new services, better utilization of equipment and facilities, more effective use of personnel, and economies of scale resulting from larger volume. The length of time can be shortened if the new cooperative has developed a carefully thought-out postmerger growth plan that takes into account the improvements that can reasonably be made and if it establishes priorities for its new ventures. By so doing, cooperatives can often overcome slowness in eliminating duplication of facilities, jobs, and transportation routes.

Garoian, Thompson, and Wentzel, in their publication *Planning and Scheduling Post-Unification Decisions for Agricultural Business*,[1] apply the PERT (program evaluation and review technique) process to postmerger decision making. By identifying key performance areas (KPAs) and critical phases in postmerger implementation (Table 20-1), they suggest (1) that the time of implementing decisions in the postmerger period can be substantially reduced, and (2) that it is necessary to identify critical activities that need top priorities if merger is to succeed.

---

[1]Leon Garoian, Stanley R. Thompson, and Roland K. Wentzel, University of California, Agricultural Extension, Berkeley, undated.

Table 20-1 Activity Occurrence by Priority Level

Key performance area	Phase I: Avoid greatest loss	Phase II: Achieve semblance of coordination	Phase III: Plug gaping holes	Phase IV: In quest of synergy
Accounting		Devise chart of accounts	Automate accounting	Generate formal accounting information
Finance and banking		Centralize funds-flow control		Secure continuing line of credit
Merchandising		Standardize price and credit policies	Devise inventory control system	Determine optimum inventory levels
Personnel	State terms of continued employment for managers; Send letters to personnel	Establish intramanagement group communication	Write job descriptions	
Insurance and public notification	Notify regulatory agencies; Select workmen's compensation insurance; Insure new office	Notify customers that bills payable should be paid to new co-op	Consolidate insurance policies with single insurer	
Facilities and equipment		Conduct facilities and equipment use study	Conduct initial pooling of facilities and equipment	Implement long-range aspects of use study
Marketing and sales	Establish uniform prices and credit terms	Establish purchasing arrangements or sales brokerage networks	Identify voids in regional marketing coverage	Coordinate production more closely with marketing; fulfill new market and product potentials.

Source: Leon Garoian, Stanley R. Thompson, and Roland K. Wentzel, *Planning and Scheduling Post-Unification Decisions for Agricultural Business,* University of California, Agricultural Extension, Berkeley, p. 124.

They have also developed the various subactivities necessary for KPAs. The scope of activities involved is indicated by their summary for one KPA, namely, personnel:[2]

> Begin survey of all employees—training, experience, and duties.
> Complete survey of all employees—training, experience, and duties.
> Begin recommendations for reclassifying employees by departments.
> Complete recommendations for reclassifying employees by departments.
> Begin to obtain personnel records.
> Complete obtaining personnel records.
> Begin to study employee benefit plans.
> Begin to standardize employee benefit plans.
> Complete employee benefit plans.
> Begin study of personnel policies.
> Complete study of personnel policies.
> Begin to unify personnel policies.
> Finish unifying personnel policies.
> Study safety programs.
> Redraft safety programs.
> Implement safety programs.
> Begin to determine and adjust manpower needs.
> Finish and implement manpower needs.
> Begin labor union renegotiations (if necessary).
> Complete labor union renegotiations.
> Begin study of nonunion employee compensation programs.
> Complete study of nonunion employee compensation programs.
> Unify nonunion employee compensation programs.

Cooperatives may also find it necessary to avoid a too-rapid expansion into new services and facilities that neither the manager nor the staff can handle because of the many additional responsibilities with which they are forced to deal.

COOPERATIVE LIQUIDATIONS

We have already suggested that not all cooperatives survive in today's business world. When cooperatives merge, consolidate, or sell out to other cooperatives or, for that matter, to other business firms, they terminate business operations. In other cases, cooperatives may be forced into involuntary bankruptcy.

Irrespective of why cooperatives liquidate their operations, the contributing factors are usually one or more of the following:

- *The need no longer exists.* Changing economic conditions, such as the urbanization of rural areas or the industrialization of urban communities, may no longer justify the operation of a cooperative.
- *Inability to realize objectives.* Some cooperatives discover that they are unable to realize their established objectives even though the need for cooperative business

[2]Ibid., p. 116.

efforts continues to exist. In view of changing member requirements, new technologies that relate to the services cooperatives provide, or improvements in transportation, many associations realize that they no longer can effectively perform the services they were designed to provide. Often these are the cooperatives that merge or consolidate with other cooperatives or sell out to other cooperatives or firms.

• *Incompetent management.* When unsatisfactory management prevails, one or more of many factors may be involved. The cooperative may have made poor choices in selecting its manager and other personnel, or it may have lacked responsible directors. As a result of incompetent management, many cooperatives have been inadequately financed, have had little or no effective communication with members, have operated with outmoded and poorly located facilities, and have failed to provide the services members needed and expected. When such situations prevail, cooperatives find it difficult, if not impossible, to adjust to changing economic conditions, and insolvency may be inevitable.

• *Expiration of the charter.* In some instances, cooperatives discontinue operations because their charter expires. This occurs if the duration of the cooperative is limited by its charter to a certain number of years, or if the incorporating state cancels the cooperative's charter owing to illegal conduct or fraud in its procurement. Most state statutes provide for the renewal of an expired charter or one that is about to expire. The courts have held that a cooperative's failure to file required reports does not necessarily result in liquidation. The state is required to act before the status of the cooperative is affected. The courts have also held that dissolution does not result because a cooperative is placed in the hands of a receiver, because it fails to elect officers, or because it ceases to carry out corporate acts.

Legal Considerations

Like any other corporation, a cooperative comes into being as the result of an agreement (a charter) between itself and the state. Therefore, the state has control over the dissolution of cooperatives. It is imperative, consequently, that cooperatives follow provisions of state statutes when they undertake dissolution proceedings.

Questions arise as to just how a cooperative can discontinue operations. If all members agree to dissolution, there is no question about taking such a step. It is not so certain, however, that a majority can force liquidation in the absence of specific provisions. If liquidation is not mentioned in state laws, it should be covered in the association's charter. For some time, there was a question of whether a cooperative, as a nonprofit organization, could be forced into involuntary bankruptcy. More recent court rulings held that because a business cooperative is a commercial corporation, such action can be taken. In many states, the directors of cooperatives at the time of dissolution continue as trustees to pay obligations and distribute any remaining assets.

Liquidations When Solvent

When a cooperative fails, its creditors obviously have first call on its assets. Therefore, the cooperative's board of directors should liquidate or transfer its assets to help meet any and all obligations. When assets are insufficient to meet the claims of all creditors, it is important to note the related provisions of state law and to avoid giving preference to any one group of creditors unless the charter has provisions to that effect.

Many factors must be considered in the liquidation of solvent cooperatives. While directors may terminate a failing cooperative in order to conserve its assets, only the members have the right to terminate a solvent cooperative. After the satisfaction of creditors, organization papers should be examined with respect to provisions for the distribution of remaining assets. For example, do these papers provide for pro rata distribution according to patronage, outstanding capital stock or other equities, or membership? Other issues to be considered are the form and time of distribution of assets. Some cooperative charters even carry the provision that in the event of dissolution, any assets are reverted to the state or may go to cooperative, public, or charitable causes.

SUMMARY

In summary, it should be emphasized that merger, especially for cooperatives that are small and not operating at maximum capacity, offers an opportunity for improved income and services for members and for increased operating efficiency. Unless the feasibility of a merger is objectively studied and unless great care in planning and implementation is exercised, merger may not improve services for members.

Mergers that are undertaken for purposes of aggrandizement of management or for little reason other than to emulate the practices of other business firms ignore the all-important interests of members. There is justification for continually raising the question: Why should mergers be undertaken? It focuses attention on two basic issues: (1) Who is the boss in a cooperative? and (2) are mergers always examined in the interests of members?

In the final analysis, it should be recognized that mergers per se do not necessarily improve business performance. Whether or not mergers can succeed in promoting the interest of members will depend on the competency and ability of management to handle the new and enlarged responsibilities growing out of a merger. Success of the merger involves (1) the effectiveness and objectivity of the educational programs that are developed to acquaint all interested groups with what can and what cannot be accomplished through merger; (2) the understanding and support that members themselves give to the merger venture; (3) the leadership of directors in dealing with the intricate and complex problems involved in merging; and (4) the willingness and ability of the manager and the staff to meet their expanded responsibilities.

Cooperative liquidations occur because these associations merge or consolidate; sell out to other businesses, cooperative or otherwise; or become insolvent. Contributing factors to liquidations are: (1) need for the association no longer exists, (2) inability to realize objectives, (3) incompetent management, or (4) expiration of their charter.

QUESTIONS

1. Distinguish among mergers, consolidations, and acquisitions.
2. Explain the differences between external and internal factors that affect mergers.
3. How do economic, social, and political forces influence the possibilities for a merger?
4. What are the special or unique aspects of cooperatives that determine how they are affected by merger forces?

5   Do rational and nonrational human traits influence prospects for mergers?
6   In your opinion, what are the principal economic benefits that may be achieved by successful merger?
7   Indicate the financial considerations that should receive attention when contemplating merger.
8   What legal precautions need to be taken into account when exploring the feasibility of a merger?
9   Describe the nature of the interests of the various cooperative publics that have an interest in mergers.
10 What are some things you would consider in undertaking a study of the feasibility of a proposed cooperative merger?
11 In your opinion, what are the main barriers to achieving merger?
12 Assuming that merger is economically feasible, what considerations might still prevent it from taking place?
13 What are the forces that contribute to the liquidation of cooperatives?
14 What are the legal considerations that should be taken into account in the liquidation of cooperatives?

REFERENCES

Abrahamsen, Martin A.: *Cooperative Growth: Trends, Comparisons, Strategy,* FCS Information 87, Farmer Cooperative Service, U.S. Department of Agriculture, Washington, pp. 12–18.

────── and J. Warren Mather: *Approaches and Problems in Merging Cooperatives,* FCS Information 54, Farmer Cooperative Service, U.S. Department of Agriculture, Washington, 1966, p. 31.

American Institute of Cooperation: "Cooperative Coordination," in *American Cooperation,* Washington, D.C., 1970, pp. 93–116.

──────: "Mergers for Stronger Cooperatives," in *American Cooperation,* Washington, D.C., 1972–1973, pp. 133–169.

Garoian, Leon, Stanley R. Thompson, and Roland K. Wentzel: *Planning and Scheduling Post-Unification Decisions for Agricultural Business,* University of California, Agricultural Extension, Berkeley, p. 131.

Haskell, James E.: *Results and Methods of Four Mergers by Local Supply Cooperatives,* FCS Research Report No. 8, Farmer Cooperative Service, U.S. Department of Agriculture, Washington, 1970, p. 46.

Kravitz, Linda: *Who Is Minding the Co-op?,* Agribusiness Accountability Project, Washington, D.C., 1974, pp. 8–21 and pp. 89–109.

Thor, Eric, Miriam Revzan, and Adrian Hutchens: *A Guide to Procedures Leading to the Consolidation of Agricultural Marketing Cooperatives,* University of California, Giannini Foundation of Agricultural Economics, Berkeley, 1967, p. 67.

Chapter 21

Cooperatives and Government Policies

Over the years, cooperatives have grappled with the problem of reconciling their relations with government. The concepts of self-help and mutual assistance have both a personal and a social orientation. They are often difficult to reconcile, however, with the business interests of cooperatives that have frequently accepted, if not solicited, state aid.

In general, governments have developed four different approaches to cooperatives. They are:

- Governments give no special recognition to cooperatives. No particular regulations apply and operations are not interfered with. A neutral attitude usually is maintained.
- Governments have a general interest in cooperatives. Assistance takes the form of advice, education, and research.
- Governments are active in organizing and controlling cooperatives. Cooperatives are registered, managerial assistance is provided, and financial statements are audited.
- Governments go "all out" in the support and use of cooperatives. As a matter of national policy, governments give grants, provide managers and directors, and use cooperatives as a means to achieve their goals.

It will help us in our discussion of the relationship of government to cooperatives to identify various relationships that exist. To this end, let us briefly review early notions that prevailed and then examine five well-established government-cooperative relationships:

- Congressional-cooperative relationships
- Federal government–cooperative relationships
- State government–cooperative relationships
- Unfavorable government action
- Government-cooperative relationships in developing countries

These government-cooperative relationships are now examined in further detail.

EARLY NOTIONS

In Chapters 3 and 4, we directed some attention to the relationships of cooperatives and government. To summarize some of the divergent views held:

- Robert Owen had no reservations about seeking philanthropic assistance for his communal colonies. The idea of looking to government for help, however, seemingly did not occur to him.
- Dr. William King, in contrast, emphasized self-sufficiency and a do-it-alone approach. He believed that cooperative effort should be voluntary and that aid would only lead to government interference that would be detrimental to cooperatives.
- After nearly a decade of operation, the Rochdale pioneers were encouraged and supported by the Industrial and Providence Societies Act of 1853. It gave legal status to the patronage refund technique and to the use of savings to promote cooperative education. Moreover, in 1862, enabling legislation was passed to permit the organization of cooperative federations. Such favorable legislation did much to strengthen local cooperatives and to establish the basis for setting up federations such as the Cooperative Wholesale Society.
- Hermann Schulze-Delitzsch is reported to have been distrustful and even hostile toward any state aid. Self-help was the key to his approach, and it was in no way compatible with state assistance.
- Quite in contrast were the views of Frederich Wilhelm Raiffeisen. Having a religious background, Raiffeisen sought assistance wherever he could obtain it, be it from philanthropists or a sympathetic government.
- The problem of government relationships proved to be a touchy one as far as the International Cooperative Alliance was concerned. In its Sixth Congress, held in 1904, there occurred a highly emotional debate on the stand of the Alliance toward state aid to cooperatives. As a result, agricultural cooperatives and many credit union associations broke away, leaving it essentially a consumer-oriented organization.
- We also know that in Sweden, Anders Orne, one of the country's leading cooperative statesmen, was actively opposed to reliance on state assistance, holding that resulting relationships would serve only to betray the cooperatives' mission and would, in effect, make them instruments of the State for carrying out its general policies.

As cooperatives gained in prominence, it often became evident that the ideas of their leaders and those of public officials were not necessarily compatible. While variations in the views on the role of government appeared in many countries, the northern European governments in general developed a neutral attitude regarding cooperatives. They looked on these associations as a part of the established economic system, and they held that cooperatives should stand or fall largely by their own efforts.

As agricultural and consumer cooperatives developed, differences arose with respect to their views on desirable relationships with government. Agricultural cooperatives, for example, often became a dominant force in the agriculture of a country, and close relationships evolved between them and their governments. They often became an instrument for carrying out national agricultural programs. In Switzerland, for example, payments were made to a number of dairy, livestock, and poultry cooperatives to implement government programs. The same relationships exist in Sweden, where cooperatives are so important that, in effect, in most fields they generally represent substantially all agricultural interests. As a result, cooperatives became involved in serving as the agency for collecting and distributing price-equalization funds for the Swedish milk industry.

In England, rural commissions have from time to time been established to study agricultural cooperatives, and they have provided encouragement for their organization and operation.

CONGRESSIONAL-COOPERATIVE RELATIONSHIPS

Cooperatives in the United States have had the benefit of a substantial degree of encouragement and public support by government. In many instances, cooperative leaders have taken the initiative and actively sought government assistance and encouragement. Such support has included favorable legislation as well as the provision of advisory assistance and the conduct of research and of promotional and educational programs.

Legal Assistance

Legislative action with respect to cooperatives has usually been favorable in the United States on both state and national levels. All states have enacted enabling legislation providing for the organization of cooperatives. Cooperative legislation in general has come to recognize the unique nature of cooperatives and the contributions they can make to various segments of society. And, through research assistance and the establishment of special financial institutions, government actions have been taken to encourage members to build stronger cooperatives. In Chapters 9, 10, and 11, the important state and federal statutes that specifically relate to cooperatives are discussed. The legal steps taken to improve the credit position of American farmers, particularly as it relates to the establishment of the cooperative Farm Credit System, are discussed in Chapter 17. Legislative support for credit unions, fishery cooperatives, and housing cooperatives, as well as diverse types of service cooperatives, is mentioned briefly in Chapters 2, 5, and 9. Supplementary information on government action in support of cooperative research, advisory services, and educational efforts is also given in Chapter 5.

More and more, farm leaders believe that, as a basic part of the agricultural economy, cooperatives have a very legitimate interest in shaping legislative policy to meet the needs of their members. They recognize, for instance, that this is the very technique used by other segments of the economy. Unless cooperative leaders are derelict in their duties, they will use the same techniques.

If they can unite on their objectives, they are in a most strategic position to influence agricultural policy. They should not stand by and passively accept unfavorable political decisions that affect cooperatives without making their views known. Certainly some cooperators are becoming more sophisticated. They recognize that the tools of government are theirs to use, and that they have a responsibility to use them effectively to present any and all legitimate issues of concern to cooperatives.

Early Studies

The first comprehensive study of cooperatives by the United States Department of Agriculture occurred in 1901 when G. K. Holmes, of the Bureau of Statistics, in an unpublished manuscript, "Farmer Cooperation," assembled basic information on types of cooperatives. He stated that the purpose in undertaking his assignment was to "present the dangers to be avoided, the requisites for success, and the actual conditions that have been encountered." During the next decade, annual reports of the U.S. Department of Agriculture indicated a growing interest in cooperatives.

We have mentioned that the establishment of the Country Life Commission by President Theodore Roosevelt in 1908 also did much to stimulate interest in agricultural cooperatives (see Chapter 5). In its report, the Commission stated: "There must be a vast enlargement of voluntary efforts among farmers themselves. It is indispensable that farmers shall work together for their common interest and for the national welfare. . . . We have only begun to develop business cooperation in the United States." It was in tune with the slogan coined by Sir Horace Plunkett: "Better farming, better business, and better living." Moreover, Plunkett suggested that better farming business was the first step in achieving this objective.

In submitting the Commission's report to Congress in a special message, President Roosevelt took a firm stand in favor of cooperatives with the statement: "The introduction of effective agricultural cooperation throughout the United States is of first importance." Although Congress refused to publish the Commission report until 1914, it gained wide attention in the meantime and was the subject of much discussion. That the President of the United States was willing to stand up and be counted on the cooperative issue gave it substantial status and indicated a high degree of intelligent backing for cooperatives.

The strong support of the Commission for cooperatives provided the grist that was to nurture cooperative development in the United States for years to come. One of the by-products, for example, was the intensification of interest in cooperative credit (see Chapter 17).

FEDERAL GOVERNMENT–COOPERATIVE RELATIONSHIPS[1]

A number of agencies of the federal government have had responsibility for assisting cooperatives. The programs of the most important ones merit discussion here.

Office of Markets

The first formalized government efforts to assist farmers in building stronger cooperatives occurred in 1913 with the establishment of the Office of Markets in the United States Department of Agriculture. As a background for setting up this agency, the Appropriations Act of 1913 directed the Secretary of Agriculture to obtain from the branches of the Department national information on marketing practices "cooperative or otherwise." The report prepared in response to this directive suggested that "a division of markets could perform excellent service in helping farmers to help themselves to organize marketing associations. . . ."

The Department of Agriculture acted with dispatch and solicited the views of cooperative leaders in the development of its cooperative program as soon as Congress appropriated $50,000 to establish the Office of Markets. G. Harold Powell, formerly chief of the Bureau Plant Industry of the Department, and then general manager of the California Fruit Growers Exchange (now Sunkist Growers, Inc.), at the invitation of the Secretary, participated in a discussion of the activities of the newly created office. In summarizing his views on assistance the Department could provide cooperatives, he stated that it might:[2]

- Determine the principles on which farmers' business organizations can be successfully founded and operated.
- Work out the principles of law which should be incorporated into state and federal legislation and which would permit the proper organization and conduct of farmers' associations.
- Study the distribution of farm crops as practiced by farmers' organizations and other agencies, in order to determine the weaknesses, the wastes in distribution, the faults and extravagances of the distributing system, and the illegal practices.

Powell's strong belief that the government should assist farmers to help themselves but not dominate them is shown by his statement that "the government should not provide a crutch for the farmer to lean on when he can walk without it."

One of the first projects undertaken by the Office of Markets was an inventory of the nature and extent of cooperative business organizations in the United States. It reported 11,000 organizations that in varying degrees operated on a cooperative basis. Findings of this project served as the basis for identifying fundamental problems that

---

[1] Material in *Agricultural Cooperation: Selected Readings* by Martin A. Abrahamsen and Claude L. Scroggs (chap. 8), and in *The Rise of American Cooperative Enterprise 1620–1920* (chaps. 8 and 9) and *The Advance of American Cooperative Enterprise 1920–1945* (chaps. 8, 14, 15, 16, and 17), both by Joseph G. Knapp, were helpful in the development of this section and the following one, "State Government–Cooperative Relationships." See "References" for full citation.

[2] Andrew W. McKay and Martin A. Abrahamsen, *Helping Farmers Build Cooperatives,* FCS Circular 31, Farmer Cooperative Service, U.S. Department of Agriculture, Washington, 1962, p. 9.

were in need of study. It became immediately obvious that cooperatives needed to improve their business practices. To this end, the Department developed a series of bookkeeping and accounting publications for different types of cooperatives—creameries, elevators, farm supply associations, and fruit and vegetable associations. In the decade that followed, informative publications were issued. Among others, they included:

Cooperative Purchasing of Farm Supplies
Cooperative Organization Business Methods
Marketing Practices of Wisconsin and Minnesota Creameries
Organization and Development of a Citrus Fruit Marketing Agency
Operating Methods and Expenses of Citrus Fruit Marketing Agencies
Sales Methods and Policies of a Growers National Marketing Agency
Agricultural Cooperation in Denmark
Cooperative Marketing of Cotton
Cooperative Marketing of Livestock in the United States by Terminal Associations

As the Office of Markets gained experience and an adequate staff, its program broadened to include studies of credit and insurance. In all studies, emphasis was on the improvement of business practices and on achieving greater business efficiency.

Division of Agricultural Cooperation

Following World War I, the cooperative program of the U.S. Department of Agriculture gained stature and momentum with the establishment in 1922 of the Division of Agricultural Cooperation in the Bureau of Agricultural Economics. This move gave renewed impetus to cooperative studies, which took the form of reports on cooperative activities along various commodity lines as well as reports on business programs and policies.

The Cooperative Marketing Act, which gave permanence to the Department's work with cooperatives, was passed in 1926. This legislation has been a basis for the Department's continuing research, advisory assistance, and educational programs for cooperatives through all the ensuing political administrations and reorganizations. The act was drafted by the staff of the then-Secretary of Agriculture William Jardine, with the advice and assistance of cooperative leaders.

This legislation changed the name of the Division of Agricultural Cooperation to the Division of Cooperative Marketing. It was authorized:

    1 To acquire, analyze, and disseminate economic, statistical, and historical information regarding the progress, organization, and business methods of cooperative associations in the United States and foreign countries.
    2 To conduct studies of the economic, legal, financial, social, and other phases of cooperation, and publish the results thereof. Such studies shall include the analyses of the organization, operation, financial, and merchandising problems of cooperative associations.
    3 To make surveys and analyses if deemed advisable, of the accounts and business practices of representative cooperative associations upon their request; to report to the

association so surveyed the results thereof; and, with the consent of the association so surveyed, to publish summaries of the results of such surveys, together with similar facts, for the guidance of cooperative associations and for the purpose of assisting cooperative associations in developing methods of business and market analyses.

   4   To confer and advise with committees or groups of producers, if deemed advisable, that may be desirous of forming a cooperative association; and to make an economic survey and analysis of the facts surrounding the production and marketing of the agricultural product or products which the association, if formed, would handle or market.

   5   To acquire, from all available sources, information concerning crop prospects, supply, demand, current receipts, exports, imports, and prices of the agricultural products handled or marketed by cooperative associations; and to employ qualified commodity marketing specialists to summarize and analyze this information and disseminate the same among cooperative associations and others.

   6   To promote the knowledge of cooperative principles and practices and to cooperate in promoting such knowledge, with educational and marketing agencies, cooperative associations, and others.

   7   To make such special studies in the United States and foreign countries, and to acquire and disseminate such information findings as may be useful in the development and practice of cooperation.

By this time, legislation had been enacted that was of special interest to cooperatives and the Department. Largely in response to the passage of the Capper-Volstead Act, Bulletin 1106, *Legal Phases of Cooperative Associations,* by L. S. Hulbert, was issued by the Department. It provided the first extensive discussion of legal problems that arise in the organization of cooperatives. It has been revised and expanded several times, the last time in 1976 when it appeared in *Legal Phases of Farmer Cooperatives* (FCS Information 100) by D. Morrison Neeley. Parts of this publication also are issued separately as: *Part I—Sample Legal Documents; Part II—Federal Income Taxes;* and *Part III—Antitrust Laws.*

During this period, too, particular attention was given to the business practices of cooperatives and to improving their operating efficiency. The results of these studies included such publications as:[3]

>   *Membership Relations of Cooperative Associations (Cotton and Tobacco)*
>   *Organization and Management Problems of Cooperative Oil Associations in Minnesota.*
>   *Business Analysis of the Tobacco Growers Cooperative Association*
>   *Agricultural Associations, Marketing and Purchasing*

Federal Farm Board

Growing concern over the low prices reflecting mounting agricultural surpluses, combined with dissatisfaction with President Calvin Coolidge's three vetoes of McNary-Haughen bills, contributed to a rising tide of agricultural discontent in the late 1920s. As a result, it was obvious that something had to be done, and President-elect Herbert

---

[3]These documents all published by U.S. Department of Agriculture, Washington.

Hoover, who was sympathetic to cooperatives, took the lead in advocating legislation to create the Federal Farm Board. This agency was established under the Agricultural Marketing Act, passed on June 15, 1929. It was described as "An Act to establish a Federal Farm Board to promote the effective merchandising of agricultural commodities in interstate and foreign commerce, and to place agriculture on a basis of economic equality with other industries." Since cooperatives handled a relatively small proportion of the total agricultural products, it should have been quite evident that cooperatives alone could not be relied upon to deal effectively with the many adverse conditions confronting agriculture.

The Federal Farm Board coined the slogan "cost of production" for farmers, and it undertook to administer the huge agricultural surpluses through a system of loans and price supports. The Board recognized the importance of cooperatives and looked on them as a vehicle for helping farmers build their own marketing system. To this end, the Board was authorized and directed: "(1) to promote education in the principles and practices of cooperative marketing . . . and (2) to encourage the organization, improvement in methods, and development of effective cooperative associations."

Board officials, after surveying the enormity of the problems facing farmers, concluded that merely to help farmers organize additional small associations would not contribute much to the solution of their problems. They believed that only strong, large-scale, national cooperatives would give the farmer increased strength in the marketplace, and they stood ready to help finance the organization and operation of such cooperatives. Cooperative leaders, in turn, developed a wait-and-see attitude toward the Board and its evolving policy regarding cooperatives. Many of them feared that instead of providing encouragement and help, the Board would seek to dominate their operations.

The Cooperative Division of the Bureau of Agricultural Economics was transferred by Executive order to the Federal Farm Board in 1929. This action substantially altered government policy regarding cooperatives by deemphasizing research. The program of the Federal Farm Board moved in two directions: (1) More emphasis was given to short-time service assistance in methods of organizing and financing cooperatives, particularly those that received loans from the Federal Farm Board (this activity involved studies largely conducted on a commodity basis—particularly for cotton, dairy, fruit and vegetable, grain, livestock, poultry, and special crop cooperatives); and (2) development of an educational program which, among other things, included the preparation of lesson outlines for the study of various kinds of cooperative marketing associations. These outlines, prepared in cooperation with the Board of Vocational Education, were used by teachers of vocational agriculture and others working with adult farmers and farm boys. In addition, radio talks, preparation of publications, and participation in cooperative meetings were a part of the educational program of the Board.

The cooperative program that developed was criticized by a number of groups. The Oregon State Council, for example, went on record as stating that cooperatives should "be built from the bottom up and not from the top down." It further held that the Board organized cooperatives too fast and with too much promotional effort.

The stabilization program of the Federal Farm Board failed to achieve its primary objectives, primarily because no effective control methods existed or were devised to deal with the mounting agricultural surplus.

The work of the Cooperative Division, however, made some significant contributions. Loan losses were held to a minimum, and the emphasis on a large-scale cooperative endeavor helped to build a better understanding of the benefits that cooperatives could bring if they had sufficient strength to make their influence felt in the marketplace. Further, the emphasis on credit operations helped to point the direction in which cooperatives should move in the years ahead (see Chapter 17). The action program of the Board also stressed the need for more attention to research if cooperative policies were to serve as the basis for the establishment of sound operation practices.

Tennessee Valley Authority (TVA)

At the close of World War I, the United States found itself with a large unused ammunition plant at Muscle Shoals, Alabama, in the Valley of the Tennessee River. What to do with this facility was a question that was debated in Congress for the next fifteen years. With the advent of the New Deal, steps were taken to deal not only with this facility but also to develop the natural resources of the Tennessee Valley and adjacent territories.

President Roosevelt, with the cooperation of Senator George Norris, was instrumental in developing legislation that established the Tennessee Valley Authority in 1933. Although this legislation did not directly authorize work with cooperatives, Dr. Arthur E. Morgan, former president of Antioch College, who was selected to serve as Chairman of the Tennessee Valley Authority, looked on these organizations as useful in helping to achieve the broad social and economic objectives of the Authority. To this end, TVA encouragement was given to various cooperative enterprises in the area. One such enterprise was the Tennessee Valley Associated Cooperatives, Inc., which included in its efforts four cannery associations in the mountain areas of North Carolina and Tennessee, a cooperative milling facility in Tennessee, a dairy cooperative in Brasstown, North Carolina, and a regional cooperative to market farm products and provide related services in Waynesville, North Carolina.

Another important development was the encouragement given to the formation of the Alcorn County Electric Power Association by TVA Director David E. Lilienthal. The Association came into being when the Wilson Dam of the Tennessee Valley Authority was able to replace the power provided by the Mississippi Power Company. The success of the Association was important because it served as a concrete example of the feasibility of cooperative power associations. As a result, several other power associations were organized in the Tennessee Valley Authority. What is more, the Alcorn and other associations subsequently organized in the area were observed by Rural Electrification Administration officials when they were considering possible approaches for the distribution of electrical power in rural areas.

The nitrogen facility at Muscle Shoals also became significant in the cooperative program of the area. The fertilizer manufactured was provided to cooperative associations and university experiment stations for demonstration purposes. This arrangement led to the formation of an independent fertilizer cooperative, Associated Cooperatives, Inc., which operated for a number of years under the control of several regional cooperatives.

The many new and unique cooperative developments in the Tennessee Valley area that followed the formation of TVA came into being as the result of imaginative and innovative government action programs. Government leaders were willing to experiment with and encourage cooperatives to achieve the specific objectives of the programs they administered. Dr. Joseph G. Knapp, in *The Advance of American Cooperative Enterprise: 1920–1945,*[4] summarized TVA contributions by stating that "the TVA became a laboratory and testing ground for the application of cooperative principles to the development of natural resources for the general social and economic welfare of the nation."

Rural Electrification Administration (REA)

Another example of how government officials have supported cooperative effort is found in the development of the Rural Electrification Administration. President Franklin Roosevelt, influenced by his experience with the New York State Power Authority as Governor of New York, was an advocate of public power. He recognized the possible contribution that such programs could make to rural America. On May 11, 1935, in response to a study that pinpointed the importance of rural electrification and to a ground swell of interest by general farm organizations, President Roosevelt created the Rural Electrification Administration under the provisions of the Emergency Relief Appropriation Act. With the passage of the Rural Electrification Act of 1936, the program achieved permanent legal status.

Spirited debate occurred as to the best method of developing a power distribution system. In the early days of REA, its administrative staff, while sympathetic to rural power needs, was primarily "private power"-oriented. It was largely by the default of private power companies and as a result of a study by Udo Rall, then chief of the Division of Self-Help Cooperatives of the Federal Emergency Relief Administration, that recommendations were made that eventually led to the use of cooperatives as the principal means of distributing rural electric power. Another factor contributing to the acceptance of cooperative power distribution was the favorable experience with power cooperatives in TVA territory. That situation prompted Clyde Ellis, for many years executive secretary of the National Rural Electric Cooperative Association, to describe the TVA as "the incubator of the rural electric system."

The REA eventually became a part of the United States Department of Agriculture, and it served as the principal financing agency for rural cooperatives.

Resettlement Administration

During early years of the New Deal era, a number of cooperative relief ventures were tried for disadvantaged groups. A very influential person at this time was Guy Rexford Tugwell, who had a strong belief that "America should be made over." To this end, he

[4]Interstate, Danville, Ill., 1973, p. 341.

and various government officials encouraged the use of cooperatives for certain social experiments. These included:[5]

- *A wide range of self-help ventures.* These undertakings were reported by the Federal Emergency Relief Administration, in December 1935, to include: "Dairying, butchering, poultry and rabbit raising, plumbing, fishing and fish processing, flour milling, logging and sawmilling, carpentry, house wrecking, graphic art work, dentistry, printing, bakeries, broom making, mattress and quilt making, furniture making and upholstery, crate making, coal mining, auto repairing, laundering, locksmithing, handicrafts such as weaving, wood carving and copperwork, making of soap and cosmetics, of cider, maple syrup, pickles, jams, shoe repairing, radio repairing, operating of barber shop, beauty shop, cafeteria, wood yard, garage, laundry, etc."
- *Subsistence homesteads organized as a "back to the farm movement."* The homesteads were organized for stranded, industrial, worker, and agricultural groups. They were described by Dr. William E. Zeuck, specialist in cooperation for the Division of Subsistence Homesteads, as "usually ideal plans for ideal people, rather than practical plans for real people."
- *The establishment of the Rural Resettlement Administration.* This agency again included a large number of cooperative ventures. They were described by Paul Conkin in his book, *Tomorrow a New World: New Deal Community Program,* as including: "farms, pasture, dairies, wood lots, greenhouses, rock quarries, poultry enterprises, hog breeding, cattle breeding, lime crushing, canneries, barbershops, cobble shops, feed grinding, gristmills, handicraft industries, orchards, vineyards, factories, tearooms, inns, restaurants, hospitals, potato-drying houses, garages, filling stations, medical associations, blacksmith shops, warehouses, cane mills, farm equipment, cotton gins, coal mines, seed houses, hatcheries, sawmills, freezing plants, and even a burial association."

Few of these ventures proved successful; in fact, many of them were resounding failures. It should be kept in mind, however, that the conditions under which these cooperative schemes were started were extremely adverse. The experience demonstrated that cooperatives could not achieve the impossible, that to be successful it was essential that they be rooted in the understanding of members, leaders, and government officials. It also became obvious that they required stronger financial resources, active member participation, and a managerial staff capable of accomplishing the jobs at hand.

The Resettlement Administration became the Farm Security Administration when it was brought under the administration of the U.S. Department of Agriculture in 1937. Cooperative programs were continued for the next ten years or so, although no new ones were initiated. These programs included ventures in industrial cooperatives, cooperative farms (more properly described as "government farms"), cooperative urban communities, and cooperatives for economic services, medical care, and land leasing. Substantially, all these ventures failed. Knapp attributed causes for failure to "lack of initial planning, weak management, extravagance, inexperienced personnel, and poor plant location." One rather substantial contribution of the Farm Security Administration to cooperative success, however, was its direct loan program to farmers

[5]See Knapp, *The Advance of American Cooperative Enterprise,* op. cit., pp. 290, 297, 301.

to enable them to purchase stock in Midwestern grain cooperatives. The recipients included nearly 200 associations that became members of reorganized regional grain cooperatives following the discontinuation of the Farmers National Grain Corporation—a cooperative organized and financed with the assistance of the Federal Farm Board.

Farmer Cooperative Service

We have traced the development of government programs for research, technical assistance, and educational contributions through several government agencies from their beginning in 1913 through the Farm Credit Administration. These agencies included the Office of Markets, the Division of Cooperatives, the Federal Farm Board, and the Cooperative Research and Service Division of the Farm Credit Administration. In 1953, the Farmer Cooperative Service was separated from the Farm Credit Administration and set up as a separate agency within the U.S. Department of Agriculture. All but the Federal Farm Board and, for a while, FCA's Cooperative Research and Service Division were a part of the cooperative program of the Department.

Throughout the existence of these agencies, emphasis was placed on helping farm people improve their economic position through building stronger cooperatives. The Farmer Cooperative Service and its predecessor agencies provided national leadership and guidance for the development of rural cooperatives. In accordance with legislative authorization, the Service has maintained a reasonably balanced program of research, technical help, and educational assistance. As resources have permitted, it has sought to adjust its program to the changing conditions confronting American farmers. Since 1965, the Administrator of the Service has been a schedule C political appointee.

In 1974, the Service described its functions and responsibilities as follows:

> Farmer Cooperative Service provides research, management, and educational assistance to cooperatives to strengthen the economic position of farmers and other rural residents. It works directly with cooperative leaders and Federal and State agencies to improve organization, leadership, and operation of cooperatives and to give guidance to further development.
>
> The Service (1) helps farmers and other rural residents obtain supplies and services at lower cost and to get better prices for products they sell; (2) advises rural residents on developing existing resources through cooperative action to enhance rural living; (3) helps cooperatives improve services and operating efficiency; (4) informs members, directors, employees, and the public on how cooperatives work and benefit their members and their communities; and (5) encourages international cooperative programs.
>
> The Service publishes research and educational materials and issues *News for Farmers Cooperatives*. All programs and activities are conducted on a nondiscriminatory basis, without regard to race, creed, color, sex, or national origin.

Great Society Programs

The period from 1952 to 1960 was one of consolidation as far as government cooperative programs and policies were concerned. In the administrations of Presidents Kennedy and Johnson, however, new, fast-moving social and political forces led to many changes. In response, government officials again looked to cooperatives as a vehicle for helping introduce these changes. In many respects, this period was not unlike the New Deal era.

The Economic Opportunity Act of 1964, for example, authorized several programs to improve social and economic conditions for people in rural areas. As a part of this act, a loan program was initiated to establish new cooperatives, predominantly for families with limited incomes. To this end the Office of Economic Opportunity (OEO) delegated responsibility for administering a loan program to the Secretary of Agriculture, who redelegated this responsibility to the Farmers Home Administration (FHA). Loans were made to assist farmers in the marketing of various agriculture products and to operate farm machines on a cooperative basis. At the time this program was discontinued (1971), 1,455 loans, totaling $21 million, had been made to some 1,300 cooperatives.

In addition to the loans received from FHA, OEO has made direct grants to the local cooperatives to help cover some organizational and administrative expenses. Special emphasis in these programs was placed on encouraging cooperative efforts of minority groups—blacks, Spanish-speaking groups, and American Indians. Substantial attention also was directed to assisting whites in Appalachian areas to improve their craft production and marketing programs.

An evaluation of these programs would lead to many of the same conclusions that were reached about some of the unsuccessful New Deal efforts. No matter how real the needs and how sincere the efforts, it is a reality of business that "hard, cool heads must replace soft, warm hearts" when permanent cooperative programs are being forged. Grants unrelated to potentials for success were often made; expensive studies frequently were contracted for, with firms having little or no understanding of the fundamentals of cooperative operation; and alternative uses for appropriated funds were often not realistically evaluated.

Many cooperative observers have frequently expressed the view that OEO assistance was provided without adequately ascertaining the economic feasibility of the proposals made. For example, OEO at one time made a $582,000 research grant to a cooperative notwithstanding the fact that the cooperative had no personnel qualified to initiate and carry on its research assignment. This grant was, in fact, a larger sum than the annual expenditures of the entire land-grant college system on specialized cooperative research at the time. Had such efforts been coordinated with an experienced research agency such as Farmer Cooperative Service, there is every reason to believe that results would have been significantly more productive.

Further indication of the support and encouragement given to cooperatives by the Department of Agriculture is seen in the policy statements it has developed. The first such statement was formulated in the 1940s. The policy was discontinued from 1952 to 1960, and reinstituted in 1960. A statement made on July 5, 1973, by the Secretary of Agriculture, enumerates the legislative laws authorizing assistance to cooperatives by the Department and describes its policy as follows:

> The Department shall maintain its policy of carrying out both the spirit and intent of these laws and offer maximum encouragement to cooperatives as a means of improving farmers' incomes and developing rural America. It is necessary that we continuously strengthen our

efforts to do so. Therefore, I hereby direct the Administrator of each Agency in the Department—to continue to reexamine each year each of his programs and,—where necessary, to reshape them to carry out the full intent of the law and Department policy so as to offer maximum encouragement to the growth and development of sound cooperatives.

It is of course recognized that a policy statement may be the basis for a carefully charted course of action, or it may be just so much rhetoric. The test comes in how well it is implemented, in the support given to it, and in the allocation of the Department resources that it receives. At all times, it must be tested not by what an administration says, but by what it does.

STATE GOVERNMENT–COOPERATIVE RELATIONSHIPS

The findings and recommendations of the Country Life Commission encouraged land-grant colleges and other state agencies to give more attention to cooperatives. No doubt this encouragement was in part due to the fact that some members of the Commission were university administrators. Cooperative courses were organized, research efforts were initiated, and extension programs that attracted considerable attention in cooperative circles were started. In a limited number of instances, state departments of agriculture also lent encouragement to cooperative ventures. We turn now to early cooperative program development in selected states, particularly as it involved their land-grant universities.

Massachusetts

The experience of Kenyon L. Butterfield, president of the Massachusetts State College of Agriculture and a member of the Country Life Commission, did much to stimulate his interest in cooperatives. As a result, he looked around for a person to assume responsibilities for work with cooperatives at the college. We have mentioned that in 1908 he employed Alexander E. Cance, a graduate of the University of Wisconsin. Cance is credited with teaching the first university course entirely devoted to cooperatives, Cooperation in Agriculture, at the Massachusetts Agricultural College in 1910. The course was described as contemplating "a somewhat comprehensive view of the principles, history, and social relations of agricultural cooperation, for profit." As Cance gained teaching experience, he emphasized more and more the business aspects of cooperatives. He stated that the stress placed on cooperative business activities was due in part to the desire to improve rural life.

Cance's efforts, however, extended beyond the teaching of cooperation. He recommended the organization of cooperatives in Massachusetts, and to this end, in 1914, he authored the publication *Farmers Cooperative Exchange*. This was followed by a publication, *Farmers Cooperation Corporations,* prepared for the Vermont Department of Agriculture, which he coauthored with L. P. Jefferson. Cance's reputation as a student of cooperation was responsible for President Roosevelt's appointing him to a committee of seven to go to Europe to study cooperative credit. He also had major responsibility for preparing the committee's report, which was published as *Senate Document* 214. That the path of cooperative pioneers did not always run smoothly is indicated by Cance's statement that on two occasions, because of the pressure from vested interests, he was nearly discharged from his college position because of his active support of cooperatives. This is the same kind of pressure that in many instances has prevented university administrators from taking a strong stand on support of cooperative teaching and research at their institutions. In Massachusetts, however, the university's support of cooperatives was further shown by the hiring of E. S. Morgan as an extension worker with the assigned responsibility of organizing communities to deal with social problems.

New York

Work with cooperatives at Cornell University was promoted by many of the same forces that arose in Massachusetts. Dean Bailey, owing to his experience on the Country Life Commission, encouraged the development of a course called Cooperation. First taught in 1911–1912 by Prof. George L. Lauman, it was oriented toward agriculture and it emphasized application of cooperative principles to farmers' business organizations. While Cornell was among the pioneers in introducing courses in agricultural cooperation, it was not until 1922 that it undertook cooperative research and developed an extension program with these organizations.

Minnesota

In 1913, the Minnesota State Legislature passed a law requiring that the Department of Agriculture of the University of Minnesota "collect statistics and information in reference to cooperative associations among farmers and the management and methods of conducting such associations." Thomas Levi Hecker, long-time head of the Dairy Department of the university, helped to set the stage for encouraging state assistance for cooperatives. He attended hundreds of farmers' meetings in the state in which he "preached" the need for cooperatives and encouraged farmers to organize their own cooperative businesses. Following Hecker's early efforts, the list of teachers and research workers in cooperation at the University of Minnesota included such nationally recognized cooperative authorities as J. D. Black, O. B. Jesness, E. Fred Koller, H. B. Price, and L. D. H. Weld. Cooperation was also taught in the classrooms of the University of Minnesota as early as 1909, when Prof. John Coulter devoted part of his course in agricultural economics, to cooperative enterprise. Concerned with the lack of an adequate textbook, he wrote *Cooperation among Farmers* in 1911.[6] Professors J.D. Black and H. B. Price prepared a landmark publication on cooperatives in Minnesota in 1924. This publication, *Cooperative Central Marketing Organization*,[7] gave a detailed evaluation of the advantages and disadvantages of centralized and federated cooperatives. In commenting on it, Prof. Black stated that "it was used more or less as a textbook on cooperatives marketing for several years. It struck at the Sapiro philosophy while the iron was hot."

[6]John Coulter, *Cooperation among Farmers*, Sturgis and Wallon Co., New York, 1911, p. 281.
[7]John D. Black and H. Bruce Price, *Cooperative Central Marketing Organization*, Bulletin 211, University of Minnesota, St. Paul, 1924, p. 112.

Wisconsin

Work with cooperatives in Wisconsin benefited from the progressive environment ushered in by such distinguished leaders as President Charles R. Van Hise of the University of Wisconsin; Profs. Richard T. Ely and John R. Commons of the Department of Economics; Profs. Henry C. Taylor and Benjamin H. Hibbard of the Department of Agricultural Economics; and Governor Robert M. LaFollette. With the encouragement of the aggressive and equally distinguished Charles McCarthy, head of the Wisconsin Legislative Reference Library and a friend of Sir Horace Plunkett, Professor Taylor, then head of the Department of Agricultural Economics, hired Professor Hibbard to teach cooperation and conduct research on the problems of cooperatives. Hibbard had given considerable attention to cooperatives at Iowa State College, Ames. He introduced the course Cooperation and Marketing at the University of Wisconsin in 1913. Prior to this time (1912), John F. Sinclair, on the staff of the Legislative Reference Library, at the request of the Wisconsin Board of Public Affairs, made a detailed four-part study of cooperatives that included agricultural cooperatives, cooperative credit, municipal markets, and distributive (store) cooperation.

It is of interest that for a time the Wisconsin Society of Equity sought to restrict the cooperative program of the university to education, rather than to stimulate cooperative effort. The latter was a prerogative that it wished to reserve for itself. However, due to the prodding of McCarthy, who advised Taylor to "get in and learn cooperation," the university was soon actively engaged in both teaching and research.

The University of Wisconsin has contributed, in addition to Hibbard and Taylor, such distinguished teachers and researchers in the field of agricultural cooperation as Profs. Henry H. Bakken, Rudolph K. Froker, Asher Hobson, Theodore Macklin, and Marvin A. Schaars.

In 1970 the university expanded its cooperative program with the establishment of the University Cooperative Education and Training Center. The Center encompassed the International Cooperative Training Center, set up in 1961, with support from the Agency for International Development, to train nationals selected by other countries to assist in the development of their cooperative programs.

Kentucky

The first course in cooperation at the University of Kentucky, Cooperation and Marketing, was offered in 1922. Kentucky contributed the Bingham Act in 1922, which for a long time served as the model for state cooperative legislation. The state university has had an active interest in teaching, research, and extension work as related to cooperatives. In 1926, O. B. Jesness, then of the University of Kentucky, presented for publication a study, *Cooperative Marketing and Price Control*.[8] This was a controversial subject, but fortunately both President Frank L. McVey and Thomas B. Cooper, director of the experiment station, were economists and understood the importance of the issues concerned.

---

[8]O. B. Jesness, *Cooperative Marketing and Price Control,* Bulletin 271, University of Kentucky, Lexington, 1926, p. 22.

In 1969, the University of Kentucky adopted a policy statement, a practice which some other universities have also adopted, to indicate the nature of its support for cooperatives. This statement reads as follows:

> The College of Agriculture of the University of Kentucky, in assuming the responsibilities established by federal and state laws, develops and conducts programs to provide a better understanding of agriculturally related cooperatives and to increase their business efficiency in the public interest. These programs include the following:
>
> **A** *Research:* The Agricultural Experiment Station, as part of its research program, conducts studies in agricultural marketing, the purchasing of agricultural inputs, agricultural finance and other economic aspects of agriculture useful to all types of agriculturally related business organizations, including cooperatives. Studies also are directed specifically to the cooperative type of business organization. Such research provides the needed understanding of the nature, history, problems, possibilities and limitations, and factors which influence the success of agricultural cooperatives.
>
> **B** *Resident Teaching:* The College of Agriculture offers resident instruction in policy, finance, marketing and agricultural prices which have applicability to a variety of agriculturally related businesses. In addition, it offers resident instruction dealing specifically with agricultural cooperatives, which includes: (a) the nature and history of cooperatives, (b) the place of cooperatives in the national economy, (c) philosophy and objectives of cooperatives, (d) problems of organization and management, (e) state and federal laws relating to cooperatives, (f) methods of financing cooperatives, and (g) other economic and business problems of cooperatives.
>
> **C** *Extension Education:* The Cooperative Extension Service provides information relating to cooperatives for people outside the classroom as part of its regular program of educational activities. Its aims in such education are similar to those of resident instruction—namely, to assist people in self-development; and to help people understand the nature, the organization and operation, and possibilities and limitations of cooperatives as integral parts of our predominantly free enterprise economy. Assistance is provided in collecting and interpreting data to help assay the economic feasibility of contemplated cooperative business ventures, including the consideration of alternatives. For existing cooperatives, information and counsel are provided in dealing with specific organization and management problems. Systematic approaches to the use of modern management techniques and practices in cooperatives as well as in other agricultural businesses have, in recent years, become increasingly important in the educational effort of the Cooperative Extension Service.

It is the policy of the College of Agriculture to include work in agricultural cooperatives as a significant part of a comprehensive program of research, teaching and extension education. The College is cognizant of the declining numbers of farms and of their increasing size. It also is mindful, however, of the relatively small size of the individual farm enterprise as part of the total agribusiness complex, and of the disadvantage of the individual farmer in an increasingly complex economy when acting alone in selling farm products or when purchasing supplies and services. While serving all forms of agriculturally related businesses, the College recognizes that the modern cooperative association is consistent with the traditional desires of people to solve problems through self-help using modern corporate organization and business practices.

California

California was noted for the especially strong cooperative program that was developed by its State Department of Markets in 1915. Under the leadership of Harris Weinstock, who was selected to head the Department, programs were developed for groups of farmers desiring to organize cooperatives. Weinstock stumped the state, speaking to and encouraging interested groups to set up cooperatives. Shortly after assuming his position, he hired Aaron Sapiro to serve as secretary and legal counsel. Between them, the commodity marketing concept developed, and California became one of the leading states in the development of agricultural marketing cooperatives. Much of this progress was due to Weinstock's contributions. He took a rather dictatorial stand on many questions, however. Lacking necessary support from the cooperative organizations, the Department of Markets was discontinued as a special agency in the 1920s and became a part of the State Department of Agriculture.

At the University of California, Prof. Henry E. Erdman, one of the early pioneers in cooperative teaching and research, made a significant contribution to cooperatives when he authored the publication *Possibilities and Limitations of Cooperative Marketing*.[9]

Activities of Other States

The Status of Cooperative Teaching In 1973, Prof. Charles Ingram of Ohio State University conducted a survey for the American Institute of Cooperation to determine the nature and extent of cooperative teaching at land-grant universities. It found that twenty-one universities offered courses in agricultural cooperation on a yearly or every-other-year basis. A number of universities also reported that selected subjects in cooperation were covered in commodity marketing and general economics courses.

In addition, some of the universities, through their extension programs, either offer or participate in specialized cooperative courses, workshops, or seminars for managers, directors, and agricultural leaders. Participating agencies in these courses often include the Farmer Cooperative Service and other agencies of the federal government, banks for cooperatives, cooperatives themselves, and the national cooperative organizations. More recently, a number of vocational schools have initiated courses that deal with the subject of cooperation either in whole or in part.

Assistance in Forming Cooperatives In many states, the early efforts of county agents made substantial contributions to the organization of cooperatives. Often, they called meetings of interested farmers, brought in specialists, helped to evaluate the feasibility of proposed cooperative ventures, and provided general advice on organization and operating problems. In some instances, their efforts were backed up by the research of their agricultural experiment stations.

---

[9]H. E. Erdman, *Possibilities and Limitations of Cooperative Marketing,* Circular 298, University of California, Berkeley, 1925 (rev. 1942), p. 19.

State Departments of Agriculture   In Chapter 11, we indicated that many state departments of agriculture were required by state law to provide technical assistance for cooperatives. These services covered participation as members of boards of directors, making feasibility studies, and providing advisory assistance.

Cooperative Month   Recognition of October as "Cooperative Month" has the support of state and national agencies and national cooperative organizations. It began on a national basis in 1964. Before that, some states, chiefly in the upper Midwest, had been observing October as "Cooperative Month" on their own. Wisconsin and Minnesota were the first states officially to hold an October "Cooperative Month" in the 1930s.

A majority of the states now have official committees directing and coordinating their efforts through the National Cooperative Month Planning Committee in Washington, D.C. The purpose of the observance is to provde a set period each year for a concerted effort to get a better understanding of what cooperatives are and how they operate to benefit members and the public.

The activities of the state committees include Governors' proclamations, special meetings and other events, educational activities with schools and universities, and arrangements for coverage in news media and on area radio and TV stations.

The National Committee—made up of federal agencies and representatives of eleven national cooperative organizations working with cooperatives—decides on a theme and symbol and provides informational and educational material to the state governments and the media. The National Committee presents national awards to outstanding leaders in cooperative work, and issues news releases and kits containing suggested advertisements, posters, feature stories, fact sheets, and other materials.

UNFAVORABLE GOVERNMENT ACTION

Congressional Conflicts

Not all government action has been favorable to cooperatives. Over the years, Congress has become more and more a battleground as the forces seeking legislation harmful to cooperatives have grown more active. In Chapters 10 and 11, we have identified specific examples of unfavorable government action on the part of both Congress and regulatory agencies as it concerns the areas of antitrust and income taxes.

A further indication of the problems confronting cooperatives at the hands of Congress, as they seek to adjust operations to a changing agriculture, is shown in the budget testimony of the Farmer Cooperative Service of the U.S. Department of Agriculture. In a discussion about cooperatives engaged in the refining of petroleum products, the late Senator Allan J. Ellender of Louisiana, of the Senate Sub-Committee on Appropriations for the Department of Agriculture and Related Agencies and representing a state with strong petroleum interests, stated: "There are complaints made that the cooperatives are going just a little too far. For instance, I had some mail showing that cooperatives went so far as to own their own oil fields, crack their own grease, and things of that nature."

Just what is "too far?" It seems obvious that an integrated petroleum service, geared to the needs of members, is exactly what a responsive cooperative would seek to provide. When cooperatives were first organized, farm power was largely provided by horses and mules and, on even more occasions than farm workers like to recall, by human muscle. Such "animal power" is in contrast with mechanized agriculture, which is dependent upon petroleum products, tractors, and electricity for its power needs. To restrict cooperatives from serving farmers by keeping them out of the petroleum business is as unrealistic as it would have been to keep them from handling oats and hay in the days of "old Dobbin."

As farmers adjusted to changing agricultural conditions, they were not content to continue to restrict the operation of their cooperatives to meeting their needs as they existed in the 1920s. Their response, for example, led to the establishment of the cooperative farm credit system and rural electric and telephone cooperatives.

As late as 1969, a member of Congress suggested at a meeting of cooperative leaders that farmer cooperatives would be less controversial and would get into less trouble if they would confine their operations to the marketing of farm products. Such a view ignores the fact that farmers answered this objection more than forty years ago when they set up regional farm supply cooperatives, and now over 5,600 of the 7,800 farmer marketing and purchasing cooperatives handle farm supplies. What is more, purchasing cooperatives have as many members as do marketing cooperatives. In essence, such backward statements say: If you are not doing the job that needs to be done, and if you don't have a significant market power in the interests of members, you may not get into much trouble.

These examples of areas of conflict serve only to emphasize the constant need of cooperative leaders to be alert to the legislative activities of Congress and the impact of proposed legislation on the operations and status of cooperatives.

Agency Conflicts

Views on the attitudes of various U.S. government agencies toward cooperatives differ widely. For example, in commenting on the attitude of the U.S. Treasury Department toward legislation relating to cooperative refunds and the return of patronage dividends that was proposed last in 1969, Kenneth D. Naden, then executive vice president of the National Council of Farmer Cooperatives, in the opening session of the forty-first annual meeting of the Association in January 1970, stated: "We found that influential persons in the Treasury are distinctly hostile to cooperative development and were willing to support the NTEA (National Tax Equality Association) ideas. The Secretary of the Treasury ignored the responsibility of the Secretary of Agriculture and the significance of these measures (proposed tax legislation) on sound farm policy."

A more recent illustration of conflicts in the philosophy of government agencies is found in a September 30, 1975, publication by the Federal Trade Commission, "A Report on Agricultural Cooperatives." Although it reached the general conclusion that "marketing cooperatives do not possess inordinate market power and are often completely overshadowed by corporations," the report stated that cooperatives dominate the milk and fruit and nut industries. The tone of the report is typical of that of poorly informed government agencies that use a static approach while attempting to deal with an institution as dynamic as cooperatives. Although published by the Federal Trade Commission it carries the astonishing disclaimer: "The remarks in this statement represent only the views of members of the Federal Trade Commission's staff. They are not intended to be or should not be construed as representative of an official Commission policy."

The report prompted Kenneth D. Naden, president of the National Council of Farmer Cooperatives, to write Lewis Engman, Chairman of the Federal Trade Commission, as follows (in part):

> After a careful study of the Federal Trade Commission staff report on agricultural cooperatives issued September 30, we regret to conclude that it does not achieve its announced objective of "contributing to an understanding of the issues related to agricultural cooperatives." Because of the bias and preconceived conclusions of the authors, it shows a fundamental lack of insight and knowledge of farm price formation, marketing costs and margins, and market power as it is used in the food industry. In its effort to boost the importance of the Federal Trade Commission in antitrust matters, it impugns the integrity of another government agency with statutory responsibility in this field.

Over the years, the Departments of Justice and Agriculture have exhibited basic differences on proposed antitrust legislation that would facilitate the merger of cooperatives and strengthen their bargaining power, as we have noted in Chapter 10.

The Justice Department has argued from time to time that such consolidations, when resulting from the merger of cooperatives and other types of business, might serve to limit competition and thus to increase prices.

Responsible Department of Agriculture representatives, in contrast, have emphasized that since cooperatives constitute a comparatively small proportion of the total business of most segments of agriculture, it is only through merger and consolidation that these organizations can strengthen their economic power so as to improve the competitive position of farmers. In effect, they have suggested that it is largely in this way that farmers can hope to achieve the countervailing power needed to bargain effectively with other segments of the industry.

Furthermore, agricultural representatives point out that there is no basis for fearing that large farm supply cooperatives have an interest in enhancing prices and exploiting their own members. The major objective of these cooperatives is to obtain production supplies at the lowest possible cost for members, and it would be the height of folly for them to try to exploit their own members by increasing prices, since all net margins must be returned to members anyway.

During the past few years, the Interstate Commerce Commission, through legal action and proposed legislation, has sought limitations on granting agricultural cooperatives exemptions from economic regulation of interstate trucking. On the other hand, the Department of Agriculture has opposed the restrictive provisions of this proposed legislation on the ground that they would adversely affect the public interest through limitations on the operating efficiency of the cooperatives concerned.

Wide variations in policy views also prevail among the independent agencies. For example, the Small Business Administration has made very few loans to cooperatives, even though its legal staff has pointed out that the "nonprofit status" of a cooperative need not be a restrictive factor in making such loans since members expect to increase their profits by belonging to a cooperative.

A review of state legislative activities and agency programs brings into focus much the same situation with respect to the initiation of actions both favorable and detrimental to cooperatives.

Political Action by Cooperatives

Cooperatives, as an important part of the nation's economy, are influenced by legislation and regulatory actions on both the federal and the state levels. During the 1920s and before, they had the protection of the farm bloc, which was a potent political force. In fact, it was described as being able to achieve for agriculture everything that was reasonable in the way of political objectives, and a good deal that was not. With important economic changes occurring in agriculture, particularly the relative decline in the total farm population since World War II coupled with the resulting marked drop in farm numbers, the farm bloc largely disintegrated and was no longer a political power to reckon with. What is more, the various general farm organizations were accused of speaking with a "babble of tongues" that frequently rang out in all directions. As a consequence, cooperatives became more and more aware of the influence of their own political action as a means of achieving their objectives.

In actual practice, cooperatives have discovered that various laws and regulations are important in determining what they can and cannot do to serve members. Sometimes these edicts have a life-and-death impact to their operations. Moreover, legislation and regulations are subject to change from day to day and year to year. This instability suggests the need for cooperatives to be constantly alert to the impact that new or amended laws and regulations can have on their operations if they want either to prevent detrimental actions or to achieve favorable ones. The problem of oil shortages and allocations that has grown with the 1972–1973 energy crunch is only a very recent manifestation of this need for alertness.

Cooperatives have learned from experience that they do not get favorable legislation or regulations because they deserve them. While it helps to have meritorious and reasonable objectives on their side, it is becoming more and more obvious that they need to supplement this with what they term "acceptability and political influence." From the standpoint of agriculture, this situation is brought into sharp focus by the fact that our agricultural population now constitutes only about 5 percent of the total population. Obviously, therefore, a favorable political action in the interest of cooperatives can be achieved only by working with allies—any group with whom they have mutual interests on any given issue.

To deal with problems growing out of the decline in farm population, national cooperative associations and some regionals, as well as the state councils of cooperatives, are active in lobbying on both national and state levels. The success of their efforts depends on their ability to influence legislation and regulatory agencies. Experience has demonstrated that they can best achieve success by getting to know legislators and their staffs, as well as administrators of government agencies. To be most effective, too, the requests of cooperatives must be reasonable, and they must share mutual interests with other groups in the economy.

Since it is impossible for legislators and regulatory agencies to have pertinent facts and information on all the issues that confront them, cooperatives have discovered that they can give invaluable assistance to legislators by providing them with timely and factual information on such subjects. Naturally, they must demonstrate a reputation for integrity in providing such information and have the political "savvy" to make it available at a strategic time.

A practical question arises as to just what lobbying procedures are acceptable and effective. Cooperatives suggest the following steps as being among the most productive techniques for building mutually advantageous relationships with either legislators or agency administrators with whom they have dealings:

- Establish personal contacts with members of Congress and administrators and their staffs. This is especially important when senators and representatives are elected or administrators selected.
- Put various senators, representatives, and government administrators on mailing lists for newsletters and releases that relate to matters of interest to cooperatives. These materials should be of special interest to legislators because cooperatives are among their legitimate constituents. Moreover, such documents can be highly useful in providing needed information for administrators of government agencies.
- Maintain files which provide information on the voting records of legislators and the decisions of administrators on specific matters of interest to cooperatives.
- Conduct legislative rallies. This step involves bringing legislative representatives together and acquainting them with legitimate cooperative interests. Such contacts can also help to establish personal relationships and contribute more to their understanding of cooperative problems.
- Encourage constituents to call on their congressional representatives whenever issues of importance to cooperatives are being considered. Experience has shown that it is most helpful for members of Congress to have a firsthand knowledge of what the thinking is at the grass roots.
- Conduct legislative workshops for cooperative officials and representatives to teach them effective techniques for presenting their case to legislators and government administrators.
- Whenever possible, arrange for legislators and administrators to speak at cooperative meetings. This suggestion applies both to those who are friendly and to those who are not. The opportunity to give them a platform upon which to express their views is often appreciated. When their appearances are handled properly, they provide a means by which cooperatives can evaluate congressional performance. They also help to develop mutual understanding and respect for the problems of both the cooperatives and the legislators whom they legitimately wish to influence.

Recently the question of the desirability of making monetary contributions to political candidates by groups or organizations sponsored by cooperatives has come to the forefront. Cooperatives, like any other corporation, are not permitted by law to donate money to political parties or candidates. However, many national cooperative organizations, as well as some of the larger regionals, have encouraged the formation of groups to carry out political action programs, including the making of contributions. In general, funds are solicited from individual members of cooperatives and support is given by political action committees to those candidates who are sympathetic to the goals and objectives of the cooperatives concerned and who are effective because of their strategic position on key congressional committees. Examples of political action by cooperatives are:

- The National Council of Farmer Cooperatives reports that it supports PACE (Political Action for Cooperative Effectiveness).
- The National Rural Electric Cooperative Association has assisted in the formation of ACRE (Action Committee for Rural Electrification).
- The Credit Union National Association has encouraged similar action through CULAC (Credit Union Legislative Affairs Committee).

Such action brings into focus a number of basic questions and issues as yet unresolved from the standpoint of cooperative associations. They are:

- Are political activities such as those listed above a means of merely helping elected friends, or do they have the sinister implication of "buying" or attempting to "buy" a member of Congress? The notorious Watergate and related scandals in which a few dairy cooperatives were involved have brought this issue into the spotlight.
- The unique and special nature of a cooperative raises definite questions in this respect. Cooperatives frequently pride themselves on being pacesetters not only in economic matters but also on ethical issues. Even though "others may do it," do they wish to "run with the pack" by participating in what some consider to be unsavory political actions, or should they be in the front rank to support and encourage political reform in contributions?
- Moreover, even on the assumption that political fund raising is desirable and legitimate in every respect and has no ethical implications, the question still prevails: Is it a game that cooperatives can afford to play? Certainly, even the larger cooperatives, when compared with the huge oil companies and other industrial giants in the United States, are relatively small business. At most, can they ever hope to come out other than second-best by seeking to influence legislators by encouraging political contributions?
- Another question relates to the reaction of members to such ventures. Taken by and large, farmer members of cooperatives usually are quite evenly divided between the two major political parties. While the political action agencies sponsored and supported by cooperatives are separate and distinct organizations, nevertheless, close and not entirely clear relationships appear to exist between them and cooperatives. Sometimes individuals have worked for both a cooperative and the political action group it has sponsored. Quite obviously, under the circumstances, farmers might have reservations about efforts to funnel financial resources to one or the other of the political parties or the individual candidates running for office. For these reasons, some national cooperative associations have concluded that they should not seek to compete with other organizations in making financial contributions to political parties or candidates. They state that, even if they could make comparable political contributions, they believe they can be much more effective by "providing ideas rather than dollars."
- While the various political action groups sponsored by some cooperatives report a very high level of success in their support of winning candidates, it also is true that in some cases they became known as contributors to the opposition. A moot

question then arises as to the reaction of candidates under the circumstances. Successful ones may be vindictive if the political action group has made contributions to their opponent. Of course such an experience may convince some candidates that they might well seek to curry favor with the contributor. As a result, they may undertake to "change their spots" by trying to develop a favorable image with a group that they consider to represent important constituents.

Government-Cooperative Relationships in Developing Countries

In the United States, the Humphrey amendment to the Foreign Assistance Act of 1971 provided assistance to cooperatives in developing nations. The act specifically declared it was "the policy of the United States to encourage the development of cooperatives, credit unions, and savings and loan associations." With its enactment, the promotion of cooperative knowledge and practices was recognized as an important way to help people achieve social and economic progress through cooperative self-help efforts.

To achieve these objectives, technicians were provided for programs of cooperative-to-cooperative assistance. Advisors were assigned to assist officials, government departments, and other agencies to develop their cooperative programs. We have observed that AID, with cooperative assistance, sponsored and supported the International Cooperative Training Center at the University of Wisconsin in Madison. The Center complemented the cooperative training programs and seminars conducted in the developing countries.

In varying degrees, somewhat similar programs have been undertaken by other developed countries, particularly Great Britain, Denmark, Norway, Sweden, Germany, France, and Israel.

In developing countries, a number of factors influence the working relationships between government and cooperatives. Experience has shown that the capability of leadership, the literacy level of members or potential members, and the employment of career program administrators and technicians—rather than using these positions to reward the politically faithful ones—are the important factors in determining the success of government programs for cooperatives in developing countries.

The importance of cooperatives in the economy of these countries was well recognized by one government official, who stated:

> Only the agricultural cooperatives are ready and in a position to hand back to producers the advantages of modern market economics. It goes without saying that a condition for this is that the cooperatives shall acquire as large a share as possible in the processing and marketing of farm products and in the supply of marketing requisites. . . .

Governments in developing countries often seek to encourage cooperative development through grants for the construction of facilities, for hiring personnel, and for conducting training programs. In turn, they may require that government officials serve on cooperative boards of directors.

There can be little objection to governments in developing countries that take these and similar steps to encourage their cooperatives. There is a justifiable objection, however, to the general idea of a government's looking upon cooperatives as instruments for maintaining and perpetuating any given government policy. Many times, cooperatives are organized and supervised by governments and no attempt is made to convert them into bona fide cooperatives that are owned and controlled by the members.

Governments, rather, should look upon cooperatives as vehicles for improving the economic position of citizens and as a training ground in educating them in the basic concepts of democracy. Henry Gerber, formerly FCS cooperative technician with the United States government's AID program in Brazil, expressed a desirable cooperative policy for governments in developing countries when he stated: "In the beginning the government should serve as a champion, later continue as a partner, and finally end up as a friend."

Governments can provide assistance to cooperatives in developing countries by:

- Enacting sound legislation to provide general guidelines for cooperative organization and development.
- Providing general support to facilitate effective operations, particularly licensing, inspection, and standards.
- Conducting research and supporting and encouraging extension programs, cooperative colleges, and other educational activities for the development of cooperative leadership.
- Assisting in the organization and early operation of cooperatives. This activity might include help in developing charters and bylaws, setting up accounting systems, providing financial assistance through the establishment of sound credit agencies, and making grants for needed facilities.
- Providing guidance in operating procedures, in selecting managers and other key employees, and in dveloping cooperative leadership.
- Providing auditing assistance. Such assistance not only can assure a businesslike keeping of records, but also can provide consultation to cooperatives in their operations and encouragement of education and training.

Except for more intensive assistance during formative periods when government officials and cooperative leaders were in a rather intensive training stage, such a program differs only a little from that developed in this country over the years on a trial-and-error basis.

COOPERATIVES AND GOVERNMENT POLICY: AN EVALUATION[10]

Government Policy Directions

A wide variety of views prevails as to the exact nature of United States government policy toward cooperatives. Some of these views are the following:

- Government is sometimes charged with supporting investor-owned business enterprise at the expense of cooperatives. Cooperative leaders, as a consequence, have

---

[10] The material in this section was orginally presented at the Fifth International Conference on Agricultural Cooperation, Oxford, England, 1973. See M. A. Abrahamsen, "The Role of Cooperatives in Implementing Government Policy," in *Yearbook of Agricultural Cooperation,* Basil Blackwell 1973, pp. 52–55.

believed at times that their interests have been ignored and that they have been subjected to various forms of anticooperative action.
- In practice, government may be a weak-kneed and ineffective bureaucracy. As far as cooperatives are concerned, it is afraid to stand up and be counted. What is more, one has only to look at the statements and pronouncements of agency leaders to see that various branches of government are often at cross purposes regarding cooperatives.
- A basic problem is that legislators and government administrators often lack the knowledge and understanding needed to make sound decisions regarding cooperatives. This limitation frequently results in poor decisions or indifference in dealing with problems of concern to cooperatives.
- Government at many times has been a friend and a legitimate supporter of cooperatives. Students of cooperation point out that when agricultural cooperative leaders agree as to the necessary and desirable action, an understanding government often enacts realistic legislation and government agencies generally provide far-reaching assistance.

Governmental Policies May Vary

Cooperatives must recognize and be alert to the fact that at any given time, government policy as to agriculture, labor, and industry may be favorable, neutral, or unfavorable. The same situation may apply to cooperatives. For example:

- Governmental policy may seek to encourage overall agricultural production or discourage it.
- Governmental price policy may be used as a tool to help achieve more or less production. In any event, it can readily result in one or the other of these possibilities.
- Legislation may be restrictive or supportive as it relates to trade, finance, grading, tariff, and related considerations.
- Government may create an environment that is encouraging or discouraging to business enterprise in general. Whatever the environment created, it may vary widely for the various business segments of the economy. The recognition given cooperatives can have an important bearing on how effectively cooperatives may serve as the representatives of agriculture.
- In actual practice, government may deliberately encourage or discourage cooperatives by measures that may help or hinder their effective operation and development.
- Government policy may be designed to keep people on the farm or to facilitate their moving off the farm.
- Depending upon a nation's stage of agricultural development, membership in an organization such as the European Common Market may be either helpful or harmful to either all of it or certain segments. For example, the objectives of increased agricultural productivity, stabilized markets which guarantee regular supplies, and a fair standard of living for the agricultural population identify areas of mutual interest for government and agricultural cooperatives. This fact explains why the European Economic Community looks with favor on well-organized cooperatives to facilitate its agricultural policy. Strong cooperatives can serve as the representatives of agriculture in effectively presenting their members' views to Common Market institutions. The member countries, in turn, have a stake in having strong cooperatives to act as their coordinating force in representing the agricultural interests of their farmers.

Mutuality of Interest as Basis for Sound Government Policy

Awareness of the possible directions that government policy can take as it relates to agriculture can have far-reaching implications for cooperatives. A fundamental question is: What is the degree of mutuality of interest that exists between cooperatives and government? It should be obvious, also, that the mutuality of interest that exists between cooperatives and the rest of the economy differs from country to country.

Cooperative development in Scandinavia, The Netherlands, and some other West European countries, serves as a case in point. The strong position achieved by cooperatives in these countries means that these organizations quite accurately reflect the interests of members. The cooperative leaders, in effect, are the leaders for all members. They belong to various boards and agencies and have an influential voice in the overall determination of national policy.

In those developing countries in which cooperatives have not achieved such a strategic position, conflicts of interest may occur between cooperatives and other segments of the agricultural economy. These conflicts may go further and involve agribusiness firms and general farm organizations. It is not unknown for the latter to attempt to manipulate and maneuver cooperatives to achieve aims and objectives that may not be those of cooperatives. Given a sympathetic and understanding government, the cooperative is generally recognized as the most effective institution through which national agricultural programs can be initiated.

When cooperatives have the support and encouragement of their government in achieving the objective of improving their members' income and thereby improving their economic and social well-being, there is every reason to believe that they can and should have an active role in implementing governmental policy. Cooperatives, however, need to be vigilant and never to fall into the trap of having to implement government policies that are not in the best interests of their members. If it is the policy of government to encourage its agriculture, one of the most realistic and effective ways to achieve this objective, quite obviously, is for the government to pursue a policy that is favorable to cooperatives and will serve to strengthen their position in the marketplace.

Policy Formation

Unless cooperatives actively participate in the formulation of national policy and are instrumental in the direction it may take, it is highly conceivable that policies of government can be detrimental to them. Government policies toward cooperatives may shift quite dramatically as political winds vary. Politically appointed administrators, for example, may be under pressure to take actions that will appear to help the fortunes of a political party, rather than to build strong and effective cooperative programs. Moreover, to keep their jobs, they may condescend to jump through political hoops for politicians rather than provide unbiased and professional assistance for the people their agencies are set up to serve. Such actions, for example, may be the result of changing economic conditions, or may be influenced by the desire of a political party in power to get more votes by temporarily juggling prices. Similarly, conflicts between political parties or changes in policy ideologies can put cooperatives in an untenable position if they have to condone policies that are not in their members' best interests.

Cooperatives should, and in most instances can, have an important role in implementing government policy when it is favorable to cooperatives. Such a role, however, does not just happen. Cooperatives need to demonstrate the ability to carry out the responsibilities involved. Those associations that advance the interests of members are likely to be the ones that (1) give due recognition to the need for building an effective educational program; (2) develop a sound financial structure; (3) draw on the research capabilities of federal and state governments, universities, and their own staffs; and (4) recognize the impact of technology on the operations of the members they serve.

If cooperatives are to be an influential tool in implementing agricultural policy, the following situations must prevail:

- Cooperatives must have a strong hand in formulating national policy.
- A high degree of mutuality of interests must exist between the objectives of cooperatives and the objectives of national policy as formulated by government.
- Government policy must be designed to build a strong economy and strong cooperatives—an economy in which cooperatives are able to withstand the impacts of economic, social, and political forces. This is an economy with a cooperative system that has developed leaders capable of taking the initiative in formulating policies that reflect the needs and interests of members. When these conditions prevail, government will find it advantageous to support and encourage the further development of cooperatives as the most effective way of implementing its national policies.

Cooperatives often have mutually advantageous ties with a competent and sympathetic government. Their objectives are much the same in that they both seek to serve members and constituents respectively. Cooperatives can also function as communication links between their members and government. They are often pacesetters and innovators of practices that are later formalized through legislation. Moreover, they serve as a training ground for directors and members in the theory and practice of democracy. As a consequence, they supply a large number of local state and national leaders. Cooperatives also provide the foundation for a team approach with government in dealing with national problems of mutual interest.

QUESTIONS

1. Identify some of the views of early cooperators relative to cooperative-government relations.
2. In what fields has the United States government supported and encouraged cooperatives?
3. Trace the development of U.S. government help to cooperatives in research, advisory assistance, and educational effort.
4. What were the contributions of the New Deal and the Great Society to cooperatives? What were the limitations of these efforts from the standpoint of cooperatives?
5. Are the policy statements of the U.S. Department of Agriculture and the land-grant colleges with respect to cooperatives desirable? What basic points should such statements include?
6. What form did early work with cooperatives at land-grant colleges take? Identify some of the universities that pioneered in cooperative work.
7. In what ways has United States government action been unfavorable to cooperatives?

8 Do you favor political action by cooperatives? If so, what form should it take? What problems have cooperatives encountered in their political action programs?
9 What noncontroversial actions can cooperatives take to develop mutually advantageous relationships with legislators?
10 Should governments in developed countries assist developing countries to establish cooperative programs?

REFERENCES

Abrahamsen, Martin A., and Claude L. Scroggs: *Agricultural Cooperation: Selected Readings,* University of Minnesota Press, Minneapolis, 1957, pp. 207–224.

Helm, Franz C.: *The Economics of Cooperative Enterprise,* The Cooperative College of Tanzania in association with the London Press, Ltd., London, 1968, pp. 232–238.

Knapp, Joseph G.: *The Rise of American Cooperative Enterprise, 1620–1920,* Interstate, Danville, Ill., 1969. See especially chaps. 6, 8, and 9.

———: *The Advance of American Cooperative Enterprise: 1920–1945,* Interstate, Danville, Ill., 1973. See especially chaps. 2, 6, 7, 8, and part 2, pp. 257–268.

McKay, Andrew W., and Martin A. Abrahamsen: *Helping Farmers Build Cooperatives—The Evolution of Farmer Cooperative Service,* FCS Circular 31, Farmer Cooperative Service, U.S. Department of Agriculture, Washington, June 1962, p. 82.

Parker, Florence E.: *The First 125 Years,* Cooperative Publishing Association, Superior, Wis., 1956, pp. 132–145.

Chapter 22

Limitations and Benefits

Many of the limitations and benefits of cooperatives are nurtured by roots that tap the same base. Cooperative personnel is an area that will serve as a case in point. When personnel is incompetent, there are pronounced boundaries on the ability of the cooperative to serve its members. On the other hand, when personnel is highly competent, members are able to realize substantial benefits from joining a cooperative.

How a cooperative conducts its communication program may also contribute to either limitations or benefits for its members. If communications are neglected, inaccurate, or poorly conducted, the cooperative may well experience marked restrictions in performance because of a lack of member, employee, and public support. But, when a communication program is effectively planned and conducted, members will know, for example, what their responsibilities and those of their cooperatives are. They also can be expected to have a realistic understanding of what their cooperative's objectives are and what it can and cannot accomplish for them.

Although many cooperative leaders are noted for a high degree of social consciousness and a willingness to act in the public interest, most cooperative members are quite pragmatic. They are likely to consider limitations and benefits in terms of what their cooperative "is doing for them now" or what it offers promise of doing in the immediate future. Thus, the time, the effort, and the financial resources involved in launching and operating a cooperative seem justified to them only when benefits promise to be real and substantial.

LIMITATIONS

In considering the limitations of cooperatives, one should be aware that these associations do not operate in a vacuum. They are subject to many of the same economic forces, laws, and human relationships that may contribute to failure in other types of business venture. Consequently, the extent of their limitations may be determined largely by whether their leaders understand the economic, social, and political environments in which cooperatives find themselves and how effectively they can operate within these environments. Let us now examine some of the more common limitations attributed to cooperatives. Some of them relate to broad, philosophical views that have prevailed over time; others may result from specific objectives that are stated in a cooperative's bylaws.

Cannot Control Production

Agricultural surpluses have been a chronic problem of commercial agriculture in the United States since the Civil War. These surpluses became particularly acute following recoveries from World Wars I and II, when the productive capacity of American agriculture was stepped up to supply food for war-ravaged countries.

We were aware, of course, that Thomas Robert Malthus's observation that population tends to outgrow food supply still applies to four-fifths of the world. Moreover, in the early days of the New Deal, we were told that one-third of our population was ill-fed. Notwithstanding the chronic hunger that stalked many areas of the world, the hungry had little purchasing power, and until recently, governments and relief agencies did little about their plight. The American farmer, therefore, was confronted with mounting surpluses in the marketplace. It was only after the economic gyrations of the early 1970s that the situation began to change drastically. For the first time, people in the United States became aware that, in the not-too-distant future, the possibility of food shortages for many products was increasingly real.

To return to a consideration of agricultural surpluses: Cooperatives have learned through bitter experience that they cannot control production to any substantial degree. The commodity marketing era of the 1920s that was ushered in by Aaron Sapiro, and the experiences of the Federal Farm Board a decade later, remind us that cooperatives are not able to initiate effective production-control programs. In fact, even if cooperatives could succeed in temporarily controlling production, they have devised no practical, long-run way to keep members and nonmembers from increasing production and flooding markets.

It became ever more obvious that if production-control programs were to be initiated, they would require the willingness and encouragement of the federal government, with its power to allocate production, to offer incentives for restricting production and to secure compliance with such programs.

Even if cooperatives had demonstrated ability to control production, such action would probably be illegal (as we have noted in Chapter 11). The lettuce growers of California, for example, contracted with their cooperative to plow up lettuce in order to eliminate excess production. While definite court action did not occur because the contract they had entered into expired before a legal decision was reached, authorities were of the opinion that such action would have been interpreted as an illegal restraint of trade. This decision is somewhat inconsistent and ironic when viewed in the light of established industrial practices. General Motors, for example, which accounts for over half the nation's automobile production and which has a volume of business substantially greater than all cooperatives combined, can restrict its production whenever it chooses. It laid off thousands of workers when it reduced production in response to the impact of the energy crunch of 1973.

Unsuccessful Production of Agricultural Products

There are inherent difficulties when cooperatives attempt to engage in the production of agricultural items. If they own and operate farms, they, in effect, are competing directly with many of their members. Obvious conflicts of interest may then arise. Under such circumstances, for example, the cooperative would compete in the farm labor market. Moreover, especially during periods of surplus production, cooperative farming operations would have a depressing effect on prices farmers would receive. Also, when individual members pool their land and other farm resources under cooperative management, experience in the United States, Canada, and other nations usually has been far from satisfactory. Over the long run, farmers almost invariably have lost interest and incentive in such ventures.

Inability to Fix Prices

Aaron Sapiro believed that, because of cooperative influence, the time would come when farmers, rather than ask the merchants what prices they would pay for their crops, livestock, and livestock products, would tell the merchants what the prices would be. Experience has demonstrated, however, that the commodity marketing programs he promoted proved ineffective as a price-fixing force. The reason was that cooperatives were unable to control production. With no control over production, cooperatives quite obviously have little prospect of effectively controlling prices. This limitation becomes even more evident when we look at the other side of the coin and observe that, although cooperatives—through emphasis on improved production, better merchandising, and more effective bargaining—may influence the demand for the particular products they market, they generally have been unable to substantially influence the overall demand for agricultural products.

There is a tendency in some quarters to refer to a near-monopoly situation among some farm cooperatives, particularly as it relates to cranberries, citrus fruits, or, more recently, milk. This viewpoint, however, does not take into account the basically inelastic nature of most agricultural consumption and the fact that consumers usually have many food choices available to them. These choices may even result from substantial competition among cooperatives. Should prices for any of these products vary too much, consumers are quite free to substitute other products. More and more, it is recognized that cooperatives cannot raise the general price level, except modestly in local areas through reductions of margins, unless they operate in conjunction with market orders that permit control of production or marketing.

Inability to Eliminate the Market Intermediary Agent

Cooperative leaders now are aware that when essential marketing functions are performed, the appearance of a cooperative on the economic scene does not eliminate the performance of these functions. A cooperative, however, may effectively coordinate these functions, determine how and when they should be performed, and improve marketing efficiency. When the cooperative undertakes to perform these functions itself, therefore, it is in a position to realize for its members the net profits that formerly resulted when other marketing agencies performed them. Moreover, cooperatives may have considerable influence on market structure and where and how marketing functions are performed. They may have this power because of their impact on the number and size of firms in the marketplace, their ability to differentiate their products (say, Land O' Lakes butter, Ocean Spray cranberries, or Diamond walnuts), their provision of market information, and the integration of their operations so that they can perform additional marketing functions. In this way, while they do not eliminate the marketing functions performed, cooperatives may improve or change inefficient marketing practices and replace the various intermediary agents who perform them.

At the same time, cooperatives cannot do the impossible or the impractical in the marketplace. They cannot always market the surplus or the poor-quality products of members to advantage. They cannot be all things to all members.

Limited Cooperative Market Power

Often, cooperative associations are unable to deal effectively with other firms in the marketplace. This is particularly true of small-scale, local associations. Therefore, it is largely only when they merge with other cooperatives, work with other cooperatives in a federated association, or integrate horizontally and vertically that they have been able to demonstrate increased market power.

In this connection, it is well to look at the position of various types of cooperatives as it relates to market power. When marketing cooperatives handle the products that appeal to consumers and to industrial firms, their market power is determined by their ability to negotiate effectively for the price of these products.

Farm supply cooperatives are in a unique, but often misunderstood, position as to market power. People who are concerned that these cooperatives may charge exploitive prices because of a possible monopoly position will see little basis for such a belief if they will critically look at the cooperatives' economic strength and methods of operation. Being organizations of users of production supplies, under no circumstances would they have an interest in exploiting their members in the use of the services they provide. It would only be in their search for such raw materials as crude petroleum products, fertilizer ingredients, feed grains, and seeds, or in their negotiations with labor unions, that they might have any chance of exerting undue economic power. A realistic appraisal of such possibilities suggests that the opportunity for gaining an exploitive position in such negotiations is very remote indeed. In fact, the situation is likely to be reversed for most supply cooperatives because of their relatively weak bargaining position when negotiating with major suppliers for raw materials and with labor unions for wage rates. The same situation prevails for retail consumer cooperatives.

Service cooperatives are in much the same position as farm supply and consumer associations. They are organized to provide services to users. As a general rule, therefore, it is only when desired services are nonexistent or ineffectively provided that the conditions necessary for the organization of this type of cooperatives arise.

Obscuring Cooperative Benefits

As cooperatives become established and provide effective competition, operating margins of all firms serving an area generally tend to narrow. Current levels of market prices for farm products increase and prices for farm inputs tend to decrease. Moreover, to the extent that agricultural cooperatives achieve greater returns for members, production tends to rise and overall prices become lower. The result is that, in the long run, consumers, rather than producers, may be the ones who indirectly realize the most substantial benefits. Another problem confronting agricultural cooperatives is that to the extent that they are successful in building markets and increasing farm income, the added returns tend to be capitalized into higher land values. Thus, cooperatives frequently find that they are contributing to the well-being of nonmembers as well as members. When it does so, the cooperative holds an umbrella over the operations of nonmembers, even though they assume no financial or patronage responsibilities. This situation places a premium on innovativeness in the cooperative. It is only when the cooperative is continually alert to the opportunity to provide new and expanded services for members that it will be able to make noticeable contributions to their continued well-being.

Deviation from Principles May Limit Cooperative Services

Cooperatives often face situations that tend to limit their success as cooperative institutions. Members may become careless in exercising their responsibilities as owners and users of their association. Directors may fail to recognize how a cooperative differs from other business firms. Managers, in the interest of expediency, may abridge unduly the maintenance of basic cooperative objectives and principles. When these situations prevail, members lose control of their cooperatives and member, employee, and public relations programs usually are ignored. Operations are not geared to member needs and interests, and persons other than members more easily become the principal beneficiaries.

Frailties of Human Nature

We have mentioned that while we in the United States pride ourselves on our high level of business literacy, the fact is that, at times, cooperative members are surprisingly illiterate regarding cooperative business activities. Cooperative members and directors may be misinformed or, at best, have little realistic knowledge of how effectively their cooperative is operating or of what it can and cannot reasonably be expected to accomplish. Likewise, directors and managers at times have been derelict in their responsibilities and have demonstrated little understanding of the economic, social, and political forces that influence the operations of their cooperative.

Cooperate illiteracy also extends to the general public, legislators, and government officials who have regulatory responsibilities for cooperatives.

Another aspect of human frailty among cooperative officials manifests itself in the vicious and unwarranted competition among cooperatives that these organizations sometimes encourage. It makes no sense for cooperative members to compete among themselves. When cooperatives duplicate services in an effort to compete with one another, it is the members who pay the additional costs and who have to put up with the poorer services that usually result. If competition is desired, there is usually more than enough to go around between cooperatives and other business firms.

Specific Operational Limitations

Members We have already suggested that members may be careless cooperative citizens. Their failure to attend and participate in annual meetings, their inclination to use cooperatives as a means to bargain with other dealers or merchants, and their disinclination to assume financial responsibilities are but some of the bad traits that limit a cooperative's ability to develop fully the potentials of an effective cooperative system. At other times, the conservative nature and the inability to overcome inertia and add new services are factors that keep members from taking the actions necessary to keep their cooperative in tune with its responsibilities for serving them effectively in the years ahead. Often members lack the commitment necessary for success; particularly, they slight their obligations to patronize and otherwise support their cooperative.

Management In addition to member responsibilities for deciding basic management policies, the directors, manager, and key staff at times lack the competence necessary for efficient cooperative operation. In some instances, a high degree of provincialism exists. Under such circumstances, the manager may assume the responsibility for determining the type of business services to provide, the market channels to use, and the source of supplies and services to obtain, even though the cooperative is a member of a regional association it helped to set up to provide needed services. The manager's decisions may prevent the cooperative from developing well-rounded services for members. In other instances, there is a tendency toward extravagance. Other people's money is being used, and on many occasions directors and managers use the cooperative to construct facilities that, in effect, are monuments to themselves rather than facilities to operate a modern business efficiently.

Financial Resources Lack of understanding of the financial resources necessary to carry on cooperative business ventures has often kept some cooperatives from achieving their true potential. At other times, members have shirked their responsibilities for providing the capital needed to get operations underway on a sound basis. The tendency to "milk the association" of cash refunds rather than to plow them back into operations designed to build necessary facilities is a further example of financial irresponsibility. On some occasions, cooperative performance has been limited because of "pinch-penny" practices in connection with salaries for competent employees, reasonable fringe benefits, and the support of other activities needed to keep an association strong, growing, and understood by farmers and the public.

Limited Services Quite often, cooperatives that have started in a comparatively simple way continue to limit business activities to one commodity, or one service, or one area, although changing conditions favor a more diversified operation. These changes, for example, often require that marketing and distribution practices move in the direction of a "one-stop service" in order to serve members effectively. Under such circumstances, if the cooperative follows a stand-pat philosophy, it could discourage (1) the development of needed field service and advisory programs; (2) the undertaking of desirable processing and manufacturing functions; (3) the diversification of operations; and (4) the presentation of effective advertising and sales programs.

Farm supply cooperatives, for example, while handling such basic items as feed, seed, fertilizer, and petroleum products, do not always provide the wide range of additional services needed in modern farming. Some associations are not aware, or have been slow to recognize, that cooperatives may need to provide such elementary services as bulk delivery of feed, the testing of soil and the application of fertilizer, a well-rounded transportation system, storage facilities, farm building services, and realistic credit policies. In the same way, retail consumer cooperatives often have only limited operations because they resist adding such items as clothing, drugs, furniture, petroleum products, and hardware and appliances to traditional grocery lines.

Semipublic Status Cooperatives, because of their special and unique business character, often are looked upon as semipublic institutions. They have a responsibility to inform members and, for that matter, the public, about their operations. As a result, their business practices are subject to continual scrutiny for information that members should have and competitors may sometimes use to advantage. Much depends on how cooperatives deal with such situations. When they are handled with understanding and competence, cooperatives may be able to improve their image by emphasizing the distinct nature of their operations. Doing so requires building member confidence in their operations and acquainting the general public with the contributions they can make to community welfare.

BENEFITS

Possible benefits of cooperatives to members and others have been mentioned or specifically suggested throughout various chapters of this book. We have noted that benefits realized by some cooperatives may stem from situations that have proved to be limitations for other cooperatives. To the extent that cooperatives have been able to achieve their basic objectives, they have benefited their members. Cooperative benefits, therefore, are closely tied to their performance. Quite obviously, any opinion as to benefits is often quite subjective. For example, people can find either the limitations or benefits they wish when they examine the operations of nearly 8,000 farmers' marketing, purchasing, and related services cooperatives or nearly 30,000 credit unions.

When benefits are examined in further detail, we see that some of them are tangible, and some of them are intangible. Put in another way, some are direct, and some are indirect. Some are general in that they apply to all types of cooperatives, whereas others are specific in that they apply only to individual types of cooperatives. General benefits tend to be more intangible and indirect than specific benefits. Benefits, too, may be examined from the standpoint of their precise effects on those who are involved. They may be largely economic in nature or social and psychological. In any event, they tend to be quite interrelated, to overlap, and not to be mutually exclusive.

General Benefits

General benefits may relate to all types of cooperatives, or to impacts that cooperatives may have on the communities in which they operate. Here, we shall consider three general benefits as they relate to all types of cooperatives. They are (1) providing a yardstick for business operations, (2) improving business performance of individuals, and (3) introducing desirable competition. Benefits to communities are identified as educational contributions and the building of better communities.

Yardstick for Business Operations When cooperatives enter into business activities, they are able to obtain quite specifically industrywide information on the costs that are involved in conducting various business operations and in providing necessary related services. Such information is useful to members in ascertaining the nature and extent of business costs and in pinpointing the specific economic advantages that they may realize by belonging to a cooperative. Moreover, cooperatives, because of their greater willingness to make operating data available, provide guidelines for determining how effectively various businesses serve the general public. Such information can be extremely useful to the cooperatives, not only in checking on the efficiency of their operations, but also in developing their member and public relations programs. In addition, information of this kind can be useful to legislators and regulatory agencies in the formulation of policies relating to general business operations.

Aid to Business Performance of Individuals Individual farmers who are operating on their own are not in a good position to obtain the many services that cooperatives can provide. For example, the individual farmer usually lacks the volume and quality of products to develop a strong marketing system. Likewise, the members who buy farm supplies and consumer goods often are at a disadvantage when attempting to buy these items by themselves. These problems have special application to small and middle-sized farmers who have inherent difficulty in operating efficiently. Through their cooperatives, however, farmers can bring together large volumes of products; they can process, market, or buy items more efficiently; and they can better provide the necessary supplementary services they desire. Besides, cooperatives provide their members with substantial assistance on production and cultural practices. As a result, it is easier for small and medium-sized farmers to stay in business. Moreover, by combining their volume of business with that of the large farmers, they are helping to build a stronger cooperative to the mutual advantage of all.

Provider of Competition It is generally recognized that if the conditions of perfect competition should prevail in the marketplace, people would have little inclination to join a cooperative and become involved in the "sweat, toil, and tears" necessary to keep such an association going. We know from experience, however, that most markets for the goods and services that cooperatives provide are not perfectly competitive. Individual farmers or consumers are in highly atomized and fragmented positions when dealing with the strongly integrated conglomerates they encounter in the marketplace. These are the basic reasons why individuals need cooperatives that will help such members achieve at least a semblance of competition with other business firms.

The competition issue raises, too, the important but unanswered question: What would be the situation in any given market if there were no cooperatives? While specific differences often would be difficult to determine, finding the answer does not take too much imagination or the reading of precooperative history. Cooperatives have catalogued numerous instances of how prices have advanced, say, 10 cents a bushel when they entered into the market or prices for feed and fertilizer have dropped as much as $5 to $10 a ton when they opened retail distribution points. It is a question that deserves to be kept in mind when members attempt to evaluate the competitive influence of cooperative business ventures.

The entrance of a cooperative business into a trade area benefits not only its members but also nonmembers. Cooperatives, by providing desirable competition, have often proved to be a salutary influence on the general tone of business activity. Thus, they make a very substantial contribution to the economic betterment of the entire area.

Community Benefits

The benefits of cooperatives extend beyond their members and patrons. Here, we examine how cooperatives may (1) serve as an educational force, (2) help build communities, and (3) benefit the general public.

Educational Force Cooperatives provide a great deal of information for members. They do so through house organs, audiovisual materials, and annual meetings. Information is supplied not only on the business operations of the cooperative but also on problems relating to business activities of members.

Members often participate in their cooperative as a family. To this end, cooperatives have developed programs that encourage and support youth activities. These programs lead to better understanding and appreciation of the cooperative system. Likewise, active women's programs have been developed. Women are important participants in the family decision-making process, and their understanding of how cooperatives work has proven highly beneficial to cooperatives.

Members, by participating in the making of business decisions, have found that it is necessary to obtain answers to basic questions confronting their cooperative. When they participate, they better understand how the economy operates and how critical social and political forces influence the operation of their cooperative business. What is more, most of the tens of thousands of directors of various types of cooperatives, because they must become acquainted with the forces that have a bearing on the business operations of their association, are much better informed community citizens.

Well-informed community citizens also serve to strengthen the democratic process. As a result of participation in cooperative activities, cooperative members have a better understanding of how to work together and how to approach community problems. By strengthening the democratic process in their communities, some 50,000 cooperatives of all kinds have a cumulative effect that is important in building a stronger nation.

Community Builders As citizens of a community, cooperatives are engaged in many activities that make contributions to the betterment of that community. One example is the contribution of Cenex, a major regional farm supply cooperative serving the Midwest and located in St. Paul, Minnesota.

In 1974, this organization gave $22,000 in scholarships to thirty-eight young men and women in the nine states in which it operates. These agribusiness vocational scholarships are awarded in the interest of expanding employment skills in rural America and to encourage and assist rural people in achieving these skills. Another example of Cenex's contributions to community development is its preparation of a manual, "What Plants Need to Grow to Feed You." This is a thirteen-lesson teaching tool for the fifth, sixth, and seventh grade science classes. Also, conscious of the energy crunch, Cenex has initiated a "Commute-a-Van" program to carry its employees to and from work. With twenty-five vans, the cooperative estimates that it has reduced the daily mileage driven from 1,925 to 364 miles, and thus has saved 166 gallons of gasoline daily.

Another example of community contributions, made by MFC Services, Jackson, Mississippi, was recognized by the Mississippi Vocational Agriculture Teachers Association. A plaque that was received by the Association in 1974 read:

> By doing things such as sponsoring judging contests, aiding our instructors and spreading the news about the educational opportunities we offer to adults and school children alike, they have helped our cause tremendously. Our cause is to produce modern and productive farmers and keep farmers abreast of new methods and innovations in agriculture.

The typical contributions of many local cooperatives to community development and improved economic well-being are illustrated by the following summary of highlights in the operations of one association.[1]

In 1914, a handful of farmers in the midwestern United States believed they could increase their income by marketing grain as a group rather than as individuals. They organized a cooperative.

Nearly 60 years later, this cooperative has 1,528 farmer owners. Annual volume of business of the cooperative exceeds $2.8 million. It has branches in three communities. Facilities include three grain elevators with a combined storage capacity of 2.7 million bushels, bulk petroleum, propane, and fertilizer storage plants, a farm supply store, a service station, and a lumber yard.

---

[1] Unpublished material prepared by Gene Ingalsbe, Director of Information, and J. Warren Mather, senior agricultural economist, Farmer Cooperative Service, U.S. Department of Agriculture.

Over the years as rural population has declined and some businesses have had to close, the cooperative has taken on new products and services to serve remaining farmers and rural residents.

The cooperative operates a furniture, carpet, and appliance store.

Custom services include grain drying, feed grinding, bulk fuel delivery, fertilizer application and pesticide spraying. Transport hauling of petroleum and fertilizer is done also for other cooperatives.

Members have nearly $1.6 million invested in their cooperative. In a recent typical year, they received 4.3 cents a bushel more for their grain than they would have received without the cooperative. By purchasing farm supplies through the cooperative, they lowered their costs 20 percent on propane, 12 percent on feed and general supplies, 9 percent on lumber, and 10 percent on service station fuel and merchandising.

These lower costs for supplies and higher prices for products amount to more than $300,000 in additional income to the cooperative's members each year. Part of this income can be attributed to the cooperative's ownership with hundreds of similar associations of regional farm supply and marketing cooperatives. The regional supply cooperative, for example, returns savings made from the basic refining of petroleum products and manufacturing of feed, fertilizer, and many farm supplies.

Members use this additional income to support their farming operations, to continue financing their cooperative, and to support the government through taxes. Of the total net saving of more than $300,000, about $38,000 was paid as dividends or interest on capital, $51,000 was retained in capital reserves, $45,000 was paid in income taxes, and $179,000 was allocated to members as a patronage refund.

The cooperative pours many dollars into the community in other ways. Each year, it pays employee salaries of $200,000, real estate and property taxes of $30,000, telephone, light, water and fuel service of $20,000, and insurance coverage of $10,000.

Public Benefactors In addition to helping to improve the welfare of farmers, cooperatives generally operate in the national interest by benefiting many segments of the general public. They are dependable users of many types of goods and services and they provide employment for many people. They also benefit consumers by providing a steady, dependable source of food and fiber; developing new products; supplying the kinds and quality of food desired; and striving for low-cost procurement and distribution systems.

Cooperatives also have benefited people in other lands by exporting products and knowledge. We have said that American cooperatives have helped train and send technicians overseas to organize cooperatives and build plants. Moreover, cooperatives have provided practical on-the-job training in the United States for many employees and leaders of foreign cooperatives.

Specific Benefits of Marketing Cooperatives

The more specific benefits of cooperatives are here examined from the standpoint of contributions that different types of associations make to their members. These contributions, directly or indirectly, are largely economic in nature. Farmer cooperatives alone had net margins or savings of about $430 million in direct benefits to members in 1970. In addition, many marketing cooperatives operating on a pooling basis had sales proceeds which exceeded average local market prices to growers. Economic benefits realized by other types of cooperatives are less precise, but they too are important. Many of these benefits, such as effects on prices, margins, and competition, while quite intangible and difficult to mesasure, may be even more significant than the tangible or direct benefits.

Increase in Member Income Marketing cooperatives, by performing a number of marketing functions and by introducing efficiencies in the performance of these functions, add substantially to the net income of their members. To the extent that these cooperatives undertake to process their members' products, transport and store products, and conduct joint sales efforts such as those of American Cotton Growers, Lubbock, Texas, they are expanding their market operations. Any resulting increase in net margins is passed on to their members.

Estimates by Farmer Cooperative Service put net margins distributed to members by cooperatives on marketing operations at about $187 million, or 1.3 percent of sales, in 1970. They no doubt have increased substantially since that time. Such an increase in annual income adds appreciably to the economic well-being of members of these cooperatives. In addition, the indirect economic benefits resulting from the increased competition provided by cooperatives, although impossible to measure, extend to all participants in the market.

Integration of Member-controlled Marketing System Cooperatives, by performing a wide range of functions, are instrumental in developing a marketing system that, under unified management, helps to move farm products from the point of production through market channels and on toward the consumers who use them. Such a coordinated approach contributes to increased marketing efficiency and to production of items of a quality that meets the needs of purchasers of foods and fibers more adequately than is usually possible through individual production. Marketing cooperatives, because they help to assemble farm products and in many instances process these products in substantial volume, are able to meet the growing needs of large-scale buyers and to maintain or expand existing markets or develop new ones that frequently would not be available to their members if they marketed their products as individuals. These new markets may be either domestic or foreign, and to the extent that they can be developed, they add appreciably to the ability of cooperatives to provide members with integrated food-production and distribution services.

Improvement in Quality of Production Because cooperative managers are more conversant than their individual members with the needs and desires of markets and the consumers they serve, they are better equipped than individuals acting alone to improve production practices. They make these improvements by coordinating their marketing operations with cooperative purchasing, either through purchasing departments within the cooperative or through independent purchasing cooperatives. In this way, they assure members of the quality and grades of supplies needed for efficient production. These efforts are supplemented with services of special field-force staffs who can advise members as to cultural and production practices needed to enable them to provide the products the market demands.

Influence on Volume of Production We have pointed out that cooperatives lack the ability to limit production during periods of critical agricultural surpluses. In an environment in which emphasis is on increased production, however, cooperatives may find themselves more at home. Among the many things that they can do to help members to expand production or to improve quality production, cooperatives can encourage members to improve cultural practices and livestock management programs. They also can alert their members to basic changes in market requirements, and they can help them in taking the steps needed to adjust to these changes.

Introduction of Realistic Grades and Standards Cooperatives have been in the forefront in introducing realistic grades and standards. Their leadership has benefited not only their members by differentiating their products but also the general public by improving the quality of food that goes to market. In this way, cooperatives have helped to stabilize markets and have increased their members income. At the same time, they have enabled consumers to obtain products of a given quality with greater assurances that such products will be available over a period of time.

Specific Benefits of Purchasing (Farm Supply) Cooperatives

In our discussion of the objectives of purchasing cooperatives, we have identified savings, improved quality, and better services as basic reasons for their organization. Let us explore these benefits a little more fully.

Substantial Savings Records provided to Farmer Cooperative Service show that purchasing cooperatives in the United States had net savings of about $243 million, or 6.5 percent, on farm supply sales in 1970. For 1972–1973, Farmer Cooperative Service reported that farm supply net margins of nineteen major regional cooperatives were 3.8 percent of sales (see *Major Regional Cooperative Supply Associations*, FCS Research Report 29, U.S. Department of Agriculture). Over the past decade, these net margins have ranged from 3 percent to 5 percent. Farmer Cooperative Service also reported that from the time of their organization through their 1972–1973 fiscal years, nine major regional supply cooperatives had net margins before income taxes of $1.4 billion. Included in these net margins were $350 million reported by Agway, Inc., Syracuse, New York, and $333 million by Farmland Industries, Inc., Kansas City, Missouri.

Also, members realize additional savings from the operation of the local retail farm supply associations. These combined savings are largely achieved through integration of business operations. We have described the fertilizer programs of purchasing cooperatives as a "mine-to-field operation." In this operation, the cooperatives not only mine the raw fertilizer ingredients but also process them, test their members' soil, and then, on a "prescription" basis, apply to their members' fields just the kinds of fertilizer needed in the amounts desired. Likewise, a substantial degree of integration exists in the milling of feeds, refining of petroleum products, and the production of seeds. Supply-purchasing cooperatives, through research farms, test feed ingredients and formulas, produce improved strains of seeds, and test many types of facilities and equipment.

Higher-Quality Products Cooperatives have been leaders in providing high-quality products that best meet the needs of their members. It is well known, for example, that in their early years of operation, cooperatives made important contributions by pioneering in the manufacture of open-formula feeds and by eliminating sand from fertilizer. The result was that cooperatives were able to significantly increase the plant food (N.P.K.) per ton of fertilizer. Cooperatives have emphasized the provision of adapted seeds of high germination and viability that are free of diseases and noxious weeds. Cooperatives have also utilized farmer's advisory panels and agricultural engineering departments to develop specifications for supplies and equipment that best meet the needs of farmers.

Dependable Services and Assured Sources of Supply Cooperatives have frequently benefited members by providing them with dependable services not otherwise readily available and with assured sources of supply. We have mentioned that farmers, through their own cooperative fertilizer-manufacturing plants, were assured of a more dependable source of supply at the very time that the prevailing price structure enabled other firms to increase profits by selling fertilizer abroad. Through bulk delivery of feed and petroleum products, farmers have benefited substantially. Farm supply cooperatives provide many related services that are important to farmers but make little margin for the cooperative. These services include, among others, erection of farm buildings; custom painting, spraying, and dusting; tractor tire repairs; and machinery repair and servicing. In this way, cooperatives provide services that save their members time and money and are not always otherwise readily available.

Benefits of Consumer Retail Cooperatives

Retail consumer cooperatives have contributed to the economic well-being of their members by lowering costs, emphasizing quality products and best buys, and providing assurances of dependable sources of supply. In addition, they have introduced such innovations as unit pricing and modern retail techniques. There is general agreement that while consumer cooperatives do not realize as spectacular savings as those realized by farm supply cooperatives, the attention they give to handling products of the quality suited to the needs of members and the advice and assistance they provide in the use of these products are important contributions to the economic well-being of members.

Moreover, Jerry Voorhis[2] mentions that in addition to expanding its retail operations, the Consumers Cooperative at Eau Claire, Wisconsin, provides credit union, check-cashing, and utility-bill-paying services for members.

Benefits of Service Cooperatives

Service cooperatives have provided many benefits for members. Often, they have made services available where none previously existed. Frequently, they can do so because cooperative emphasis on providing services for members does not require meeting business goals that may keep profit-oriented firms from attempting to serve

[2]*Cooperative Enterprise,* Interstate, Danville, Ill., 1975.

many communities with limited volume potential. In other instances, cooperatives have supplied the competition necessary to improve existing services or to offer additional ones. Voorhis also mentions that the Ferndale Cooperative Credit Union, Ferndale, Michigan, in response to soaring housing costs, has developed its own home improvement program. It has hired its own craftworkers and opened a showroom. "New rooms are added to homes, new, modern kitchens installed, new insulation provided, garages built, new heating systems installed, all at costs considerably below what they would otherwise be." Ferndale has also established a travel-service department and plans tours for its members. Voorhis further points out that, as a benefit to policyholders rather than as a means of making money for itself, Nationwide Insurance Company is a supporter of no-fault insurance, and that the Twin Pines Savings and Loan Association, Twin Pines, California, besides financial services, provides a prepaid legal service.

SUMMARY

The limitations and benefits of cooperatives may stem from the same situations. The many factors which contribute to good or poor cooperative performance will determine limitations or benefits that prevail for members. Cooperative limitations include inability to control production, to determine or fix prices, or to eliminate functions performed by market middlemen; limited market power; a tendency for benefits to become obscure; deviation from cooperative principles; the special vulnerability of cooperatives, people-oriented as they are, to the frailties of human nature; and operational failure traceable to shortcomings of members, directors, and employees.

In contrast, good performance can result in pronounced benefits by cooperatives. Some of these benefits are general and apply to all types of cooperatives. They include providing a yardstick for business operations; improving the business performance of individuals; providing desirable competition; functioning as an important educational force; and building stronger communities.

Direct benefits are usually economic in nature. They apply to marketing, farm supply, consumer retail, and service cooperatives. The benefits of belonging to these associations center on increased income for members, higher prices for products or services sold, or lower costs for goods and services purchased. Also, benefits result because markets are expanded or developed, because new services are provided where none was previously available, and because existing services are improved and expanded.

QUESTIONS

1. What is meant by the statement: "Both the limitations and the benefits of cooperatives may be alloyed in the same situations?"
2. What are the principal limitations of cooperative business enterprise?
3. Why do cooperatives have difficulty in controlling production? In fixing prices?
4. What opportunities do cooperatives have for eliminating the intermediary agent?
5. Do you think that American cooperatives possess effective market power?

6 What is meant by the statement: "Cooperative benefits tend to become obscure?"
7 What operational limitations do cooperatives have?
8 Identify the different ways in which marketing, purchasing, consumer, and service cooperatives benefit members.
9 How can we distinguish between direct and indirect benefits of cooperatives?
10 What is meant by the educational contributions of cooperatives?
11 Balancing possible limitations and benefits of cooperatives, what is their future?
12 What criteria would you set up for cooperatives to achieve further significant growth?

REFERENCES

Abrahamsen, Martin A., and Claud L. Scroggs: *Agricultural Cooperation: Selected Readings,* The University of Minnesota Press, Minneapolis, 1957, pp. 421–542.

Erdman, Henry E.: *Possibilities and Limitations of Cooperative Marketing,* Circular 298, University of California, Agricultural Experiment Station, Berkeley, 1942.

Knapp, Joseph G.: "Are Cooperatives Good Business?" *Harvard Business Review,* January–February 1957.

———: *Farmers in Business,* American Institute of Cooperation, Washington, D.C., 1963, pp. 337–432.

———: *Can Cooperatives Meet the Challenge?* FCS Information 5, Farmer Cooperative Service, U.S. Department of Agriculture, Washington, 1966.

Knutson, Ronald D.: "Cooperative Strategies in Imperfectly Competitive Market Structures," *American Journal of Agricultural Economics,* December 1974, pp. 904–912.

Schaars, Marvin A.: *Cooperative Principles and Practices,* University of Wisconsin—Extension, Madison, 1973.

Chapter 23

Cooperative Opportunities

We have previously identified areas in which cooperative management, through good performance, can improve opportunities for providing the services their members desire. These opportunities include care in organization; special aspects of cooperative management; development of effective communications (including member and public relations); establishment of sound financial programs; and diligent attention to such activities as bargaining, pooling, and mergers. Legal problems and government relations are other areas that require constant attention if cooperatives are to maximize opportunities for improved performance in the future.

There are, in addition, other areas where cooperatives have made only limited progress or at least are far from reaching their full potential. As cooperatives turn their efforts to ways to serve members more effectively, they may well benefit by giving special consideration to opportunities for improving their future performance. Depending upon the cooperative and how and where it operates, the number of such areas that might be identified are legion.

For example, among other existing opportunities are those of (1) obtaining a larger share of the market for many commodities in many communities; (2) developing more complete farm service centers, including arrangements for providing custom services; (3) merging or coordinating federated effort at local and regional levels; and (4) reaping benefits that result from long-range planning.

The recognition of the opportunities inherent in cooperative operation have been identified on a nonpartisan basis by our Presidents and other public figures (see Appendix B).

We shall here, however, consider four areas that offer substantial opportunities for many cooperatives to serve members better in the years ahead. They are: increased emphasis on economic integration, expansion of foreign trade, greater attention to research, and recognition of cooperatives as a tool for economic development.

INCREASED EMPHASIS ON ECONOMIC INTEGRATION

From time to time, we have mentioned economic integration as it relates to cooperatives. We have stated, too, that it is not a new concept for cooperatives. As early as the 1920s, for example, both Knapp and Black recognized the importance of integration as an economic process that might have special application to cooperatives. Moreover, in the 1950s and 1960s, increased emphasis on integration resulted from the far-reaching impact of changing economic conditions on how cooperatives might serve members. Prior to that time, the cooperative was viewed as the farmers-off-the-farm buying, selling, and service agency. Integration by cooperatives was considered largely a process by which these associations undertook to perform additional functions in marketing their members' products, or in providing them with the necessary production supplies for their farm operations.

It has become generally recognized, however, that for farmers and their agricultural cooperatives, integration might start with the production process and continue on through the performance of the various marketing functions and services. This chain of activities has been described by some cooperative leaders as providing "one-stop service." The implications of these developments for cooperatives and their members were subjects of much discussion. In the late 1950s too, Carroll Streeter, then the editor of the *Farm Journal,* in an article with the catchy title "Who is Going to Control Farming?" was successful in bringing into sharper focus the far-reaching implications of economic integration as it related to American agriculture.

In the 1970s, interest in the topic, while less dramatic, has continued. In Chapter 3 we mentioned that Ronald Knutson called attention to the role of integration in enabling farmers to compete more capably and to improve their economic situation.

Kinds of Integration

Before considering integration further, we should examine the different forms it has taken and how it relates to the marketing structure in which members and their cooperatives have found themselves. It will be helpful in bringing integration into proper perspective if we recognize that, irrespective of the type of integration taking place, the basic motivating force behind it is to add to the profits of the individual or the firm doing the integrating. To achieve these profits, it is necessary to maintain a greater degree of control over a wide range of production and market operations.

To the extent to which integrators produce their own products and package, transport, finance, store, and carry them on through wholesale and retail operations,

a Mechanical harvesting of Concord grapes at the vineyard of a member of Welch Foods, Inc. b Processing Welch grape juice for the retail trade at the North Pennsylvania plant of Welch Foods, Inc. Integrated activities of this cooperative start with the production of grapes on member farms and continue on through processing operations. *Courtesy of Welch Foods, Inc.*

they can realize for themselves the savings that are made in performing these marketing services. They can do so because the individuals or firms doing the integrating are the ones who make the business decisions involved in operating additional units or in performing additional marketing functions or service activities.

Economists generally identify three types of integration—horizontal, vertical, and conglomerate.

Horizontal Integration As the term implies, horizontal integration means adding or bringing together certain business units of the same type. In the case of a farmer this might mean operating two or three farms instead of one. For the local or centralized regional cooperative, it may mean adding branches at different locations to receive grain or distribute farm supplies. For the federated regional cooperative, it may require adding member associations that provide essentially the same services. In each case, additional units that operate in substantially the same way as the original one are brought under one management.

Vertical Integration Vertical integration means the taking of one or more products through more than one stage in the process of marketing or buying. When applied to marketing cooperatives, it is sometimes termed *forward integration*. If carried to its entirety, it would involve, for example, a dairy cooperative's providing necessary production supplies for members to produce milk and then processing this milk and selling it to the eventual consumer. In the case of farm supply cooperatives, the term *backward integration,* or *becoming basic,* is frequently used to describe the process involved.

In actual practice, it is well illustrated by a mine-to-field application for fertilizers, as provided by some farm supply cooperatives. In other words, the cooperative not only applies the fertilizer to its members' fields but, through their regional associations, goes back in the production process to the point of manufacture, and in some cases to operating its own mines for the production of rock phosphate or potash. A simple illustration of a 100 percent vertically integrated activity is a farmer's operation of a roadside market in which all functions from production to sales to eventual consumers are performed. In many instances, however, integration is partial, and in such circumstances the cooperatives involved perform only a limited number of functions and services in a total operation.

Conglomerate Integration Conglomerate integration involves adding or assembling a number of different types of enterprises or activities. As far as cooperatives are concerned, it may occur when a marketing cooperative expands its operations to include additional products. To illustrate, a grain cooperative might enter into the processing and marketing of broilers, the handling of production supplies, the pelleting of alfalfa, and the distribution of consumer goods.

Related Concepts

Two concepts that have far-reaching implications for cooperatives have come into being since the mid-1950s. These are contract farming and joint ventures. They are especially relevant to cooperative integration.

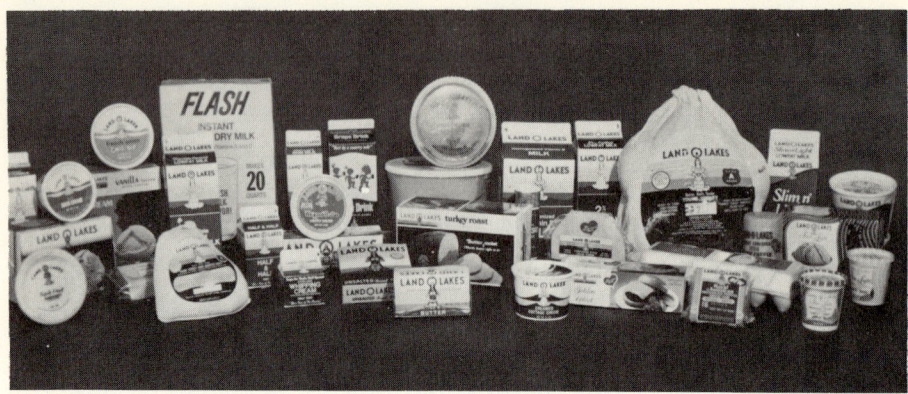

Land O' Lakes processed dairy and poultry products. Land O' Lakes engages in highly integrated processing operations that package farmers' dairy and poultry products for the retail trade. *Courtesy Farmer Cooperative Service.*

Contract Farming Contract farming has come to mean a contractual agreement between farmers and the various kinds of firms buying their products. The contract often specifies cultural or production practices to follow, some measure of volume to be delivered, and certain quality specifications. The firm frequently provides field services, seeds, fertilizers, or broilers, depending on the type of production for which it contracts. The net result is that many management functions are transferred from the farmer to the integrating firm, and the farmer occupies a role not too different from that of a hired hand. The farmer has certain assurances as to income but forgoes most of the risks and the financial benefits that exist when managing his or her own business.

Individual farmers may have several available options. They may deal with firms other than cooperatives and largely turn the management function over to them. On the other hand, they may integrate their operations through their cooperative and in this way realize the resulting losses or benefits, depending on how competently the cooperative performs.

If members can work out effective contract arrangements through their cooperative, these arrangements can enable them to use their cooperative to develop an integrated marketing system of their own. In this way they can improve their marketing position, add stability to marketing arrangements, and strengthen their commitments as members. To the extent that farmers contract with private firms, however, they may foreclose their opportunity to join a cooperative and realize for themselves the economic benefits of an integrated business operation. Contracting farmers may, of course, organize bargaining cooperatives to negotiate with private firms.

Joint Ventures Another form of integration that has received considerable attention from cooperative leaders in recent years is the establishment of joint business ventures. Joint ventures, in effect, are a form of integration. They have been defined as "an association of two or more participants, persons, partnerships, corporations, or cooperatives to carry on a specific economic operation, enterprise, or venture, but with

Ham canning operations of Farmland Industries, Inc., Carroll, Iowa. Modern processing operations are greatly accelerating capital needs of cooperatives. *Courtesy Farmer Cooperative Service.*

the identity of participants remaining apart from their ownership or a going participation in the venture."[1]

It is obvious that joint venture activity may involve cooperatives in dealing with other cooperatives. This type of activity has been commonplace for a number of years among regional cooperatives marketing cotton, grain, and fruits and vegetables. Regional supply cooperatives also have formed jointly owned associations to manufacture feed and fertilizer or to refine petroleum products. The establishment of Farmers Export Company, a federation of seven grain regionals, and Universal Cooperatives, Inc., a federation of some thirty regional farm supply cooperatives in the United States, Canada, and Puerto Rico, are examples of joint ventures by cooperatives. Also, a local cooperative is actually a joint venture of farmers, and a federated regional cooperative is a joint venture of local cooperatives.

More recently, cooperatives have become increasingly involved in joint ventures with other types of corporations. The much-publicized joint venture of Allied Grape Growers with Heublein, Inc., in 1969 illustrates some of the problems that may result when cooperatives and other firms undertake such ventures. The main features of the arrangements were that Heublein would acquire an 82 percent interest in United Vintners, which was the marketing arm of the Allied Grape Growers, a farmers' marketing cooperative. Allied Grape Growers was to provide grapes to United Vintners, which became a wholly owned subsidiary of Heublein Allied Vintners, a newly created firm. It was further agreed that not less than 40 percent of the directors of United Vintners would represent Allied Grape Growers, which would also own 18 percent of the stock in United Vintners and share 20 percent of the profits of that firm.

---

[1]Fred E. Hulse and Michael J. Phillips, *Joint Ventures Involving Cooperatives in Food Marketing*, Marketing Research Report 1040, Farmer Cooperative Service, U.S. Department of Agriculture, Washington, 1975, p. 2.

In 1972, the Federal Trade Commission charged that Heublein violated section 7 of the Clayton Act when it acquired controlling interest in United Vintners, and that this action eliminated actual or potential competition. In 1975, Allied Growers brought suit to rescind the merger with Heublein because of alleged fraudulent and misleading statements to the cooperative as to business intentions, and because Heublein had "systematically mismanaged" Allied's share of the enterprise. As of November 1975, no final agreements or decisions had been reached on either the Federal Trade Commission charge or the Allied suit.

Hulse and Phillips found that, in 1975, cooperatives had established twenty-two joint ventures involving fifty participants and including twenty-eight cooperatives. Of these ventures, twelve operated as separate entities, and ten were conducted as contractual or sales arrangements. Of the twelve operating as separate entities, seven represented cooperative-cooperative ventures; four were cooperative–investor owned–corporation ventures; and one was a cooperative–large-scale farmer venture.

Of the contractual arrangements, three represented cooperative-cooperative ventures, and seven cooperative–other corporation ventures. Usually such services as processing and marketing, sales and sales promotion, transportation, and storage are provided by separate entity ventures. Contractual arrangements relate to one firm's providing another with products for processing or retail distribution.

In general, joint ventures may enable cooperatives to expand their services, increase their efficiency, and control operating costs and margins. Joint ventures also may permit cooperatives to utilize additional alternatives for procuring needed services. Cooperative-cooperative ventures have demonstrated that they can be successful in achieving these major objectives. However, cooperative–other corporation ventures often are more complex and are somewhat more difficult to evaluate. Usually the success of such joint ventures depends upon the degree of mutuality that exists between the participating firms. Knutson, in "The Role of Cooperatives in Future Agriculture,"[2] suggests that the extent to which mutuality of interest may exist depends to a considerable degree upon whether the associations undertaking joint ventures are of comparable size. If they are, they are more likely to strike a balance as to both benefits and the risks and responsibilities involved.

While joint ventures with other corporations may benefit some cooperatives, it is obviously important for the cooperatives involved to consider the legal or antitrust implications of such ventures. Moreover, they will need assurance that they are not being exploited by the firms with which they are dealing. Under no circumstances should they permit themselves to be in a position comparable to that of chickens when a fox guards the chicken coop.

IMPLICATIONS FOR COOPERATIVES

If we ask ourselves why integration is so important for cooperatives, the answer is likely to be found in the imperfect market structure that exists for most firms handling agricultural products. As a result of both technical and economic research, very sub-

---

[2]Ronald D. Knutson, in *Journal of Agricultural Economics,* December 1974.

stantial changes have been introduced in the production and marketing processes. These changes have put individual farmers at a great disadvantage in dealing with large conglomerate firms that desire a given volume of products of specified grade at a certain time. By themselves, they often lack the capital, the bargaining ability, and the necessary knowledge of production and marketing practices to operate efficiently.

Unless farmers join together in cooperatives to meet these market needs, the conglomerates may very well enter into contractual arrangements with individual producers, such as have already developed in large segments of the broiler industry. When this happens, atomistic competition still prevails among farmers. This situation explains why the cooperative offers the individual farmers an opportunity to develop their own integrated business to deal with the changing market situation that confronts them. Only in this way can they marshal the resources to operate efficiently. As we have suggested previously, it is only through cooperatives that farmers can gain some of the bargaining and market power enjoyed by the highly concentrated business firms with which they deal. Membership in a cooperative, then, can be the farmers' response to the changing market structure in which they find themselves. Through their cooperatives, members can integrate their business operations and thus deal more effectively with other market firms.

Vertical integration, therefore, has special implications for cooperatives. These vertical, integrated associations become the vehicle through which their farmer members can achieve increased control over their products and perform more marketing or distribution functions. This approach contributes to more stability on the part of the marketing cooperative. The net margins that the cooperative realizes by performing each marketing function or service accrue to its members. When farmers integrate their operations with firms other than cooperatives, the farmers in effect trade their opportunities for management profits for financial security; but often it is financial security at only the level of a farm laborer.

Cooperatives, however, may find that they are faced with additional problems of substantial magnitude as they further integrate their operations. For example, do they have the capital to engage in the various additional functions that vertical integration requires? Even if we grant that they have adequate capital, do they have the managerial ability to undertake and effectively perform more market functions and the increased services that integration will require? Moreover, are members willing to make the necessary commitments to assure success for their cooperative? The need for commitment by cooperatives is emphasized in a 1975 FCS study, "Grain Marketing Patterns of Local Cooperatives," by Charles A. Kraenzle and Francis P. Yager, which showed that local cooperatives sold 31 percent of their grain to dealers other than cooperatives. Finally, if an established supply cooperative with 1,000 members desires to expand operations, for example, by starting an integrated broiler operation for 100 of its producer members, can it undertake such an enterprise on a basis that preserves equitable treatment for the 900 other members with respect to financial obligations, risks undertaken, and benefits obtained?

As cooperatives integrate their operations, there are still more problems they may encounter. In a local community, the nonmember producers may find themselves essentially foreclosed as far as market outlets are concerned. In the future, cooperatives will need to give increased attention to determining their possible responsibilities to such nonmembers and how, for example, they can meet the needs of nonmember patrons on a basis that is equitable both to them and to the members who originally organized the cooperative. It may be that under these circumstances, a cooperative, through well-planned member and public relations programs, can demonstrate to nonmembers the advantages of becoming members.

Integrating cooperatives are today being faced, too, with such basic questions as: What does and does not constitute an agricultural producer, and should a cooperative admit corporate members? Corporate members may vary from incorporated family farms to large conglomerate enterprises producing the same types of products that the regular members do. An example is the membership status of corporations in the National Broiler Marketing Association and the implications that such membership has for possible antitrust involvements of cooperatives (see Chapter 10).

Cooperatives can open the door of opportunity to farmers by providing them with their own integrated business. While farm supply and some fruit and vegetable cooperatives have made substantial progress in this direction, it is obvious that these cooperatives, as well as grain, cotton, and livestock cooperatives, have as yet great potentials for developing more highly integrated business operations. In addition, there are virtually untapped opportunities for further integration of effort through joint sales agencies, coordinated operation of transportation and storage facilities, and the development of jointly owned insurance and service programs.

EXPANSION OF FOREIGN TRADE

It is only natural that with the increased national emphasis on foreign trade, cooperatives will be interested in exploring opportunities for expanding their share of such trade. For cooperatives, foreign trade actually is an extension of their integration activities because they assume additional marketing or purchasing functions. When they market farm products abroad, they move these products closer to the eventual consumer. When they buy production supplies abroad, they go back farther toward the basic sources of these supplies.

In general, cooperatives have not developed their foreign trade to the same extent as their domestic trade. For example, in fiscal year 1970, while 26 percent of all agricultural products were marketed by cooperatives, at one stage or another, the total exports of these associations accounted for only 21 percent of total United States exports of agricultural commodities. Of the cooperative exports, 14 percent were sold direct to foreign buyers and 7 percent were indirect, i.e., to other firms that did the actual exporting. Since cooperatives have control of the direct sales only, most references in this section are to such sales.

It is obvious that cooperatives must assume additional market responsibilities if they are to engage effectively in foreign trade.

To expand their foreign trade, they must first of all take steps to provide the types of products in the form that foreign markets desire. In some instances, foreign demands may vary substantially from those in domestic markets. Secondly, they will need to give more attention to developing long-range and continuing trade relationships. Stable foreign markets cannot be developed on a hit-or-miss basis, active in some years and inactive in others. This works both ways, in terms of foreign demand as well as United States supply. The market gyrations caused by Russia's large purchases of grain in 1972 and 1975 illustrate the problems that arise when market requirements are unknown until we Americans start to harvest our grain. More attention also should be directed to servicing customers and having sales representatives in areas where the customers are.

Nature and Extent of Cooperative Foreign Trade

Farmer Cooperative Service has studied the extent of foreign trade conducted by the 101 largest cooperatives in the United States.[3] It found that in fiscal year 1970 the total volume of exports of agricultural commodities by these cooperatives was $1.2 billion ($782 million direct and $417 million indirect). Of the firms reporting, 95 percent engaged in export operations and only 75 percent in importing. Figure 23-1 shows the area export markets and the ten largest co-op export markets for the fiscal year 1970. In that year, Asia accounted for over half of area export sales, with lesser volumes going to Europe, Canada, and Latin American countries. Japan provided the largest export market and was followed by India, the Republic of Korea, and Canada.

Figure 23-2 shows the important types of products exported by cooperatives in 1970. Grains and preparations were the most important, followed by oilseeds and products, fruits and preparations, cotton and cotton linters, and vegetables and preparations.

The values of direct exports and imports by cooperatives are shown in Table 23-1. Grains and fruits and their preparations were the principal exports. Vegetables and preparations were the principal imports. About two-thirds of the total came from the Philippines and one-fourth from Mexico.

In fiscal year 1970, direct exports of farm supplies by cooperatives amounted to $6.9 million dollars. The principal items were fertilizers, oils and grease, and farm machinery and tools. About 70 percent of these sales went to Canada and Mexico. Imports of farm supplies by cooperatives totaled $46 million in 1970. About half this amount came from Canada. Venezuela, Japan, and Belgium were other important sources of supplies. Fertilizers, oils and grease, steel products, twine, and gas were the principal products imported by American cooperatives. Some of the important exporting cooperatives in the United States are identified on pages 99–100.

Problems Encountered and Suggestions for Improvement

Cooperatives encounter a number of problems in developing and maintaining their foreign trade programs. The most important of these are dock strikes, nontariff and tariff barriers, transportation arrangements and costs, and foreign competition.

Cooperatives have identified a number of opportunities for improving their foreign trade. Farmer Cooperative Service reported that most of these related to joint efforts and that cooperatives may, among other activities,

---

[3]Henry W. Bradford and Richard S. Berberich, *Foreign Trade of Cooperatives,* FCS Information 88, Farmer Cooperative Service, U.S. Department of Agriculture, Washington, 1973, p. 38.

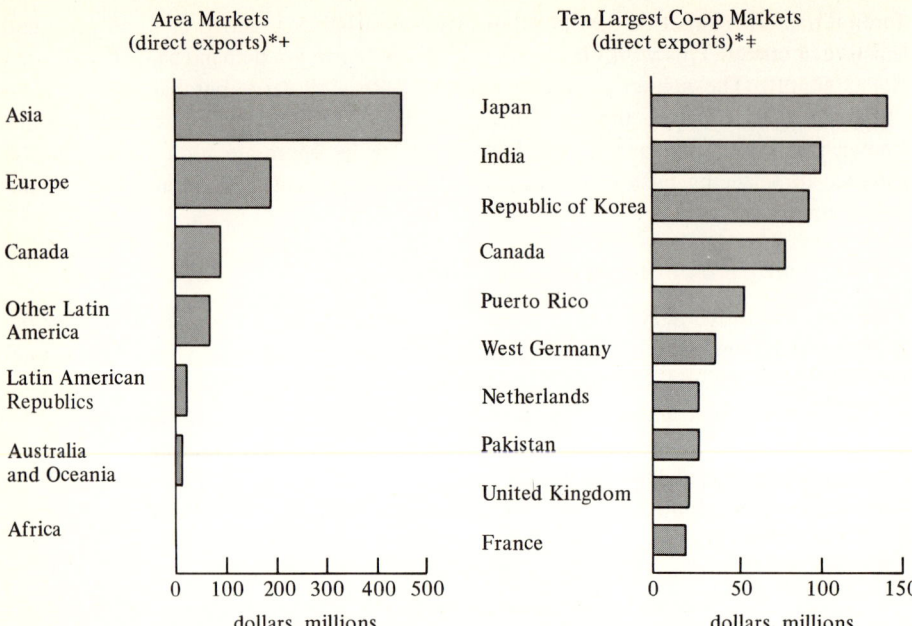

*Part estimated.
†Excludes $40.6 million of direct exports not specified by area.
‡Excludes $32.3 million of direct exports not specified by country. Part of this volume probably was exported to these ten countries.

Figure 23-1 Major export markets of cooperatives, fiscal year 1970. (*Source: Henry W. Bradford and Richard S. Berberich,* Foreign Trade of Cooperatives, *FCS Information 88, U.S. Department of Agriculture, Washington, 1973.*)

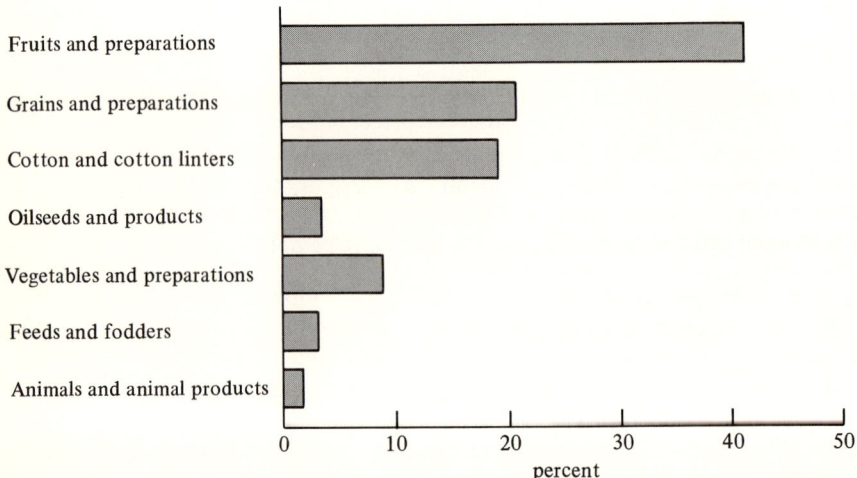

Figure 23-2 Cooperative share of agricultural commodities going overseas, fiscal year 1970. (*Source: Henry W. Bradford and Richard S. Berberich,* Foreign Trade of Cooperatives, *FCS Information 88, U.S. Department of Agriculture, Washington, 1973.*)

Table 23-1 The Value of Cooperative Commodities in Direct Foreign Trade, 1970

Type of trade and item	Value (in millions)
Export	
Grains and preparations	$474
Fruits and preparations	162
Cotton and cotton linters	68
Oilseeds and products	44
Vegetables and preparations	18
Animals and animal products	12
Feeds and fodders and misc.	4
Farm supplies	7
Total	$789
Import	
Vegetables and preparations	$ 2.8
Animals and animal products	0.3
Fruits and preparations	0.1
Feeds and fodder	0.1
Farm supplies	45.6
Total	$48.9

Source: Henry W. Bradford and Richard S. Berberich, *Foreign Trade of Cooperatives,* FCS Information 88, Farmer Cooperative Service, U.S. Department of Agriculture, Washington, 1973.

    1 Make a study through the Grain Division of the National Council of Farmer Cooperatives regarding feasibility of cooperatives exporting grain through one organization.
    2 Coordinate foreign sales with other cooperatives that export.
    3 Organize more of the Webb-Pomerene type of sales agencies for foreign trade.
    4 Keep commodity prices competitive.
    5 Develop a marketing program to give more attention to reducing price fluctuations.
    6 Strive for better arrangements and outlets for a wider range of products.
    7 Improve trade by keeping abreast of foreign markets, including increasing knowledge about necessary forms and procedures and competitive situations through foreign contacts and trips.
    8 Improve foreign representation by increasing the number of overseas branch offices and working more closely with foreign buyers and brokers.
    9 Pursue export business aggressively on co-op terms. An example is selling co-op branded products overseas.
    10 Develop more advertising and educational programs with the Foreign Agricultural Service, U.S. Department of Agriculture.
    11 Obtain a more favorable balance of trade through effective government export incentives.
    12 Encourage foreign countries to accept grading, labeling, and packaging requirements of the U.S. Department of Agriculture.
    13 Encourage freer trade and lower protective tariffs.

14 Consider chartering modern freight vessels.
15 Improve the East Coast terminal situation.
16 Develop working agreements with foreign cooperatives.
17 Bring in foreigners for training in American export programs.

These suggestions identify many opportunities for cooperatives in the development of their foreign trade programs. To summarize, the important areas where opportunities for expanded foreign trade for cooperatives exist are: (1) systematic identification of countries and commodities where trade can be increased; (2) careful study of long-term market needs and market practices; (3) improved member discipline and commitments; (4) greater emphasis on developing cooperative-to-cooperative trade relationships; and (5) establishment of coordinated joint sales programs.

INCREASED ATTENTION TO COOPERATIVE RESEARCH[4]

Cooperatives have long demonstrated an interest in using research techniques to improve their operations.[5] As one cooperative manager expressed it, research is "a compass for policy determination." In 1925, the first issue of *American Cooperation,* the proceedings yearbook of the American Institute of Cooperation, contained some early articles on research. One was a paper, "Commercial Research As An Aid to Management," by L. D. H. Weld, then manager of commercial research for Swift and Company and formerly chief of the Division of Agricultural Economics, University of Minnesota. In 1924, he was the author of one of the first comprehensive marketing textbooks, *The Marketing of Farm Products.*[6] Another article, "Business Analysis for Cooperatives," was presented in the same 1925 yearbook by A. V. Swarthout, marketing economist, Division of Agricultural Cooperation, Bureau of Agricultural Economics, of the United States Department of Agriculture.

Types of Cooperative Research

Research as used by cooperative associations may be classified into two types—business and technical.

Business Research The term *business research* comprises one or more of such subjects as economic research, market research, operations research, and financial research—as well as legal and tax inquiries. It also may include planning and sociology (human relationships), involving members, employees, directors, and the general public. The important feature of this type of research is that it entails all aspects of social

---

[4]Much of the material for this section is adapted from two previous studies of cooperative research by the author (see References at the end of this chapter).

[5]*Webster's New International Dictionary* defines the term *research* as a "careful or critical inquiry or examination in seeking facts or principles; diligent examination in order to ascertain something." Research is described by the *Encyclopedia of Social Sciences* as "the manipulation of things, concepts, or symbols for the purpose of generalization to extend, correct, or verify knowledge." These definitions place special emphasis on such terms as *critical inquiry, principles,* and *facts,* and on *extended, corrected,* and *verified knowledge.*

[6]L. D. H. Weld, *The Marketing of Farm Products,* Macmillan Company, 1924, rev., p. 483.

science as they relate to the business operations of a firm. As such, it is broader than marketing or economic research.

Business research may apply to all types of business organizations—cooperatives and other firms—or it may focus on problems of specific interest to cooperatives. For example, recent studies at land-grant universities, such as "Returns, Costs, and Profits for Family Type Sugar Cane Farms in Louisiana—1971 Crop Year"[7] and "Who Will Control United States Agriculture?"[8] are general economic studies that have application to all firms, cooperative or otherwise, as well as to all individuals interested in economic aspects of agriculture.

Sometimes general economic studies may have special or unique relevance for cooperatives. Usually cooperative researchers and officials are better able to bring these studies into proper perspective. For example, the study of family-type sugar-cane farms in Louisiana may suggest new services that can best be provided by cooperatives. Such studies as "Cooperative Research: Problems and Practices"[9] and "How Members Feel about Cooperatives"[10] are economic in nature and have specific application to cooperatives. Findings, however, may also be useful to other firms as well.

Technical Research This research relates largely to product development. It includes various aspects of processing farm products, and quite generally it involves laboratory experimentation and analysis. It often encompasses production investigations that involve experimental or field tests to develop improved crop varieties, better use of fertilizers, and superior feeds. It may also be concerned with all aspects of livestock breeding and improvement. In some instances, technical research relates also to facilities, equipment, and processing techniques.

Most of the technical research that applies to cooperative associations has come out of the land-grant colleges. Specific examples relate to practical research in such areas as development of better seed varieties, pasture improvement, swine and sheep breeding, communicable diseases of domestic animals, and nutritional problems. The development of tomato- and other fruit-harvesting equipment is a further example of important technical research findings. Such developments quite generally are useful to other firms as well as to cooperatives.

Research by Cooperatives

Cooperatives have been conducting research, both business and technical, for over thirty-five years. We will have a better basis for understanding the opportunities of cooperatives for using research more effectively if we briefly review the nature and

---

[7]Joe A. Campbell and Daniel Morris, *Returns, Costs, and Profits for Family Type Sugar Cane Farms in Louisiana,* 1971 crop year, B.A.E. Research Report 452, Louisiana State University Agricultural Experiment Station, Baton Rouge, 1971, p. 35.

[8]North Central Public Policy Education Committee, *Who Will Control United States Agriculture,* North Central Regional Extension Publication 32, Cooperative Extension Service, University of Illinois, Urbana—Champaigne, 1972, p. 56.

[9]Martin A. Abrahamsen, *Cooperative Research: Progress and Problems,* FCS Research Report 26, Farmer Cooperative Service, U.S. Department of Agriculture, Washington, 1973, p. 37.

[10]David W. Cobia and Luis A. Navarro, *How Members Feel about Cooperatives,* Agricultural Economics Statistical Series 11, North Dakota University Agricultural Experiment Station, Fargo, p. 26.

Economic research has become a vital tool for cooperative decision making. *Courtesy Southern States Cooperative, Inc.*

extent of the research they have conducted. Eight regional cooperatives were known to have initiated research by 1940, and another eight regionals did so in the decade that followed. Nineteen cooperatives had technical research departments, and another six had combined business and technical research departments.

Ever since 1956, regional farm supply and marketing cooperatives have maintained an informal organization of research personnel (Economic and Market Research Personnel). This group meets yearly to exchange information, to report on research practices and findings, and to explore possibilities for coordination of research efforts.

Early Research Programs Early cooperative research efforts are reflected in the minutes of the first annual meeting of research directors of farm supply regionals in 1956. C. H. Becker, then general manager of the Illinois Farm Supply Company (now F S Service), Bloomington, Illinois, emphasized the importance of marketing research, brand-position analysis, farmer opinion surveys, market trends, public opinion and employee opinion surveys, and price analysis. He went on to point out that, in view of the changes then occurring in agriculture, "small organizations were endangered unless they did a lot of research."

In their reports, research directors attending this first annual meeting emphasized the following points: (1) commercial research farm panels were used by Illinois Farm Supply Company; (2) the research function at Cooperative GLF Exchange (now Agway Inc., Syracuse, New York) was highly decentralized, with emphasis on agronomic and technical research through grants to land-grant colleges; (3) Eastern States

This aerial view of the new Land O' Lakes Answer Farm near Fort Dodge, Iowa, focuses on the cluster of eleven buildings that have been constructed on the 535-acre site. Pictured are: (1) Office and reception area, (2) agronomy greenhouse and seed laboratory, (3) seed storage building, (4) maintenance and machine storage, (5) swine gestation, (6) farrow and nursery, (7) growing finishing unit, (8) turkey research, (9) dairy production, (10) beef confinement, and (11) animal milk research building. Shown at the top of the photo are the cow-calf shelters and the overwintering lots. *Courtesy Land O' Lakes.*

Farmers Exchange (now part of Agway Inc.) indicated that one-half of 1 percent of its sales income was directed toward its research, which was entirely technically oriented; (4) research at Consumers Cooperative Association (now Farmland Industries, Kansas City, Missouri) was just getting under way, and its economic research was expected to be broader than market research; and (5) research at Missouri Farmers Association, Columbia, included analysis of audit reports, credit control, considerable consultation with other cooperatives, and frequent launching of new ventures under the research department. Incidentally, this cooperative was the first regional to establish a business research department—back in 1945.

During the same period, technical research by cooperatives was also progressing. In feed manufacture, special attention was given to vitamin and protein supplements and mineral deficiencies. The use of soybeans and fish meal in feeds was also being explored. In fertilizer, research stressed high analysis formulation, demonstration plot checks, and equipment design. Other areas undergoing research were plant-breeding and cultural practices, machinery design, and paint formulation.

Advances in Cooperative Research

Cooperatives have improved remarkably in their research efforts since 1956. In 1972–1973, a study by Farmer Cooperative Service, based on responses from 80 of the 100 largest cooperatives in the United States, determined that 55 of them conducted research.[11] These associations accounted for 45 percent of the net business volume of all cooperatives. Thirty-four of these associations maintained formal research departments. Of this number, twenty-one had business research departments and twenty-three had technical research departments. In addition, twenty-eight cooperatives reported conducting business research in other than business research departments and twenty-three reported conducting technical research in other than technical research departments. Twenty-seven cooperatives contracted research out to the federal government, universities, research firms, and other organizations. Twenty of the thirty-four formal research departments were in cooperatives having a net annual volume of business of over $100 million.

The seventy cooperatives reported an annual expenditure on research of over $10 million and the employment of about 250 research workers and 230 full- or part-time assistants.

The types of research conducted by cooperatives and the distribution of their research expenditures for the fiscal years that ended between July 1, 1971, and July 1, 1972 are shown in Table 23-2. These findings indicate that most cooperative research was conducted internally by cooperative staffs, but, depending upon the research philosophy of the various associations, substantial additional support was given to grants to universities and contracts to research firms. The total research expenditures reported in 1972 were about 110 percent higher than five years previously.

Cooperatives reported that the principal areas covered in their research programs were: (1) distribution of farm supplies, including market potentials; (2) marketing of farm products with emphasis on special commodities, brands and market acceptance, and foreign trade; and (3) functional studies with emphasis on planning, operations, feasibility and facility investigations, processing, mergers and acquisitions, local cooperatives and member service, and general economic studies.

There is reason to believe that cooperatives could improve services to members by directing more attention to pilot-test studies. The opportunities for such efforts are limitless because of the number of unanswered, or inadequately answered, questions that challenge cooperatives. Areas where more pilot tests might be made, to mention a few, are cultural practices, effectiveness of various types of facilities, new marketing techniques, and distribution practices.

Establishing and Operating a Research Department

Cooperatives are faced with special problems both when they wish to establish a research department and when they are interested in strengthening their ongoing research programs. Their capability in dealing with these problems to no little degree may determine the opportunities they can realize through carefully planned research programs. Some of these problems are here examined briefly.

Convincing Management of the Need for a Research Department Cooperative management is serious about research only when it sees the benefits to be derived

---

[11]Martin A. Abrahamsen, *Cooperative Research: Progress and Problems,* Research Report 26, Farmer Cooperative Service, U.S. Department of Agriculture, Washington, 1973, p. 38.

Table 23-2 Cooperative Expenditures for Research, by Type of Research

Type of research and method used	Expenditures during business year ending between July 1, 1971, and June 30, 1972		
	Cooperatives	Amount (in thousands)	Percentage of total
Business			
With own staff	28	1,936	63
Jointly with other cooperatives	3	70	2
Grants to universities	7	204	7
Grants to federal government	1	2	0
Contracts with commercial firms	11	847	28
Total	28*	3,059	100
Technical			
With own staff	32	6,491	87
Jointly with other cooperatives	6	398	5
Grants to universities	16	408	6
Grants to federal government	3	50	1
Contracts with commercial firms	7	80	1
Total	36*	7,427	100
Total	*	10,486	*

*Not additive.

Source: Martin A. Abrahamsen, *Cooperative Research: Progress and Problems*, FCS Research Report 26, Farmer Cooperative Service, U.S. Department of Agriculture, Washington, 1973, p. 37.

from a well-functioning research department. While management support and encouragement for cooperative research have increased substantially in the past quarter-century, it still lags behind that of most other agribusiness firms. For example, a tabulation by the National Science Foundation shows that total expenditures of the United States government in 1975 for basic and applied research was $12.1 billion,[12] of which about 35 percent was for basic research. As closely as can be determined, only about 4 percent of this amount was for economic and related social science research, with expenditures for such research at $48 million.

Another measure of the extent of social science research is that reported by the Current Research Information System (CRIS) of the U.S. Department of Agriculture. It estimates that, in 1974, a total of $62.5 million was directed to social science research by the U.S. Department of Agriculture, other federal agencies, and nonfederal resources. About 85 percent of these funds were for economic research, 8 percent for sociological research, with the remainder divided among such areas of investigation as anthropology, education, information and communication, history, law, political sci-

---

[12] See National Science Foundation, "National Patterns of R and D Resources: Funds and Manpower in the United States, 1953–1975," Washington, 1975.

ence, psychology, and art and architecture. Approximately 70 percent of these funds were from federal sources, primarily the U.S. Department of Agriculture. Social science research, in turn, accounted for only 8 percent of the total research expenditures reported by CRIS in 1974.

In 1975, CRIS reported expenditures for cooperative research at $1.4 million, with 87 percent of these funds coming from the Department of Agriculture. Cooperative research funds in 1975 supported thirty-three scientist years, or 2.5 percent of the man-years devoted to social science research as reported by CRIS.

To some extent, the lag in cooperative research may be due to management's reliance on the research done by state and federal agencies. It may also reflect inadequate appreciation of just how cooperative research can help to provide basic information needed in reaching better decisions on a wide range of operating problems.

In some instances, it is difficult to convince management of the merits of establishing a research program, because the contributions of such a department are hard to measure. The costs of operating a research department or conducting a research study are quite specific and obvious. What are not so specific and obvious are the benefits of having better information and knowledge upon which to evaluate the merits of a proposed business venture. These benefits are often quite intangible and difficult to recognize and measure.

Management, for example, may tend to look on a $50,000 budget for initiating research as just an added expense—a questionable addition to overhead. In reality, the study may provide basic information that will enable management to make the best possible decision when considering whether to undertake a project. A better basis for reaching a "no" decision when evaluating an unsound project may save members of a regional cooperative many times $50,000. On the other hand, sound information leading to a "yes" decision may initiate action resulting in benefits for members amounting to many times the cost involved. Arriving at a better answer in evaluating just one proposed undertaking may very possibly cover all the annual costs of operating a research department.

Setting Up a Research Department Once management is convinced that a research department should be established, a number of practical questions arise. Depending on the nature of cooperative effort, the first question to consider may well be: Should research emphasize business or industrial programs, or both? Some cooperatives have found that the establishment of a research advisory committee is helpful in setting up priorities and in determining the nature and direction of a research program and its overall emphasis.

The structure and organization of a research department should also receive thorough consideration when cooperatives initiate a research program. For example, should the research director report directly to the manager, or to an assistant manager or a department head such as the director of sales?

Research directors state that the opportunity to achieve success in their research programs is closely related to the appreciation and support given them by the manager and other key officials of the cooperative. The stature a research department has in a cooperative depends to a considerable extent on the level in the management hierarchy to which the director reports. Reporting to the higher levels, too, could assure a greater degree of objectivity in the use of research. Often it is only when the research director reports directly to the general manager or assistant general manager that management can most objectively use research to evaluate the effectiveness of some of the operating programs of various division and department heads.

More important than the specific niche the research department may occupy on an organization chart, however, is the environment in which the director functions. It is recognized that, depending on how effectively research directors work, they may be able to shape, or at least influence, the research environment once they are given a chance to prove their usefulness. Such an environment must reflect understanding, appreciation, and support. As one research director phrases it, it is important to "operate at the heartbeat of the cooperative."

Staffing a Research Department Staffing a research department is an essential consideration if cooperatives are to develop effective research programs. Indications are that much progress has been made in selecting competent research personnel. Currently, a number of cooperative research directors have Ph.D. degrees in their respective fields and have demonstrated on-the-job competence in initiating and developing valuable research programs. Some cooperatives report that they require an advanced degree for employment as a professional in their research departments.

One research director, when stressing the need for professional training for the research worker, emphasized this same point when he said: "Management . . . should also be made aware of the problems of trying to make researchers out of former line management personnel or former salesmen."

Identifying Responsibilities of Management and Research Directors The effectiveness of a cooperative's research program is likely to be determined, to a large measure, by how well cooperative management and research directors assume responsibilities for its operation. Any progressive research program will be more successful when the manager fully accepts it as an important management tool. The responsibilities of general managers in realizing the full potential of a cooperative research program include:

- Selecting a research director with proper training and experience
- Supporting the employment of competent assistants
- Furnishing needed facilities and funds
- Giving the department proper status within the association, and encouraging efforts of research personnel to gain professional recognition outside the cooperative
- Developing and maintaining a spirit of "research consciousness" among key association officials
- Building morale in the department by letting research channel its energies into main problems of policy determination; and, once findings are determined, permitting research personnel to participate in discussions relating to policy decisions

If management assumes these responsibilities, it is in a good position to demand performance. Maintaining an effective research program, however, is as much the responsibility of the research director as of the manager. Given a favorable environment within the cooperative, the research director will, to a large degree, determine by his or her performance how effective research will be in guiding policy decisions of cooperatives.

The following points are important in contributing to the development and maintenance of a good research program by regional cooperatives:

- Encouraging the use of research and project committees, budgets, and proper facilities and equipment
- Maintaining high professional standards, both in caliber of work and in professional relationships with research workers in other cooperatives, and in federal and state agencies
- Establishing research programs that relate to the major operating problems of associations
- Insisting on effective presentation of research findings
- Arranging working schedules to allow sufficient time for considering association problems objectively

The suggestions advanced for improving the research operations of cooperatives also pinpoint opportunities for cooperatives to improve their research programs. It is evident that the federal and state funds directed to cooperative business research are a mere pittance when compared with the relatively small federal and state expenditures for research. While cooperative recognition of and expenditure for research have shown encouraging progress, cooperatives have a long way to go when compared with firms other than cooperatives. The fact that only 21 of the 100 largest cooperatives in the United States have business research departments is indicative of the opportunities ahead for the development of useful research programs.

COOPERATIVES AS A TOOL FOR ECONOMIC DEVELOPMENT[13]

Economists generally agree that the term *economic development* means a sustained improvement in living standards as reflected by an increasing flow of goods and services to consumers. It focuses on the interaction between people, natural resources, capital formation, and technology, though recognizing the possible importance of other factors.

Most of the human population lives in what we call the developing or underdeveloped countries. As of 1975, only about one-fifth of the world's population lives in the so-called developed countries in which per capita annual income amounted to $1,800 or more.

The terms *underdeveloped nation* or *developing nation* do not imply any value judgments. Both refer solely to the economic and technical development of a country and not to its cultural, religious, ethnic, political, or social background.

---

[13]The initial draft of this section was prepared by Abraham Avidor, research assistant, Department of Agricultural and Resource Economics, University of Maryland.

The Concept of Economic Development

Dulfer considers development from the standpoint of the individual and the nation.[14] He suggests that the individual, as a member of a motivated group and under favorable legal and institutional conditions, may seek on-the-job training and the necessary credit to apply new production techniques and to develop improved processing and marketing facilities. The individual's development contributes to increased modified production, quality control, and improved marketing practices. With the increased and stabilized income that results, individuals are able to improve their nutrition, modernize their social and technical standards of living, and become motivated to participate in national activities.

Dulfer also advances the idea that national policies, once having established targets, emphasize the mobilization of human resources and the reform of legal and institutional structures. There is increased emphasis on diversified agricultural production and improved marketing systems. This stress contributes to higher GNP, stabilized production, fewer imports, and more exports. Increased per capita income follows, tax receipts rise, and foreign exchange makes possible the importation of needed technical equipment. The consequences are improved public health and a better technical and cultural foundation. From a national standpoint, these developments are building blocks for political and financial independence and equality with other nations.

Criteria for Evaluating Progress[15] Our discussion of individual and national progress suggests that to measure or evaluate a country's level of economic development, it is necessary to establish realistic criteria and goals. Often, per capita national income is used for this purpose. Since it ignores the distribution of income, however, by itself it may be a misleading index of the level of development or the economic welfare of a country. Other more concrete criteria that frequently are used as measures of achieving individual and national targets are:

- The standard of nutrition as measured by protein and calorie intake
- The standard of health as measured by life expectancy, frequency of various diseases, and infant mortality
- The standard of education as measured by percentage of illiteracy and number of years of schooling
- The standard of technology as measured by the number of cars, telephones, and owner-occupied houses

In whichever combination these indicators are selected, one finds that a group of countries, including the United States, Canada, most nations in Western Europe,

---

[14]Eberhard Dulfer, *Operational Efficiency of Agricultural Cooperatives in Developing Countries,* Food and Agricultural Organization of the United Nations, Rome, 1974, pp. 18 and 19.

[15]While fully aware of the important contributions cooperatives can make to economic development, some cooperative representatives see a larger role for them. Disenchanted with the efforts of diplomats and politicians to achieve peace, they are examining the contributions cooperatives may make. Jerry Voorhis, for example, in *Cooperative Enterprise* (Interstate, Danville, Ill., 1975, p. 221), states: "But more fundamentally the hope for peace depends upon how well people learn to live together in a crowded, deeply divided, and rapidly changing world." He believes that, through cooperatives, the idea of mutual aid and recognition of our interdependence can grow out of people's working together through cooperatives. This experience, he believes, is a legacy to the next generation that will help it to develop better political and economic institutions to "create a better world for all."

Australia, and New Zealand, have the highest standard of living, while most nations in Asia, Africa, and South America have considerably lower levels of living.

The eradication of poverty and unemployment and the redistribution of income are the real objectives of a national economic development program. Such a program contributes to the improvement of both individual welfare and national growth. We have suggested that the attainment of a higher GNP growth rate alone is not enough since it can be accompanied by deepening poverty, extreme income disparity, and the accumulation of wealth by a few. A true development program should be attuned to the needs of the masses, and it should attack the worst forms of poverty. Its primary goal in the realization of individual and national goals should be the progressive reduction and eventual elimination of hunger, malnutrition, disease, illiteracy, squalor, and unemployment.

To achieve these goals, the national planning and organizing of future production and investment should be adapted to the requirements of the masses. Only the satisfaction of basic needs can guarantee minimum living standards for all the people, a higher level of productivity, employment, and growth, and a better distribution of income for the nation. In this way, the benefits of progress will be more widely shared and more equally distributed, and economic improvement in individual and national welfare can be achieved at the same time.

Cooperatives' Role in Economic Development

The effort to achieve individual and national targets brings into focus the role of cooperatives in furthering these objectives. It raises the crucial question: Is the role of cooperatives *complementary* or *competitive* in achieving these objectives? To answer, we should ascertain whether cooperatives can function as a motivating force for individuals and serve as an effective tool in helping people achieve projected national targets. Likewise, we should seek to determine whether the role of cooperatives in mobilizing resources, building markets, and increasing per capita income through better production practices is also compatible with basic national objectives.

The effectiveness of a cooperative as a development tool should be examined from the standpoint of its capacity to fulfill the objectives of a national economic development program. As such, the success of a cooperative should be measured in terms of its ability to improve the living standard of all members and its ability to promote the better distribution of income and the economic growth of the nation. Experience in the developing and the developed countries alike has shown that cooperatives are uniquely qualified to assist in economic development. What makes cooperatives so suitable for this role are their basic characteristics.

- Cooperatives provide service at cost, distribute refunds in case of operating margins, and take over the functions of the market intermediary agent, thus improving members' income and quality of life.
- Cooperative members are the owners, the participants in establishing broad business policies, and above all, the beneficiaries. As such, they are in the midst of the development process, and they are able to get first-hand experience in democratic action.

- Cooperatives can be organized for almost any form of business enterprise, be it agriculture (marketing, supply, processing, credit), rural electrification, housing, health care, credit unions, savings and loan institutions, consumer services, or small industries. As business institutions, they involve such practical and operational skills as management, administration, accounting, and policy making.
- Cooperatives constitute an effective link between local initiative and the nation's economic plan. This is especially so when they are organized on a national or regional basis. Cooperatives can be an efficient tool for implementing government policy by linking individual members to a national economic program. Cooperatives can also be a useful channel for the flow of information, the distribution of ideas, and the dissemination of knowledge among members, state and federal agencies, and the general public.
- Cooperatives, as nonprofit enterprises, pay only a limited return on equity capital. This factor encourages the buildup of a wide popular membership, and it discourages the establishment of a narrow elite who may regard the cooperatives as a means of financial investment.

Cooperatives, in addition to the inherent features which make them highly qualified for the development function, must also be able to adjust to the local social, political, and economic conditions. This is especially true as it relates to the difference between cooperative effort in the developing and in the developed countries.

In the Developing Countries In the developing countries, most people have a low standard of living, and many suffer from the worst forms of poverty. Survival for many, therefore, depends on the rapid progress of an effective development program. Cooperatives, organized by and for the people, can help to guarantee the success of such a program if accompanied by educational programs for members, managers, and directors. Development through cooperatives can bring about an improved social and economic order, based on democratic foundations where the benefits of progress are widely shared. For the great majority of the people of the developing countries, cooperatives represent the most practical mechanism through which they can produce and consume the things they need and obtain the services they require. When such people organize a cooperative to buy feed, to market rice, or to obtain credit, they are essentially creating economic units that enable members to improve their standard of living; acquire economic strength, purpose, and hope; and have a voice in their own destinies.

Agriculture in the developing countries is the main economic activity, and its planning, therefore, should be the basis of the general economic development program. Most of the people live on small family farms which are traditionally producing merely for their own consumption. It seems obvious that if the growing population of the poor nations is to be fed and if the farm families are to earn better incomes, ways must be found to increase the productivity of these farms. Cooperatives have shown that they are among the most effective institutional forms for carrying out this task. They can introduce modern techniques in agriculture, integrate vertically, and better employ productive resources, thus improving farmers' incomes and standard of living.

It is also a characteristic of developing countries that labor is cheap and capital is dear. Only naturally, then, a strong emphasis should be placed on the development of credit cooperatives. Such institutions can, for example, help meet the urgent needs of peasant farmers for investment and working capital. Production, marketing, or supply facilities require large amounts of capital which local credit associations are often unable to provide. International financial agencies such as the World Bank and the Inter-American Development Bank can help alleviate the pressure by providing debt capital for sound cooperative ventures.

In the Developed Countries In the developed countries, most people enjoy an acceptable living standard as measured by income, health, education, and technology. For some nations, the development process has been slow, gradual, and undisturbed (e.g., Sweden, Switzerland), whereas in others it has been shorter and more vigorous (e.g., Japan, Israel, West Germany). We have shown that in almost all countries, cooperatives have had an important part in past economic development efforts. The current development goals of most advanced nations include:

- Closing the gap between the high personal incomes of the secondary and tertiary sectors (industry and services) and the lower incomes of the primary sector (agriculture and natural resources)
- Maintaining an acceptable economic growth rate
- Attacking selectively pockets of poverty, either in urban slums or in rural areas

Cooperatives can contribute considerably, and are doing so, to the accomplishment of these goals. They serve members reliably, increase their bargaining power, and provide the services performed traditionally by intermediary agents in integrating vertically toward the eventual consumer and toward sources of supply. Thus, they improve members' income and standard of living. As modern and efficient economic units, cooperatives contribute to national growth and to a more equitable distribution of income. And, as a democratic and self-help tool which distributes economic benefits widely to all participants, cooperatives can effectively attack existing pockets of poverty.

Strengthening Cooperatives for Development Opportunities

It is important to identify objectives of various groups of cooperatives to determine where assistance may most effectively be directed. Once the needs have been ascertained, the programs of assistance, depending upon the status of development for any given type of cooperative, will be much the same.

When public agencies perceive cooperatives as desirable instruments for achieving broad national objectives and serving the public interest, they can set in motion forces that will both encourage and strengthen these organizations. Such a public program should recognize that members need not necessarily be the victims of uncontrolled economic forces. We have learned that these forces can be shaped and molded to achieve desired economic and social change and that cooperatives can be an important means for achieving it.

To be most effective, programs to facilitate the growth of cooperatives must be geared to the stage of development in any country as well as to established customs and the main aspects of national policy. Such programs should identify limiting or strategic factors in cooperative development and should have as their basic tenet the philosophy that "sound policy must precede practice" if substantial results are to be achieved.

The following five-point approach is suggested for public agencies in developing a program of cooperative assistance.[16] These points are not unique. They do, however, emphasize fundamentals and reflect the distillation of worldwide experience. They are: (1) assuring a favorable climate, (2) encouraging and conducting research, (3) providing technical assistance, (4) developing realistic educational programs, and (5) building financial strength.

Assuring a Favorable Climate The distinct nature of cooperatives is not always appreciated. As economic tools of members, they can make significant contributions toward the improvement of their economic positions. They can do so because (1) the economic benefits of cooperation go directly to the users of the cooperative, and (2) the social and political benefits of participating in policy-making decisions in business organizations help train members in the functions of a democracy.

A favorable climate for cooperatives depends upon:

- Having responsible government officials who understand basic cooperative objectives and what can and cannot be accomplished through cooperative effort.
- Developing sound cooperative legislation that provides broad guidelines, spells out government and member responsibility, and is in tune with national customs and legal structure.
- Achieving general support. Such support may include, among other things, government trading through cooperatives; creation of the right psychological climate which recognizes that people working together can accomplish more than people working as individuals; financial assistance; and realistic help in licensing, inspecting, and providing guidance during formative periods.

Encouraging and Conducting Research A realistic program of research, including economics as well as other social science disciplines, is essential in order for a country to develop effective cooperatives. For example, a national body of statistics can provide basic information on trends in principal commodities and geographic areas as they relate to volume of business, membership, and number of cooperatives. Likewise, studies of such distinctly cooperative features as financing, business operations, management, and membership can be extremely helpful. Research on operating problems might include preparing practical case studies on successful cooperatives and on how various operating practices can be, or are being, carried on effectively.

Providing Technical Assistance Cooperatives are confronted with a large number of operating problems. Through appropriate programs of technical assistance, it is possible, for example, to use research findings to improve living conditions in rural villages. Better answers often can be found on ways to raise capital; on where to locate

[16]Martin A. Abrahamsen, "The Role of Public Agencies in Assisting Industrial Cooperatives in Developing Countries," a paper prepared for the International Symposium on the Role of Group Action in Industrialization of Rural Areas, Tel Aviv, Israel, March 24, 1969.

facilities; on how to provide new services needed by members; and on methods of holding annual meetings, keeping accounts, and auditing association records.

Developing Realistic Educational Programs It has become axiomatic that cooperatives are able to go no further than the educational level of their members and leaders allows them to go. Helping members realize that cooperatives can assist them in dealing with their unfulfilled needs is important. To develop such understanding, printed and audiovisual materials on the nature of cooperatives and on member responsibilities in supporting their associations are needed. In developing countries, it is wise, when cooperatives are introduced, that local, state or provincial, and central government officials receive training for their specific responsibilities. As in developed countries, the general public, too, needs to be informed about cooperative potentials.

Building Financial Strength Public agencies can strengthen the financial position of cooperatives in developing countries in at least three ways: (1) They can help develop specialized banking and credit facilities geared to the specific needs of cooperatives; (2) they can encourage government programs to provide low-interest loans for certain types of cooperatives; and (3) through a program of outright grants and subsidies, they can help initiate and support needed cooperative activity.

Opportunities for Cooperative Contributions

The actual growth and development of cooperatives in the United States were traced in earlier chapters from the economic, legal, and historical standpoints. Here, we shall focus on the special opportunities for cooperatives to contribute to the economic progress of low-income rural communities. We have indicated that the number one objective is the eradication of poverty and the widely shared expansion of rural incomes. In pursuing this objective, cooperatives can do many things that contribute to the economic and social improvement of the communities of which they are a part. In general, they can be especially influential in economic development by:

- Strengthening and expanding local business enterprises
- Broadening services to members
- Assisting in organizing other cooperatives
- Providing effective local leadership
- Improving communications among rural and urban communities
- Building needed plant facilities
- Providing needed services such as selling handicraft products, processing locally produced food, or improving the water supply
- Assisting other groups in challenging rural development problems
- Contributing significantly to the promotion of democratic principles and practices
- Integrating vertically, thereby realizing greater per capita income for members
- Improving the bargaining power and terms of sale for individual members
- Disseminating scientific findings or any other useful information to members

Evaluation

Some essential considerations are necessary if cooperatives are to function as important development tools. They may be summarized thus:

Economic and Political Environment   Cooperatives have learned from experience that they need not accept as inevitable the unplanned working out of economic and political forces. Rather, by taking purposeful action, they can change and modify their economic and political environment to achieve their objectives. This opportunity places even greater emphasis on determining the critical or limiting factors in the business economy and then on having economic and political leaders who can identify the times when cooperatives can be helpful in meeting major needs and in initiating the actions necessary to cope with them.

Public Agency Guidance   There is need for the public officials in developing countries to understand the contributions cooperatives can make to their people. Given such understanding, public agencies, local, state or provincial, and national—through programs of cooperative research, technical assistance, and education—can help guide and shape cooperative development. To be most effective, such programs must be coordinated and taken directly to operating cooperatives. This means transforming research findings reported in publications and pamphlets into action programs by individuals competent and willing to work directly with cooperative members and leaders. These types of support should be provided on a basis that will eventually leave cooperatives free from government control and domination.

Competent Government Leaders and Officials   Competent government direction and encouragement mean guiding, developing, and sustaining but never usurping leadership as cooperatives develop. There is no substitute for selecting and developing competent local officials, achieving support of government agencies, building a practical program centered on sound finance, capable management, and realistic information, and then taking such a program directly out to members and potential members.

Self-Help Aspects   In the long run, cooperatives will be successful only to the extent to which they become truly self-help organizations. This responsibility calls for planning necessary supporting educational programs, developing a sense of financial responsibilities among members, and making a deliberate plan to have government agencies and their officials turn over to cooperatives the responsibility for more and more operation and control just as soon as they demonstrate ability to carry it.

Recognition of Uniqueness   When successfully operated, cooperatives are a very effective self-help tool. One explanation is that the persons who belong to cooperatives are the ones who benefit from their business efforts and the ones who have a voice in their operation and control. For example, imagine, if you will, the difference in motivation of Indian villagers who deal with moneylenders and motivation of those who benefit from owning their credit cooperative. In the first instance the villagers work largely for others, whereas the owners of the cooperative work for themselves and benefit in direct proportion to the business they do with their cooperative, the support and encouragement they give it, and the competency of management.

SUMMARY

Areas of activity that offer special, and in some instances largely untapped, opportunities for cooperatives are: (1) increased emphasis on integration; (2) expansion of foreign trade; (3) greater attention to research; and (4) recognition of cooperatives as a tool for economic development.

Increased Emphasis on Integration

Integration is a process that brings the performance of more production and marketing functions and services under the control of one management. Although not a new development as far as cooperatives are concerned, the idea of filling production needs and providing services, together with performing marketing functions, is comparatively recent.

Three types of integration are generally recognized—horizontal, vertical, and conglomerate. Integration may be partial (performing some enterprise functions) or complete (performing all enterprise functions). Closely related to integration, and having definite implications for cooperatives, are (1) contract farming, and (2) joint ventures. The latter may involve cooperative-cooperative relationships or cooperative–other corporation relationships. Farmers find that integrating certain production and marketing services through their cooperatives constitutes one of the most effective ways for them to maintain control of their own farm operations. To perform integrating functions for their members, cooperatives require highly competent management, strong financing, and well-planned member relations programs.

Expansion of Foreign Trade

Cooperatives have a growing interest in exploring opportunities for foreign trade. Although cooperatives handle 27 percent of all United States products at one stage or another in the marketing process, they account for only 14 percent of all foreign trade. In 1970, direct foreign trade by cooperatives totaled $782 million. Over half this volume went to Asia, with lesser volumes going to Europe, Canada, and Latin American countries. Fruits and vegetables and their preparations were the most important export items, followed by grains, cotton and linters, and oilseeds and products. Imports of agricultural products and farm supplies were of relatively little significance. This was also true for farm supplies, although imports at $46 million were over 6 times exports. To expand foreign markets further, cooperatives must (1) provide the types of products in the form that these markets desire; (2) develop long-range and continuing market relationships; and (3) carefully study foreign marketing techniques and practices and coordinate their foreign trade programs with other cooperatives.

Greater Attention to Research

Research involves a careful and critical inquiry to ascertain facts and establish principles in order to learn something. Research, from the standpoint of cooperatives, may be classified into two broad categories: *business research,* which covers broad aspects of social science investigations—economic, sociopsychological, political, and legal; and *technical research,* which relates largely to product development. It includes laboratory experimentation and analysis, product testing, processing, plant and animal breeding, and facilities and equipment.

In establishing research departments, managers of these departments reported that success depended on such factors as (1) convincing management of the need for research, (2) effective department structure and organization, (3) competent staffing, and (4) identifying the responsibilities of management and research directors. It should also be emphasized that research is not an end in itself. The objective of research, as applied to cooperatives, is to improve operations. It is, therefore, a tool to be used by decision makers, and as such, it can make important contributions to cooperative development.

Recognition of Cooperatives as a Tool for Economic Development

Economic development is measured by the ability to achieve certain goals or targets. These goals or targets relate to both a nation and its individual citizens. When mutuality of interests between the nation and its citizens prevails, the opportunity for success is greatest. For cooperatives to make their maximum contribution to economic development, they must be complementary to, rather than competitive with, the interests of the nation and its citizens. The citizens also are the actual or potential members of cooperatives. Because these associations benefit those who use their services, they are in a strategic position to contribute to economic development. They can be a substantial force for improved production, marketing, and general business practices, as well as an educational vehicle for the strengthening of democratic institutions. The direct and indirect benefits to members provide the means for improving nutrition, establishing better health standards, and raising standards of education and technology. These direct contributions to their individual members also strengthen cooperative opportunities to help in the achievement of national goals.

QUESTIONS

1. What is economic integration? Differentiate between the three types of economic integration.
2. How are contract farming and joint venture related to economic integration?
3. How can members benefit from increased integration by their cooperatives?
4. What speical problems should an integrated cooperative be prepared to deal with?
5. Consider the foreign trade of American cooperatives from the standpoint of principal areas and countries involved; products exported; and relative importance of trade in farm products and farm supplies.

6. Why is the proportion of products sold in foreign trade by American cooperatives less than their domestic market share of sales of these products?
7. What are the principal problems cooperatives encounter in developing foreign markets?
8. What steps should cooperatives take to increase their foreign trade?
9. Distinguish between business and technical research.
10. How does each of these types of research relate to problems that have industrywide implications as compared with those that are of special interest only to cooperatives?
11. What considerations should cooperatives take into account in deciding whether to start their own research program?
12. Why is it difficult to determine the benefits of research?
13. Why is it important to consider the targets or goals of nations and their citizens when considering economic development? Are these targets or goals the same for the nation as for its citizens?
14. How do these goals or targets differ in developed and developing countries? What are the implications for cooperatives?
15. What role can cooperatives have in economic development in developing countries? In developed countries?
16. How can public agencies strengthen the role of cooperatives in economic development?

REFERENCES

General

American Institute of Cooperation: *American Cooperation,* Washington, D.C. These annual yearbooks contain articles on a wide range of subjects including future opportunities for cooperatives. See particularly part II, 1974–1975, pp. 54–254, and 1972–1973, pp. 23–56.

Knapp, Joseph G.: *Farmers in Business: Studies in Cooperative Business Enterprise,* American Institute of Cooperation, Washington, D.C., 1963. See particularly part V, pp. 337–431.

Knutson, Ronald: "A Policy Perspective on Cooperatives," *News for Farmer Cooperatives,* Farmer Cooperative Service, U.S. Department of Agriculture, Washington, June 1975, pp. 4–5.

Kravitz, Lina: *Who's Minding the Co-op?* Agricultural Accountability Project, Washington, D.C., 1974, pp. 53–66.

Integration

Hulse, Fred E., and Michael J. Phillips: *Joint Ventures Involving Cooperatives in Food Marketing,* Marketing Research Report 1040, Farmer Cooperative Service, U.S. Department of Agriculture, Washington, 1975, p. 30.

Mather, J. Warren, and John Bailey: *Integrated Petroleum Operations of Farmer Cooperatives,* Farmer Cooperative Service, Research Report 21, U.S. Department of Agriculture, Washington, 1971, p. 19.

National Agricultural Library, "Contract Farming and Vertical Integration, 1953–1963 (A List of Selected References)," Library List No. 64, rev., U.S. Department of Agriculture, Washington, 1963, p. 77.

Foreign Trade

American Institute of Cooperation, *American Cooperation,* Washington, D.C. See particularly part IV, 1973–1974, chap. 3, pp. 352–362; and 1972–1973, pp. 197–240.

Bradford, Henry W., and Richard S. Berberich: *Foreign Trade of Cooperatives*, FCS Information 88, Farmer Cooperative Service, U.S. Department of Agriculture, Washington, 1973, p. 39.

Research

Abrahamsen, Martin A.: *Business Research of Regional Farm Supply Co-ops,* FCS General Report 13, Farmer Cooperative Service, U.S. Department of Agriculture, Washington, February 1955.
———: *Cooperative Research: Progress Problems,* FCS Research Report 26, Farmer Cooperative Service, U.S. Department of Agriculture, 1973, p. 38.
American Institute of Cooperation, *American Cooperation,* Washington, D.C. Annual yearbooks contain numerous articles on research. See particularly 1971, pp. 58–69; 1970, pp. 171–201; 1969, pp. 317–323; 1966, pp. 390–418; and 1965, pp. 611–630.

Development Tools

Anschel, Kurt R., Russell H. Brannon, and Eldon D. Smith: *Agricultural Cooperatives and Markets in Developing Countries,* Praeger, New York, 1969, p. 373.
Dulfer, Eberhard: *Operating Efficiency of Agricultural Cooperatives in Developing Countries,* Food and Agriculture Organization of the United Nations, Rome, 1974, p. 188.
Englemann Konrad: *Building Cooperative Movements in Developing Countries,* Praeger, New York, 1968, p. 238.
Klatzmann, Joseph, Benjamin Y. Llan, and Yair Levi: *The Role of Group Action in the Industrialization of Rural Communities,* Praeger, New York, 1971, p. 599.
McCabe, Robert: "The Role of Cooperation in the Third World," *Canadian Journal of Public and Cooperative Economy,* January–December 1973, pp. 121–132.
The Plunkett Foundation for Cooperative Studies, *Yearbook of Agricultural Cooperation,* Blackwell's, Oxford, England. These yearbooks contain a number of articles relating to cooperatives in developing countries. See especially 1972, and also 1970, pp. 230–250.

Appendix A

Terminology[1]

Over the years, a body of terms and captions unique to financial statements of cooperatives has developed. While some of these terms are quite useful in that they may describe a particular type of transaction or financial relationship for which no parallel exists in accounting for other concerns, a great many of them developed for reasons of ideology rather than from a lack of appropriately descriptive terms in general use. In recent years, there has been a trend away from the specialized terms, back to those in general use. Many cooperatives do employ such special terminology, however, and therefore some of the common terms of this type are included in the following glossary (the National Society of Accounts for Cooperatives has not taken a position as to preferred usage of general or specialized terminology):

Term	Description
Products marketed Produce marketed Merchandise marketed for patrons Marketing volume Sales	Any of these terms may be used to describe sales of a marketing cooperative.

[1]Excerpts from *Accounting and Financial Reporting for Agricultural Cooperatives,* published by the National Society of Accountants for Cooperatives, 1973.

TERMINOLOGY[1]

Term	Description
Purchases by patrons Patrons' purchases Sales to patrons Patrons' volume Sales	Any of these terms may be used to describe sales of a purchasing cooperative.
Gross proceeds	A special term created to describe sales, less opening inventory, plus closing inventories of a marketing cooperative, thus (theoretically) reflecting volume attributable to the current year's pool.
Payments to producers (growers) Advances to producers (growers) Cost of products marketed	Terms used to describe payments for produce in a marketing cooperative.
Purchases for patrons Cost of patrons' purchases Cost of sales	Cost of sales of a supply cooperative.
Gross margins Gross savings	Sales, less cost of sales, of a supply cooperative.
Net realization	A special term applicable to a marketing cooperative, representing the amount remaining after deduction of all cost and expenses from gross proceeds, but before payments to producers.
Net proceeds Net proceeds available for distribution Net undistributed proceeds Net margins Net savings	Terms used by marketing cooperatives to describe the final figure on the operating statement, approximately comparable to net income of a conventional corporation where advances to producers approach the prevailing market price.
Net margins Net savings	Terms used by supply cooperatives to describe the figure approximately comparable to net income of a conventional corporation.
Statement of operations and margins Statement of operations and net proceeds Statement of operations	These terms, or variations thereof, are in common use among cooperatives and are preferable to "income statement," "statement of earnings," and similar terms used by other corporations.

Term	Description
Stockholders' and patrons' equity Capital stock and patrons' equity Members' and patrons' equity Capital, patrons' equity, and retained margins	Terms used, depending on circumstances, to describe the equity section of the balance sheet.
Revolving fund certificates Revolving capital certificates Equity certificates Participation certificates Certificates of ownership Allocated patrons' equity Allocated reserves Patronage capital credits	Typical balance sheet terms referring to allocated patrons' equities of various kinds.
Reserve for contingencies Reserve for working capital Statutory reserve General purpose reserve	Typical balance sheet terms describing general reserves of various types. Such reserves may be allocated, but often are merely apportioned to patrons, or subject to apportionment, although technically they are patrons' equity rather than stockholders' equity.
Retained margins Retained earnings Undistributed margins Earned surplus	Usually, these terms refer to tax-paid, unallocated retained margins. Normally shown as last item in equity section of balance sheet.
Patronage refund Patronage distribution Patronage dividend	Terms used to describe the distribution of annual net margins or net proceeds to patrons, whether in cash or scrip.

Appendix B

Quotations from Leaders on Cooperatives[1]

Senator George Aiken

The cooperative is rooted in the concept of dispersal of ownership and control—the opposite of monopoly. The cooperative is the regulator—the great leavening influence—in our economy.... The cooperative method is the one organized economic force which demonstrated that it has within itself the facilities for stemming the tide of our economic system from one of tenancy and dependency to one of ownership and responsibility.

Senator Clinton P. Anderson

Cooperatives are the very essence of free enterprise.... Nothing could be more American in basic spirit and purpose.

Calvin Coolidge

I have many times declared my conviction that the development of a powerful cooperative movement in this country is one of the needs of this period of economic readjustment.

Senator Paul H. Douglas

In preservation and extension of democracy, the cooperative movement has a great part to play.

---

[1]Most of these quotations are excerpts from a pamphlet issued by the Cooperative League of the U.S.A., *They All Endorse Cooperatives.* Others are published statements from other sources.

Dwight D. Eisenhower

The role of farm cooperatives is increasingly important in our national economy. Over the years they have proved a major means for assisting farmers to meet the problems and opportunities of modern agriculture. . . . Farmer cooperatives are shining examples of the self-help pioneering spirit that has made this Nation great.

Fortune Magazine

Cooperatives . . . bring social responsibility along with self-interest.

Orville L. Freeman

To me the workings of our farmer cooperatives represent one of the great fulfillments of our democratic free enterprise system. . . . Cooperatives must become ever more effective instruments through which farmers can operate in our free enterprise system with greater benefits for themselves and their families.

Dag Hammarskjöld

Cooperatives aim not at making maximum profits for a few but at rendering maximum service to the community at large.

Warren G. Harding

I know of no single movement that promises more help toward the present relief and permanent betterment of agriculture than the cooperative movement.

Herbert Hoover

Today business organization is moving strongly toward cooperation. There are in the cooperative great hopes that we can even gain in individuality, equality of opportunity and an enlarged field for initiative, and at the same time reduce many of the great wastes of overreckless competition in production and distribution . . . indeed this phase of development of our individualism promises to become the dominant note of its twentieth century expansion. . . . This cooperative system is self government outside of government. It is the most powerful development among free men that has taken place in all the world.

Hubert H. Humphrey

Cooperatives, in essence, are doing things for themselves. This embodies the basic spirit of our freedom. Cooperatives help preserve our American heritage of a man with an independent spirit who is yet sensible enough to work together with others for his own common good.

National Council of Churches of Christ in the U.S.A.

The churches should encourage full membership participation in organization of mutual aid and cooperation.

Lyndon B. Johnson

I know of no partnership (cooperatives) which affects so many areas of national life—marketing, consumer purchasing, credit, housing, and insurance are only a few. Nor do I know of a partnership which results in such a productive sharing of knowledge, manpower, money, and even equipment with people here and abroad. . . . I have seen cooperatives grow up. Their performance over the past half a century is reason for great pride. Their future success lies in their ability to assume new responsibilities with the same self-reliant spirit of the past, to explore their capacity to help in America's war on poverty, to broaden their programs to bring hope to areas of need, and to advance the general economic and social well-being of our society.

John F. Kennedy

Cooperative and mutual business has been a very important and constructive part of our free economy ever since Benjamin Franklin organized the first mutual insurance company in Philadelphia in 1752. It is one of the finest expressions of the American spirit. Here groups of people, faced with common needs, invest their capital and organize their own cooperatives to meet these needs. This is self-help at its best.

George Meany

By patronizing and joining cooperatives, workers can obtain high quality goods and services at the lowest cost. At the same time, they are participating in and building consumer-owned, democratically-operated enterprises. The American Federation of Labor strongly supports cooperatives in recognition of their fundamental contribution to the democratic way of life.

Pope John XXIII

Rural workers should feed a sense of solidarity one with another and should unite to form cooperatives, which are necessary if they are to benefit from scientific and technical progress. . . . They need to organize to have a voice, for today almost nobody hears, much less pays attention to isolated voices.

Pope Pius XII

Small and medium holdings in agriculture, the arts, trade and industry must be guaranteed and supported. Cooperative unions must provide them with the advantage of big business.

New York Times

One of the world's most peaceful, most constructive economic reform movements.

Franklin D. Roosevelt

The weavers of Rochdale who founded modern cooperative enterprise balanced independence with interdependence, self-interest with good will, and action with foresight. The cooperative movement belongs to no one nation but has its roots in the traditions of all democratic peoples. I look forward with confidence to the contribution that cooperative organizations will make to the years of peace that lie ahead.

Theodore Roosevelt

Wherever farmers themselves have the intelligence and energy to work through cooperative societies, this is far better than having the state undertake the work. Community self-help is normally preferable to using the machinery of government for tasks to which it is unaccustomed.

Walter P. Reuther

Consumer cooperatives are one of the economic foundations on which the American people must build for the future.

Adlai E. Stevenson

Cooperatives . . . stand today the zealous guardians of genuine economic freedom and individual enterprise, so essential in a truly democratic society. They have preserved variety in our economy and encouraged self-reliance through broad, responsible, local ownership of business and industries.

Senator Robert A. Taft

The farmer cooperative is a multiple corporate partnership of America's basic capitalists—the farmers. They are essential because the number of farmers and the small size of the farm unit deprive the farmer of the bargaining power enjoyed by other businessmen.

Harry S. Truman

We support the right of free enterprise and the right of all persons to work together in cooperatives for the purpose of carrying out any proper business operations free from any arbitrary and discriminatory restrictions.

Washington Post

The cooperative movement has made an exceedingly valuable contribution to American democracy. . . . It has demonstrated the feasibility of applying democratic controls to economic as well as political affairs.

Index

Index

AAMA (*see* American Agricultural Marketing Association)
Abrahamsen, Martin A., 394*n*., 449*n*., 452*n*., 461*n*.
Acquisitions (*see* Mergers)
Action Committee for Rural Electrification (ACRE), 413
Adjustments to change:
   growth and, 105–107
   integration intensified, 98
   (*See also* Economic integration)
Agricultural Adjustment Act of 1933, 218
Agricultural Cooperative Development International (ACDI), 170
Agricultural Credits Act of 1923, 322, 340
Agricultural Fair Practices Act (*see* Bargaining)
Agricultural Marketing Act of 1929, 95, 322
Agricultural Marketing Agreement Act of 1937, 218–219
Agway, Inc., 39

Allied Grape Growers, 441
   (*See also* Joint ventures)
American Agricultural Marketing Association (AAMA), 350–352
American Cotton Growers, 365
American Farm Bureau Federation, 93, 168
   affiliated cooperatives, 93
American Institute of Cooperation (AIC), 159–161
AMPI (*see* Associated Milk Producers, Inc.)
Antitrust decisions, 205–211
   Cape Cod Food Products v. National Cranberry Association, 207
   federal court decisions, 206–207
      Cape Cod Food Products v. National Cranberry Association, 207
      Case-Swayne Co. v. Sunkist Growers, Inc. 210
      Connolly v. Union Sewer Pipe Company, 206

477

Antitrust decisions:
   Liberty Warehouse Company v. Burley Tobacco Growers Cooperative Association, 206–207
   Sunkist v. Winckler and Smith Citrus Products, 209–210
   Tigner v. Texas, 207
   Treasure Valley Potato Bargaining Association v. Ore-Ida Foods, Ind., 210–211
   United States v. Associated Milk Producers, Inc., 211
   United States v. Borden Company, 207–208
   United States v. Maryland Cooperative Milk Producers and Maryland and Virginia Milk Producers Association, Inc., 208
   United States v. Maryland and Virginia Milk Producers Association, Inc., 208–209
   Justice Felix Frankfurter and, 207
   Chief Justice Charles E. Hughes and, 207
   state court decisions, 205–206
     Burns v. Wray Farmers Grain Company, 206
     Reeves v. Decorah Farmers Cooperative Society, 205
Antitrust legislation:
  Capper-Volstead Act, 193–197
  Clayton Antitrust Act, 192–193, 205
  Sherman Antitrust Act, 191–192, 205
  status of cooperatives, 212–216
Appleby, Paul H., 328
Arkansas Grain Corporation, 365–366
Arnold, C. R., 328, 336
Assistance in organizing cooperatives, 254–256
  banks for cooperatives, 255
  federal government, 255
    Bureau of Census, 255
    Department of Commerce, 255
    Economic Research Service, 255
    Small Business Administration, 255
  national cooperative associations, 255
  regional cooperatives, 255
  state cooperative councils, 255
Associated Milk Producers, Inc., 211, 214
  Judge John W. Oliver and, 211

Associated Press, 34
Avidor, Abraham, 456n.

Backward integration, 439
  (*See also* Economic integration)
Bailey, John, 340
Bailey, Liberty Hyde, 404
Bakken, Henry H., 50, 53, 405
Banks for cooperatives, 117, 118, 294, 329–332
  (*See also* Cooperative Farm Credit System)
Bargaining, 84, 344–362
  Agricultural Fair Practices Act and, 360–361
  areas of confusion, 347–348
    bargaining is marketing, 347–348
    bargaining function and bargaining cooperatives, 347
  bargaining cooperatives, 346
  bargaining groups, 345–348
    firms, 345
    individuals, 345
    labor unions, 345–346
    nations, 345
    operating cooperatives, 346
  Capper-Volstead Act and, 360
  expansion of, 99
  extent of, 349–352
  importance of, 348–349
    individual farmers at a disadvantage, 349
    institutional changes and consumer preferences, 349
    plague of surpluses, 349
    specialized markets, 348
    technology and market structure, 348
    traditional markets avoided, 348
  multicommodity, 350–352
  operating practices, 352–355
    contract relationships, 352–353
    methods of payment, 355
    negotiating representatives, 354
    ownership of product, 354
    price negotiations, 353
  problem areas, 355–361
    achieving member discipline, 356
    extent of potential gains, 356–357

INDEX

gaining recognition, 355
identifying areas of mutual interest, 357
legal status, 360–362
production control, 357–359
relationship with operating cooperatives, 359
role of government, 359–360
Treasure Valley Potato Bargaining Association v. Ore-Ida Foods, Inc., 84
Bargaining Cooperatives, Selected Agri-Industries, 353n.
Barnes, Stanley H., 213
Becker, C. H., 450
Benefits of cooperatives, 426–435
community benefits, 428–430
Cenex and, 429
community builders, 429–430
educational force, 428–429
MFC Services and, 429
public benefactors, 430
consumer cooperatives, 433
general benefits, 427–428
business performance improved, 427
competition provided, 427–428
yardstick for operations, 427
marketing cooperatives, 430–433
improvements in production, 431
increase in member income, 431
influence on volume of production, 432
integration of member-controlled marketing system, 431
realistic grades and standards introduced, 432
purchasing cooperatives, 432–433
assured sources of supply, 433
dependable service, 433
higher quality products, 433
substantial savings, 432
service cooperatives, 433–434
Ferndale Cooperative Credit Union, 434
Nationwide Insurance Company, 434
Twin Pines Savings and Loan Association, 434
Berberich, Richard S., 445n.
Bergengren, Roy F., 166
Biggs, Gilbert W., 350
Black, Justice Hugo, 209

Black, John D., 78–79, 404, 437
Blanc, Louis, 74
Bonner, Clyde, 62, 67
Bradford, Henry W., 445n.
Brandeis, Justice Louis, 203
Brandow, George E., 358
Breimeyer, Harold, 84
Buckez, Philippe, 74
Bureau of Agricultural Economics, 395
Bureau of Indian Affairs, 296
Bureau of Reclamation, 296
Burns v. Wray Farmers Grain Company, 206
Business enterprise, 12–17
corporations: cooperative, 15–16
other firms, 16
individual proprietorships, 12–14
partnerships, 14–15
Business persons' cooperatives, 34
business services, 34
grocery chains, 34
Business research, 448–449
Butterfield, Kenyon L., 403
Butz, Earl, 214

California Canning Peach Association, 346
Campbell, Joe A., 449n.
Cance, Alexander E., 94, 403
Cape Cod Food Products v. National Cranberry Association, 207
Capper-Volstead Act, 84, 95, 193–197, 212–216
and bargaining, 360
modifications considered, 212–216
Capper-Volstead Cooperatives, 207
Case-Swayne Co. v. Sunkist Growers, Inc. 210
Changes in agriculture, 105–107
changes in other business sectors, 106
farmers gain sophistication, 106–107
improved services, 106
mechanization, 106
technical and economic research, 106
Clayton Act, 192–193
Clearwaters, Keith I., 215
Cobia, David W., 449n.
Commercial banks, cooperative financing and, 297

Commissioner v. B. A. Carpenter, 230
Commodity Credit Corporation, 296
Communications (cooperative), 274–287
    communicators identified, 277–278
    cooperative publics, 278–280
        outside the cooperative, 279–280
        within the cooperative, 278–279
    effective programs, 280–283
        knowing what to communicate, 282–283
        reliance on research, 282–283
    Farmland Industries, Inc., 284–286
        techniques used by, 284–285
    Frank Groves and, 276–277
    J. H. Heckman and, 275
    International Cooperative Alliance and, 274
    measuring results, 286–287
    member relations and, 283–287
    methods of, 280
        audiovisual, 280
        personal contact, 280
        printed material, 280
    need for, 275–277
        creating a favorable image, 276
        dollar value of, 276–277
        growth and, 275–276
        new developments, 276
        new publics and, 276
        unique nature of cooperatives, 275
    Rochdale principles and, 274
    techniques for, 284–285
    what to communicate, 282–283
Communism, 7–9
    Arnold P. Aizsilnieks and, 8
    Bolshevik Revolution, 8
    Charles Fournier and, 7
    Sir Thomas Moore and, 7
    Robert Owen and, 7
    Plato's *Republic* and, 7
    Joseph Stalin and, 8
Conklin, Paul, 400
Connolly v. Union Sewer Pipe Company, 206
Consolidation (*see* Mergers)
Consumer cooperatives, 28–31, 238
    types of, 27–31
Coolidge, President Calvin, 396
Cooper, Ken, 301

Cooper, Thomas B., 405
Cooperative Central Marketing Organization, 404
Cooperative credit corporations, 340
Cooperative Democracy, 76
Cooperative Farm Credit System, 24–25, 117–119, 237–238, 323–337, 341
    banks for cooperatives, 117, 118, 329–332
        capitalization, 330–331
        Central Bank for Cooperatives, 330
        operations, 331–332
        services provided, 331
        structure, 330
        trends, table, 118
    control of, 324–326
    expanded activities of, 327–328
    Farm Credit Act of 1937 and, 325
    Farm Credit Act of 1953 and, 325
    Farm Credit Act of 1959 and, 329
    Farm Credit Act of 1971 and, 325
    Farm Credit Administration districts, 324–325
    federal land banks, 117, 118, 332–334
        Agricultural Credit Act of 1923 and, 333
        Emergency Farm Credit Act and, 334
        Emergency Farm Mortgage Act of 1933 and, 332
        Farm Credit Act of 1971 and, 334
        Federal Farm Loan Act of 1916 and, 332–333
        Federal Farm Mortgage Corporation and, 334
        operations, 334
        trends, table, 118
    formulation of, 323–324
        Henry Morganthau and, 323
        William I. Myers and, 323
        President Franklin D. Roosevelt and, 323–324
    nonpartisan status of, 328–329
        Paul H. Appleby and, 328
        C. R. Arnold and, 328
        F. F. Hill and, 328
        William I. Myers and, 328
        United States presidents and, 329
        Henry A. Wallace and, 328–329

INDEX 481

operations, 327–328
  decentralization emphasized, 327
  normal value and, 327
production credit associations, 118, 119, 335–337
  background, 335–337
  operations, 337
  trends, table, 118
structure, 324
Cooperative finance associations, 321–342
Cooperative growth, 104–125
  consumer cooperatives, 121
    membership, numbers, volume, table, 121
  Federal Trade Commission studies and, 113
  general service cooperatives, 117–121
  marketing and purchasing cooperatives, 105–117
    business, 108
    dairy products, 111–113
    financial comparisons, figure, 116
    GNP, 110
    market share, 109–110
    membership, 107–108
    numbers, 107
    petroleum, 113–114
    relative and absolute comparisons, 115–116
    ten largest cooperatives and other firms, 114
  strategy for, 122–124
    facilitating growth, 123–124
    identifying elements of, 122
    selecting methods for, 122–123
Cooperative League of the U.S.A. (CLUSA), 94, 164–165
Cooperative legislation:
  benchmarks in, 183–200
  special problems of, 202–221
  taxation, 223–241
Cooperative Marketing Act of 1926, 95, 212, 395
Cooperative month, 408
Cooperative principles, 47–69
  antecedent ideas, 48–49
    Lennoxtown Society, 49
  basic principles reexamined, 53–63
    duty to educate, 61–63
    limited returns on equity capital, 60–61

member control, 56–59
member ownership, 59–60
operation at cost, 54–56
cash trading, 67
control of facilities and service institutions, 67
definitions of, 47
evaluation of, 49–50
  Henry H. Bakken and, 50
evolutionary development, 49–53
  Henry H. Bakken and Marvin Schaars, 51
  Ward W. Fetrow, 51
  International Cooperative Alliance and, 53
  Edwin G. Nourse and, 53
  "Penny Capitalists," 49
  Marvin A. Schaars, 51
other principles and practices, 63–68
  cooperation among cooperatives, 67–68
  exclusive trading with members, 64–65
  financing in proportion to capital, 65–66
  indivisable capital reserves, 65
  open or selective membership, 63–64
  political, religious, and racial neutrality, 64
  selling at market prices, 66–67
  single or multiple-business services, 66
principles and practices compared, figure, 52
Rochdale contributions, 47–50
  antecedent ideas, 48–49
  Paul Lambert and, 48
  Catherine Webb and, 48
Cooperative Research and Service Division (see Farmer Cooperative Service)
Cooperative trade organizations, 165–170
  Agricultural Cooperative Development International (ACDI), 170
  Credit Union National Association, Inc. (CUNA), 166–167
    Roy F. Bergengren and, 166
    CUMIS Insurance Society, Inc., 167
    CUNA Service Group, Inc., 166
    Edward A. Feline and, 166
  Foundation for Cooperative Housing (FCH), 167
  National Association of Housing Cooperatives, 167–168

Cooperative trade organizations:
  National Federation of Grain Cooperatives, 168
  National Livestock Producers Association, 168–169
  National Milk Producers Federation (NMPF), 169
  National Rural Electric Cooperative Association (NRECA), 169
  National Telephone Cooperative Association (NTCA), 170
  state cooperative councils, 170–172
Cooperatives:
  basic features of, 3–5
  and capitalism, 5–6
  and communism, 7–9
  cooperation and cooperative business enterprise contrasted, 1–3
  definitions of, 3*n*.
  and fascism, 9–10
  forms of business enterprise and, 12–16
  and the isms, 10–12
  nature and place in the economy, 1–17
  in other countries, 126–156
    Brazil, 149–152
    Denmark, 137–138
    factors influencing development, 155–156
    Finland, 142–143
    Great Britain, 127–134
    Iceland, 143–144
    India, 152–155
    Israel, 144–146
    Japan, 146–149
    Norway, 141–142
    Sweden, 138–141
    Switzerland, 134–136
  in the political economy, 5–12
  and socialism, 6–7
  types of, 19–45
    areas served, 35–37
    cooperative service and trade associations, 42
    factors influencing type established, 42–44
      capital requirements, 42
      institutional factors, 43
      management, 42–43
      need, 42
      preemption of field, 43
      problems of workers' cooperatives, 43
      services desired, 43
      understanding, 43
    farm supply cooperatives (*see* production supply cooperatives *below*)
    financial structure, 41
    functions performed, 37
    groups served, 21–35
    legal status, 40–41
    marketing cooperatives, 21–23
    membership, 39
    problems of classification, 19–21
    production supply cooperatives, 23, 24, 37
    purchasing cooperatives (*see* production supply cooperatives *above*)
    quasi-cooperatives, 41–42
    size, 37–38
    summary of, 44–45
Corporations:
  cooperative, table, 13, 15–16
  other than cooperative, 13, 16
Coulter, John, 404*n*.
Country Life Commission, 94, 322, 403
Credit cooperatives, 29
  types of, 24–27
  (*See also* Cooperative finance associations)
Credit Union Legislative Affairs Committee (CULAC), 413
Credit Union National Association, Inc. (CUNA), 166–167
Credit unions, 341
CUMIS Insurance Society, Inc., 167
Cuna Service Group, Inc., 166–167

Dairy-herd improvement associations, 26
Davidovic, Georg, 81
Digby, Margaret, 131
Directors' responsibility for cooperative success, 264–265
Division of Agricultural Cooperation, 95, 395–396
  (*See also* Farmer Cooperative Service)
Donoghue, John H., 189
Dulfer, Eberhard, 457

Early American cooperative thinkers, 76–82
Early cooperative exploration (up to 1870), 89–90

INDEX 483

  in agriculture, 89–90
  Mayflower Compact, 89
  in urban and industrial communities, 89–90
Economic development, 456–465
  concept of, 457
  cooperative role in, 458–460
    developed countries, 460
    developing countries, 459–460
  cooperative role strengthened, 460–462
    educational programs, 462
    favorable climate, 461
    financial strength, 462
    research, 461
    technical assistance, 461–462
  evaluating cooperative progress, 457–458
  evaluating cooperative role, 463–464
  opportunities for, 104, 462
Economic integration, 437–442
  kinds of, 437–439
  related concepts, 439–442
Economic Theory of Cooperation, 81
Eidam, John, 331
Ellender, Allen J., 408
Ellis, Clyde, 399
Emelianoff, Ivan V., 81–83
Engberg, Russell, 340
Engman, Lewis, 410
Erdman, Henry E., 407
Evolution of cooperative thought, 71–86
  early American, 76–83
  European-post-Rochdale, 74–75
  European-pre-Rochdale, 72–74
  Edwin G. Nourse, 53
  Robert Owen, 72
    associated effort, 72–73
    democratic control, 72
    service to members emphasized, 72
    voluntary approach, 72
  recent views, 83–85
    antitrust laws, 84
    income tax treatment, 84
Exchange Lemon Products Company, 209

Farm Bureau's Committee of Fifteen, 168
Farm Credit Administration, 237–238, 323–337
Far-Mar-Co, Inc., 365
Farmer Cooperative Service, 401

  (*See also* Cooperative principles; Government policies and cooperatives; Historical development of cooperatives)
Farmer's Alliance, 91
Farmer's Educational and Cooperative Union of America, 91–93
  affiliated cooperatives, 92
Farmers Grain Dealers Association, 23
Farmers Union Central Exchange (CENEX), 429
Farmers Union Merchantile Co., 35
Farmland Industries, Inc., 284–286
FCA (*see* Farm Credit Administration)
Federal Farm Board, 322, 396–398
Federal Farm Loan Act of 1916, 322
Federal Housing Administration, 298
Federal income taxes, 225–238
Federal Intermediate Credit Bank, 322
Federal Trade Commission, 213, 322, 409–410
Feline, Edward A., 166
Financial controls, 301–306
  implementations of, 305–306
  ratios, 302–305
    efficiency, 303–305
    liquidity, 302–303
    solvency, 305
Financing, 289–306
  balanced agriculture with industry, 297
  borrowed capital sources, 294–298
  capital sources, 290–298
  financial planning and management, 300–301
  government agency sources, 295–298
Fishery cooperatives, 33–34
Food and Agriculture Organization (FAO), 172–173
Foreign Assistance Act of 1971, 414
Foreign market ventures, 99–100
Foreign trade of cooperatives, 444–448
  nature and extent of, 445
  problems encountered, 445–448
  suggestions for improvement, 445–448
  value of, table, 447
Forward integration, 439
  (*See also* Economic integration)
Foundation for Cooperative Housing (FCH), 167
Fourier, Charles, 48, 73

Franklin, Benjamin, mutual insurance companies and, 25
Froker, Rudolph K., 405
Frost v. Corporation Commissioner, 203

Gardner, Kelsey B., 262
Garoian, Leon, 384–386
General farm organizations, 172
    (*See also* American Farm Bureau Federation; Farmers Alliance; Farmers Educational and Cooperative Union of America; National Grange)
George, Henry, 187
Gerber, Henry, 415
Gide, Charles, 49, 75
Gold Kist, Inc., 98–99
Government policies and cooperatives, 390–418
    congressional, 392–393
        early studies, 393
        legal assistance, 392–393
    early notions about, 391–392
    evaluation of, 415–418
        cooperative role, 417–418
        mutuality of interest required, 417
        policies may vary, 416
    federal government, 394–403
        Division of Agricultural Cooperation, 395–396
        Farmer Cooperative Service, 401
        Federal Farm Board, 396–398
        Great Society programs, 401–403
        Office of Markets, 394–395
        Rural Electrification Administration (REA), 399
        Tennessee Valley Authority (TVA), 398–399
    government cooperative relationships in developing countries, 414–415
    New Deal, 398–401
        Resettlement Administration, 399–401
        Rural Electrification Administration, 399
        Tennessee Valley Authority, 398–399
    Office of Economic Opportunity and, 402–403
    Oregon State Council and, 397
    unfavorable government action, 408–411
        Department of Justice and, 204

Griffin, Nelda, 291*n*.
Group Health Association, Inc., 29

Hall, F., and W. P. Watkins, 128*n*.
Hard Winter Wheat Pools, The: An Experiment in Agricultural Market Integration, 81
Health care cooperatives, 29
Hearings on Monopolistic Practices and Concentration in the Food Industry, 214
Hecker, Thomas Levi, 404
Heinz, J. H., III, 214
Helmberger, Peter, 82
Hill, F. F., 328
Historical development of cooperatives, 88–103
    adjustment to change (1945 to date), 98–101
        additional services, 101
        bargaining activities, 99
        consolidations and mergers, 99
        education and research, 100
        employee and director training, 100–101
        facilities and equipment, 101
        financial structure, 100
        foreign market ventures, 99
        Great Society motivations, 101
        integration, 98
    age of experimentation (1870–1920), 90–94
        American Farm Bureau Federation, 93
        Farmer's Alliance, 91
        Farmer's Educational and Cooperative Union of America, 91–93
        National Grange, 90–91
    business improvement (1933–1945), 95–98
        Cooperative Farm Credit Administration, 97
        modern business techniques, 97
        New Deal assistance, 97–98
        processing expansion, 96–97
        research and educational assistance, 96
    cooperative commodity marketing (1920–1933), 94–95
        legislative benchmarks, 95
        Aaron Sapiro and, 94
    early cooperative explorations (up to 1870), 89–90

in agriculture, 89
in urban and industrial communities,
89–90
federal and state government
encouragement, 93–94
Country Life Commission, 94
Federal Farm Loan Act, 94
Office of Markets, 94
President Theodore Roosevelt and, 94
Smith-Lever Act, 94
Great Society motivations, 101
Kennedy-Johnson Administrations, 101
urban and industrial communities, 89–90
Benjamin Franklin and, 89
Journeyman and Cordwainers of
Philadelphia, 90
New Harmony Indiana Cooperative
Colony, 90
Robert Owen and, 90
Philadelphia Contributionship for
Insurance of Houses from Loss by
Fire, 89–90
Hobson, Asher, 405
Holmes, G. K., 393
Hoos, Sidney, 82
Horizontal integration, 439
(*See also* Economic integration)
Housing Act of 1950, 30
Housing cooperatives, 30
How Cooperatives Use Credit Agencies to Meet Patron's Needs, 340
Hulbert, Lyman S., 3n., 202, 206, 396
Humphrey Amendment, 414

ICHDA (*see* International Cooperative
Housing Development Association)
Industrial and Provident Societies Act, 129,
183
Ingalsbe, Gene, 429n.
Ingram, Charles, 407
Insurance companies and cooperative
financing, 298
Integration (*see* Economic integration)
Inter-American Development Bank, 165
International cooperative organizations,
172–179
Food and Agriculture Organization
(FAO), 172–173

Inter-American Cooperative Finance
Development Society
(SIDEFCOOP), 173
International Cooperative Alliance (ICA),
177–178
International Cooperative Bank Company,
Ltd. (INGEBA), 176–177
International Cooperative Housing
Development Association (ICHDA),
174
International Federation of Agricultural
Producers (IFAP), 178
International Labor Organization (ILO),
174–175
International Research Center on Rural
Cooperative Communities
(CIRCOM), 175
Joint Committee for Promotion of Aid to
Cooperatives (COPAC), 175–176
Organization of Cooperatives of America
(OCA), 176
Plunket Foundation for Cooperative
Studies, 178–179
World Council of Credit Unions, Inc.
(WOCCU), 179
International Cooperative Petroleum
Association, 36
International Cooperative Training Center
(Wisconsin–Cooperative Education and
Training Center), 405, 414
Interstate Livestock Producers Association,
23

Jerry Voorhis Memorial Library, 165
Jesness, O. B., 404
Joint Committee for the Promotion of Aid to
Cooperatives (COPAC), 173, 175–176
Joint ventures, 440–442
Allied Grape Growers and, 441
Heublein, Inc., 441
(*See also* Economic integration)

Kauper, Thomas E., 214
Kefauver, Senator Estes, 213
Kennedy, President John F., 401–403
Key Performance areas (KPA), 384
King, Dr. William, 49, 73

Knapp, Joseph G., 80, 88*n*., 324*n*., 365, 399, 400*n*., 437
Knutson, Ronald D., 84, 442*n*.
Koller, E. Fred, 404
Kraenzle, Charles A., 443

Lambert, Paul, 49, 65
Land O' Lakes, Inc., 346
Lauman, Professor George L., 404
Leasing and leveraged leasing financing, 298–300
   leveraged lease, 300–301
   single investor lease, 299–300
Legal Phases of Cooperative Associations, 396
Legal Phases of Farmer Cooperatives, 202, 206, 396
Legal Phases of Farmer Cooperatives: Part I—Sample Legal Documents, 249*n*., 396
Legal Phases of Farmer Cooperatives: Part II—Federal Income Taxes, 225*n*., 396
Legal Phases of Farmer Cooperatives: Part III—Antitrust Laws, 396
Legal problems, 202–222
   Capper-Volstead Act and Peter Radino, 203
   legislative and regulatory environment, 202–205
   (*See also* Antitrust decisions; Antitrust legislation; Marketing agreements and orders; Marketing contracts)
Legislation, 183–201
   Capper-Volstead Act (1922), 193–197
      basic provisions of, 195
      benefits of, 196
      President Warren G. Harding and, 194
      Lyman S. Hulbert and, 197
      limitations of, 196
      National Cooperative Milk Producers Federation and, 193–195
   Clayton Act, 192–193
      Senator Robert M. LaFollette and, 193
   common law background, 190–191
   consumer cooperatives, 189
   Federal Trade Commission and Clayton Act, 192–193
   Industrial and Provident Societies Act of 1852, 183
   nonstock cooperative legislation, 186–187
   other federal legislation, 197–199
      Agricultural Fair Practices Act, 199
      Agricultural Marketing Act, 197
      Agricultural Marketing Agreements Act, 199
      Civil Rights Act, 199
      Cooperative Marketing Act, 197
      District of Columbia Consumers' Cooperative Act, 197
      Federal Credit Union Act, 198
      Federal Housing Acts, 198
      Federal Legislation Authorizing the Chartering of Cooperative, 197
      Fishery Cooperative Marketing Act, 197
      Future Trading Act, 198
      Income Tax Statute, 198
      Motor Carrier Act, 199
      Packers and Stockyards Act, 198
      Rural Electrification Act, 197
      War Revenue Act, 198
   Sapiro Law, 188
   Sherman Antitrust Act, 191–192
      Miller-Tydings Act and, 191
   special state assistance to, 189–190
      appointment of public directors, 190
      colleges of agriculture, 190
      departments of agriculture, 189
   Standard Marketing Act, 188
      Aaron Sapiro and, 188
      Colonel Harris Weinstock and, 188
   state laws, 184–190
   stock corporations, 185–186
Liberty Warehouse Company v. Burley Tobacco Growers Cooperative Association, 206–207
Limitations of cooperatives, 420–426
   benefits obscured, 424
   cannot control production, 421–422
   cannot eliminate market intermediaries, 423
   deviation from principles, 424
   frailties of human nature, 424–425
   inability to fix prices, 422
   limited market power, 423–424
   operating practices, 425
      financial resources, 425
      management, 425

members, 425
  semipublic status of, 426
  services, 426
Liquidation of cooperatives, 386–388
  legal considerations, 387
  reasons for, 386–387
  when solvent, 387–388
Long Poultry Farms, Inc. v. Commissioner,
  230–231

McCarthy, Charles, 405
MacIntyre, Everett, 213–214
McKay, Andrew W., 394*n*.
Macklin, Theodore, 405
McReynolds, Justice James, 203
Madison, President James, 62
Major export markets, figure, 446
Malthus, Thomas Robert, 421
Management, 261–272
  Kelsey B. Gardner and, 262
  Frank J. Smith, Jr., and, 265
  special considerations, 269–271
  success as a business, 267–269
  success as a cooperative, 262–267
  title of chief executive officer, 270–271
  Robert A. Wilson and, 265*n*.
Marketing agreements and orders, 218–220
  Agricultural Adjustment Act of 1933, 218
  Agricultural Marketing Agreements Act of
    1937, 218–219
  conditions for success, 219–220
  secretary of agriculture and, 218–219
Marketing contracts, 216–218
  general provisions of, 217–218
  Willard F. Mueller and, 217
  Aaron Sapiro and, 218
  Marvin A. Schaars and, 216
  types of, 216–217
Marketing cooperatives, 21–23, 37, 109,
  111, 113
Marketing orders and cooperatives, 220
Marx, Karl, 8
Maryland and Virginia Milk Producers
  Association, 22, 208–209, 346
Mather, J. Warren, 38, 255*n*., 429*n*.
Matteson, Bill, 284*n*.
Member investment in rural cooperatives,
  119, 121

Membership structure illustrated, figure, 40
Mergers, 376–388
  adjustments resulting from, 381–383
    financial considerations, 382
  Capper-Volstead Act and, 379–380
  Clayton Antitrust Act and, 379
  definition of, 376
  external considerations, 377–380
    economic factors, 377–379
    human relations, 379
    legal and regulatory considerations,
      379–380
  feasibility of, 383–384
  Federal Trade Commission and, 379
  local and internal considerations, 380–381
    economic factors, 380–381
    personal implications, 381
    postmerger considerations, 384–386
  role of management in, 382–383
  Sherman Antitrust Act and, 380
Mid-American Dairymen, Inc., 214
Migros, 66, 135
Mischler, Raymond J., 189, 202, 206,
  212–213
Morgan, Arthur E., 398
Morgan, E. S., 404
Morganthau, Henry, 323
Morris, Daniel, 449*n*.
Mutual insurance companies, 25–26, 30
Mutual irrigation companies, 26
Mutual savings banks, 341
Myers, William I., 323–324, 328

Naden, Kenneth D., 409–410
National Association of Housing
  Cooperatives, 167–168
National Broiler Marketing Association, 444
National Commission on Food Marketing,
  215, 356
National cooperative organizations, 159–165
  American Institute of Cooperation (AIC),
    159–161
    AIC Newsletter, 160
    National Institute on Cooperative
      Education, 159
  Cooperative League of the U.S.A.
    (CLUSA), 164–165

National cooperative organizations:
   Association for Cooperative Educators (ACE), 164
   Cooperative Editorial Association (CEA), 164
   Cooperative Management Development (CMD), 164
   Inter-American Development Bank and, 165
   Organization of Cooperatives of America and, 164
   National Council of Farmer Cooperatives, 161–164, 410, 447
   National Council of Farmer Cooperative Associations, 161
National cooperatives, 36
National Farmers Organization (NFO), 351
National Federation of Grain Cooperatives, 168
National Grange, 90–91
   Grange supply house, 90
   Oliver Hudson Kelly and, 90
   Montgomery Ward and Company and, 90
National Grape Cooperative Association, Inc., 39
National Livestock Producers Association, 168–169
National Marine Fisheries Service (NMFS), 297
National Milk Producers Federation (NMPF), 94, 169
National Rural Electric Cooperative Association (NRECA), 169
National Rural Utilities Cooperative Finance Corporation (CFC), 337–338
   membership, 338
   Rural Electrification Administration (REA) and, 337–338
   source of funds, 338
   staffing, 338
   structure, 338
   types of loans, 338
National Telephone Cooperative Association (NTCA), 170, 339–340
Nationwide Corporation, 30
Navarro, Luis A., 449n.
Neely, D. Morrison, 225n., 249n., 396
New Deal, 398–401, 421
   political systems and, 10

New Deal era, 415–418
New York State Power Authority, 399
Nourse, Edwin G., 79, 184n.

Ocean Spray, 23
Office of Economic Opportunity, 297
Office of Markets, 401
Organization of Cooperatives of America (OCA), 164, 176
Organizations serving cooperatives, 158–181
Organizing a cooperative, 243–259
   assistance available, 254–255
   identifying need, 243–250
   legal documents, 249–250
   precautionary organizational measures, 250–253
   strengthening structure, 255–258
   structure comparisons, 255–258
Owen, Robert, 48, 61, 72, 128
   Brook Farm and, 7
   New Harmony and, 7

Packel, Israel, 2n.
Pakucah and Illinois Railroad Company, 230n.
Patronage refunds, 308–312
   cash and noncash, 309
   distinct from dividends, 310
   distinct from pooling settlements, 310
   distribution of, 310
   how determined, 311–312
   investment or retains, 309
   legal status of, 309–310
Peace Corps, 165
Per unit capital investments, 312–313
PERT (*see* Program evaluation and review techniques)
Peteet, Walton, 187
Phillips, Richard, 81
Plunkett, Sir Horace, 178, 393
Plunkett Foundation for Cooperative Studies, 178–179
   Agricultural Cooperation, 179
Political Action for Cooperative Effectiveness (PACE), 413
Political action by cooperatives, 411–414

INDEX 489

Political systems:
   capitalism and, 5–6
   communism and, 7–9
   contrasted and, 5–12
   cooperatives and, 5–12
   fascism and, 9–10
   human nature and, 5, 6, 8, 9
   private property and, 6–10
   socialism and, 6–7
   the state and, 5, 7–9
   Laszlo Volko and, 12
Pooling, 364–374
   advantages of, 370–371
   American Cotton Growers and, 365
   American Rice Growers Cooperative Association, 364
   Arkansas Grain Corporation, 365–367
   comparison with other methods of sale, 373–374
   disadvantages of, 371–372
   early efforts, 365
   nature of, 365–367
Pooling operations, 364–370
   allocation of costs, 370
   duration and number, 370
   grades to establish, 368
   illustrated, 367–370
   patron relationships, 368
   pools to establish, 368
   Riceland Foods, Inc., and, 364–367
Powell, G. Harold, 394
Price, H. Bruce, 78, 404
Production credit associations (*see* Cooperative Farm Credit System)
Program evaluation and review techniques (PERT), 384
Purchasing cooperatives, 23, 37
Pursell, Arthur, 340

Quasi-cooperatives, 41–42

Raiffeisen, Friedrich Wilhelm, 75
Railway Express Agency, 34
Rall, Udo, 399
REA (*see* Rural Electrification Administration)
Recreation cooperatives, 30–31
Reeves v. Decorah Farmers Cooperative Society, 205

Regional cooperatives, 35–36, 39, 297
Report of Inquiry on Cooperative Enterprise in Europe, 2n.
Research (cooperatives), 448–456
   advances in, 451–452
   Current Research Information System (CRIS), 453–454
   expenditures for, table, 453
   National Science Foundation, 453
   research departments, 452–456
   types of, 448–449
Revolving capital financing, 313–319
   advantages of, 317
   equitable treatment of members and, 318
   noncash patronage refund investments, 313–314
   per unit capital investments, 315–317
   problem areas, 317–319
   (*See also* Patronage refunds)
Riceland Foods, Inc., 364–367
Robotka, Frank, 77, 81
Rochdale pioneers, 47–50, 74, 128–130
Roosevelt, President Franklin D., 97, 323, 398, 399
Roosevelt, President Theodore, 94, 322, 393
Rural credit unions, 25
Rural electric and telephone cooperatives, 238
Rural Electrification Act of 1936, 399
Rural Electrification Administration, 25, 296
Rural Telephone Bank, 297, 339–340
   operation, 339–340
   structure, 339
   types of stock, 339
Rust, Irwin W., 254n.

Samuels, J. Kenneth, 350
Sapiro, Aaron, 61, 78, 188, 407, 422
Savage, Job K., 81, 82
Savings and loan associations, 341
Scandinavian Cooperative Wholesale Society, 36
Schaars, Marvin A., 51, 216, 266, 405
Schulze-Delitzsch, Herman, 75
Scroggs, Claude L., 394n.
Securities and Exchange Commission, 240
Senate Document 214, 403
Sequoia Farm Labor Association, 33

Service cooperatives, 23–27, 37, 145, 433
    types of, 23–27
Share of export market, figure, 446
Sherman, Senator Arthur, 192
Sherman Antitrust Act, 191–192
Simon, Saint, 73
Sims, Melvin E., 240
Sinclair, John F., 405
Size of cooperatives, 37–38
    number distribution by volume and type, table, 38
Small Business Administration, 298, 410–411
Smith, Adam, 5
Smith, Frank J., Jr., 265n., 301
Socialism, Saint Simon and, 6
Southern States Cooperative, Inc., 35, 36, 39, 80
Special organizational problems of limited resource cooperatives, 258–259
"Special treatment" and "exceptional privileges," 83
Standard Marketing Act, 188–189
State cooperative councils, 170–172
State court decisions, 205–206
State government (role of):
    assistance in forming cooperatives, 407
    California Department of Markets, 407
    cooperative relationships, 403–408
    Massachusetts, 403–404
    New York, 404
    state departments of agriculture, 408
    status of cooperative teaching, 407
    Wisconsin, 405
        (See also cooperative relationships above)
Stokdyk, E. A., 79–80
Streeter, Carroll, 437
Sunkist Growers, Inc., 209–210, 346
Sunkist System (see Sunkist Growers, Inc.)
Sunkist v. Winckler and Smith Citrus Products, 209–210
Swarthout, A. V., 448

Taft, President William Howard, 332
Taxation of cooperatives, 223–242
    basic income tax issues, 239–241
        elimination of Section 521, 239–240
        taxation of patronage refunds, 239
        uninformed legislators and regulators, 240–241
    early legislation, 225–226
        1951 Revenue Act as amended in 1954, 226–227
        Revenue Acts of 1913, 1916, 1921, 1924, 1926, and 1934, 226
    federal income taxes, 225–241
        alternatives, 234–236
        basic income tax issues, 239–241
        Commissioner v. B. A. Carpenter and, 230
        consumer cooperatives, 238
        Farm Credit Administration Units, 237–238
        Long Poultry Farms, Inc., v. Commissioner and, 230–231
        "look through" provisions, 233
        patronage refunds, 231–232
            on cooperative level, 231
            on member level, 231
            to members and nonmembers, 234–236
            to members only, 234–236
            tax status of, 229–230
        per unit capital investments, 236
        requirements for Section 521 tax status, 228
        Revenue Act of 1962 as amended in 1966 and 1969, 230–231
        rules for Section 521 cooperatives, 228
        rural electric and telephone companies, 238
        Section 501 certain cooperatives and other organizations, 237–238
        Section 521 cooperatives, 232–234
        Section 522 tax on farmers' cooperatives, 228–229
        ways of obtaining patron consent, 231–232
    franchise, sales, and other related taxes, 225
    property taxes, 224–225
    state income taxes, 238–239
Taylor, Carl C., 77
Technicoop (TCI), 167
Tennessee Valley Authority (TVA), 398–399

INDEX

Arthur E. Morgan and, 398
Senator George Norris and, 398
Guy Rexford Tugwell and, 399–401
Terminology:
  for accounting, 468–470
    National Society of Accountants for Cooperatives and, 468
  misunderstood terms, 223–224
Thompson, Stanley R., 384
Tigner v. Texas, 207
Treasure Valley Potato Bargaining Association v. Ore-Ida Foods, Inc., 210–211, 348
TVA (*see* Tennessee Valley Authority)

Unfavorable government action, 408–414
  agency conflicts, 409–411
    Federal Trade Commission, 409–410
    Interstate Commerce Commission, 410
    Justice Department, 410
    "A Report on Agricultural Cooperatives," 409–410
    U.S. Treasury Department, 409
  congressional conflicts, 408–409
    Senator Allan J. Ellender, 408
  political action by cooperatives, 411–414
    Action Committee for Rural Electrification (ACRE), 413
    Credit Union Legislative Affairs Committee (CULAC), 413
    National Rural Electric Cooperative Association, 413
    Political Action for Cooperative Effectiveness (PACE), 413
    relationships with agency administrators, 412–414
    relationships with legislators, 412–414
    unsolved issues, 413
  views expressed, 214, 215, 410
Unique nature of cooperatives, 275
United Cooperatives, 36
United States v. Associated Milk Producers, Inc., 211
United States v. Borden Company, 207–208
United States v. Maryland and Virginia Milk Producers Association, Inc., 203, 208–209, 217
  Embassy Dairy, Inc., and, 208–209

United States v. Maryland Cooperative Milk Producers and Maryland and Virginia Milk Producers Association, Inc., 208
United Vintners (*see* Joint ventures)
Universal Cooperatives, Inc., 36
University Cooperative Education and Training Center, 405

Vertical integration, 85, 439
  (*See also* Economic integration)
Virginia Seed Services, 35–36
  (*See also* Southern States Cooperative, Inc.)
Voorhis, Jerry:
  cooperative benefits and, 433, 434
  cooperative principles and, 62

Wallace, Henry A., 328–329
War Finance Corporation, 322
Warbasse, James Peter, 76–77
Watergate scandals, 214
Webb, Beatrice, 74–75
Webb, Catherine, 48
  Industrial Cooperation —Story of a Peaceful Revolution, 48
Webb, Sidney, 74
Weinstock, Colonel Harris, 188, 407
Weld, L. D. H., 404, 448
Wentzel, Roland K., 384–386
Who Will Control United States Agriculture, 449n.
Wilson, Robert A., 265n.
Wilson, President Woodrow, 94, 332–333
Wisconsin Legislative Reference Library, 405
Worker cooperatives, 31–33
  types of, 31–33
Workman's Protective Association, 25
World Council of Credit Unions, Inc. (WOCCU), 179

Yager, Francis P., 443

Zeuck, William E., 400